The World in the 20th Century

The World in the 20th Century:
A Thematic Approach

Stephanie A. Hallock

PEARSON

Boston Columbus Indianapolis New York San Francisco Upper Saddle River
Amsterdam Cape Town Dubai London Madrid Milan Munich Paris Montréal Toronto
Delhi Mexico City São Paulo Sydney Hong Kong Seoul Singapore Taipei Tokyo

Editorial Director: Craig Campanella
Editor-in-Chief: Dickson Musslewhite
Executive Editor: Jeff Lasser
Editorial Project Manager: Rob DeGeorge
Editorial Assistant: Julia Feltus
Director of Marketing: Brandy Dawson
Senior Marketing Manager: Maureen Prado Roberts
Marketing Assistant: Samantha Bennett
Senior Managing Editor: Ann Marie McCarthy
Project Manager: Cheryl Keenan
Manufacturing Manager: Mary Fischer
Operations Specialist: Alan Fischer
Art Director, Text and Cover: Maria Lange
Cover Art: National Archives and Records Administration/National Archives and Records Administration/Library of Congress/Perspectives/Glow Images
Director, Digital Media: Brian Hyland
Media Editor: Emsal Hassan
Composition and Full-Service Project Management: Integra
Printer/Binder: Edwards Brothers
Cover Printer: Lehigh-Phoenix Color Corp
Text Font: 10/12 Times

Credits and acknowledgments borrowed from other sources and reproduced, with permission, in this textbook appear on appropriate page within text or on pages 313–314.

Library of Congress Cataloging-in-Publication Data

Hallock, Stephanie A.
The world in the twentieth century : a thematic approach / Stephanie A. Hallock.
p. cm.
Includes bibliographical references and index.
ISBN-13: 978-0-13-603253-3
ISBN-10: 0-13-603253-2
1. History, Modern—20th century—Textbooks. 2. Military history, Modern—20th century—Textbooks. 3. World politics—20th century—Textbooks. 4. International relations—History—20th century—Textbooks. I. Title.
D421.H26 2013
909.82—dc23

2011049052

10 9 8 7 6 5 4 3 2 1

ISBN-10: 0-13-603253-2
ISBN-13: 978-0-13-603253-3

To my students at HCC for making me want to write this book,
Alice Barr for making me believe I could actually do it,
Avery Ward for making it possible, and Jeff, Julia, Kristin,
and Mirella for making it all come together.

Contents

Maps

Chapter 7

Chapter 8

Chapter 9

Chapter 10

Chapter 11

Chapter 12

Chapter 13

Chapter 14

MySearchLab Connections

Chapter 1

Read the Document

Watch the Video

Chapter 2

Read the Document

Watch the Video

Chapter 3

Read the Document

Watch the Video

Chapter 4

Read the Document

Watch the Video

Chapter 5

Read the Document

Watch the Video

Chapter 6

Read the Document

Watch the Video

Chapter 7

Read the Document

Watch the Video

Chapter 8

Read the Document

Watch the Video

Chapter 9
Read the Document

Watch the Video

Chapter 10
Read the Document

Watch the Video

Chapter 11
Read the Document

Watch the Video

Chapter 12
Read the Document

Watch the Video

Chapter 13

Read the Document

Watch the Video

Chapter 14

Read the Document

Preface

Understanding the events and issues of the twentieth century is vital to any student who hopes to make sense of the world he or she lives in today. It was an eventful century during which technological progress led to dramatic changes in concepts of identity that spread rapidly around the globe in a fairly messy fashion. The entire process was, of course, all driven by humans making decisions based on their interests and goals, which created a lot of conflict. Making sense of it all is no easy task, and one that is certainly open to interpretation.

During the past ten years of teaching the history and politics of the twentieth century, I have struggled to find a textbook that provides a holistic narrative of the century in a user-friendly format. Most texts on the subject tend to be very detail oriented and verbose, rendering them inaccessible and difficult to read for students who may be approaching the material for the first time. Students quickly become frustrated at what appears to be a daunting challenge, and I spend most of our classroom time together simply explaining the text. I have tried teaching solely from primary source documents, but that approach lacks a cohesive, overarching storyline that students need to organize the information. Perhaps most disturbingly, in focusing so heavily on dates and details, many texts do not encourage students to link the events and people of the past to current events and global conditions. The "past" becomes something that happened "back then" and is irrelevant to their lives today.

I have written this book for those students who may not have a strong background in history but do have a strong desire to understand the story of the twentieth century. I know many young people who have heard of particular events or individuals but do not exactly understand what happened or why the events and individuals are important. Taking cues from my students, I have developed a thematic approach to the study of the twentieth century that focuses on elucidating connections in specific areas as the century progresses and asking students to continue tracing those patterns into their current lives. To engage students in the story, the narrative is less formal than that found in typical academic texts.

This textbook is born from more than a decade of classroom experience and a love of teaching. It is not based exclusively on extensive research, nor is it narrowly focused on particular elements of twentieth-century life. The primary and perhaps only goal of this text is to help instructors guide students through the process of learning (how and why), using the historical events (who, what, when, and where) of the twentieth century. Students learn best when they perceive that their instructors are facilitators and guides, not interpreters or preachers. When a choice has been made, you will notice a sacrifice of detail (which instructors can easily fill in if need be) in exchange for a stronger emphasis on student engagement with the material. Synthesis activities in which students are asked to apply what they read, see, and hear (based on text, maps, photographs, primary source documents, websites, and film clips) are embedded in each chapter to demonstrate comprehension of a particular concept. There are also evaluative activities in which students will connect the events and concepts to the overarching course themes and/or their personal experiences.

Recent advances in both educational research and technology allow instructors to present information to students in ways that will accommodate all types of learners, and studies suggest that students learn better when they are visually and actively engaged. Likewise, instructors are more enthusiastic about their subject and energetic in presenting it when they have the tools they need to create an interactive learning environment. With this straightforward and brief textbook, reading assignments will not be onerous—students will come to class with a basic background, prepared to dig deeper into the analysis of the events. Instructors can then use classroom time to creatively foster that analysis and "fill in the blanks" with primary source documents, maps, interactive websites, simulation games, films, and other activities related to the topics they want to highlight in their own courses. This textbook is not designed as a stand-alone source of information on the twentieth century; rather, it is a cornerstone of a well-rounded and flexible learning environment in which instructors create their courses to meet their students' needs without sacrificing important elements of the overall story.

I encourage instructors to take advantage of the online materials available on the MySearchLab website for *The World in the Twentieth Century: A Thematic Approach.* All of the primary source documents and video clips noted in the chapter margins are there for you to access at no additional charge. Because this text is designed to facilitate the learning process, I have also worked with an instructional technology specialist to pull together suggestions for classroom activities and simulation games that we think are useful for each chapter. We have created an Instructional Resource Center blog, where instructors can share classroom activities and ideas for instruction that are linked to the textbook and supplements. We will continue to update the resources as new ideas come to us and ask that you do the same. The intention is not that every one of these resources will be utilized throughout the semester, but rather that instructors will select which pieces to embed based on their blueprints for the course and their teaching styles.

I hope you enjoy teaching and learning about the world in the twentieth century as much as I have enjoyed the process of writing about it. It was a much more difficult task than I envisioned it would be when I developed the first proposal three years ago. Although I am cited as the sole author, this text could not have been written without the professional and loving support of my editor/husband Joe Cooney and educational specialist and dear friend Lisa Twiss. The quality of the final project is a result of the collaborative efforts of the incredibly thorough editors and assistants at Pearson, anonymous reviewers who provided crucial feedback as the text unfolded, and my students and colleagues at Harford Community College who continue to guide and challenge me in my professional development. I am deeply grateful to Katey Cooney for her love and patience with me, as well as PJ Burns, Sarah Cooper, and my friends and family for making sure I kept my life in balance throughout the project.

—Stephanie A. Hallock

Introduction

The very ink with which history is written is merely fluid prejudice.

—Mark Twain

History is a story about people—the story of our past, present, and future. All of the decisions and actions that came before us shape the world of today, some obviously influencing more directly than others. But history is a complicated and messy story, in which one person's hero is another's enemy, and conflict and human progress are inextricably linked as they propel each other forward through time. This is particularly true by the time we get to the end of the twentieth century and there are roughly 195 nation-states and 6 billion people engaging with one another in real time via satellites orbiting Earth. Trying to understand the story can be confusing—it's easy to get bogged down in the details and overwhelmed by the sheer volume of interaction. But it is vital to make the effort, because without an understanding of the choices that were made in the twentieth century, we have no context for the world we live in today. And without that, we cannot make informed choices to shape the future.

Using the Thematic Approach

To help you sift through the many events and concepts that unfolded in the twentieth century, the content is structured around four broad themes that are intended to help you keep your eye on the big picture as you dig into the specifics within each chapter. Think of the themes as the skeleton that holds the body together—you will flesh out the details as you develop a deeper understanding of how individual events fit together. The purpose of a thematic approach to studying history is not to divide events into discrete categories. As you will quickly realize, most of the events of the twentieth century will fall into more than one of these broad themes.

You will find a brief timeline at the beginning of each chapter, but it certainly does not include all events that occurred in that time period, and it will often include events that are covered in other chapters to remind you that global events juxtapose one another. When looking at the big picture, you cannot easily connect one event to the next in a linear fashion, although it is tempting to try. In doing so, you lose an accurate understanding of the interconnectedness of people, ideologies, experiences, and actions across the globe. This is where the themes will guide you. The beginning of each chapter also includes a set of boxes called "Working with the Themes," which contain a very brief overview of what you will read in that chapter with regard to the specific themes. The overview is purposely brief because it is your job to tie the events to the larger themes in a way that makes sense to you. To guide you, there are specific questions related to each theme at the end of the chapter to help you place the individual events in larger contexts. As you go through the chapters, you will be building a storyline based on the broad themes, one that focuses not on dates but instead on the causes and consequences of events. As you link these events together, you will be weaving a story of the twentieth century that emphasizes that the decisions people make resonate throughout the world, throughout the century and into the next.

The Themes

1. **The Effects of Technology:** This is probably the easiest theme to follow throughout the entire century. Technological advances happen often and evolve very quickly into the next generation of technology. Every part of human society is affected from medical advancements and household conveniences to transportation and communication. By the end of the twentieth century, even intellectual property is recognized as a tradable good.

New technologies are driven by demand, particularly with regard to consumer goods. But the research and development behind them is frequently based on a military application. From World War I communications equipment for trench warfare, we get the radio. From Cold War satellite technology for espionage, we get mobile telephones and television. Because of this relationship, the technology that evolves can be somewhat of a double-edged sword. Nuclear power plants can provide relatively inexpensive renewable sources of energy, but nuclear weapons can destroy the planet. Technology's effect on society is easily seen, but don't overlook the linkage between technology and political decision-making, which often has social ramifications as well.

2. **Changing Identities:** The twentieth century witnessed a remarkable shift away from the social structure of the conservative order. The end of the Victorian Era in the West gave rise to political movements to restructure society, such as liberalism and feminism. As these political movements gave way to democracy, alternative political ideologies appeared that demanded the entire global structure be remade to reflect fascism or communism. Nationalist movements ripped apart empires and created nation-states, but there was still ethnic conflict because of the way those nation-states were created. Decolonization had a dramatic impact on people throughout Africa and Asia as they struggled, often violently, to re-identify themselves in light of the colonial experience. And the creation of Israel in Arab territory gave rise to Islamic fundamentalism as religious warfare continued into yet another century.
3. **Shifting Borders:** As the twentieth century opened, the world was still largely structured by vast empires, some of them stretching back to ancient times. As empires disintegrated, they were replaced by independent nation-states, which then continued to fight against one another for control of territory and resources. By the end of the century, these sovereign states had formed regional and even international organizations in an attempt to mitigate the worldwide conflict and distribute resources more justly. But the territorial imperative persists, as evidenced by the ever-increasing refugee crisis and migrations stemming from ethnic, civil, and economic strife.
4. **Globalization:** Of the four themes, this may be the most difficult to work with because so many definitions of the term have been offered in the past decade, many of them value-laden. Globalization is political, economic, environmental, and sociocultural. Despite the focus on globalization in the last half of the twentieth century, it is a process rooted much deeper in history and has been driven by migration, evangelization, exploration, technology, and trade since humans began interacting with one another. In today's world, globalization tends to focus on consumerism and the uneven patterns of distribution of goods and money around the world, made all the more tangible by the rapid increase in communications technology. But a particular form of globalization has been met with a cultural backlash—a desire to slow down the process and protect and preserve identity. For our purposes, globalization exists wherever the choices made in one country or region limit or shape the choices made by others.

Brief Overview of the Twentieth Century

The world in 1900 did not function as one global entity—not politically, culturally, economically, or in any sense of the word. But by the end of the century, we became aware—sometimes painfully aware—that we are essentially one large machine even if the parts do not agree with one another about how the machine should function. As you can imagine, this ongoing shift from separateness to togetherness is not a smooth, peaceful transition.

Our story must begin in the late nineteenth century with a brief look at the roots of the major changes that will create the twentieth-century world. As we go through these events, we will focus on what causes these connections and what specifically pushes us forward and together. Immediately, technological development will jump right out at you, but there are also broad cultural trends that have a dramatic impact on identity. So not only will we be looking at how particular events shape events in other parts of the world but how they shape the world and humanity itself. And what you will notice more than anything else as this process takes place is the extraordinary amount of conflict.

During the twentieth century, we see the late stages of a shift away from the ancient power structure of wealthy monarchs over poor and powerless people through internal revolutions. We also witness the early stages of a shift away from wealthy imperialists over the poor and resource-lacking nations; this shift was generally achieved through warfare. A world structure begins to emerge in which power lies in the hands of the people to a much greater extent than ever before. That shift rapidly creates a whole new set of problems for societies internally, and social and cultural norms are reevaluated. At the global level, the shift does not happen quite so fast and comes at the expense of millions of lives in global wars. Many argue it still has a long way to go—imperialism has not disappeared—it now structures the world economically through transnational corporations and international organizations.

Of course, history did not end on December 31, 1999. As we move forward into the twenty-first century, we carry with us our understandings of the past to guide us as we make decisions for the present and the future. Where we go is in your hands, but you cannot make good decisions without understanding, reflection, and the sense of empowerment that comes from knowledge. As Winston Churchill once said, "History will be kind to me, for I intend to write it."

About the Author

Stephanie A. Hallock is Associate Professor of Political Science at Harford Community College in Bel Air, Maryland, where she chairs the college's International Education Initiative. Her primary work has been in the area of global curriculum development and study abroad, consulting and presenting in Bulgaria and the United States. These experiences led to her current exploration of various pedagogical approaches to promote student engagement, both in the classroom and in larger communities in which they live. She received her B.A. from Roanoke College, M.A. from Virginia Tech, and Ph.D. from the University of Miami.

1 Setting the Stage: Overview of the Nineteenth Century

CHAPTER OUTLINE

- Empires Structure the Globe
- New Imperialism
- The Direct Effects of Industrialization
- Ideological Revolutions against Conservatism
- The World in 1900

CHAPTER TIMELINE

1800

1804
Haiti is the first colony to achieve independence

1830s
The typewriter is invented
The telegraph is invented

1848
Communist Manifesto is published
Nationalist revolutions occur in Europe

1859
On the Origin of Species is published

January 1901
Queen Victoria passes away

Photos from left to right: Suffragette parade, New York City, ca. 1912; Specification of Letters Patent and Patent Drawings; *From the Cape to Cairo*, by Udo J. Keppler; Farmer, ca. 1890.

1860s	1867	1870s	1888	1898	1900
The Gatling machine gun is invented **Dynamite is invented** **Torpedoes are invented**	**Meiji Restoration occurs in Japan**	**The first usable light bulb is invented** **The telephone is invented** **The first usable combustion engine is invented**	**Wilhelm II ascends to the German throne**	**Spanish-American War**	**The Open Door Policy is created** **The Boxer Rebellion and retaliation occur** **Paris Exposition Universelle opens**

To understand the significance of the twentieth century, we must first look carefully at the revolutionary events of the late 1800s that reshaped political, economic, social and religious perceptions of the world. Among the most notable changes was the large-scale shift in productivity from agricultural-based societies to industrial ones. This process had very serious ramifications: it led to wealth, which translated to power, and it expanded technology, which also translated to power when applied to advancing weaponry. It is obvious why political leaders were anxious to industrialize, but there were other effects of industrialization they had not anticipated—a comprehensive change in the way people produced and consumed naturally led to major changes in the way they lived, which required political and social change as well. Existing governments were not eager to accept this "side effect" of industrialization and were violently unwilling to do so in some cases. Industrialization and all that came with it set the stage for external conflicts between governments seeking to expand their power and wealth, as well as internal conflicts between conservative rulers and the people they ruled.

WORKING WITH THE THEMES

THE EFFECTS OF TECHNOLOGY Industrialization has dramatic effects on individuals, social class structure, domestic and international economies and concepts of power.

CHANGING IDENTITIES Four major ideological movements appear to challenge the existing conservative order—feminism, liberalism, Marxism, and nationalism.

SHIFTING BORDERS Territorial empires become unstable as sea-linked empires rise in economic and geostrategic power. New Imperialism carves up Africa and Asia.

GLOBALIZATION Sea-linked empires connect people and natural resources across continents. Social Darwinism creates an artificial hierarchy in and across human civilizations. Increased industrialization requires international markets.

Empires Structure the Globe

empire
a large expanse of territory comprised of multiple cultures ruled by one emperor, generally called a monarch by the 1800s

divine right
kings are the natural leaders by birthright (ancestry) and are answerable only to God (not the people)

Since ancient human civilizations began, the ultimate goal of most political leaders was to expand their own territory by conquering others, thus creating an **empire.** That was still largely true throughout the 1800s, although the methods of accomplishing this goal changed as a reflection of ever-improving technology. By the nineteenth century, monarchs had applied the scientific advances of the industrial revolution to increase their power through wealth and better weaponry. And as that power grew, they did the only thing they knew to do with it—build an empire.

An empire differed from a country in that an empire encompassed many different smaller countries. Leaders of the constituent countries were overthrown after a physical invasion by another country, and the territory and people within them were co-opted into the empire. The goal of the monarch was to stay in power and gain glory and wealth, so the goal of the empire was to expand—the more territory, the more people answering to the monarch. The monarchs who controlled these empires came from a long tradition of rule by **divine right** and had no self-perception of serving the people or responsibility to them. Of course there were variations according to culture, but this was the basic structure of governments in the nineteenth century.

Territorial Empires

The earliest form of empire building was the territorial empire, built over centuries through the conquest of land surrounding the core region. By the 1800s, the building of territorial empires had led to large expanses of land that were difficult to defend from neighbors pursuing the same kind of expansion and which often contained multiple ethnic and religious identities who did not always culturally mesh with one another or the ruling family.

In the 1800s, one of the oldest territorial empires was the Ottoman Empire, bridging the Muslim-dominated Middle East and Christian-dominated Europe. It was established by Turkish nomadic tribes in the eastern part of the Byzantine Empire in the fifteenth century and reached its height in the sixteenth and seventeenth centuries when it covered parts of three continents. The steady territorial expansion of the Ottoman Empire and Russia's aggressive attempts to gain control of the Black Sea put the two empires in frequent military conflict throughout the eighteenth and nineteenth centuries. In the mid-1800s, Ottoman leaders allied with the British and French to prevent Russia from expanding into their territory. This relationship led to a wave of European political and cultural influence that was met with resistance by the Muslim leaders. The combination of external warfare with Russia, internal political conflict over **westernization** and increasing ethnic **nationalism** put the empire in a weakened position, and by the end of the nineteenth century it was clear that the Ottoman Empire could not hold together much longer.

westernization the application of Western government, culture, religion, economics, language, etc., to non-Western culture

nationalism the self-perception that one is part of a nation, defined as a community with its own language, traditions, customs and history that distinguish it from other nations; a sense of identity that often becomes the primary focus of one's loyalty

The rise of the Russian Empire under Peter the Great in the early eighteenth century coincided with the decline of its territorial rival to the south, the Ottoman Empire. Its rapid and aggressive expansion throughout the eighteenth century made Russia the second-largest empire in the world in terms of territory (behind Great Britain), and the Russian military's defeat of Napoleon in the early nineteenth century secured its powerful political position in European affairs. As in the Ottoman Empire, attempts to westernize Russian political, economic and social life were met with resistance by the nobility and Orthodox Christians, and opposition to the tsar (the Russian monarch) grew increasingly violent throughout the nineteenth century. Given this internal political violence and Russia's lack of industrial capability (particularly notable in terms of military technology), the Russian empire did not present a credible threat to Europe. But European economic interests in China were certainly at risk if Russia decided to take advantage of its geographic position and expand to the east.

The third major territorial empire of the nineteenth century was China. Its strength came from its relative geographic isolation, and although Chinese dynastic leaders always suffered challenges from internal disunity, they did not face major external threats until they began trading with Europe in the late eighteenth century. The **Qing** dynasty took control of China in the mid-seventeenth century and dominated all of Asia during the eighteenth century through aggressive

Qing (ch'ing) also known as the Manchu dynasty, it was the last dynasty of China

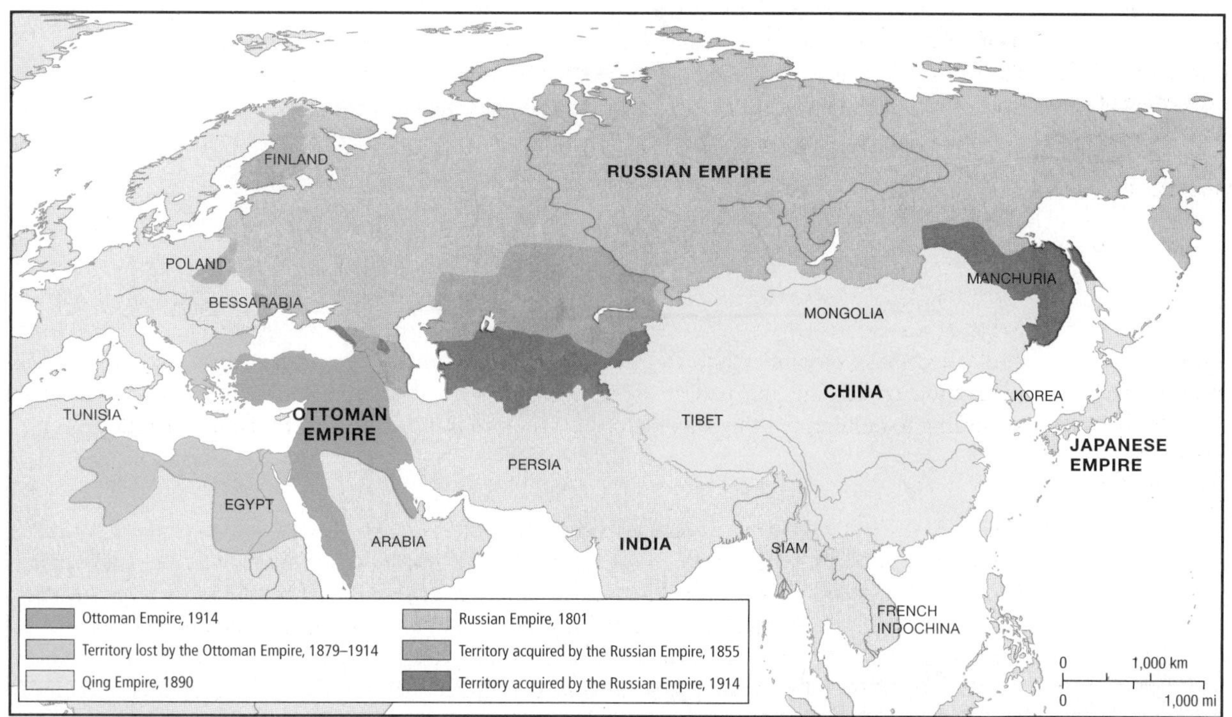

MAP 1.1 Ottoman, Russian, and Chinese Empires in the Mid-1800s

military campaigns. While increased trade with Europe in the early nineteenth century led to wealth for China, it also led to the Opium Wars during which Great Britain easily defeated China, took control of its economy and redirected production and trade to benefit the West.

Taiping Rebellion large-scale revolt against the Qing dynasty demanding social reform; lasted from 1850–1864 and resulted in 20–30 million deaths

As economic conditions for the Chinese people worsened, internal rebellions against the Qing leadership increased, culminating in the **Taiping Rebellion,** which required British and French military assistance to quell. Sensing that the Qing dynasty was vulnerable, both Russia and Japan attacked China separately and gained territory in the late nineteenth century. There was immense wealth to be gained by controlling Chinese raw materials and human resources, and all of the world's powers wanted a piece of the action. At the end of the nineteenth century, the Qing dynasty was politically, militarily and economically dysfunctional—the only question was which world power would deliver the final blow and take control of China's vast resources.

Sea-Linked Empires

economic theory of mercantilism because there is a finite amount of wealth in the world, a country should export more than it imports, thereby accumulating bullion (gold)

As patterns of production and consumption changed with increasing industrial capabilities, countries that excelled in naval power created sea-linked empires, built by acquiring colonies and territories during the eighteenth and nineteenth centuries in Asia, Africa and the Americas. The ultimate goal of the sea-linked empire was the same as the territorial empire—to expand territory and generate wealth. But industrialization changed the way wealth was generated as well. Whereas the economies of traditional territorial empires were grounded in agriculture and population, the massive wealth of sea-linked empires was built upon access to inexpensive raw materials and labor and markets of consumers who would be forced to purchase the ever-increasing supply of manufactured goods. Built on the **economic theory of mercantilism,** sea-linked empires built a network of colonies around the globe through which all wealth flowed to the imperial power at the expense of the economic health of the colonies.

The first country to build a sea-linked empire was Spain, which dominated Central and South America and the Caribbean from the sixteenth century to the eighteenth century. When

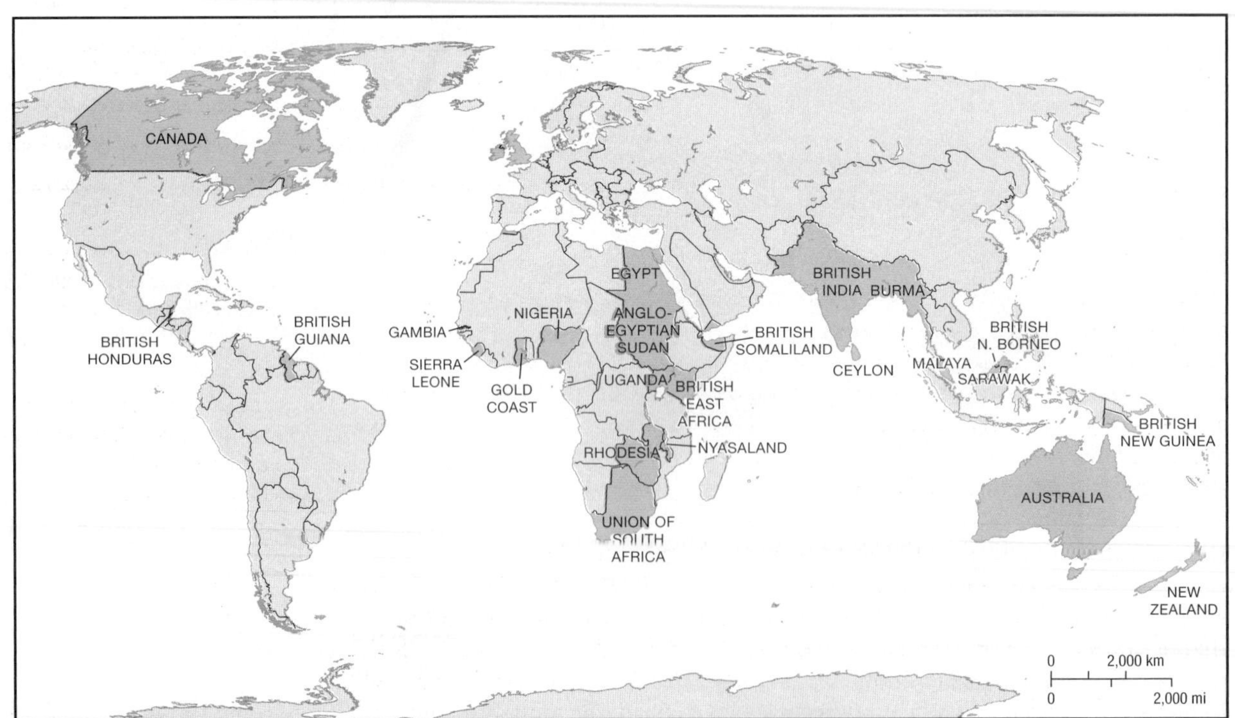

MAP 1.2 The British Empire, 1900

rival European powers Great Britain, France, Portugal and the Netherlands (and eventually Belgium, Germany and Italy) realized the vast potential for wealth, they too began seeking colonies around the world. This competition for growth and wealth put them in direct conflict with one another, and naval wars, piracy and smuggling became common in the eighteenth century. Because of its industrial and technological superiority, naval power and strategic military and corporate alliances, Great Britain clearly dominated the others and was the largest empire in modern history at the turn of the twentieth century, controlling roughly 20 percent of the world's total landmass and 23 percent of the human race.

The colonies created by sea-linked empires varied, depending on how and why they were created. Most of the colonies, particularly in Africa, Asia and the South Pacific, were tropical dependencies. That is, a small of group of Europeans (including their militaries) kept control over the large populations of "others" (the nonwhites) who were used for labor and considered quite expendable. But there were also settlement colonies, places where European citizens actually moved, set up homes, raised families and, to some extent, became part of the local culture. In places such as Canada and Australia (called White Dominions by the British), the westerners basically moved in and took over—it was relatively easy because most of the indigenous people already had been killed. But in other places, such as South Africa, New Zealand, Hawaii, and much of the Caribbean, the Europeans came to settle and moved in next door to the existing indigenous populations. These settlements were called mixed-settler colonies because many different cultures were living together in the same communities. In most cases there was a lot of conflict, and the Europeans set the rules that all must live by; but in other cases (particularly in the Caribbean) there was a true sharing or blending of the cultures that created a new and unique culture altogether. Either way, in all of the colonies there was a prevailing sense of racial (white), religious (Christianity) and cultural (civilized) superiority of the westerners over all others, supported in large part by their technological superiority (weapons).

U.S. imperialism sparks debate, as demonstrated in this 1899 issue of *Life* magazine.

ANALYSIS

What prompted Professor John Wilson to write in 1829: "His Majesty's dominions, on which the sun never sets. . ."?

From a geographical perspective, why was India considered "the Jewel in the Crown of the British Empire"?

In 1776, Scottish theorist Adam Smith published *An Inquiry into the Nature and Causes of the Wealth of Nations*, a sharp criticism of the mercantilist practices of the eighteenth century. Smith particularly challenged the notion that a country could only get wealthy at the expense of others, and he believed the "invisible hand" (rational self-interested behavior) operating in a "system of natural liberty" (the free-market economy) would lead to economic well-being for all. Smith's work became the foundation of the Classical School of economic

laissez-faire
in economics, the belief that government should not intervene in economic affairs beyond the minimum necessary to keep the peace and protect property rights

economic capitalism
an economic system based on private ownership of the means of production and open competition in a free market where the goal is profit

Read the Document *Reflections on Revolutions* on mysearchlab.com

theory, which focuses on economic freedom, **laissez-faire** and free competition, hallmarks of **economic capitalism.**

The first evidence that the sea-linked imperial system was vulnerable occurred in Latin America (where it all began) in the late eighteenth century. Although at one time Spain, Portugal, Britain, France, the Netherlands and the United States controlled colonies in Latin America, they fought so much over the territory that they weakened one another. Add to that angry indigenous people who did not want to be colonized and a huge population of Africans who were imported as slave labor and often treated brutally, and the result was a volatile situation. Led by the example of the British colonies in North America that won their independence in the late 1700s, the Latin American colonies rebelled against imperial power. Haiti was the first to achieve independence (from France) in 1804, and by the mid-nineteenth century almost all of the former colonies of the western hemisphere had earned their independence. Most of the newly created independent countries were geographically small, economically disadvantaged and stuck with political connections from the old days of colonialism, leaving them vulnerable to continued economic domination.

New Imperialism

Despite the wave of successful colonial independence movements in the early nineteenth century, the imperialists of the world made yet another push to expand their power in the late nineteenth century. Termed *New Imperialism* because of the subtle shift in goals and the more blatant shift in the methods used to achieve the goals, the imperialist movement dramatically changed the power structure in the world in a remarkably short amount of time.

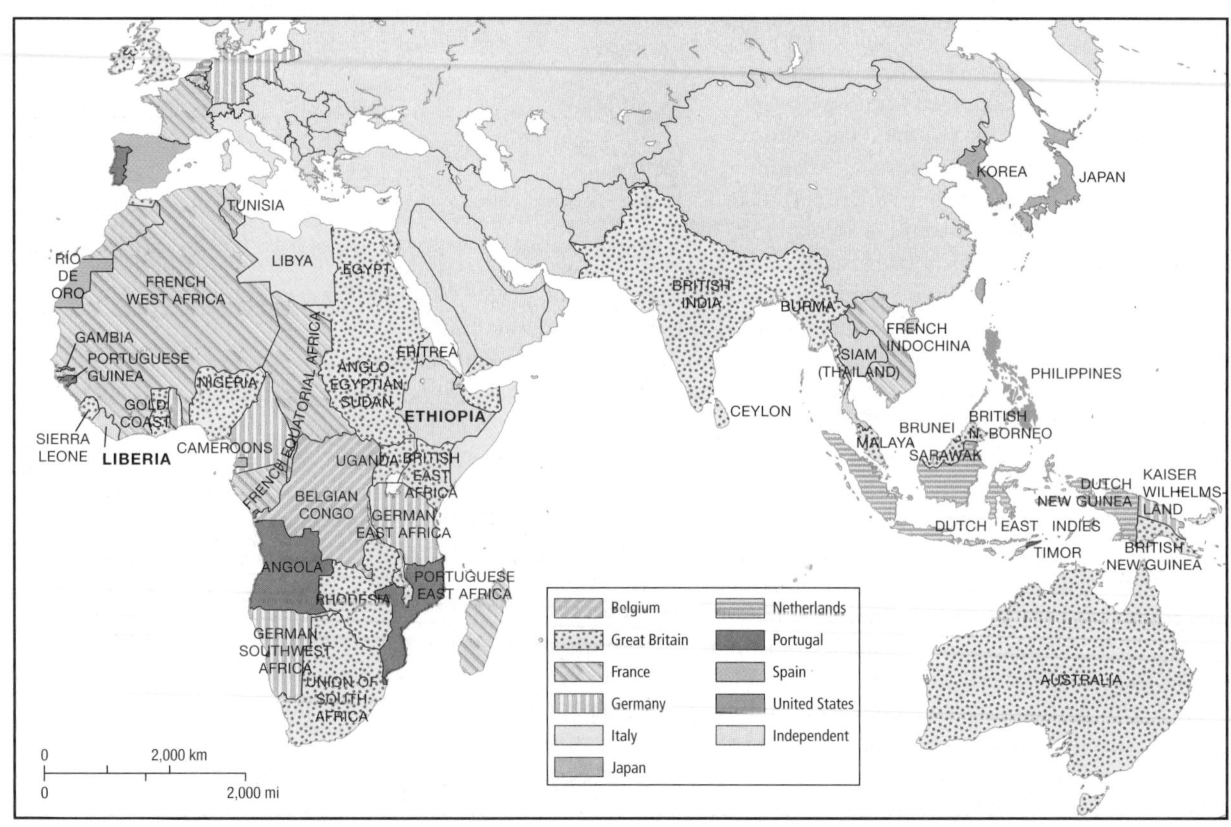

MAP 1.3 Africa and Asia, 1900

Certainly, imperial powers in the late nineteenth century were seeking to expand their control of territory and generate wealth, as they had always done. But because industrialization had progressed so dramatically in these countries during the 1800s, the focus was now also on finding markets in which to sell surplus goods as much as it was on acquiring access to inexpensive raw materials. That element was still relevant, which explains in part why New Imperialism targeted Africa and Asia, but it was not nearly as important as having trading partners that were dependent on importing your manufactured goods because they lacked the industrial capacity to create them on their own. And the competition for these markets was more intense because there were more imperial powers going after them. In the eighteenth century, Great Britain was far ahead of the others in terms of industrial capacity, but by the end of the nineteenth century, many other countries had caught up, most notably Germany, Japan and the United States.

Watch the Video *The Origins of Modern Imperialism and Colonialism* on mysearchlab.com

This competition extended beyond securing markets in which to sell goods. New Imperialism was driven by strategic and political considerations as well. On the one hand, New Imperialism was about establishing a physical (military) presence throughout the world to prevent others from expanding, and on the other the movement was about blocking competitors from doing the same. It became very important to hedge others in by making sure you controlled their neighbors. This focus on **geostrategic positioning** was very important in the early twentieth century. Perhaps most notably, it was during this wave of New Imperialism that two new participants entered the competition and very quickly moved to the forefront.

geostrategic positioning control of a territory based on how it's geographic and political factors meet your political and military goals

MAKE THE CONNECTION

Using the map below and your understanding of geostrategic positioning, identify which empires you think are the most powerful in 1900. What makes them powerful?

Japan

Like China, Japan was relatively isolated from the rest of the world until Great Britain, Russia and the United States began sending both trade ships and warships in the mid-nineteenth century. The Japanese rejected foreign intervention (sometimes violently)

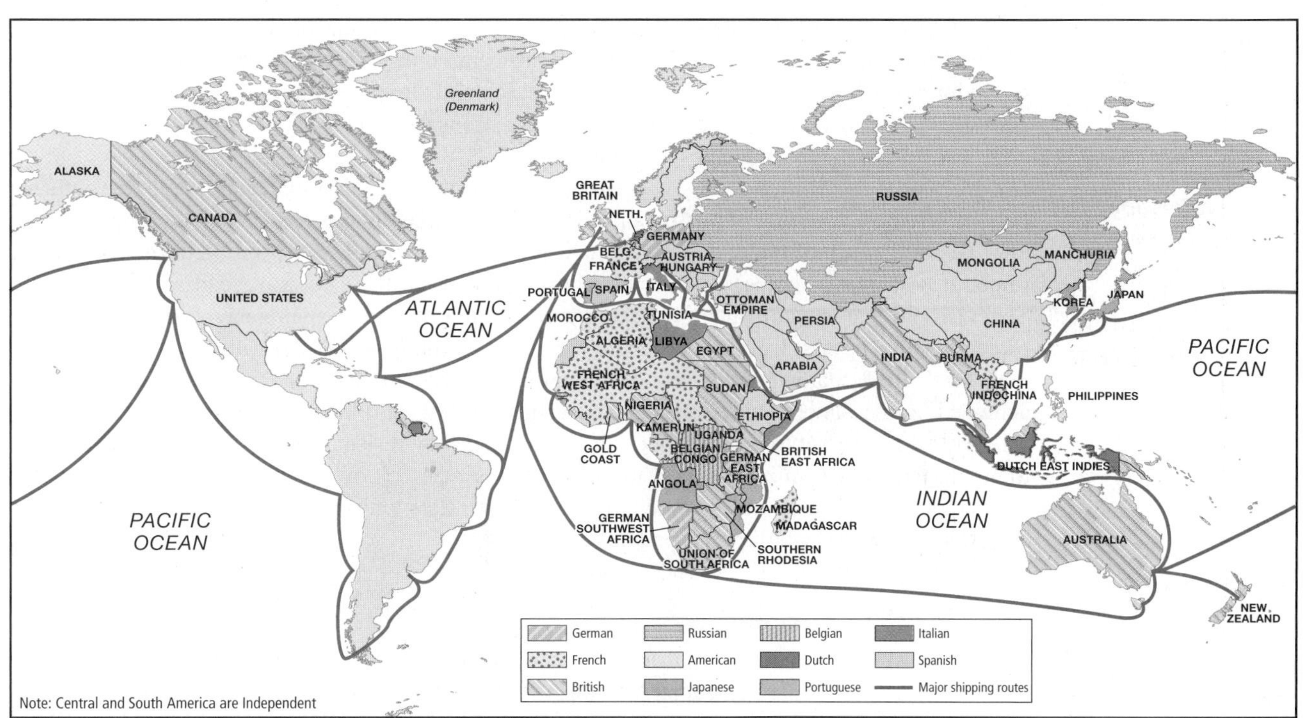

MAP 1.4 The Colonized World, 1900

shogun
the top military commander of Japan prior to the Meiji era

samurai
military social class of Japan; became the Imperial Army Officer Class during the Meiji era

Read the Document *Meiji Constitution* on mysearchlab.com

and were concerned about the increasing control the West held over China. Commodore Matthew C. Perry of the U.S. Navy regularly visited Japan in the 1850s to establish a U.S. presence in the Pacific, leading to a political crisis in Japan. In 1868, the leaders in the provinces decided they didn't trust what was going on between the U.S. Navy and the Japanese **shogun.** They feared that the government was developing agreements with the United States and demanded a return to strong imperial rule that would preserve Japanese independence by resisting interaction with the United States. Called the *Meiji Restoration* (after the new emperor Meiji took over in 1867), it was essentially a revolution that transformed the Japanese economic, social and political systems, abolishing feudalism and the **samurai** class in order to create a national imperial army. Although the Meiji Restoration clearly functioned as a centralized imperial government, there were many Western elements in the Meiji Constitution, including capitalism focused on aggressive industrialization. The wealth and technology created was invested into the military, and a powerful Japanese Empire was born.

At the turn of the twentieth century, Meiji Japan was a rising imperial power, demonstrated by its relatively effortless defeat of the Qing in the Sino-Japanese War of 1894–1895 over control of the Korean peninsula. This act of aggression signaled to the United States and Europe that Japan was clearly intent on building an empire in the Pacific, and this would most certainly require taking Chinese territory. This presented two challenges to the United States and European powers: (1) They were not willing to give up the economic benefits they were getting from China, and (2) Japan was becoming a formidable military rival.

.... the right of our manifest destiny to over spread and to possess the whole of the continent which Providence has given us for the development of the great experiment of liberty and federaltive development of self government entrusted to us.

—John O'Sullivan, 1845

The United States

In the late nineteenth century, the United States was completely different from just about every other country in the world in terms of its democratic political structure. After achieving independence in the late eighteenth century, the United States, throughout the nineteenth century, focused on rapid industrialization that was geared primarily toward generating wealth and a high standard of living for its citizens. Imperial expansion came in the traditional territorial sense as the United States moved across the North American continent, gaining land by militarily defeating the indigenous Native American tribes and Mexico and signing diplomatic treaties with France and Great Britain. The biggest challenge to the strength of the United States was an internal civil war fought in the mid-nineteenth century.

Manifest Destiny
American philosophy and movement arguing that the United States had a responsibility to God to spread its ideals of liberty and government across the North American continent

Spanish-American War
brief military conflict of 1898 that occurred in the Caribbean and the Pacific; the U.S. victory marked the end of the Spanish Empire and the U.S. acquisition of Puerto Rico, Guam and the Philippines

Militarily, the United States was isolationist for most of the nineteenth century, venturing outside of North America in pursuit of allies and trade agreements rather than conquering territory. But at the turn of the twentieth century, it was clear to the U.S. government that expanding imperial powers, particularly Japan, presented a potential threat to American soil. The United States would need to consider geostrategic positioning to limit Japan's aggressive growth and protect itself. The first truly imperialistic war (beyond the **Manifest Destiny** of North America) that the United States fought was the **Spanish-American War** of 1898. Among the gains achieved by the American victory was the acquisition of the Philippines in the Pacific. But the Filipinos did not want to be an American colony, and they resisted fiercely, requiring the United States to use heavy military action to hold onto its new colony. Within the United States, the Anti-Imperialist League was formed to oppose the military action in the Philippines and the new direction U.S. foreign policy seemed to be taking.

The "Rules" of New Imperialism

Clearly, the most successful countries in this age of imperialism were the sea-linked empires—Britain, the United States and Japan. But this represented a major change from the "rules" of previous imperialist activities. New Imperialists wanted to *transform* the entire economy and culture of the dominated area to their own benefit (economic and military). In the past, imperialists would have invaded the declining empires (the Qing and the Ottomans) and weak, unindustrialized territories (Asia and Africa), but conquering them required a lot of financial and military investment. It was more convenient, New Imperialists decided, to simply *control* them through trade by making agreements and treaties at major trading ports (for example, Istanbul in the Ottoman Empire and Canton and Shanghai in the Qing Empire). The weaker country generally had no choice but to comply in the face of potential war with a technologically superior military. Known as **gunboat diplomacy,** this tactic enabled the imperial countries to get all the economic and strategic benefits without incurring the costs of building and maintaining colonies. Rather than physically occupy a territory itself, the imperial power provided the elements needed for political and military reform and industrialization in the newly acquired territories—weapons, advisors and financial loans—so the governments of these territories were immediately in debt. The territory retained its own name, government and economy, but a foreign power was making all the decisions. And those decisions were clearly designed to benefit the imperial powers. By the turn of the twentieth century, between the colonies they held and the territories they influenced and dominated, the sea-linked imperial powers had control of the globe.

gunboat diplomacy pursuing foreign policy objectives by demonstrating and/or threatening to use overwhelming force; putting gunboats (warships) in the harbor of weaker powers was often enough to convince them to cooperate

The Direct Effects of Industrialization

In the nineteenth century, new discoveries were made in the fields of science that led to new technology—the Industrial Revolutions. First came the use of steam and iron—machines that could produce large quantities of consumer goods faster and more cheaply than human beings could. The Second Industrial Revolution delivered societal progress in the form of steel, chemicals and electricity. When the new science and technology that came with industrialization was applied to military power, the countries that did not possess industrial capability were at an obvious disadvantage in world affairs. Of course, the wealth gained from these resources and the technologies created by them were not equitably distributed within countries either, so the Industrial Revolutions and the vast wealth they created dramatically changed society.

The most pervasive internal consequence of the shift to cash-based economies caused by industrialization was the rise in size and power of the middle class. While the traditional wealthy elites owned the land, factories and shipping fleets, they certainly were not interested in working in them. So they hired educated people to do the accounting, to oversee shipping and transportation, to manage the daily operations and deal with the laborers. Managers, accountants, lawyers, importers, exporters and bankers all earned profit from the wealth that was generated. They used that money to buy things, so the demand for luxury goods and services increased. Restaurants and department stores opened; doctors and lawyers set up shops. Despite their access to the finer things in life, there was a clear distinction between the middle and upper classes. Middle class people had to go to work to earn their money, whereas the upper class did not work—they enjoyed the profits generated by other people working for them. Yet the middle class was clearly far better off than the poor laborers who dug in the mines and worked in the factories. Those people were paid the absolute minimum amount possible in order to increase profits so that the wealthy could afford to pay this expanding middle class. As the middle class gained a higher standard of living and fully integrated themselves as essential to industrial life, they demanded the privileges they believed came with wealth. The lower classes resented their upward mobility, and the upper classes viewed them as a threat to their power.

The evolution of scientific inquiry that led to the Industrial Revolutions also had a dramatic effect on how people viewed the world and their place in it. By the end of the nineteenth century, public education systems available to all social classes were in place in the advanced, industrialized countries of Great Britain, the United States and Germany. With the advent of the rotary printing press in the mid-nineteenth century, there were many relatively inexpensive sources of information for those who could read. People were exposed to the radical new understandings of natural and human existence coming from the fields of physics (Albert Einstein and Max

theory of natural selection
when change occurs in an environment, those organisms best suited to the new circumstances will thrive and those that are not ideally suited will die out completely; over time, this could result in a species changing enough traits to eventually become a totally different creature

Planck), philosophy (Friedrich Nietzsche), psychology (Sigmund Freud), and social and political theory (Max Weber). But these new theories about how the world functioned and humanity's role in the world were frequently inconsistent with the religious explanations that people had regarded as truth for centuries. This created an opening for debate—if we were wrong about the relationship between matter and time, perhaps we are also wrong about what happens to human matter after death! People began to question religious doctrines, morality and the human unconscious and social class systems.

One of the most controversial debates to spring from scientific inquiry in the nineteenth century centered on the work of an English naturalist and geologist, Charles Darwin. Based on fossils and specimens he collected during a five-year expedition to chart the coastline of South America, Darwin noticed how species evolved into other species, and he began developing his **theory of natural selection.** Darwin and other scientists investigated this premise throughout the mid-1800s; the investigations culminated in the publication of *On the Origin of Species by Means of Natural Selection, or The Preservation of Favoured Races in the Struggle for Life* in November 1859. The basic idea of this very popular text was succinctly stated in the opening:

> *As many more individuals of each species are born than can possibly survive; and as, consequently, there is a frequently recurring struggle for existence, it follows that any being, if it vary however slightly in any manner profitable to itself, under the complex and sometimes varying conditions of life, will have a better chance of surviving, and thus be naturally selected. From the strong principle of inheritance, any selected variety will tend to propagate its new and modified form.*

Caricature showing English naturalist Charles Darwin as a monkey hanging from the Tree of Science.

Darwin's theory referred to all animal species, which raised a major debate with regard particularly to the origin and evolution of human beings. All major religions assumed it to be divine, but Darwin's theory seemed to suggest otherwise, drawing a deep schism in the Western world that pitted church against science.

At the end of the nineteenth century, a very aggressive form of nationalism called Social Darwinism spread throughout the industrialized world. Although popularly named after Darwin's work, the concept of "survival of the fittest" among social and political communities first appeared in the work of philosopher Herbert Spencer before *Origin of the Species* was published. Spencer, along with political demographer Thomas Malthus and eugenicist Francis Galton, focused on competition between individuals as "the law of life." Those who possessed the skills necessary to excel in the competition (the "fittest") would survive and pass on those skills to future generations. According to Spencer, individuals who did not possess superior skills should "not be prevented from dying out;" hence, the phrase "survival of the fittest." Although the theory focused on individuals, it translated into larger communities just as easily. To Social Darwinists, the increasingly industrialized world around them was evidence that they were right—nations

MAKE THE CONNECTION

On January 9, 1900, U.S. Senator Albert J. Beveridge made a speech regarding the U.S. acquisition of the Philippines as a territory. In his speech, Beveridge stated:

> *Mr. President, this question is deeper than any question of party politics: deeper than any question of the isolated policy of our country even; deeper even than any question of constitutional power. It is elemental. It is racial. God has not been preparing the English-speaking and Teutonic peoples for a thousand years for nothing but vain and idle self-contemplation and self-admiration. No! He has made us the master organizers of the world to establish system where chaos reigns. He has given us the spirit of progress to overwhelm the forces of reaction throughout the earth. He has made us adepts in government that we may administer government among savage and senile peoples. Were it not for such a force as this the world would relapse into barbarism and night. And of all our race He has marked the American people as His chosen nation to finally lead in the regeneration of the world. This is the divine mission of America, and it holds for us all the profit, all the glory, all the happiness possible to man. We are trustees of the world's progress, guardians of its righteous peace... (Congressional Record. 56th Cong., 1st sess. Vol. XXXIII, pp.705, 711.)*

- Based on Spencer's explanation of Social Darwinism and Beveridge's interpretation of how it applies to foreign-policy decision making, do you think Social Darwinism provides an explanation as to why imperialism naturally occurred in human civilizations? Or do you think Social Darwinism was created to justify imperialist actions taken by powerful countries against weaker ones?
- Can you think of any historical examples in which the theoretical concepts of Social Darwinism were applied in practice? Can you think of any examples in the world today?

that possessed superior industrial technology had superior weapons and wealthier economies and thus controlled more territory than nations that did not. To ensure this kind of ongoing progress, those nations that could not adapt to the industrialized world should "not be prevented from dying out."

Read the Document *Social Darwinism* on mysearchlab.com

For Spencer and his contemporaries, competition naturally pushed social evolution in a direction that would lead to ever-increasing prosperity and personal liberty. Critics of Social Darwinism charged that it would create a violently self-interested world of constant conflict among nations. Arguing from political, social, economic and religious perspectives, they believed that Social Darwinism was fundamentally racially motivated and meant to justify the wave of New Imperialism tearing through Africa and Asia at the end of the nineteenth century. At its worst, it created a sense of European (white, Christian, industrial) superiority over all others in the world.

Ideological Revolutions against Conservatism

The establishment of what is called the "conservative order" in Europe in the nineteenth century goes all the way back to the French Revolution of the late eighteenth century. That violent event (along with the rise of American democracy) seemed to indicate that people wanted to live without emperors, monarchs and hereditary royal families. In reaction, those royal families spent much of the nineteenth century trying to firmly establish their power and legitimate rule. The methods of doing so varied by culture: Russia was clearly the most oppressive and violent in crushing revolutions, while Great Britain was the most willing to compromise to prevent potential revolutions from beginning. **Conservatism** in the nineteenth century refers to the desire, primarily on the part of those already in power, to maintain the monarchical/imperial system and prevent internal revolutions. But at the turn of the twentieth century, there were several ideological revolutions challenging the power of monarch in the Western world. Although each had its own particular goals, they shared a common commitment to destroying the structure of the existing conservative order and re-creating Western society.

conservatism political philosophy that favors the preservation of tradition over rapid change

Feminism

The first wave of modern political feminism appeared in Great Britain and France in the late eighteenth century and focused on gaining property rights and equal standing under the law. In 1791, French playwright Olympe de Gouge wrote *Declaration of the Rights of Woman and of the Female Citizen* in reaction to the *Declaration of the Rights of Man and of the Citizen* (1789), which defined the goals of the French Revolution and notably omitted the legal status of women. In 1792, Mary Wollstonecraft's *A Vindication of the Rights of Women* pointedly argued that women did not exist simply for the pleasure of man, and as equals they ought to be accorded such status in education, politics, and employment opportunities:

> *Probably the prevailing opinion, that woman was created for man, may have taken its rise from Moses's poetical story; yet as very few, it is presumed, who have bestowed any serious thought on the subject, ever supposed that Eve was, literally speaking, one of Adam's ribs, the deduction must be allowed to fall to the ground; or, only be so far admitted as it proves that man, from the remotest antiquity, found it convenient to exert his strength to subjugate his companion, and his invention to shew that she ought to have her neck bent under the yoke; because she, as well as the brute creation, was created to do his pleasure.*

suffrage the right to vote

abolitionism nineteenth- and twentieth-century movement in the Western world to outlaw slavery

Feminism did not become a truly organized movement until the nineteenth century when the focus shifted toward **suffrage.** In the United States, women such as Elizabeth Cady Stanton and Susan B. Anthony, who were leading the fight for **abolitionism,** demanded that concepts of liberty and freedom be applied to all Americans, women included. In the early twentieth century, British suffragette Emmaline Pankhurst and American suffragette Alice Paul increased the pressure on their governments as the feminist movement became increasingly radical and demonstrative. Although suffragettes in Russia were the first in the western world to achieve their goals of national political equality in 1906, most of the western industrialized countries followed suit within the first quarter of the twentieth century.

Liberalism

Enlightenment eighteenth-century intellectual and philosophical movement in the West focused on the power of human reason

propertied classes the upper and middle class who owned businesses, land, homes, etc.

Directly born from the political theories of the **Enlightenment,** liberals demanded an end to absolute monarchy. This was primarily a middle-class movement, led by men who had achieved wealth and consumer goods through employment but were still denied legal equality and access to government. Liberalism called for representative government dominated by the **propertied classes** and argued that the legitimacy of the government comes from the freely given consent of the governed. There should be an elected legislative body that limits the power of the monarch against individual citizens. But it is important to note that this was not democracy as we consider it today—the only people who would have representation in the government would be the propertied classes. Liberals also demanded minimal government interference in the economy, essentially overturning mercantilism, to increase the power and profit of the business owners. As for society, liberals believed in legal equality, religious toleration and freedom of the press. These were educated and relatively wealthy people, usually professionals who were excluded from the existing political process by virtue of social class standing. This was the new middle class that didn't have the family heritage to be nobility but certainly considered themselves to be above the laborers and peasants.

The specific issues addressed by liberalism differed according to the circumstances of each country's culture, but liberals all shared the common goal of acquiring political power by overturning the conservative order of the nineteenth century. Monarchs and the upper class dealt with the demands of liberals in different ways as well, ranging from compromising with them, as Queen Victoria did in Great Britain, to politically marginalizing them, as Russian tsars Alexander III and Nicholas II did.

Marxism

Another major change to the social class structure of industrial societies was the demand for unskilled labor to work in the factories. This demand drew peasants from the agricultural and artisan sectors into the towns, where payment for their services was guaranteed. In this way, the Industrial Revolutions led to the process of what German socialist Karl Marx called the **proletarianization** of the worker. In the **barter economy** that preceded industrialization, people traded finished goods, physical labor and services to others in exchange for their finished goods, physical labor and services. The goal was that each party got what they needed or wanted to support themselves and their families. In the industrial age, the goal of factory owners was to make a profit, which came only from selling their finished goods at high prices. They didn't want to trade for labor; they wanted to pay people the least amount of money possible to provide the labor to produce a large quantity of goods to be sold for profit for the factory owner. So when workers entered the **wage economy** created by industrialization, the only way they could support themselves and their families was to sell their labor for money. People were paid to show up at work and perform laborious tasks, but they no longer owned the means of production (tools, equipment, etc.); therefore, they no longer had control over their own trades—they made no decisions, and they made no profit. They simply worked for their paychecks while someone else owned and controlled the business. While this seems normal to us now, it was a huge change that had dramatic effects on the economy and society.

proletarianization downward social mobility, whereby people move from self-employment to working for someone else; they join the proletariat class of wage workers

barter economy the exchange of goods or services for other goods or services without the use of money

wage economy payment in the form of money to a worker in exchange for labor or services

In the *Communist Manifesto*, published in 1848, Karl Marx and his partner Friedrich Engels explained why the changes created by the proletarianization of the worker would develop into a huge problem for industrial societies. The *Manifesto* contends that human history is the story of humankind's learning to live with physical nature in order to produce the goods necessary for human survival. Historically, the organization of the means of production (getting what we need to survive) has always involved conflict between the classes who owned and controlled the means of production and those classes who worked for them. Marx believed that, in the nineteenth century, class conflict had become simplified into a struggle between the bourgeoisie (middle class) and the proletariat (workers), a struggle that the proletariat would eventually win. Because of their struggles (and presumably reading Marx's *Manifesto*), the proletariat would understand that the ongoing historical process of class conflict would continue unless there was a radical social transformation to eliminate the inherent social and economic evils in the structure of production. To avoid social class conflict, they would have to create a society in which everyone had what they needed and wanted to support their families, but no one had more than others. Everything society produced would be a public good to be distributed equitably to all who participated in the production system; if no one owned private property, there would be no social class distinctions and therefore no social class conflict. This, said Marx, is the culmination of human history, and it will happen not just for some people in some countries, but for all people in all civilizations.

Read the Document *The Communist Manifesto* on mysearchlab.com

According to Marx, this worldwide proletarian revolution is inevitable, and he provided historical and economic evidence to "prove" that it would happen when the workers of the world united to free themselves from the many oppressions of capitalism. Some nineteenth-century economic reformers used Marx's evidence as support for their platforms, but what made Marxism ultimately attractive to the lower classes was the promise of human liberation. Notice that major social and economic change comes from the people, by the people and for the people. No matter what kind of government you lived under, according to Marx, it is inevitable that the people will prevail. This was, of course, a major challenge to the conservative order of the nineteenth century.

Nationalism

Although nationalism in its most basic sense had certainly existed throughout human civilization, it became a major political movement in the nineteenth century, in large part because of centuries of imperialism. As countries expanded their borders through warfare and colonialism, the map of the world was completely redrawn. Geographic lines were shifted to create political

indigenous populations
the people originally born and living in a particular area

state
a territory with defined physical borders and a single recognized government that rules over the population

nation
a group of people who self-identify as a community connected by language, tradition, etc.

entities based on the "winners" and "losers" of conflicts rather than based on ethnic lines of **indigenous populations.** The world was drawn up according to which monarch took which territory from another, and by the mid-1800s the political entity of the **state** had very little relationship to the **nation(s)** of people living within it. According to nineteenth-century nationalists, people who are joined together by culture, history, language, etc., ought to also be joined together politically under the same form of government that best meets their unique needs. The nationalists wanted to once again redraw political and geographic lines to more closely coincide with groups of people, cultures or civilizations.

As a political movement, nationalists demanded no less than the destruction of imperialism, which led directly to colonial wars for independence and civil wars within countries comprised of multiple nations. Clearly, monarchs were not willing to arbitrarily give up territory and power, so they generally chose resistance over compromise. Another problem for nationalists was that it was often difficult to determine exactly where some ethnic groups began and others ended, which led to conflict between nationalities living together within a country. By the turn of the twentieth century, nationalist movements threatened to tear apart the established empires and the world order the empires had created.

The World in 1900

As the twentieth century began, monarchs were under attack internally by dissatisfied subjects and externally by countries challenging their power. The monarchs did what they could to hold on, compromising where necessary and exerting force where possible, making treaties and forging alliances. Because of their technological capacity and its military applications, the sea-linked empires were clearly in a stronger position than the territorial empires. In 1900, it was evident that the Ottoman and Qing empires lacked the stability, wealth and weapons to survive into the twentieth century.

Paris Exposition Universelle

The World's Fair in Paris opened on April 15, 1900, and closed on November 12. Seventy-six thousand exhibitors from fifty-eight countries participated in this event to mark the progress of human civilization at the turn of the century. More than 50 million people attended to witness such dramatic technological advances as the first talking films, moving sidewalks, the "aesthetic engineering" of steel architecture, and the diesel engine, all illuminated by strings of electric lights. Colonized countries were not allowed to design their own pavilions; instead, French architects recreated indigenous villages and temples to give visitors a taste of the "uncivilized" world. As the opening event of the twentieth century, this exposition quite clearly demonstrated the varying levels of scientific ingenuity among the countries of the world. With pavilions named the Palaces of Machinery, Industry, Civil Engineering and Transportation, and Mining and Metallurgy, there was no doubt as to who possessed superior technology entering the twentieth century.

While the United States had the most exhibits and won the most awards at the exposition, Germany clearly had the most imposing pavilions. Nonetheless, upon his return to the United States at the end of the exposition, Ferdinand W. Peck, Commissioner General of the United States to the Paris Exposition, told the *New York Times*:

> *It was admitted on all sides that the display of America was the most prominent of any of the foreign countries.... A much larger number of awards were allotted to Americans than to exhibitors of any other nation outside of France, thus showing the quality of their exhibits.... The commission received every courtesy and consideration from the French government and the representatives of other nations. They manifested at all times the fact that they recognized the greatness of America.* (December 23, 1900)

MAKE THE CONNECTION

Countries participate in world's fairs in order to show off their cultures and products, hoping to expand trade and promote their civilizations. How might Social Darwinist theories of the time affect how one viewed the exhibits at the Paris Exposition? Do you think Commissioner Peck was influenced by such theories as he assessed the exposition?

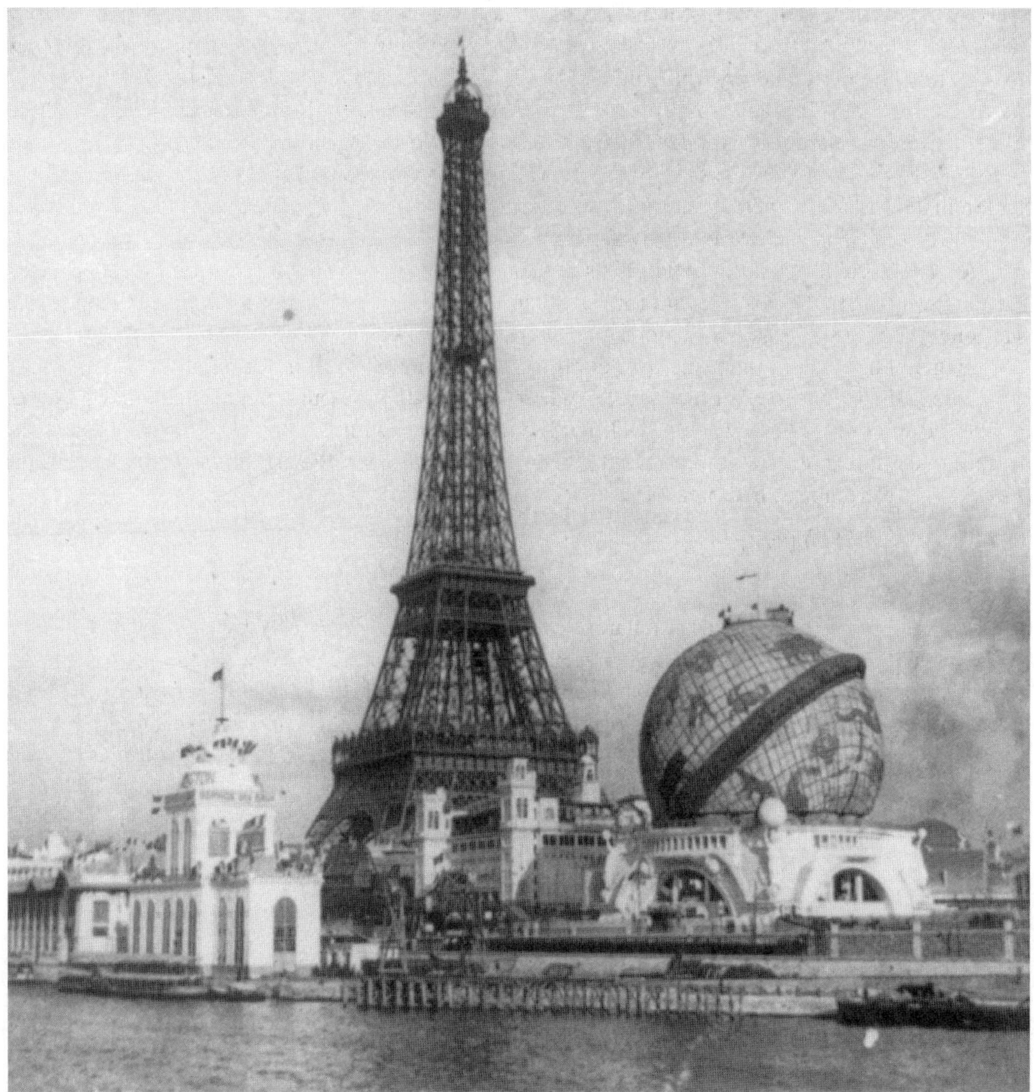

Forrestry [sic] Building and the globe from Point Passay, Paris Exposition, 1900.

The Boxer Rebellion

The pressures of internal disunity and heavy Western intervention had become too much for the Qing dynasty to deal with effectively by the end of the nineteenth century. The final blow to its power came when the Japanese Imperial Army successfully invaded Korea in 1894 and regional power shifted to Meiji Japan. It was obvious that Japan intended to continue its expansion and the Qing was unable to stop them. Although the Europeans and Americans were not happy about this shift, neither were they ready to risk an almost certain all-out war in the Pacific. In the fall of 1899, U.S. Secretary of State John Hay proposed to Great Britain, Japan, Russia, Germany, France and Italy what became known as the **Open Door Policy** in China. This was basically an agreement that no single country would attempt to conquer the weakened Qing dynasty, thus guaranteeing everyone access to economic gain without the cost of a war to maintain it. The agreement was, of course, primarily intended to limit Japan from further military action, and the Meiji regime was well aware of this. But Japan wasn't ready to risk war either, so all of the major powers consented to the concept of the Open Door Policy in the summer of 1900 and continued to challenge one another for control of **spheres of interest** in China.

Open Door Policy
an agreement among the world's major powers to respect the territorial integrity of China

spheres of interest
a region within a country that is economically dominated by an outside power

Chinese "boxer," 1900.

The people of China were deeply troubled by the Western economic and religious domination of Chinese culture and the seeming inability of their government to prevent it. Secret societies formed in the late 1890s to oppose the Qing dynasty, but Empress Dowager Cixi was able to redirect their anger toward the Western interventionists and began channeling aid to the secret societies in 1898 to oppose Christian activities in Chinese temples. By early 1900, the Empress openly supported a group called "The Righteous and Harmonious Fists," a predominantly religious society that believed ridding China of foreigners would usher in a new Golden Age of Chinese culture. In the West, these men became known simply as "the Boxers" because of their martial arts training.

In June 1900, 140,000 Boxers attacked the foreign embassies located near the Forbidden City in Peking, murdering foreign diplomats, Christian missionaries and even Chinese people who had converted. Empress Dowager Cixi allied with the Boxers, committing Imperial troops and declaring war against the West on June 21, 1900. The West responded quickly, sending an international force called the Eight-Nation Alliance that captured Beijing within months and forced the Qing dynasty to accept the Boxer Protocol of 1901, requiring massive political reform and allowing Western military forces to occupy China. This was the end of the Qing Empire.

Read the Document *Kaiser Wilhelm's Speech to His Troops* on mysearchlab.com

The Eight-Nation Alliance consisted of 50,000 troops from Japan, the United States, Great Britain, France, Germany, Russia, Italy and Austria-Hungary. The alliance was led by British commanders but comprised primarily of Japanese soldiers. Despite the differences between the world powers that participated in the alliance, they shared the common overarching goal of controlling China and, perhaps more importantly, preventing one another from doing so. The alliance also had the strong support of the European people, who were anxious to punish these "uncivilized" barbarians who killed Christian missionaries. The alliance's retaliation was brutal because it was grounded in outrage, revenge and nationalism, as evidenced by German Kaiser Wilhelm II's words as he sent his soldiers into battle: "Thus I send you now to avenge injustice, and I shall not rest until the German flag, united with those of the other powers, waves victoriously over the Chinese, planted on the walls of Peking, and dictating peace to the Chinese."

Queen Victoria's Funeral

Queen Victoria of England died on January 22, 1901, after serving as the British monarch for sixty-three and a half years in what has become known simply as the Victorian era. Many of the remarkable events and revolutionary movements discussed in this chapter occurred during her reign over the largest empire of the nineteenth century. She had nine children and thirty-four grandchildren who survived into adulthood, all of whom were married into European royal families, extending her influence throughout the Western world and earning her the nickname "the grandmother of Europe." In hindsight, Queen Victoria's death reflects the death of the conservative order in the West, ushered in by many of the changes she witnessed in her life.

Conclusions

Major changes occurred in the nineteenth century that dramatically impacted how people lived. Where the Industrial Revolutions took hold, social class systems were completely restructured by marked shifts in patterns of production and consumption. The scientific revolutions that accompanied these technological changes led to alternative and often competing perspectives on humanity's relationship with the natural and social worlds, shaking the foundations of long-held religious "truths."

In the face of such dramatic change, the conservative order led by monarchs came under fire, facing opposition from dissatisfied groups within society. Women, the new middle class, laborers and ethnic minorities became increasingly aware that their identities had been determined by a very small group of powerful men, and they demanded redress. Forced to respond to maintain their territory and power, governments either compromised with the demand for change or attempted to brutally crush it.

Technological advances also encouraged continuing imperialism, although the methods by which countries expanded and controlled others began to change. The direct correlation between industrial capacity, wealth and the size of an empire became clearer, allowing new players such as the United States and Japan to catch up quickly. Countries without technological capacity were at an obvious disadvantage in the shifting world order, and the powerful countries focused on geostrategic positioning to prevent their competitors from further expansion.

WORKING WITH THE THEMES

THE EFFECTS OF TECHNOLOGY What effect did the Industrial Revolutions have on internal economic and social class structures in the West? How did the Second Industrial Revolution affect the goals and methods of imperialism?

CHANGING IDENTITIES What was conservatism, and how was it challenged in the nineteenth century? What factors led to the rise of nationalism in the nineteenth century? In what ways did the United States struggle with its decision to become a sea-linked empire? How did Social Darwinism explain the international hierarchy?

SHIFTING BORDERS What factors led to the decline of territorial empires? How did New Imperialism of the late nineteenth century differ from imperialism of the fifteenth to eighteenth centuries? What happened in the Latin American colonies in the nineteenth century, and what lessons did it offer imperialists?

GLOBALIZATION Where did Karl Marx predict the proletarian revolution would occur? Why? What was the Open Door Policy, and how did it affect international relations at the turn of the twentieth century? How did the sea-linked empires structure the international economy?

Further Reading

TO FIND OUT MORE

Images et Savoirs: The Map as History. Available online at http://www.the-map-as-history.com
ExpoMuseum: Exposition Universelle. Available online at http://www.expomuseum.com/1900
Les Fearns: Casahistoria, Imperialism. Available online at http://www.casahistoria.net/imperialism.htm
Stuart Joseph Woolf: *Nationalism in Europe, 1815 to the Present*, Psychology Press (1996)

GO TO THE SOURCE

Edward Augustus Freeman: *Race and Language* (1879)
Carl von Clausewitz: *Principles of War* (1818)
John Stuart Mill: *On Liberty* (1869)
Mary Wollstonecraft: *A Vindication of the Rights of Woman* (1792)
Karl Marx and Frederich Engels: *Communist Manifesto* (1848)
Rudyard Kipling: *The White Man's Burden* (1899)
Charles Darwin: *On the Origin of Species* (1859)
Albert Einstein: *Relativity: The Special and General Theory* (1916)

MySearchLab Connections

Read the **Document** on **mysearchlab.com**

1.1 Jose Rufino Echenique, *Reflections on Revolutions*. The proliferation of Latin American caudillos (military leaders) in the post-independence era added to the fledgling republics' fragility. The most successful caudillos, like Peru's José Rufino Echenique, moved skillfully through multiple layers of society and built their alliances on personal, as opposed to strictly political, loyalties.

1.2 *Meiji Constitution*. Leaders of the early Meiji period in Japan sent several embassies abroad to Europe and the United States to study the Western political institutions and economic system. In their effort to modernize their country, the reform-minded Japanese wrote their first modern constitution.

1.3 Herbert Spencer, *Social Darwinism*. In the 1870s and 1880s, the theory of social Darwinism was devised by Herbert Spencer. It took the concept of evolution from Darwinism and applied it to the hierarchy of social classes. Many used the idea to exploit the poor and laboring classes.

1.4 Karl Marx and Friedrich Engels, *The Communist Manifesto*. Designed primarily as a propaganda piece, the Manifesto outlined modern socialism. Marx believed that laws governed both scientific and historical events. He predicted that the unequal distribution of wealth between different social classes would finally lead to open class conflict—revolution—in which eventually the working classes would seize power and create a classless society.

1.5 *Kaiser Wilhelm's Speech to His Troops*. The Boxer Rebellion in China sparked heated nationalistic rhetoric all over Europe. During the siege of Peking, some Europeans, including the German envoy and several missionaries, were killed by Chinese forces. When a military force was assembled in Germany for a punitive expedition. Kaiser Wilhelm made this impromptu speech to the soldiers.

Watch the **Video** on **mysearchlab.com**

1.1 *The Origins of Modern Imperialism and Colonialism*

2

The Great War: 1914–1918

CHAPTER OUTLINE

- Changes in Europe
- Surprise and Stalemate
- Revolutions Restructure Russia
- The United States Enters, and the Great War Ends

CHAPTER TIMELINE

1882	1890	1904	1905	1907
Triple Alliance is formed	German Chancellor Bismarck resigns	Russo-Japanese War begins	Einstein's *Theory of Relativity* is published	Triple Entente is formed Hague Convention establishes rules of war

Photos from left to right: German Machine Gunners in a trench; WWI gas mask; Vladimir Lenin; Woodrow Wilson.

1912	1914	1917	1918	1918
Balkan Wars begin	June: Austrian archduke is assassinated	March: Russian revolution establishes the provisional government	British women gain suffrage	November: The Great War ends
	July: War declarations are made in Europe	April: United States declares war on Germany	Russia exits war with the Treaty of Brest-Litovsk	
	August: Germany enacts Schlieffen Plan	November: Lenin takes over Russia in the Bolshevik revolution	Wilson announces his Fourteen Points	
	The gas mask is invented	Russian Civil War begins	The first U.S. troops are shipped out to Europe	

At the close of the Victorian era, Europe was changing. Nationalist and liberalist demands had given way to revolutions, and monarchs were increasingly forced to sacrifice absolute power to some form of oligarchic legislature. The largest of the European powers, Great Britain, sought continued expansion in the East. As the Ottoman Empire showed signs of weakness, the Russian Empire saw an opening for expansion to the south and east. In the center of Europe, the recently united German Empire tried to position itself for consideration as one of the world's great powers. The innate sense of competition for territory among these European powers was fueled by two factors: (1) staggering advancements in military technology as a result of investment in scientific inquiry and industrial capacity, and (2) a Social Darwinist interpretation of the world that alleged only the strongest nations would survive and the others must necessarily perish. As these factors came together in the early part of the twentieth century, the result was a war of unprecedented magnitude.

WORKING WITH THE THEMES

THE EFFECTS OF TECHNOLOGY Advanced military technology and weaponry leads to devastating casualties in the first Great War.

CHANGING IDENTITIES Nationalist violence sparks the creation of new countries in Central Europe. Communism takes over in Russia after Lenin's Bolshevik Revolution. Woodrow Wilson's *Fourteen Points* demand decolonization and self-determination for all.

SHIFTING BORDERS Nationalist tensions in the Balkans lead to regional violence that becomes the Great War. At the end of the Great War, the German, Austro-Hungarian, Ottoman, and Russian Empires no longer exist.

GLOBALIZATION Global alliances lead to worldwide conflict. Colonies and territories around the world are forced to participate, contributing troops and supplies.

Changes in Europe

Although colonists and the embittered Chinese people considered the West to have one identity, there were actually a lot of political, socioeconomic and nationalist divisions within the countries of Europe. Each handled the liberalist challenges to its rule differently, resulting in varying forms of democracy beginning to take hold in former absolute monarchies. Some countries suffered from deep nationalist divisions within their borders that grew increasingly violent. Furthermore, these nations had been competing with one another over territory for centuries and, by the turn of the twentieth century, had built powerful militaries to defend themselves from that ongoing and seemingly inevitable conflict.

The Rise of Wilhelm II

While the New Imperialists were working on their sea-based empire building in the late 1800s, Germany was quietly growing into a territorial empire under the leadership of the Prussian Prime Minister Otto von Bismarck, who achieved the growth through secret deals, alliances, economic incentives and outright war where necessary. Often considered the most important political development in Europe in the nineteenth century, the creation of a unified German Empire totally transformed the balance of economic, military and international power.

The German Empire was largely born out of Wilhelm I of Prussia's efforts to block the growing power of liberalism in the mid-1800s and his desire to industrialize and modernize to maintain power parity in Europe. Building on popular nationalist sentiment, Wilhelm I utilized the force of the very powerful Prussian army and the political cunning of Bismarck to conquer surrounding territory through the Danish War of 1864, the Austro-Prussian War of 1866 and the Franco-Prussian War of 1870. In 1871, Wilhelm I was crowned emperor of the German Empire, and he named Bismarck the Imperial Chancellor.

Between 1871 and 1890, Bismarck dominated Europe's diplomacy, successfully weaving a web of alliances to protect Germany. His first strategic move was to establish the Three Emperors' League in 1873 to bring together the three great conservative empires of Germany,

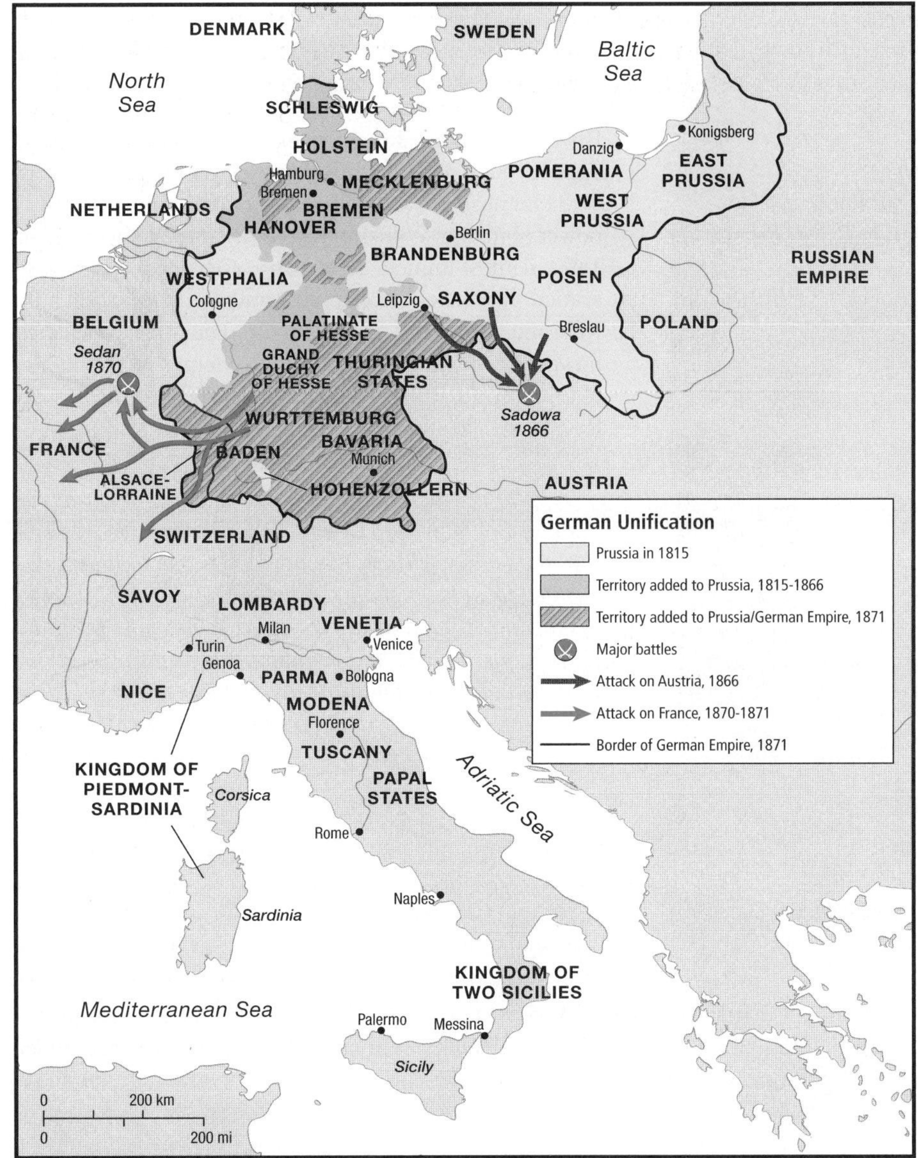

MAP 2.1 German Unification

Austria-Hungary and Russia. Although this alliance collapsed when Russia invaded the Ottoman Empire in 1877, Bismarck managed to maintain a defensive alliance with Austria (the Dual Alliance) and a neutrality agreement with Russia (the **Reinsurance Treaty**). Italy, recently united in 1870 and anxious to become a major player in European affairs, asked to join the Dual Alliance, and the **Triple Alliance** was formed in 1882.

When Wilhelm II became emperor in 1888, Bismarck found himself at odds with the new young leader when it came to foreign policy. As a teenager, Wilhelm (grandson of Wilhelm I) was an intelligent egomaniac with a bad temper. Perhaps due to his physically deformed arm or the mental illness that ran in the family, Wilhelm II was totally focused on proving his strength and power. Bismarck trained him to be a military-style leader so that he would rule the German Empire according to Bismarck's wishes. But Wilhelm was not satisfied with being the emperor of a powerful territorial empire—he believed Germany should expand its naval capabilities to become not only a sea-linked empire but to challenge Great Britain's status as the most powerful empire in the world.

Reinsurance Treaty
an 1887 agreement in which Russia and Germany both agreed to remain neutral should the other go to war with a third party; the agreement did not apply if Germany attacked France or Russia attacked Austria-Hungary

Triple Alliance
an 1882 alliance between Germany, Austria-Hungary and Italy promising *defensive* military support to one another

Wilhelm II, Germany.

I had a peculiar passion for the navy. It sprang to no small extent from my English blood. When I was a little boy. . . I admired the proud British ships. There awoke in me the will to build ships of my own like these some day, and when I was grown up to possess a fine navy as the English.

—Kaiser Wilhelm II, from the autobiography, *My Early Life*

In early 1890, the conflict between Bismarck and Wilhelm reached a turning point over domestic policies. Bismarck was adamantly pushing anti-Socialist legislation that ran counter to Wilhelm's social policies. Bismarck interfered both openly and behind the scenes to oppose much of Wilhelm's domestic policy platform, and Wilhelm pushed back with legislation to limit Bismarck's power. Finally, Wilhelm forced Bismarck to resign in 1890. Almost immediately, many of Bismarck's carefully crafted alliances collapsed, most dangerously the Reinsurance Treaty with Russia. The Triple Alliance, however, remained intact, as did Wilhelm's foreign policy objectives. In 1901, Wilhelm told the North German Regatta Association:

> *In spite of the fact that we have no such fleet as we should have, we have conquered for ourselves a place in the sun. It will now be my task to see to it that this place in the sun shall remain our undisputed possession, in order that the sun's rays may fall fruitfully upon our activity and trade in foreign parts, that our industry and agriculture may develop within the state and our sailing sports upon the water, for our future lies upon the water.*

Though his uncle Edward VII ruled the British Empire, Wilhelm aggressively pursued the development of a German navy specifically designed to rival Britain's. Wilhelm publicly declared that he did not want war with Britain; his intent was to create enough of a threat in the North Sea to force Britain to give in to German demands in international affairs. But Edward VII, viewing Germany's naval buildup as a direct threat to Britain's military and trade security, responded by building up Britain's Royal Navy, leading to a naval arms race in the North Sea in the early 1900s.

The End of the Ottoman Empire

The beginning of the twentieth century was particularly difficult for the rapidly declining Ottoman Empire. As a result of a series of wars with Russia and nationalist independence movements in the 1800s, the empire was territorially smaller, politically weaker, and financially indebted to the British and French, with whom the Ottoman government had formed partnerships in an effort to modernize the military and protect its borders. Internally, the empire was sharply divided by religion, ethnic nationalism, culture and socioeconomic status, creating ongoing civil unrest.

Young Turks
a coalition of military, nationalist and political groups that demanded reform in the Ottoman Empire

Balkan League
an alliance of Bulgaria, Montenegro, Greece and Serbia, countries that had earned their independence from the Ottoman Empire

In July 1908, a reform movement led by the **Young Turks** and supported by the military staged a revolution in the Ottoman Empire, forcing the Sultan to restore constitutional government and reconvene the Parliament. Unfortunately for the revolution, ethnic nationalism made it almost impossible for the democratic government to compromise. Capitalizing on the instability, Austria-Hungary annexed Bosnia and Herzegovina (the Bosnian Crisis) in October 1908; Italy seized Ottoman provinces in North Africa in 1911 (the Italo-Turkish War); and the **Balkan League** declared war against the Ottoman Empire in 1912 to free Macedonia, Albania and Thrace (First Balkan War). The following year, the members of the Balkan League turned against one another

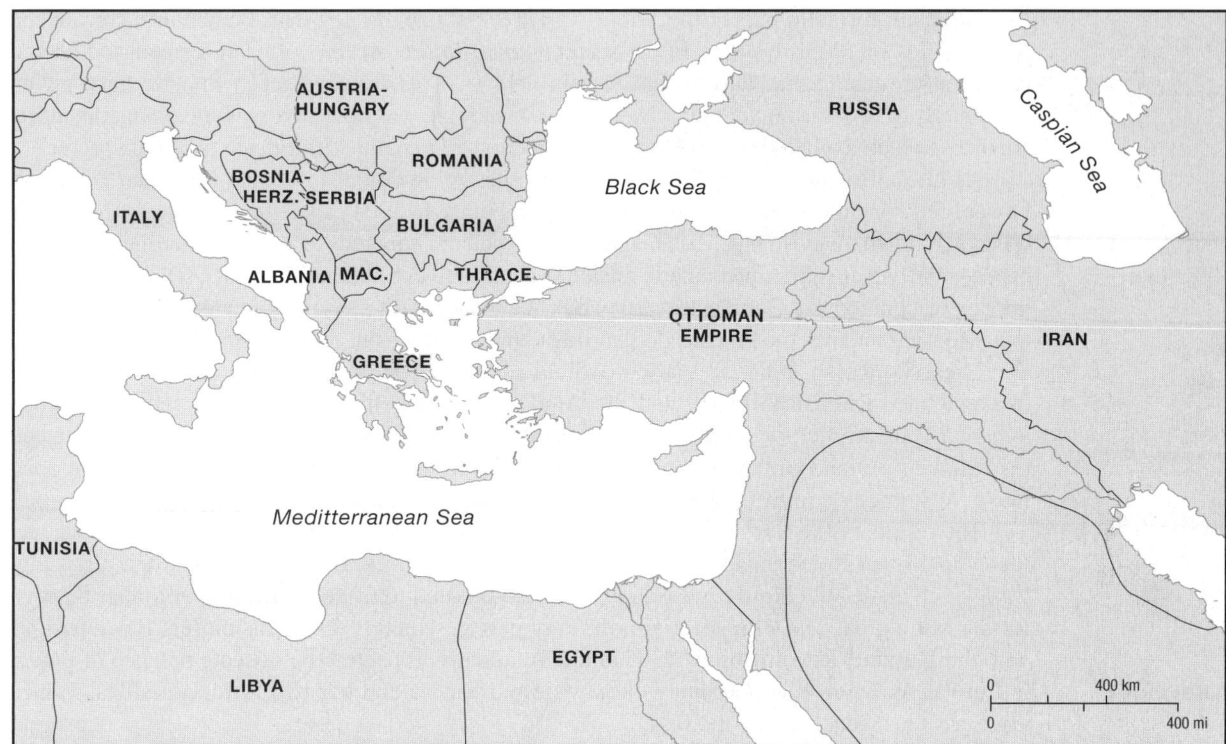

MAP 2.2 Ottoman Empire and the Balkans

over the division of the territory they gained in the Second Balkan War. These attacks, combined with the Young Turks' political revolution and nationalist uprisings in Bosnia, Morocco, Macedonia, Turkey, Bulgaria, Albania and Serbia, clearly signaled the end of the Ottoman Empire.

The "great powers" of Europe had very particular goals when it came to the dissolution of the Ottoman Empire. Russia had always sought access to the Mediterranean Sea and supported Serbia and Bulgaria in their efforts. Great Britain wanted to prevent Russia from expansion as well as maintain access to the oil fields in the Middle East, where France was also hoping for territory. Austria-Hungary needed the Ottoman Empire to survive—if nationalism could destroy the Ottoman Empire, the same could happen to Austria-Hungary. It also had a vested interest in preventing Serbia from gaining territory and power. Germany was hoping to keep the Ottoman Empire intact simply so that Germany could colonize the entire region and prevent Great Britain access to the oil fields. As a young nation, Italy was hoping to gain territory and become a power player in European affairs. None of these countries was about to let the Ottoman Empire fall apart without interfering to secure its own goals.

LINING UP FOR WAR

Triple Alliance	1882
Franco-Russian Alliance	1894
Anglo-Japanese Alliance	1902
Franco-Italian Accord	1902
Entente Cordiale	1904
Russo-Japanese War	1904
First Moroccan Crisis	1905
Anglo-Russian Entente	1907
Triple Entente	1907
Bosnian Crisis	1908
Second Moroccan Crisis	1911
Italo-Turkish War	1911
First Balkan War	1912
Second Balkan War	1913

Alliances

Wilhelm II's aggressive imperialism and the Triple Alliance of Germany, Austria-Hungary and Italy worried the nations that surrounded them. As early as 1894, France and Russia signed the *Franco-Russian Alliance*, a military alliance designed to increase each nation's power and limit Germany's expansion. Under Queen Victoria, Great Britain remained isolationist in European affairs but was concerned about Russia's expansion in the Pacific after Russia moved into China. In 1902, Edward VII of England concluded an alliance with Japan, the *Anglo-Japanese Alliance*, worded so that it applied to the defense of British interests in the Far East (Australia, New Zealand and islands throughout Polynesia, Micronesia and Melanesia) against Russia. In response, Russia strengthened its relationship with France; and China and the United States vocally opposed what they perceived as Britain's support of Japanese imperialism.

Although formally part of the Triple Alliance, Italy negotiated with France over territory in North Africa in 1902, resulting in the secret *Franco-Italian Accord*. This agreement included a condition promising that Italy would remain neutral if Germany attacked France. Italy, trying desperately to become an integral power player in Europe, was now clearly involved in competing alliances, which explains why the Italians wanted the agreement with France to remain secret.

As Great Britain emerged from several decades of isolationism on the European continent, Edward VII concluded a series of agreements with France in 1904 called the *Entente Cordiale*. This was not a formal treaty so much as an agreement to end the hundreds of years of intermittent conflict between the two countries, particularly related to respecting one another's colonies. There was also an implicit recognition that German expansion must be blocked, but no explicit military alliance was tied to it. Most importantly, the Entente Cordiale kept both countries out of the impending war in the East.

The 1904 Russo-Japanese War put Britain and France at opposite ends of the table because of the Franco-Russian Alliance and the Anglo-Japanese Alliance. Although most of Europe assumed Russian victory against the fairly new Meiji military machine, the Japanese defeated the Russians on land and at sea in a year and a half. In just three decades, Japan had developed into a Western-style industrial powerhouse that clearly dominated the Pacific.

The results of the Russo-Japanese War were dramatic. Russia lost its territory in China, and Japan controlled Korea unchallenged. Neither France nor Great Britain followed their allies into war, which made Wilhelm II question just how committed to these alliances everyone truly was. Russia lost a great deal of respect as a military power, which had serious internal repercussions with the **Russian Revolution of 1905** and dramatically impacted the delicate balance of power in Europe. Wilhelm II of Germany clearly viewed Russia and her two European allies, France and Serbia, as weakened by the loss.

Wilhelm II decided to test how strongly Britain and France were committed to their Entente Cordiale by directly challenging France's **protectorate** of Morocco in North Africa (*First Moroccan Crisis*). Wilhelm himself traveled there in March 1905 to promote Moroccan independence from French control, but he seriously miscalculated Europe's reaction. Britain, Russia, Spain, the United States and even his ally Italy strongly supported the French, driving them even closer together in opposition to Germany and its only supporter, Austria-Hungary. This made it very clear to Wilhelm that his plans for expansion might result in a potentially devastating two-front war against France and Great Britain to the west and Russia to the east. The Schlieffen Plan, named after the general who created it, was devised in December 1905 to enable Germany to initiate and win a two-front war. Relying on incredible speed and good timing, the German military would invade the neutral states of Luxembourg and Belgium, surprise France and force them into surrender (all within six weeks), then swing back across Germany via a newly created rail system to the eastern front, where the notoriously slow-moving Russian army would just be mobilizing. As Wilhelm put it, he would have "Paris for lunch, St. Petersburg for dinner."

Germany's intervention in Morocco proved Wilhelm's imperialistic goals and required surrounding empires to work together. In 1907, it made sense for Britain to get along with France's other major ally, Russia, and the *Anglo-Russian Entente* created an agreement regarding imperial borders, particularly in the Middle East. The result was the **Triple Entente,** an informal but very powerful association of Great Britain, France and Russia to counterbalance the power of the Triple Alliance of Germany, Austria and Italy.

By 1911, the competing alliances were firmly in place. Nationalism was turning to widespread violence in the Balkans and Ottoman Empire. The naval arms race between Great Britain and Germany had escalated since the launching of the ***HMS Dreadnought*** in 1906, requiring Germany to intensify its efforts to compete with the British navy. A 1911 rebellion in Morocco provided the perfect opportunity for Germany to show what she had accomplished. When the people revolted against the Sultan, France and Spain sent in troops to put down the rebellion. The *Second Moroccan Crisis* was ignited by the arrival of a German gunboat (the *SMS Panther*) in the Port of Agadir. Germany argued it was there to protect German citizens and financial interests in Morocco, but it was a classic example of gunboat diplomacy attempting to intimidate France into negotiating with

Russian Revolution of 1905
revolution and reform movement against the Romanov dynasty; though the tsar stayed in power, he made many political concessions, including the creation of a legislative branch (the Duma)

protectorate
a weaker country under the partial military control of a superior power in the name of "protecting" them from others

Triple Entente
1907 informal alliance between Great Britain, France and Russia that encircled Germany and Austria-Hungary in an attempt to block their expansion

HMS Dreadnought
a British battleship utilizing remarkably advanced technology; required all other navies to catch up quickly to remain in the naval arms race

MAP 2.3 Alliance Systems in 1914

Germany over control of North African territory. Great Britain sent warships to the region in support of the Entente Cordiale and to prevent Germany from establishing an unchallenged naval presence in Morocco. The resulting treaty allowed France to seize full control over Morocco but gave much of the Congo to Germany. More importantly, this incident strengthened the Triple Entente and further deepened the hostilities between Great Britain and Germany.

Europe finally exploded in 1914. Decades of aggressive imperialism, competing alliances, rampant militarism and demands for social and political change culminated in an intensely competitive environment in which, according to Social Darwinist interpretations of civilization, only the strongest would survive. While all of these factors were certainly in play at the time, it was the exceedingly complex and violent nationalism in the Balkans that provided the spark for war.

Surprise and Stalemate

Nationalist-driven violence was certainly nothing new in the Balkans and what was left of the Ottoman Empire, so it was somewhat surprising that a politically motivated assassination in the region could lead to such large-scale warfare. Indeed, even as the fighting began, no government involved thought it would take much longer than six months to wrap up, because each believed its alliance was clearly superior to the other. Instead, the violence dragged into one of the deadliest conflicts in human history.

The Trigger

On June 28, 1914, a Bosnian nationalist named Gavrilo Princip, from a group called Young Bosnia, assassinated the heir to the imperial throne of Austria, Archduke Franz Ferdinand, and his wife, Sophie. Although this was certainly a terrible crime, the impetus for war was not obvious until Princip's subsequent interrogation, which revealed that the assassination was probably not the act of a lone, angry Bosnian but rather part of Serbia's ongoing efforts to foster nationalist revolutions in Eastern Europe.

Many nationalist and independence movements had appeared in Bosnia since Austria-Hungary took it over in 1908, but the Young Bosnia movement in particular was directly linked to the **Black Hand,** a well-established antigovernment group in Serbia. So it was the Black Hand operating out of Serbia that provided the weapons, plans and coordination for the assassination of Archduke Ferdinand. This put the Serbian government, which clearly could not control the Black Hand, in a difficult position.

Black Hand
an antigovernment group in Serbia led by Serbian military officers; it fostered nationalist revolutions in Serbia, Bosnia and Herzegovina and Macedonia

From Austro-Hungarian Emperor Franz Josef's perspective, the destabilizing force of Serbian nationalist movements in the Balkans had to be stopped, and if the Serbian government couldn't do it, he would have to. But action against Serbia was dangerous. Russia was opposed to the expansion of both the Austro-Hungarian and Ottoman Empires, and Russia supported Serbia's efforts to encourage Slavic nationalist movements in the Balkans. Austria-Hungary would most certainly need the military help of its ally Germany if Russia came to Serbia's defense. Wilhelm was so confident that his Schlieffen Plan and powerful navy would ensure victory that he promised full German military support, but under the condition that it be kept secret lest the European leaders think he was

The arrest of Gavrilo Princip.

MAKE THE CONNECTION

- How does the assassination of Franz Ferdinand relate to internal problems the conservative order faced at the turn of the century? Why do you think Franz Josef felt compelled to send a letter of explanation to royal families of Europe?
- When you read Document 2.1, do you get the feeling Austria-Hungary was looking for a way to rectify the situation or for an excuse to declare war? Does Serbia's response surprise you?
- How do the problems of the nineteenth century shape the first war of the twentieth century?

trying to incite war. It took weeks for the Austro-Hungarian government to decide on the best path to pursue, but it finally issued a harsh ultimatum to the Serbian government on July 23, 1914, blaming it directly for the many acts of terrorism committed by "subversive movements" within Austria-Hungary. The Serbian government was clearly offended to be implicated in the assassination, stating that it "cannot be held responsible for manifestations of a private character," and mobilized its army on July 25, 1914. In response, Austria-Hungary declared war on Serbia on July 28.

Read the Document *Austria-Hungary's Ultimatum to Serbia* on mysearchlab.com

The Balkan Conflict Spreads Worldwide

What was supposed to be a regional conflict to settle aggravated territorial disputes, and nationalist demands quickly became a full-blown war due to the entangling alliances in place:

- Russia was committed to supporting Serbia and announced on July 31 that it would begin the process of mobilizing its military. Underneath the nationalist-rallying flag, of course, was Russia's obvious desire to position its military in the Balkans in case territory from the crumbling Ottoman Empire became "available," giving Russia full control of the Black Sea.
- As Germany promised, it came to Austria-Hungary's aid and declared war on Russia on August 1 and followed with a declaration of war against France (Russia's ally) on August 3. On August 4, practically as it invaded, Germany declared war on the neutral country of Belgium.
- Germany's invasion of Belgium forced Great Britain to support a long-standing treaty with Belgium, so Great Britain declared war on Germany on August 4.
- On August 6, Austria-Hungary officially declared war on Russia.
- Honoring the treaty with Great Britain, Japan declared war on Germany on August 23, and two days later Austria-Hungary declared war on Japan.
- In August 1914, under pressure from the German government, the Ottoman Empire formalized its support of Germany with the Turco-German Alliance; however, the Ottomans did not actually enter the war until Turkey bombed Russian ports on the Black Sea on October 28. Russia, Britain and France declared war on Turkey on November 4.
- By extension of alliances, all declarations of war against Germany also included Austria-Hungary. The war further extended throughout the globe as colonies and dominions were pressed into providing military and financial support to the direct participants.
- Although it was formally part of the Triple Alliance, Italy remained neutral at the outset of war due to its interpretation of the agreement and its secret alliance with France. Italy argued that the language of the Triple Alliance very clearly stated that countries were committed only to *defend* one another if they were attacked. Because both Austria-Hungary and Germany initiated the declarations of war against others, these were offensive actions, and Italy was, therefore, not bound by the Triple Alliance.
- President Woodrow Wilson declared absolute neutrality for the United States, based both on his personal stance and public opinion in the United States.

ALLIES

British Empire
France
Belgium
Serbia
Russian Empire (until November 1917)
Italy (April 1915)
Greece (October 1915)
Romania (August 1916)
Albania
Montenegro
Portugal (March 1916)
Algeria
Empire of Japan

CENTRAL POWERS

German Empire
Austro-Hungarian Empire
Ottoman Empire
Bulgaria

NEUTRAL COUNTRIES

Switzerland
Netherlands
Norway
Sweden
Denmark
Spain
United States (until April 1917)

Once it became obvious that this was not going to be a local Balkan conflict settled between Serbia and Austria-Hungary, all participants mobilized their militaries and initiated their war plans. Serbia's plan was quite simple: get everyone you can, and put them on the border against Austria-Hungary. Austria-Hungary's plan also was narrowly focused on Serbia, with only a few units in place to prevent Russian aid to Serbia; it was assumed that Germany would handle the Russian military. Russia had two plans prepared; one was based on a full German assault against Russia, and the other assumed (correctly) that Germany would go after France first and foremost. Russia mobilized for the first plan then followed the second plan after Germany made its initial move.

On August 4, 1914, Germany enacted its Schlieffen Plan, invading the neutral country of Belgium in a surprise attack. Conquering Belgium quickly was essential to the success of the plan, but Belgian troops engaged Germany at the Battle of Liege for almost two weeks (August 5–16), slowing down Germany's progress and earning their country the nickname "brave little Belgium." The French knew that the German military was obviously headed for them, but they made a major miscalculation about Germany's goals, assuming that going through Belgium was a ploy to draw French forces north while Germany launched a full-scale invasion farther south. But as France sent its troops to the French-German border, German troops entered France through Belgium, split into two units and stopped outside of Paris to wait for supplies. This hesitation, a deviation from the Schlieffen Plan, may have cost the Germans the easy victory they planned for in the west. French troops had time to turn around and engage the German army at the first Battle of the Marne from September 5–10. By the middle of September, the German army was stopped, the first trenches were dug, and the western front was established.

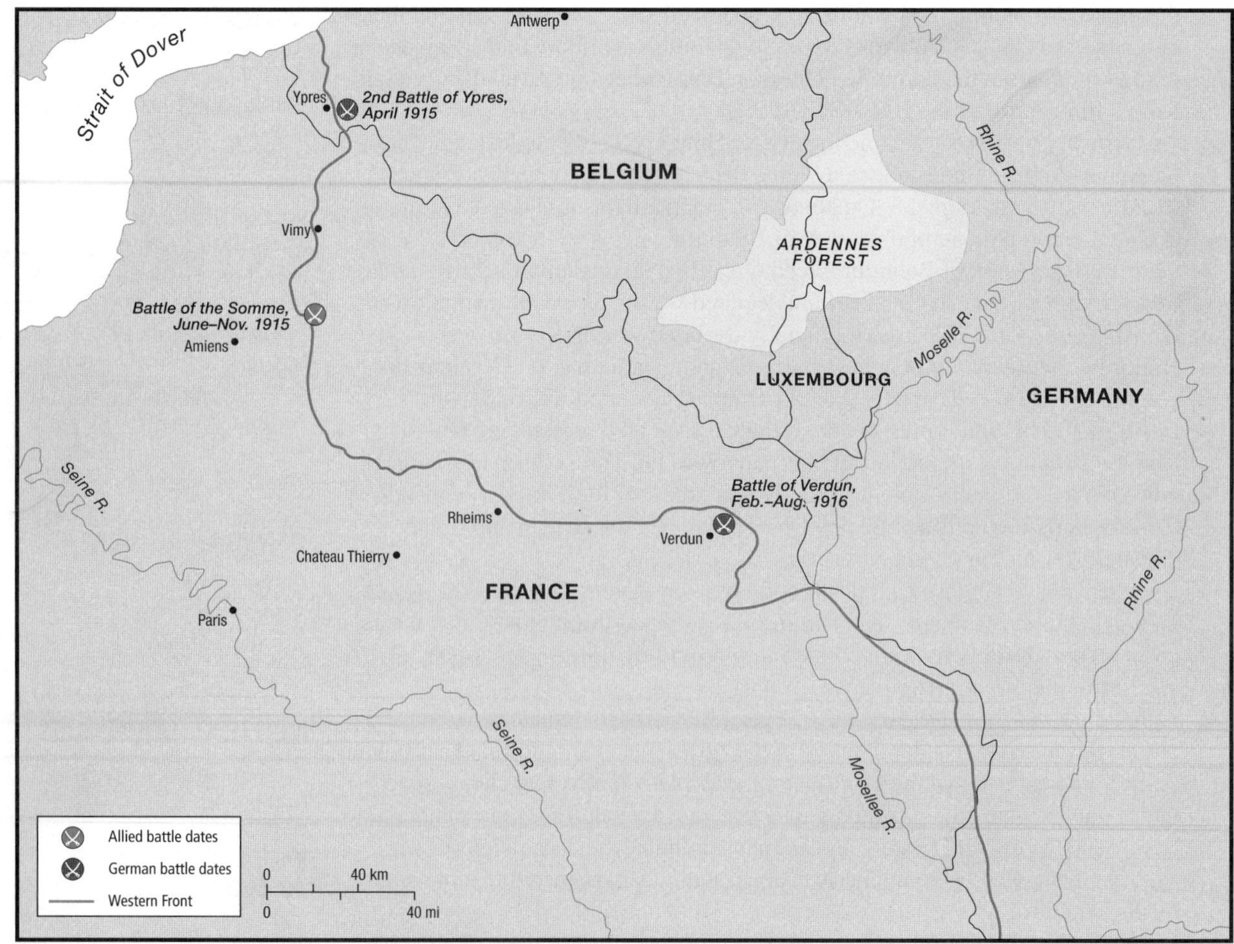

MAP 2.4 Stabilization of the Western Front, 1914

On the southern front, Austria-Hungary began invading Serbia on July 29, but Serbia put up an excellent (and somewhat surprising) defense for the first year of the war. Unfortunately for Serbia, two things came together in the fall of 1915 that guaranteed its demise. First, the Serbian military was struck with a typhus epidemic that killed many and weakened the rest of the troops. Then, in October 1915, Bulgaria entered the war for the specifically stated purpose of gaining territory from Serbia after its defeat. The following month, Austro-Hungarian, German and Bulgarian forces invaded Serbia, and they fully occupied it by November 15, 1915.

On the eastern front, the military activity between the Germans and Russians began in mid-August with Russia's unexpected invasion of East Prussia. The German High Command thought that Russia would be slow to mobilize, giving the German military time to defeat France. When Russian troops crossed into Germany on August 17, 1914, German strategists were forced to rethink their plans. They recovered well, and the largest victory the Germans had on any front during the war occurred on August 26, 1914, at the Battle of Tannenberg, where they decisively defeated a Russian force of 350,000. The Russian military was pushed completely out of Germany and off its war plan.

Stalemate on Land

The Allies had a definite advantage in numbers, financial resources and command of the sea. But the Central Powers had the advantages of internal supply lines and of having struck and positioned themselves first. So both sides were relatively equally matched, and because of the new long-range weapons created by the technology of the Second Industrial Revolution, the key feature of the "Great War" was **stalemate.** The entire western front quickly became a quagmire of very ugly and very deadly trench fighting, which basically lasted throughout the entire war.

stalemate
an unresolved situation in which it is impossible for either side to move forward; a deadlock

trench warfare
a stalemated situation in which both sides are in fortified positions (ditches); sometimes viewed as a military tactic or weapon to demoralize the enemy

Trench warfare was not a particular strategy of any side nor really a position in which any military wanted to find itself. Trench warfare was a matter of survival given the long-range artillery and chemical weapons used during the Great War. The best protection from long-range artillery was to take shelter from it, either underground or as close to the ground as possible to minimize vulnerability. In the first six months of the war, nearly 6,250 miles of trenches were dug on the western front alone. By the end of the war, approximately 12,000 miles of trenches crisscrossed eastern and western Europe.

The Allies constructed open-air trenches in three parallel but zigzagged rows: the frontline trench for firing, the support trench behind it with backup men and weapons and the reserve trench several hundred yards behind in case of emergency. Communications trenches connected these three rows, and the men rotated between the rows throughout roughly one month so that a person never spent more than one week at a time in the firing trench unless a major offensive was underway. Allied trenches were built to be temporary because they assumed they would break through the German lines quickly and move forward. Unfortunately for the soldiers, particularly on the western front, trench warfare lasted from fall 1914 through spring 1918. Life in these trenches was brutal: the trenches were open to all weather conditions, which lead to "trench foot," and infested with rats and lice, which led to "trench fever." The labor was difficult, living conditions were terrible, food supplies were sometimes scarce and the stench was overwhelming. There were unpredictable sniper attacks, enemy shelling and poisonous gas infiltrations, which resulted in dead bodies that could not be properly buried. One-third of the Allied casualties on the western front were killed or wounded in the trenches.

Watch the Video *The Outbreak of World War I* on mysearchlab.com

Between the Allied and the German trenches was a space called "no-man's land." This space was filled with barbed wire and patrolled by snipers and machine gunners from both sides to prevent the enemy from moving into it.

Conditions in the German trenches were much better because German trenches were built as relatively permanent structures, with large underground spaces for shelter. The Germans too built a frontline trench, a support trench and a reserve trench, but their communications trenches generally were underground tunnels. The Germans were in a defensive position and knew they would be there awhile (if all went well for them), so their trenches were built with luxuries such

ANALYSIS

Using the database at Poets.org, read the following poems about the Great War:

"The Soldier" was written by British soldier Rupert Brooks in 1914 as the war began.

"Dulce et decorum est" ("It is Sweet and Fitting to Die for One's Country") was written by British soldier Wilfred Owen in 1917.

Compare these two poems. What is different about them? Why? If you could respond to each poet, what would you say?

as electricity, toilets and beds. Concrete reinforcements prevented the muddy mess that Allied trenches often became. Of course the Germans still suffered from rats, lice, trench fever, improperly buried bodies, sniper attacks, shelling and the horrible effects of mustard gas.

The western front was not the only stalemate to develop during the Great War. In the secret Treaty of London in April 1915, the Allies promised Italy territorial gains at the end of the war in exchange for Italian entry into the war to defeat Austria-Hungary. So on May 23, 1915, Italy ended its neutrality and entered the war on the side of the Allies. Italian and Austro-Hungarian troops were almost immediately stalemated along their mostly mountainous, shared border, and there were ongoing battles for control of the Isonzo River that lasted through the end of 1917.

On the eastern front, the Austro-Hungarian army was weak and lost ground quickly, but the Russian army was poorly supplied and couldn't hold onto what it gained. In the spring of 1915, the Germans took command of the eastern front for the Central Powers. Their first offensive against Russia was so successful it triggered the collapse of an entire Russian front line; the German military moved far into Russian territory, and the Russian military was in disarray. Tsar Nicholas II stepped in and took personal command of the army. He reformed the front line, but two million Russian troops

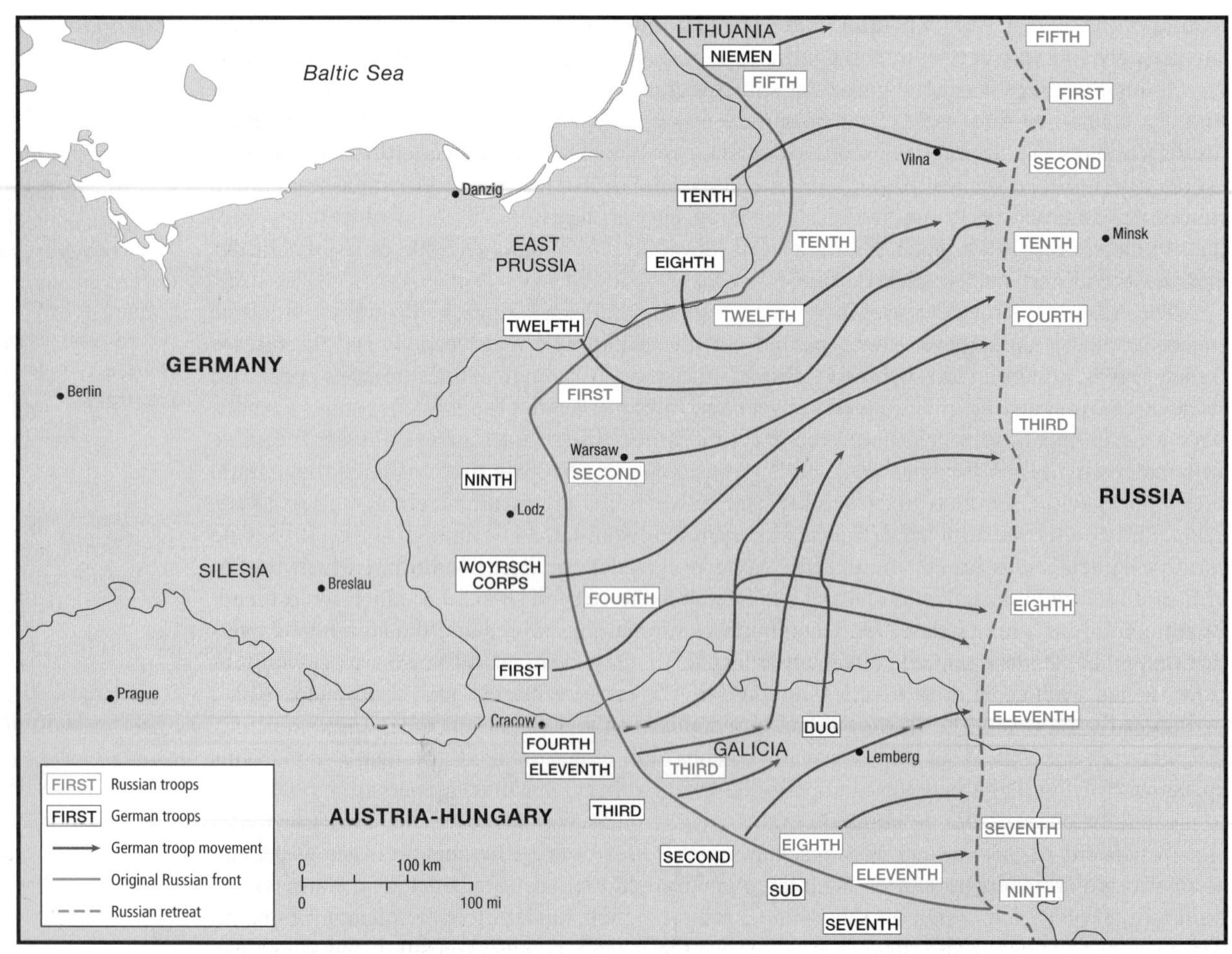

MAP 2.5 The Eastern Front, 1914

were lost in 1915, and public support for the war dropped dramatically. In August 1916, Romania entered the war to help the Allies on the eastern front but was quickly crushed by Germany.

It was the Balkan conflicts in and around the weakening Ottoman Empire that led in part to the beginning of the war. Each of the European powers was determined that, if the Ottoman Empire fell, it would be in a position to gain territory. As the war dragged on and the stalemate continued throughout Europe, Allied troops (primarily British) invaded Turkey (the Gallipoli front), Gaza from the Suez Canal to Jerusalem (the Palestine front) and the Middle East (the Mesopotamian front) to secure military control of the territory. British and Indian forces also invaded Germany's colonies in Africa, spreading the Great War across continents.

Stalemate at Sea

Another often-cited cause of the Great War was the naval arms race between Germany and Great Britain of the early 1900s. Cousins Kaiser Wilhelm II and King George V (Commander of the Royal Navy before taking the throne after his father's death in 1910) were each eager to prove that his navy was superior. Both navies consisted primarily of battleships and battle cruisers, and also included torpedo boats and destroyers to defend against them. The latest in naval technology was the submarine (called the U-boat in Germany), and Germany clearly held the advantage in this category.

To protect Great Britain, the English Channel was filled with minefields. As a result, no major naval battle occurred there, shifting the front line in the naval war to the North Sea. The first naval battle of the war occurred at the end of August 1914 when the British attacked the northwest German coast, creating a blockade to prevent German military and trade ships from moving in and out of port. Germany tried to break this blockade, resulting in what some consider the largest naval battle in history to date, the Battle of Jutland, from May 31 to June 1, 1916. Germany's ships were superior in battle (Great Britain lost more ships than Germany did), but in the end the German military retreated to safe harbor and remained there for the rest of war, enabling Great Britain to continue to economically strangle Germany by closing off its seaports.

With the German High Seas Fleet blockaded in the North Sea, the primary danger to the British Grand Fleet was German U-boats. The U-boats patrolled the Atlantic Ocean and attacked merchant vessels to prevent the Allied powers from trading and importing needed supplies, in effect creating their own very successful blockade of Great Britain. But U-boats could not always distinguish between merchant ships and passenger ships (and many ships served both purposes simultaneously), so the civilian casualty rate was high. To the Allies, this seemed a direct attack on civilians and nonmilitary targets, proving German brutality and further casting Kaiser Wilhelm as a barbarian.

Although there were not many battles in the Mediterranean Sea, where German and Austro-Hungarian navies faced French, British, Italian and even a small contingent of Japanese forces, one of the most catastrophic losses for the Allies occurred at the Battle of Gallipoli (a peninsula of Turkey) from April 1915 to January 1916. With the help of Australia and New Zealand, British and French forces launched a combined naval and ground assault to capture the capital city of Turkey, Constantinople, and open access to the Black Sea to get much-needed military supplies into Russia. From the beginning, the Allied attempt suffered from poor planning and even worse execution both on sea and land. Battle casualties were extremely high on both sides as the Gallipoli front stalemated for nine months until the Allies were forced to withdraw without achieving their goal.

The large Russian navy struggled for control of the Black and Baltic seas against German and Ottoman forces. These seas, too, were stalemated as both the Allies and Central Powers settled into defensive positions and relied on minefields to prevent significant movement. Other naval military action took place in the south Atlantic Ocean, to support Allied troops in seizing German colonies, and in the Indian and South Pacific Oceans, where both sides sought to close down the trade routes of the other.

Sinking of British ships Hogue and Aboukir.

Total War

In retrospect, the Great War is often considered the beginning of an era of **total war** in terms of its geographic scope and the ways in which technology was applied to military applications. The development and use of long-range artillery, **chemical weapons,** U-boats and airplanes extended military conflicts across three continents, into the seas and through the air.

The stalemated condition of the eastern and western fronts led to some of the deadliest battles in history. During the Battle of Verdun (February to December 1916), 300,000 French and German troops were killed and another 750,000 wounded. At the end of the battle, the front line remained almost exactly where it was when the fighting began. The Battle of the Somme (July to November 1916) included the single worst day in terms of casualties in British military history—20,000 men dead and 40,000 wounded out of 100,000 who began the battle. More troops came, and when the battle ended four months later, British, French and German casualties numbered 1.1 million and the Allies had gained seven and a half miles of ground.

Although specifically outlawed by the **Hague Convention,** more than 124,000 tons of chemical weapons were produced and almost 51,000 tons used during the Great War. The French used chemical weapons first, employing tear gas in the trenches on the western front; but the first full-scale chemical warfare occurred at the Second Battle of Ypres on the western front in April 1915 when the Germans used chlorine gas. By the end of the war, chemical weapons caused about 85,000 fatalities and 1.2 million injuries to military personnel on both sides.

When the Great War began, aviation was a brand new field (the first flight occurred in 1903) and certainly not seriously integrated in any nation's military. Initially, planes were used by the British, French, Russians and Germans but only for reconnaissance missions to figure out

total war
a conflict that is unlimited in scope and in which each combatant uses every possible resource imaginable to completely destroy its enemies, including propaganda that demonizes the enemy to gain citizen support for the war

chemical weapons
the use of toxic chemicals to injure or kill enemies; in the Great War the chemical weapons were primarily tear gas, chlorine gas and mustard gas

Hague Convention
peace conferences of 1899 and 1907 that outlined the rights and duties of belligerents during wartime

German aeroplane at Huj, Palestine, 1917.

exactly where the enemy lines were. These were very dangerous missions because the planes had to fly low to capture useful photographs, putting the planes in range of antiaircraft artillery. Because the air was about the only front that was not stuck in stalemate, countries began pursuing aviation technology for military use. By October 1915, the French had the first fighter planes in the air (with fixed machine guns); and after capturing one of the French planes, Germany quickly improved upon the model. By 1916, custom fighter planes routinely engaged in air battles to defend air space for each country. Offensive airplanes, bombers, were developed in 1914 and used by the Germans, Russians, British, Italians and French. Bombers enabled the fighting to move behind the stalemated fronts, attacking the civilian population of the enemy to cause confusion and fear.

Many elements of this war specifically targeted civilians. Naval blockades and U-boats cut off trade, leading to poverty and starvation across Europe and Russia. All vital resources were directed for military use, leaving civilians with limited access to coal, oil, medical supplies and transportation equipment. Colonists were shipped from their home countries to trenches on the western front, and women and children across Europe left home and school to work in factories. In the Ottoman Empire, where nationalism ran high, the government led by the Young Turks took advantage of the worldwide war to engage in ethnic cleansing at home. From 1915 to 1918, an estimated 1.5 million ethnic Armenians (out of approximately 2.5 million in the Ottoman Empire in 1914) were deported or died as a result of the twentieth century's first **genocide.**

genocide
the mass extermination of a national, racial, religious or ethnic group

And this is how it dragged on until 1917, when two events occurred that completely changed the war: (1) the Russian revolution in March ignited a period of political unrest, and (2) the United States officially entered the war in April.

Revolutions Restructure Russia

The Russian Revolution

One of the major factors that turned the tide in the Great War was the Russian Revolution in March 1917. People in Russia had finally had enough with the dictatorship of the tsar, his brutal repression and his incompetence in governing. There was widespread famine and poverty, soldiers were sent into battle ill-equipped for warfare, and the middle and upper classes were frustrated by their lack of political power. The revolution that occurred on March 15, 1917, was totally spontaneous—not planned, incited or executed by any political faction. As revolutionary leader Vladimir Lenin pointed out in his *April Theses*, it was primarily a bourgeois revolution (the middle class wanting control of government), and Tsar Nicholas II was simply too weak to govern any longer. Military and domestic failures produced massive war casualties, widespread hunger, strikes by workers and disorganization in the army. In 1916, Nicholas had disbanded the Duma (Parliament) and once again seized absolute power. So in March 1917, as labor strikes and hunger demonstrations erupted, the army refused to fire on them, and the tsar ran for his life, abdicating his throne. The Duma reconvened and formed a temporary provisional government, popularly led by Alexander Kerensky and comprised of mostly Western European sympathizers.

The goal of the provisional government was to create a stable democratic government in Russia. The provisional government immediately announced there would be elections for political office with universal suffrage but did absolutely nothing to alleviate the widespread hunger of the peasantry or to get Russia out of the war. The provisional government was in a tough spot—to build democracy, it would most certainly need financial and political support from the West, which at the time was embroiled in the Great War and very much needed Russia to keep the eastern front open. So to get help from the West, the provisional government had to stay in the war, which made the government increasingly unpopular with its own people.

The Bolshevik Revolution

soviet
a local town council comprised of soldiers and workers

At first, the socialists let the provisional government rule, neither supporting nor challenging it while they focused on organizing themselves into **soviets.** But the socialist movement itself was not united. The Menshaviks (a minority group of socialists) were hard-core Marxists who believed they must wait for the bourgeoisie stage of development to occur before the spontaneous proletarian revolution could take place. But the Bolsheviks (the majority group) believed in the leadership of their own central committee—they would determine when the time was right for revolution.

In 1917, Lenin was living in Switzerland, exiled by Nicholas II for his radical politics. Lenin wanted to return to Russia to rejoin the Bolsheviks and shape the ongoing revolution, but he would have to cross enemy territory to do so. The German government, however, was more than willing to assure Lenin safe passage across the war zone, hoping that, upon his return, he would lead the Bolsheviks in overthrowing the provisional government and pull Russia out of the war, closing the eastern front and allowing the German military to focus on the west. Indeed, Lenin arrived in Russia in April, published the *April Theses* and asserted his control of the Bolsheviks. His comments sparked the **July Days,** forcing Lenin back into hiding briefly (in Finland) to avoid arrest.

July Days
Bolshevik-led riots against the provisional government in Petrograd

Read the Document *Bolshevik Seizure of Power, 1917* on mysearchlab.com

In September 1917, a prominent Bolshevik, Leon Trotsky, became president of the Petrograd Soviet, the most powerful network of soviets. His first order was that all soviet members (soldiers and workers) refuse to follow any command of the provisional government unless he approved it. This effectively placed the provisional government under the power of the Petrograd Soviet. In October 1917, Lenin returned to Russia and directed the overthrow of the provisional government and the storming of the royal Winter Palace. The Bolsheviks ruled Russia.

Lenin addressing crowd during Russian Revolution, 1917.

Once in power, the Bolshevik government became somewhat of a paramilitary organization, using violence to suppress dissenters (the middle and upper classes as well as other socialist groups) and maintain control. The Bolsheviks **nationalized** the land and turned it over to the peasants. They also got Russia out of the Great War, signing an armistice with the Central Powers in March 1918 called the Treaty of Brest-Litovsk. Russia lost a lot of territory, one-third of its total population, one-half of its industrial capacity and nearly all of its coal mines. Furthermore, when the war was finally over, Russia would be forced to accept harsh conditions imposed at the Paris Peace Conference. But Lenin was not concerned about the short-term losses because he was focused on modernizing Russia and establishing absolute control.

nationalized when the government seizes ownership of privately owned assets

The United States Enters, and the Great War Ends

U.S. President Woodrow Wilson was an idealist, preferring isolationism and limited material help for the Allies to directly participating in conflict. Furthermore, joining the war meant joining the Allies, which included Russia, and he was absolutely adamant about not becoming allies with the decidedly antidemocratic regime of Nicholas II. But a few events took place in 1917 that made it difficult for the United States to justify staying out of the war.

Watch the Video *American Entry into World War I* on mysearchlab.com

On January 31, 1917, Germany declared that it would wage unlimited submarine warfare, sinking all ships in the war zone, including America's. This openly defied U.S. neutrality; but to be fair, the United States had been shipping the Allies weapons and supplies throughout the war, so Kaiser Wilhelm didn't really consider the United States to be neutral. Kaiser Wilhelm's position was that, if the United States was indeed neutral, the U.S. ships had no reason to be in the war zone. In 1916, after German U-boats sunk U.S. merchant ships and passenger ships with American citizens on board, Wilson forced Wilhelm to sign the **Sussex Pledge,** promising to respect U.S. neutrality. Within a year, Germany violated that agreement, and Wilson had no choice but to end U.S. diplomatic relations with Germany in February 1917.

Sussex Pledge agreement in which Germany promised to search merchant ships and sink only those containing "illegal" war supplies after removing the crew and passengers

On February 24, Great Britain gave President Wilson a telegram it had intercepted and decoded. The telegram was sent by German foreign secretary Arthur Zimmermann to the president of Mexico. The telegram basically proposed a German-Mexican alliance and promised that, after the Great War was over, a victorious Germany would help Mexico go to war against the United States to take back Texas, New Mexico and Arizona. When the U.S. press published this telegram on March 1, 1917, Americans were outraged. Kaiser Wilhelm had once again shown his ruthlessness, and public support shifted toward war.

Read the Document *The Zimmerman Telegram* on mysearchlab.com

In March, German U-boats sank four unarmed American merchant ships, killing everyone on board, and the news of the Russian Revolution that overthrew the tsarist regime reached the American press. By April 1917, President Wilson had little choice—the United States had been directly threatened by the Zimmermann note, U.S. ships had been destroyed and Americans had been killed. The United States declared war on Germany on April 6, 1917.

Preparing for War

When the United States declared war in April 1917, the military was far from ready to actually mobilize and send troops. The necessary resources to fight the war simply were not available. Because the government had focused on staying out of the conflict, it was completely unprepared in terms of trained men, equipment, weapons and ammunition. Any supplies and equipment the United States had produced during the preceding few years had already been shipped to Europe. Full-scale efforts to prepare the U.S. military to go to war, including a draft that enlisted 2.7 million men, did not begin until Congress declared war in April 1917, and it was almost a year before the full extent of U.S. combat troops was prepared and shipped out to Europe.

For President Wilson, the problem was even deeper. A man who was generally opposed to war as a tool of foreign policy was now faced with the job of whipping up American support for the war and serving as commander in chief. In Wilson's mind, American soldiers were not being sent into battle to gain territory or resources—if American lives were put at risk, it would have to be for something more important than material gain. To Wilson, this was "a war to make the world safe for democracy." It was about creating a world where democracy and capitalism would flourish, where all people everywhere would be free to choose their government representatives and the laws that governed them. This freedom, of course, would result in democratic countries all around the world, because Wilson could not imagine a situation in which, given the choice, people would choose any form of government other than democracy. And if all countries were democracies, there would be no need for war because democratic governments would negotiate with one another to solve their minor differences. When Wilson spoke to the American people, it was not to rally support for the war itself but for the wonderful worldwide peace that would result from it.

When the U.S. government declared war in April 1917, the provisional government in Russia was trying to establish a Western-style democracy. By the time the first U.S. troops were prepared to go to battle, Lenin had established his Soviet regime, heavily supported by the Red Army and secret police. This had a dramatic impact on Wilson, because he was now allied with exactly the kind of government that he intended to erase from the world. On

For the Freedom of the World (Wilson addresses Congress in April 1917).

Think of what it was that they were applauding. My message today was a message of death for our young men. . . .

—Woodrow Wilson

January 8, 1918, just before the first U.S. troops shipped out to Europe, Wilson announced his *Fourteen Points* as sort of a justification for U.S. intervention in Europe. Wilson's intent was that his points would be the blueprint to structure the postwar world. The *Fourteen Points* were a platform of peace: freedom of the seas, removal of economic barriers to trade, reduction of armaments spending, decolonization, abolishing secret deal making in international politics and his favorite—**self-determination** for all peoples of the world. This last piece was aimed directly at the nationalistic violence that Wilson believed started the mess the world was in. All groups of people throughout the world would be free to establish their own governmental systems instead of being subsumed by larger, imperialistic countries (as long as the people chose democracy, of course). Point fourteen explained just how Wilson thought all of this would work—it called for the establishment of the League of Nations, an international organization of which all countries were members and they made decisions in unity. The concept is called **collective security**—everyone comes together to work out potential conflicts, thus guaranteeing the peace. Unfortunately for Wilson, his allies were the major imperial powers of the world, and the *Fourteen Points,* specifically the ones about decolonization and self-determination, required his allies to change their political and economic structures to more closely match the United States' way of doing things. Did Wilson really believe that they would do that? Openly, the Allies said basically nothing in response to the *Fourteen Points* because they really needed American support to win the war. But in the royal palaces of Europe, Wilson was somewhat of a laughing stock. They certainly didn't have the same vision of the postwar world as Wilson, and even if they did agree with some of his postwar plan in principle, how would they actually accomplish his goals?

Read the Document *The Fourteen Points* on mysearchlab.com

self-determination
the right of nations (based on ethnic lines) to rule themselves

collective security
each nation's security depends on that of all the member nations; the goal is universal peace

U.S. Military Participation

The U.S. military decided that it had the best chance of defeating Germany on the stalemated western front. In the one year U.S. troops were directly involved in conflict, approximately 2 million American soldiers were sent overseas, one-half of them to the trenches of northern France, where fighting was the most intense and Allied and civilian morale the lowest.

Led by General John "Black Jack" Pershing, a small group of American Expeditionary Forces (AEF) first arrived in France in June 1917, although the bulk of the combat troops did not arrive until the following spring. Small groups of soldiers also were sent to Belgium, Italy and Russia. Their initial goal was to support the British and French troops, so they fought mostly in localized battles until the full American fighting force arrived in the summer of 1918. By then, Russia had left the war and Germany was quickly shifting its troops to the western front. It was a race against the mobilization of the U.S. troops—Germany went on the offensive in the spring of 1918 in an attempt to gain control of the front before fresh American troops and weapons arrived.

The first major campaigns for U.S. troops on the western front occurred in July and August 1918 at the Battle of Aisne-Marne. This battle turned out to be a key victory for the Allies and Germany's last offensive campaign. As was typical on the western front, casualties were high on all sides, but the Germans were forced to retreat and lost ground. This led directly to the American-led Meuse-Argonne offensive from September to November 1918. During the course of this forty-seven day battle, 1.25 million American soldiers drove forty-three German divisions back thirty miles. It was the largest gain of territory on the western front in years, and it was this overwhelming victory that drove the Germans to surrender.

Repairing frontline trench after bomb explosion, fifty yards from enemy trenches.

When the war ended, American soldiers had experienced heavy combat for only about six months, compared to the previous four years their Allied counterparts spent mired in the trenches. During that time, U.S. troops captured 49,000 Germans, 1,400 guns and, most importantly, 101 miles of the western front (23 percent of its total line). Of course, these numbers are small compared to what the British and French accomplished in their years of combat, but these American victories came at a time when both Allied and German troops were too physically and materially exhausted to gain control over the other. French Marshal Henri Philippe Petain believed that the most vital thing the American troops delivered to the western front was their "mere presence." As the German military grew smaller and weaker during the last year of the war, the Allied forces grew larger and stronger because of the American troop influx. Perhaps most important, the Americans delivered morale that the British and French desperately needed to lift themselves up out of the trenches.

The Great War Ends

By the end of the Battle of Meuse-Argonne, fresh American troops strengthened the Allied lines daily as the German lines disintegrated. By the end of September 1918, Bulgaria was defeated, and the Balkans were liberated in October. That same month, the German navy revolted, and Germany's top General (Lundendorff) acknowledged that "the condition of the army demands an immediate armistice." Germany asked the Allies for armistice on October 3, 1918, but the Allies put conditions on the agreement that Germany refused to sign. The people of Germany, however, were finished with the war, and antigovernment revolutions quickly spread throughout Germany. The Ottoman Empire signed an armistice with the Allies on October 30, and Austria-Hungary signed one on November 3. With no allies, no public support and a very minimal military, Wilhelm II had little choice left but to abdicate his throne on November 9, 1918, and flee his beloved Germany for exile in the neutral Netherlands. Field Marshal Paul von Hindenburg stepped in and quickly approved an armistice with the Allies on November 11, 1918, that basically required German soldiers to drop their weapons where they stood and retreat to Germany.

Conclusions

The so-called Great War propelled humanity into an extended global conflict with far-reaching implications. Although it is impossible to get an exact count, battle fatalities were around 8.5 million men (an average of 5,800 per day every day for four years), 21 million wounded and 7.75 million missing or imprisoned. The 22 million Allied casualties represented about 52 percent of the men they sent into battle, and the 15.5 million casualties of the Central Powers represented about 67 percent of the men they sent into battle. These numbers do not include civilian deaths, which are virtually impossible to tally accurately. All told, the war cost an estimated $186 billion (calculated in 1914 dollars) to fight, with the Allied Powers ($125.5 billion) outspending the Central Powers ($60.5 billion) two to one. Of course, no one had that kind of cash on hand, so everyone went deep into debt that would have to be paid back after the war. Unfortunately, economic recovery was made especially difficult because much of the working class had been killed or wounded in battle, and the factories and farmland of Europe were destroyed by trenches and the residue of chemical warfare. Much of the money was spent on technology—the new weapons of this war (tanks, submarines and airplanes) would be improved upon for the next. Perhaps most dramatically, the Great War led to the end of the era of empires: The German, Austro-Hungarian, Russian and Ottoman empires all ceased to exist. By the end of 1918, the United States had clearly demonstrated its military might as President Wilson traveled to Paris to transform the world according to his *Fourteen Points*.

WORKING WITH THE THEMES

THE EFFECTS OF TECHNOLOGY What is the connection between weapons technology and the concept of "total war"? Did weapons and communications technology in the early 1900s make warfare more efficient as intended?

CHANGING IDENTITIES For each country involved in the Great War, what is the link between nationalism and political decision making? Were nationalist tensions in Europe eased by the war? Why or why not? Why did Wilson formulate and publicly announce the *Fourteen Points*?

SHIFTING BORDERS What effect did internal nationalist differences have on European and Asian empires? How did external wars of aggression lead to the demise of empires in the early 1900s?

GLOBALIZATION How did the alliance system in place in 1914 affect the outcome of the Great War? Why were the sea-based empires in a better position to fight and win the Great War than the land-based empires? Why was collective security a radical idea in 1918?

Further Reading

TO FIND OUT MORE

PBS: The Great War and the Shaping of the Twentieth Century. Available online at http://www.pbs.org/greatwar/

Michael Duffy: A Multimedia History of World War One. Available online at http://www.firstworldwar.com

Marxists Internet Archive: Lenin Internet Archive. Available online at http://www.marxists.org/archive/lenin/index.htm

Philip J. Haythornthwaite: *The World War One Source Book*, Brockhampton Press (1992)

MATRIX, the Center for Humane Arts, Letters and Social Sciences Online: Seventeen Moments in Soviet History—1917. Available online at http://www.soviethistory.org

GO TO THE SOURCE

Charles F. Horne (ed.): *Source Records of the Great War* (Volumes 1 to 7) (1923)

John Dos Passos: *One Man's Initiation: 1917; A Novel* (1920)

Vladimir Ilyich Lenin: *Imperialism: The Highest Stage of Capitalism* (1916)

Leon Trotsky: *The War and the International (The Bolsheviks and World Peace)* (1914)

Captain F. C. Hitchcock: *Stand To: A Diary of the Trenches 1915–1918* (1936)

Erich Maria Remarque: *All Quiet on the Western Front* (1929)

MySearchLab Connections

Read the **Document** on **mysearchlab.com**

2.1 *Austria-Hungary's Ultimatum to Serbia.* This exchange between the Austro-Hungarian and Serbian governments one month after the assassination of Archduke Franz Ferdinand shows that they clearly did not trust one another. Given that the German Empire supported Austria-Hungary and the Russian Empire supported Serbia, neither was willing to back down.

2.2 *Bolshevik Seizure of Power, 1917.* These documents chronicle some of that momentous year in Russia: overthrow of the Provisional Government, and efforts by Lenin and the Bolsheviks to put down opposition through censorship of the press and establishment of a secret police force.

2.3 *The Zimmermann Telegram.* On January 19, 1917, Germany's foreign secretary sent a telegram to the German ambassador in Mexico. It was intercepted by British intelligence agents, transmitted to U.S. President Wilson, and shared with the American public. The resulting outrage contributed to the U.S. declaration of war against Germany and its allies later that year.

2.4 Woodrow Wilson, *The Fourteen Points.* As the end of World War I approached, U.S. President Woodrow Wilson issued his plans for a permanent peace in Europe.

Watch the **Video** on **mysearchlab.com**

2.1 *The Outbreak of World War I*

2.2 *American Entry into World War I*

3

The Interwar Years

CHAPTER OUTLINE

- The Treaty of Versailles
- Imperial Demise and Restructuring
- The Great Depression
- Technological Advancement

CHAPTER TIMELINE

November 1918
The Great War ends

1919
Paris Peace Conference opens
Weimar Republic is formed in Germany

1920
Treaty of Versailles is finalized
The first commercial radio broadcast
League of Nations is founded
Women in United States gain suffrage

1921
Washington Naval Conference is held

1922
Egypt earns independence
Treaty of Rapallo is signed
USSR is created
Irish Civil War begins

1930
United States enacts Hawley-Smoot Tariff

1935
Government of India Act is enacted

Photos from left to right: Migrant mother; Albert Einstein; Flapper, 1925; Jewish re-settlement ad.

1923	1924	1925	1927	1928	1929
France invades Germany's Ruhr Valley	League of Nations issues *Mandate for Palestine*	The Treaty of Locarno settles borders	Lindbergh flies across the Atlantic Ocean	Kellogg-Briand Pact outlaws wars of aggression	U.S. stock market crashes
	Lenin passes away	The Scopes Trial is held			
	U.S. Immigration Act and U.S. Dawes plan take effect				

Each participating country had its own particular reasons for being involved in the Great War, ranging from specific (gaining territory) to broad (proving superiority over others) to downright unattainable (making the world safe for democracy). Naturally, when the victors sat down at the Paris Peace Conference to settle the disputes, each had his own agenda. The decisions made at that conference had a significant impact on economic and political events to come. Victorious political leaders redrew the global map to meet their needs, while the governments that lost the war watched from the sidelines as their empires were dismantled. Citizens and subjects throughout the world suffered the tremendous human costs of the Great War, and the more pervasive societal costs incurred as the decisions made by their governments reverberated through the international economy. The twenty-year period from 1919 to 1939 is more accurately termed "interwar" than "postwar" because it was certainly fraught with conflict. The frustrated nationalism created by the Treaty of Versailles, the societal effects of the Great Depression and ongoing investment in military technology would provide the roots of the next armed conflict.

WORKING WITH THE THEMES

THE EFFECTS OF TECHNOLOGY The technology of the Great War is translated into consumer goods (radios, automobiles, etc.) and the aviation industry. Einstein, economists, and geneticists change how people view the world.

CHANGING IDENTITIES Colonists and Zionists demand self-determination. German nationalism is crushed. Arab–Jewish violence increases in Palestine.

SHIFTING BORDERS The Treaty of Versailles redraws the map of Eastern Europe and the Middle East with the creation of successor states and mandates. Lenin creates the USSR.

GLOBALIZATION The decrease in production and trade spreads worldwide to create the Great Depression. The League of Nations is created but without U.S. membership.

The Treaty of Versailles

When the Great War ended, many people in the world had idealistic hopes of "peace without victors" as U.S. President Wilson envisioned. But Wilson's idealism was in direct opposition to the European governments still trying to hold on to their domestic and international power. When Wilson went to the postwar peace conference in Paris in 1919 to explain to the imperialist powers why they should decolonize and adopt self-determination for all people of the world, they did not at all agree with him.

Read the Document *French Demands at the Peace Conference* on mysearchlab.com

The Paris Peace Conference opened on January 18, 1919, a deliberate slap in the face to Germany because January 18 marks the date of the birth of the German Empire in 1871. Representatives from thirty countries attended, although the "big four" clearly dominated the decision making, and the Central Powers and Russia were notably banned from the negotiations. Whereas President Wilson's goal was the implementation of his *Fourteen Points*—most notably the democratization of Europe based on the concept of self-determination and the creation of a powerful League of Nations to block Soviet expansion—his European Allies had very different goals. Italian Prime Minister Vittorio Orlando was there to claim territory and respect by participating as an equal in world events. British Prime Minister David Lloyd George hoped to seize control of Germany's navy and make the German government pay (financially) for the damage it caused. He also intended to seize Germany's colonies in Africa and as much of the territory of the former Ottoman Empire as possible. French Prime Minister Georges Clemenceau's goal was nothing short of revenge for the financial, military and human costs Germany had inflicted on France since Bismarck's unification process in the late 1800s. He was rightfully concerned about French security and sought to completely dismantle Germany's military, industrial capacity, economy and nationalist pride, making France a comparatively stronger power in Europe as a by-product of the process. Clemenceau was particularly annoyed that the U.S. president thought his voice should matter so much in European affairs, half joking that "God was satisfied with Ten Commandments; Wilson gives us fourteen."

The "big four": Lloyd George of Great Britain; Orlando of Italy; Clemenceau of France; Wilson of the United States, outside the Hotel Crillon, Paris, France, May 1919.

The formal settlement of the First World War (WWI) consisted of five separate treaties between the victors (the Allies) and the defeated Central Powers. The first and most famous, the Treaty of Versailles, was signed on June 28, 1919, and the last on August 10, 1920. In the end, very few of the concepts in Wilson's *Fourteen Points* were included.

Punishing the "Losers"

First and foremost, what to do with Germany? It had only unified in 1871 and, in the minds of the victors, almost immediately proceeded to cause the most devastating war ever known. France was justifiably nervous about letting a united Germany stay strong, but Great Britain and the United States were also nervous about allowing France to become the dominant power on the European continent. Nor did they want Germany so economically devastated that it could not become a healthy trade partner, or so bitter that it would not participate in the important task of limiting the spread of communism. In what is often called "the unhappy compromise," the "big four" drafted the treaty and presented it to Germany for signature. Germany, outraged that its delegation was banned from negotiations, felt that the treaty was unduly harsh and responded with some suggested alternatives. Clemenceau replied personally: "The protest of the German Delegation shows that they utterly fail to understand the position in which Germany stands today." Not only was Germany's protest completely ignored, the German government was given the choice of either signing the treaty as written or risking an Allied invasion and occupation of Germany to force its compliance.

Read the Document *Henry Cabot Lodge Objects to Article 10 of the Treaty of Versailles* on mysearchlab.com

Of the 440 clauses in the Treaty of Versailles, more than 400 of them dealt with punishing Germany. In terms of territory, Germany lost 13.5 percent of its total territory (roughly 7 million people) and all of its overseas colonies. France, Belgium and Denmark gained the territory taken from the western border (including much of Germany's industrial capacity), and parts of the eastern borderlands were taken to create the new country of Poland. The Sudetenland, a region of the German Empire in which ethnic Czechs outnumbered ethnic Germans two to one, was carved out and given to the newly created Czechoslovakia. Finally, Germany was expressly forbidden to reunite in any way with Austria.

WAR GUILT CLAUSE

The Allied and Associated Governments affirm and Germany accepts the responsibility of Germany and her allies for causing all the loss and damage to which the Allied and Associated Governments and their nationals have been subjected as a consequence of the war imposed upon them by the aggression of Germany and her allies.

—Treaty of Versailles, Article 231

Militarily, the German army was limited to 100,000 men. Germany could not produce nor own any form of heavy artillery, chemical or gas weapons, tanks or airplanes. The navy was restricted to six ships and absolutely no U-boats. A **demilitarized zone (DMZ)** was created in German territory to separate it from France and Belgium. The DMZ was occupied by Allied troops for ten years, and the German military was not allowed to enter the zone.

One of the hardest parts of the treaty for the German people to accept was Article 231, the *War Guilt Clause*, which required that Germany take full responsibility for starting the war. Given that, it only made sense to the Allies that Germany should pay for the entire cost of the war. These war reparations were paid primarily to France and Belgium to rebuild the infrastructure destroyed by the surprise assault and drawn-out trench warfare on the western front; the reparations included payment for replacing all the military equipment France and Belgium used during the war. The specific dollar amount of war reparations was not included in the treaty when Germany was forced to sign it. In April 1921, Germany received a bill for $33 billion to be paid in cash or commodities (coal and steel), an amount far beyond its means to pay. An initial payment of $250 million was made in September 1921, but that was all the German government could ever come up with before a serious economic crisis developed in Germany.

demilitarized zone (DMZ)
a defined area in which it is prohibited to station military troops or build military installations

Weimar Republic
Democratic federal republic in Germany with nineteen states; included popular elections for president and Reichstag (parliament) with universal suffrage

The German government during this era, the **Weimar Republic,** was created by constitution in August 1919, two months after the acting government accepted the Treaty of Versailles. It was a parliamentary republic led by the Social Democrats, a liberal political party representing the interests of the working class. During the early years of the republic, there were frequent communist uprisings attempting to establish a soviet republic, as well as violent right-wing revolutions intended to return authoritarianism to Germany. Devastated by the loss of the war, the Versailles restrictions and the economic devastation that followed, the German people never really supported the government, and political violence became the norm in Germany.

The League of Nations

sovereign
the right to rule a territory and its people without outside interference

Integral to President Wilson's vision of a peaceful world was the creation of a League of Nations—a body of **sovereign** countries that agreed to pursue common policies and cooperate with one another in the common interest of preventing war. Articles one through twenty-six of the Treaty of Versailles established the League of Nations and its structure, goals and operating principles. The Treaty also specifically named the original signatories and who was eligible to be considered for membership. Only democratic governments could be trusted in an endeavor requiring collective security, so Lenin's Russia would not be invited to participate. Neither would the Weimar Republic of Germany initially; although it was democratic, it was not historically cooperative with others. The limited parameters for membership meant that only forty-five countries qualified to be members (and only forty-two of them actually joined), which was not exactly what Wilson had in mind.

Truly the worst part for Wilson was that the United States Senate refused to ratify the Treaty of Versailles, thereby preventing the United States from joining the League of Nations. Although politics certainly played a part (Republicans held the Senate majority and were led by Wilson's political enemy Henry Cabot Lodge), the heart of the disagreement was Article 10, which stated:

> *The Members of the League undertake to respect and preserve as against external aggression the territorial integrity and existing political independence of all Members of the League.*
>
> *In case of any such aggression or in case of any threat or danger of such aggression the Council shall advise upon the means by which this obligation shall be fulfilled.*

Lodge interpreted Article 10 as *requiring* the United States to commit economic or military aid to any nation in the League. He was concerned that it would pull the United States into wars around the world that it neither needed nor desired to be involved in. Wilson, who had actually written Article 10 himself, insisted that it did not necessarily require the United States to do anything because the United States enjoyed veto power in the League Council. To Wilson, though, the United States would be morally obligated to help other nations, and that was much more important than any legal requirement. Because Wilson considered it "a very grave and solemn obligation," he refused to negotiate with Lodge. The Senate refused to ratify the treaty, and the United States never joined the League of Nations.

So the League of Nations was created, but it suffered from some pretty serious handicaps. First was the heavy focus on moral obligations, which are interpreted differently by all people everywhere, rather than dealing with specific issues in a practical manner. Another problem stemmed from the League's consequences for violating world peace—economic sanctions would end up hurting everyone because they slowed down trade, and any credible military threat would have to include the United States, which wasn't a member. This left the League of Nations with little power to enforce anything.

But that does not mean that the spirit of **internationalism** wasn't present in the world, or that the United States was prepared to let the world make political decisions without its input. Because the League of Nations was so weak, the real work in international relations in the post-war period came from conferences dealing with specific issues rather than the general goal of maintaining peace. In 1921, the United States held the Washington Naval Conference to determine the balance of power in the Pacific. The conference resulted in an agreement to set the ratio for large naval vessels to 5:5:3 for Britain, the United States and Japan. To get Japan to agree to this second-best position, Great Britain and the United States allowed Japan to keep control of Manchuria so long as Japan promised not to go farther into China.

internationalism
a policy of cooperation among nations

To settle problems created by the Treaties of Brest-Litovsk and Versailles, the Treaty of Rapallo was made between Germany and Russia in 1922. The Treaty of Rapallo basically restored diplomatic relations between the two countries and settled territorial disputes on Germany's eastern border. Both of these countries had been excluded from the postwar negotiations at the Paris Peace Conference, and the Treaty of Rapallo was a sign that they fully intended to participate in world affairs whether the West wanted to include them or not.

In Europe, the Treaty of Locarno in 1925 was an agreement between Germany, France, Belgium, Great Britain and Italy that settled the territorial disputes along Germany's western border created by the Treaty of Versailles. The treaty was designed to reduce the high tension and occasional outright aggression that marked postwar relations in Europe. Germany agreed to respect the DMZ in the Rhineland, so the Allies agreed to remove their troops (completed by 1930). Everyone agreed not to use military force against the others, and Germany was allowed to join the League of Nations in 1926.

Despite these agreements, France was still nervous about Germany and worried that the United States would not be of any help because it had not joined the League of Nations. French Foreign Minister Aristide Briand approached U.S. Secretary of State Frank Kellogg with a bilateral proposal of peace; the proposal basically promised that the two countries would not go to war against one another. The U.S. government was worried that this would essentially form an alliance that might require the United States to get involved in Europe again, so Kellogg suggested that this proposal be extended to all nations of the world. The Kellogg-Briand Pact (sometimes called the Pact of Paris) of 1928 declared wars of aggression to be illegal under international law and required that signatories settle their disputes by peaceful means. It was a very popular idea in a world still recovering from the devastation of the Great War, and the fifteen original signatories were soon joined by another forty-seven countries. That so many governments were willing to participate in this idealistic hope for world peace demonstrated that **pacifism** was a much more powerful influence after the war than the **militarism** that preceded it. While the Kellogg-Briand Pact didn't actually prevent

pacifism
the moral opposition to war or violence as a means of settling disputes

militarism
the policy of aggressive military preparedness

future wars of aggression, it did form an important foundation for international law that has carried through to the present, and it happened outside the realm of the League of Nations.

The Direct Consequences

The Treaty of Versailles is one of the most controversial treaties in modern history. In retrospect, many historians claim that it was too tough on Germany and created the conditions that led directly to the rise of Adolf Hitler. Others believe that it was too easy on Germany because the treaty didn't prevent Germany from rebuilding into a powerful state. Still others say the treaty was fine; it just was never enforced well, and that is why World War II (WWII) developed.

ANALYSIS

Was the Treaty of Versailles too harsh on Germany? Based on Document 3.2 and your understanding of the treaty, which elements do you think impacted Germany the most? Why?

One thing is clear—the Treaty of Versailles was unsatisfactory in several important ways. The Treaty of Versailles did not end imperialism; in fact, instead of decolonization, the Allies gained more territory as they divvied up Germany's colonies and the former Ottoman lands. The postwar world certainly was not "peace without victors" as Wilson imagined, because the resulting peace treaties made it painfully clear who the losers were. And, although new countries were indeed created, the process by which this happened totally violated the principles of self-determination, reigniting nationalist movements rather than stopping them. That nationalism spilled over into China, Turkey and other countries around the world—these countries thought they would gain freedom and self-determination from the Treaty of Versailles, but they did not. One of the most glaring problems was the refusal to let Russia or Germany participate in the postwar negotiations. Like it or not, these two countries did play, and would continue to play, a major role in European politics, so they really should have been allowed to participate in the postwar restructuring. The effects on Germany were devastating and absolutely led to what came next for them: the Weimar government was unstable, the German people were completely stripped of their nationalist pride, and the reparations and provisions of the treaty left Germany basically unable to defend or even feed itself.

Even the victors were dissatisfied with the outcome of the Treaty of Versailles. Wilson's *Fourteen Points* were largely ignored, some even ridiculed, and he could not participate in his own League of Nations. Clemenceau was concerned that Germany was left with more territory and, therefore, potential power than it should have been. And Lloyd George remarked, "We shall have to fight another war again in twenty-five years time."

The Unarmed Cop, 1930.

Imperial Demise and Restructuring

At the end of the Great War, territorial empires were all but gone physically, and the concept itself had really been discredited. The Great War had just proven that technological advancements dramatically changed the way countries could gain (or lose) territory. Traditional ground troops spent almost the entire war stalemated. U-boats played an enormous role in the outcome of naval battles, and, for the first time ever, the only real movement during the war happened in the air. So, while the territorial empires disappeared altogether or shifted to a different form of governance, the sea-based empires (the victors of the war) actually expanded their reach around the globe.

The Successor States and Mandates

With the German, Austro-Hungarian and Ottoman empires defeated, the map of Europe had to be redrawn to meet the goals of the victors. But the victors had different goals: the European victors intended to gain territory, while the United States, which promoted self-determination as a means to create stable democracies, hoped to form a strong buffer zone across Eastern Europe to isolate communist Russia. Agreeing on where territorial lines would be drawn was an impossible task given the disparate views of the Allies, each of which made many secret and contradictory agreements during the war to secure support from other countries. In the end, the former empires were carved up and new countries created with little regard for ethnic populations, despite all the rhetoric about self-determination.

successor state a country created out of territory taken from a previously well-established state

As punishment for their parts in the war, the Austro-Hungarian and Ottoman empires were completely dismantled. Austria-Hungary was carved into four **successor states**—Austria, Hungary,

MAP 3.1 Successor States in Eastern Europe

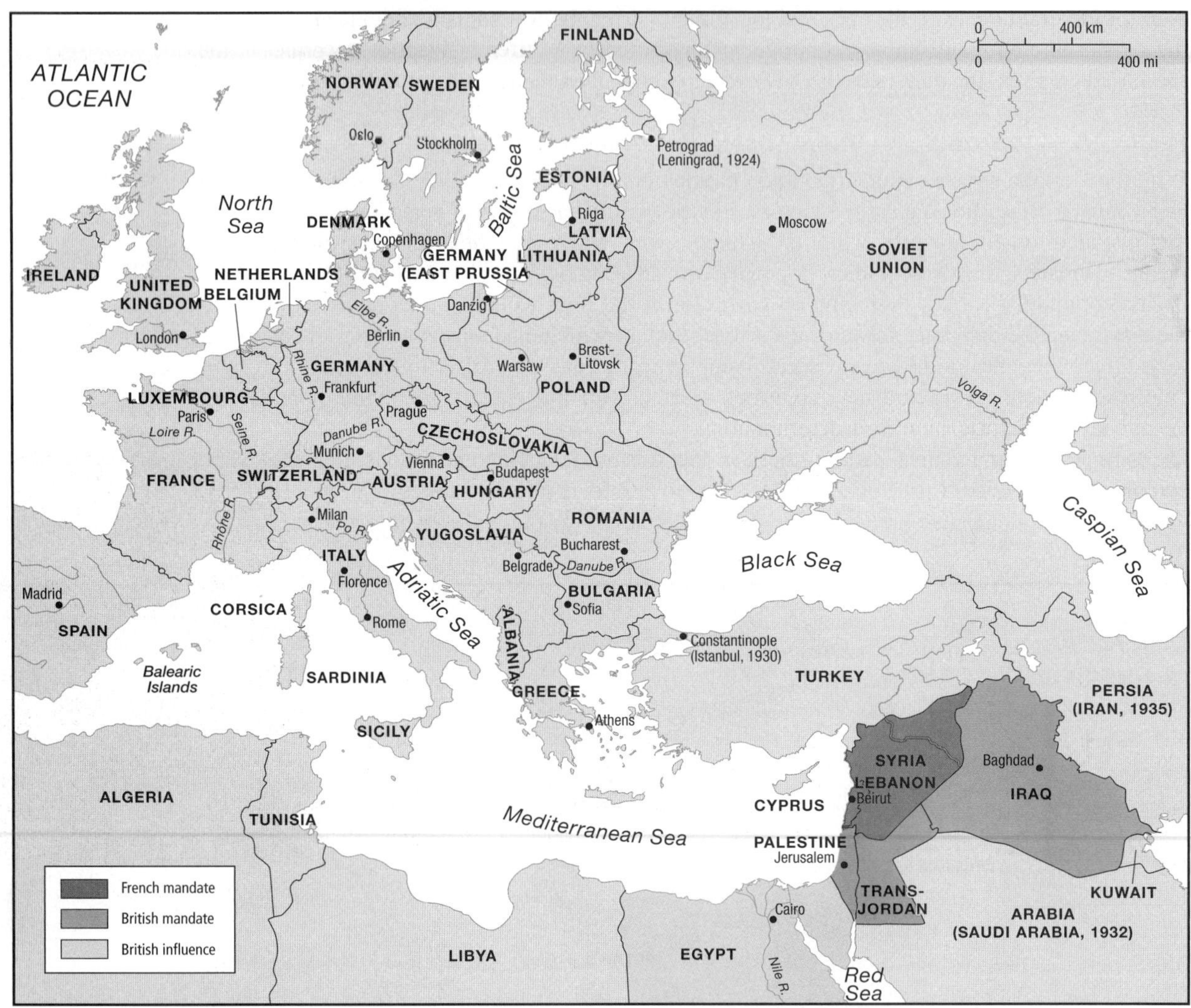

MAP 3.2 Mandates in the Middle East

Czechoslovakia and Yugoslavia—each of which was comprised of multiethnic populations. The Ottoman Empire, which had been suffering from internal challenges for years, completely disintegrated. In its place, only the Republic of Turkey stood as a recognized, independent country. The rest of the territory, weakened by nationalist and religious differences, fell victim to the ambitions of the European powers. The former Ottoman Empire was divided into separate territories, called League of Nations **mandates,** which were then given to Great Britain and France as protectorates. This essentially expanded the imperial power of Great Britain and France into the oil-rich Middle East. The new countries of Finland, Estonia, Latvia, Lithuania and Poland were created out of the territory the Russian Empire was forced to cede to Germany in the Treaty of Brest-Litovsk.

mandate
a territory granted to a League member for the purpose of establishing a government

Watch the Video *The Continuing Legacy of World War I in the Middle East* on mysearchlab.com

The successor states faced several problems: (1) they were new and had no tradition of ruling themselves; (2) they were established by the United States, Great Britain and France and were therefore expected to follow democratic and capitalist principles; (3) they were financially devastated from the beginning, and no one had the money to help them develop healthy economies; (4) they were multiethnic states, which made it difficult to form internal political alliances or consistent foreign policy; and (5) they had large groups of nationalists within their borders fighting for self-determination. Poland's problem was that it was comprised of significant pieces of

Germany, Austria and Russia, and it just couldn't get those different experiences and outlooks coordinated into one government. Hungary's economy was totally reliant on agriculture, so the postwar economic depression destroyed Hungary. In southern Europe (particularly Yugoslavia), ongoing nationalist disagreements between the Serbs, Croats and Albanians prevented any internal or external peaceful political relationships from developing. Czechoslovakia came closer than any of them to actually becoming a stable country but was ultimately taken over by extreme German nationalism in the Sudetenland, a region that was carved out of the former German Empire. None of these successor states was able to establish a stable democratic regime, which left Eastern Europe just as volatile after the Great War as it was before the war began.

MAKE THE CONNECTION

- Why were independent countries created in Eastern Europe but mandates created in the Middle East?
- Does the creation of the successor states solve the problems that led to the Great War?
- What might be the long-term effects of creating mandates in the Middle East?

The USSR

The Bolshevik Revolution of November 1917 and the Treaty of Brest-Litovsk led directly to the Russian Civil War from 1918 to 1921, which pitted the Reds (Bolsheviks) against the Whites (anticommunists). During the civil war, the Russian Empire ceased to exist and broke into several independent republics (Russia being the largest). Each of these republics was eventually controlled by a Bolshevik-led Soviet as the Red Army advanced and defeated the Whites. In December 1922, these independent Soviet republics were rejoined together to form the Union of Soviet Socialist Republics (USSR).

When Tsar Nicholas II and his family were executed in July 1918, Russia was no longer an empire. The USSR established a one-party political system under the Communist Party led by Vladimir Lenin. He began the process of completely restructuring the political, economic and social systems according to communist ideology, which was a direct affront to Wilson and the principles of democracy he held to be sacred. For the United States and, to a lesser extent, Great Britain, the establishment of stable, capitalist democracies in Eastern Europe was essential to create a buffer zone between them and Lenin's communist USSR.

The Flag of the Soviet Union.

The Demand for Self-Determination

Wilson's *Fourteen Points* promised decolonization—by definition, colonies were breeding grounds of poverty, injustice and violence, all of which could lead to communism. But after the devastating war, the European victors (Great Britain, France and Belgium) still needed the financial support the colonies provided and were not about to let them go. In fact, during the Paris Peace Conference and subsequent negotiations, they gained even more territory through the seizure of Germany's former colonies in Africa and the former Ottoman territory, all of which were declared to be League of Nations mandates but put under the direct control of either Great Britain or France.

But in the colonies and **dominions,** the colonists heard Wilson's promise of self-determination loud and clear. When they did not receive political independence from the Paris Peace Conference, many tried to achieve it on their own. The result was often violence and bloodshed because most colonies lacked the internal nationalist leadership to put together a successful independence movement. France and Belgium in particular were adamant about holding onto these colonies for economic gain, exploiting the land and labor of Africa and Asia in an effort to rebuild Europe. They utilized all the technology developed prior to the Great War to keep control through fear and military domination.

dominions autonomous communities under the authority of the British Empire (monarch)

Clearly the most successful imperial power in terms of territory and wealth, Great Britain had invested a lot of money into making its colonies operate efficiently. Great Britain built railroads, schools and local court systems, and in many cases relied on local elites to maintain a political and social hierarchy for stability. Many of Britain's colonies participated willingly in the Great War, sending supplies, laborers and troops. So after the war, they felt like they earned respect, which to them meant being treated as equals rather than subordinates. But the British government did not offer equality, sparking protests, labor strikes and boycotts on the part of

Sinn Fein
Irish Republican political party whose goal was to end British rule in Ireland and create a unified and independent Ireland

Read the Document *Irish National Identity* on mysearchlab.com

caste system
the pattern of social classes in Hinduism, with five hierarchical levels into which people are born, marry and die

Indian National Congress
political party founded in 1885 that became the leader of the Indian independence movement

home rule
a constituent's right to self-government within the larger administrative structure

the colonists. British troops cracked down, which only intensified the opposition to their presence. The primary difference between the way Great Britain handled these independence movements and the violent conflicts in other imperial colonies was Britain's willingness to compromise.

IRELAND Closest to home, nationalists in Ireland had been fighting for independence from Great Britain for many years. The Irish government fulfilled its obligations to Great Britain during the Great War, conscripting Irish men into battle for the Allies. This only exacerbated the nationalist issue. In 1918, **Sinn Fein** announced Ireland's independence, organized the Irish Republican Army, and fought a war of independence against a limited British military. In 1922, the British ratified the Anglo-Irish Treaty, which did not make Ireland an independent republic as Sinn Fein had hoped but instead granted Ireland dominion status in the British Empire and established the Irish Free State as a constitutional monarchy. Immediately, Northern Ireland chose to "opt out" and rejoin Great Britain. This issue, along with the assassination of several key Irish statesmen, split Sinn Fein and led to the Irish Civil War of 1922–1923. Those who supported the treaty (the Irish Free State Army) defeated those who wanted to continue to fight for full independence (the Irish Republican Army), and the Irish Free State was born as a British dominion.

INDIA Britain's most geostrategically important and lucrative colony was India, but it suffered from internal religious and social divisions. Politically, two-thirds of the region was under direct British control, and the rest was divided between traditional Indian maharajahs. Although the British government and military certainly held a distinct technological advantage over India, the British primarily maintained control by working through the existing hierarchical social structure. The British allowed Indian elites to maintain their prestigious social positions at the top of the **caste system,** which gave them the respect and support of wealthy local populations, who in turn kept the lower classes in place. The British also fueled religious disputes between Muslims and Hindus to prevent the population from uniting against the British.

India had participated heavily in the Great War, providing troops, supplies and airstrips. After the war, the **Indian National Congress** asked for dominion status, which would give them **home rule.** The local elites didn't want major change that could destabilize the caste system and create disorder; but in the wake of WWI, like most other colonies, India experienced widespread famine, disease, violence and falling prices for goods as the international economy collapsed. This gave rise to an independence movement led by Mohandas Gandhi, a member of the Indian National Congress who demanded that independence be achieved through nonviolent methods. Gandhi's goal was self-rule, and he meant both politically and personally for each individual. He went so far as to argue that technology did more harm than good in communities and the Indians should return to manual labor and artisan craft to regain control of their own productive capacities. This message had broad appeal, and Gandhi picked up local, national and international support that crossed social and religious dividing lines. Through the Indian National Congress,

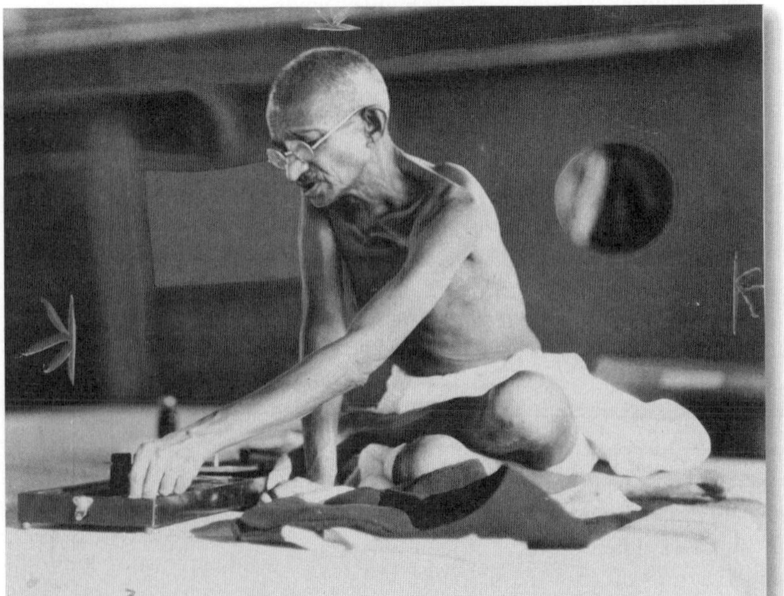

Gandhi spinning cotton by hand.

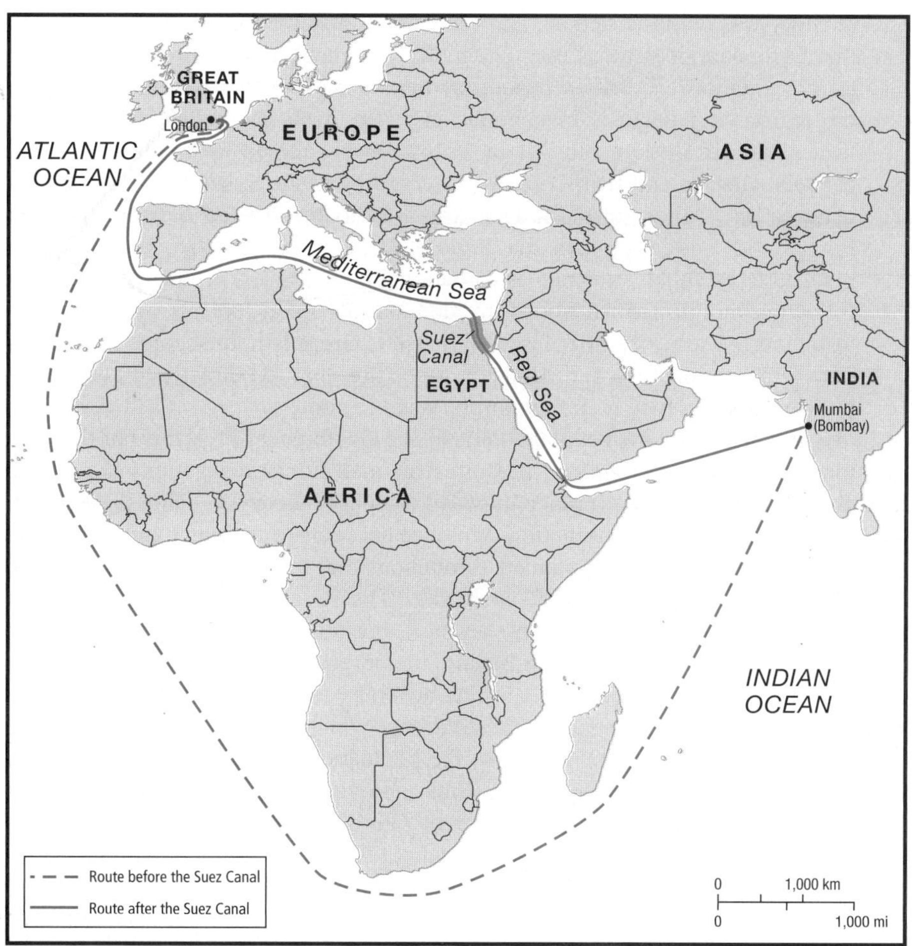

MAP 3.3 The Impact of the Suez Canal

Gandhi was able to achieve a series of successes toward Indian independence, culminating in the Government of India Act of 1935, which gave India a degree of self-rule at the local level but not dominion status.

Read the Document *Gandhi Speaks against the Partition of India* on mysearchlab.com

EGYPT Although Egypt never became a full colony of Great Britain, it had been militarily occupied and its government controlled by the British since the late 1800s. Control of Egypt was crucial because of the Suez Canal, built by British and French private investors to provide direct access between the Mediterranean and India. Nationalist movements were common, particularly among the Muslim population. During the Great War, the British government declared Egypt a protectorate to use it as a military base of operations against the Muslim Ottoman Empire and forced half a million peasants into military service against the empire. At the Paris Peace Conference, the Egyptian delegation demanded independence, but the British would not even listen to the request. As a result, violent nationalist demonstrations and labor strikes swept through Egypt. In February 1922, Great Britain granted Egypt its independence under the conditions that the British maintain absolute control over the Suez Canal (with a military force to protect it) and all Egyptian foreign policy decisions be consistent with Great Britain's.

Zionism
a nationalist movement to establish a homeland for the Jewish people in Palestine, centered around Jerusalem for historical and religious reasons

PALESTINE Based on **Zionism** of the late 1800s, European and Russian Jews began moving to Palestine (part of the Ottoman Empire) in the early part of the twentieth century, where they promptly encountered Muslim Arabs who did not want the Jewish settlers. To the Arabs, the

THE BALFOUR DECLARATION

His Majesty's Government view with favour the establishment in Palestine of a national home for the Jewish people, and will use their best endeavours to facilitate the achievement of this object, it being clearly understood that nothing shall be done which may prejudice the civil and religious rights of existing non-Jewish communities in Palestine, or the rights and political status enjoyed by Jews in any other country.

—November 2, 1917

territory was both their ethnic and religious homeland. One of the goals for all the European powers as the Great War opened was control of Ottoman territory, and Great Britain began negotiating with different groups to secure the region of Palestine. In negotiations with Arab nationalist (and Muslim leader) Sharif Husayn bin Ali in 1915, Britain agreed to divide the region between Husayn and British control. According to the Sykes-Picot Agreement between the Allies in 1916, Palestine was to be divided between Britain, France and Russia. And in the *Balfour Declaration of 1917,* Great Britain pledged to establish Palestine as a "national home for the Jewish people." The following month, British troops invaded and occupied Jerusalem. In its effort to secure the territory of Palestine for itself, Great Britain seemed to support both Arab nationalism and Zionism, a position that led directly to conflicting policies and violence in the region for years to come.

When the victors met at the Paris Peace Conference, 11 percent of the population of Palestine was Jewish. Both Arab and Zionist delegations showed up to remind Great Britain of its promises; France intended to uphold the Sykes-Picot Agreement, and Wilson kept talking about self-determination. Violence between Arabs, Jews and occupying British troops began in Palestine and continued throughout the 1920s and 1930s. The U.S. Congress weighed in with its 1922 statement supporting "The Re-creation of Palestine as the National Home of the Jewish Race." It was no easy task, but in 1923 the League of Nations issued the *Mandate for Palestine*. According to Britain, the purpose of the mandate administration was to create a peaceful co-occupation of Palestine by Arabs and Jews under British control. The government would include representative institutions, which would certainly favor the Arabs because they comprised almost 90 percent of the population. Indeed, the first legislative body of Palestine consisted of ten Arabs (eight Muslims and two Christians) and two Jews. But Jewish immigration was also permitted, and thousands of Zionists moved to Palestine and established large collective farms in the late 1920s and throughout the 1930s (particularly once Adolf Hitler came to power in Germany). By 1936, Jews represented almost 30 percent of the population of Palestine. But Arab immigration to Palestine from surrounding countries also increased during this time, as noted in the 1937 Peel Commission assertion that "the shortfall of land is, we consider, due less to the amount of land acquired by Jews than to the increase in the Arab population." The possibility of peaceful co-occupation was destroyed by Arab–Jewish violence that intensified throughout the interwar years as both populations increased. In 1939, Britain gave in to Arab demands and limited Jewish immigrants to 75,000 over five years, after which the immigration would stop altogether as Palestine worked toward becoming an independent Arab state.

The Great Depression

boom-bust cycle
an economy does well (the boom) when it can sell its goods to foreign markets, but is absolutely devastated (the bust) when it cannot

inflation
rising consumer prices, which reduce the purchasing power of a currency

Although the period known as the Great Depression did not officially begin until 1929, the conditions that caused it were direct results of the Great War and decisions made by governments immediately afterward. From 1914 to 1918, the major powers of the world were mired in the war, devoting their entire natural, financial and human resources to winning it. When the war was over, farmland and factories were destroyed, governments were in billions of dollars of debt and 37.5 million men were dead or wounded, not including civilians. And these were the developed countries—the poor countries of the world that relied on primary agricultural products for export had no one to sell to as demand dropped and prices collapsed. International trade had led to a **boom-bust cycle,** and this economic fluctuation aggravated social conflicts within a country because the boom increased social class divisions and the bust led to blame.

In short, three factors combined to make the economic depression severe and long: (1) the Great War burdened most European nations with massive **inflation,** and reparations payments and war debts added further problems; (2) a worldwide decline in production and trade that stemmed from an agricultural depression, a lack of demand for consumer goods due to high unemployment and competitively high **tariffs** on imports; and (3) poor economic planning and decision making by the governments of Europe and the United States. There were problems in Europe and Latin America throughout the 1920s, but the collapse of the U.S. economy in 1929 created a truly worldwide economic crisis.

tariffs
a tax on goods coming into a country imposed by the government of that country as a way to raise revenue and discourage imports

Europe

Even though France and Great Britain had won the war, they were economically devastated and lost their vital workforce of young men. In both countries, the political system was unstable with coalition governments switching back and forth between conservatives and liberals ruling over the democratic system. The conservatives were accused of not helping the people enough in dire economic times, and the liberals were accused of trying to foster a communist revolution. Unemployment in Great Britain remained above 10 percent, and the socialist-leaning Labour Party challenged the authority of the conservatives. The French government fell into financial ruin and was forced to raise taxes on its citizens at the same time inflation was on the rise and the value of the French currency was dropping. In the twenty years following the Great War, France had forty different governments as the fascist, socialist and communist parties battled for control. Unfortunately, this political instability happened at the exact time when the people needed political, economic and social stability.

Germany was even worse off—on top of the regular internal debt from war, Germany was supposed to be paying reparations to Great Britain and France. After the initial payment, the German government stopped sending money. France insisted Germany must pay immediately, and Great Britain tried to compromise by reducing the amount of the payments. Frustrated that Germany was getting away with nonpayment, French and Belgian troops moved out of the DMZ and invaded Germany's Ruhr Valley in January 1923. The goal was to occupy the vital coal and steel industries, thus taking all the profits for themselves. The outraged German government called for passive resistance, essentially a state-sponsored labor strike throughout the occupied area. But because the German government called the strike, it had to somehow pay the striking laborers even though it had no money. The government decided to print more currency, which destroyed its

Family in crowded living quarters in Essen, Germany, during French Occupation.

hyperinflation
a rapid increase in the price of goods as the currency loses its value

already weak value, leading to **hyperinflation.** The German currency was literally not worth the paper it was printed on. The middle class, whose savings and investments were wiped out, suffered more than any other group. It was this traumatic experience on top of everything else that led to the German people's desire for order and security (and revenge against France) at any cost.

Although Great Britain disagreed with the Ruhr occupation, the League of Nations did nothing. The United States stepped in to solve the crisis, putting together the Dawes Plan of 1924. Under the Dawes Plan, the United States restructured Germany's banks and loaned them money. Germany then used those loans to make reduced reparations payment to Britain and France. It was a short-term fix that got France out of Germany (the troops left in August 1925) and stabilized the German economy. The loan also enabled Great Britain, France and Belgium to pay off the outstanding debts they owed to the United States from the Great War, which is really why the United States put together the plan. Unfortunately for all nations involved, the long-term consequence of the Dawes Plan was that it tied Europe's economies to the United States—Germany through foreign loans and Britain and France through trade. So when the U.S. economy failed in 1929, so too did everyone else's.

ANALYSIS

- What does the Dawes Plan say about U.S. foreign policy? Was the U.S. isolationist as it claimed to be?
- What does the Ruhr occupation and France's ultimate acceptance of the Dawes Plan say about France?

Immigration Act of 1924
established a national origins quota that provided immigration visas to 2 percent of the total number of people of each nationality in the U.S. in 1890 and completely excluded immigrants from Asia (which angered Japan); according to the State Department, its most basic purpose was "to preserve the ideal of American homogeneity"

The United States

After the Great War, the American people wanted nothing to do with the rest of the world. They basically closed off America—physically by putting an end to immigration with the **Immigration Act of 1924,** politically by ignoring or breaking diplomatic commitments and participating in world affairs only when it was in their best interest to do so, and culturally by shunning anything anti-American. This led to a drop in demand for foreign consumer goods. Despite essentially separating the American economy from the rest of the world, America thrived and prospered due to the growth of domestic consumer industries. Unemployment was low, the standard of living was high, and new technologies such as the automobile, radio and talking movies were introduced, which made life easier and more fun. It was the booming economy that earned this era's nickname, the "roaring twenties."

Most of this mass consumerism was built on credit. Coming out of the Great War, people did not have money in savings to purchase homes, cars and appliances. Industries realized that if they wanted to sell their goods, earn profits and keep people employed, they would have to find a way to help people buy their products. Credit was extended well beyond individuals' means to repay it; the unregulated stock market fluctuated wildly, and the government was in debt from overspending on military research and development. Like all good things must, the economic boom of the twenties came to an end. The first sign there was a problem occurred when local banks starting closing because borrowers stopped making payments on their debts. Subsequently, the people who lost their savings and investments when the banks closed were unable to pay back their debts. The crisis deepened by the late 1920s as people stopped buying consumer goods and factories and stores had to lay off employees, further reducing everyone's abilities to pay back their debts.

Hooverville in Portland, Oregon.

In an effort to protect and promote America's industries, as well as raise money for the indebted government, the United States continued to push tariffs higher throughout the 1920s, culminating in the Smoot-Hawley tariff of 1930 that raised the tax to 60 percent on some categories of imported goods. Critics have charged that this was essentially economic warfare—as the Great Depression began to impact the U.S. economy, people would not pay extra for imported goods. This dramatically reduced trade from Europe, and in retaliation, the European economies raised their tariffs on goods imported from the United States, leading to an overall decline in world trade by 65 percent in just five years (1929–1934). And this is how economic recession in several countries became a worldwide Great Depression.

Americans were wrapped up in the frenzy of consumerism, while the rest of the countries of the world were unable to recover from war and the U.S. government was sinking deeper in debt. The U.S. stock market crash of October 29, 1929, brought a dramatic end to the "roaring twenties" and plunged America and the rest of the world into a deep economic depression. Fearing the spread of communism to the United States, President Herbert Hoover decided that the American people would have to "pull themselves up by the bootstraps." The government would not take the responsibility of bailing everyone out by providing welfare, leading to the criticism that Hoover did "too little too late" and paving the way for a major political shift in the United States.

The USSR

Lenin's attempt to establish a fully communist economy under the policy of **War Communism** involved the nationalization of all land, banks, foreign trade, food distribution, private residences, and any factory that employed more than ten workers. Money was outlawed for most transactions and bartering encouraged, leading to massive inflation and the demise of the Soviet currency on the international market. It was a disaster that led to famine, poverty and unemployment—the West even sent humanitarian aid (food and medicine) to the communist country. In February 1921, Lenin admitted that War Communism was "a grievous error." The problem, he believed, was that Russia was still primarily an agrarian economy that relied on peasants and, according to Marx, the shift to communism required an industrial base with an urban labor force. In an attempt to go backward, toward socialism, which could then progress smoothly to communism over the next few generations, Lenin established the **New Economic Policy (NEP).** Limited private ownership was restored, agricultural output increased and factories began producing consumer goods. As inflation began to rise, the government stepped in to fix prices. At the same time, the government focused on building the industrial infrastructure of the USSR but was unable to catch up to the West because the NEP simply didn't generate enough revenue for the government.

War Communism
Russia's economic system from 1918–1921 during the civil war

New Economic Policy
Lenin's early Soviet economic system that allowed for some private ownership

Read the Document *Five-Year Plan* on mysearchlab.com

When Stalin took over after Lenin's death, he abolished the NEP and instituted a series of Five-Year Plans to raise both agricultural and industrial output. The result was the **collectivization of agriculture,** which did lead to increased agricultural output but at the expense of the lives of 6 million peasants through famine, execution or suicide. Similarly, the expansion of the coal, steel, electricity, engineering and military industries was astounding in terms of real numbers, but it came through violent and coercive control of a labor force kept in constant fear for their lives. Still, because the USSR was not integrally linked to the U.S. or European economies through trade or loans, when the Great Depression hit in 1929, it did not hit the Soviet Union. That fact, coupled with an extensive propaganda machine, made the communist ideology appear to be the only viable answer to the economic problems faced by the majority of the world's citizens.

collectivization of agriculture
under Stalin, all small private farms were united into massive state-owned farms to increase productivity

The Underdeveloped World

The existing and former colonies and the newly created successor states in the 1920s simply could not compete with the wealthy countries in the world and became especially vulnerable to economic depression. They had a lot of agricultural and/or mineral resources, but they did not have the technology (or money to buy the technology) to turn them into manufactured goods to sell at a profit. As a result, they were stuck providing cheap labor and cheap raw materials to the industrialized countries that made the profit, which had a serious effect on political and social development as well. For these countries, their entire economies depended on the performance of one or two commodities—when that commodity was in demand, there was overall growth, but when that commodity failed for whatever reason, it led to immense poverty. Because most of the

Watch the Video *Life During the Great Depression* on mysearchlab.com

world slipped into economic decline after the Great War, demand for these commodities dropped. Colonies were somewhat protected, but the countries of Latin America were devastated by this, particularly Cuba's sugar industry and the banana industry in Central America. The economic "bust" led to political and social upheaval throughout Latin America, Africa and Asia. What all of these revolutions had in common was that they were basically fought in reaction to Western-style economic development. In one way or another, almost all of the countries of the world were directly reliant on the economies of the West by the end of the 1920s. It is what made the Great Depression worldwide, and it is what led many peoples of the world to seek alternatives.

Technological Advancement

Western economies became the linchpin for the international economic system for the simple reason that they were technologically advanced. They produced more goods and, therefore, generated more profit. This extended their economic reach around the world in search of consumer goods. In the worst-case scenarios, their search for goods led to direct colonization or mandates; in the best circumstances, it created a trade dependency for countries that relied solely on exports for their economic well-being.

Technology is often one of the causes cited for the Great War—countries had invested money into science and technology to create new weapons and communications equipment, and they wanted to test them out. As evidenced by the naval arms race between Germany and Great Britain, having military technology gave a country a sense of superiority and confidence that it could exert its power, and war is generally how a country proves its superiority. From the beginning of the twentieth century, it is clear how intricately technology and politics are intertwined.

Charles Lindbergh working on the Spirit of St. Louis.

By the end of the Great War, the link between science (understanding) and technology (usable products) was clear and could be consistently reproduced. Science shifted from being a theoretical field of study for intellectuals into something that people could replicate, control and use to shape the world around them. A whole new class of scientists appeared—electrical, chemical and mechanical engineers; psychologists; economists—people who provided the physical products to link the theories and experiments going on in the academic world with the problems and solutions of people's everyday lives. Governments in Europe, the United States and Japan invested heavily in education to train these people, including the establishment of government-subsidized public schools and universities to ensure that talented individuals were educated regardless of socioeconomic status. At the beginning of the Great War, the United States had more scientists and engineers than any other nation in the world, but Germany led the way in national research laboratories and was the first to focus on diversification (applying the same basic technology to many different fields). Germany led in chemistry and electricity, but the United States jumped ahead early in oil research. The

Great War produced brand new technologies: U-boats, airplanes, tanks and chemical weapons.

In the 1920s, military engineers in all countries took what they learned about weapons technology in the Great War and went back into the research labs to improve upon what they had. In an effort to prevent the debilitating stalemate that erupted on all fronts, the focus was squarely on improving airplanes as the ideal weapons-delivery system. The world would not see what these military engineers produced until the late 1930s, but civilian aviation engineers began developing airplane technology for commercial use. The commercial aviation industry was limited by the financial restraints of the Great Depression, and the most famous flights were taken by individuals rather than corporations. Charles Lindbergh saved up $500 to buy a WWI-surplus biplane in 1923 and became the first pilot for the U.S. Post Office to deliver airmail. Lindbergh designed and built his own airplane, the *Spirit of St. Louis*, and in May 1927 became the first person to successfully fly across the Atlantic Ocean (New York to Paris). Amelia Earhart was the first woman to fly across the Atlantic solo in 1932; in 1937 her plane disappeared while attempting the first-ever flight around the world.

Ford Motor Company assembly line.

Scientific research was also translated into consumer goods, particularly in the United States, in an effort to rebuild the economy and raise the standard of living after the war. The ultimate example is the radio—key communications technology during the Great War and an affordable luxury for civilians around the world afterward. In the 1920s, radio broadcasts filled homes with news, entertainment and advertising, as well as provided a direct link between governments and their citizens. Another popular consumer good was the automobile, which certainly existed before the Great War but, in the 1920s, became more like the car we recognize today because it pulled together and combined the oil, electrical, textile and communications technologies into one powerful and more luxurious machine. Thanks to Henry Ford's assembly line production and the advent of credit, the car was also more affordable.

On a darker note, uncovering the secrets of **genetics** and DNA provided scientific "evidence" for Social Darwinism and the desire to create technology to control it. The result was **eugenics,** which was basically a breeding program to produce humans with all the good qualities and none of the bad qualities (breeding programs were most prominent in Germany). On the flip side, people who were genetically inferior would have to undergo sterilization so that they couldn't reproduce. The United States was the first country with a government-sponsored compulsory sterilization program (for individuals who were mentally ill, deaf, blind, epileptic or physically deformed), and many countries followed suit from the 1930s through the 1970s.

genetics
a branch of biology that deals with hereditary and variation in organisms

eugenics
science that deals with the improvement of hereditary qualities in a race or breed

The ability to translate science into tools to shape and control nature also had a dramatic impact on the societies that were being controlled and shaped. When people looked at the human toll of the weapons used in the Great War, they wondered if advanced technology had really made war "better." In 1921, Albert Einstein published his theory of relativity, claiming that there is no fixed frame of reference to chart the absolute location of an object. In other words, everything is relative (time, our physical beings, gravity) and may not actually exist outside of how we perceive it. That was a disconcerting thought, and combined with the political, economic and social instability of the 1920s, it led to a Christian revival in the West, where some feared that scientific explanation had replaced religious understanding. The question of science versus religion was actually litigated in July 1925 in Dayton, Tennessee, when John Scopes, a biology teacher, was arrested for teaching Darwin's theory of evolution in science class. The trial, dubbed the "Monkey Trial" by the press, was a media circus engineered by evolutionists to challenge what they viewed as America's fundamental Christian approach to education and legislation.

During the interwar period, people around the world struggled to make sense of their role in a world they felt they could not control. Increasingly, their lives (and deaths) were controlled by science and machinery. Industrialization had led to consumerism and trade dependency, which contributed in large part to the Great Depression. Neither science nor religion could fix that problem—it would have to be governments.

Conclusions

The Great War led to the Treaty of Versailles, which directly resulted in frustration, poverty, ongoing imperialism (albeit by a different name), nondemocratic governments and increased investments in military research and development—the exact opposite of the world that Wilson hoped to create. The frustration stemmed from what many felt was an unsatisfactory end to the armed conflict of the Great War—Germans and Russians felt they were punished far too harshly; Italians, colonists and even the citizens of the newly created successor states and mandates felt they were ripped off by promises made but not kept. At the end of the armed conflict, economic conflict continued as debts; reparations and high tariffs led to a financial standoff between the wealthy countries of the world who dragged every other economy down with them as they sank into a deep and pervasive Great Depression. The money governments did have was being heavily invested in military research and development in preparation for the next conflict, leading to a further division in the world between the "haves" and "have-nots." Whether power is defined as military strength, economic strength or a combination of the two, countries in Latin America, Africa and Asia simply had none and were getting comparatively weaker as the others became more powerful. The League of Nations was far too weak to deal with a worldwide economic depression and the social consequences of it, so people started looking for another answer. They would find it in authoritarian governments.

WORKING WITH THE THEMES

THE EFFECTS OF TECHNOLOGY How did consumers benefit from the technology created to fight the Great War? Was eugenics the logical "next step" of Social Darwinism? How did science challenge religion in the early 1920s? Why was it particularly noticeable in the postwar era?

CHANGING IDENTITIES How did the Treaty of Versailles affect German citizens? What effect did the treaty's realignment of borders in Eastern Europe have on nationalism? How and why did Great Britain deal with nationalist demands differently in the postwar era than before the Great War?

SHIFTING BORDERS Why did the segments of the former Ottoman Empire become mandates while European nations were granted independence? What are the roots of the Arab–Israeli conflict in Palestine?

GLOBALIZATION What caused the onset of the Great Depression? Why did it take longer for the Great Depression to reach the United States? What prevented the depression from reaching the USSR? Why didn't the League of Nations work as Wilson envisioned it?

Further Reading

TO FIND OUT MORE

The Library of Congress Manuscript Division: *American Life Histories: Manuscripts from the Federal Writers' Project,* 1936–1940. Available online at http://lcweb2.loc.gov/ammem/wpaintro/wpahome.html

The World at War: From Versailles to the Cold War. Available online at http://worldatwar.net/

PBS: A Science Odyssey—People and Discoveries Databank. Available online at http://www.pbs.org/wgbh/aso/databank/

Neil A. Hamilton (ed.): *Lifetimes: The Great War to the Stock Market Crash: American History Through Biography and Primary Documents* (2002)

GandhiServe Foundation: Mahatma Gandhi Research and Media Service. Available online at http://www.gandhiserve.org/

GO TO THE SOURCE

John Maynard Keynes: *The Economic Consequences of the Peace* (1920)

The Covenant of the League of Nations (1924)

Frank B. Kellogg: *The Pact of Paris and the Relationship of the United States to the World Community (An Address Delivered over the Columbia Broadcasting System)* (October 30, 1935)

Mahatma K. Gandhi: *Hind Swaraj or Indian Home Rule* (1938)

MySearchLab Connections

Read the **Document** on **mysearchlab.com**

3.1 George Clemenceau, *French Demands at the Peace Conference.* French Premier, George Clemenceau, as one of the chief negotiators at the Versailles peace treaty after World War I ended, had an important influence on its final terms. Despite U.S. President Woodrow Wilson's hope for a peace without victors, Clemenceau demanded compensation for French losses and security against future German aggression.

3.2 *Henry Cabot Lodge Objects to Article 10 of the Treaty of Versailles.* Senator Henry Cabot Lodge of the United States objected to many details of the Treaty of Versailles, particularly the League of Nations. He believed that membership in the League of Nations would entangle the United States in foreign affairs and prevent the country from acting independently in such matters.

3.3 *Irish National Identity.* Several years after the bloody Easter Rising of 1916, Ireland split in two—the independent Republic of Ireland in the South, and Northern Ireland, still part of the United Kingdom. The division resulted in decades of political agitation and violence between Irish Republicans, Ulster Unionists and the British troops in Northern Ireland.

3.4 *Gandhi Speaks against the Partition of India.* In the transition from British colony to independent nation, long-standing tensions between Hindus and Muslims returned to the surface. Some more extreme leaders on both sides of the issue had called for separate countries for the two groups but many Indian leaders pleaded against division and in favor of unity. Indian nationalist Mohandas Gandhi believed that a successful nation included both, and pleaded for a unified India.

3.5 Joseph Stalin, *Five-Year Plan.* In an effort to realize rapid industrialization, Stalin initiated a plan to build heavy industry funded by the state. Under the plan, the government forced peasants into collectivized farms in order to increase agricultural yields; the surplus revenue from agriculture then financed government-owned factories and industries.

Watch the **Video** on **mysearchlab.com**

3.1 *The Continuing Legacy of World War I in the Middle East*

3.2 *Life During the Great Depression*

4 Political Ideologies of the Interwar Years

CHAPTER OUTLINE

- Democracy
- Authoritarian and Military Regimes
- Communism
- Fascism
- The Rise of Nazi Germany

CHAPTER TIMELINE

1921
The Treaty of Versailles restructures Europe

1922
Mussolini becomes Prime Minister of Italy

1925
Hitler writes *Mein Kampf*

1927
Stalin seizes leadership in USSR

Shanghai Massacre in China ignites civil war

1930
USSR collectivizes agriculture

1939
The Pact of Steel is signed

Germany invades Czechoslovakia

The Nazi-Soviet Pact is signed

The helicopter is invented

September 1, 1939
Germany invades Poland, igniting WWII

'Kristallnacht'
1938
Heute schüren sie das Feuer neu

Photos from left to right: Adolf Hitler and Benito Mussolini in Munich; Joseph Stalin; Chinese Communist rally; Kristallnacht propaganda poster.

1933	1934	1935	1936	1937	1938
Roosevelt launches the New Deal in the United States Hitler becomes chancellor of Germany The first concentration camp opens in Germany	CCP is forced on Long March in China	Italy invades Ethiopia Nuremburg Laws pass in Germany	Spanish Civil War begins Stalin initiates the Great Purge Socialist government sets up in France	Japan invades China The first jet engine is built Hitler remilitarizes the DMZ on the French border	The *Anchluss* reunites Germany and Austria The Munich Conference is held *Kristallnacht* takes place

The world created after the Great War was one of economic depression and political instability. People were looking for radical solutions to these radical problems, and many began to believe that the answer could be found in ideology. As Chapter 3 addressed, nationalism was still prevalent throughout the world as colonies sought independence, successor states struggled to establish legitimate governments, mandates were created, and Zionism moved into the Middle East. Wilson's goal was the spread of democracy, but many people held the capitalist economy associated with democracy responsible for the Great Depression. In the relatively strong countries, governments stepped in to provide relief for their citizens, shifting many democratic governments decidedly toward socialism. In the weaker countries, the military took control of the government to provide security. For the poor, communism seemed to be an answer to their poverty because one of its basic core beliefs was that wealth should be shared equally by the citizens. But communism and the equal sharing of wealth was exactly what the middle and upper classes feared most, and they started looking for a government to protect them against the communist revolution. After years of war and economic depression, they wanted security and stability, and fascism was just the ideology to give it to them. The result of these ideological "isms" was the rise of authoritarian governments around the globe—the exact opposite of the world Wilson envisioned.

WORKING WITH THE THEMES

THE EFFECTS OF TECHNOLOGY Communications and weapons technology developed during the Great War are used to solidify political power within countries.

CHANGING IDENTITIES As the economic depression deepens, people turn to radical political ideologies to address their problems. Democracy is in decline as communism, fascism, and authoritarianism spread. Women in democracies gain suffrage.

SHIFTING BORDERS Germany grows as Hitler seizes the Rhineland, Austria, and Czechoslovakia in pursuit of *Lebensraum*.

GLOBALIZATION The economic devastation of the Great Depression creates political turmoil. The Comintern fosters communist political parties around the globe.

Democracy

Although President Wilson died in 1924, his vision of a peaceful world filled with self-determined, democratic governments did not. Nationalists and colonists around the world continued to fight for their right to participate in governmental decision making. Ironically, this often forced governments to crack down even harder to prevent revolutions and civil wars and preserve domestic stability. Similarly, democracy and the capitalist economic theory it espoused were blamed for exacerbating the Great Depression. Throughout the 1920s and early 1930s, as the economic depression deepened, democratic governments continued their laissez-faire approach and refused to intervene in the economy. But as living conditions worsened and life became less stable and predictable, democracy appeared to be unable to provide what people needed.

Women living in democracies had been arguing about the hypocrisy of democracy since the mid-1800s. If indeed a democracy is "rule by the people," then shouldn't all the people be included? Although some women enjoyed suffrage in a few local elections in a few parts of the world prior to the Great War, a debate in the British House of Commons exemplified the prevailing attitude toward extending the right to vote to women:

> *...women had their own honourable position in life, that that position had been accorded to them by nature, and that their proper sphere was the home...Women would be neglecting their homes if they came into the House of Commons, and when they would be compelled to attend public meetings and to read all the newspapers and Blue-books and other dry documents, so as to fit themselves for the franchise...There were times and periods in women's lives when they required rest not only for mind but for body, and to drag them into the political arena under those conditions would be cruel indeed.* (Sir Samuel Evans in Parliament, April 25, 1906)

Allied women suffragists at the Paris Peace Conference.

During the Great War, women kept the factories and farms producing necessary supplies, maintained functioning homes and held their families together, clearly proving that they were physically and mentally capable of taking care of both domestic and civic life. Suffragist demonstrations resumed with vigor after the war, and it became increasingly difficult for democratic governments to refuse to acknowledge women's rights to participate in government. The Netherlands granted suffrage in 1917, and many other countries followed suit. In 1918, women's suffrage was granted in Austria, Czechoslovakia, Poland, Sweden and Great Britain (but only to women over the age of thirty, until that was changed in 1928). In 1919, Germany and Luxembourg extended women's suffrage, and the United States passed the Nineteenth Amendment to its Constitution in 1920, granting American women the right to vote. For women in France, Belgium, Italy, Romania and Yugoslavia, suffrage did not happen until the 1940s.

Great Britain

Parliamentary democracy in Great Britain had deep roots and was never seriously challenged by right-wing fascist politics or left-wing communist politics. Although the centrist Conservative and Labour parties disagreed on the role the government should play during the Great Depression, both parties agreed wholeheartedly that communism must be stopped. The British Communist Party, founded in 1920 by Lenin's **Comintern,** was relatively small and never a real revolutionary threat.

Comintern
nickname for the *Communist International*, a political movement started by Lenin to establish communist political parties around the world directly connected to the USSR

Economic, political and social recovery from the Great War was not yet achieved when the full force of the Great Depression hit in 1930. As demand for British goods dropped, unemployment rose as high as 30 percent in some areas. The Conservative Party was blamed for the war and its economic consequences, paving the way for the dominance of the Labour Party in the late 1940s.

France

Throughout the 1920s, France was physically, economically and emotionally devastated and absolutely reliant on loans from Great Britain and the United States and German reparations for money to rebuild. By the time the Great Depression hit in the 1930s, the Allied troops were gone, the Locarno Treaty was in place, and the French people had lost faith in their government. Although one segment of the French Socialist Party joined Lenin's Comintern in 1920, others did not, splitting the party into several factions that frequently pressured the government of the **Third Republic.**

Third Republic the republican parliamentary democracy of France, created in 1870 after the monarchy was destroyed by the Franco-Prussian War

In 1934, fascist-led riots convinced the various strands of socialist and communist parties to ally and form a coalition known as the Popular Front. Leon Blum became France's first socialist president in 1936 and began work on some bold reforms to help the working class get through the economic depression, including the Matignon agreement that legalized labor unions and provided national rights to workers. Nonetheless, France suffered from tremendous internal political divisions, leading to instability.

The United States

The dramatic poverty brought on by the Great Depression was absolutely unprecedented in the United States. As a constitutional democracy, the government was supposed to stay far removed from individual citizens' lives, which is exactly how the Hoover administration initially responded. As the depression worsened, it appeared that American democracy was failing.

The Communist Party of the United States was founded in 1919 when the Socialist Party of America joined Lenin's Comintern. State and federal authorities did everything they could to destroy the party, driving it underground throughout the **red scare** of the early 1920s. Although membership continued to grow through connections to many labor unions, communist leadership in the United States was frequently` divided, particularly after Lenin's death.

red scare U.S. government response to the fear of a Bolshevik revolution in America that included censorship, unconstitutional raids and arrests, and the deportation of foreigners

In 1932, the American people elected Franklin Delano Roosevelt, a Democrat who promised them a "New Deal." His radical three-pronged economic policy was aimed at providing short-term relief to the people and economic recovery for industry, as well as restructuring the American economic system. In the first three months of 1933, Roosevelt and Congress enacted a record number of laws, all of which involved heavy government participation in the economy. Although the New Deal leaned further toward socialism than past American economic and social policies and required a planned economy, the administration's philosophy was that the government had a responsibility to solve problems for its people. In doing so, the U.S. government expanded its political reach in ways that violated both the fact and the spirit of the U.S. Constitution. On the other hand, the New Deal restored Americans' faith in their government, perhaps preventing radical political ideologies from taking root in the United States as they did elsewhere in the world. In economic terms, the New Deal did not directly end the depression; it would take a national effort at rearmament and war preparations to achieve that.

The U.S. Socialist Party campaign poster.

Authoritarian and Military Regimes

The countries that lacked the internal political or ethnic unity required to form democratic governments suffered from political and social instability during the 1920s.

Once the Great Depression hit in 1930, there was no hope of developing a coordinated economic, political and social response. The most effective way to prevent internal chaos was to form an authoritarian regime, either ruled directly or heavily supported by the military.

Read the Document *FDR's First Inaugural Address* on mysearchlab.com

Successor States

Although the Republic of Austria was set up as a parliamentary democracy, it was basically ruled as a League of Nations mandate throughout the 1920s because of outstanding financial debts. In 1933, in an attempt to prevent Nazism from spreading into Austria, the chancellor dissolved the Parliament, outlawed the Social Democrat Party and established authoritarian rule, igniting civil violence.

In Poland, a group of former military officers created the *Sanacja* movement and led a coup against the corrupt government of the Second Polish Republic in 1926. Led by Jozef Pilsudski, all political parties except *Sanacja* were outlawed, and all government leaders required Pilsudski's approval before taking office.

Watch the Video *Hitler and Roosevelt* on mysearchlab.com

At the Paris Peace Conference, the Allies combined the independent countries of Serbia and Montenegro with chunks of former Austro-Hungarian territory to create the Kingdom of Serbs,

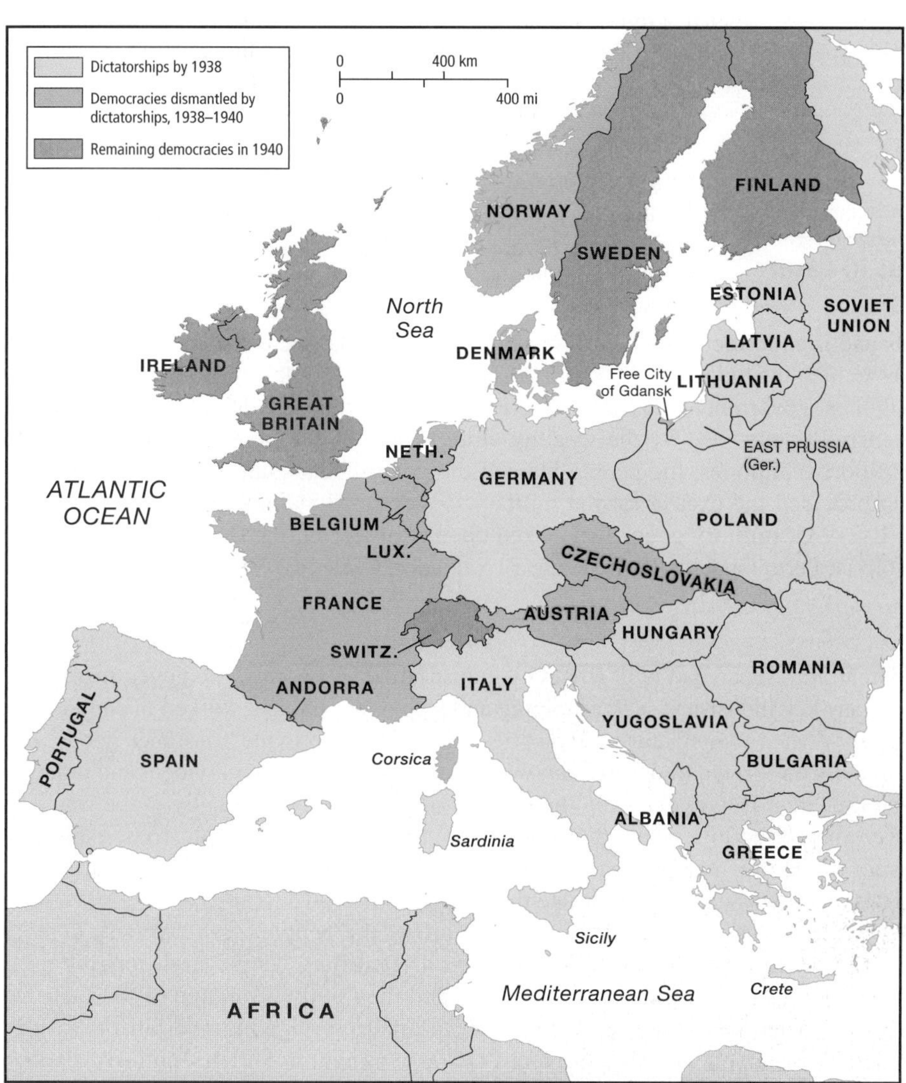

MAP 4.1 Europe, 1940

MAKE THE CONNECTION

Why didn't the Western European governments do anything to prevent authoritarian regimes from replacing weak democratic governments throughout Eastern Europe?

MAP 4.2 Authoritarian Regimes in Latin America, 1940

Croats and Slovenes. The nationalist rivalries crippled the political system, so in 1929 King Alexander banned all political parties and created his own country, Yugoslavia, which he ruled as a dictator.

Estonia, Latvia and Lithuania fought wars against Russia to earn their independence, and each initially established a democratic government in the 1920s. A military coup in Lithuania in 1926 led to an authoritarian regime marked by nationalist education and radical land reform. Estonia and Latvia remained democracies until 1934, when political coups in each country established nationalist dictatorships.

Probably the most robust of the successor states, Czechoslovakia was a democratic republic with a comparatively healthy industrial sector, but it suffered from serious internal ethnic divisions. The Czech majority ran a highly centralized political and economic system that disenfranchised the Slovak, German and Hungarian minorities. These minority populations never fully acknowledged the authority of the Czech government and frequently worked against it.

Latin America

Because Latin American countries relied almost solely on the exportation of primary goods, the Great Depression thoroughly destroyed their economies. Furthermore, many large industries were owned by foreign (mostly U.S.) corporations over which the governments had no control. During the 1920s, most Latin American governments defaulted on their foreign debts and tried to focus on their domestic economies, but there was no money for welfare measures to help the citizens.

Although most governments in Latin America were constitutional democracies by design, they were generally controlled by the wealthy elite. As the Great Depression ravaged these commodity-export economies, the people blamed the governments, and internal violence increased. That provided the excuse for the military to step in to maintain control and prevent civil unrest. By 1935, military coups had seized control of Argentina, Brazil, the Dominican Republic, Bolivia, Peru, Guatemala, Ecuador, El Salvador, Chile and Venezuela.

Japan

Prior to the Great War, Japan had built a heavily industrialized economy. The government itself had financed many key industries, such as mining and shipyards, and had worked in conjunction with large family-owned manufacturing industries and banks to provide consumer goods. But Japan relied heavily on foreign trade, so it too was vulnerable to the unemployment and inflation brought on by the Great Depression even though it participated only minimally in the war. The Japanese government tried to regulate the economy by financing military industries, exploiting its territories for cheap raw materials and artificially depressing the prices of domestically manufactured goods, but it was unable to alleviate the people's suffering.

Because of these measures and the dissatisfaction of the people, parliamentary democracy in Japan fell victim to a series of assassinations and military coups. High-ranking military officers ran the government and the economy, and they took advantage of the fact that the world's governments were focused on domestic affairs to engage in imperialist invasions of Manchuria and China. They shifted the focus of the economy to military industries above all else, including food and consumer goods. When the League of Nations condemned Japan's militaristic actions, the Japanese government simply quit the League of Nations.

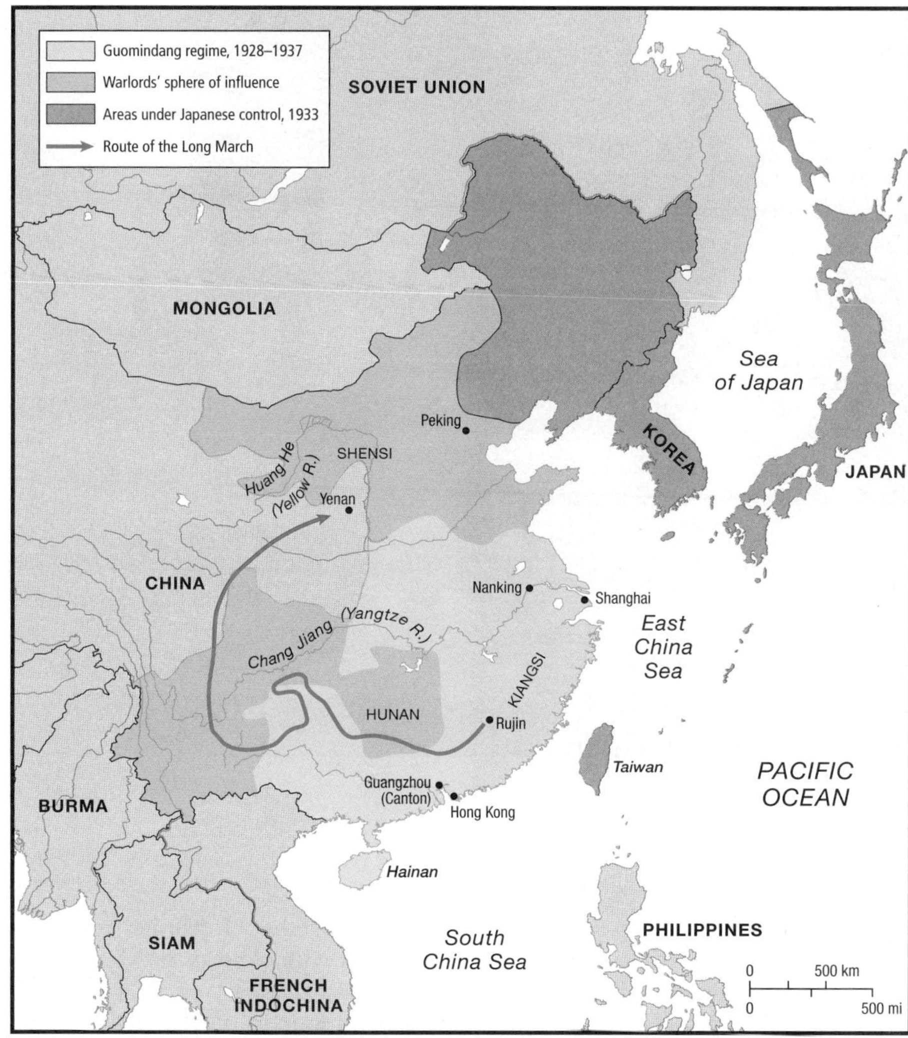

MAP 4.3 Japanese Expansion

Communism

Many of the decisions made by the U.S. government at the Paris Peace Conference and in the two decades that followed were, in large part, driven by the desire to block communist expansion. As poverty grew, so too did the appeal of communist ideology. With established communist political parties throughout Europe and the United States, an expanding Comintern movement worldwide and Mao Zedong's peasant revolution in China, communism was quickly becoming a viable political alternative to democracy.

The USSR

Under the Bolsheviks, the USSR was ruled by the heavy and harsh hand of the General Secretary of the Communist Party (initially Lenin) and its Red Army. When Lenin died in 1924, the Communist Party was split at first between two factions: Leon Trotsky's followers, who called for rapid industrialization at the expense of the peasantry, and Josef Stalin's followers, who wanted to conduct industrialization slowly and concentrate on "socialism in one country." By 1927, Stalin had won the struggle for power and evicted Trotsky first from

Stalin (front row, fourth from the right) with Great Purge survivors.

ANALYSIS

This is a photograph of the top echelon of the Communist Party after the Great Purge. What does Stalin's body language tell you? What else is notable, for 1938, about this picture?

the Communist Party, then from the USSR altogether. To further prove his victory, he sent out assassins, who caught up with Trotsky in Mexico and brutally murdered him with an ice pick.

Traditional Bolshevik ideology (grounded in Marxism) called for a permanent international revolution, which is why Lenin formed the Comintern to support revolutions in other countries. Marx predicted that the proletarian revolution would be worldwide and spontaneous, but Lenin's Comintern strayed from the spontaneity requirement. Stalin's focus on "socialism in one country" marked a complete shift in party ideology and practice. With this motto and his Five-Year Plans, he made it clear to the Soviet people, who were tired of civil war and struggling with famine, that he was more concerned about their well-being than he was about spreading the communist ideology around the world. While this made him popular with his people, he was not one to leave his power to chance.

gulags
forced labor camps in remote regions of Siberia; the Soviet economy became reliant on their labor for major infrastructure projects and mining, but conditions were extremely harsh

Between 1936 and 1938, Stalin consolidated his absolute control of the USSR with the "Great Purge," which he started after one of his closest comrades was assassinated. There is, of course, no way to know what really happened before and after the assassination. Publicly, Stalin declared that he was expelling "opportunists" and "counter-revolutionary infiltrators" from the party. In reality, he imprisoned and executed anyone he believed might pose a threat to his leadership, including government officials, Communist Party members, military officers and ethnic minorities. Conservative estimates put the death toll of the Great Purge at 1 million people (of the approximately 1.5 million who were detained). Almost 700,000 of them were executed (shot), an average of 1,000 per day. The rest died in **gulags** during their imprisonment. By the end of the 1930s, Stalin clearly controlled the USSR.

China

In the wake of internal disorder at the beginning of the century, a popular uprising in the city of Wuchang against the Qing Empire led to the empire's demise and the eventual creation of the Republic of China in 1912, although there was no true centralized government and the country was essentially run by warlords in different regions of the territory. In 1922, Sun Yat-sen, founder of the Guomindang (Nationalist Party), received financial assistance from the Comintern to build a military to defeat the warlords and reunite China. This forced the Guomindang into an alliance with the newly formed Chinese Communist Party (CCP), led by Mao Zedong. But when Sun Yat-sen died in 1925, Chiang Kai-shek seized control of the Guomindang and launched the **Shanghai Massacre** against the CCP. He established an authoritarian nationalist government with one-party rule by the Guomindang, which, because communism was what the West feared most, was recognized by the West even though the government was decidedly nondemocratic.

Chiang Kai-Shek.

Shanghai Massacre the Guomindang army attacked their communist allies (executing 5,000 to 6,000) in April 1927, igniting civil war in China

The Great Depression hit China particularly hard because it was an agrarian economy. Debilitating poverty attracted China's peasants to communism, enabling Mao Zedong to build a guerilla military force to rival the Guomindang army. Civil war throughout the early 1930s culminated in the "Long March" of 1934, when the Guomindang army forced 100,000 CCP guerillas 6,000 miles across the mountains of China, killing 90 percent of them along the way. Despite the ongoing civil war, the 1936 Japanese invasion of Manchuria forced Chiang Kai-shek's Guomindang and Mao's CCP into a very uneasy and temporary alliance in an attempt to defeat Japan and preserve China's territorial integrity.

Fascism

Fascism was a right-wing political ideology that appeared during the interwar years as the primary opponent to the spread of communism. Relying on an authoritarian government structure to provide much-needed stability for citizens, fascism was antidemocratic, anti-Marxist and racist. But it was fiercely nationalistic, and it promised to hold back the spreading communist revolution, so it appealed to the middle and upper classes in Europe.

Italy

Although Italy had joined the Great War on the Allied side, the Italian delegation was not allowed to participate equally with the other victors at the Paris Peace Conference. The government (a constitutional monarchy) viewed this as disrespectful, particularly after the final version of the Treaty of Versailles denied Italy much of the territorial gain it felt it was promised. Within Italy, the people were suffering from the consequences of the war and did not believe their government was representing their interests either domestically or internationally. Almost immediately (from 1919 to 1921), there was considerable social turmoil, and the politically deadlocked Parliament could not agree on a single piece of legislation to help the people. The Italian middle and upper classes feared that the poverty and social turmoil would lead to a communist revolution.

Portrait of Benito Mussolini.

In stepped Benito Mussolini, an educated man from the middle class. He was an active socialist and journalist before he enlisted and fought in the Great War (earning the rank of corporal). After the war, he used the newspapers he owned to explain his newly developing fascist ideology to the Italian people, and in 1919 he established the National Fascist Party. To win their support, he formed a volunteer paramilitary group called the National Security Volunteer Militia (more commonly known as the "Black Shirts" because of their uniforms) to intimidate the communists and assure the people that someone was paying attention to security in their neighborhoods. The Black Shirts tapped into the frustration and outright anger of the Italian people following the war; and the group attracted nationalists, former military officers and soldiers and young middle-class men as volunteers. Promising to prevent the communists from seizing control of the government, Mussolini's fascist ideology was exactly what the Italian people wanted to hear, and he was one of thirty-five fascists elected to the Italian Parliament in 1921.

In August 1922, the Socialist Party and the unions it represented organized a labor strike across Italy. Recognizing opportunity, Mussolini ordered his Black Shirts to replace the striking workers to keep the Italian economy running and maintain social order—he was a hero to the middle and upper classes. The strike lasted only four days, after which Mussolini emerged as the most popular politician in Italy. To avoid a civil war, King Victor Emmanule made him the Prime Minister of Italy in October 1922. In the following years, Mussolini staged a very popular and completely legal revolution that left Italy a one-party state ruled by the National Fascist Party under his dictatorial control. Mussolini's regime stayed in power because of effective anticommunist propaganda, censorship, the Black Shirts and the support of the Catholic Church (in exchange for maintaining control of the Vatican).

Read the Document *"The Political and Social Doctrine of Fascism"* on mysearchlab.com

To deal with the financial aftermath of the war and the Great Depression, Mussolini undertook a program of public works, subsidized the shipping industry, introduced protective tariffs to help Italian industry, and expanded wheat farming. He made agreements with leaders of industry and agriculture and all but destroyed labor unions. Under the policy of **Corporatism,** private industry was subordinated to state guidance but not total control—Corporatism was sort of a hybrid between capitalism and a planned economy. Still, Corporatism was unable to solve the economic crises affecting the people.

Corporatism
Mussolini's plan for social revolution and national cohesion in which everyone is united, each with a particular role to play, in strengthening and glorifying Italy

Mussolini became "Il Duce" (revered leader) to the Italian people and even gained worldwide respect from governments that feared the spread of communism. But he had dreams of building a new Roman Empire around the Mediterranean, which led him to attack the Greek island of Corfu and set up a puppet regime in 1923 and eventually to invade Albania and colonize Libya. In 1935, he invaded Abyssinia (now called Ethiopia) and drew criticism and a painful economic embargo from the League of Nations for his aggression. But he didn't let it alter his foreign policy choices, and in 1936 Mussolini began supporting the fascist overthrow of the Spanish government. By the end of the 1930s, as the world was lining up for yet another war, Great Britain and France viewed Mussolini as an uncooperative aggressor, pushing him closer to Hitler.

Spain

In 1931, the King of Spain was exiled when the Spanish people voted to establish a republic form of government. In the first elections, the Socialist Party won an overwhelming victory and controlled the government until a coalition of right-wing parties took over after the 1933 elections. The Socialist, Communist and other left-wing parties formed the Popular Front coalition to oppose the right-wing National Front coalition. In the 1936 general election, the Popular Front defeated the National Front by only one percentage point and then upset the conservatives with the leftist policies they enacted when they took office. They released all leftist political prisoners, outlawed the *Falange Espanola* (a political party that followed Mussolini's model of fascism) and sent right-wing military leaders to serve outside of Spain. They introduced agrarian reforms that financially hurt the landed aristocracy and granted the region of Catalonia autonomy. Fearing that communism was on its way to Spain, the upper class sent its money out of the country to protect it, leading to an economic crisis. The currency declined in value while prices rose, leading to labor strikes across Spain. The Spanish military, which supported the National Front, began planning to overthrow the Popular Front government.

Because we are no longer an isolated minority group fighting hopelessly against an immense giant. Because, my dear, we have joined with, and become an active part of, a great progressive force, on whose shoulders rests the responsibility of saving human civilization from the planned destruction of a small group of degenerates gone mad in their lust for power. Because if we crush Fascism here we'll save our people in America, and in other parts of the world from the vicious persecution, wholesale imprisonment, and slaughter which the Jewish people suffered and are suffering under Hitler's Fascist heels. . .

—Canute Frankson, American volunteer in Albacete, Spain, July 6, 1937

The Spanish Civil War began in July 1936. The war was fought between the Nationalist military, led by General Francisco Franco and supported by Germany and Italy, and the Republican army, which consisted of ethnic minorities, various left-wing paramilitary groups supported by the USSR and the **International Brigades.** The civil war, which lasted through 1939, was a classic ideological confrontation between communism and fascism. Interestingly, the powerful democracies in the middle of the political spectrum (Great Britain, France and the United States) did not participate, although volunteers from these countries joined the International Brigades. They were not necessarily communists, but they felt compelled to help fight fascism because their governments were not doing so.

International Brigades organized by the Comintern, 59,000 communist and antifascist volunteers (men and women) from fifty-five countries were militarily trained and fought for the Republican cause

By February 1939, General Francisco Franco's Nationalist military clearly controlled Spain. During the course of the civil war, roughly 500,000 people including civilians died, 10,000 of them foreign soldiers fighting to spread either fascism or communism. The fact that the U.S., British and French governments—the victors of the Great War—were unwilling to participate to spread their own ideology (democracy) sent a message to both fascist and communist governments in Europe. As a result of the Spanish Civil War, Germany and Italy solidified their "Rome-Berlin alliance" into a **Pact of Steel** in May 1939.

Pact of Steel ten-year total military commitment between Germany and Italy with regard to war

The Rise of Nazi Germany

Throughout the 1920s, Germany struggled economically, socially and politically under the democratic Weimar government. The suffering German people blamed the regime for accepting the terms of the Treaty of Versailles, which brought about disastrous effects. Extreme poverty led to political unrest as people were increasingly attracted to communism and other radical political alternatives. By the 1930s, antigovernment sentiment was high—the only question was, who would emerge to replace the Weimar regime?

The Nazi Party

Adolf Hitler, head of the National Socialist German Workers' Party (better known as the Nazis), believed that his political party had the answers to Germany's problems. Although they did not call themselves a fascist party, they certainly had a lot in common with Mussolini's ideology, including militant anti-Marxism, brutal racism in the form of **anti-Semitism** and intense nationalism (preserving Germany for pure Germans only), all defended by legions of

anti-Semitism prejudice or hostility against Jews

Read the Document *Twenty-Five Points* on mysearchlab.com

ANALYSIS

- How many of the Twenty-Five Points related directly to the Treaty of Versailles?
- How many of the twenty-five points dealt with treatment of Germany's Jewish population?
- How many of the twenty-five points expanded the powers of government?

paramilitary volunteers in the *Sturm Abteilung* (called the SA, Stormtroopers or Brownshirts). The party's platform was explained in the *Twenty-Five Points*, which made demands such as the end of the conditions imposed by the Versailles Treaty, the unification of Austria and Germany, the exclusion of Jews from German citizenship, agrarian reform and various other measures to benefit the working class. The more the Nazis talked, the more support they gained from German citizens who were completely fed up with feeling inferior to the rest of Europe. The people loved the Nazi message of nationalism and hoped the promise of economic growth was true. They even loved the SA—because the Treaty of Versailles had banned a substantial German military, someone needed to provide security.

Watch the Video *Conformity and Opposition in Nazi Germany* on mysearchlab.com

Hitler's Early Career

How did Hitler move from being a regional political party member to becoming *"der führer"* (the leader) of Germany? Hitler's rise to leadership happened through the gradual growth of the Nazi political party, the support of the German people and Hitler's legitimate appointment to German political office.

Before the Great War, Hitler was living in poverty in Vienna (the capital of Austria-Hungary), which suffered from political upheaval because of high nationalist tensions. On the eve of the Great War, he moved to Munich, his German Fatherland, and enthusiastically volunteered for the Bavarian military. Hitler was a good soldier, earning the rank of corporal and the Iron Cross first class medal, rarely awarded to foot soldiers. As the war dragged on, Hitler was disgusted by his fellow soldiers' low morale in the trenches and the antiwar sentiment among the German citizens. When the German government admitted defeat, he remarked, "I knew that all was lost . . . in these nights hatred grew in me, hatred for those responsible for this deed." He blamed the Weimar government and the Jews for subverting his beloved, Christian monarchy.

Hitler Youth at a Nuremburg Rally, November 9, 1935.

Hitler first became associated with the German Workers' Party in 1919, which he saw as a nationalist working class movement more than anything else. He was put in charge of propaganda and membership because of his fiery nationalist and anti-Semitic tirades. He drew in a lot of ex-military colleagues who were disgusted at the terms of the so-called peace treaty. He drew middle- and upper-class people who feared a communist revolution, and he drew Christians who wanted to stamp out Judaism. By the end of 1920, the Nazi Party had about three thousand members, primarily due to Hitler's marketing. In 1921, he took control of the party leadership.

As economic conditions worsened in Germany, particularly after France's invasion of the Ruhr Valley, Hitler made his first attempt at a government coup with the Beer Hall Putsch. In November 1923, he and his SA troops seized a beer hall in Munich while three top Bavarian government officials were there. The coup did not go at all as planned, and Hitler was arrested and tried for treason in a month-long public event that received heavy press coverage. Hitler used the trial as an opportunity to spread the Nazi message, and support for the party grew. Even the judges liked what he said, so Hitler received a minimal sentence in a low-security prison, with the promise of early parole. During the nine months Hitler was imprisoned, he ranted and raved about the problems of the world and how to solve them while his personal secretary wrote it all down. The result was a political tirade entitled *Mein Kampf* (My Struggle), which contained Hitler's views on Aryan supremacy and Jewish and Slavic inferiority, including specifics on what he would do about it. He declared that ***Lebensraum*** would be acquired by force and specifically referred to seizing Russian territory and seeking revenge against France. In 1925, *Mein Kampf* laid out exactly what Hitler planned to do when he gained control of Germany, but hardly anyone read the published book.

Read the Document *Mein Kampf* on mysearchlab.com

Lebensraum
literally "living space"; to Hitler the term meant the acquisition of territory to the east (Russia) to allow for the growth of the superior race (Aryan)

After the Beer Hall Putsch, Hitler decided to take control of Germany by election rather than force. He completely reorganized the Nazi Party, creating one group focused on undermining the Weimar government and a second group that was essentially a "government-in-waiting" to take over when the Weimar government fell, as he knew it would. The party divided Germany into thirty-four districts (sort of like soviets in the USSR) and the Hitler Youth group was formed to bring adolescents on board. Hitler also created an elite guard unit within the SA, called the Schutzstaffel (SS), to do the dirty work.

With the Dawes Plan of 1924, the German economy began to pick up. But after the U.S. stock market crash in 1929 and the onset of the Great Depression, Hitler knew his time had come. The Weimar government lost support, and when new elections were held in September 1930, the Nazis won 18 percent of the vote, which entitled them to 107 seats in the 577 seat **Reichstag.** When the elected Nazis entered the Reichstag, they wore the Brownshirt uniform and at roll call responded, "Present! Heil Hitler!". Hitler became a national hero and an international political figure. The second largest political party in Germany, the Nazis went after their political opponents (Social Democrats and Communists) viciously, disrupting parliamentary proceedings and rendering the Reichstag totally ineffective.

Reichstag
the German Parliament

Hitler Takes Control of Germany

As the economy worsened, civil unrest grew, and the government was unable to help. In March 1932, Hitler ran for president of Germany and forced a **runoff** against the aging incumbent, Paul von Hindenburg (Hindenburg received 49 percent of the votes, Hitler received 30 percent). Despite the vigorous efforts of the Nazi propaganda machine, Hindenburg received 53 percent of the votes in the final election that April and narrowly retained the office of president. But there was no doubt that Hitler was incredibly popular with the people—13.5 million Germans had voted for him.

runoff
in an election with several candidates running, if no candidate receives a majority of the votes, a second election is held between the top two candidates only

At eighty-five years old, the odds were that Hindenburg would not be able to serve out his seven-year term, and men within the administration began fighting for control of his government. After six months of political backstabbing, scandal, four failed governments and civil violence led by the Nazi Brownshirts, a state of martial law was declared in Germany—there was no working government in place. Fearing a communist revolution in the midst of German civil rioting, the country's most influential corporate and industrial leaders pushed Hindenburg to allow Hitler to try to establish a government. Left with no other choice, Hindenburg reluctantly named Adolf Hitler the chancellor of Germany on January 30, 1933, although his cabinet was limited to only two additional Nazis in an attempt to keep his power in check.

Whatever happens, mark what I say. From now on Germany is in the hands of an Austrian, who is a congenital liar [Hitler], a former officer who is a pervert [Röhm], and a clubfoot [Goebbels]. And I tell you the last is the worst of them all. This is Satan in human form.

—Gregor Strasser, December 1932 (Strasser was a founder of the Nazi Party but was removed in 1932 after disagreeing with Hitler over Nazi policies.)

By appointing Hitler Chancellor of the Reich you have handed over our sacred German Fatherland to one of the greatest demagogues of all time. I prophesy to you this evil man will plunge our Reich into the abyss and will inflict immeasurable woe on our nation. Future generations will curse you in your grave for this action.

—General Erich Ludendorff, who participated with Hitler in the Beer Hall Putsch, to Hindenburg in January 1933

But Hitler's power came less through elected political office than through the 500,000 Brownshirts who supported him. He never intended to share power through a coalition government—Hitler's plan called for a dictatorship. Although the German army stayed in place, SA and SS members replaced high-ranking local police officials throughout Germany and began attacking communists and other Nazi enemies. On February 27, 1933, a known Dutch communist set fire to the Reichstag building. The arsonist was convicted and beheaded, and Hitler used the incident to incite fear of a communist revolution. Hindenburg signed the following emergency decree:

Enabling Act called the "Law to Remedy the Distress of the People and the Nation," it gave Hitler the power to pass laws without the consent of Parliament, even if the laws were unconstitutional

> *Restrictions on personal liberty, on the right of free expression of opinion, including freedom of the press; on the rights of assembly and association; and violations of the privacy of postal, telegraphic and telephonic communications and warrants for house searches, orders for confiscations as well as restrictions on property, are also permissible beyond the legal limits otherwise prescribed.*

The SA and SS sprang into action, rounding up, imprisoning and executing suspected communists, social democrats and liberals. Anyone speaking against the Nazi Party was a suspect, and political enemies were quickly silenced. Still, in the March election, the Nazis did not win the majority of the Reichstag, forcing to Hitler to seek the **Enabling Act** to seize absolute control, essentially ending democracy in Germany.

I swear by God this sacred oath: I will render unconditional obedience to Adolf Hitler, the Führer of the German Reich and people, Supreme Commander of the Armed Forces, and will be ready as a brave soldier to risk my life at any time for this oath.

On August 2, 1934, President Hindenburg died, and Hitler passed a law combining the offices of chancellor and president, becoming the *Führer* of Germany. Each military officer in Germany was required to take an oath of obedience. Hitler created a police state and ruled by force, purging the Nazi Party of anyone not totally on board, purging the government of anyone not Nazi, and purging society of anyone not German (by his definition). He justified this anti-Semitism based on Social Darwinism—if he was to create a strong Germany, only the fittest could participate.

Domestic Affairs in Nazi Germany

Under the Enabling Act, the government instituted a massive program of public works and spending, mostly related to rearming Germany, restoring its military strength and rebuilding the infrastructure. The government guided the decisions of private industry and crushed trade unions. Although this kept wages low, it reversed the spiraling unemployment. Women returned to their traditional German responsibilities in the home, and by 1935 German agriculture and industry were on the rise. Despite its destruction of personal liberty, the Nazi regime did achieve economic security for the German people.

Jewish people in Germany represented less than 1 percent of the population, came from all economic backgrounds, and were members of a variety of political parties (except, of course, the Nazis). But to Hitler, the Jewish people were all enemies of the Germans, despite the fact that 80 percent of them were German citizens and many others were married to ethnic Germans. In the twelve years Hitler was in power, more than four hundred laws were created specifically to hurt Jews. Stripping Jews of their legal rights began with a boycott of Jewish businesses just a week after the Enabling Act was signed. The boycott was a Nazi reaction to negative stories about Hitler in the British and American press, which he blamed on the "international Jewry." From there, Jews were banned from working as government employees, lawyers, doctors, dentists, teachers, professors, journalists and entertainers.

In 1935, the Nuremburg Laws stripped Jews of their German citizenship and specifically outlawed sexual relations and marriage between ethnic Jews and Germans. But it was very difficult to distinguish exactly who was legally a Jew and who was not. The government decreed that a "full Jew" was a person with at least three Jewish grandparents; those with fewer than three were designated **mischlinge** in the first (two Jewish grandparents) or second (one Jewish grandparent) degree. Many of the mischlinges were even Christian. To help officials identify Jews, the Nazis produced instructional charts that measured facial features and distinguished between Jewish and non-Jewish eye and hair color.

The persecution of the Jews was temporarily suspended while the world watched as Berlin hosted the 1936 Olympic Games. Afterward, however, Jews were required to register their property and relinquish their businesses and jobs to ethnic Germans. They carried identity cards marked with a red "J" stamp and were eventually required to wear a "Star of David" insignia on their clothing to make it even easier for the police to identify them. Localized, violent assaults on Jews were common, but a nationwide attack took place on November 9 and 10, 1938, in what is now called *Kristallnacht* ("Night of Broken Glass"). Led by the SA and Hitler Youth, Germans destroyed and burned Jewish synagogues, homes and businesses.

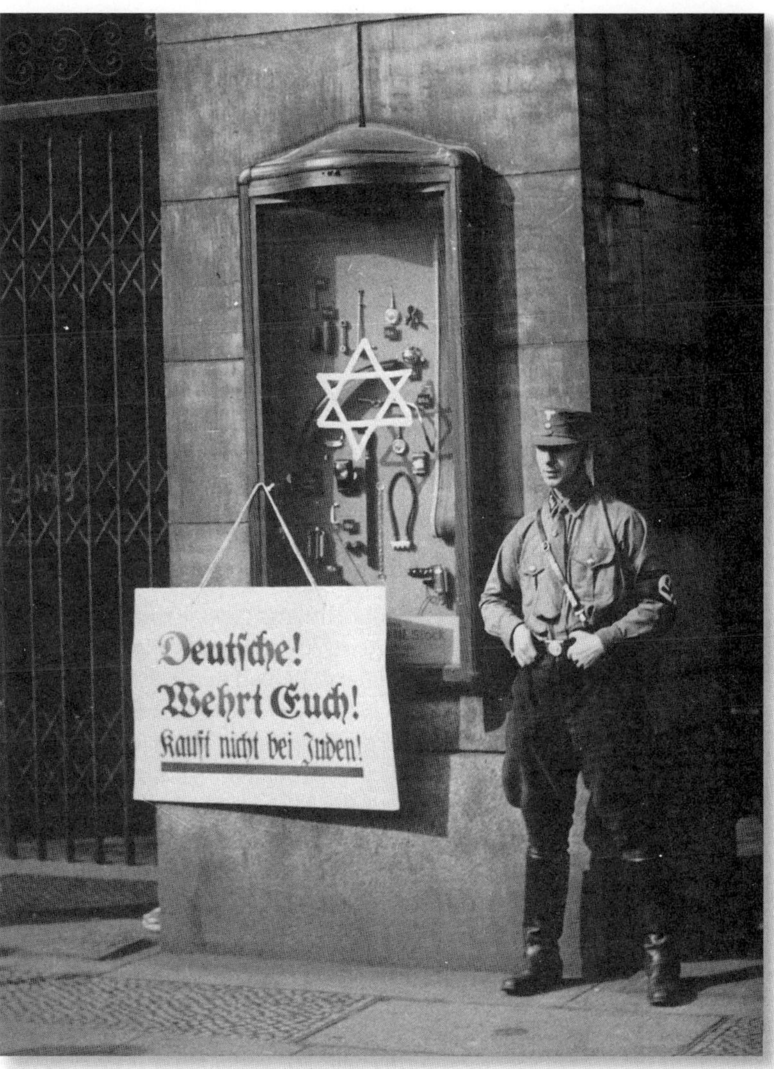

On April 1, 1933, the Nazi boycott began. Placard reads, "Germans, defend yourselves, do not buy from Jews," at the Jewish Tietz store in Berlin.

Another important goal for the Nazis was the reeducation of German citizens. In Hitler's mind, they had been exposed to devastatingly non-German perspectives that needed to be purged. Strict adherence to Nazi propaganda in education at all levels was nonnegotiable. Book burnings demonstrated the outright hatred for non-German ideas, and all teachers and professors were required to take the Nazi oath to keep their jobs. Those who could flee the country did, most famously Albert Einstein, depriving Germany of intellectual richness and diversity. Between the Nazi curriculum in schools and the Nazi Youth for after-school activities, education was focused on preparing German children for service to the German state. For adults, the Nazis held religious-like rallies (best captured in Leni Riefenstahl's 1934 documentary film, *Triumph of the Will*) and created extensive propaganda to indoctrinate Germans in the Nazi ideology. Refusing to conform to Nazi standards exacted a high price.

The **Gestapo** was created to ensure that Nazi laws were followed. Because the Gestapo operated outside of the court system (by decree), there was no legal oversight or appeal for Gestapo activities, which included interrogation, incarceration and execution. The first **concentration camp** at Dachau was opened in 1933 to reeducate Germans who did not comply with Nazi ideology. Because of prison overcrowding due to the new laws in place, there were fifty camps by the end of the year, each run by either the SA or the SS. Initially, the camps were barbed-wire stockades within which the "enemies of the state" were denied sleep, forced into hard labor and fed little more than Nazi ideology. The goal was to reform them and send them

mischlinge
half-breed

Gestapo
plain-clothes police force

concentration camp
Nazi prisons first opened in 1933 in remote locations where people were kept in one location to increase efficiency—a camp complex would have separate facilities for hard labor, experimentation and eventually extermination

back to be productive members of Nazi society. The motto was: "There is one way to freedom. Its milestones are: obedience, zeal, honesty, order, cleanliness, temperance, truth, sense of sacrifice and love for the Fatherland."

To simplify matters of domestic law, in 1938 Hitler declared: "All means, even if they are not in conformity with existing laws and precedents, are legal if they subserve the will of the *Führer*."

Hitler's Foreign Policy

Throughout his career, Hitler based his actions on the belief that all the ethnic Germans should be united in Europe's strongest nation. Hitler never lost sight of this goal; he was, nonetheless, an opportunist, willing and able to change tactics when the situation changed. He recognized that achieving his goal would almost certainly require a major war, one that Germany, of course, must be prepared to win.

The first step for Hitler was to free Germany from the military restrictions of the Treaty of Versailles. In 1935, he formally denounced the treaty's disarmament provisions and began to rebuild the Germany military, reinstating **conscription** until he had an army of half a million men. Although Hitler had clearly violated the treaty, the League of Nations did not respond. In fact, Great Britain even negotiated an agreement allowing Germany to build its naval power to 35 percent of Britain's.

conscription
compulsory enrollment for military service, also called "the draft"

How did Hitler get away with this? The short answer is that he was a really good liar. Hitler was a gifted orator, and he convinced the League of Nations that his actions were simply to prepare Germany to defend herself within Europe. He told them horror stories of his experiences in the trenches of the Great War and assured them that he would never instigate matters in Europe that could lead to such devastation. The truth is that Great Britain recognized that a weak Germany could never successfully block the spread of communism across Eastern Europe, leaving Western Europe vulnerable.

What they did not know, however, was that Hitler's war plans were already underway. In November 1937, Hitler convened a secret meeting of his most trusted followers and laid out his plans for expanding *Lebensraum* based on the simple fact that the German people were entitled to more living space than any others in Europe. This would only be gained through force—Hitler presented three possible military strategies against France and Britain but ultimately focused on the Soviet Union. Clearly, he had been planning this for awhile.

Hitler's first step—sort of a test to see how France and Great Britain would react—was to remilitarize the Rhineland (the DMZ between Germany and France) in March 1936. This action violated both the Treaty of Versailles and the Locarno agreements. The League of Nations had every reason and right in the world to react but did not, mostly because its membership could not agree on how to respond. France was justifiably angry but militarily incapable of responding on its own. Poland, which had just signed a border agreement with Germany, decided it was probably a legitimate action given Germany's position. Great Britain agreed with France that the action was wrong but did not view it as a threat in any way. So the League of Nations did not react and instead sent Hitler the subtle message that they were not willing (or perhaps not prepared) to defend the Treaty of Versailles. This led to one of the most controversial foreign policies in modern history—**appeasement.** The League of Nations would not stop Hitler as long as his goals seemed limited and reasonable. Neville Chamberlain, the Prime Minister of Great Britain, actually came to trust Hitler, or at least believed Hitler was a reasonable man with whom he could negotiate. After all, Hitler promised Europe that he was satisfied after the Rhineland:

appeasement
literally, "to pacify" or "conciliate"; in Chamberlain's words, "As long as war has not begun, there is always hope that it may be prevented, and you know that I am going to work for peace to the last moment" (September 1938)

> *First, we swear to yield to no force whatever in the restoration of the honor of our people, preferring to succumb with honor to the severest hardships rather than to capitulate. Secondly, we pledge that now, more than ever, we shall strive for an understanding between European peoples, especially for one with our Western neighbor nations... We have no territorial demands to make in Europe!... Germany will never break the peace.*

Austrians welcome Hitler during the *Anschluss*.

Emboldened by a 99 percent approval rating from the German citizens and the lack of response from the League of Nations, Hitler continued toward his goal of *Lebensraum*. In 1938, Hitler made use of his alliance with Mussolini to expand Germany's borders and bring the 7 million ethnic Germans living in Austria home to the Fatherland. Hitler called it the *Anschluss* (the union) of Germany and Austria, and indeed there was no violence, bloodshed or Austrian military resistance as Germany's tanks and troops invaded Austria in March 1938. In fact, ethnic Germans were lined up on the side of the road, cheering and waving Nazi flags to celebrate Hitler as their new *Führer*. Invading a sovereign country was clearly yet another violation of the Versailles Treaty, but by now it was obvious that no one was going to uphold the treaty. Mussolini supported Hitler; Chamberlain thought it seemed reasonable because the Austrian people were happy about it, and the Austrian government never even asked for help.

After the *Anschluss*, Czechoslovakia found itself surrounded by Germany on three sides and still in possession of the Sudetenland, home to 3 million ethnic Germans. Clearly, Czechoslovakia was next on Hitler's "to-do" list. As Nazi supporters in Czechoslovakia created civil unrest, Hitler planned a full-scale military invasion. A group of high-ranking German officers even sent a secret envoy to Great Britain to warn of the impending attack, hoping that the League of Nations would take a threatening stance against Hitler and the German army could overthrow him, but Chamberlain thought it was a trick. Instead, he would meet with Hitler personally. Britain and France had decided to negotiate with Hitler, allowing him to seize and occupy the Sudetenland as long as he promised he would go no farther into Czechoslovakia. The agreement was signed into treaty by Great Britain, France, Italy and Germany at the Munich Conference on September 30, 1938. The government of Czechoslovakia was not even invited to attend. On October 1, German troops invaded the Sudetenland and the British press announced Chamberlain's triumphant declaration that the Munich agreement would bring "peace for our time." In March 1939, Hitler violated the Munich agreement and invaded and occupied the rest of Czechoslovakia. Perhaps appeasement was not the way to handle Hitler after all.

MAP 4.4 German Territorial Expansion, 1933–1939

Read the Document *The Nazi-Soviet Pact* on mysearchlab.com

By now, the British Parliament had enough of Chamberlain's appeasement policy and pushed him to respond more forcefully. The British and French announced that they would guarantee the security of Poland, Hitler's next territorial goal. As the governments of the world quickly formed their alliances in preparation for the war that was now certain to come, the only real question was what would Stalin do? He was, quite frankly, a little offended that he had been left out of European negotiations up to this point and questioned if perhaps Chamberlain and Hitler were actually working together against him. Would Stalin remain neutral, because both alliances were anticommunist, or would someone convince him to get involved?

The primary problem for the West was that it did not trust Stalin. Poland absolutely refused to allow Soviet troops into its territory, even to protect it against a German invasion. Plus, every bit of rhetoric in the West was aimed squarely against communism and Stalin himself, which did not make Stalin excited at the prospect of having to trust them. Of course, Hitler and Mussolini were violently anticommunist, so Stalin was not terribly trusting of them either. But Hitler and Stalin had two things in common (other than being ruthless dictators): their countries were arbitrarily carved apart in the Treaty of Versailles, and they both wanted that land back.

When the Nazi-Soviet Pact was signed on August 28, 1939, the world knew that war was inevitable. The pact was simply one of nonaggression, which meant the two leaders promised not to take aggressive action against the other. But this essentially handed Poland over to the German military because Hitler had no threat of a two-front war. To get Stalin to agree to this neutrality agreement, Hitler added a secret provision—as Germany invaded Poland from the west, the Soviet military would move into the region and regain the territory it lost in the Treaty of Versailles. For Germany and the USSR, the "wrongs" committed at the Paris Peace Conference that closed the Great War would be corrected. Now the rest of the world would have to decide how to respond.

Conclusions

By the end of the 1930s, there were far more nondemocratic governments among the leading world powers than democracies. Strikingly, almost all of these nondemocratic governments enjoyed the support of the citizens. The dramatic effects of the Great War, coupled with the crippling poverty created by the Great Depression, forced people to think about what their government actually did for them. A very tangible fear of spreading communist ideology and violent governments (Stalin's) made people seek security, which, given the chaotic destruction of the Great War, could only come through a strong military force such as fascism. In Germany, the restrictions imposed by the Treaty of Versailles added another layer of despair for the common people. All of these authoritarian governments were successful because: (1) they provided stability for the people (and most also offered a way out of economic depression), and (2) they employed very effective propaganda machines to convince the citizens to "buy in." By the end of the 1930s, the spread of communism seemed to be stopped, but so too did the spread of democracy.

MAKE THE CONNECTION

Of the major powers of the world, which ideology controlled the most governments? Which controlled the fewest?

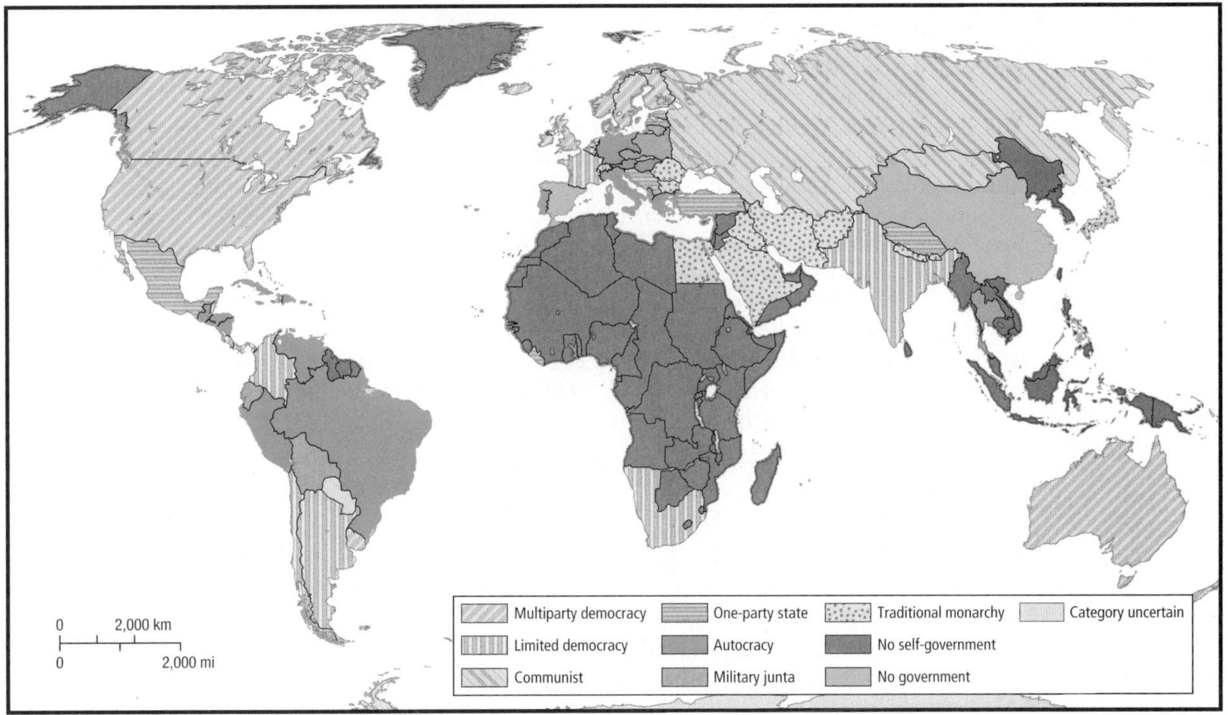

MAP 4.5 Political Systems, 1939

WORKING WITH THE THEMES

THE EFFECTS OF TECHNOLOGY How did advancements in communications equipment help governments establish control over their borders? How did political leaders use technology to achieve their domestic goals?

CHANGING IDENTITIES Why did Western governments extend suffrage to women from 1917 to 1928? Why did the German people love Hitler and the Italian people love Mussolini? Why wasn't the Comintern able to gain a larger following in the West, even during the Great Depression? What problems in the successor states led them away from democracy?

SHIFTING BORDERS What was Hitler's reasoning for expanding German borders in the 1930s? How did Germany's expansion affect nationalism in Europe? How particularly did the Nazi-Soviet Pact of 1939 signal the onset of WWII?

GLOBALIZATION Why wasn't the League of Nations able to prevent military conflicts in central Europe and China? How did the worldwide economic depression affect foreign-policy decision making in the 1930s?

Further Reading

TO FIND OUT MORE

Roosevelt Institute: New Deal Network. Available online at http://newdeal.feri.org

Hitler Historical Museum: Hitler's Speeches. Available online at http://www.hitler.org/speeches/

Marxists Internet Archive: Josef Stalin Internet Archive. Available online at http://www.marxists.org/reference/archive/stalin/index.htm

Marxists Internet Archive: Mao Zedong Internet Archive. Available online at http://www.marxists.org/reference/archive/mao/

Les Fearns: Casahistoria—Spanish Civil War. Available online at http://www.casahistoria.net/civilwar.htm

Open Society Archives: Forced Labor Camps. Available online at http://www.osaarchivum.org/gulag/

MATRIX, the Center for Humane Arts, Letters and Social Sciences Online: Seventeen Moments in Soviet History—1921, 1924, 1929, 1934. Available online at http://www.soviethistory.org

GO TO THE SOURCE

Adolf Hitler: *Mein Kampf* (1925)

Aldous Leonard Huxley: *Brave New World* (1932)

Benito Mussolini: *What Is Fascism?* (1932)

Ernest Hemingway: *For Whom the Bell Tolls* (1940)

Commission of the Central Committee of the C.P.S.U.(B.): *History of the Communist Party of the Soviet Union (Bolsheviks)* (1938)

MySearchLab Connections

Read the **Document** on **mysearchlab.com**

4.1 *FDR's First Inaugural Address.* Franklin Roosevelt took office during the worst economic depression the nation had ever experienced. This speech is famous for his statement that Americans had *"nothing to fear but fear itself."* It also began to give shape to a program that would require powers no previous U.S. president had ever wielded.

4.2 Benito Mussolini, from *"The Political and Social Doctrine of Fascism."* Mussolini was perhaps fascism's most articulate spokesman. He believed that the twentieth century was a new historical epoch that required a different political premise based on popular loyalty to the state and supported by violent force.

4.3 *Twenty-Five Points.* The Twenty-Five Point Program was the official platform of the NSDAP (National Socialist German Workers' Party). Adapted from the political platform of the Austrian Worker's Party by Adolf Hitler in 1920, the platform very clearly spelled out what the NSDAP stood for.

4.4 Adolf Hitler, *Mein Kampf.* Hitler wrote the book *Mein Kampf* ("My Struggle") nearly twenty years before the Holocaust. In this selection, he evaluates the contributions of the Aryans and cloaks his racism, including his slander of the Jewish people, in the garments of pseudoscience.

4.5 *The Nazi-Soviet Pact.* In an effort to avoid a two-front war, Adolf Hitler proposed to Josef Stalin that they forge a "Treaty of Non-Aggression between Germany and the Soviet Union." It stipulated that each would remain neutral in the event that either was engaged in war against a third party, and that neither of them would participate in a group "directly or indirectly aimed at the other."

Watch the **Video** on **mysearchlab.com**

4.1 *Hitler and Roosevelt*

4.2 *Conformity and Opposition in Nazi Germany*

5

World War II

CHAPTER OUTLINE

- The War Begins in Europe: 1939–1941
- Opening the Eastern Front: 1941–1942
- War in the Pacific: 1941–1943
- The North African Theater
- Germany on the Defensive: 1943–1945
- The Final Phase in the Pacific: 1944–1945
- The Human Cost of the War

CHAPTER TIMELINE

September 1, 1939

Germany invades Poland, igniting World War II

The first ghettos are built in Poland

1st phase is marked by "The Phoney War"

1940

Churchill becomes prime minister of Great Britain

April: Germany invades Western Europe

June: France surrenders

Germany launches the London Blitz

Lend-Lease Act is signed

Italy invades Greece

Tripartite Pact is signed

1941

Hitler sends Afrika Korps to North Africa

Hitler launches Operation Barbarossa

The first computer controlled by software is invented

Japan and USSR sign nonaggression pact

The Atlantic Charter is signed

Japan bombs United States at Pearl Harbor

Japan subjects U.S. troops to Bataan Death March

1942

Manhattan Project begins

First extermination camps are built in Poland

Operation Torch is launched in North Africa

The Battle of Stalingrad destroys German troops

Roosevelt issues Executive Order 9066

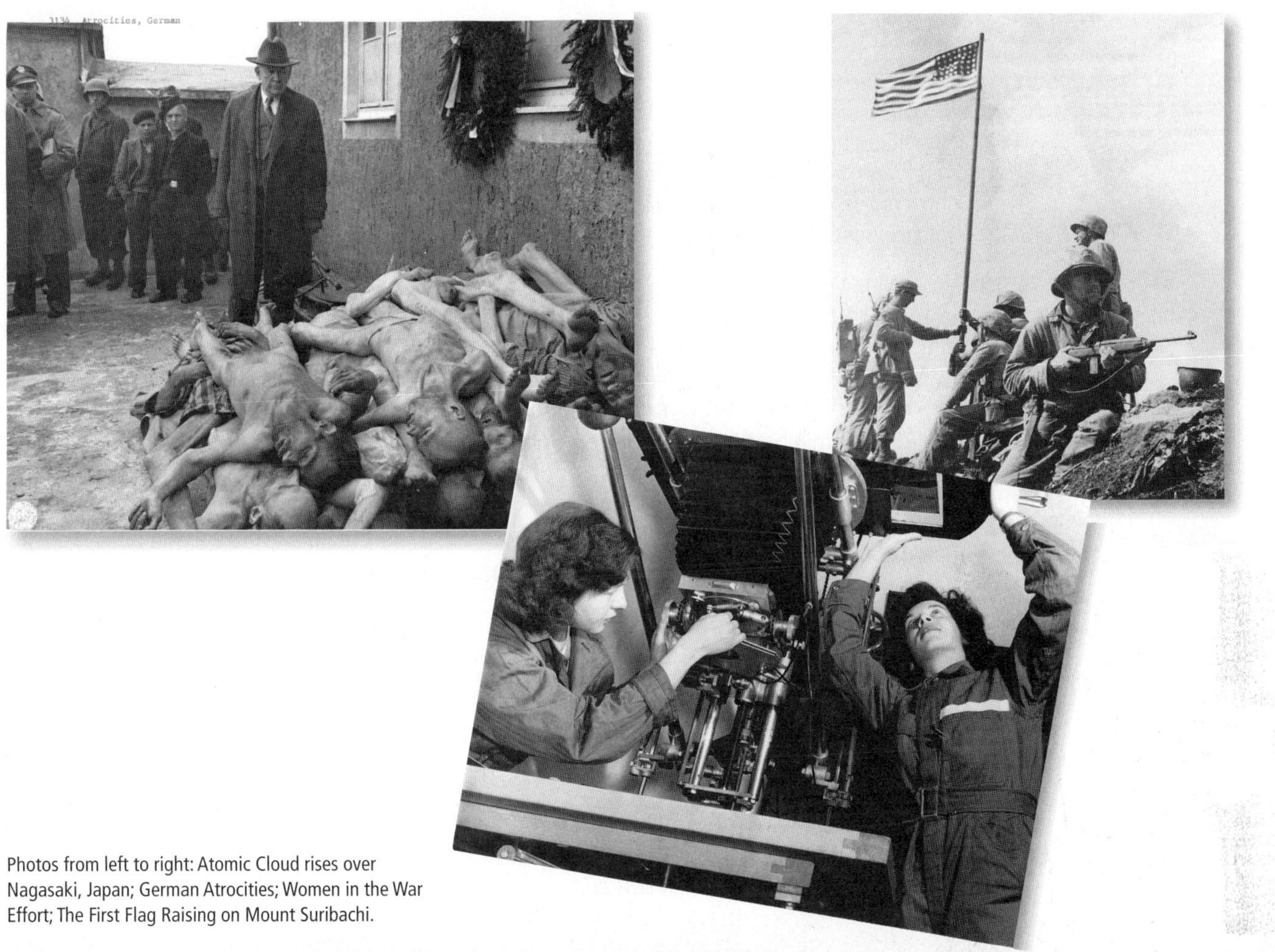

Photos from left to right: Atomic Cloud rises over Nagasaki, Japan; German Atrocities; Women in the War Effort; The First Flag Raising on Mount Suribachi.

1943

Operation Cartwheel changes the Pacific war

Tehran Conference is held

Mussolini is removed from power

Italy surrenders

1944

Allies secure the Pacific in the Battle of Leyte

The Battle of the Bulge opens the road to Berlin

D-Day launches Operation Overlord

1945

The "big three" meet in Yalta

Roosevelt dies

Hitler commits suicide

May 8: VE Day ends the fighting in Europe

Welfare state is established in Britain

U.S. and Japan fight for Iwo Jima

Potsdam Declaration

The first atomic bombs are used

The United Nations is founded

September 2, 1945

VJ Day ends WWII

On the eve of World War II, democracy was in danger. Weakened by the physical and economic devastation of the Great War and the subsequent Great Depression, people around the world had chosen what they hoped would provide stability in an attempt to quell their insecurity. There were many more communist, fascist and authoritarian governments than democratic ones, most enjoying the full support of their citizens. Unfortunately, the focus on militarism within these regimes created seemingly inevitable conflict between them. The two regional wars that came together to create the second world war were connected by the political consequences of the Treaty of Versailles, the economic devastation of the Great Depression and the development of radical political regimes in the 1930s. One regional war was in Europe, where authoritarian governments had taken over most of the continent and were headed straight for the last democratic strongholds, Great Britain and France. The other war was in East Asia, where China struggled both internally, as nationalists and communists fought for control, and externally, against the very aggressive and imperialistic Japan. Bolstered by advanced weapons technology, these regional power struggles merged into World War II, and both the United States and the Soviet Union were drawn in. Radical political ideologies had pulled the world into war, and peace could only be achieved by forging a very uneasy alliance between the two least likely to share power.

WORKING WITH THE THEMES

THE EFFECTS OF TECHNOLOGY World War II takes place at sea, in the air, and on the ground with more power but less precision, increasing civilian casualties. The atomic bomb is invented and used. Rapid advances are made in communications.

CHANGING IDENTITIES Germany launches a mass extermination of Jews, Slavs, "unfit" Germans, and others, seeking to create a "perfect" Aryan race. The United States struggles with its self-perception versus national security interests.

SHIFTING BORDERS Hitler occupies most of Europe as he ignites World War II. Japan expands its empire in the Pacific, drawing the United States into the war. The USSR occupies territory in Eastern Europe and negotiates to keep it.

GLOBALIZATION Most countries around the world are drawn into World War II because of location, alliance or colonial status.

The War Begins in Europe: 1939–1941

As he wrote in *Mein Kampf* in 1925, Hitler's ultimate goal was *Lebensraum*—living space for the German people. His first steps toward that goal required regaining territory that had been stripped from Germany in the Treaty of Versailles, and until Hitler violated the Munich agreement in March 1939 by invading Czechoslovakia, he seemed to be well on his way to doing so with ease. Although Great Britain threatened to stop his military machine, Hitler approached Poland with greater confidence after the signing of the Nazi-Soviet Nonaggression Pact in August 1939.

Poland

Germany invaded Poland at dawn on September 1, 1939. In Britain, Prime Minister Neville Chamberlain addressed the Parliament:

> *The time has come when action rather than speech is required...It now only remains for us to set our teeth and to enter upon this struggle, which we ourselves earnestly endeavored to avoid, with determination to see it through to the end...We have no quarrel with the German people, except that they allow themselves to be governed by a Nazi Government. As long as that Government exists and pursues the methods it has so persistently followed during the last two years, there will be no peace in Europe.*

These words led to declaration of war against Germany on September 3, 1939, by the British Empire and her allies Australia, New Zealand, France, Canada and South Africa. World War II

German troops parade through Warsaw, Poland, September 1939.

had officially begun, although no foreign power sent troops to help defend Poland. The German military pushed the Polish military toward the east, where the Poles ran directly into Soviet troops who had entered Poland on September 17. The Polish military was quickly defeated. Soviet and German troops met in Brest-Litovsk on September 28 to reaffirm their previously arranged territorial agreement, and Poland surrendered the following day. Germany immediately annexed the Polish cities and lands along its border—where many German nationalists lived—and established the rest of Poland as an occupied territory.

The *Blitzkrieg*

From the first hours of the invasion of Poland, it was clear to all observers that this war would not be fought like the Great War just twenty-five years before. Military applications and weapons technology had improved vastly, and Germany was clearly at the forefront of this new style of fighting. Trench warfare had been a debilitating and ultimately unsuccessful way to seize territory, and engineers and scientists had been working in earnest to find a more efficient way to fight. World War II would not be fought below ground in trenches, which led to stalemate; it would be a fast-paced war of infantry and armored vehicles moving across land, with bomber planes clearing their paths.

The German military called it *Blitzkrieg* ("lightning warfare") because it centered on rapid advances into enemy territory with columns of air support, preferably with the element of surprise to throw the enemy into disarray. The fighting was loud, fast and came at you from several different locations at once. The basic requirements for this kind of fighting were first developed at the end of the Great War, and all powerful countries had been working on the advancing technology of motorized vehicles, airplanes and bombs. Because Germany's military had been almost completely destroyed as a requirement of the Treaty of Versailles, Germany was forced to rebuild from the ground up with the latest technology, and it did so quickly under Hitler.

Watch the Video *The German Army: U.S. Air Force Analysis of Captured German News Reels* on mysearchlab.com

Germany's *Blitzkrieg* was initially successful because it was a new way of waging war. It combined highly mobilized tank units and mechanized infantry units with massive yet precise aerial bombardment, all in constant contact with one another through radio communications. And *Blitzkrieg* strategy was basically simple—it relied on surprise attacks and allowed flexibility for the commanders in the field. Some militaries, such as those of Poland and France, still relied on the outdated technology and strategy of the Great War. Great Britain had improved its technology but was unable to coordinate the different branches of the militaries as *Blitzkrieg* required. It would take a few years for these militaries to figure out how to effectively combat *Blitzkrieg*.

Phoney War
the nine-month period of relative inactivity on the part of Great Britain and France immediately following their declarations of war against Germany; the Germans referred to this period as the "Sitzkrieg"

armistice
an agreement to temporarily suspend hostilities between belligerent powers so that a peace agreement can be negotiated

The Western Front

In the months following the occupation of Poland, the USSR occupied the Baltic states (Estonia, Latvia and Lithuania) and invaded Finland. The USSR was expelled from the League of Nations for these acts of aggression, but once again, no one sent troops to Eastern Europe. A small contingent of British troops was sent to the continent, but it did not attack German troops. This period of World War II, from Germany's invasion of Poland and the declarations of war in September 1939 through the spring of 1940, is often called the **Phoney War.** Despite their declarations of war, neither Great Britain nor France was militarily prepared to actually engage in combat. They knew it, and they spent these nine months putting things in order to take action in the summer of 1940. Unfortunately for them, Hitler knew it too, and he took full advantage of this time to further prepare his military and formulate his plans.

In April 1940, without warning, Germany invaded Denmark and Norway, securing air and naval bases closer to Britain and encircling Sweden (with the Soviet-occupied Finland). This prompted harsh criticism of Neville Chamberlain and his Phoney War from the British Parliament and people. Chamberlain was forced to resign, and Winston Churchill, a prominent member of the War Cabinet, became prime minister on May 10, 1940. That same day, the German military made its move against the Netherlands, Luxembourg and Belgium, capturing them all in two and a half weeks. Still unprepared for Hitler's *Blitzkrieg*, the French army quickly collapsed. Churchill ordered the evacuation of 330,000 British and French troops in the first week of June as Hitler's military was poised just outside of Paris. The Phoney War was over.

Eager to show his Axis ally support, as well as seize long-desired territory along the French–Italian border, Mussolini declared war on France and Great Britain at midnight on June 10 as his troops invaded southern France and headed toward Paris. Facing certain defeat, Paris surrendered on June 14, and the German troops moved in. Former World War I hero Marshal Henri Petain took over the government of France and asked Germany for an **armistice.** Hitler presented Petain with humiliating terms of surrender on June 22 in the same railway car in which the Germans were forced to surrender at the end of the Great War. To celebrate both his immediate military and symbolic nationalist victories over France, Hitler had the railway car destroyed.

According to the terms of the armistice, the French would stop fighting the Germans immediately in the occupied northern half of the country. In exchange for this cooperation, Petain would be allowed to set up a puppet government in unoccupied southern France at Vichy. No German soldiers would be

Hitler in Paris.

MAP 5.1 Alliances and Areas of Occupation as World War II Begins

MAKE THE CONNECTION

What was Hitler's goal? Why did Hitler invade and occupy the countries of Europe in the order he did? Did his strategy work in terms of meeting his goals? Why or why not?

stationed there, so long as the Vichy government allied with the Nazis. Petain established a fascist-style dictatorship that collaborated with Hitler and applied many of his domestic policies to Vichy France, including anti-Semitic laws and censorship. For many French, this was the only way to secure a good position in what they viewed as an inevitable German-controlled European continent. But Charles de Gaulle, a French army officer who was evacuated to England just before France's surrender, spoke out in opposition to the Vichy regime. His inspirational speeches led Churchill to denounce Petain's Vichy government as unofficial and instead recognize de Gaulle as the leader of France in exile. The Free French Movement (which grew stronger as it unified various French Resistance forces) was based in London, and the Vichy regime, which extended into France's colonial holdings in North Africa, became a German ally.

Great Britain was clearly in trouble. Germany's *Blitzkrieg* had just moved through Denmark, Norway, Belgium, the Netherlands, Luxembourg and France in only four months! Between the territories he controlled directly and the territories controlled by his allies, Hitler's empire in spring 1940 was the largest in the history of the world. Given his demonstrated military superiority and Britain's lack of capable allies (the United States was still adamantly neutral), Hitler fully expected Churchill to approach him seeking armistice. But when Chamberlain left the office of prime minister, the days of appeasement went with him. Churchill was determined to keep Germany from taking over all of Europe. As Paris was preparing for surrender at the end of June, Churchill warned his Parliament, "...the Battle of France is over. The Battle of Britain is about to begin."

The Battle of Britain

Although the U.S. government and most of its citizens were officially committed to isolationism, Churchill convinced U.S. President Franklin Delano Roosevelt to help where he could by sending military supplies and warships. While running for reelection in 1940 for an unprecedented third term, Roosevelt repeatedly promised the American people, "Your boys are not going to be sent into any foreign wars." Nonetheless, he recognized the grave danger democracy faced with the rapid spread of fascism and communism across Europe. He felt compelled to act to save democracy, so when Churchill requested military supplies (but not troops), Roosevelt quickly agreed. Sparking a major debate in the U.S. Congress, Roosevelt developed the **Lend-Lease Act** to provide Britain with much-needed supplies while technically maintaining U.S. neutrality.

Lend-Lease Act
Congressional act that gave President Roosevelt almost unlimited freedom in directing supplies, tanks, aircraft and ammunition to the war effort in Europe and Asia

Knowing that help was on the way, Churchill refused to negotiate with Hitler and began scrambling to prepare his Royal Air Force (RAF) for the inevitable German attack. This forced Hitler to reassess his strategy—he never thought he was going to have to actually invade Britain. Once he realized Churchill was not backing down, he developed Operation Sea Lion—a plan to send 260,000 German troops ashore on the English coast and march into London. But to get those troops ashore, Germany first had to gain control of the air.

The German air force (the *Luftwaffe*) began attacking merchant ships in the English Channel in July 1940 in an attempt to draw the RAF into battle, but the real Battle of Britain began on August 13 when the *Luftwaffe* started bombing airfields and radar stations in southern England. The goal was to destroy the RAF on the ground, which was much more efficient and less risky than engaging in dogfights in the air. In the first two weeks, the RAF lost 25 percent of its pilots, raising the very real fear that it would lose this important battle and be forced to negotiate with Germany. To prevent that, military supplies came from the United States, and reinforcement pilots were sent by the British Dominions (Australia, New Zealand, South Africa, India and Canada).

Watch the Video *The London Blitz* on mysearchlab.com

The Battle of Britain changed on August 24, 1940, when a German bomber made a critical mistake. Missing his strategic target on a foggy night, the German pilot dropped his payload over downtown London, killing civilians. The RAF Bomber Command responded with an attack on Berlin the following night, marking the first time that the fighting struck German soil. Infuriated, Hitler ordered that London be destroyed, and the Blitz began on September 7.

Children of an eastern suburb of London, who have been made homeless by the random bombs of the Nazi night raiders, waiting outside the wreckage of what was their home.

German bombs fell on London every night for fifty-eight nights straight, killing 15,000 civilians and all but destroying the city. The bombing runs were timed to coincide with low tide of the Thames River so that there would be less water available to fight the fires. But the Blitz did not destroy the RAF, and Londoners all pitched in to repair the nightly damage to the infrastructure so that industry (particularly military industry) would not be interrupted. The Blitz actually strengthened the resolve of the British people to defend England and democracy. Without control of the air, Hitler could not even contemplate invading Britain. On September 15, 1940, Operation Sea Lion was postponed indefinitely.

Opening the Eastern Front: 1941–1942

Because Hitler could not force Great Britain to surrender, he turned his attention toward the east for two reasons: one of his goals had always been *Lebensraum* for the German people; and, despite the Nazi-Soviet Nonaggression Pact, he hated everything that communism represented.

Operation Barbarossa

Hitler had the plans for attacking the USSR drawn up in the summer of 1940. After the failed attack on Great Britain, and as foreign relations with the Soviets became difficult by the end of 1940, Hitler made the decision in January 1941 to put Operation Barbarossa into effect. Set to begin on May 15, the carefully designed plan for this ten-week campaign would have to be closely followed to succeed.

It was a risky move for Hitler, as his generals had warned him. First, the USSR was a huge and cold expanse of land. German troops would have to negotiate across 635 miles of enemy territory to get to Moscow, and they would have to do it quickly before the Russian winter set in.

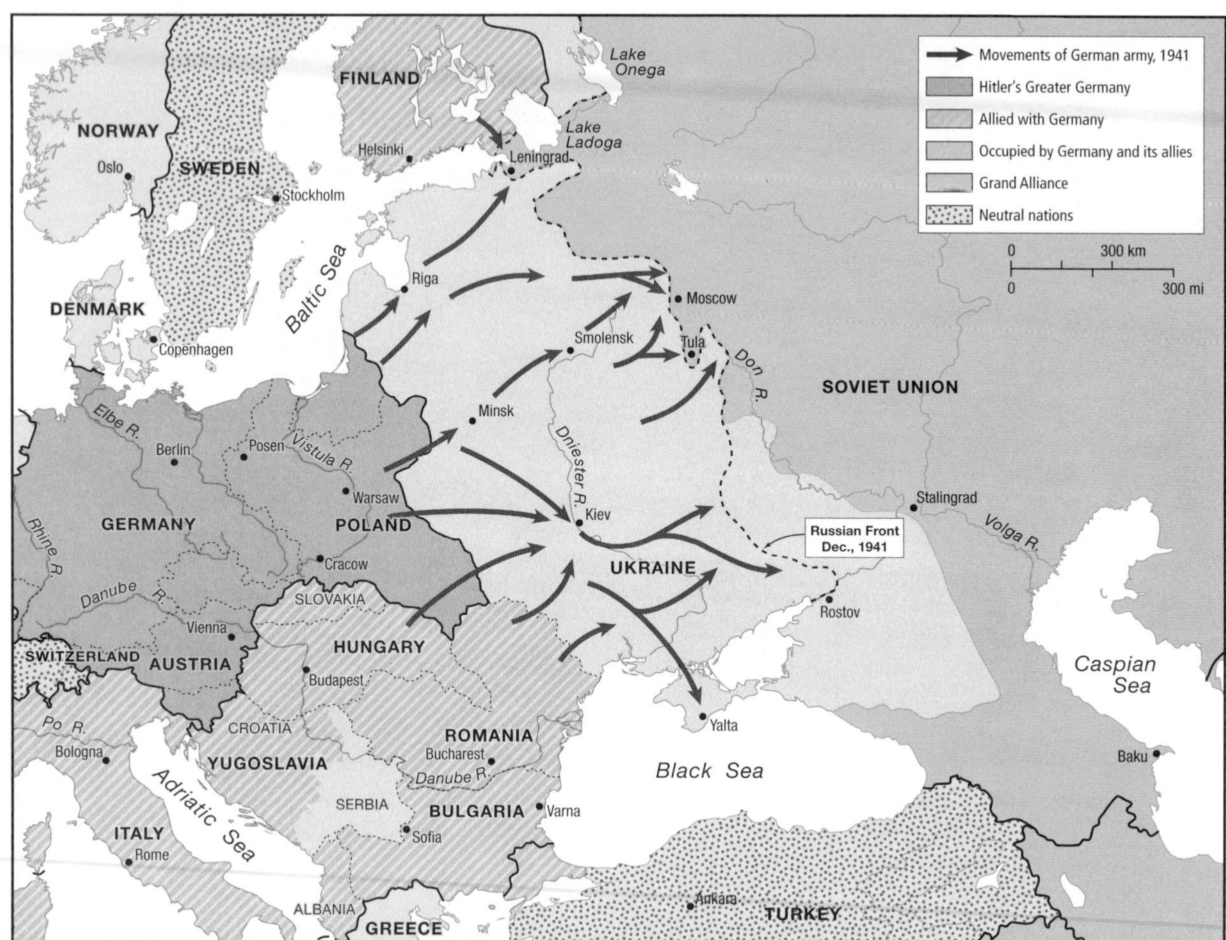

MAP 5.2 Germany's Invasion of the USSR

Second, putting Operation Barbarossa into effect meant opening up a two-front war for Germany. Hitler would not have his full military available should things not go as planned, and a German military spread too thin would be vulnerable to attack from both eastern and western borders. And while *Blitzkrieg* strategy and technology was outstanding, the USSR far outnumbered Germany in sheer number of troops. Finally, though Napoleon came close, no military strategist/leader in history had been able to conquer Russia, which is precisely why Hitler was determined to proceed.

Unfortunately for Hitler, Mussolini interfered with his plans. Since coming to Germany's aid in southern France the summer before, Italian troops had not really participated in the war. Mussolini was frustrated and anxious to pick up more territory for Italy. At the end of October 1940, Italy attacked Greece from its base in Albania. Within a few weeks, not only had the Italian military failed to conquer Greece, but the Greek military had pushed the Italians back into Albania and was headed for its capital city, with the British support troops on their way. This presented a major problem for Hitler, as it gave British troops momentum to swing north and threaten the southern border of the German Empire. Hitler was enraged at Mussolini (who had not discussed his military plans beforehand) but sent German forces to take back Albania and occupy Greece. They did so quickly and easily, but it cost Operation Barbarossa five weeks of precious warm weather.

Hitler began his invasion of the USSR on June 22, 1941. It has been called the greatest land–air attack in the history of war, primarily because the Germans launched 3.5 million troops,

3,500 tanks and 1,900 aircraft along an 1,800-mile front. Even though Stalin had been warned by both his intelligence service and the British that the attack was coming, he did not really believe Hitler would do it. When his commanders noticed the massive buildup of German troops on the border and asked for defensive plans, Stalin explicitly told them not to take any action that might provoke the Germans. So the Soviet troops were wholly unprepared to face the German *Blitzkrieg*. In the first week of battle, the Soviet front line fell apart as German troops pressed two hundred miles into the Soviet Union. In the city of Kiev alone, the Germans took 650,000 Soviet soldiers prisoner, the most in any single battle in history. Hitler expected to be goose stepping though Moscow by the end of the summer.

German Colonel General Heinz Guderian, the strategist who developed *Blitzkrieg* and successfully led the invasion of Poland to start the war, was in charge of German troops in Operation Barbarossa. He disagreed with Hitler over the invasion strategy from the outset, warning him that the plan contained serious miscalculations regarding timing, conditions and troop movement. After their brief, initial success in June 1941, the German military very quickly and painfully experienced the obstacles Guderian foreshadowed.

The first problem was the terrain—to get to Moscow, the German troops had to seize control of 635 miles of enemy territory from west to east and 1,865 miles north to south, crisscrossed with rivers, marshes and mountains. Travel was made even more difficult by the lack of Soviet transportation infrastructure, and anything the Germans could have used was destroyed by the Soviet troops in the first few months of the battle. Travel alone was difficult, and keeping supply and communications lines open behind them was almost impossible. The German troops frequently found themselves isolated from one another and lacking critical medical, food and military supplies. Morale plummeted as health problems, mostly related to the harsh Russian climate, such as typhus and frostbite arose. The initial summer months of the invasion were marked by scorching, dry heat that kicked up dust and led to dehydration. When the rain finally came at the end of September, the dust turned to mud so thick even the Panzer tanks could not get

German troops in High Caucasus Mountains, Russia, November 1942.

through it. The winter of 1941–1942, the worst in central Asia in over a hundred years, began in early October, and the snow fell through March. Temperatures dropped as low as -55C (-67F), and everything froze, including the weapons, vehicles and troops. By November, the German army was at a standstill on all fronts, hunkered down in hopes of surviving the winter with few supplies. Guderian sent a message to Hitler: "We have seriously underestimated the Russians, the extent of the country and the treachery of the climate."

An Uneasy Alliance

The temporary halt in the German offensive gave the Soviet army time to pull itself together, and it did so with the aid of Great Britain and the United States. Hitler's invasion of the USSR put Churchill, Stalin and Roosevelt in a difficult position. Obviously, Churchill and Roosevelt did not want Hitler to succeed, yet neither were they excited about allying with the communist dictator. Similarly, Stalin did not consider the United States or Western European countries to be "friends," but his military would certainly need help to turn things around and expel the Germans from the Soviet Union.

In August 1941, Roosevelt and Churchill met aboard a ship anchored in international (therefore neutral) waters off the coast of Newfoundland. Both were concerned about Hitler's growing power and clearly expansive ambitions. Despite the continued official neutrality of the U.S. government, Roosevelt and Churchill developed common goals, a coordinated strategy for combating Germany and the Axis powers and a vision for the postwar world. Spelled out in the **Atlantic Charter**, the vision included many of the principles of democracy that Wilson expressed in his Fourteen Points as the United States poised to enter the Great War—self-determination, decolonization, freedom of the seas and basic human rights. To solve the more immediate problem, the Atlantic Charter also included an offer of military aid to the Soviet Union. Stalin accepted it, and a Soviet–British–U.S. conference was held in October in Moscow to work out the details.

Read the Document *The Atlantic Charter* on mysearchlab.com

The Battle for Stalingrad

As things began to thaw out in the USSR in April 1942, there was massive flooding and more mud. With limited supplies and troops available, Hitler focused the German offensive on three cities in the south in an attempt to seize the Soviet oil fields in the Caucasus. German troops were successful in two of the three in June and July and entered the third target, Stalingrad, in August 1942. The Soviet military was under strict orders to protect this city, named after its leader, at all costs, and the German military was clearly told that there would be "no withdrawal." By October, the battle for Stalingrad had become a vicious, house-to-house operation that neither the Germans nor the Soviets could decisively control. With yet another brutal Russian winter underway and their supply lines cut off, the Germans were encircled by a Soviet offensive in November 1942 that trapped the entire German 6th Army (more than 250,000 German troops) in the city. Field Marshal Friedrich von Paulus requested assistance or permission to retreat—neither was granted. On January 31, 1943, he surrendered, violating direct orders and sending Hitler into a rage. This was the beginning of the end for the German army in Europe. The Soviets were able to turn the victory at Stalingrad into a complete reversal along the eastern front, thanks in large part to the aid of a new participant in the war, the United States.

War in the Pacific: 1941–1943

Although the Pacific theater did not officially become part of World War II until late 1941, military conflict had been ongoing in the region throughout the 1930s due to Japan's aggressive expansionism. The United States considered Japan a rival because of its political and economic strength.

Captured German Generals at Stalingrad.

Japanese Aggression

Japan took advantage of Europe's obsession with Germany and U.S. neutrality during the 1930s to pursue its goals, beginning with the occupation of Manchuria (northeast China) in September 1931. The United States responded with the **Stimson Doctrine** but no military threat or economic sanctions. So the following year, Japan went after Shanghai. This time the Western powers had financial interests at stake, and Japan backed down in the face of a potential military response. But Japan also quit the League of Nations, and the West lost the opportunity to participate in foreign policy discussions with the aggressive nation. In July 1937, without an official declaration of war, Japan invaded China and occupied Peking. The United States continued to ship weapons to support the Chinese nationalist government in its defense but officially maintained neutrality.

Stimson Doctrine
U.S. policy of nonrecognition of any territorial or administrative changes the Japanese imposed upon China; supported by the League of Nations, but ignored by Japan

In summer 1940, the Japanese military staged a successful coup against its own government. When Japan invaded the Hong Kong peninsula and moved toward Indochina (controlled by the French), the United States and Great Britain warned Japan to end its aggression in the Pacific and sent Allied troops to the Dutch West Indies. Hoping to prevent the Allies from taking action, Japan signed the **Tripartite Pact** (also called the Axis Pact) with Germany and Italy in September 1940. Hungary, Romania, Slovakia, Bulgaria and Yugoslavia also signed this pact, securing the Axis alliance. Stalin was also interested in participating, but Hitler ignored his request because the plans for Operation Barbarossa were already underway.

Tripartite Pact
established an alliance between Germany, Italy and Japan that promised economic and military assistance to one another for ten years

For security reasons, Japan negotiated a separate nonaggression pact with the USSR in April 1941 and began trading for much-needed supplies. This relationship became difficult to maintain once Germany launched Operation Barbarossa at the end of June. In July, the United States and the Allied powers froze all Japanese assets and cut off oil supplies to the island. Japan's military machine would grind to a halt without that oil. War now seemed inevitable.

To buy some time, and hopefully gain the element of surprise, a Japanese delegation was sent to the United States in the fall of 1941 under the ruse of negotiating a settlement. Meanwhile, the Japanese military-led government began preparing for war. If Japan waited for an attack by the United States, it would be entrenched in a defensive position in its homeland. Admiral Isoroku Yamamoto presented a plan to strike first with an attack on a U.S. strategic military target—the naval base at Pearl Harbor, Hawaii, a U.S. territory in the Pacific Ocean that housed the U.S. Pacific fleet and several airfields. Yamamoto reasoned that, with the element of surprise, the Japanese military could destroy the Pacific fleet while in harbor. It would take weeks for the U.S. Atlantic fleet to mobilize and get to the Pacific Ocean, allowing Japan time to seize control of the Pacific island territories to its east, particularly the U.S.-held territories of Guam and the Philippines, and keep the war away from the Japanese mainland. This strategy was approved in November 1941.

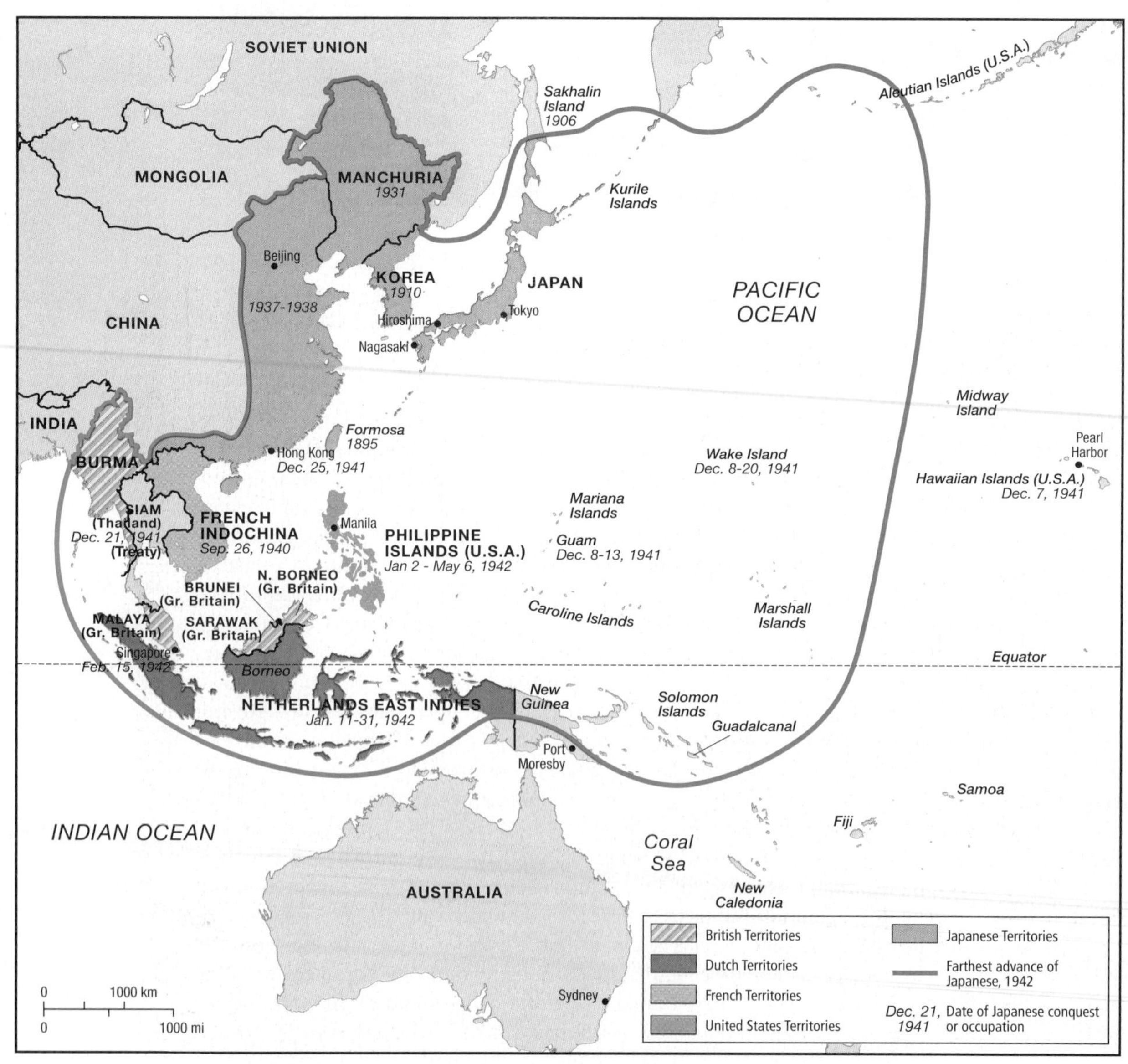

MAP 5.3 The Pacific, 1941

The U.S. ambassador in Japan warned Roosevelt that war was imminent, and the U.S. Pacific forces in Malaya, the Philippines, the East Indies and China were put on alert. On December 3, 1941, the Japanese navy was given its war orders and began to move into striking position, but the Japanese government assured the United States that its troop movements were precautionary actions only. Unconvinced, President Roosevelt sent a personal appeal to Emperor Hirohito on December 6 to maintain peace between the two nations. By then, thirty Japanese submarines had formed a ring around the Hawaiian Islands, and a Japanese fleet with six aircraft carriers was on a high-speed run to Pearl Harbor.

Early Sunday morning, December 7, 1941, an inexperienced army radar station operator on Oahu reported an "unusually large blip" approaching from the north, but the operator was told by his commanding officer to ignore it because it was assumed to be a U.S. air force squadron of B-17s. It was actually the first of two waves of Japanese carrier attack planes—384 torpedo, high-level, dive bomber and fighter planes in all. In approximately two hours, the Japanese sank five battleships, three destroyers and two light cruisers and damaged many other ships in the harbor, as well as destroyed 180 planes on the ground. The death toll was 2,335 American servicemen and sixty-eight civilians, along with 1,178 wounded. Japan lost twenty-nine aircraft, with fifty-nine men aboard, and five mini-submarines. The same day, Japan also launched successful airstrikes against the Philippines, Guam, Hong Kong and the Wake Islands in the Pacific.

Pearl Harbor Naval Base, Hawaii.

Read the Document *Roosevelt's Request for a Declaration of War* on mysearchlab.com

The United States Enters the War

Japan officially declared war on the United States on December 8, 1941. That same day, President Roosevelt delivered one of his most moving speeches to Congress, asking for a declaration of war against Japan. Congress and the American people supported him wholeheartedly, as did the British government, which also declared war on Japan. Three days later, Germany and Italy declared war on the United States, and Congress responded immediately with war declarations against them. The war was now truly global and the lines were clearly drawn: the Axis powers of Germany, Italy, Japan and their allies faced the significantly enhanced Allied powers of Great Britain, the USSR, the United States and their allies.

In the Pacific, the U.S. army was taken by surprise. The United States was not ready for war of this type or magnitude. By the spring of 1942, Japan had basically taken what it wanted in the Pacific. In the first few months of the Pacific war, the Allies lost a lot of troops and many ships, while Japan regained access to valuable oil and rubber supplies as it seized Pacific islands.

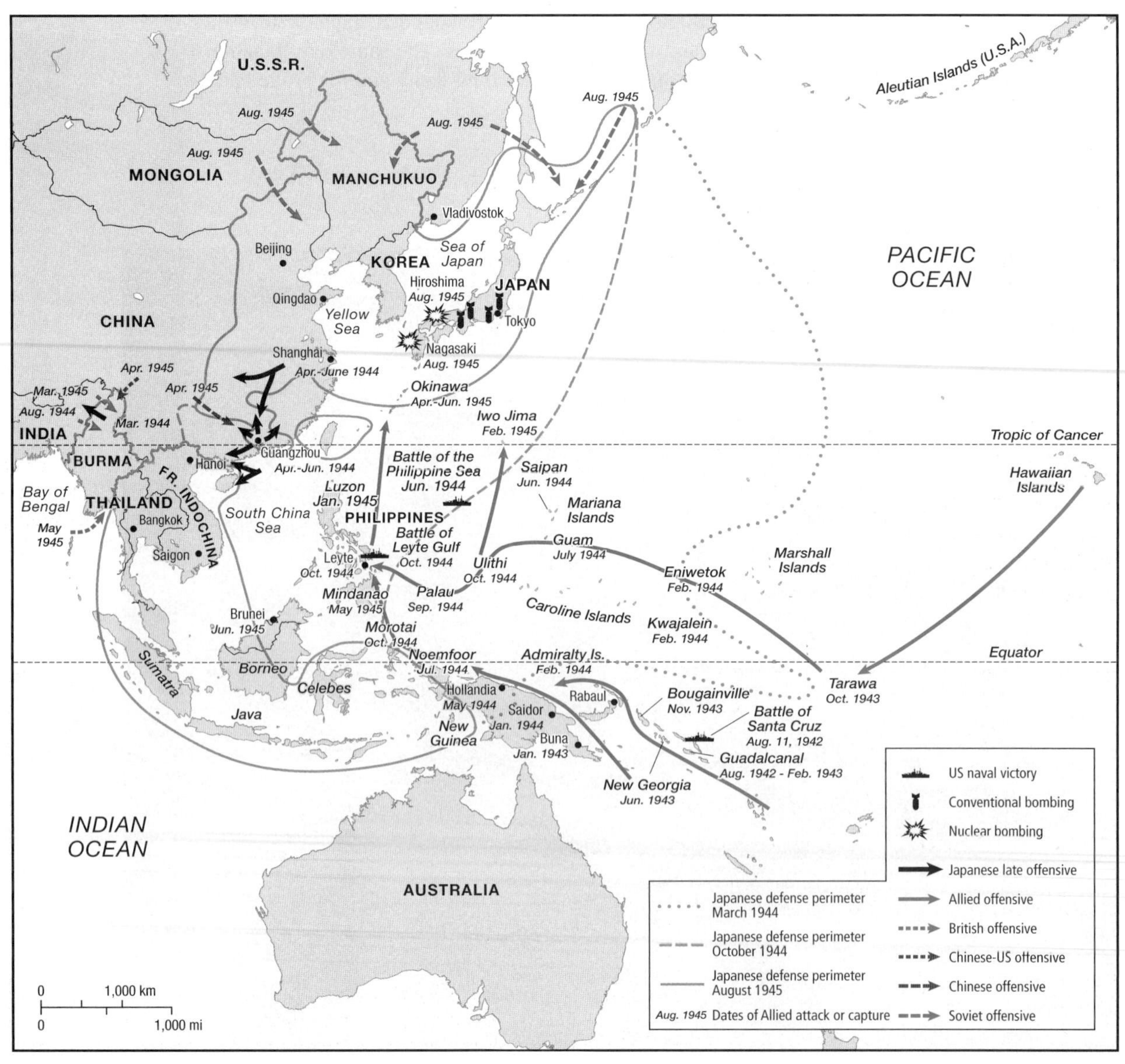

MAP 5.4 The Pacific Theater

Perhaps most devastating to the U.S. military and morale, the Japanese conquered the Philippines in May, leading to the single largest surrender in U.S. history (76,000 Filipino and U.S. troops). The Allies developed a broad offensive strategy originating from bases in Australia, Alaska and India, and the Japanese navy was spread thin to maintain such a wide defensive line. A decisive battle at Midway in early June 1942 between Yamamoto and U.S. Admiral Chester Nimitz finally put the Allies on equal military footing with the Japanese and marked the end of Japanese expansion in the Pacific. After Midway, the Japanese regrouped into a defensive position as the Allies began fighting their way toward the Japanese mainland.

In what would become the longest battle in the Pacific and a turning point in the war for the United States, the battle for Guadalcanal began in August 1942 and lasted through February 1943. Guadalcanal was difficult for several reasons: it required the U.S. navy, army and marines to work together collaboratively; communications technology was lacking; malaria ravaged the Allied troops; and they simply did not have enough planes and small ships to protect the island. But the lessons learned at Guadalcanal translated into a strategic initiative that guided the U.S. offensive for the remainder of the war.

A New Strategy for the United States

In 1943, the U.S. forces began "island hopping" across the Pacific toward Japan. The strategy, first employed in Operation Cartwheel led by General Douglas MacArthur, involved bypassing the strongly held Japanese islands where potentially devastating battles could occur and instead targeting strategic sites along Japan's supply line that fed those bases. These sites were easier to capture, and the result was that the major base would be cut off from supplies and ammunition, eventually making it easier to invade. Though island hopping took a bit longer, it cost the United States far fewer casualties (both men and equipment). Using island hopping, U.S. troops captured the Gilbert Islands by the end of 1943 and the Marshalls and the Marianas in 1944. The United States began construction on large airbases to launch a raid on Japan.

The North African Theater

The fighting in North Africa began in June 1940 when Italy first entered the war. In response to Italy's declaration of war, Great Britain attacked Italian forces in Libya. It was as much a show of presence as anything else—the 40,000 British troops in North Africa at the time were vastly outnumbered by Italy's 200,000 troops in Libya and 250,000 troops in Ethiopia. But Mussolini was over-confident and ordered his troops into Egypt in early fall 1940, spreading them thin. He did not expect a British response,

> **MAKE THE CONNECTION**
>
> Why did World War II extend into North Africa? What made Libya and Egypt geostrategically important territories in World War II?

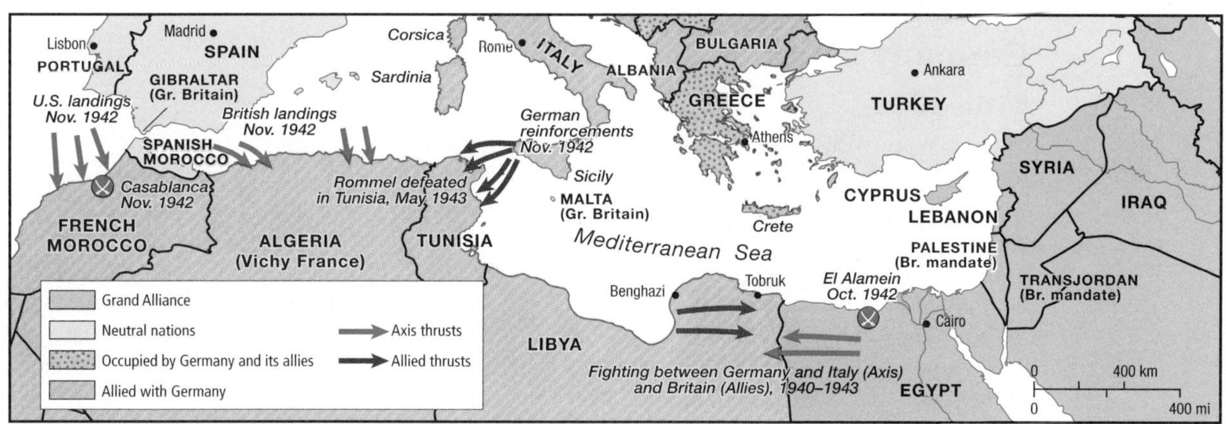

MAP 5.5 The North African Theater

which allowed the British military to take the Italians by surprise and seize control of a large piece of territory spanning both sides of the Egypt/Libya border. By the end of the year, British, French, Indian, African and Australian troops were in control of Egypt and Libya, and Mussolini requested help from Hitler. In February 1941, Hitler sent the Afrika Korps—German troops and Panzer divisions led by Field Marshal Erwin Rommel. Nicknamed "the Desert Fox," Rommel was a brilliant strategist and heroic field commander. Focused on speed and mobility, Rommel's Afrika Korps quickly spread the fighting all the way across West Africa to Morocco and into the Middle East.

Operation Torch

Once the United States was committed to the war in early 1942, Allied strategists developed several possible scenarios for offensive action against Germany, most in response to Stalin's insistence that a western front be opened to alleviate the pressure on the Soviet troops who were fighting the bulk of the German offensive forces and incurring heavy casualties. The Americans wanted to concentrate troops in England, move across the English Channel to invade occupied France, and then sweep into Germany. The British feared the potential consequences if the operation was unsuccessful. They preferred to launch an invasion against the German troops in North Africa, then move north through Italy into Germany. When the logistics of the cross-channel plan seemed too difficult to work out, the Allies began preparing for an invasion of North Africa to start in late 1942. The benefits to this approach included freeing French troops stuck in Morocco, Algeria and Tunisia, who would then participate in the continental invasion, and regaining access to the Suez Canal in Egypt. Controlling North Africa meant first defeating Rommel's Afrika Korps—success would require simultaneous multiple attacks and the element of surprise.

The goal of Operation Torch, which began in October 1942, was to squeeze German and Italian troops from both sides: the British, under Field Marshal Bernard Montgomery, attacked from El Alamein in Egypt; and an Anglo-American force led by U.S. General Dwight Eisenhower invaded from three landing sites in French North Africa. The advantage gained from the surprise attacks was lost quickly, as Vichy French forces fought against the invading Allied troops until they were forced to cooperate in November. This gave Rommel time to bring 150,000 troops in to secure Tunisia and assume the offensive position in early 1943. That changed in the spring, when U.S. troops under General George Patton and British troops under Montgomery surrounded the Germans and cut off their supply and communication lines. Though Hitler refused to allow the Afrika Korps to surrender, he did move Rommel into France just before the Allies captured 240,000 Axis troops on May 13, 1943, gaining control of the North African theater. From this position, Patton began preparations for the invasion of Sicily.

Germany on the Defensive: 1943–1945

Battle at Sea

Though World War II is noted for its extensive air battles and bombing, some of the most dramatic sea battles in military history occurred in the battles of the Atlantic and Mediterranean, where Germany used its U-boats from the beginning of the war to cut off shipments of military and merchant supplies to Great Britain. For Churchill, keeping these supply lanes open for his troops and blocking the supplies and movements of the Axis powers was crucial. Germany's U-boat production outstripped the British and American naval production of new ships, and those in the water were sunk by the U-boats at an alarming rate. To combat the German U-boats, the Allies employed the **convoy** system, but it wasn't until early 1943 that the Allies were in control of the seas, which was vital in order to open a western front.

convoy
neutral merchant vessels sailing with the protection of an armed escort

By 1943, Allied shipbuilding surpassed the losses they were incurring in the sea battles, and a strategic bombing campaign on German industrial targets reduced the production of new

First test of radar on board ship: the USS Leary (DD-158) in April 1937.

U-boats. The success of Operation Torch in North Africa had taken away Axis ports in the Mediterranean Sea, and the Allies developed technology such as radar, sonar and the Leigh Light (a huge searchlight) to detect and destroy U-boats when they encountered them, rendering the German navy useless by the summer of 1944.

Italy

Once the United States and Great Britain secured North Africa and the Mediterranean, it was clear they would use their position to attack Italy. There were several benefits to this strategy: (1) although the Italian military was not a huge threat, taking it off the battlefield would put more pressure on Germany's military; (2) opening a front in Italy would draw German troops, alleviating the pressure on Soviet troops along the eastern front (as Stalin had demanded); (3) invading Italy would be easier than invading France to gain a foothold on the continent and create free-flowing supply lines for that eventual invasion; and (4) the Allies would control the Mediterranean.

The king of Italy, Victor Emmanuel, knew that the Allied invasion was imminent. He fired Mussolini and had him arrested and began seeking peace negotiations with the Allies to save his country. When the Germans intercepted one of these requests for a negotiated surrender, Hitler became even more determined to hold onto Italy, whether the country's government went along with his plan or not. Because the negotiations were taking place in secret, the Allies proceeded with their invasion plans, gaining control of Sicily in early August 1943 and landing British forces on the Italian mainland on September 3, the same day the Italian surrender was signed. When the armistice was publicly announced on September 9, 1943, the Italian military fell apart. Some units surrendered to the Allies and others joined the German military buildup, making the road to Rome a very difficult one for the Allied troops. It took nine months from the Italian surrender for the Allies to actually seize control of Rome on June 4, 1944; and brutal fighting with German troops continued in the north for almost another year.

Mussolini, who had been rescued from prison by German paratroopers, tried to establish his own little country in German-held northern Italy but was once again arrested by the Italians in

April 1945. He and his mistress were shot to death and hung (upside down as a show of disrespect) in a town square in Milan along with fifteen other executed fascists.

D-Day

In November 1943, Stalin, Roosevelt and Churchill met in Tehran, Iran, to discuss how to proceed with the final stages of the war in Europe. Stalin refused to launch another major offensive on the eastern front unless the United States and Great Britain agreed to open the western front they had been promising. The result was a highly secretive and logistically complicated invasion plan code-named **Operation Overlord.**

Operation Overlord the Allied invasion of German-held France, under the command of U.S. General Eisenhower, involving landings on five separate beaches to establish an Allied foothold on the continent

Read the Document *General Eisenhower's D-Day Message* on mysearchlab.com

Operation Overlord required Allied troops to travel across the English Channel and board amphibious landing craft that would take them in waves to five Normandy beaches heavily fortified and guarded by the Germans. To support the operation, ships would transport troops and supplies and bombard the German beach defenses, while fighter planes would take on the *Luftwaffe* in the air. Because the element of surprise was absolutely crucial for the success of Operation Overlord, the Allies set up deception campaigns in the spring of 1944 to throw the Germans off track. A series of fake plans were released, indicating that the invasion would come from the Balkans, Norway or different parts of France. General Patton was even sent to southeast Britain to lend credibility to a potential attack on northern France, where a fake camp was established with trucks, inflatable tanks and camp facades to convince the German spy planes that the attack would be further north. The night before the actual invasion, dummy paratroopers were dropped over Le Havre to divert the German's attention.

Due to bad weather conditions, Operation Overlord was postponed a day and began just before dawn on June 6, 1944. An advance wave of 12,000 paratroopers were dropped near Caen on the Cotentin Peninsula; and at 6:30 a.m. 156,000 troops and 30,000 vehicles landed along a fifty-mile stretch of Normandy beaches. They were supported by roughly 5,000 ships and 4,000 landing craft; and Allied aircraft flew 14,674 sorties the first day alone. Allied troops faced five German infantry divisions under Rommel's command, consisting of 50,000 men with assault weapons and about 100 tanks in a heavily fortified defensive position called the **Atlantic Wall.** The fighting on D-Day was brutal and deadly for both sides—Allied casualties are estimated at 10,000 (4,414 of those dead), and German casualties are estimated at 4,000 to 9,000. But D-Day, the first stage of the Battle of Normandy, was a turning point in World War II. All together, nearly four million men in 47 divisions were deployed for the Allied invasion of France, and from the moment they crossed the beaches and opened that western front, they were fighting their way toward Berlin.

Atlantic Wall Germany's coastline defense, which included reinforced concrete pillboxes housing machine guns, antitank guns and artillery, 6 million landmines and antitank obstacles on the beaches and underwater just offshore, and sharp poles in potential landing spots for paratroopers

Watch the Video *D-Day* on mysearchlab.com

Read the Document *"The Toughest Beachhead in the World"* on mysearchlab.com

By the end of June, the Allies had landed 920,000 troops and fought their way inland from the Normandy beaches, seizing the deep-water port of Cherbourg, vital to maintaining their supply lines. The plan called for Allied troops to stop at the Seine River and bypass the city of Paris, but when French Resistance fighters took on their German occupiers within the city, Allied troops led by General de Gaulle himself entered Paris on August 25 to help them. After four years of occupation, Paris was liberated.

The Battle of the Bulge

By September, Allied troops in the north and south had joined forces to create a formidable front line that moved east into Belgium, and the Germans were on the run. The Allies swept across northern France and Belgium, liberating civilians and opening ports to keep their supply lines open. Hitler refused to accept defeat and ordered a counteroffensive in Belgium for December 1944 against the advice of his generals. Thirty German divisions, really all that was left on the western front, attacked the Allied lines in the Ardennes on December 16, 1944. The Allies were taken by surprise, and the Germans pushed into the front line, causing a bulge (hence the name Battle of the Bulge). But the casualties were high, almost 100,000 for the Germans, and there were no reinforcements left. The Allies regained all of the ground they had lost in the battle by the end of January 1945 and crossed the Rhine River into Germany in March.

MAP 5.6 Allied Victory in Europe

Germany

In 1943, the Allies began a massive, round-the-clock aerial bombardment of Germany, with Americans flying precision bombing missions aimed at military and industrial targets during the day and the British picking up the night runs aimed at the general destruction of German cities and infrastructure (in retaliation for the Blitz of London). Though targeting civilians was controversial, by 1945 the Allies had pretty much wiped out the *Luftwaffe* and many of the war industries within Germany, paving the way for the Allied troops to enter Germany in March 1945 with little resistance.

Even before the Battle of the Bulge, it was clear to most of Germany's high command that Germany would not win World War II. They urged Hitler to negotiate a peace with the Allies that would save the German people and territory, and some even launched an internal conspiracy against Hitler when he refused to accept their advice. Hitler became increasingly paranoid and had many of his advisors and strategists killed, including the very popular Field Marshal Rommel, whose death was reported to the German people as a suicide. With the Allies approaching from the west and the Soviets from the east, Hitler demanded that Berlin be defended to the death by the people of Berlin, while he retreated to the safety and isolation of an underground bunker. There, he convinced himself that the Soviets, Americans and British would turn against one another, and the love of the people for their great nation would protect Berlin.

Read the Document *Hitler's Will* on mysearchlab.com

U.S. and Soviet troops together in Berlin.

The USSR launched its invasion of Germany in the summer of 1944 to coincide with the D-Day landings, and Soviet troops moved very quickly across Eastern Europe in just nine months. On April 23, 1945, the first Soviet troops entered Berlin with over 1 million men and 20,000 pieces of artillery. They outnumbered the Germans 5:1 in men, 15:1 in guns, 5:1 in tanks and 3:1 in planes. A few days later, the Soviet troops were joined by U.S. troops.

The Battle for Berlin was bloody and spiteful, fought from house-to-house throughout the city. On April 30, 1945, Hitler committed suicide in his bunker, and his successor, Grossadmiral Karl Donitz, immediately sent diplomatic envoys to the Allies to negotiate terms for peace. U.S. President Roosevelt had died on April 12, so it was Churchill, Stalin and Harry Truman who accepted Germany's **unconditional surrender** on May 8, 1945, now known as VE Day (Victory in Europe Day).

unconditional surrender
the country surrendering is given no guarantees and cannot set any limits on the actions of the victors

The Final Phase in the Pacific: 1944–1945

By 1944, island hopping had paid off in the Pacific—the United States was closing in on the Japanese mainland. For General MacArthur, retaking the Philippines was not only a matter of strategic importance but a personal vendetta as well ever since U.S. troops had been forced to surrender the U.S. territory in May 1942. The Battle of Leyte in October 1944 destroyed what was left of the Japanese navy and left Allied naval forces clearly in control of the Pacific. Two more months of ground battles at Leyte, combined with successful Allied invasions of Luzon in early 1945, secured the Philippines and established U.S. air superiority as well.

By 1945, American troops were poised for an invasion of Japan's home islands, which appeared necessary to force the Japanese to surrender. The first island they attacked, in February and March 1945, was a barren strip of land called Iwo Jima. Heavily fortified with 21,000 Japanese soldiers, hidden artillery and eleven miles of tunnels winding through Mt. Suribachi, Iwo Jima was the home of vital airstrips that would put the United States within striking distance of Japan. The Americans seized the island, but the Japanese fought ferociously to the death

(20,000 of the 21,000 died defending the island), and it cost the Allies 20,000 casualties to do so. The invasion of Okinawa from April to June produced a similar result, costing the United States 35,000 casualties (12,000 dead) to gain control of an island within 300 miles of mainland Japan. To defend Okinawa, the Japanese launched the largest **kamikaze** raid of the Pacific war, destroying twenty-six U.S. ships and damaging 168 others. Forty percent of the U.S. soldiers killed on Okinawa died in kamikaze attacks.

kamikaze
literally, "divine wind"; refers to Japanese pilots who flew their planes into enemy targets (usually U.S. naval vessels), committing suicide but ensuring damage to the target

Once within striking distance in the summer of 1945, the United States began firebombing Japanese cities in an attempt to force Japan into surrender. In six months, conventional bombing killed nearly 300,000 civilians and left 8 million more homeless. The survivors faced starvation because the supply lines into Japan were completely cut off. And there was little the Japanese military could do about it—the navy was all but destroyed and the air force was reduced to kamikaze missions rather than organized sorties. Still, the Japanese government would not surrender.

Operation Downfall

The Allies began developing strategic plans to invade Japan, code-named Operation Downfall, beginning with the southernmost island of Kyushu in November and reaching Tokyo by March 1946. Based on what happened at Iwo Jima and Okinawa, U.S. military strategists predicted that the United States could successfully conquer Tokyo, but it could take up to two years and would require 3.5 million troops to do so. They would have to use the existing Pacific troops, whose morale was low due to high casualties and drawn-out campaigns, as well as bring in troops from Europe, whose morale would be even lower because they had already fought and won in "their" theater. They may even have to rely on Soviet troops, which meant trusting Stalin, who was already displeased that his military had suffered disproportionately to the United States. And in the five months it would take for the Allies to prepare this invasion, the remaining 250,000 Japanese soldiers on Kyushu would dig in and prepare their defense as they had done on Iwo

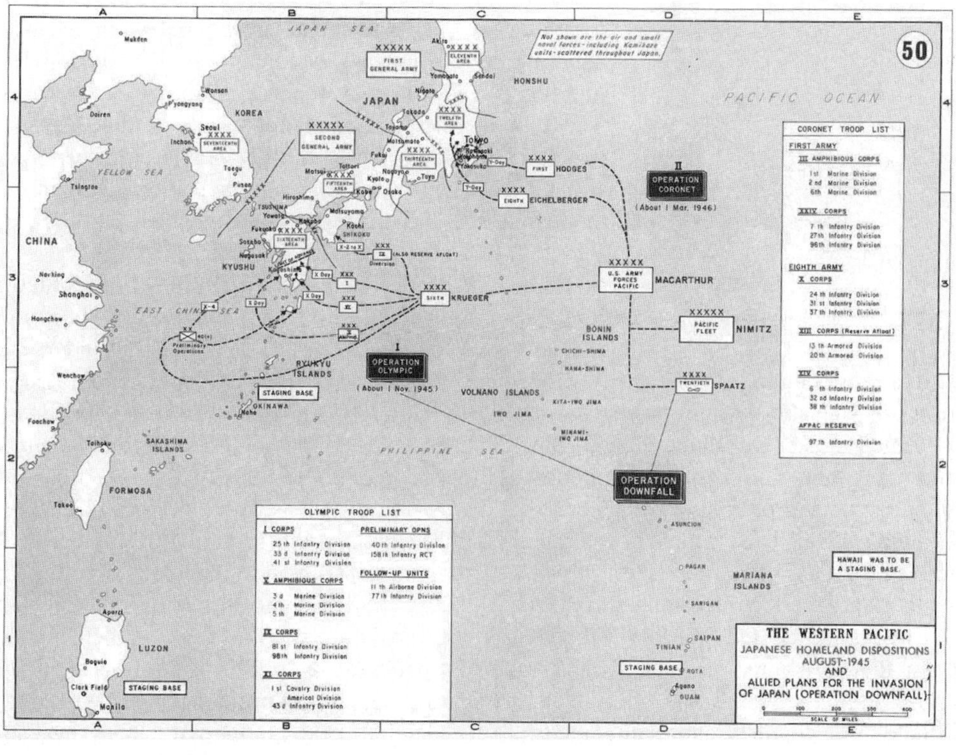

Map of Operation Downfall.

Jima and Okinawa. U.S. government agencies prepared many estimates of the potential casualty rate, and although no one knew for sure how many soldiers would possibly die in Operation Downfall, everyone agreed it would be a lot. The report from the secretary of war was the highest at 1.7 to 4 million American casualties with up to 800,000 dead.

When Harry Truman, a combat veteran of the Great War, became president of the United States in April 1945, he faced both the best and worst parts of wartime decision making. In Europe, the Allies were weeks from a hard-fought but clearly won victory. To win in the Pacific, however, it appeared as though he would have to approve Operation Downfall, a devastating loss of life in order to win the war. But technological advancements during the course of the war had yielded an alternative that would not result in such high American casualties—the atomic bomb.

Fat Man shake test at V site.

The Atomic Bomb

The atomic bomb was the product of a top-secret military research and development laboratory set up in Los Alamos, New Mexico, code-named the Manhattan Project. In August 1939, Albert Einstein, a German scientist who fled to America to avoid Nazi persecution, wrote a letter to President Roosevelt, warning him that German scientists were investigating the use of enriched uranium to create "extremely powerful bombs." That fall, Roosevelt created a "Uranium Committee" of American scientists to look into the project, which became a government office in 1941 when it became apparent that the United States was going to join the war. On December 28, 1942, the project, led by J. Robert Oppenheimer and five of the leading scientists in the United States, became top priority (and top secret). Spanning three years and costing $2 billion, the project pushed the limits of physics. The initial idea was that the bomb would be used against Hitler, who was developing a similar weapon; but the bomb was not ready for testing until July 16, 1945, two months after Germany's defeat. Even the scientists working on the project could not predict with certainty what the consequences of an atomic explosion might be; nonetheless, before the tests were conducted, a bomb was sent to the Pacific to be used in battle.

On July 26, 1945, Great Britain, the United States and China issued the **Potsdam Declaration,** clarifying the terms of the unconditional Japanese surrender and warning that anything else would result in Japan's "prompt and utter destruction." Although Stalin did not sign the declaration, he did cancel the nonaggression pact he had with Japan. Japan's Prime Minister Danshaku Suzuki responded: "We will do nothing but press on to the bitter end to bring about a successful completion of the war."

Potsdam Declaration called for Japan's unconditional surrender, including limited territory occupied by Allied troops, prosecution of war criminals, and democratic government

Truman agonized over his choices—Operation Downfall, which would certainly kill hundreds of thousands of U.S. troops, or the atomic bomb, which would certainly kill hundreds of thousands of civilians. The secretaries of war and state urged Truman to use the atomic bomb, not only to save American lives and end the war quickly, but as a demonstration of U.S. power. Not only would the United States win the war, but they would send a message to their hostile ally, Stalin, that the United States held clear military superiority. Other advisors warned Truman that the use of atomic weapons would violate the basic humanitarian principles upon which the United States was founded and encouraged him to negotiate peace terms with Japan instead. Ultimately, Truman's decision to drop the bomb on Hiroshima was based upon his desire to end

Read the Document *Excerpts from Truman's Papers* on mysearchlab.com the war quickly and save American lives. Although Truman was clear that it was to be used on military targets only and spare civilian lives as much as possible, the bombing order issued by General Carl Spaatz identified the city itself as the target.

The first bomb was dropped by a B-29 bomber (the *Enola Gay*) on Hiroshima on August 6, 1945, killing and wounding 150,000 people upon impact. In a public announcement, Truman placed the blame for the attack squarely on the shoulders of the Japanese government:

> *We are now prepared to obliterate more rapidly and completely every productive enterprise the Japanese have above ground in any city...Let there be no mistake; we shall completely destroy Japan's power to make war. It was to spare the Japanese people from utter destruction that the ultimatum of July 26 was issued at Potsdam. Their leaders promptly rejected that ultimatum. If they do not now accept our terms they may expect a rain of ruin from the air, the likes of which has never been seen on this earth...* (White House press release, August 6, 1945)

Watch the Video *Hiroshima* on mysearchlab.com

Still, Japan did not surrender. On August 9, Stalin declared war on Japan and invaded Manchuria. The Japanese Cabinet met but disagreed about terms of surrender. They believed the United States had more bombs to drop and knew that they could not defend themselves against a joint Soviet and U.S. invasion, but the Cabinet did not want the nation to be disgraced by an unconditional surrender. In the middle of the meeting, they received news that a second atomic bomb had been dropped on the city of Nagasaki, instantly killing or wounding another 75,000 civilians. Emperor Hirohito recommended to the Cabinet that Japan accept the terms of surrender, and after much disagreement within the government, the surrender was announced on August 15, 1945. General MacArthur arrived in Tokyo to oversee the surrender and occupation of Japan, and the formal peace agreement was signed on September 2, 1945, now known as VJ Day (Victory in Japan Day).

Photograph from the ground, A-Bomb blast, Nagasaki, Japan.

The Human Cost of the War

World War II represented an effort of total war on the part of all belligerents and was truly fought all over the world. More than fifty countries and dependencies (dominions, territories or colonies) were directly involved. All home fronts were affected, and the battlefields extended from deserts to mountains and forests, across the oceans and seas and into the air. Most of European civilization was repeatedly bombed, burned, invaded and occupied. Although it is difficult to know exactly how many people died because of World War II, recent estimates run as high as 70 million people when civilian deaths from starvation, disease and homelessness created by the refugee crises are added. The greatest loss of life (military and civilian combined) occurred in the USSR and China.

Military

Roughly 20 million troops died or went missing in World War II, with another 28 million wounded. The Allied powers (seventeen countries and dependencies) suffered 32.8 million killed, missing or wounded, and the Axis powers (seven countries) suffered 9.5 million killed, missing or wounded.

Most of the military deaths occurred in battle, whether on the ground, at sea or in the air. Approximately 5 million military personnel died as prisoners of war (POW), often in brutal conditions (torture, beatings and starvation were the norm in all camps). Some of the worst atrocities of the war occurred in German POW camps, where French, British, American and Soviet soldiers were sent into forced labor to work literally to their deaths, or, as the camps got full, the prisoners simply were executed. The Germans were particularly brutal to the Soviet POWs—of the 5 million captured, only 1 million lived, while almost 75 percent of the Allied POWs survived. The Soviet POW camps were built in Siberia or other remote regions of the USSR, where the likelihood of being rescued was slim to none. The German and Japanese POWs were reeducated in communist ideology, and those who survived the Soviet camps during the war were held for an additional ten years after the war ended.

Bataan Death March Japanese soldiers forced the captured Filipino and U.S. soldiers to walk sixty miles to their POW camp

The Japanese were not prepared for large numbers of POWs, and they generally just shot Allies on sight, publicly beheaded them in a display of power, or threw them in the holds of their ships with no food or air. When the ships were destroyed in battle, so were the POWs. The Japanese POW camps that did exist were mining and construction forced labor camps, and only about one-half of the Allied POWs sent there survived. One of the most notorious incidents of Japan's treatment of Allied POWs occurred in May 1942 during the **Bataan Death March** in the Philippines, where three thousand Americans and ten thousand Filipinos died within the first few days. Allied POW camps in the Pacific were also labor camps, but 95 percent of the Japanese POWs survived them. In Japanese culture, it was dishonorable to be taken prisoner, so most soldiers would fight to the death or commit suicide rather than surrender. When Japanese soldiers were taken prisoner, it was reported to their families as a death in battle to preserve their dignity, so the POWs had nothing to go home to anyway. Most Japanese POWs willingly participated in camp life if they were unable to commit suicide. Germans held in Allied POW work camps in England and the United States often had more food and better medical care than their citizens suffering in the war zone but were sometimes mistreated by guards in retaliation for Hitler's brutality.

Civilian

An estimated 47 million civilians died as a result of World War II, and another 6 million were wounded. Direct civilian deaths were primarily due to the bombing and shelling of European, Soviet and Japanese cities and the resulting starvation and homelessness. The two atomic bombs are the most well-known civilian attacks, in which the death toll five years after the blasts (including deaths from initial impact, radiation sickness and cancer) was 340,000, and subsequent generations have been born with serious birth defects. But "traditional" bombing was every bit as destructive and deadly for civilians. For example, firebombing raids over Tokyo alone in March 1942 resulted in an estimated 100,000 dead, 1 million wounded and 1 million homeless, and the raids continued throughout the war. More than 50 percent of Tokyo had been destroyed by VJ Day.

The routine bombing during the air war over Germany resulted in about 300,000 deaths, 800,000 wounded and probably 7.5 million homeless, many of whom ultimately died from exposure, disease or famine. By the end of the war, Berlin was 70 percent destroyed by bombing. One of the most controversial raids occurred over the city of Dresden, Germany, in February 1945. In the span of fourteen hours, the city was firebombed and destroyed, killing one-third of its population (an estimated 30,000 people in one night). There was no military target except for a hospital for wounded soldiers, yet more than 700,000 phosphorus bombs were dropped on the city of 1.2 million people (approximately one bomb for every two people).

The firebombing of Dresden, 1945.

At the outset of the war, Germany's attacks on Polish cities led to 40,000 civilian casualties; and the bombing of Rotterdam, Holland, left 1,000 dead and 80,000 homeless. As the war progressed and *Blitzkrieg* swept across Europe and into the USSR, most Europeans suffered from German shelling and bombing. The most well-known example is the London Blitz, which killed 15,000 civilians in two months. It is estimated that 500,000 Soviet citizens were killed by German bombs during Operation Barbarossa.

Though the Japanese conducted raids on military targets in the Philippines, northern Australia and Pearl Harbor, they also flew bombing missions over the Chinese cities of Shanghai, Nanjing and Canton at the beginning of the war simply to destroy the population and the will of the people to resist. An estimated 20,000 Chinese civilians were killed in the first nine months of the attacks. Between 1942 and 1945, the Japanese engaged in biological warfare, dropping germ bombs carrying bubonic plague in China's eastern provinces and infiltrating the water supply in Manchuria with typhus. Civilian deaths from disease in Chinese villages were not recorded accurately, so it is difficult to know how many civilians suffered. All told, perhaps as many as 20 million Chinese civilians were killed or wounded during the war.

The Holocaust

Certainly the most infamous example of civilian casualties in World War II is the genocide known as the **holocaust.** Hitler's desire for *Lebensraum* and his hatred of the Jewish people was evident early in his political career. In October 1939, the first **ghettos** were built in Poland to round up and segregate the Jewish population while the Nazi regime developed a plan to deal with them. Thousands of ghettos were established across Eastern Europe and in the USSR before Hitler came up with "the Final Solution" in late 1941—to exterminate all Jews. He began in the USSR as a component of Operation Barbarossa, sending along mobile killing units called the *Einsatzgruppen* in vans reconfigured to gas Jews with carbon monoxide. Operation Reinhard, the extermination of the Jews in occupied Poland, was set in motion to accomplish what

holocaust
literally, "sacrifice by fire," refers to the systematic, state-sponsored persecution and murder of Jews in Germany by the Nazis

ghettos
enclosed districts of a city here the Jews were forced to live in terrible conditions

Hermann Goering called, "the complete solution of the Jewish question." The first permanent extermination camps were established at Chelmno, Belzec, Sobibor and Treblinka (all located in occupied Poland) in late 1941 and early 1942. Jewish men, women and children were deported from Germany and the ghettos in the occupied territories to concentration camps; the Nazis also used the camps to rid Germany of the Romani and Sinti people (so-called gypsies), non-Germans, Jehovah's Witnesses, ethnic Slavs (considered to be "subhuman") and political opponents (Communists and Socialists). Because of its loyalty to Hitler, a paramilitary and political unit called the *Schutzstaffel* (SS) was given the task of overseeing the camps, which grew in number as the war dragged on.

Within the camps, living conditions were terrible, and food was scarce. Those who could work were put to hard labor to assist the Nazi war effort until they died. Nazi doctors used prisoners as subjects in some of the most outrageous medical experiments on record. Prisoners who were not useful to the Nazis in some way were executed, and mass executions took place when the camps got too crowded. The Birkenau extermination camp (at the Auschwitz complex), for example, was designed for efficiency, with four gas chambers—at its peak as many as six thousand prisoners were gassed per day. It is estimated that, between 1933 when Hitler took office and 1945, more than 10 million people died in the Holocaust, mostly civilians, including German citizens.

Group	Deaths
European Jews	6,000,000
Polish Catholics	3,000,000
Serbians	700,000
Romani and Sinti	240,000
Germans (enemies of the state)	80,000
Germans (handicapped)	70,000
Homosexuals	12,000
Jehovah's Witnesses	2,500
Total	**10,104,500**

(http://www.holocaustchronicle.org/holocaustappendices.html)

In his quest to preserve land and resources for the ideal German people, Hitler initiated a euthanasia program called Aktion T4. Launched on the same day Germany invaded Poland to ignite World War II, patients who were "considered incurable according to the best available human judgment of their state of health, [were] granted a mercy death." The ultimate expression of Social Darwinism, Hitler called T4 a "racial hygiene" program, necessary to preserve the strength of the Aryan race. The program began with mandatory sterilizations in the mid-1930s (about 360,000 people in all) and resulted in the establishment of T4 centers in 1939 to kill children (5,000 in all) and adults diagnosed by Hitler's T4 doctors as "unworthy of life." The program targeted mentally and physically disabled children and adults and homosexuals.

As Germans realized the extent of the T4 program, they began to pull their relatives out of nursing homes, hospitals and asylums. Although death certificates were falsified and staff members were ordered to secrecy, citizens living around the T4 centers knew exactly what was happening there. A strong popular protest movement began, and the Catholic Church formally opposed the program. In a rare move, Hitler chose to end the program in the fall of 1941 rather than risk losing public support. By then, approximately 275,000 "socially undesirable" and "unfit" Germans had been killed under T4.

Watch the Video *Nazi Murder Mills* on mysearchlab.com

The Holocaust was driven by Nazi ideology and carried out by the SS with government funding, so Hitler and his top commanders can certainly be held accountable for crafting the policies and procedures of the genocide. The more intriguing question is why the German people went along with it (with the notable exception of T4). From the beginning of Hitler's regime and the establishment of the Nuremberg Laws, Germans supported the Nazi Party because it promised to free Germany from the Treaty of Versailles restrictions and took active steps to do so. People went back to work when Hitler took office, and they did not want that to change. They were proud of their leader for standing up to the unfair Versailles restrictions. If the government needed to detain people who were threats to the state, most citizens supported the action. Certainly some non-Jews in Germany opposed the persecution of the Jewish people and helped them whenever possible, but the punishment for doing so was severe and included deportation or imprisonment in a concentration camp. Once Germany was at war and the Final Solution was in place, Hitler changed his approach to policy making, hiding the policies and practices of concentration camps from the citizens. By then, the nation was focused on the problems associated with life during wartime.

Outside of Germany, people in the occupied territories, particularly Poland and the USSR, certainly knew about the Final Solution. Many citizens of these countries cooperated with the Nazis, either out of immediate fear or in the hope that Germany would respect them and grant them independence. And fascism was a popular political ideology throughout Europe, so many people followed Nazism willingly. In democratic countries such as Great Britain and the United States, war correspondents reported on Hitler's policies and the "Final Solution," although the details were not always accurate. But again, most citizens at the time were struggling with their own war-related problems and, even in democracies, they understood that governments take actions during wartime to protect national security.

Read the Document *The Buchenwald Report* on mysearchlab.com

U.S. Executive Order 9066

In January 1942, President Roosevelt ordered all noncitizens living in the United States to register with the government. The fear was that Germany, Italy and Japan had spies and saboteurs living within the United States and reporting back to their home governments. U.S. intelligence, particularly during wartime, could not accurately identify them and feared sabotage on U.S. soil. On February 19, 1942, President Roosevelt signed Executive Order 9066, authorizing the U.S. military "to prescribe military areas in such places and of such extent as. . .the appropriate Military Commander may determine, from which any or all persons may be excluded." The citizens removed were put in internment camps throughout the United States.

The majority of those targeted, about 120,000, were of Japanese descent, many of them second-generation immigrants born in the United States or naturalized citizens. Additionally, 3,200 Italian residents were arrested, 300 of whom were interned, and 11,000 German residents were arrested, 5,000 of whom were interned. Many others were relocated outside of the United States. All were required to leave their homes, jobs, schools and property. It is estimated that they lost $400 million in property and assets.

ANALYSIS

Were the Great War and World War II separate wars, with distinct causes and consequences, as often classified by historians? Or was the period of 1914–1945 really one long global war, carried out in military conflict from 1914–1920, economic warfare from 1920–1939, and military conflict from 1939–1945?

Read the Document *Japanese Relocation Order* on mysearchlab.com

Conclusions

Any way you measure it, World War II was the most destructive war in world history and certainly a turning point in the twentieth century. The physical and human devastation that resulted would cause world leaders to think differently about foreign policy making, everyone agreeing that a third world war should be avoided at all costs. Technologies in weapons, transportation, communications and medical advances developed at a faster rate than even the military strategists and planners could keep up with. Technology changed the world and, once again, the way we fight. But the underlying passions and political goals that led the nations to war remained stubbornly consistent. The desire for territory (empire building) and access to resources was a driving force. Nationalism was certainly a part of this, fueling atrocities, particularly by the Germans and Japanese, but also affecting Soviet and American policies and actions. And although militaries had settled the question of who "won" and who "lost," questions of governance, ideology and territory loomed large. How would the so-called "winners" redesign the world? Would they create another Treaty of Versailles? How would they prevent the horrific economic crisis that followed the Great War from reoccurring? They were unsuccessful in preventing World War II—could they prevent World War III? And how would the Allies answer these questions, absolutely vital for maintaining peace, when they were working from combative political ideologies?

WORKING WITH THE THEMES

THE EFFECTS OF TECHNOLOGY How was *Blitzkrieg* different from the fighting in the Great War? Should combatants have refrained from air raids and bombing campaigns once they realized the civilian costs? Did Truman make the right choice in using the atomic bombs? Given the advancements in weapons, communications, and medical technology, why did World War II last longer and kill more people than the Great War?

CHANGING IDENTITIES Could the Holocaust have been prevented? By whom and at what point could the intervention have occurred? Did Roosevelt do the right thing by signing Executive Order 9066?

SHIFTING BORDERS How was Hitler able to rebuild a military and seize control of most of Europe in fewer than ten years? Should Churchill and Roosevelt have included Stalin as an ally? What were the positive and negative consequences of doing so? Would the United States have switched from economic sanctions to military intervention against Japan if they had not attacked Pearl Harbor?

GLOBALIZATION Should the United States have entered the war earlier than it did? Whose responsibility was it to uphold the requirements of the Hague Convention, particularly with regard to the treatment of POWs?

Further Reading

TO FIND OUT MORE

The World War II Multimedia Database. Available online at http://www.worldwar2database.com

PBS: Behind Closed Doors. Available online at http://www.pbs.org/behindcloseddoors/

The Churchill Centre and Museum. Available online at http://www.winstonchurchill.org/

Wright Museum of WWII History. Available online at http://www.wrightmuseum.org/

British Broadcasting Corporation: World War Two. Available online at http://www.bbc.co.uk/history/worldwars/wwtwo/

Yad Vashem—The Holocaust Martyrs' and Heroes' Remembrance Authority. Available online at http://www.yadvashem.org

UK National Archives: The Art of War. Available online at http://www.nationalarchives.gov.uk/theartofwar/

Portsmouth Museum and Records: D-Day Museum and Overlord Embroidery. Available online at http://www.ddaymuseum.co.uk

MATRIX, the Center for Humane Arts, Letters and Social Sciences Online: Seventeen Moments in Soviet History—1939, 1943. Available online at http://www.soviethistory.org

GO TO THE SOURCE

Tom Fletcher: Civvy Street in World War 2. Available online at http://www.rin-fs.com/

William Burr (ed.): The National Security Archive: The Atomic Bomb and the End of World War II. National Security Archive Electronic Briefing Book No. 162. Available online at http://www.gwu.edu/~nsarchiv/NSAEBB/NSAEBB162/index.htm

Museum für Kommunikation Berlin: War Letters in the Second World War. Available online at http://www.feldpost-archiv.de/english/index.html
Anne Frank: *The Diary of a Young Girl* (1952)
Saburo Ienaga: *The Pacific War, 1931–1945: A Critical Perspective on Japan's Role in World War II* (1968)

MySearchLab Connections

Read the **Document** on **mysearchlab.com**

5.1 *The Atlantic Charter*. President Roosevelt's concern over the war in Europe sharply increased in 1940 with the collapse of France and the potential expansion of Hitler's empire to the New World. After taking steps that led the U.S. closer to war, he and Churchill met in summer, 1941, and forged a closer alignment with their joint statement known as the Atlantic Charter.

5.2 *Roosevelt's Request for a Declaration of War.* The day after Japan attacked Pearl Harbor, President Roosevelt addressed a joint session of Congress, referring to December 7, 1941 as "a date which will live in infamy." He intended to stir the emotions of Americans by portraying the United States as a peaceful nation unprepared for the "dastardly attack" by Japan.

5.3 *General Eisenhower's D-Day Message.* On the morning of June 6, 1944, General Eisenhower addressed the troops of the Allied Expeditionary Forces as they were about to embark on the invasion Normandy, France.

5.4 Ernie Pyle, *"The Toughest Beachhead in the World."* War correspondent Ernie Pyle cabled this report of D-Day.

5.5 *Hitler's Will.* Adolf Hitler's will and political testament, written before committing suicide, are perhaps the best source of information we have about Hitler's state of mind in the final weeks of World War II.

5.6 *Excerpts from Truman's Papers.* These documents reveal some of the information that President Truman had while making the decision whether to invade Japan as planned or make use of the new atomic bomb technology.

5.7 *The Buchenwald Report.* At the end of the war, the world finally had to confront the horrific reality of Hitler's "final solution." Reports of the shocking conditions at the camps and the gruesome deeds committed in them began to spill out as Allied troops liberated areas under German control.

5.8 *Japanese Relocation Order.* After the Japanese attack on Pearl Harbor, the U.S. War Department urged Roosevelt to order the evacuation of all Japanese and Japanese-Americans on the West Coast to relocation centers. This action was debated openly in government and in California before it was implemented with the full knowledge of the American people.

Watch the **Video** on **mysearchlab.com**

5.1 *The German Army: U.S. Air Force Analysis of Captured German News Reels*
5.2 *The London Blitz*
5.3 *D-Day*
5.4 *Hiroshima*
5.5 *Nazi Murder Mills*

6 Conflict and Convergence: 1945–1950

CHAPTER OUTLINE

- Worldwide Conflict
- Western Europe on the Front Line
- Regional Conflicts
- International and Regional Convergence

CHAPTER TIMELINE

1941	1943	1945	1946	1947
United States and USSR join the Allies	Sartre's *Being and Nothingness* is published The "big three" meet at Tehran conference	Yalta conference is held VE Day ends the war in Europe Potsdam conference is held VJ Day ends the war in the Pacific Ho Chi Minh "decolonizes" Vietnam Korea is divided into occupation zones The United Nations is founded	The first Indochina war begins Bretton Woods system goes into effect Kennan writes the "Long Telegram" Churchill makes "Iron Curtain" speech	India is decolonized India and Pakistan are created UN Partition Plan for Palestine is approved Truman Doctrine, Marshall Plan, and National Security Act go into effect in United States The "Red Scare" takes hold in the United States

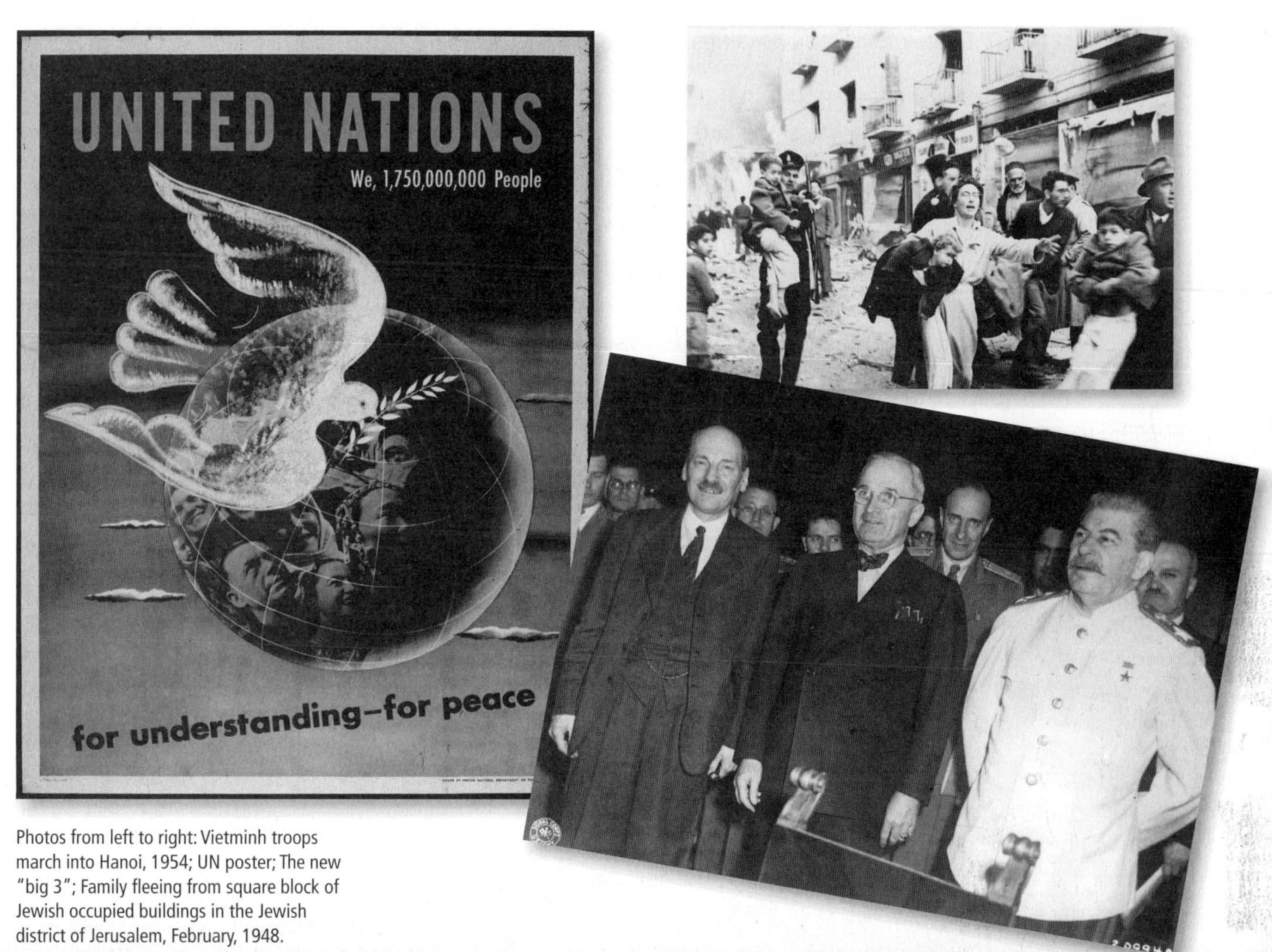

Photos from left to right: Vietminh troops march into Hanoi, 1954; UN poster; The new "big 3"; Family fleeing from square block of Jewish occupied buildings in the Jewish district of Jerusalem, February, 1948.

1948

Congress of Europe meets

Gandhi is assassinated

USSR blockades Berlin, and United States flies airlift around it

The OAS is established

State of Israel is created and recognized

The first Arab-Israeli War begins

1949

Mao wins civil war in China and establishes PRC

Chinese nationalists flee to Taiwan

The German Federal Republic is created

NATO is established

1950

Sino-Soviet Treaty is signed

U.S. government issues NSC-68

1955

Moscow creates the Warsaw Pact

The victors of the second world war were anxious to avoid the mistakes made at the end of the Great War, particularly those that contributed to the worldwide economic depression. This required cooperation, which led to convergence in several key economic and political areas in the latter half of the twentieth century. But different views on who should dominate the postwar political, economic and social cultures led to regional and international conflicts. It was in these immediate postwar years, 1945–1950, that the patterns of conflict and convergence that would structure the rest of the century, as well as shape the twenty-first century, were established.

WORKING WITH THE THEMES

THE EFFECTS OF TECHNOLOGY The "total war" era of the first half of the twentieth century gives way to a "Cold War," driven by the ongoing development of weapons technology.

CHANGING IDENTITIES Thirty years of war in Europe greatly impacted its citizens. Two new issues evolve that will remain dominant features for the remainder of the twentieth century: the implications of the Cold War on people throughout the world and the short- and long-term consequences of decolonization.

SHIFTING BORDERS Because the Allies cannot agree on political ideology, their division of the postwar world into occupation zones has serious worldwide ramifications. The creation of new independent countries in the late 1940s through decolonization leads to regional violence.

GLOBALIZATION Two seemingly contradictory paths emerge: international political and economic division created by the Cold War and unprecedented convergence in the creation of the United Nations and Bretton Woods system, as well as the development of regional organizations.

Worldwide Conflict

The defining structural characteristic of the latter half of the twentieth century was the conflict between the two "superpowers" that emerged at the end of World War II. After thirty years of war and its consequences in Europe, Germany's and Italy's military capacities were almost completely destroyed and Great Britain's and France's had been greatly diminished. What was left of Japan's military was being dismantled by the United States during the **Occupation,** and China was engaged in an intermittent civil war from April 1927 through May 1950. By 1945, only the United States and USSR were capable of fielding effective military machines, and the United States was clearly leading in terms of military technology, proven by its use of the atomic bombs in Japan. The military alliance these two countries forged to defeat fascism in World War II was not strong enough to overcome the ideological differences between them.

Occupation
after the Japanese surrendered at the end of the WWII, the Allied military, led by General MacArthur, supervised the political, economic and social reconstruction of Japan from 1945–1952

The Roots of the Cold War

Patterns of war in the twentieth century (really throughout the history of humankind) were based on technological growth: close-range combat of the late 1800s led to long-range weapons (grenades, mortar, nerve gas) for total war in World War I, which led to airplanes and bombing in World War II. With the advent of the atomic bomb and rapidly expanding nuclear technology, it became obvious that waging a total war would have destructive consequences worldwide. This led to the **Cold War,** which does not mean "no war"; it simply means that the primary combatants never engaged in direct military conflict against one another. As long as the two superpowers with the nuclear weapons did not go to war, the world could survive. Somewhat ironically, it was because of the advancements in military technology that the United States and USSR could not engage one another in traditional military warfare without potentially destroying the world.

Cold War
describes the conflict between the United States and USSR between 1945–1991, when the two primary combatants never engaged in direct military conflict against one another

In many ways, the goals of the two main contenders in the Cold War followed the very traditional goals of combatants throughout history—each side was fighting for control of territory. The Cold War is often referred to as an **ideological war,** implying that the two sides were fighting over beliefs. On some level, that is certainly true—the stated goal of the USSR was to spread communism, and the stated goal of the United States was to contain the spread of communism (which is a less aggressive way of saying, "to spread democracy"). In order to accomplish its goal, however, each side would have to control a territory, or control the government of that territory at the very least.

ideological war conflict rooted in differing world views; to win, one ideology would become dominant over all others

How did the world get to this somewhat artificial divide between democracy and communism, with each ideology outright vilifying the other to prove to the rest of the world that its political and economic system was the better one? Thanks to the actions of Mussolini and Hitler, fascism had essentially been discredited as an ideological form of political governance (not that it ended it in reality, of course). During World War II, the democracies and communist USSR joined together to defeat those fascist regimes. Interestingly, it is in this military alliance to defeat fascism that the Cold War took shape.

The "Big Three"

When Hitler broke his nonaggression pact with Stalin and invaded the USSR, he forced the Soviet Union into a military alliance with the Allies. The Soviets proved to be absolutely vital in the final defeat of Berlin and Germany, which created a bit of a problem after the war because the Red Army physically occupied all of Eastern Europe and one-half of Germany. Driving out the Soviets would require military action, which the United States and Britain could not even contemplate at that point. But the alliance between the USSR and the Allies was a military one only and had nothing to do with achieving political harmony. Predictably, when it came time for all the winners to sit down at the table and bring the war in Europe to its conclusion, the USSR wanted to install communist governments in Eastern Europe that would be subordinate to Moscow. And predictably, Great Britain and the United States opposed such expansion.

The "big three": U.S. President Franklin D. Roosevelt, British Prime Minister Winston Churchill and Soviet Premier Josef Stalin.

The first meeting of the "big three" was in Tehran, Iran, in November 1943, before the war even ended. They agreed to keep fighting together and pursue unconditional surrender from Germany and Japan in an effort to avoid the diplomatic messes created by the negotiations at the end of World War I. Churchill and Roosevelt agreed to open a second front in France (leading to D-Day), and in return, Stalin promised to join the war in the Pacific after Germany was defeated. But as the Soviets moved through Eastern Europe on their way to Germany, they held onto the territory for themselves. Churchill opposed Stalin's actions, and in October 1944 they talked and tentatively agreed on how they would divide up control of the Balkans after the war. There was a lot of tension over the countries of Eastern Europe occupied by the Soviet military—Stalin wanted them all to be communist under his control, while the United States and Great Britain still had hopes of freely elected democratic governments everywhere in the world. Stalin agreed to let the citizens decide (self-determination), knowing that he would violate the agreements anyway and establish communist regimes. When it came to Germany, all three men agreed that it would be stripped of its government and military and would be divided into four occupation zones (one for each of the Allied powers, including France).

ANALYSIS

Look carefully at the body language in this photograph. What does it tell you about each man? What does it tell you about the relationship between them?

The next time the "big three" met was in February 1945, in Yalta, just before Germany fell. Roosevelt's goal was to encourage the USSR to get involved in the war against Japan after

Germany was defeated, so he and Churchill promised Stalin he could control significant regions in the Pacific after Japan was defeated. Roosevelt expressed his idea of a United Nations (UN) organization to ensure peace after the war—sort of a League of Nations, but with more muscle. Because Stalin agreed to participate, the United States made some more concessions to him, allowing the USSR to essentially control all of Eastern Europe, assuming the people were allowed to choose their own governments. Stalin was relentless in "convincing" them to "choose" communism.

The last time the Allied leaders met was in the Berlin neighborhood of Potsdam in July 1945. Germany was defeated, Roosevelt had passed away and had been replaced by Truman, and the British people had replaced the very conservative Churchill with Clement Attlee and his Labour Party. The leaders confirmed past agreements, expanded Soviet control in Eastern Europe, and carved Germany into four separate occupation zones until they could figure out a better arrangement (which did not come until 1990). Rather than creating an unsatisfactory, overarching peace treaty like the Treaty of Versailles that ended World War I, they left Potsdam with no treaties at all. Such agreements would come slowly in following years. When the Allied leaders left Potsdam, the world had been divided into two unfriendly camps: the West (led by the United States) and the East (led by the USSR).

Behind the Iron Curtain

In a speech to the Soviet people in early 1946, Stalin made a statement implying that capitalism made future wars inevitable:

ANALYSIS

These words were taken from Stalin's "Two Worlds" speech of 1946. Why did the U.S. government react to these words with concern?

> *It would be wrong to think that the Second World War broke out accidentally, or as a result of blunders committed by certain statesmen, although blunders were certainly committed. As a matter of fact, the war broke out as the inevitable result of the development of world economic and political forces on the basis of present-day monopolistic capitalism. Marxists have more than once stated that the capitalist system of world economy contains the elements of a general crisis and military conflicts, that, in view of that, the development of world capitalism in our times does not proceed smoothly and evenly, but through crises and catastrophic wars.*

Read the Document *Long Telegram* on mysearchlab.com

The U.S. Department of State asked George Kennan, a U.S. diplomat in Moscow since 1933, for his view on Stalin's intentions. His now-famous response, *The Long Telegram* of February 22, 1946, warned that "in the long run, there [could] be no permanent, peaceful coexistence" with the Soviet Union. In Kennan's mind, the conflict stemmed from Stalin's belief in Marxism and his fear that Western capitalism would affect his people; therefore, the American way of life had to be destroyed. Probably the most important feature of this Long Telegram is Kennan's conclusion regarding how best to handle the situation. Although Stalin would never negotiate or compromise, the problem could be solved "without recourse to any general military conflict." Ultimately, Kennan said, the Soviet system of government is weaker than the American system of government and American success "... depends on health and vigor of our own society... Every courageous and incisive measure to solve internal problems of our own society, to improve self-confidence, discipline, morale and community spirit of our own people, is a diplomatic victory over Moscow..." The United States should firmly guide other countries in developing political, economic, and social well-being "and unless we do," Kennan warned, "Russians certainly will." Kennan's words became the cornerstone of American foreign policy for most of the remainder of the twentieth century.

A few weeks after Kennan's telegram, Winston Churchill, the former British prime minister, spoke at a college in Fulton, Missouri. His speech was not well received at the time—many people viewed Churchill as a warmonger trying to drag the United States into another military conflict—but the speech coined the phrase that best described the political and ideological divide between the Soviets and the West as the Cold War began:

> *... From Stettin in the Baltic to Trieste in the Adriatic an iron curtain has descended across the Continent. Behind that line lie all the capitals of the ancient states of Central and Eastern Europe. Warsaw, Berlin, Prague, Vienna, Budapest, Belgrade, Bucharest and Sofia; all these famous cities and the populations around them lie in what I must call the Soviet sphere, and all are subject, in one form or another, not only to Soviet influence but to a very high and in some cases increasing measure of control from Moscow.*

MAP 6.1 Soviet Sphere of Influence by 1948

Churchill was referring to the divide across Eastern Europe between free countries with Western-style democratic governments and the Eastern bloc countries with communist governments that answered directly to the USSR. Stalin, of course, perceived Churchill's speech as a threat, particularly the opening phrases in which Churchill seemed to challenge America to act against communism: "... The United States stands at this time at the pinnacle of world power ... with this primacy in power is also joined an awe-inspiring accountability to the future." Churchill may well have been trying to provoke the United States to stay involved in European affairs rather than return to isolationism as it did after World War I, but there was good reason for him to be concerned about the future of democracy in Europe.

Read the Document *Iron Curtain Speech* on mysearchlab.com

As agreed upon during the Tehran, Yalta and Potsdam conferences, the Soviet military occupied the territory it conquered on the way to Berlin to defeat Hitler, including Poland, Romania, Bulgaria, Hungary and parts of Czechoslovakia, Austria and Germany. In violation of those same agreements, however, Stalin refused to allow democratic elections in those countries, and each was ruled by a communist government supported by the Red Army. With the exception of Yugoslavia, where the communist yet fiercely nationalist leader Josip Broz Tito refused to comply with Stalin's domination, each of these communist countries fell under the Soviet **sphere of influence**. They became known as the satellite states because they resolutely duplicated Stalin's political and economic models, although they were technically independent countries. Additionally, a civil war between democratic and communist forces in Greece threatened to replace the democratic government there, and the USSR clearly hoped to add Turkey to the satellite bloc to secure the Soviet border.

sphere of influence a geographic region over which one country directly or indirectly controls political, economic, social, and/or military decision making

The U.S. Response

After thirty years of war and economic hardship, Europe was in shambles politically, economically, industrially, commercially and socially. Much had been destroyed, leading many Western Europeans to wonder if communism was a way out of the hard life and injustices they suffered. President Truman believed that if the United States did not step in to help, communist movements underfoot in Western Europe would be successful. After studying Kennan's *Long Telegram*, Truman made three key announcements:

Read the Document *National Security Council Memorandum Number 68* on mysearchlab.com

1. The official U.S. policy of containment, eventually formalized in *NSC-68* to prevent the spread of communism to noncommunist countries

Read the Document *The Truman Doctrine* on mysearchlab.com

2. The Truman Doctrine to support "free people who are resisting attempted subjugation by armed minorities or by outside pressures" (primarily targeted toward Greece and Turkey)
3. The Marshall Plan to provide money for the rebuilding of Europe

Read the Document *The Marshall Plan* on mysearchlab.com

Under the Marshall Plan, any European state was invited to submit a request to the United States to receive funding for reconstruction programs. At first, Poland and Czechoslovakia tried to sign up, but Stalin quickly realized the political aspect of this economic program and blocked participation from countries within the Soviet sphere of influence. Taking money from the U.S. Congress would certainly place a country squarely within the U.S. sphere of influence.

In four years, the Marshall Plan provided aid to sixteen countries in the total amount of $13.2 billion. The Allies received the largest shares: Great Britain got $3.2 billion to rebuild its oil industry; France got $2.7 billion to modernize industry and transportation; and West Germany used its $1.5 billion to create a free-enterprise industrial system that worked so well it boosted German production 50 percent within four years. Overall, the Marshall Plan achieved its economic goals—the nations of Western Europe rebounded economically, enabling them to trade with the United States. And economic well-being in the Western world provided the

MAKE THE CONNECTION

Using the map on the right as a guide and documents 6.3, 6.4, and 6.5, what connections can you make between the policy of containment, the Truman Doctrine and the Marshall Plan?

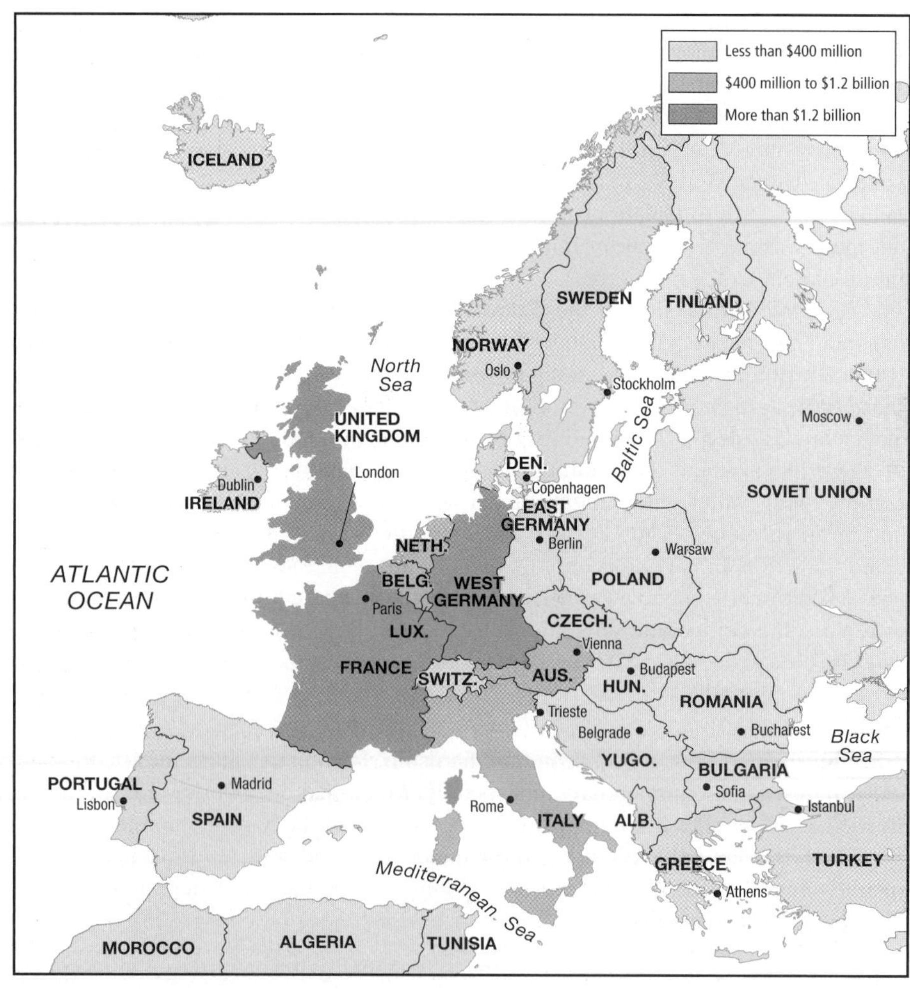

MAP 6.2 Marshall Plan Aid to Europe, 1948–1952

"proof" that democracy generated wealth for all, leading to a high degree of political stability in the United States and Western Europe.

The mental image of the iron curtain across Europe, the language of the containment policy and the bold political and economic promises of the Truman Doctrine and Marshall Plan solidified the divisions, differences and distance between the East and the West—the Cold War had begun and both sides had made their positions clear. But was the United States prepared to follow through? Not quite yet.

The National Security Act of 1947 created the Department of Defense and included the army, navy and air force as equals within it. The act also created the National Security Council to advise the president of foreign policy matters and the Central Intelligence Agency (CIA) to collect and analyze intelligence information and conduct covert operations outside of the United States. The Federal Bureau of Investigation (FBI) would continue to handle internal affairs. One of the first actions of the National Security Council was to recommend increasing military spending by 400 percent. The military budget jumped from $13 billion in 1949 to more than $40 billion in one year. To prevent communist influences from surfacing within the United States, Executive Order 9835 in March 1947 revoked governmental security clearances for people who were considered politically "leftist." The Taft-Hartley Act, which passed in June 1947 despite a presidential veto, restricted the power of labor unions. In 1949, Congress instituted a peacetime draft to make sure the military was trained and ready to go at moment's notice. Congress also revived the **House Committee on Un-American Activities** and went after America's film industry, academicians, and eventually even members of the U.S. military and top State Department officials. Republican Senator Joseph McCarthy led this Red Scare and held Senate hearings that accused people of sympathizing with communists. At the least, many people lost their jobs and friends; at the worst, they faced contempt citations, criminal trials, and even prison sentences.

House Committee on Un-American Activities
a standing committee of nine representatives who investigated suspected communists in influential positions in U.S. society

The First Conflict of the Cold War: the Berlin Airlift

For the U.S. government, 1947 was a busy year; and Stalin decided to test the new policies—he wanted to gauge how committed the United States was to containment. In June 1948, Stalin tried to push the line between the communists (supported by the USSR) and the Western democracies (supported by the United States), which ran right down the middle of Germany. Even though the city of Berlin was located 110 miles inside of East Germany (controlled by the USSR), it too was divided into four sectors—one part to each of the victorious Allies. The French, British and American sectors combined to form West Berlin, and the USSR agreed to allow access through East German territory to and from West Berlin.

Watch the Video *President Truman and the Threat of Communism* on mysearchlab.com

But in June 1948, the Soviets cut off all power to West Berlin and closed all transportation access, completely forming a blockade around it. Although U.S. troops were stationed nearby, using them against the Soviet troops who were upholding the blockade would most certainly result in armed conflict, escalating the Cold War just as it got underway. Truman decided the better way to handle this was to bypass the blockade and show the Soviets that they could not "beat" the United States. For almost one year, basic necessities were consistently flown into West Berlin via the Berlin Airlift. At the peak of the Berlin Airlift, Western cargo planes were landing at one of Berlin's three airports at a rate of one plane every sixty-two seconds. In May 1949, the Soviets realized that the United States was not going to simply surrender West Berlin and discontinued the blockade, but not before 275,000 flights had carried a staggering 2.3 million tons of supplies into West Berlin. The point was made—the United States would take action to contain the spread of communism.

Watch the Video *The Berlin Airlift* on mysearchlab.com

Stalin's aggression in Berlin led to the birth of the German Federal Republic in 1949, created by a constitution written by Germans under Allied supervision. Germany was no longer one country divided into occupation zones; it became two independent states—familiarly known as West and East Germany—that formed the front line of the Cold War.

MAP 6.3 German Occupation Zones, 1947

Western Europe on the Front Line

For almost the entire first half of the twentieth century, Western Europe had been torn apart by war, and the results were absolutely devastating. The physical destruction was almost unimaginable; an estimated 70 percent of Europe's industrial infrastructure was destroyed. From the largest cities on the continent to the smallest rural villages, farmland, factories and all methods of transportation were unusable and, in many cases, simply gone. People suffered through bombings, military occupations, war crimes, forced labor camps and the Holocaust. Approximately 37 million Europeans were dead, which included almost twice as many civilians as military. For those left to survive in what American journalist William Shirer described as an "utter wasteland," famine and poor living conditions were rampant. Unemployment, food rationing and a coal shortage led to civil unrest and violence. In an effort to find homes, jobs and their families, people migrated and relocated across the continent. An estimated 50 million refugees were homeless.

Rebuilding England.

The emotional and psychological toll on the people of Europe cannot be underestimated and is perhaps most eloquently expressed in the writings of French philosophers Jean-Paul Sartre and Simone de Beauvoir. In developing **existentialism,** these writers (and others) combined the scholarly work of previous philosophers such as Nietzsche and Heidegger with the experiences of war and poverty that the people of Europe lived through in the first half of the twentieth century to create philosophical essays, fictional novels and theatrical performances that expressed the raw emotions of postwar European life. The basic premise of existentialism is that "existence precedes essence," which means that humans are defined by their existence and nothing more. Trying to give meaning to your existence is absurd—there is no god and no established set of ethics or morals to compare yourself to. Who you are, who you become, is all a matter of choices you make in a state of perfect freedom. Sartre's most famous work, the one that really formulated the existentialist movement of the 1940s and 1950s, is an essay entitled "Being and Nothingness: An Essay on Phenomenological Ontology," published in 1943. His companion, de Beauvoir, blended existentialism and **liberal feminism,** a quickly growing movement in the late 1940s, when women were not anxious to give up the jobs and independence they had gained while their husbands were gone. Her 1949 best seller, *The Second Sex*, argues that, throughout history, women have been defined as the "other" sex, implying they are not the "normal" sex.

Governments knew they had to respond to the people's needs, but they were trapped in political conflict. In Great Britain, the Labour Party, under Attlee, took over government just at the end of the war in 1945. In an attempt to alleviate the problems associated with thirty years of war and poverty, Attlee established a **welfare state** with the passage of the National Insurance Act, the National Assistance Act and the National Health Service Act on July 5, 1948. This comprehensive program provided "cradle to grave" services for all citizens, a sort of compromise between democracy and communism. In France, the Fourth Republic (the postoccupation government) was controlled by a powerful parliament filled with communists and socialists who refused to allow a strong president. This led to instability—there were twenty-four

existentialism
a philosophical movement of postwar Europe that emphasizes individual decision making as the sole source of one's identity

liberal feminism
a philosophy and activist movement that seeks political, legal and social reform on the premise that men and women are equal

welfare state
a system in which the government provides certain public services (health care, education, unemployment insurance, social security, etc.) as a right of citizenship, regardless of personal wealth

MAKE THE CONNECTION

Sartre was drafted into the French army in 1939, captured by Germans in 1940 and spent nine months in a prisoner of war camp. After negotiating his release, he returned to Paris and began working for the French Resistance. Sartre's experiences during World War II reflect the conundrum most Europeans faced during those years—do I collaborate with the Nazis, join the Resistance or focus solely on self-preservation? Solving this question for himself led Sartre to one of the fundamental tenets of existential philosophy—*freedom is what you do with what's been done to you*. Why did this philosophy gain popular appeal in Europe following World War II?

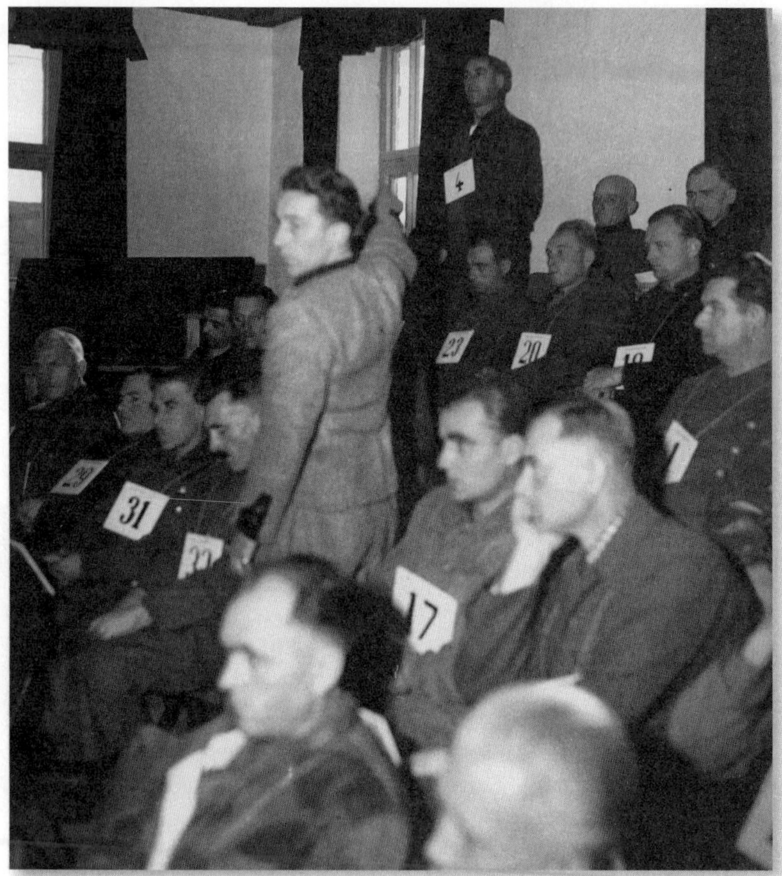

German War Crimes Tribunals, 1945.

governments in just twelve years. In West Germany, the government was initially ruled by the Allied High Commission, comprised of four commissioners from the United States, three from the United Kingdom and one from France. Germans regained control of their government in September 1949. In Italy, a threat of impending civil war led to a referendum in June 1946 to decide whether to maintain the monarchy or move to a republic form of government. With only 54 percent of the vote in favor of republicanism, in a hotly contested election with charges of corruption, Italy officially became a republic on January 1, 1948.

The Denazification of West Germany

Although the war was officially over, throughout Europe Germans were still popularly regarded as the enemy. The hatred and distrust extended to all German people, although the official Allied policy toward Germany was focused on the denazification and demilitarization of the state. Across Europe and the United States, there was a sense of the need for retribution for the death and destruction that Germany had initiated, particularly because Hitler was unavailable to publicly suffer for the misery he created. On August 8, 1945, *The London Charter of the International Military Tribunal* was published, providing the legal basis for conducting trials for individuals accused of committing **war crimes, crimes against peace,** and/or **crimes against humanity** during the war, and it spelled out the procedures that would be followed in doing so. From November 20, 1945, to October 1, 1946, the International Military Tribunal (IMT), comprised of judges from the four Allied countries, tried twenty-four of the highest-ranking Nazi officials who were captured at the end of the war. The United States also held its own tribunal for war criminals, including specific ones for doctors and judges. Collectively, these tribunals were known as the Nuremberg Trials because they were held in the city of Nuremberg, Germany, the site of some of the largest Nazi rallies before and during World War II. Of the twenty-four high-ranking Nazi officials tried by the IMT, twelve received the death sentence (by hanging), seven received prison time ranging from ten years to life, three were acquitted, one had his charges dropped to lesser crimes and was sent to a U.S. tribunal, and one committed suicide before his trial began. The Nuremberg Trials became the foundation for the ongoing development of international criminal law through UN conventions and the creation of international courts.

war crimes
violations of the laws of war, including murder, slave labor, abuse of prisoners of war, wanton destruction of cities, towns, or villages

crimes against peace
planning, initiating or participating in a war of aggression

crimes against humanity
murder, extermination, enslavement, deportation and other inhumane acts done against any civilian population, or persecutions on political, racial, or religious grounds

Between the U.S. military presence throughout Europe and the money coming in through the Marshall Plan, American citizens, corporations and culture spread throughout Europe. Unlike the end of World War I, when the American troops went home and the country became isolationist, the United States established military bases in West Germany to keep a close eye on the encroaching communist regimes in Eastern Europe. The European countries were simply too weak militarily to handle the occupation of Germany and protect themselves from the Soviet Red Army without the help of the United States. Similarly, they were too financially drained to rebuild their own economies and had to rely on aid from the United States to do so. This was a tough spot for the European governments, who were on the one hand thankful the United States was willing to stay involved and participate in establishing economic, political and military stability; but at the same time painfully aware of the **Americanization** of Europe.

Americanization
U.S. influence on the culture of another country, generally spread through consumerism and/or militarization

Regional Conflicts

While the beginning of the Cold War was certainly the most divisive conflict of this era, it was by no means the only one. Some of the most dramatic conflicts in the latter half of the twentieth century also began in these postwar years as a result of issues associated with migration and decolonization. Because of the bipolar structure of the world during this time, many of these regional conflicts became key battles in the Cold War (and are discussed in future chapters). Indeed, many of them remain heated regional conflicts in the twenty-first century.

India and Pakistan

After years of working toward self-rule, India gained its independence from Great Britain in August 1947. Unfortunately, the people of India disagreed (often violently) on religion and government. Muslims believed that religion should be an integral part of the governance system, while Hindus wanted to establish a democratic republic with a separation of church and state. Because they could not agree, they could not create a single government for the newly

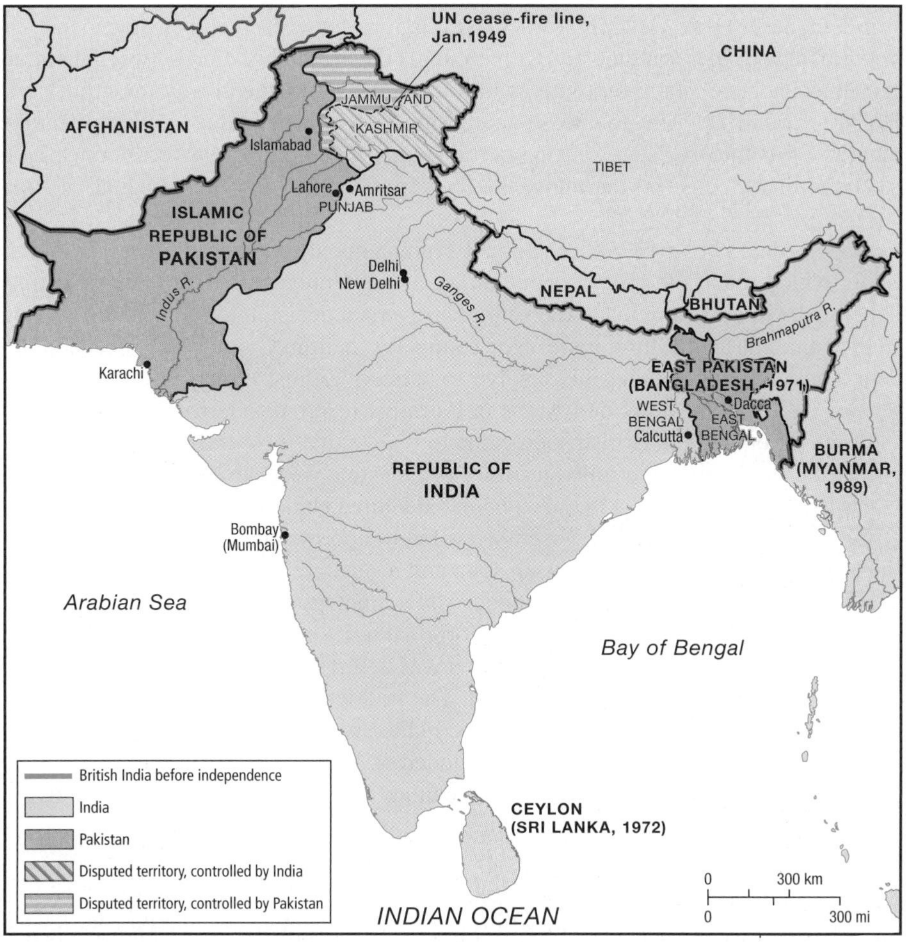

MAP 6.4 India and Pakistan, 1947

decolonized state, and India was partitioned into two separate nations: India for the Hindus and Pakistan for the Muslims. This partition led to violence as approximately 14.5 million people rushed the border—the Muslims in India heading for Pakistan and the Hindus in Pakistan heading for India. They met in the Punjab region, where an estimated 500,000 were killed in rioting.

Mohandas Gandhi, by then the most powerful figure in the Indian National Congress, opposed the partition, but his closest advisors convinced him that it was the only way to avoid civil war, so he reluctantly agreed. After the partition, he became focused on Hindu–Muslim unity, engaging in a fast-unto-death unless financial aid from India that had been promised to Pakistan was delivered. The money transfer was made; but despite Gandhi's efforts, in October 1947 the first of what would be four wars broke out between the newly created India and Pakistan over the territory of Kashmir. In 1948, Gandhi was assassinated by a radical Hindu who was angered by Gandhi's efforts at Hindu–Muslim unity.

Israel versus Arab Nationalism

Jewish immigration to Palestine from Germany and the rest of Europe increased dramatically throughout the 1930s as a result of Hitler's actions, further angering the Arabs living in Palestine and igniting violence. The Arabs demanded an end to immigration, warning Great Britain that "no room can be made in Palestine for a second nation except by dislodging or exterminating the first." In other words, give us our independence, but the Arabs must rule it. The Jews, however, also claimed the right to rule an independent Palestine.

In March 1945, six Arab countries formed a regional intergovernmental organization (IGO) called the Arab League in order to "draw closer the relations between member States and coordinate their political activities with the aim of realizing a close collaboration between them, to safeguard their independence and sovereignty, and to consider in a general way the affairs and interests of the Arab countries." The goal was to create an Arab homeland that would respect the sovereign authority of its member states but support one another politically and economically in world affairs. The primary focus was to remove the Jews from Palestine and restore it as an Arab territory.

After Roosevelt's death in April 1945, President Truman openly supported Jewish immigration to Palestine, which made the Arab League angry at the United States. As the Holocaust camps were liberated, Great Britain made the very controversial decision to refuse the survivors admittance to Palestine, instead setting up refugee camps for them in Cyprus. This decision angered President Truman, strengthening his resolve to support Zionist efforts at establishing a homeland in Palestine. Both the Jews and Arabs in Palestine resorted to terrorism to get rid of the British and each other, and the British soon came to realize that the 1 million Arabs and the 400,000 Jews sharing the British-controlled territory of Palestine were never going to get along peacefully. Great Britain decided to let the newly created United Nations step in and take over.

Arab Nationalism
a self-rule movement based on the assertion that all Arabs are united by a common cultural, historical, linguistic heritage

recognized
to be a legitimate state in the international system, you must have a well-defined territory with a permanent population and a single government to engage in relations with other states

In November 1947, the UN General Assembly voted to approve the *UN Partition Plan for Palestine*, which would create a separate Jewish state and a separate Arab state, leaving a small territory containing Jerusalem and Bethlehem under UN administration. According to the plan, the Arab state would receive about 43 percent of its original territory and the Jewish state would receive approximately 56 percent (although much of it was desert) to accommodate the expected rise in immigration once a Jewish state was created. The problem was not the land itself, however; it was the population living within those borders. In the process of trying to include most of the Jews in the Jewish state, a lot of Arabs were included as well. As a result, the Jewish state ended up with only a 61 percent majority of Jews, meaning that 39 percent of the people living in the Jewish state were Arab, most of them Muslims.

The response of the Jewish leadership was mixed, but they accepted the partition plan. The Palestinian leadership disagreed with it for a variety of reasons, arguing first and foremost that partition only represented the will of one-third of the overall Palestinian population (the Jewish people). Leaders in the surrounding Arab countries, concerned about the large numbers of Arabs who would be living as a minority group inside what was historically their own land, got involved as well. **Arab nationalism,** which first appeared in force after the fall of the Ottoman Empire, grew into an organized anticolonial movement after the Treaty of Versailles turned the territory of the Middle East into British and French mandates. Now that the Western powers were once again determining state boundaries and who could dominate them, Arab nationalists were eager to help Palestinian Arabs maintain control of their territory. In December 1947, Syria established the Arab Liberation Army with 6,000 volunteers, Arabs primarily from Syria, Iraq, Lebanon, Transjordan and Egypt. But the Jews also had their own army and paramilitary organizations, with many World War II veterans, and violent conflicts and terrorist attacks occurred daily.

The British wanted nothing to do with Palestine once the violence began and announced that they would leave Palestine on May 15, 1948, refusing to participate in the implementation of the plan. On May 14, 1948, the leader of the provisional government of Israel, David Ben-Gurion, announced the establishment of the state of Israel, basically enacting the UN Partition Plan. Arabs throughout the Middle East denied his ability to do so, arguing that Israel was stealing land that belonged to Palestine. President Truman immediately **recognized** Ben-Gurion's government as the leadership of the new state of Israel. As the now-declassified documents show, Truman knew in advance of Ben-Gurion's plan, and Ben-Gurion knew that he had U.S. support. The UN was angry that Truman did not discuss his plans with the Security Council before publicly announcing his support for Israel, but it too followed suit in recognizing Israel as a legitimate state.

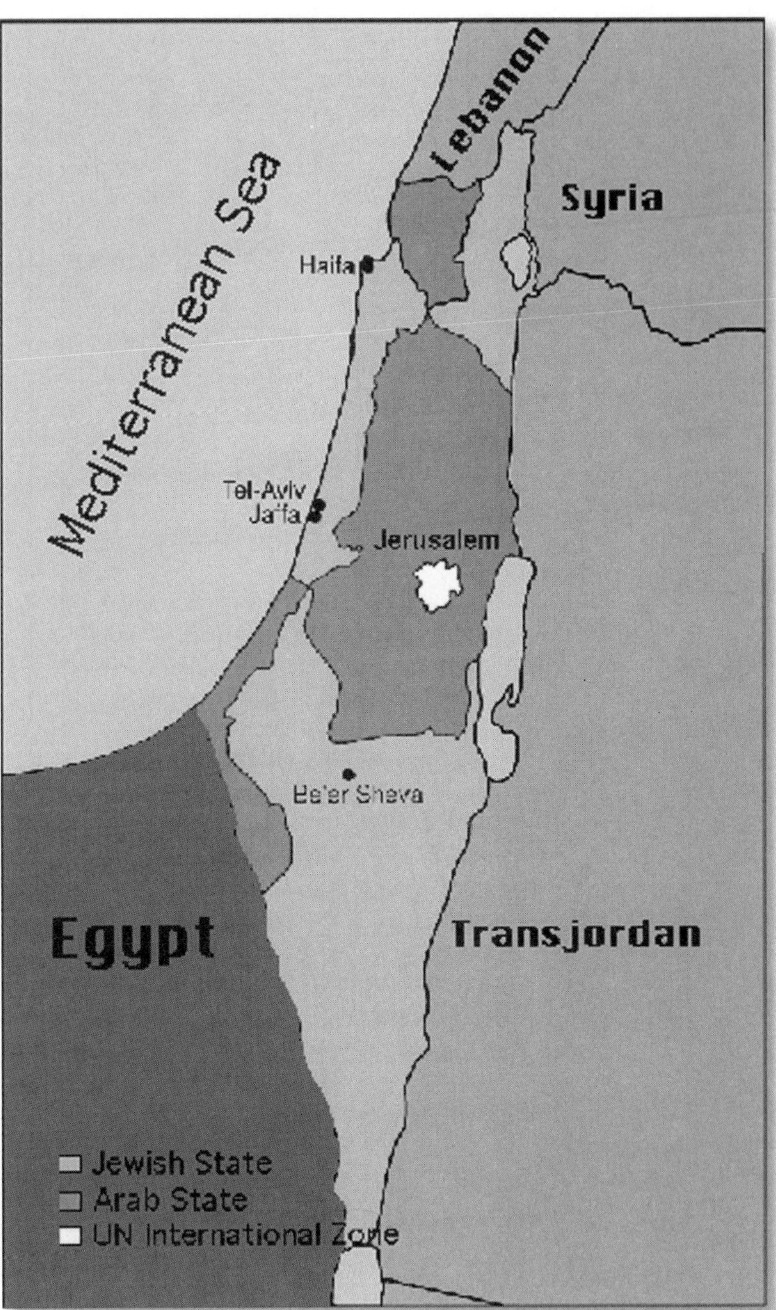

UN Partition Plan for Palestine, 1947.

The very next day, May 15, 1948, state militaries from Egypt, Transjordan, Syria, Lebanon and Iraq joined with the Arab Liberation Army and invaded Palestine. This was the first Arab–Israeli War, and it lasted until January 1949. The Jewish people successfully held onto the territory they were originally allotted under the Partition Plan, gained almost half of the land designated for Palestine, and also captured part of Jerusalem. At the end of this war, Israel controlled approximately 78 percent of the original state of Palestine. Egypt gained the territory known as the Gaza Strip, and the West Bank went to Transjordan. One of the most severe effects of the war was the incredible refugee crisis throughout the Middle East. Palestinian refugees fleeing Israeli control were estimated at anywhere from 360,000 to 711,000, and most

Read the Document *Israel's Proclamation of Independence, 1948* on mysearchlab.com

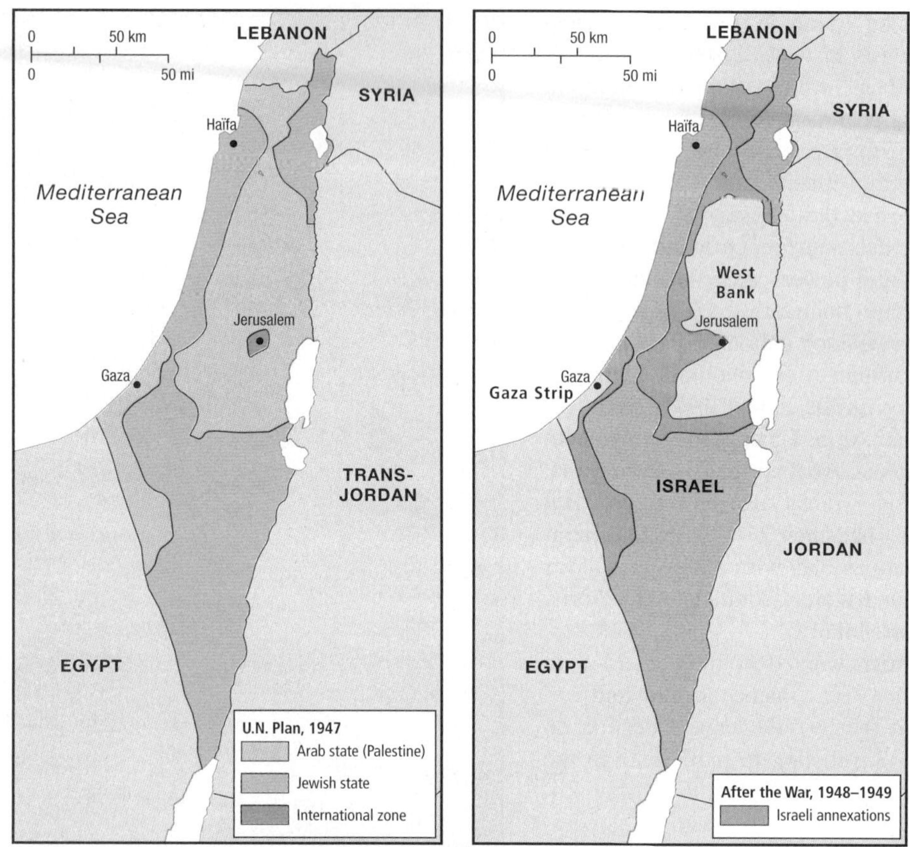

MAP 6.5 Consequences of the First Arab-Israeli War

surrounding Arab countries were not financially, politically or geographically equipped to accommodate them. Another 758,000 to 900,000 Jewish refugees fled from Arab nations, most of them to Israel. The war also made the Arabs determined to seek revenge, not just against the Jews, but also against the West, which had clearly provided Israel with political support, financing and military technology.

Once Israel was established, the population grew rapidly due to immigration, doubling in just three years. Unfortunately, the economic situation was bleak due to the boycott by all surrounding Arab states and high taxes to keep the military running for much-needed defense. Some help arrived when Israel became a member of the UN in May 1949; but to survive, Israel relied heavily on direct financial and military aid from the West, particularly from the United States.

Two Communisms

In China, the Guomindang (Nationalist Party) government and Communist Party had temporarily united to help defend the country from Japan's attacks. But Japan's defeat in World War II meant its conquered territory was returned to its rightful owners, and China was geographically restored, so the struggle for political power between the Guomindang and Communist Party resurfaced in the form of a civil war. Chiang Kai-Shek, the leader of the Guomindang and a member of the Allied Powers in WWII, officially ruled the Republic of China, according to its constitution, but Mao Zedong and his communist forces made substantial territorial gains in the immediate postwar era. Despite almost $2 billion in aid from the United States, the Guomindang was no match for the popular Communist Party. By the fall of 1949, Chiang Kai-Shek and the nationalists fled, reestablishing the Republic of China on the island of Taiwan with the full support of the United States. Mao took over mainland China and, on October 1, 1949, renamed it the People's Republic of China (PRC) to reflect its communist ideology. He called his government the "People's Democratic Dictatorship."

Stalin was cautious about the establishment of a communist state that was not under his direct control. Mao quickly made it very clear that he would not be considered a satellite state of the USSR—Mao had his own brand of communism, rooted deeply in the unique cultural and historical experiences of China. After a few months of difficult negotiations, the Sino-Soviet Treaty of Friendship, Alliance and Mutual Assistance was signed in February 1950. The treaty included a mutual defense pact, an agreement to consult on international affairs that involved both countries, moderate economic assistance (roughly $300 million) from the USSR to the PRC and a promise of nonintervention in the domestic affairs of the other. Nationalism, it seemed, was stronger than communism.

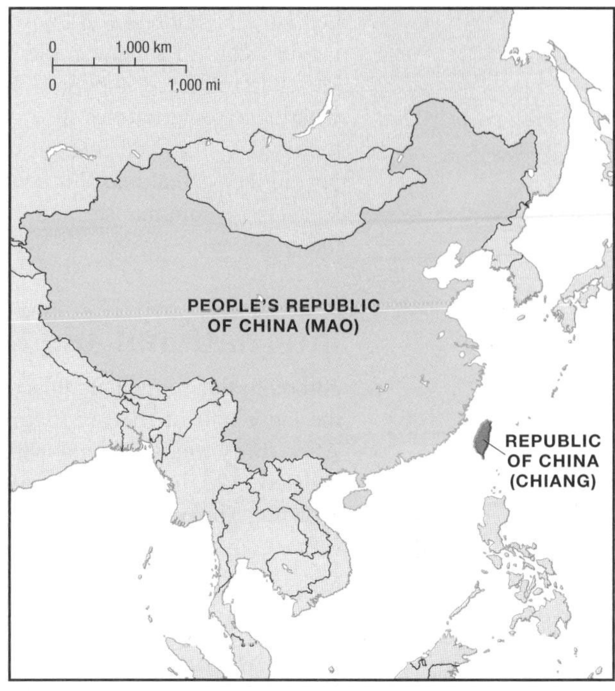

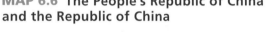

MAP 6.6 The People's Republic of China and the Republic of China

Vietnam

When Germany controlled France during World War II, Japan began supervising France's Asian colonies, including Vietnam. Though guerilla resistance failed against the powerful Japanese military, the independence movement in Vietnam grew even stronger. After Japan's defeat in 1945, the Vietnamese people tried to negotiate for their independence, but the French refused. Led by Ho Chi Minh, the people decided to fight.

Born in Vietnam under French colonialism, Ho Chi Minh spent his early adult years in London and Paris (he even attended the 1919 Paris Peace Conference), where he helped establish the French Communist Party. He attended East Moscow University in the USSR and, as a member of the Comintern, traveled through China and Indochina establishing regional communist political parties. In 1941, he brought nationalists and communists together as the Vietminh, an organization devoted to Vietnamese independence. Ho was certainly a communist, but he was first and foremost a nationalist.

Ho Chi Minh at the Versailles Peace Conference, 1919.

On September 2, 1945, Ho Chi Minh announced the establishment of the Democratic Republic of Vietnam, ironically using language from both the U.S. *Declaration of Independence* and the French revolutionaries of the late 1700s to proclaim the Vietnamese people free from outside domination. The French responded, and the First Indochina War began in December 1946. For eight years, Vietnam was a battleground as France struggled to fight off a nationalist movement led by the Vietminh.

But as much as the Allies believed in decolonization, the Cold War mentality had taken hold, and Ho Chi Minh was a known communist. With good reason, the Allies did not trust that he would establish a democratic state in Vietnam. By 1950, the U.S. policy of containment had kicked in full force, and the United States began providing military and financial aid to the French with the expectation that they would stop the communist takeover. At about the same time, Mao took over China and began providing military support to Ho Chi Minh. The French suffered a major military defeat and lost control of Vietnam in 1954. They were forced to negotiate with the Vietnamese communists, and the resulting "independence" agreement created far more problems than it solved.

International and Regional Convergence

Although this immediate postwar period served as a sort of incubator for the major conflicts of the latter half of the twentieth century, it was also a period of cooperation in many respects. After thirty years of total war, it was apparent that the nation-states of the world were not isolated. The linkages between them—economic, ideological and political—were great and growing. The powerful countries in 1945 recognized that, if they could harness those linkages to create convergence in several key areas, most notably trade, they could control the international system without the expense of colonization.

International Agreements

It was no mystery why the League of Nations failed to prevent World War II. Without the participation of the United States, the League was virtually ineffective outside of Western Europe (and barely credible there). Before the United States was even officially involved in World War II, President Roosevelt was determined that the United States should take its rightful

Flag Day Ceremonies at the White House.

place in a new international organization dedicated to many of Wilson's original goals for the League of Nations. When creating the Atlantic Charter in 1941, Roosevelt and Churchill used the phrase "united nations" to describe their alliance. Roosevelt liked the term and suggested to Churchill that it should be the name of the postwar organization they would create to establish stability and peace. At the first meeting of the "big three" in Tehran in 1943, Roosevelt proposed the creation of the United Nations with five core members: the United States, the United Kingdom, the USSR, France, and China (at the time still under one-party rule by the Guomindang). Representatives from those countries spent the fall of 1944 working out the general parameters for the international organization, and in the spring of 1945 the UN Conference on International Organizations brought together the governments of fifty nations and several nongovernmental organizations to create the UN Charter. Once this charter was ratified by the five original members, who retained permanent positions on the Security Council, and by a majority of the other forty-six nations involved, the United Nations was officially established on June 26, 1945.

There was no doubt why the UN was created—the first line of the preamble reads: "We the Peoples of the United Nations Determined ... to save succeeding generations from the scourge of war, which twice in our lifetime has brought untold sorrow to mankind ..." The stated goal was to prevent World War III. The United Nations was established to do what the League of Nations was supposed to do but could never accomplish; much of Wilson's language even appears throughout the text. The primary differences lie in the structure and membership, giving the UN far more power to carry out its goals than the League of Nations ever possessed.

One of the major reasons World War II started was economic depression and the fear that poor people would turn to communism as an answer. To provide an alternative other than fascism or Nazism to prevent this, representatives from all forty-four Allied nations met in Bretton Woods, New Hampshire, at the United Nations Monetary and Financial Conference (more commonly referred to as the Bretton Woods Conference) in July 1944 to figure out how to stabilize the world financial system and prevent a repeat of the economic disaster that occurred post-World War I. The goals of the representatives were to create rules and institutions that would regulate the international monetary system to prevent another worldwide depression and to help the poorest countries of the world get stronger to prevent a communist takeover. They established a **liberal economic system** to provide "economic security," which would be maintained through two newly created institutions. The International Monetary Fund (IMF) was established to oversee currency exchange rates, promote economic growth and employment and provide emergency loans to countries in severe debt. Working as an agency under the UN, the International Bank for Reconstruction and Development (IRBD), more commonly referred to as the World Bank, began with $10 billion to loan to governments of countries most in need of postwar reconstruction.

liberal economic system
a set of international agreements and rules designed to promote free trade, open markets and monetary stability

THE PURPOSES OF THE UNITED NATIONS ARE

1. To maintain international peace and security, and to that end: to take effective collective measures for the prevention and removal of threats to the peace, and for the suppression of acts of aggression or other breaches of the peace, and to bring about by peaceful means, and in conformity with the principles of justice and international law, adjustment or settlement of international disputes or situations which might lead to a breach of the peace;
2. To develop friendly relations among nations based on respect for the principle of equal rights and self-determination of peoples, and to take other appropriate measures to strengthen universal peace;
3. To achieve international co-operation in solving international problems of an economic, social, cultural, or humanitarian character, and in promoting and encouraging respect for human rights and for fundamental freedoms for all without distinction as to race, sex, language, or religion; and
4. To be a centre for harmonizing the actions of nations in the attainment of these common ends.

Bretton Woods system
the institutions created and controlled by the wealthy democratic countries to encourage worldwide prosperity and counter political extremism

The **Bretton Woods system** was officially established in 1946 after ratification by a majority of the Allied nations at the conference. An international trade organization was originally proposed, but the idea never made it past the U.S. Senate, so it never went on for consideration by the other Bretton Woods members. Instead, the General Agreement on Trade and Tariffs (GATT) was put in place to regulate trade issues. Although a Soviet representative attended the initial conference, the USSR refused to join the IMF or sign the GATT because the goals of a liberal economic system ran exactly counter to the goals of a communist economy.

Regional Agreements

Western European governments were reliant on Marshall Plan aid to rebuild their shattered economies. And as the UN demand for decolonization grew, they were also faced with the prospect of completely revamping their economies, which had been built on mercantilism. Without colonies, they would have to pay for natural resources and labor and sell their goods at a fair price. In 1948, a Congress of Europe was held to look at the options for opening up cooperative trade opportunities between the six participants: France, Italy, West Germany, Belgium, Netherlands and Luxembourg. Over the next few years, they established the Organization of European Economic Cooperation, the European Coal and Steel Community and the European Economic Community, all of which eventually merged into the European Community in 1967. Instead of competing over limited resources and colonies, Europe would work together to support one another's economies. In part, this was an economic necessity, but many realized that it was a political necessity as well in the face of clearly increasing U.S. dominance over Europe. Tying the success and failures of these six major European economies together also linked them politically, and the European Parliament was established in 1957 as part of the European Economic Community. Eventually, other Western European powers joined, creating the basic structure for European unity that continued to converge throughout the century.

As the Cold War began, the countries of Latin America realized that the United States would once again seek them out for political and economic support. In part because of the heavy U.S. financial investment and in part because of geostrategic positioning, the United States would never allow a communist foothold to develop in Latin America. Given the high poverty rates and U.S. intervention in their leading industries over the years, left-wing political regimes were relatively popular with the people of South America. The U.S. government realized that these regimes were vulnerable to accepting financial and military support from the USSR in exchange for a jump just a little further left on the political spectrum. Eager to prevent this, the United States once again approached the countries of Latin America, offering support. The 1947 Rio Pact placed the twenty-one countries of Latin America in a security alliance supported by the United States. In April 1948, this alliance was formalized as the Organization of American States (OAS), a collective security arrangement "to achieve an order of peace and justice, to promote their solidarity, to strengthen their collaboration, and to defend their sovereignty, their territorial integrity, and their independence." One of the stated goals was to "promote and consolidate representative democracy," so the United States channeled money, direct military assistance and covert CIA aid to help prevent left-wing regimes from gaining power in Latin America.

After the experience of the Berlin blockade, it was apparent to the United States and Western Europe that the USSR was serious about spreading communism and would perhaps even resort to violence to do so. To prepare for this possibility, they established a collective self-defense organization in April 1949 under Article 51 of the United Nations Charter. They called it the North Atlantic Treaty Organization (NATO), and it essentially told the world that an attack on one member was equivalent to an attack on all members. In response, the Eastern European states, controlled by Moscow, created COMECON (Council of Mutual Assistance), supposedly to integrate their economies (sort of a Marshall Plan for the eastern bloc), but also very much as an informal military alliance. The Soviets formalized this when they established the Warsaw Pact, an Eastern European defense organization, on May 14, 1955.

In an effort to prevent the further spread of communism in Southeast Asia, the United States, France, Great Britain, New Zealand, Australia, the Philippines, Thailand (where the headquarters were located) and Pakistan created the Southeast Asia Treaty Organization (SEATO) in September 1954. Its membership included only two Southeast Asian countries—the rest were not terribly concerned that communism presented a threat to their internal stability. The United States viewed SEATO as an essential tool in containment; France and Great Britain were financially invested in the region; New Zealand and Australia joined because of their close proximity; and Pakistan was trying to build international support and marginalize India. Given its membership and lack of military forces, SEATO's ability to take action was restricted only to meet U.S. interests (particularly during U.S. involvement in Vietnam).

Conclusions

In the first fifty years of the twentieth century, the combination of technology and economic growth built advanced militaries, while nationalism, Social Darwinism and consumerism tore apart existing empires, leading to roughly thirty years of total war and global economic depression. In the aftermath, during the years 1945–1950, the leaders of the world's most powerful countries were determined to prevent what seemed to be a downward spiral for humanity. They sought new ways to cope with the results of their actions, seeking a convergence of political ideals and military control wherever possible to prevent large-scale warfare and extensive cooperation in economic matters to prevent another worldwide depression. The people of the world also chose new responses to what they perceived as the same problems they had been facing since the century began. They had been promised self-determination before and were frustrated when the political leaders they trusted to deliver it had failed to do so. This time they would fight for independence and create their own identities through civil war, political revolutions, and migration. With ongoing nationalistic-driven, postcolonial, and identity-related violence marking almost every region of the world and a "cold war" prevailing on a global level, the structure for the latter half of the twentieth century was established.

WORKING WITH THE THEMES

THE EFFECTS OF TECHNOLOGY What were the ramifications of the United States utilizing its atomic bombs against Japan? How did the use of the bombs lead to a "cold war"?

CHANGING IDENTITIES How did WWII affect European civilians? What were the implications of the East/West divide into "spheres of influence"? What were the immediate effects of decolonization for people in the Middle East, India, and Southeast Asia?

SHIFTING BORDERS How did the victorious Allies settle land disputes at the end of WWII? What were the short-term effects of occupation zones? What were the geographic consequences of decolonization from 1945–1950?

GLOBALIZATION Why was the United Nations created after the failure of the League of Nations? How did the Great Depression of the 1930s lead to the Bretton Woods system? Why was there an increase in regional organizations in the postwar era? What were the ramifications of the linkage between cold-war politics and economics?

Further Reading

TO FIND OUT MORE

Library of Congress: For European Recovery: The Fiftieth Anniversary of the Marshall Plan. Available online at http://www.loc.gov/exhibits/marshall/

PBS American Experience: The Berlin Airlift. Available online at http://www.pbs.org/wgbh/amex/airlift

MATRIX, the Center for Humane Arts, Letters and Social Sciences Online: Seventeen Moments in Soviet History—1947. Available online at http://www.soviethistory.org

Imperial War Museum: Through My Eyes—Stories of Conflict, Belonging and Identity (Indian Partition). Available online at http://www.throughmyeyes.org.uk/

James L. Gelvin: *The Israel–Palestine Conflict: One Hundred Years of War* (2007)

NATO: NATO Declassified 1949–1959. Available online at http://www.nato.int/ebookshop/video/declassified/#/en/home/

GO TO THE SOURCE

Yale Law School/The Avalon Project: The Nuremberg Trials Collection. Available online at http://avalon.law.yale.edu/subject_menus/imt.asp

Yale Law School/The Avalon Project: The Bretton Woods Agreements. Available online at http://avalon.law.yale.edu/20th_century/decad047.asp

Library of Congress: Revelations from the Russian Archives. Available online at http://www.loc.gov/exhibits/archives/intro.html

Harry S. Truman Library & Museum: Ideological Foundations of the Cold War. Available online at http://www.trumanlibrary.org/whistlestop/study_collections/coldwar/index.php?action=docs

MySearchLab Connections

Read the **Document** on **mysearchlab.com**

6.1 George F. Kennan, *Long Telegram.* In 1946, the wartime alliance between the United States and the Soviet Union was falling apart. U.S. Foreign Service officer George F. Kennan argued that the systems of the United States and the Soviet Union were incompatible and that Soviet security depended on destroying the American way of life.

6.2 Winston Churchill, *Iron Curtain* Speech. After World War II, Churchill toured the United States alongside President Harry S. Truman. In a speech at Westminster College in Missouri, he coined the phrase "Iron Curtain" to describe the lack of clarity in the west for what was going on in Soviet-dominated Eastern Europe.

6.3 *National Security Council Memorandum Number 68.* The emerging Cold War led some U.S. officials to view the world as dividing into two hostile spheres. A major issue concerned nuclear weapons in the Soviet-dominated sphere and the need to maintain the American lead in the arms race.

6.4 Harry S. Truman, *The Truman Doctrine*. World War II left Europe economically devastated and politically unstable. Early in 1947, it appeared that Turkey and Greece would fall under Soviet influence. In this speech, Truman outlines his support for a policy of aggressive containment of the Soviet Union not only in Turkey and Greece, but all over the world.

6.5 George Marshall, *The Marshall Plan*. In 1947, U.S. Secretary of State Marshall articulated a plan for American aid to Europe. The plan was designed to fill the power vacuum in Europe and to help Europe reconstruct itself after the devastation of war.

6.6 *Israel's Proclamation of Independence, 1948*. One day before the termination of the British mandate for Palestine, the Provisional State Council (a forerunner of the Israeli Parliament) declared the independence of Israel on May 14, 1948.

Watch the **Video** on **mysearchlab.com**

6.1 *President Truman and the Threat of Communism*

6.2 *The Berlin Airlift*

7

The Cold War Begins

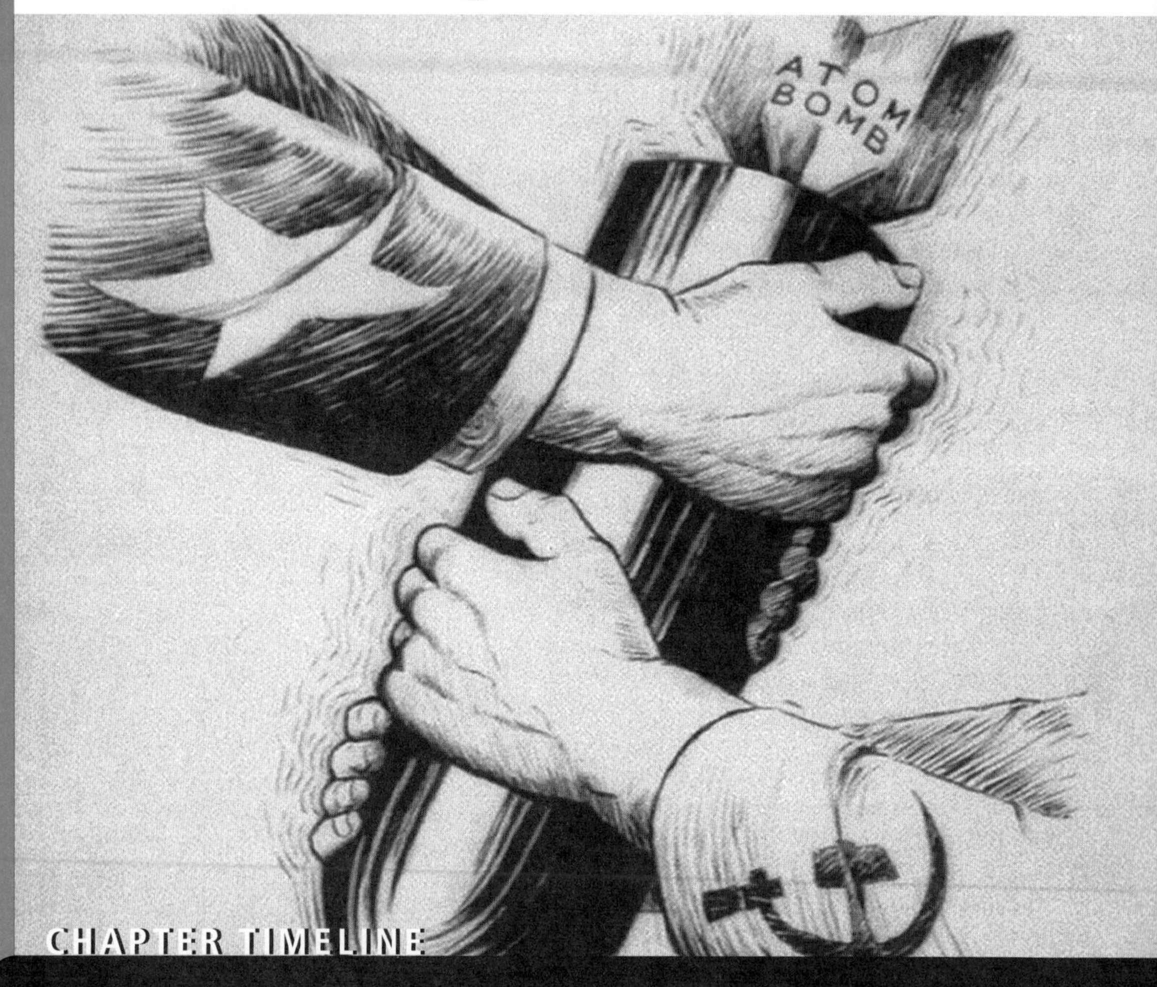

CHAPTER OUTLINE

- U.S. Occupation of Japan
- The "Other" Communism: Mao's People's Republic of China
- Conflict in Korea
- The Arms Race
- Battle by Proxy

CHAPTER TIMELINE

1945
United States uses atomic bombs
VJ Day–U.S. occupation of Japan begins
Korea is divided into communist north and democratic south

1947
Japan approves democratic Constitution

1949
Mao wins Chinese Civil War and establishes PRC
United States recognizes Taiwan
Sino-Soviet Treaty is signed
USSR detonates atomic bombs

1950
Korean War begins

1953
Stalin dies
The transistor radio is invented
USSR and United States invent hydrogen bombs

1964
Quotations from Chairman Mao Zedong is published
The PRC becomes a nuclear power

1965
Mao's Great Proletarian Cultural Revolution begins

Photos from left to right: Political cartoon depicting the arms race; Korean War; Diagram of a fallout shelter; Mao and Khruschev, 1958.

1954	1957	1958	1960	1961
Vietnam wins independence from France	USSR and United States invent ICBMs	Khrushchev becomes premier of the USSR	The Sino-Soviet Split changes the Cold War	USSR and United States develop ABMs
Geneva Accords divide Vietnam	USSR launches Sputnik	Mao launches the Great Leap Forward		

While the roots of the Cold War were certainly planted in the agreements made between the Allies toward the end of World War II and the immediate decisions made by both Stalin and Truman, the Cold War itself really took shape in the late 1940s and throughout the 1950s as the United States and the USSR scrambled to secure ideological supporters without risking World War III. Rather than building traditional militaries, the two superpowers financed espionage (the CIA and KGB), funded civil wars and political coups around the world, and hoped that the existence of ever-increasing stockpiles of technologically advanced nuclear weapons would be enough to demonstrate power without having to actually detonate them. To a great extent, the Cold War was driven by the personalities and goals of the many political leaders who participated over the years. In the first phase of the conflict, Stalin was still firmly in control of the USSR, and the United States was led by Truman, who knew all too well the difficult decision-making processes of the nuclear era. Truman was followed by WWII General Dwight D. Eisenhower. Their decisions established the foundation of the Cold War.

WORKING WITH THE THEMES

THE EFFECTS OF TECHNOLOGY The escalating arms race and related space race make WWIII potentially devastating for all participants, so the superpowers use battle by proxy in an attempt to keep warfare conventional.

CHANGING IDENTITIES The Sino-Soviet split creates a schism in the communist world. The Japanese Meiji constitution is replaced with democracy under U.S. occupation.

SHIFTING BORDERS Korea is divided into occupation zones, and the superpowers fight a battle by proxy to establish control. Korea becomes two separate countries.

GLOBALIZATION The arms and space races expand the potential theater of WWIII to the entire globe. Through proxy battles, the world becomes increasingly divided into spheres of influence.

U.S. Occupation of Japan

Japan was an active, aggressive player in world affairs from the late nineteenth century until it was defeated in August 1945. Because of the terms of surrender, Japan was unable to play a dominant role during the Cold War, but it certainly served several important functions in helping the United States maintain its interests in the East.

The Occupation

For seven years immediately following WWII, Japan was occupied by Allied forces (primarily U.S. troops) led by U.S. General Douglas MacArthur, Supreme Commander of the Allied Powers (SCAP). To MacArthur and the U.S. government, a thorough military occupation was required for three reasons: (1) to prevent future aggression, which was so deeply ingrained in Japanese Meiji culture, (2) to make sure that the desired changes actually occurred (unlike what happened in Germany after WWI), and (3) to provide a democratic safe haven in a region of growing communist dominance. During the occupation, Japan was thoroughly demilitarized and politically, socially and economically restructured through SCAP directives that the Japanese leaders and people had no choice but to accept.

MacArthur had spent a lot of time in the Pacific and studied Japanese culture, which was very focused on obedience to a hierarchical chain of authority. He knew that the occupation would meet significantly less internal resistance if the emperor (at the top of the chain) supported U.S. policies, so he made sure during the surrender negotiations that Emperor Hirohito kept his position as a figurehead, though not as a divine leader. To pave the way for democracy, MacArthur had to remove the authoritarian military government, which he did through war crimes tribunals. Almost 6,000 Japanese military and government officials were put on trial in Tokyo for war crimes associated with Japan's treatment of civilians and POWs, including mass killings, the use of biological and chemical weapons, torture, cannibalism and sexual slavery. The Tokyo Tribunal began in May 1946, and the verdicts were announced in November 1948: 984 were sentenced to death (920 of whom were actually executed), 3,419

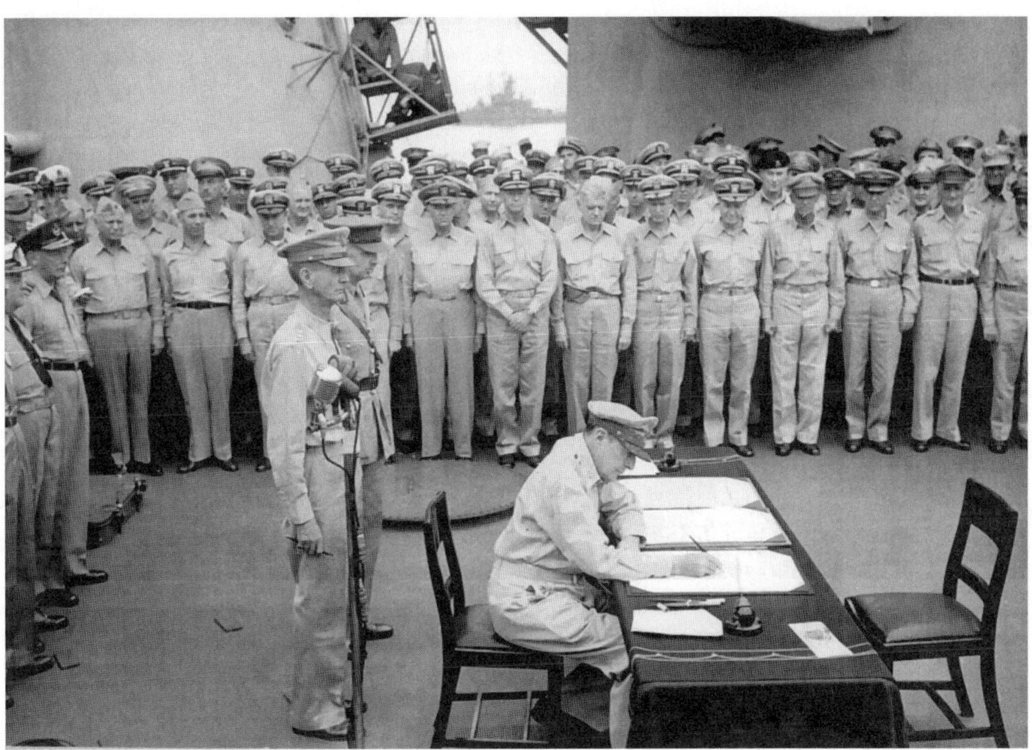

MacArthur signs Japanese Surrender.

were sentenced to prison (475 for life), and 1,018 were acquitted. Another 5,500 Japanese officials and soldiers were tried in other countries: 4,400 were convicted, 1,000 of whom were executed. And although the structure of the new government under SCAP was democratic, the focus on authority and hierarchy remained to remind the Japanese people that they were indeed living under a military occupation. For example, SCAP practiced strict censorship to prevent antidemocratic rhetoric that opposed the U.S. occupation and tried to keep communist ideas from infiltrating Japan.

The 1947 Constitution

To democratize Japan, the Meiji Constitution from 1889 obviously had to be changed. After Japanese officials submitted a draft that was essentially a rewording of the existing Meiji Constitution, MacArthur realized that the Japanese would not understand or agree with democratic principles that did not exist in the Meiji culture. As a result, he and a committee of U.S. military officials wrote a new constitution for Japan in just six days in February 1946. The constitution was presented to Japanese government officials in March, and although the officials tried to negotiate, they achieved only minor revisions. It helped MacArthur that Emperor Hirohito endorsed the constitution and even personally took it to the Diet (Japanese Parliament). The constitution was voted into law by the new Diet in fall 1946 and went into effect in May 1947.

The 1947 Constitution was grounded in the principles of British and American democracy, devoted to **popular sovereignty** and a parliamentary system of government. The emperor, stripped of his former powers, became a constitutional monarch, and MacArthur himself handpicked the first prime minister with the emperor's "consent." The Diet was turned into a bicameral legislature, with a weak upper chamber to represent the entire country and a powerful lower chamber to represent the people. Most importantly, members of the Diet were elected by popular vote. Almost one-third

popular sovereignty the concept that government is created by and subject to the will of the people of the articles of the Constitution were devoted to ensuring civil liberties and individual rights for Japanese citizens. These "basic human liberties," as MacArthur called them, included the fundamental freedoms expressed in the U.S. Bill of Rights, but go even further, adding universal adult suffrage, workers' rights, a right to property and education, and specific marriage and property rights for women. The requirements of the 1947 Constitution forced a complete restructuring of Japanese education and business systems, as well as altered social norms.

Read the Document *The Constitution of Japan* on mysearchlab.com

The most unique element of the constitution, and the one that earned it the nickname "MacArthur Peace Constitution," was Article 9, which stated: "aspiring sincerely to an international peace based on justice and order, the Japanese people forever renounce war as a sovereign right of the nation and the threat or use of force as means of settling international disputes." This article was essentially the prohibition of war, which no other nation before or since has agreed to as a component of its constitutional structure. Article 9 also forbade Japan from maintaining land, sea or air forces, but federal laws passed a few years later allowed them to create the National Police Reserve, a small paramilitary force to defend the Japanese islands. The amendment process defined in the constitution was rigorous. As a result, although there is often debate, no amendments have ever been made. The constitution of Japan stands today as it was written by SCAP during the occupation in 1946.

Consequences of Article 9

Article 9, also called "the peace clause," met a few important needs of the United States. First and foremost, it prevented Japan from rearming itself and becoming a threat to world peace again. The article also created a situation that essentially required Japan to allow U.S. military bases to remain intact even after the occupation ended—a strong U.S. presence might be the only thing that prevented surrounding aggressive nations from invading Japan. And although this was marginally important to the United States when the constitution was written in 1946, it very quickly became vital for several reasons: Stalin grew openly hostile toward the United States, Mao seized control of China and established the PRC (1949), communist North Korea invaded South Korea (1950), and Ho Chi Minh earned Vietnam's independence from France (1954). For the United States, it was imperative that its military remain stationed in Japan to protect against communist threats, as well as to maintain a U.S. military presence in the region.

With the new constitution in place, Japan and the United States began negotiating the end of the occupation in 1951. The United States agreed to a peace treaty that would fully restore Japan's sovereignty, and Japan agreed to a Mutual Security Treaty that allowed U.S. forces to be stationed in Japan for the defense of the region and also to intervene in Japanese domestic affairs if the government requested assistance. Both agreements went into effect simultaneously in April 1952, with the support of both governments and most of the Japanese citizens; although a vocal minority in Japan as well as the Soviet government protested the Mutual Security Treaty. The occupation officially ended in April 1952, but the United States maintains military bases in Japan to this day.

The democratic structure that MacArthur created in Japan allowed the nation to excel politically and financially. When the occupation ended, there were some political clashes between the left- and right-wing political parties, but the economy superseded everything. Because the infrastructure of the country was destroyed during the war, the government and private enterprise formed a mutually beneficial partnership to rebuild the country's industrial capacity and put people to work. During the occupation, the Japanese government was aided financially by the United States, and when the Korean War started, Japan was able to produce just about everything needed by the UN troops. Because Japan fell under U.S. military protection and the constitution prevented Japan from building an offensive military machine, Japan invested all of its income in technological research and development and established trade relationships around the world. The connection between government and industry made for a very lucrative and well-coordinated economic plan for the country, and the economy took off. By the end of the 1960s, Japan had the second largest economy in the world (behind the United States).

MAKE THE CONNECTION

Why did the United States want military bases in Japan? What are the long-term costs or consequences for both Japan and the United States of having military bases there?

MAP 7.1 East and South Asia in 1945

The decisions MacArthur made during the occupation were vital in establishing Japan as a solid democratic and capitalist nation in an increasingly communist-dominated region of the world. Because of its economic dominance, its democratic political regime, and the presence of U.S. military bases, Japan held a very important geostrategic position for the United States throughout the Cold War.

The "Other" Communism: Mao's People's Republic of China

When Mao seized control of China in October 1949, Chinese citizens were exhausted and poor after decades of warfare with European imperialists, competing warlords, the Japanese invasions during WWII and the internal civil war for control of the government. China had been under attack for one hundred years, and the Chinese citizens were looking to Mao and the Communist Party to provide political stability, economic well-being and peace.

"Democracy" in China

To provide stability for the citizens, Mao established what he called a "democratic dictatorship," in which all four social classes were represented in decision making by elected officials in local assemblies (the democracy part), but the central government maintained strict control over those local assemblies and all citizens to prevent a counterrevolution (the dictatorship part). To solidify the power of his government, which Mao claimed ruled by the "Mandate of Heaven," he established prisons to reeducate political opponents and forced labor camps to punish those who were deemed beyond help. He also executed an estimated 5.5 million "enemies of the people" in the first five years of his regime.

The central government consisted of one body that held all political power in the PRC: the Central People's Government Council, led by Chairman Mao. Though there were several committees and councils under this central council, there was no question about who was in charge of decision making at the national level. The first local assemblies were established in 1954, and everyone over the age of eighteen (except counterrevolutionaries and landlords) could vote for their representatives. The primary job of the local assemblies was to elect members to serve in provincial assemblies, and the provincial assemblies elected representatives to the National People's Congress (which pretty much did whatever Mao said). The PRC's constitution included rights of all citizens, except those who were deemed to be counterrevolutionaries. In other words, you could vote, say and do anything you wanted in Communist China, as long as you did not disagree with the government. National social organizations were created specifically to educate everyone—youth, laborers, women—about their specific roles in Chinese society. Ultimately, each citizen was reponsible for the well-being of the PRC overall and carried a duty to put the interests of the state above the individual. Mao firmly believed that the strength of the PRC lay in the masses—peasants and workers who were committed to faithfully following his ideology.

Mao Propaganda Poster.

Following Stalin's Economic Model

The biggest problem Mao faced was the largely agrarian economy, which was all but destroyed after years of war. Communist economic policy assumed tight control of currency, inflation and wages in an effort to stabilize prices. To deal with the daunting economic problems, Mao largely followed the economic policies that Stalin implemented in the USSR, including the 1950 Agrarian Reform

Law that ended all private land ownership in the PRC. The peasants suffered by the unequal distribution of land that resulted from the law, and when they complained about it, they were executed. In 1953, the government established **collective farms,** which were turned into **communes** with almost 1,000 people living on each by the end of the 1950s. Mao also used Five Year Plans to rebuild the industrial capacity of the PRC, focusing on factories and infrastructure. The first one doubled industrial output in just two years, although at the expense of the rural peasantry.

collective farm
a group of farms organized and managed as one, worked cooperatively by a group of laborers under state supervision

commune
structure for pooling labor and income to coordinate all activities of a village with joint responsibility for all projects

In 1958, the government launched the Great Leap Forward in an effort to catch up with the rest of the world. The educational system was reformed to focus on science and engineering, and everyone in the country was required to participate in expanding the production of steel, electricity and coal. People were literally building steel furnaces in their backyards, so the quantity of steel produced increased, but the quality of what they produced rendered it basically unusable. The focus on industrial output meant less time and fewer resources for agriculture, which made it nearly impossible to feed the 660 million people living in the PRC in 1960. The Great Leap Forward helped precipiate the Great Famine, and between the two, an estimated 20 to 43 million Chinese citizens died. Economically, the Great Leap Forward was a disaster that threatened to turn back all the progress the PRC had made in the previous decade.

The Great Proletarian Cultural Revolution

The failure of the Great Leap Forward led to divisions within the ruling elite of the Communist Party. A splinter group led by Deng Xiaoping actually questioned Mao's decision making, arguing that collectivization and industrialization had been pursued too quickly. They also questioned his ability to lead—Mao was 71 years old and suffering from Parkinson's disease. In 1965, to regain his authority, Mao initiated the Great Proletarian Cultural Revolution to rid the government and the PRC of counterrevolutionaries. To do so, he relied on the faithful masses, requiring every citizen to report to local committees anyone, even family members, who they believed might hold counterrevolutionary ideas. The entire process was carried out in the provinces by the newly created Red Guards, a paramilitary force of students responsible for purging counterrevolutionaries. These students took their jobs very seriously, and anyone who challenged their authority was immediately arrested, so they enjoyed absolute power. What started as a student-led revolution grew into a proletarian movement as the Red Guards spread out across the countryside and pulled peasants, laborers and military into the revolution, targeting educated citizens, teachers and high-ranking Communist Party officials. They were guided in an almost cult-like fashion by *Quotations from Chairman Mao Zedong*, a collection of Mao's quotations published in 1964 that was required reading for every citizen of the PRC. The only group capable of stopping the Red Guards was the military (People's Liberation Army), so the

ANALYSIS

The *Little Red Book*, as it is known in the West, contains 427 quotations on thirty-three different topics that define Mao's ideology. What do these quotes tell you about Mao's leadership style?

- If there is to be revolution, there must be a revolutionary party. Without a revolutionary party, without a party built on the Marxist-Leninist revolutionary theory and in the Marxist-Leninist revolutionary style, it is impossible to lead the working class and the broad masses of the people in defeating imperialism and its running dogs.
- People of the world, be courageous, and dare to fight, defy difficulties and advance wave upon wave. Then the whole world will belong to the people. Monsters of all kinds shall be destroyed.
- Ideological education is the key link to be grasped in uniting the whole Party for great political struggles.
- The principle of diligence and frugality should be observed in everything.
- One requirement of Party discipline is that the minority should submit to the majority. If the view of the minority has been rejected, it must support the decision passed by the majority.
- Liberalism is extremely harmful in a revolutionary collective. It is a corrosive which eats away unity, undermines cohesion, causes apathy and creates dissension.

A propaganda poster for the Red Guard.

only way Mao could end the revolution he started was to call in the troops against it, initiating violent clashes across the country. The Great Proletarian Cultural Revolution certainly reaffirmed Mao's authority in the PRC, but it also weakened the unity of the Chinese Communist Party and slowed industrial progress. And on the international front, the revolution escalated the growing tension between the PRC and the USSR.

The Sino-Soviet Split

As far back as the 1930s, Stalin had served more as an advisor to Mao than a provider. Mao listened, but he mostly ignored the advice, particularly when Stalin suggested that Mao and Chiang Kai-Shek acquiesce to U.S. attempts to force a compromise between them to govern China after WWII. But once Mao seized control and established the PRC in 1949, he needed financial and military support. Although he feared a loss of independence, he sought the Sino-Soviet Treaty and followed most of Stalin's economic advice. Stalin was driven into the alliance with Mao by his need to keep the United States away from the growing power. Particularly once the North Atlantic Treaty Organization (NATO) was created in 1949, Stalin wanted to secure his alliances in the Pacific to control the region. So the relationship between the USSR and the PRC was not really about communist ideology, nor was it grounded in mutual trust; rather, it was very clearly about what Mao and Stalin each perceived to be best for his national security interests. Still, Mao respected Stalin's authority as the leader of one of the world's superpowers, and Stalin did stand up for Mao at the UN, boycotting the Security Council when the seat for China went to Chiang Kai-Shek instead of Mao.

ANALYSIS

From a "containment" perspective, why is a communist China dangerous to the United States? Is it dangerous to the USSR?

By 1960, a lot had changed. Stalin died in 1953, and Mao did not respect Stalin's successor, Nikita Khrushchev. Khrushchev harshly criticized Stalin's leadership and Mao's Great Leap Forward, and in 1959 he traveled to the United States to meet with Eisenhower about improving communication between the two countries. In Mao's mind, the only thing that would bring these two enemies together was their mutual desire to reduce his power in Asia. Mao's fears were confirmed when Khrushchev returned from the United States and publicly warned Mao to stop provoking U.S. military action with his ongoing attacks against the nationalist regime in Taiwan.

Khrushchev and Mao verbally attacked one another repeatedly, and the struggle for preeminence in the communist world was clearly out in the open. In 1960, the USSR stopped providing financial aid to the PRC, and in 1962 the USSR did not hold up its promise of military support in the PRC's border dispute with India. In 1964, the PRC became a nuclear power, and Mao decided he did not really need the USSR anymore anyway. Both countries began heavily building up their military presence on either side of the Sino-Soviet border in the PRC's northwestern Xinjiang province, territory that Russia had seized from China in the nineteenth century. In 1969, military clashes broke out, although both countries agreed not to resort to their nuclear arsenals.

The border disputes continued intermittently throughout the Cold War, forcing the Western democracies to reevaluate their perceived sharp ideological divide between democracy and communism. Communism itself was clearly divided in two, and both the USSR and the PRC certainly presented credible military threats to the United States. The PRC was a populous country with a big military, and in 1964, when it became the third country in the world to acquire nuclear

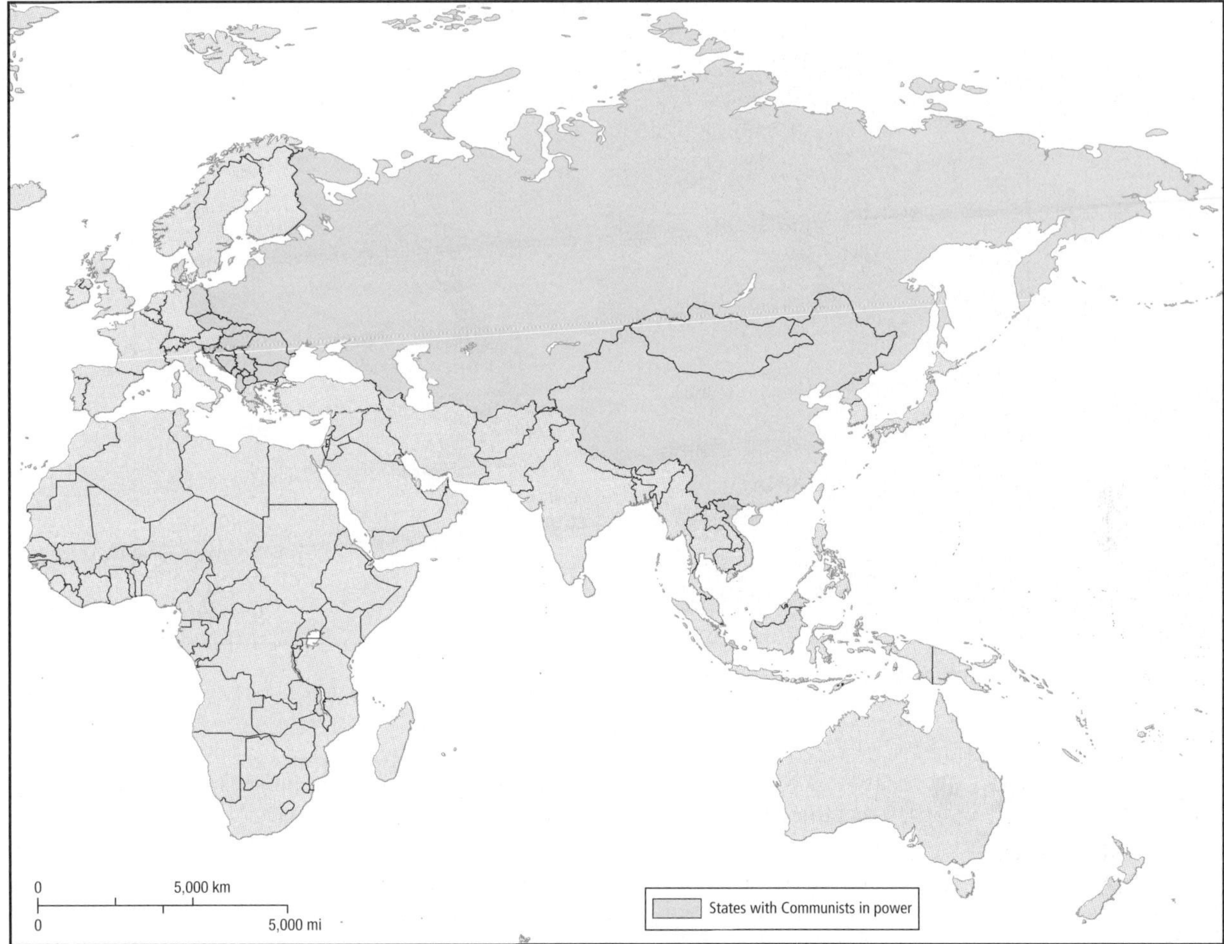

MAP 7.2 The Cold War in the Pacific

weapons, it also became a superpower. Even so, the Americans' fear of communism was largely driven by the brutality of the communist governments. Although it is hard to know exactly, experts estimate that Stalin's purges and famines killed 30 to 40 million Russians and that Mao's regime can be held accountable for 40 to 80 million Chinese deaths. What was most staggering to citizens in the West was that these governments killed so many of their own citizens.

Conflict in Korea

Japan's defeat in World War II "freed" its colonies, which did not necessarily bring them independence, as evidenced by what happened to Korea. In August 1945, the USSR declared war on Japan and invaded Manchuria, liberating the northern half of Korea from Japanese control to the 38th parallel, where Soviet troops met up with U.S. troops moving in from the Pacific islands. But just as it had in Eastern Europe, the Soviet military held onto the territory it conquered as part of the Soviet sphere of influence. Because the United States was still focused on defeating Japan and thought it may still need Stalin's help to do so, the two Allied powers divided the Korean peninsula into occupation zones and sent the matter to the newly created United Nations to handle. In early 1948, the UN established a temporary commission to oversee elections to reunite the country in May. But the Soviet military refused to allow UN workers into the north, making it clear that Korea would not be reunited under a democratic regime. The Korean people were not consulted, and they absolutely hated the idea of dividing their country, particularly

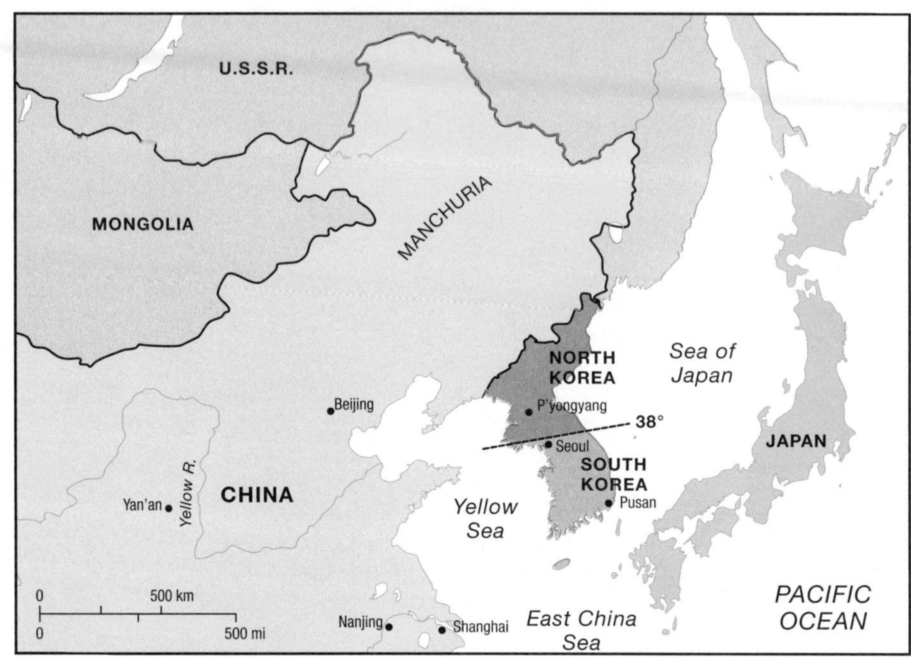

MAP 7.3 Korea Divided along the 38th Parallel

MAKE THE CONNECTION

What is the relationship between the U.S. foreign policies of containment and decolonization?

because this was their first taste of independence since the Japanese colonized them in 1910, but there was little they could do to prevent the division.

In keeping with the Cold War, a communist government was established in North Korea under Kim Il-Sung, who enjoyed full political, military and financial support from the USSR and used the support to build a powerful military state. Satisfied that Kim Il-Sung was in full control, Soviet troops withdrew from North Korea in December 1948. In South Korea, elections were held to establish a democratic government. But because this was the Cold War, the United States supported the most avid anticommunists they could find to take over the government rather than the left-wing candidates who were more popular with the Korean people. When the U.S.-educated, anticommunist Syngman Rhee won the election, most South Koreans viewed the election as fraudulent and protested violently against both the "puppet" government they were saddled with and the U.S. military supporting it. In June 1949, just as Mao's Communist Party was gaining the upper hand in the Chinese civil war, the U.S. troops left. Korea was now in the hands of Kim Il-Sung and Syngman Rhee, each of whom was determined to reunite Korea under his leadership.

Kim Il-Sung acted first, requesting military help from the USSR. Initially, Stalin rejected the idea of invading South Korea for fear that it would undermine his bargaining position with the United States, but the potential gains in terms of Korea's natural resources and geostrategic positioning in the region, particularly once the communists seized China in October 1949, were too great to pass up. Stalin agreed to *secretly* help Kim Il-Sung reunite the country, and on June 25, 1950, the North Korean army rolled south in a surprise assault.

For President Truman, North Korea's military action against South Korea was a clear threat to the U.S. containment policy. Although South Korea itself was not particularly important to U.S. security interests, a failure to enforce containment policy in this case could set a dangerous precedent that would lead to conflicts around the globe and the expansion of communism. The United States immediately went to the UN and called a meeting of the Security Council to decide an appropriate response to North Korea's aggression. Because the Soviet Union was boycotting the UN in a show of solidarity with Mao, Stalin was unable to exercise his veto power to prevent a UN military response, which is exactly what Truman wanted.

There were reasons to be concerned about military conflict just five years after WWII ended with the detonation of atomic weapons. Now that these weapons existed, was it possible to have a **conventional war,** or would Truman have to again resort to nuclear weapons? Could this war be geographically limited to Korea, or would the USSR and/or the PRC get involved, leading to WWIII? With these questions looming, the Security Council authorized a UN force that included soldiers from sixteen nations, with the largest contingent coming from the United States, all under the command of General MacArthur. Chiang Kai-Shek's offer to commit Chinese troops (from Taiwan) was rejected for fear that they would invade North Korea just to get to the PRC, instigating WWIII.

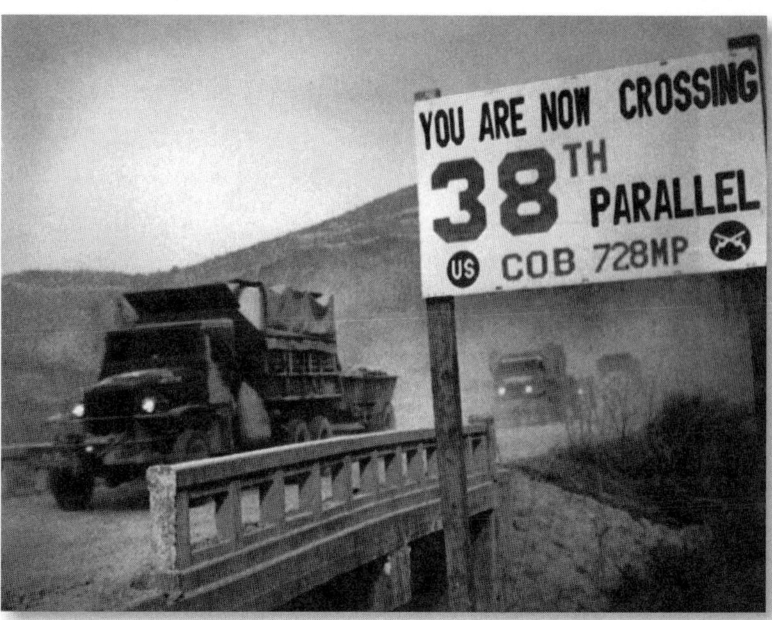

UN forces crossing the 38th parallel.

Initially, UN troops were able to provide limited help to the South Korean military from its tiny toehold position in Pusan in summer 1950. MacArthur engineered a daring attack behind North Korean lines at the port of Inchon in September that cut off the North Korean supply lines and forced their troops to retreat. UN forces drove the North Koreans out of the South and reached the 38th parallel in just two weeks. Truman thought MacArthur should stop at the 38th parallel to begin peace negotiations rather than risk inciting the PRC or the USSR, but he agreed to give the very successful general leeway to do what he thought was best so long as it did not lead to WWIII. MacArthur did not believe that the PRC or the USSR would send in troops, and he viewed stopping at the 38th parallel as a failed military opportunity to do some harm to the PRC's industrial base in Manchuria, so he sent two American armies into North Korea. He miscalculated—Mao was concerned about the presence of UN troops on his border, and he was also angry because neither Kim Il-Sung nor Stalin had bothered to tell him that North Korea was going to initiate the war. Mao did not trust any of them, and rather than risk the end of communism in Korea and having UN forces within attack range, Mao prepared the People's Volunteer Army, ill equipped but battle ready from years of civil war, to enter North Korea.

conventional war warfare conducted by states without the use of nuclear, chemical or biological weapons

In November 1950, after repeated warnings through diplomatic channels, the PRC attacked, sending the surprised UN forces reeling southward. By January 1951, the UN troops were able to reestablish a front line just south of the 38th parallel that stopped the advance by North Korean and Chinese forces, and the war developed into a long and difficult stalemate. MacArthur was frustrated that Truman would not bring in Taiwanese troops for support and go after the PRC, and he made several statements to that effect to the media. In March 1951, General MacArthur wrote a letter to the U.S. House of Representatives, hoping to receive support for his plans. In the letter, MacArthur warned, "if we lose the war to communism in Asia the fall of Europe is inevitable, win it and Europe most probably would avoid war and yet preserve freedom." Truman considered MacArthur's actions insubordination, and the Pentagon was angered by the media war MacArthur was waging against his own government. Truman fired MacArthur, ending his military career and his leadership of the Japanese occupation. Stalin agreed to support Mao but would not commit Soviet troops. In summer 1951 armistice talks began, but it was not until July 1953, after years of fighting and the death of Stalin, that a cease-fire was finally negotiated. The armistice permanently divided the Korean peninsula into two countries separated by a UN-controlled demilitarized zone that remains in place today.

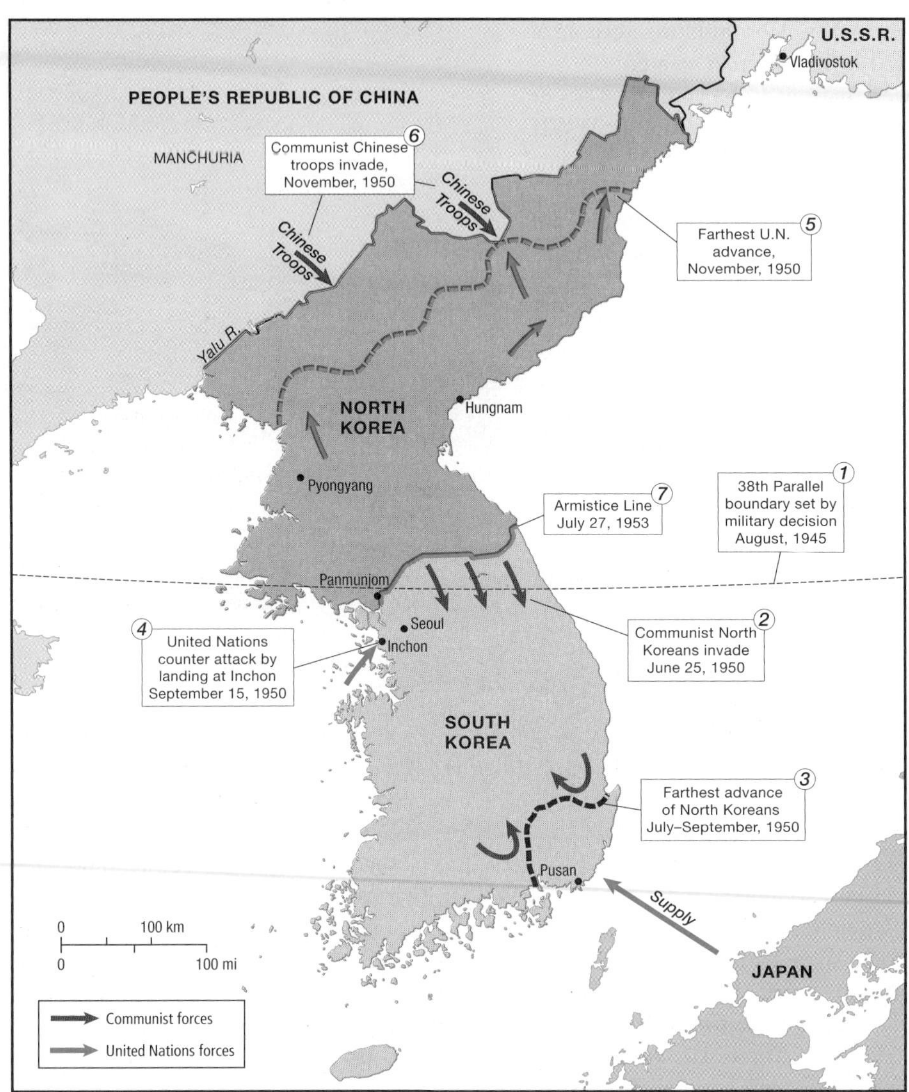

MAP 7.4 The Korean War

The Korean conflict was the first major military battle of the Cold War between democracy and communism, and it did not result in WWIII or nuclear annihilation. But neither did it result in a clear victory for either side.

The Arms Race

Truman's desire to fight a limited, conventional war in Korea was driven by his fear that the ideological conflict between the United States and USSR would turn into a military conflict. And although the United States had demonstrated its technological and military superiority at the end of WWII by detonating the atomic bomb, the USSR was close behind, and Truman could not be sure just how close. The Soviet bomb project began shortly after the United States initiated the Manhattan Project, but the Soviet project had far fewer scientists and resources devoted to it. Stalin increased support for the project after he returned home from the Potsdam conference, where Truman had hinted at U.S. weapons superiority; and Stalin made the project a top priority after the United States dropped the bomb on Hiroshima. Stalin did not want the United States in a dominant position in postwar negotiations for territory.

On August 29, 1949, the USSR detonated its first atomic bomb, demonstrating technological parity with the United States. From there, both countries began research on the next level—the thermonuclear bomb. In 1952, the United States exploded an H-bomb, smaller than the atomic bomb used on Hiroshima but 2,500 times more powerful. The Soviets exploded their first H-bomb in 1953, and the **arms race** was on. While improving the technology of nuclear weapons was a high priority, creating delivery systems to get them where you want them without risking pilots' lives was equally important and led to the **space race.**

The Soviets tested the first intercontinental ballistic missile (**ICBM**) in May 1957. The United States had developed the B52 bomber, which could deliver a nuclear payload 6,000 miles away, but the United States did not have an equivalent to the ICBM until December 1957. On October 4, 1957, the Soviets surprised the world by launching Sputnik, the first satellite. Sputnik was a shock to U.S. government officials, who feared it provided the USSR a delivery system for its missiles. The United States built the **DEW line** around the Arctic and kept working on its own satellite technology. In January 1958, the U.S. Explorer satellite was fired into space on top of a military Redstone missile.

The arms race put both the United States and the USSR in a state of constant vigilance. Both sides assumed that WWIII would be a nuclear war. America still remembered the surprise attack at Pearl Harbor and did not want to be surprised again—U.S. intelligence estimated that, if the Soviets attacked with their full nuclear capability, it would result in 20 million dead and 22 million injured American civilians. In 1958, the U.S. government created the National Aeronautics and Space Administration (NASA) to provide federal funding to compete in the ongoing arms and space races. The United States focused on producing high-quality missiles with rapidly expanding technology, while the USSR produced a higher quantity of low-tech missiles overall. By 1960, the United States and the USSR combined had enough nuclear missiles to destroy the world.

arms race
the buildup of military weapons (particularly nuclear) by the United States and the USSR

space race
developing technology to conquer outer space to demonstrate scientific superiority and military strength

ICBM
a long-range missile designed to carry nuclear warheads

DEW line
(**D**efense and **E**arly **W**arning system) a system of radar stations around the arctic to detect incoming Soviet bombers and missiles

Watch the Video *Duck and Cover: School Bomb Drill* on mysearchlab.com

MAD versus NUTS

The arms race itself was not so different from the military buildup that happened in the early 1900s when Great Britain and Germany engaged in the escalating naval race that led to the Great War. And expanding weapons technology in the 1930s created *Blitzkrieg* and gave Hitler the military confidence to begin WWII. The lesson from the first half of the twentieth century is that, when powerful countries build militaries with a technological edge over others and form alliances to extend their power base, the result is worldwide war. So in the 1950s, the United States and the USSR were clearly headed for WWIII and, due to the advancements in weapons technology, it would be nuclear and everyone would die.

When President Eisenhower, a WWII general, became president of the United States in 1953, the nuclear arms race was just getting underway. He and a team of advisors shaped what would stand as U.S. foreign policy for the remainder of the Cold War: contain Soviet expansion without military engagement, apply political pressure to encourage countries to choose democracy, and rely on **nuclear deterrence** to win the Cold War. Eisenhower knew this would require a lot of time and money, but it was better than the alternative. His assessment: "The only way to win WWIII is to prevent it."

nuclear deterrence
the theory that an enemy will choose not to use nuclear weapons if it believes that doing so will result in its own destruction as well; requires a credible threat of second-strike capability

In the United States, nuclear deterrence took the form of Mutual Assured Destruction (MAD) theory. Essentially, so long as both the United States and the USSR maintained equilibrium in the nuclear arms race, neither side could actually use the weapons it created without destroying itself as well. Each side had the capacity to destroy the other, and each side had a radar system in place to detect incoming missiles; so when one side fired, the other would know it and launch a nuclear response, thus ensuring that everyone was destroyed. Of course, the nuclear fallout from a large-scale war would destroy the rest of the world as well. For the United States, there was a strange comfort to MAD. All it had to do was keep building more and better nuclear weapons, and the U.S. government was pretty confident that it had the money and scientific ability to at least keep

MAP 7.5 The DEW Line

up with the USSR, if not surpass it. Indeed, in the last half of the twentieth century (1945–1996), the United States spent an estimated $5.8 trillion on nuclear weapons (research, developing warheads, delivery systems technology, defense and intelligence). The United States built more than 70,000 nuclear bombs and warheads in sixty-five different configurations and developed 116 different kinds of delivery systems. Much of this was driven by a lack of precise knowledge about Soviet capabilities, as well as a belief that the promise of MAD would prevent WWIII.

The Soviets did not fully buy the MAD theory—they were preparing to fight and win a nuclear war. In the United States, that approach was called NUTS (Nuclear Utilization Targeting Strategy), which contends that it is possible to engage in a limited nuclear war that does not result in worldwide destruction. The Soviets focused their weapons research on the tools they would need to win a limited nuclear war, creating defensive weapons called antiballistic missiles (ABMs) that could intercept and destroy U.S. missiles in flight. The introduction of ABMs destabilized the concept of MAD because it took away second-strike capability. The USSR could launch a nuclear attack against the United States but prevent a successful U.S. retaliatory attack with ABMs. U.S. scientists came up with a countermeasure: Multiple Independently Targeted Reentry Vehicles (MIRVs). One single missile carried ten warheads, each capable of destroying a separate city. NUTS led to the creation of entirely new kinds of offensive and defensive nuclear weapons.

Both the technology and sheer number of nuclear weapons expanded quickly in the early years of the Cold War. Great Britain, which collaborated with the United States on the Manhattan Project, successfully tested its first nuclear weapon in 1952 in an effort to demonstrate that it was an independent power player in the Cold War. France quickly began a nuclear weapons program to maintain relevancy, joining the "nuclear club" in 1960. When the PRC developed a nuclear weapons program in 1964, the fear of **nuclear proliferation** became a reality. The ability to destroy the world lay in the hands of a few men, and none of them trusted the others. Each was operating under a different worldview, and each was relying on theories and espionage to prevent WWIII. The world would become an increasingly unstable place as this power spread.

nuclear proliferation the spread of nuclear weapons capabilities to more countries

Battle By Proxy

In retrospect, we know that both the United States and the USSR wanted to avoid initiating WWIII. In the years immediately following WWII, neither superpower had the financial or human resources to commit to winning a war of that magnitude. The most viable option to win WWIII would be using nuclear weapons, but the arms race had progressed so quickly that resorting to nuclear war would certainly mean the destruction of the entire world, and no one would win in that scenario. The biggest problem was a lack of communication—neither side was sure who was winning the arms race, nor could they be sure of the true intentions of the other. In an atmosphere of distrust, a willingness to negotiate would surely be seen as weakness—the other side might assume it had the upper hand, ideologically or militarily. And that rhetoric, combined with a lack of information, is what made the Cold War so potentially dangerous.

Because the Cold War could not be fought in a traditional way between the primary combatants, it was impossible to measure progress toward their goals (spreading ideology) in a traditional way. Instead, successes and failures in the Cold War were measured by the extent of ideological, political and financial influence each side exerted over the other countries of the world. To "win" a territory, both sides engaged in similar tactics: they provided financial incentives to political leaders who agreed to adopt their ideology; they maintained military bases in geostrategic locations; and they created formal alliance blocs that divided the world into East versus West. But they absolutely could not go to war directly against one another for fear of WWIII.

proxy a substitute with the authority to act on behalf of another person; in the Cold War, a battle by proxy refers to a war in which the country that instigated the war is not a direct participant

This competition between the United States and the USSR for control of governments was not at all "cold." Some of the nastiest little wars of the twentieth century were the **proxy** battles of the Cold War (as opposed to the total wars of the first half of the century). Korea was the first example of a battle by proxy, and although the Korean War ended in a draw, both superpowers realized that they could fight for control of a territory as long as they did so carefully. A battle by proxy looked like a civil war, where competing interests within a country or sometimes between neighboring countries were fighting one another for control of the government. One group wanted to establish a communist regime, and the other a democratic one. But because each side was financially and militarily supported by one of the two superpowers, they were

Cold War Tally Sheet

U.S.	U.S.S.R.
卌 I	卌

Each country that fell within the U.S. or Soviet sphere of influence represented another "win" for one side or the other.

The Cold War "Tally Sheet."

essentially proxies for the larger battle between the United States and the USSR. Throughout the Cold War, money and weapons flowed freely from the two superpowers all around the globe in support of these proxy battles. As we will see, in Asia, Africa and Latin America, this practice incited civil wars where existing political discontent could be exacerbated by large sums of money and free weapons. Local entities gained political power, and the superpowers gained hash marks on the tally sheet, spreading democracy and communism to other countries. Where the stakes were high (usually because of geostrategic position and/or access to natural resources), the United States or the USSR might also send in troops. This is where proxy battles became potentially dangerous—only one side could have troops on the ground or the world risked having Soviet soldiers and U.S. soldiers firing on one another, which would most certainly have led to WWIII.

Conclusions

Stalin, Truman, and Eisenhower established the parameters for the Cold War in the 1950s—the Cold War was an ideological conflict in which each side used its growing military technology and alliance systems to stop the spread of the opposing ideology, thereby spreading its own ideology around the globe. Because no one wanted a nuclear holocaust, the superpowers relied on others (proxies) to engage in battles for them. The first battle by proxy, the Korean War, ended in a draw, demonstrating that the Cold War would be long and expensive for both the United States and the USSR. The Korean War also sent a clear message to the citizens in countries where proxy battles would be fought that the ultimate goal was not to help them achieve their political desires but rather to meet the strategic interests of the superpowers. Most notably, the Korean War demonstrated to both the United States and the USSR that Mao Zedong and his version of communism had to be taken seriously.

The Sino-Soviet split in the 1960s changed the Cold War. For the USSR, the PRC became a practical problem with a large military and nuclear weapons on its border. For the United States, the split was a serious blow to the idea that the Cold War was an ideological war. If alliances weren't based on ideology and decisions were instead being made out of pure national interests, then this was actually a traditional war with a traditional enemy (the USSR) that could be fought in a traditional way. But that might lead to WWIII.

WORKING WITH THE THEMES

THE EFFECTS OF TECHNOLOGY Should the United States and the USSR have invested so much money in expanding nuclear technology that they could not use without worldwide devastation? Which theory is more viable to you—MAD or NUTS? Why are the arms and space races interconnected?

CHANGING IDENTITIES Did the United States have the right to create Japan's 1947 constitution? What are the domestic and international long-term effects of the 1947 constitution? What were the differences between Stalin's version of communism and Mao's? How did the Sino-Soviet split affect U.S. decision making?

SHIFTING BORDERS Why wasn't Korea granted full independence immediately following WWII? Should UN troops have stopped at the 38th parallel or tried to reunite Korea? Should Korea be allowed to reunite now?

GLOBALIZATION Was battle by proxy a reasonable way to prevent WWIII? How did the arms race affect national security concerns in Europe and Asia?

Further Reading

TO FIND OUT MORE

University of Maryland Libraries—Gordon W. Prange Collection: Rebuilding a Nation: Japan in the Immediate Postwar Years 1945–1949. Available online at http://www.lib.umd.edu/prange/html/exhibit/index.jsp

Society for Anglo-Chinese Understanding: About China. Available online at http://www.sacu.org/communisthistory.html

Korean War National Museum. Available online at http://www.theforgottenvictory.org/

Stefan R. Landsberger/Chinese Posters Foundation: Chinese Posters. Available online at http://chineseposters.net

National Science Digital Library: The Atomic Archive. Available online at http://www.atomicarchive.com/

GO TO THE SOURCE

Marxists Internet Archive: The "Great Debate" Documents of the Sino-Soviet Split. Available online at http://www.marxists.org/history/international/comintern/sino-soviet-split/index.htm

Harry S. Truman Library: The Korean War and its Origins. Available online at http://www.trumanlibrary.org/whistlestop/study_collections/koreanwar/index.php

Douglas MacArthur: *Reminiscences* (1964)

Kim Il Sung: *Reminiscences With the Century*, Volumes 1–8 (1994)

Mao Zedong: *Quotations from Chairman Mao* (1964)

Taiwan Documents Project. Available online at http://www.taiwandocuments.org

Central Intelligence Agency: The China Collection. Available online at http://www.foia.cia.gov/nic_china_collection.asp

MySearchLab Connections

Read the **Document** on **mysearchlab.com**

7.1 *The Constitution of Japan.* Following Japan's surrender at the end of World War II, Allied occupation forces, know as the SCAP (Supreme Commander of Allied Powers), began its task of remaking a new Japan that would be an American ally in the Pacific The constitution drafted by SCAP would reshape Japan in all aspects.

Watch the **Video** on **mysearchlab.com**

7.1 *Duck and Cover: School Bomb Drill*

8 Khrushchev's Cold War

CHAPTER OUTLINE

- Changes in the USSR
- Peaceful Coexistence
- Challenges in the Satellite Bloc
- The Soviet Sphere of Influence Reaches the Western Hemisphere

CHAPTER TIMELINE

1953	1956	1958	1959	1960
Tito becomes president of Yugoslavia Stalin dies United States and USSR invent hydrogen bombs	Khrushchev delivers "secret speech" Civil war erupts in Vietnam Polish Uprising occurs Hungarian Revolution sparked by Polish uprising	Khrushchev becomes premier of the USSR	Castro's Cuban Revolution succeeds United States institutes trade restrictions against Cuba Khruschev and Nixon square off in the "Kitchen Debate" Khrushchev visits United States	U.S. spy plane is shot down by USSR Non-Alignment Movement is created Paris Summit takes place USSR and Cuba ally Sino-Soviet split deepens

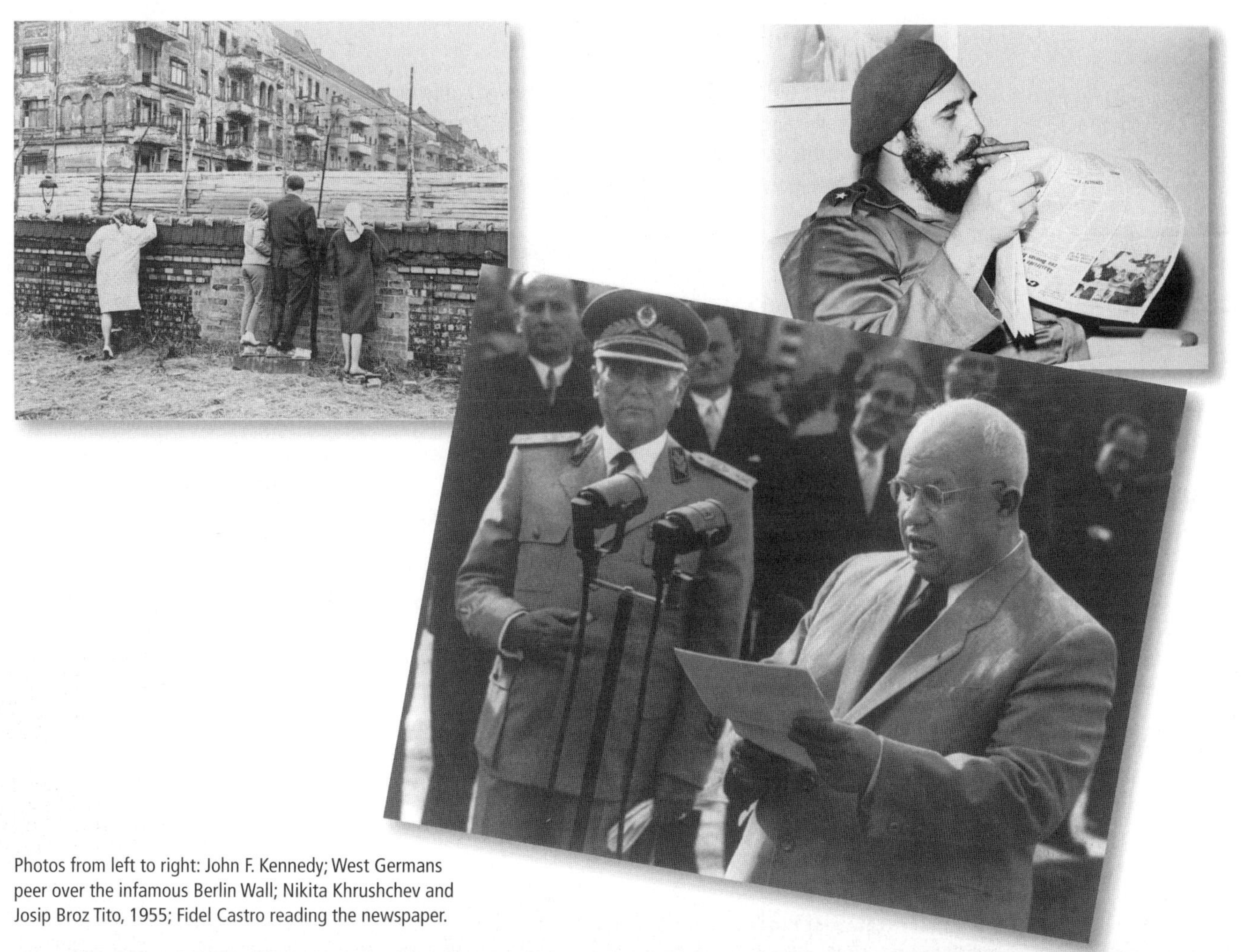

Photos from left to right: John F. Kennedy; West Germans peer over the infamous Berlin Wall; Nikita Khrushchev and Josip Broz Tito, 1955; Fidel Castro reading the newspaper.

1961	1962	1963	1964	1965
United States and USSR develop ABMs U.S. launches Bay of Pigs invasion Berlin Wall is built	Cuban Missile Crisis heats up the Cold War Operation Mongoose goes into effect	Kennedy and Diem are assassinated	The PRC becomes a nuclear power U.S. Congress passes the Gulf of Tonkin Resolution	The first U.S. ground troops arrive in Vietnam Khrushchev resigns from office

To Stalin, the Cold War was a "zero-sum" game—only one side could win. Either the world would be politically and economically structured according to communism, with the USSR firmly in charge, or the world would operate according to democratic principles and a free-market economy. Because the goals and requirements of each ideology were so different, certainly both could not function simultaneously. But the Cold War was not only about ideology—there were some very practical issues regarding territorial expansion and military superiority that required compromise between the superpowers to ensure the continued survival of all. That desire to expand (ideologically and territorially) while preventing direct conflict, coupled with the inherent financial limitations of a communist economy, led to a shift away from the "zero-sum" game approach in the latter part of the 1950s. Stalin's successor, Nikita Khrushchev, took a different philosophical approach to fighting the Cold War—peaceful coexistence. In practice, it was not terribly peaceful. Khrushchev used violence to maintain the Soviet grip over the satellite states, and, in a risky move that came dangerously close to World War III, aggressively spread communism into the western hemisphere.

WORKING WITH THE THEMES

THE EFFECTS OF TECHNOLOGY The United States moves far ahead of the USSR in consumer technology, prompting changes in Khrushchev's approach to expanding communism. The USSR finds a way around the U.S. missile defense system by placing missiles in Cuba.

CHANGING IDENTITIES Stalin's death leads to Khrushchev's Thaw and revolution in the satellite states. The people of Cuba reject the United States and accept communism.

SHIFTING BORDERS The Berlin Wall divides the capital city of Germany, leading to concern in the West that World War III could begin in Europe.

GLOBALIZATION Peaceful coexistence attempts to reframe the Cold War and leads to cultural exchanges between the United States and the USSR.

Changes in the USSR

Stalin's Death

On the evening of February 28, 1953, Josef Stalin and his four closest advisors shared a meal at Stalin's country home just outside of Moscow. After Stalin went to bed, his bodyguard instructed the guards that Stalin was not to be disturbed under any circumstances. So the next morning, when Stalin did not come out of his room, the guards were afraid to enter. Finally, late in the evening of March 1, a guard went to check on Stalin and discovered that he had suffered a debilitating stroke that paralyzed the right side of his body. The guards immediately called the members of the **Politburo,** but they did not show up until the next day (March 2). The day after that (March 3), someone finally called for medical help, and Stalin died at 9:50 p.m. on March 5 from a cerebral hemorrhage.

Politburo the supreme decision-making body of the Communist Party; a small but powerful group

Stalin's death remains a historical debate. Many historians believe that, while it is certainly plausible that a seventy-four-year-old man would suffer a cerebral hemorrhage, it is not likely that Stalin's occurred naturally. They believe that KGB Chief Lavrenty Beria gave Stalin warfarin (rat poison) to induce the hemorrhage, which is certainly supported by the uncharacteristic "do not disturb" order and the fact that the Politburo waited two days to call a doctor. And because it was widely known that Stalin was about to begin another round of political purges and Beria's name was on the list, Beria certainly had motive. Other historians believe that Stalin died of completely natural causes, mostly because there would not have been opportunity to poison him. Stalin was incredibly suspicious and cautious—he always made others sample food and drinks that were presented to him. So why did the Politburo members wait to call a doctor? They said they just thought he was drunk and needed to sleep it off. Still, each member of the Politburo stood to gain political power from Stalin's death.

Josef Stalin, lying in state.

Within the USSR, Stalin's death brought an end to his "**cult of personality.**" The citizenry was split—people suffering in gulags around the country were quietly hopeful that things would change for the better, but many openly grieved. Stalin's body was embalmed and placed on display next to Lenin's in the Hall of Columns near Moscow's Red Square. In the first three days, several million people traveled to see him, waiting in line for hours to pass by the body. On the last night, they stampeded to get in, and it is estimated that several hundred people were crushed to death in the crowd.

cult of personality public adoration of a political leader who is viewed as infallible, created largely by his or her control over the mass media; occurs in totalitarian regimes

From a Cold War perspective, Stalin's death opened the door for potential change. U.S. President Dwight D. Eisenhower had only been in office for two months and was committed to fighting the Cold War with what he called "strength and civility." He made a speech to the Soviet people, encouraging them to take advantage of this opportunity to embrace change in the USSR, and made it clear that the United States would not attack the USSR in its time of mourning. Then he waited to see who would emerge as the next Soviet premier and how that man would choose to fight the Cold War.

Nikita Khrushchev

Stalin's death led to a fierce power struggle between the top Communist Party officials for the position of premier of the USSR. From March 6, 1953, to February 8, 1955, Georgy Malenkov filled the position. Although he was allied with Lavrenty Beria, Malenkov agreed to Beria's execution as a traitor in December 1953. Nikita Khrushchev and Nikolai Bulganin worked together to oppose Malenkov's administration, and they used his relationship with Beria to force him to resign in February 1955. Bulganin took over as premier but then turned away from Khrushchev when the more conservative and powerful Vyacheslov Molotov offered to support him. The power struggle between Molotov and Khrushchev was about the future of the USSR—Molotov represented a continuation of Stalin's policies and methods, and Khrushchev sought major reform. On March 27, 1958, the battle ended as Khrushchev became the premier of the USSR and named Molotov the Soviet ambassador to Mongolia.

Khrushchev's Thaw policies designed to liberalize Soviet life politically, economically, culturally and socially

Although Khrushchev used Stalinesque methods to achieve power, once he gained power he was focused on reforming the USSR. He truly believed in communism and that it would triumph over capitalism when executed properly. **Khrushchev's Thaw** was aimed at easing the rigid political and social climate of the USSR created by Stalin so that people could simply enjoy the benefits of communism. He switched economic production toward consumer goods to provide a higher standard of living for the people and built housing in cities, encouraging people to move around the entire satellite bloc. A Soviet popular culture was created, and people enjoyed art, music, fashion and sporting events. Censorship laws were relaxed, and Khrushchev personally encouraged the publication of Solzhenitsyn's *One Day in the Life of Ivan Denisovich*, detailing the horrors of life in a gulag. While they remained underground, a generation of dissident intellectuals began to write and speak without fear of execution. Khrushchev also released millions of political prisoners from the gulags.

ANALYSIS

Solzhenitsyn served in the Soviet army at the beginning of World War II but was arrested in 1945 when a letter he wrote to a friend in which he criticized Stalin was intercepted by censors. Solzhenitsyn was sentenced (without a trial) to eight years in prison, part of which was served in a gulag. While there, he wrote his experiences, which would later become *One Day in the Life of Ivan Denisovich*, on scraps of paper, memorized them, and then destroyed them. Upon his release from the gulag, he was exiled to Kazakhstan, where he began writing. Although Khrushchev allowed *One Day in the Life of Ivan Denisovich* to be published as part of his de-Stalinization campaign, Solzhenitsyn was again censored and harassed by the government after Khrushchev resigned.

The primary themes of *One Day in the Life of Ivan Denisovich* are the struggle for human dignity, the outrage of unjust punishment and the importance of faith, experiences that transcended the gulags and extended throughout Soviet life under Stalin's regime. Explain what Solzhenitsyn meant when he wrote: "freedom is found only when a [person] has been stripped of everything." Why do you think Khrushchev wanted this novel to be published?

Still, Khrushchev maintained absolute power in the Soviet government. Convinced that the USSR could "beat" the West in every way, he launched the Virgin Lands Campaign, an effort to increase agricultural production by using technology to grow new kinds of crops on unusable land in Kazakhstan and Siberia. Despite considerable evidence that it could not work, Khrushchev forced nearly a half million "volunteers" to the area, many of whom died from famine. And while censorship was relaxed, it certainly did not go away. Khrushchev was particularly opposed to organized religion and had many churches closed or destroyed.

De-Stalinization

Khrushchev's biggest political move domestically was the de-Stalinization of the USSR. In retrospect, he was not saying anything terribly earth shattering, and his sharp criticism of Stalin's brutality was certainly warranted when you consider the millions of Soviet citizens who died at the hands of their own government. But to many citizens and loyal Communist Party members, Stalin was a hero, and hearing the premier speak of him disparagingly was shocking.

In February 1956, when he was the leader of the Communist Party but not yet the premier of the USSR, Khrushchev delivered a speech to the Twentieth Congress of the Communist Party called "The Personality Cult and its Consequences." The speech became known as the "secret speech," because Khrushchev delivered it to a closed session of high-ranking party officials in the turbulent political climate that followed Stalin's death. His goal was to divide the top ranks of the party, alienating Stalin's supporters and drawing support for himself. The speech, which went on for more than four hours, detailed the horrors of Stalin's regime against the party, focusing on the Great Purge that led to the arrests and executions of so many members of the Communist Party. In his speech, Khrushchev evoked Lenin's dreams for the USSR and emphasized how Stalin brutally destroyed them in creating his own cult of personality. He presented detailed evidence that the purges and gulags targeted Bolsheviks, the true followers of Lenin's ideology. In conclusion, Khrushchev specifically blamed his political rivals—Beria, Molotov and Malenkov—for planning and actively participating in Stalin's purges (but downplayed his own role).

Read the Document *Nikita Krushchev's Secret Speech* on mysearchlab.com

As Khrushchev intended, the top echelons of the Communist Party were indeed divided. The split deepened when the text of the so-called "secret speech" was read at all Communist Party meetings throughout the USSR and eventually distributed throughout the satellite states and leaked to the Western press as well. The speech led to protests and riots, particularly in the Georgian Republic, where Stalin was born and raised. But Khrushchev's gamble paid off when he became premier in 1958 and initiated the policies of the "thaw," winning the support of many Soviet citizens. In 1961, he had Stalin's body removed from public display in Lenin's mausoleum and buried nearby with a simple marker that read: "J. V. Stalin 1879–1953." With the following decree, Khrushchev completed de-Stalinization:

> *The further retention in the mausoleum of the sarcophagus with the bier of J. V. Stalin shall be recognized as inappropriate since the serious violations by Stalin of Lenin's precepts, abuse of power, mass repressions against honorable Soviet people, and other activities in the period of the personality cult make it impossible to leave the bier with his body in the mausoleum of V. I. Lenin* (Khrushchev, quoted in Robert Payne, *The Rise and Fall of Stalin*, New York: Simon and Schuster, 1965, p. 682).

Peaceful Coexistence

The philosophy of Khrushchev's "thaw" extended into his foreign-policy decision making, ushering in a new phase of the Cold War. Whereas Stalin believed that the Cold War was a zero-sum game, Khrushchev believed that communism and democracy/capitalism could both exist in the world without requiring World War III to settle the ideological dispute. He based this philosophy on Lenin's principle of peaceful coexistence, again drawing the distinction between Stalin's violent approach to world affairs and the true principles of Soviet communism as established by Lenin's revolution. Khrushchev's use of peaceful coexistence to guide his foreign-policy decision making was largely a product of his faith in communism as the superior ideology. He believed that workers around the world would *choose* a communist way of life and that it was his responsibility as the leader of the communist world to help them in their revolutionary struggles to establish communist governments.

There was, of course, a very practical side to peaceful coexistence as well. Khrushchev wanted to avoid World War III and slow down the arms race. He recognized that a nuclear holocaust would destroy the world, and he could not be sure that the USSR was winning the arms race, so he really wanted to avoid direct conflict with the United States. He feared that aggressive and violent rhetoric like Stalin's would incite the United States to strike, particularly if President Eisenhower believed the United States was winning the arms race.

Khrushchev hoped that the concept of peaceful coexistence would alleviate the United States' fears of a Soviet attack and slow down the arms race. This would allow him to divert money away from defense spending and instead devote resources to fostering communism around the world, which was the ultimate goal of communist foreign policy. This meant increased spending on domestic industry to convince

> *...We shall never take up arms to force the ideas of communism upon anybody. We do not need to do that, for the ideas of communism express the vital interests of the popular masses. Our ideas, the ideas of communism have such great vitality that no weapon can destroy them, that not even the nuclear weapon can hold up the development of these progressive ideas. Our ideas will capture the minds of mankind. The attempts of the imperialist to arrest the spread of the ideas of communism by force of arms are doomed to failure.... for forty years now ... the capitalists have been reiterating that...private ownership is omnipotent. We affirm that the ideas of communism are incomparably stronger, that these ideas will ultimately prevail. Therefore, we repeat again and again: let us compete, let us coexist peacefully...*
>
> —Khrushchev, speech to Albanian embassy, spring 1957

MAKE THE CONNECTION

How does "peaceful coexistence" fit in with Marxist theory? With Lenin's view of the "struggle"? With Stalin's execution of the Cold War?

people that communism provided for its citizens. He was also obligated to militarily support the satellite states, which were located in crucial geostrategic positions that buffered the USSR from Western aggression. And to support communist revolutions around the world, Khrushchev had to provide financial incentives for political leaders in Latin America, Asia and Africa. He preferred to finance "splashy" projects such as stadiums and buildings that would draw the attention of the international press, but these projects were very expensive.

Domestic Consequences

Because the goal of peaceful coexistence was to minimize the use of military force to spread communism and compete for peoples "minds" instead, Khrushchev had to make the USSR look better than the West. His domestic policies were focused on catching up with, and eventually overtaking, capitalist countries in terms of economic development, thereby proving that communism was superior. People would demand communist governments, and democracy/capitalism would fade away.

But ideology aside, a communist economy was not designed to generate excess profits. The goal was for every citizen to produce what he or she can, and the products of the process would be distributed equitably throughout the population. Everyone worked, and everyone shared in the profits generated by the entire community. No one paid taxes, because the government was not providing for the citizens; the citizens were providing for one another. In fact, a true communist society (according to Marx) would not even have a government—the state would wither away because it would be unnecessary when the people worked together to produce what they needed. This, of course, was not how the Soviet economy was designed. Everyone worked in state-owned enterprises, but the government then siphoned off the money it needed to run the country and fight the Cold War.

So the primary problem Khrushchev faced was how to feed the more than 214 million people in the USSR in 1960, provide them with as many consumer goods as in the West, and maintain the country's infrastructure (things such as roads, buildings, dams and power); but he also had to pull enough money out of the economy to maintain an active military, keep up (at least) in the arms race, and provide financial assistance to spread communism around the world. To maintain superpower status and prove the superiority of communism, those last three foreign-policy goals absolutely had to be met. Unfortunately, meeting those goals did not leave enough money for domestic affairs. Under Khrushchev, the USSR developed a major food crisis, the black market took over the domestic economy for almost all consumer goods, and the infrastructure began to crumble.

Foreign Affairs

To Khrushchev, peaceful coexistence meant avoiding World War III, but it certainly did not mean abandoning superpower status. He was always very clear that he maintained absolute authority within the USSR, and he was a powerful player in world affairs. Although Khrushchev was not a tall man, he made a big impression on people—he was talkative, loud and spoke aggressively. His formal education was limited, but he was clever and certainly ambitious. And by the time he gained the top position in the USSR, he did not control his temper well. Khrushchev was angry at Stalin for subverting Lenin's vision for the USSR and angry at the United States for its insistent criticism of communist ideology. Though he wanted to avoid World War III, Khrushchev had an unwavering faith in his ideology and would not compromise its success. Drawing on his Marxist teachings, in November 1956 he vehemently told Western diplomats: "Whether you like it or not, history is on our side. We will bury you!"

As part of peaceful coexistence, the United States and the USSR attempted to promote understanding between their citizens with a cultural exchange in 1959, although there were certainly heavy political undertones as well. The Soviets presented an exhibit in New York that depicted daily life in the USSR, and the United States took its American National Exhibit to

Khruschev and Nixon in Moscow.

Moscow that July. Designed to show off America's superiority, the exhibit was basically a recreation of the "typical" American suburban home, featuring the latest appliances, luxury amenities, high fashion and recreational vehicles. As U.S. Vice President Richard Nixon gave Khrushchev a tour of the "home," Khrushchev commented: "You Americans expect that the Soviet people will be amazed. It is not so. We have all these things in our new flats." This sparked a debate between the men on the merits of capitalism versus communism that ended with Khrushchev threateningly pointing his finger in Nixon's face and challenging: "Who is giving the ultimatum?" Still, the so-called "Kitchen Debate" remained friendly, and Khrushchev even allowed Nixon to speak out against communism on Soviet national television before Nixon left the USSR in August.

Read the Document *The Kitchen Debate* on mysearchlab.com

Khrushchev's trip to the United States did not go quite as well. He arrived on September 15, 1959, and was escorted around the country by President Eisenhower and a huge contingent of international media. At the top of Khrushchev's itinerary was Hollywood, California. Touring 20th Century Fox Studios, Khrushchev met his favorite movie star, John Wayne (who was an avid anticommunist) and had lunch with Frank Sinatra, Kirk Douglas, Gary Cooper and Marilyn Monroe. But Khrushchev was angered when other actors, including Ronald Reagan, refused to meet with him, and Khrushchev blamed the studio chief and President Eisenhower for the many protestors who followed him around Los Angeles. Khrushchev's largest public outburst came when he was told he could not visit Disneyland for security reasons, but he enjoyed visits to New York, San Francisco, Iowa and Pittsburgh during his two-week stay in the United States. Although Khrushchev and Eisenhower spent the last two days in high-level discussions at Camp David, no concrete agreements or policies regarding peaceful coexistence were made. The leaders of the superpowers agreed to maintain open lines of communication as they competed for worldwide political and economic dominance.

The open relationship between the United States and the USSR came to an end on May 1, 1960, when a U-2 spy plane from the United States was shot down by a Russian missile 850 miles east of Moscow flying at an altitude of about 68,000 feet. Although the United States denied it was a spy plane, the Soviets produced the captured pilot, Francis Gary Powers, and photographs and films he had taken of Soviet military installations and important industrial

Wreckage of Gary Powers' plane on display in the USSR.

targets. According to Powers's arrest records, the evidence the Soviets collected from the plane's wreckage and the pilot's testimony "left no doubt that it was a deliberate intrusion into the air space of the Soviet Union with hostile purposes." Eisenhower was forced to admit that he approved the mission, but he refused to apologize for invading Soviet airspace. Powers, a civilian, pleaded guilty to spying for the CIA and was sentenced to ten years in a Soviet military prison (although he was freed in February 1962 in exchange for the release of a Soviet spy, Rudolph Abel). The entire event occurred just as the **Paris Summit** was opening on May 14, 1960. In the days preceding the meeting, both Eisenhower and Khrushchev took increasingly rigid stances on the U-2 incident. Khrushchev, who refused to attend the private meetings and only spoke when the international media was present, used language such as "aggressive, treacherous and incompatible" to describe the United States and declared: "When the government of one of the great powers declares bluntly that its policy is intrusion into the territory of another great power with espionage and sabotage purposes…it is clear that the declaration of such a policy dooms the summit conference to complete failure in advance." He demanded that Eisenhower apologize and punish members of the U.S. government who planned, approved and executed the mission.

Paris Summit meeting between Eisenhower (United States), Khrushchev (USSR), Harold Macmillan (Great Britain) and Charles de Gaulle (France) to discuss nuclear dearmament, China, and the division of Berlin

Evoking the memory of Pearl Harbor, Eisenhower responded that Khrushchev's "fetish of secrecy and concealment…is a major cause of international tension and uneasiness…" He upheld the United States' right to engage in espionage, calling it "a distasteful but vital necessity," and refused to apologize for protecting his citizens against the Soviet threat. This was not the response Khrushchev was looking for—he rescinded the invitation for Eisenhower to visit the USSR and refused to negotiate with the United States until another administration was in place. The summit was cancelled, and the open communication between the United States and the USSR came to an end.

The following September, Khrushchev traveled to the United Nations in New York City to celebrate the UN's fifteenth anniversary. Fearing for his safety after thousands of death threats, Khrushchev did not leave the city. Eisenhower also attended the event but steered clear of

Khrushchev, so the two never confronted one another directly. Throughout the meetings, Khrushchev was disruptive, pounding his desk and interrupting speakers in angry outbursts. He was displeased with UN actions around the world and demanded that UN Secretary Dag Hammarskjöld resign his position. Khrushchev gave a two and a half hour speech calling for decolonization and disarmament, accusing the West of preventing progress in those areas. He laid out his plan for the complete reorganization of the UN, which he felt should certainly not meet in the United States. Khrushchev's behavior throughout the week was aggressive and erratic, culminating in a now-infamous incident in which he allegedly pulled off his shoe and banged it on the table in a fit of rage as he called the head of the Philippine delegation "a jerk, a stooge and a lackey of imperialism."

Khrushchev's change in behavior in 1960 confirmed U.S. suspicions that de-Stalinization and peaceful coexistence were simply more Soviet rhetoric and that the Cold War was as potentially hot as ever. But why the change from open communication and competition to actions that would bring the world to the brink of nuclear war in 1962? Top-ranking Communist Party officials within the USSR did not approve of Khrushchev's approach to fighting the Cold War, as evidenced by an attempted coup against him in May 1957. They were concerned that he was too soft on democracy and capitalism, and Khrushchev had to demonstrate to them that he was not if he wanted to keep his position of power. Additionally, Mao's frustrations with Khrushchev over de-Stalinization led to the Sino-Soviet split in 1960, highlighting the divisions and power struggles within the communist world. Anxious to prove his absolute authority, Khrushchev seized on the U-2 incident to reassert an anti-American stance and silence internal challenges. In doing so, he also escalated the Cold War.

Challenges in the Satellite Bloc

The front line of the Cold War between East and West ran right through Europe. The Eastern Bloc countries, or satellite states (what Churchill called the Iron Curtain), were completely controlled by the USSR politically, socially and economically. They were pro-Soviet communist states expected to emulate Stalin's USSR in every respect: five-year plans, collectivization, industrialization, and frequent political purges. When Khrushchev's "thaw" and de-Stalinization reached these satellite states, some government leaders saw an opportunity to redefine communism for themselves, which was not exactly what Khrushchev had in mind.

Poland

Under the communist government of Boleslaw Beirut, life in Poland in the early 1950s followed Stalin's model very closely. But Khrushchev's "thaw" and Beirut's death in 1956 (under mysterious circumstances while attending the Twentieth Party Congress in Moscow) led to turmoil as pro-Stalinists tried to prevent the reformists, led by Wladyslaw Gomulka, from taking control of the Communist Party and the government.

Polish laborers had been dissatisfied for years about low wages and long workdays but never dared do much about it during Beirut's reign. As reforms began in Poland following Beirut's death—for example, 28,000 political prisoners were freed from the gulags—the laborers became more vocal about their concerns. On June 28, 1956, the

MAP 8.1 The Soviet Satellite Bloc

situation turned into an all-out protest as 100,000 workers and their families from all industries in the city of Poznan gathered in the town square. Things got out of hand quickly—demonstrators attacked the prison, police station and Communist Party headquarters, seizing weapons, as the Polish army fought to restore order with bombs and guns. It took two days, 10,000 troops and 400 tanks to end the revolt, which killed approximately eighty people, but the point was made, and the Polish government allowed workers to elect councils in the factories to negotiate reforms.

While Khrushchev talked about reforming communism, he feared losing control of the process. In October, the Politburo dispatched Russian troops to Warsaw, and Khrushchev traveled there himself to reassert Soviet authority over the government. The workers were prepared to battle the Russian army for their freedom, but Gomulka was able to convince Khrushchev that even a reformist Polish Communist Party would remain loyal to the Warsaw Pact. In late October, Gomulka demanded an end to the protest rallies and demonstrations. Once in power, he shut down the radical newspapers that had surfaced to support him months before, reasserted the illegality of labor strikes, and put an end to the workers' councils. Gomulka recognized that Khrushchev would not allow another independent leader (like Tito) in the satellite bloc, and fell back in line to retain his power.

Hungary

Throughout the early 1950s, Hungary was one of the most oppressive countries in Europe under the authoritarian leadership of Matyas Rakosi and his Security Police. As a consequence of Khrushchev's de-Stalinization program, Rakosi was removed from power in July 1956 and replaced by reformist Erno Gero. Intellectuals and students in Hungary began openly debating and discussing reform, developing a list of sixteen demands for reform of government policies. In solidarity for the reform movement happening in Poland at the same time, 200,000 student protestors gathered in Szeged and read their demands aloud. When Gero rejected them and called for an end to the demonstration, the students toppled a statue of Stalin and cut the communist coat of arms out of the national flag of Hungary. The demonstration turned into a revolution as the Secret Police attacked and the fighting became widespread.

On October 24, Soviet tanks and troops entered Budapest to put an end to the revolution, which only outraged Hungarians even more. Workers, police and even Hungarian soldiers joined the student revolutionaries to fight the Russians. Popular reformist leader Imre Nagy stepped forward to encourage the revolutionaries to stop fighting and allow negotiations to begin. Satisfied that Gero was out of power and the Russian military would leave, the violence ended while Nagy attempted to establish order, suspended the Secret Police, and laid out his plans to build a multiparty social democracy. Nagy appealed to the UN Security Council for assistance, but of course the USSR exercised its veto power to prevent it, and the United States was unwilling to risk World War III by intervening in a Warsaw Pact state. Hungary was on its own to develop a democratic government.

The Politburo was divided on its response—a few hard-liners wanted to invade immediately, but most assumed that the Communist Party would regain control of Hungary, as it had in the labor strikes in Poland. It was not until Hungary announced its neutrality in the Cold War and withdrew itself from the Warsaw Pact on November 1 that the Politburo realized the Hungarian Revolution was truly a revolution against communism itself. Losing an ally, particularly one along the buffer zone against the West, was absolutely unacceptable. The Soviet military launched an invasion of Budapest in the evening of November 3, 1956. After a week of violence, a Soviet-controlled government was reinstated in Hungary on November 10. By the end of the Hungarian Revolution, more than 2,500 Hungarians had died, and 13,000 more were wounded. More than 200,000 Hungarians became refugees, and 26,000 were put on trial by the new communist government (13,000 of whom were imprisoned). The Soviet military remained in Hungary for the duration of the Cold War.

Yugoslavia

Josip Broz Tito, a communist, was a World War II hero in Yugoslavia for his role in organizing the military to defeat the Axis powers. After the war, he was overwhelmingly elected prime minister and served as president from 1953–1980. Because Tito was a communist, the United States considered him Stalin's ally; but because he preferred to make his own leadership decisions, Stalin did not trust him. When establishing his government in Yugoslavia in 1948, Tito told Stalin: "We study and take as an example the Soviet system, but we are developing socialism in our country in somewhat different forms." In response, Stalin expelled Tito's Yugoslav Communist Party from the **Cominform.**

Tito was not what Stalin was looking for in a Cold War ally, and he sent several assassins to Yugoslavia in an attempt to solve his "Tito problem." They were never successful, and Stalin settled for a smear campaign throughout his satellite states—anyone suspected of practicing "Titoism" was sent to the gulag. Tito used this open split with Stalin to gain U.S. financial support through the Marshall Plan, but he refused to fall under the American sphere of influence, remaining neutral in the Cold War. When Khrushchev launched de-Stalinization, he assumed that it would bring Yugoslavia into the Soviet sphere of influence. The two men met several times, although initially Tito would not travel to Moscow and made Khrushchev visit him in Belgrade instead. Tito insisted on maintaining independence for Yugoslavia in all matters and criticized the Soviet invasion of Hungary in 1956. Khrushchev was unable to convince Tito to rejoin the communist bloc, and Tito remained persistently neutral throughout the remainder of the Cold War.

Cominform (Communist Information Bureau) international organization to create and spread communist solidarity

brain drain when skilled labor and/or intellectuals leave their country to seek more favorable political or economic conditions; results in primarily unskilled labor in the country

The Berlin Wall

East and West met in the divided city of Berlin, 155 miles inside the borders of the Soviet-controlled German Democratic Republic (GDR). This was where Khrushchev hoped to demonstrate the economic superiority of the Soviet model over capitalism in the U.S.-supported Federal Republic of Germany (FRG). Unfortunately, even with heavy subsidies from the USSR, the standard of living in the GDR steadily dropped lower than the FRG throughout the 1950s, leading to a "**brain drain**" from the GDR to the FRG through the open border in the city of Berlin. And by 1958, Khrushchev began to fear that the FRG, a member of NATO, was preparing to launch some sort of military intervention into the GDR. In hopes of securing even more financial and military support for his government, the communist leader of the GDR, Walter Ulbricht, convinced Khrushchev that something had to be done or the GDR would most surely succumb to the FRG from internal and/or external pressures. Particularly after the Sino-Soviet split of 1960, Khrushchev could not afford another "loss" on the Cold War scorecard, and diplomatic measures had failed to stop the United States from strengthening the FRG through rearmament. After the failure of the Paris Summit in 1960, Khrushchev attempted to negotiate with the new U.S. President, John F. Kennedy, but Kennedy too refused to compromise on Berlin.

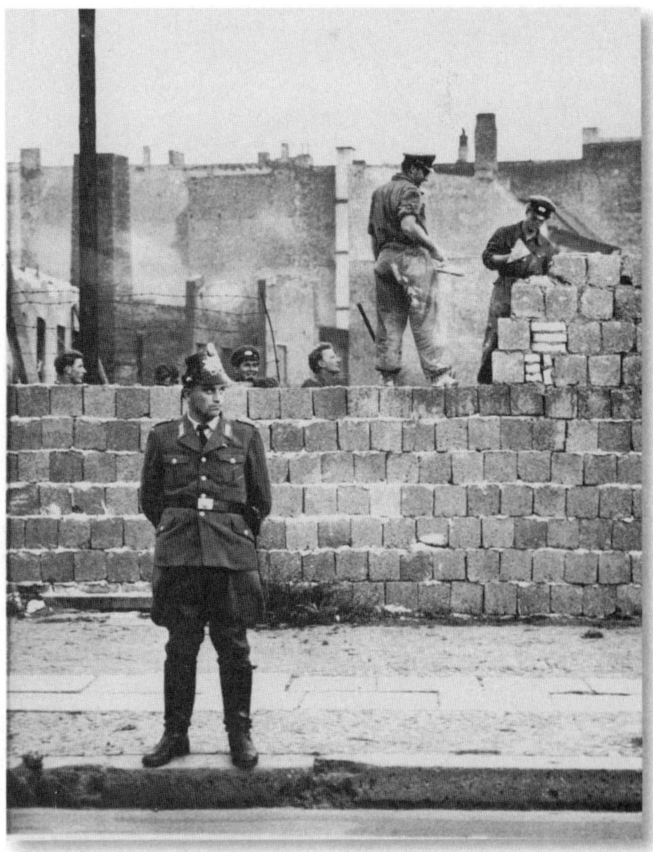

The Berlin Wall going up, 1961.

By spring 1961, the refugee crisis from the GDR had become an international embarrassment, and the economic situation had worsened. In just one year (1960), an estimated

200,000 East Germans fled for the FRG. On August 1, 1961, Ulbricht and Khrushchev met to discuss putting "an iron ring around Berlin." Two factors were crucial: (1) the East German people must be convinced that the action was to protect them from the FRG, and (2) there must be no warning before the border was sealed to prevent a further "brain drain." That same week, another 15,000 people fled the GDR.

On the morning of August 13, 1961, Berliners awoke to a divided city. Overnight, East German and Soviet troops had closed crossing points and erected six-feet-high barbed-wire fences, cut off train service between East and West Berlin, and armed border guards with the "shoot to kill" command. Despite verbal protests from the West, the lack of a military response signaled to Khrushchev that he had won this battle. The wall continued to go up, eventually becoming a 103-mile stretch of concrete and barbed wire, twelve feet high on average, guarded by three hundred watch towers and loaded with booby traps and landmines. Khrushchev said it was necessary to protect the people of the GDR against espionage, economic disaster and potential military aggression, but the Berlin Wall did not just prevent Westerners from entering East Berlin. Anyone caught leaving East Germany was killed—almost two hundred of them in the twenty-eight years the wall was there.

Watch the Video *Escaping the Berlin Wall* on mysearchlab.com

Though a very real physical border, the wall also became the symbol of the ideological divide between East and West as the Cold War began to heat up in the late 1960s. In June 1963, U.S. President Kennedy spoke to a crowd of 120,000 people in West Berlin, noting their crucial role on the front line of the Cold War and promising international support:

> *...the wall is the most obvious and vivid demonstration of the failures of the Communist system, for all the world to see...it is...an offense not only against history but an offense against humanity, separating families, dividing husbands and wives and brothers and sisters, and dividing a people who wish to be joined together...All free men, wherever they may live, are citizens of Berlin, and therefore, as a free man, I take pride in the words, 'Ich bin ein Berliner.'*

MAP 8.2 Cuba in Relation to U.S. Border

The Soviet Sphere of Influence Reaches the Western Hemisphere

Ever since the United States freed Cuba from Spanish colonial status in 1898, the economy of the independent island nation was largely controlled by U.S. interests. By the 1920s, U.S. corporations owned two-thirds of all Cuban farmland (primarily sugar plantations), all of its large mines (containing iron ore and copper) and the entire tourist industry, thus reaping the profits from all of Cuba's export commodities. The Cuban people worked for Americans but owned nothing and so retained no profits to reinvest in their own economy or infrastructure. Why did the government of Cuba allow U.S. corporations to control the national economy in their best interests and to the detriment of the Cuban people? In exchange for allowing the U.S. control to happen, Cuban government officials became personally wealthy.

From the mid-1930s, decision making in the Cuban government was controlled largely by Fulgencio Batista serving in one official capacity or another. When he staged a coup and became president in 1952, Batista suspended civil rights, enacted censorship and used brutality to enforce his policies. Student rioting and political protests became commonplace and were always met with violence by the police. With Batista's help, U.S. corporations expanded their ownership of the export industries to include local transportation (highways, trains and the airport) and the power company. His most personally lucrative deal was with the American mafia, which

Fulgencio Batista (far right) and Richard Nixon (far left).

built many casinos and used Havana as an international drug port. But it was the Cold War, so a dictator who prevented left-wing political policies and who also met the interests of U.S. corporations enjoyed the full support of the U.S. government. Under Batista, Cuba became totally dependent on the United States—71 percent of Cuba's imports were from the United States, and 67 percent of its exports were sent to the United States. When Batista was reelected president of Cuba in 1955 in what was obviously a rigged election (he was the only candidate on the ballot), a group of Cuban nationalists had had enough.

The Cuban Revolution

In December 1956, brothers Fidel and Raul Castro and professional revolutionary Ernesto "Che" Guevara led a group of eighty-two nationalist revolutionaries in an unsuccessful coup attempt against the Batista regime. Most were captured within three days, but the Castro brothers, Guevara and eight others escaped into the Sierra Maestra Mountains, where they regrouped and were joined by more revolutionaries (mostly university students) during the next two years. In May 1958, Batista sent 10,000 troops into the Sierra Maestras to find the revolutionaries—by the end of the summer, the Cuban military had been defeated, and Castro's rebels were well armed. The rebels began fighting their way to Havana that fall, arriving in the capital on January 1, 1959. With the widespread anti-Batista movement splashed across U.S. newspapers and growing sympathy for the Cuban revolutionaries, Eisenhower realized that Batista's military could not hold on. In December 1958, he sent an ambassador to inform Batista that the United States would no longer support his regime, nor could he seek exile in the United States (even though Batista owned a home in Daytona Beach, Florida). With Castro's revolutionaries at the edge of Havana on New Year's Eve, Batista and 180 of his supporters fled to Spain with over $300 million.

Though the Cuban Revolution technically had control of the Cuban government on January 1, 1959, Castro stopped in the towns and villages along the way to speak to the people, building support for the revolution. When Castro entered Havana on January 8, he was escorted by hundreds of revolutionaries, what remained of the Cuban military, and hundreds of thousands of cheering citizens. To the Cuban people, Castro and his revolutionaries were heroes who freed them from Batista's brutality and who would solve the huge urban–rural disparities created by U.S. "colonialism."

Fidel Castro, a lawyer, was a smart man who recognized that, to the people of Cuba, the ideological bantering of the Cold War was the least of their concerns. He promised not to rule by ideology: "Not Communism or Marxism is our idea. Our political philosophy is representative democracy and social justice in a well-planned economy." So the Cuban people—rich and poor, urban and rural—were united in their support of Castro's revolution. He was careful to establish a government led by intellectuals rather than revolutionaries. He initially served simply as the leader of the Rebel Army, but he was certainly pulling the strings behind the scenes. As they gained political power, the revolutionaries began to disagree on exactly what the policies of their new government should be. Some clearly embraced communism while others were opposed to it. Unwilling to let the revolution fall apart from within, Castro gradually assumed central leadership and imprisoned or executed those against him.

Read the Document *Fidel Castro Defends the Revolution* on mysearchlab.com

In April, Castro visited the United States, hoping to meet with President Eisenhower to discuss financial aid to help Cuba's economy. Eisenhower's administration was undecided on how to respond to the Cuban Revolution—some wanted to offer Castro the same deal Batista had to keep him firmly within the U.S. sphere of influence, but others wanted to take a hard line against what they feared were communist elements in his regime. Eisenhower refused to meet with Castro, but Vice President Nixon did spend three hours talking with him. Nixon came to the

The Castro Brothers and Che Guevara.

conclusion that Castro did not really have a good grasp on the realities of communism and the Cold War, and the United States refused aid to Cuba.

That spring, Castro's regime began returning Cuban land and resources to the Cuban people. The government nationalized the power and telephone companies. The May 1959 Agrarian Reform Act banned land ownership by foreigners—the government nationalized farms larger than 1,000 acres (all held by U.S. corporations) and titled the land to 200,000 Cuban peasants. U.S. corporate executives demanded that the Eisenhower administration do something, so the United States put trade restrictions on Cuban imports.

Castro and Khruschev at the UN.

In this competitive Cold War environment, if the United States would not help Castro, the USSR would. In February 1960, Castro negotiated a trade agreement in which the USSR would purchase five million tons of sugar from Cuba over five years, and Cuba would receive oil, grain and money from the USSR. But when the Soviet crude oil arrived in Cuba in April, the U.S.-owned oil refineries (Texaco, Esso and Shell) refused to refine it. In Castro's mind, the United States had declared economic war on Cuba, so he nationalized the refineries. In response, Eisenhower expanded the trade restrictions, cutting off 80percent of Cuba's total sugar exports. The USSR stepped in and agreed to buy the sugar, and Cuba and the USSR established formal diplomatic relations in May 1960. That June, Castro nationalized $850 million in U.S. property, and he seized all U.S. banks in Cuba at the end of the summer. At the United Nations General Assembly in September 1960, Castro and Khrushchev were clearly allied. The Soviet sphere of influence extended into the West.

With Castro and Khrushchev allied and Cuba just ninety miles off the U.S. coast, Eisenhower had to choose his actions extremely carefully. He clearly needed Castro out of power, but how to accomplish it and keep U.S. involvement hidden? Eisenhower's $13 million plan was called Operation Zapata. When approved in February 1960, the plan ignited a chain of events that came as close to World War III as the Cold War ever got.

The Bay of Pigs

When John F. Kennedy became president of the United States in 1961, he vowed to be a new kind of "Cold War warrior." He would be tough on communism, of course, but hoped to negotiate an end to ideological hostilities rather than risk World War III. While campaigning for office, Kennedy had blamed Eisenhower and Nixon (against whom he was running in the 1960 election) for "neglecting" Castro and allowing him to "slip behind the Iron Curtain." Yet immediately after taking office, when presented with the Eisenhower administration's plan to oust Castro, Kennedy agreed to it.

Read the Document *John F. Kennedy and Cuba* on mysearchlab.com

In preparation for Operation Zapata, CIA agents had been secretly training Cuban **exiles** at several military facilities throughout the southeast United States and a few Latin American countries to prepare them to invade their homeland on the southeast coast of Cuba at Playa Giron. They would travel to Havana, picking up supporters along the way, overthrow Castro's regime and establish a U.S.-friendly provisional government in Cuba. From the planning of the invasion right through its execution, the CIA made some serious miscalculations that doomed the operation's success.

exile
a citizen involuntarily living outside of his or her country

The Cuban government knew the attack was coming, through its contacts in Miami and with KGB agents, so it prepared a defense of the coastline. The success of the plan also relied heavily on the 1,300 invaders picking up the support of anti-Castro revolutionaries in Cuba, but most of them had been arrested or executed by April 17, 1961, when the invasion began. And particularly in the countryside, most Cuban people supported Castro. Finally, to combat the Soviet-supplied Cuban military, the invaders would need significant help from the U.S. military, and President Kennedy was simply unwilling to commit that level of support.

At 6:00 a.m. on April 15, 1961, eight U.S. bombers painted to look like Cuban aircraft took off from Nicaragua and attacked three Cuban airfields in an attempt to destroy the planes while on the tarmac, but they caused only minimal damage. Immediately after the attack, the Cuban foreign minister went to the UN and accused the United States of launching the attacks, which of course the United States denied. But, worried that the UN might look into it, Kennedy canceled all remaining air attacks on Cuba, leaving the Cuban air force intact. Castro arrested hundreds of thousands of civilians that he did not quite trust on April 15 and 16. On April 17, the CIA-trained force of 1,300 exiles landed on Playa Giron, about 125 miles south of Havana, where they and the supply ships were immediately attacked by the Cuban air force. Without American air support or supplies, the invasion force was quickly outnumbered and outmaneuvered—all of them captured or dead within the week.

The failed Bay of Pigs invasion was a disaster for the Kennedy administration. The United States looked weak militarily, which was a dangerous perception in the middle of the Cold War. And Kennedy had been obviously lying in a press conference on April 12 when he clearly stated: "First, I want to say that there will not be, under any conditions, an intervention in Cuba by the United States Armed Forces." Kennedy's political opponents in the United States exploited his weakness as commander in chief and his ability to carry out tough choices to fight the communist presence in the western hemisphere. The invasion changed things in Cuba, too. People who opposed Castro were in prison or dead, leaving only ardent Castro supporters among the population. Che Guevara sent a note to Kennedy thanking him for making the revolution stronger than ever. But perhaps

MAKE THE CONNECTION

- Did Castro ally with the USSR for political, financial or national security reasons?
- Did Eisenhower push Cuba behind the Iron Curtain, as Kennedy alleged?
- Did Kennedy escalate the Cold War through his reactions to Castro?

The Kennedys Greet the Cuban Invasion Brigade Members, December 1962.

most dangerous in terms of the larger Cold War, the invasion made Castro realize that the United States would indeed use military force to remove him from power, and he needed help to prevent that from happening.

Operation Mongoose

Kennedy was even more determined to remove Castro from power, but he did not want to be embarrassed again, so he relied heavily on the CIA to handle the problem covertly. In January 1962, Kennedy told his closest advisors that getting rid of Castro was "the top priority of the U.S. government—all else is secondary—no time, money, effort, or manpower is to be spared." The CIA decided that Castro had too much support to be overthrown from within, so it launched Operation Mongoose, a series of small-scale secret sabotage and assassination attempts planned by CIA operative General Edward Lansdale. The sabotage missions went after strategic communication and transportation targets in an attempt to incite a popular uprising against Castro. Far more bizarre were the attempts to get rid of Castro directly. Fabian Escalante, head of the Cuban secret service throughout Castro's regime, alleges that there were 638 assassination attempts made on Fidel Castro's life. Because it was imperative that U.S. government involvement be hidden, the creative attempts ranged from exploding cigars and seashells to pen syringes and bacteria-laced coffee.

The Cuban Missile Crisis

With the Bay of Pigs invasion and the assassination attempts, the United States made it clear that it intended to oust Castro, so he turned to Moscow for military support. Khrushchev was delighted to help, deploying Soviet military support and nuclear missiles to Cuba in the summer of

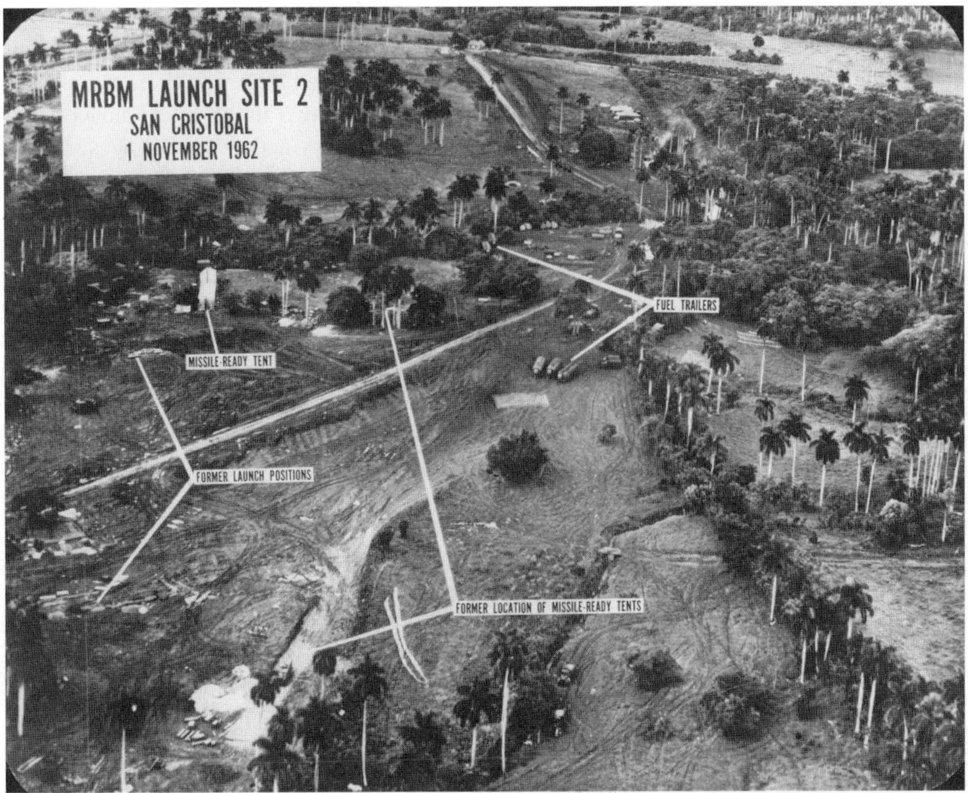

Aerial Photograph of Medium Range Ballistic Missile Launch Site Two at San Cristobal, November 1962.

1962. Because Cuba lies well south of the DEW line, a nuclear attack launched from Cuba would not be detected until the missiles were in U.S. airspace. For the USSR, this was certainly an edge in the arms race, although military experts in Kennedy's administration were not too concerned that the Soviets would actually use the missiles. They were far more worried about the impression of power the situation created—that Khrushchev could brazenly expand the Soviet sphere of influence to the United States' backyard and Kennedy could not do a thing about it. Particularly because of the Bay of Pigs fiasco, it was vital that Kennedy demonstrate his willingness and ability to contain communism.

The United States first had evidence that the USSR was sending military aid to Cuba in the summer of 1962. By mid-October, U-2 spy planes flying over Cuba brought back pictures of nine ballistic missile sites under construction. On October 16, Kennedy called together the Executive Committee of the National Security Council (EXCOMM) to figure out how to deal with a Soviet nuclear threat ninety miles offshore. Council members discussed several options, including doing nothing at all or using diplomacy to negotiate with Khrushchev. They considered surgical strikes on the missile sites, but that was a dangerous gamble because they were not sure whether the missiles were operational or if they knew the locations of all the sites. The Joint Chiefs of Staff called for a full-scale invasion of Cuba, but Kennedy resisted because he feared one of two things would happen: either the Soviets would let the United States seize Cuba and then invade West Berlin in retaliation; or there would be Soviet troops on the ground in Cuba, which would ignite World War III.

Watch the Video *President John F. Kennedy Addresses the Nation* on mysearchlab.com

By October 19, EXCOMM was fairly confident that four of the missile sites were operational—the situation was getting worse, and something had to be done. Kennedy decided to put a quarantine around Cuba (in international waters) that would require suspicious ships heading for Cuba to be stopped and searched by the U.S. navy. This was clever language because, under international law, a **naval blockade** is considered an act of war. Kennedy argued that this was not an actual blockade because of its limited nature—the United States would only stop ships it suspected carried offensive weapons to be used against them. On October 22, 1962, President Kennedy announced to the American people that the Soviets had built tactical missile sites in Cuba and that the United States (with full support from the OAS) would erect a quarantine around the island nation. He demanded that the USSR remove its missiles and bombers from Cuba and explicitly warned Khruschev not to take retaliatory action against West Berlin. Then the world waited to see what Khruschev would do.

naval blockade the use of ships at sea to surround and cut off a place from the movement of goods or people, usually to compel a surrender or achieve a political goal

For thirteen days, the world held its collective breath as the United States and the USSR appeared to be moving toward direct conflict. U.S. forces, including bombers with nuclear weapons, were put on alert. In Cuba, work on arming the missile sites continued around the clock. On October 24, two Soviet ships approaching Cuba stopped just short of the quarantine and stayed there, in a standoff with the U.S. navy, while Soviet oil tankers and merchant vessels steamed right through. Both Kennedy and Khrushchev continued to issue public statements with strong language and threats, but behind the scenes, aides to both men worked diligently to negotiate a peaceful end to the potential crisis. On October 26, with tensions increasing, Kennedy received an offer from Khrushchev. The USSR would withdraw its missiles from Cuba under two conditions: (1) the United States must never invade or attack Cuba; and (2) the United States must remove all of its missiles in Turkey aimed at the USSR.

The fact that the United States had missiles on the border of the USSR was supposed to be top secret. The missiles were old and were slated for decommission anyway, but their presence helped justify Khrushchev's actions in Cuba and made Kennedy's public outrage at the USSR seem a bit hypocritical. Kennedy was anxious to end the ordeal peacefully, but he certainly could not admit to having missiles in Turkey. As EXCOMM deliberated over its response, a U-2 spy plane was shot down over Cuba on October 27. EXCOMM assumed the Soviets were initiating a military "solution" to the crisis and pushed Kennedy to order a U.S. military response. Kennedy hesitated—he wanted to be sure that it was

ANALYSIS

Why is the Cuban Missile Crisis considered the closest the Cold War came to getting "hot"? Consider the map on the right, as well as Khrushchev's and Kennedy's personal attributes, in your explanation.

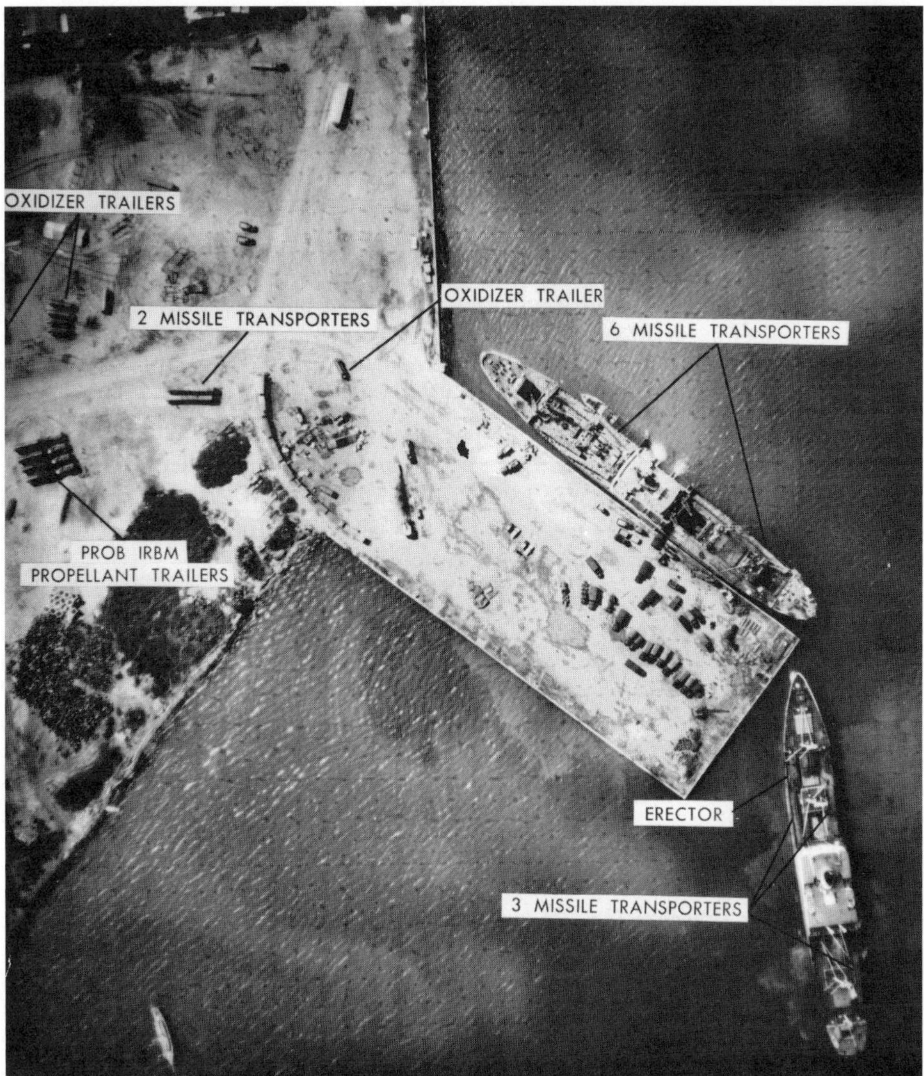

Cuban Missile Crisis: U.S. reconnaissance photo of Soviet missile site at Mariel Naval Port, Cuba, November 8, 1962.

Khrushchev's decision to shoot down the plane rather than Castro's. In last-minute negotiations, Khrushchev (who had not ordered the attack) and Kennedy were able to strike a deal that prevented further military escalation: Soviet missiles would be removed from Cuba in return for the *unpublicized* removal of missiles from Turkey. And the United States agreed to leave Castro alone.

Castro was angry about the entire course of events. Although Khrushchev had placed forty-two nuclear weapons in Cuba, he never entrusted Castro with control over any of them. Nor did he consult Castro at all during the thirteen days of negotiations. Khrushchev made it clear to Castro that he and his country were simply pawns in the larger game of the Cold War. And from that perspective, the Cuban Missile Crisis revealed just how dangerous that game had become. EXCOMM had significantly underestimated Soviet military capabilities in Cuba and overestimated Khrushchev's desire for direct conflict with the United States. Furthermore, the Cuban Missile Crisis made it apparent to everyone that the potential nuclear annihilation of the world rested in the temperaments of a few men, their interpretations of one another's actions, and flawed and incomplete intelligence gathering. Both Kennedy and Khrushchev realized how close they had come to a nuclear exchange, and the pair began working toward agreements such as the 1963 Test Ban Treaty and the 1968 Non-Proliferation Treaty in an attempt to limit the potential damage of nuclear weapons research and testing. In this so-called Cold War, a single miscalculation or misinterpretation could be catastrophic.

Conclusions

Khrushchev viewed the West as a rival to be defeated rather than an evil entity to be destroyed. While he certainly engaged in endeavors to expand communism and denounce democracy and capitalism, he believed that communism would naturally defeat the West because the people would prefer it. This peaceful coexistence approach changed the nature of the Cold War. The cohesion of the communist ideology began to fall apart—first with the revolutions in the satellite states that believed they could craft their own versions of communism, then with the outright Sino-Soviet split in 1960 that opened the door for a relationship between the United States and the PRC. But Castro's popular revolution in Cuba, and both the U.S. and Soviet reactions to it, reminded everyone that the number-one priority for each of the superpowers was to expand its sphere of influence. And the Cuban Missile Crisis, perhaps the hottest period of the Cold War, demonstrated that each side would pay *almost* any cost to win.

WORKING WITH THE THEMES

THE EFFECTS OF TECHNOLOGY What was Khrushchev trying to prove in the "Kitchen Debate"? How did the U-2 spy plane incident affect intelligence gathering? Why were Soviet nuclear missiles a bigger threat to the United States when placed in Cuba?

CHANGING IDENTITIES What did Khrushchev hope to gain with "de-Stalinization"? Did he succeed? What effect did it have on nationalism in the satellite states? Why were the Cuban people willing to follow Castro, even into communism?

SHIFTING BORDERS What were the short- and long-term consequences of the Berlin Wall? Why did the United States believe that World War III would begin in Berlin?

GLOBALIZATION Why did Khrushchev support "peaceful coexistence"? Did it change the Cold War as he hoped? How might the U.S. embargo and quarantine of Cuba affect its image across Latin America?

Further Reading

TO FIND OUT MORE

Stalin's Death. 1953. Available online at http://stalin.narod.ru/

Senate Chancellery Berlin: Berliner Mauer, 1961–1989. Available online at http://www.berlin.de/mauer/index.en.html

MATRIX, the Center for Humane Arts, Letters and Social Sciences Online: Seventeen Moments in Soviet History—1954, 1956, 1961. Available online at http://www.soviethistory.org/

John F. Kennedy Presidential Library and Museum: The World on the Brink. Available online at http://microsites.jfklibrary.org/cmc/

GO TO THE SOURCE

The Current Digest of the Soviet Press: Government Announcement. Available online at http://chnm.gmu.edu/worldhistorysources/sources/stalinsdeath.html

Alexander Solzhenitsyn: *One Day in the Life of Ivan Denisovich* (1962)

Nikita S. Khrushchev: On Peaceful Coexistence (Foreign Affairs, October 1959)

Latin American Network Information Center/University of Texas at Austin: Castro Speech Database. Available online at http://lanic.utexas.edu/la/cb/cuba/castro.html

National Security Archive/Peter Kornbluh (ed.): Bay of Pigs Declassified: The Secret CIA Report on the Invasion of Cuba (1998)

National Security Archive/Laurence Chang and Peter Kornbluh (eds.): The Cuban Missile Crisis, 1962 (1998)

National Security Archive/Vladislav M. Zubok and Constantine Pleshakov (eds.): Inside the Kremlin's Cold War—From Stalin to Khrushchev (1996)

MySearchLab Connections

Read the **Document** on **mysearchlab.com**

8.1 *Nikita Krushchev's Secret Speech.* In 1956, Khrushchev delivered a speech to the Communist Party of the Soviet Union in which he denounced Stalin's crimes against the Soviet people and the 'cult of personality' surrounding Stalin.

8.2 *The Kitchen Debate.* In July 1959, U.S. Vice President Richard Nixon attended the opening of an exhibition in Moscow, hosted by Soviet Premier Nikita Khrushchev. The exhibition showcased the latest cultural and technological advances from the U.S. and Soviet Union. Shadowed by the press from both nations, Khrushchev and Nixon engaged in a series of staged conversations, one of which took place in a model U.S. home.

8.3 *Fidel Castro Defends the Revolution.* In July 1953, Fidel Castro's first attempt to overthrow Cuban dictator Fulgencio Batista was a failure. He was put on trial where he delivered his "History Will Absolve Me" speech that explained his vision for a post-Revolution Cuba.

8.4 *John F. Kennedy and Cuba.* U.S. President Kennedy took a hard line on Communism during his campaign in 1960. After his election, he authorized the disastrous Bay of Pigs invasion of Cuba with the hopes of overthrowing the island's communist dictatorship under Castro.

Watch the **Video** on **mysearchlab.com**

8.1 *Escaping the Berlin Wall*

8.2 *President John F. Kennedy Addresses the Nation*

9 The Problems of Decolonization

CHAPTER OUTLINE

- The Forces behind Decolonization
- Africa
- Southeast Asia
- The Non-Aligned Movement

CHAPTER TIMELINE

1954
France loses Vietnam at Dien Bien Phu
FLN launches war in Algeria
Geneva Conference divides Vietnam

1956
Reunification elections in Vietnam canceled
Civil war erupts in Vietnam

1960
Non-Aligned Movement forms
Sino-Soviet split deepens
Congo wins independence; Lumumba is killed

1961
United States and USSR develop ABMs
Bay of Pigs invasion fails
Berlin Wall is built

1963
Diem is assassinated
Kennedy is assassinated
Organization of African Unity is created

1975
Operation Frequent Wind removes last U.S. personnel from Vietnam
Vietnam is reunited under a communist regime

1977
Ogaden War in Africa shakes up the Cold War

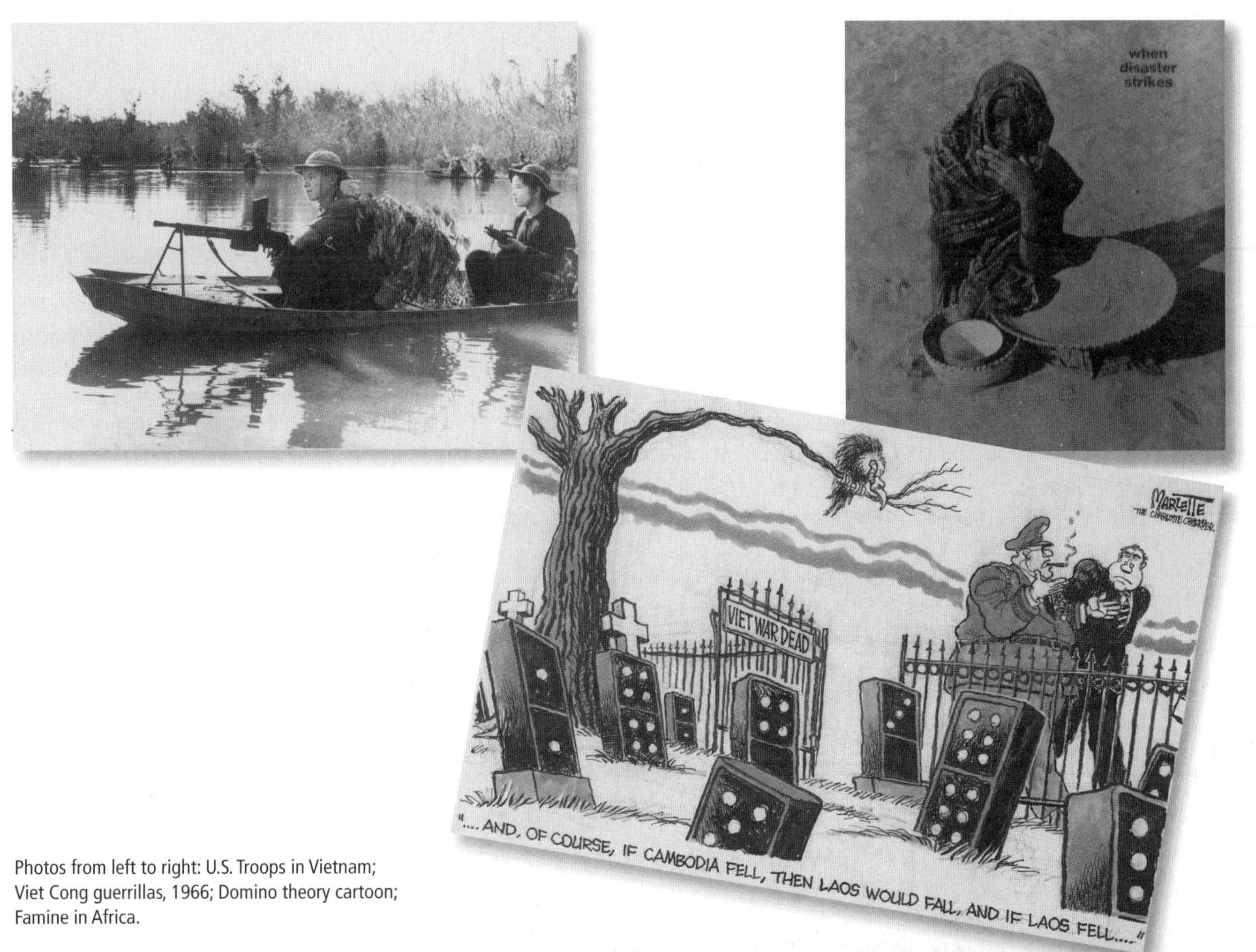

when
disaster
strikes
VIET WAR DEAD
MARLETTE
THE CHARLOTTE OBSERVER
"... AND, OF COURSE, IF CAMBODIA FELL, THEN LAOS WOULD FALL, AND IF LAOS FELL...."

Photos from left to right: U.S. Troops in Vietnam; Viet Cong guerrillas, 1966; Domino theory cartoon; Famine in Africa.

1964	1965	1968	1973	1974
PRC becomes a nuclear power Gulf of Tonkin incident takes place and Congressional Resolution passes	The first U.S. ground troops arrive in Vietnam	Nuclear Non-Proliferation Treaty (NPT) is signed Nixon is elected U.S. president Tet Offensive, Battle of Khe Sanh, and My Lai Massacre stun the United States	Treaty officially ends the conflict in Vietnam	Haile Selassie is overthrown by Marxists in Ethiopia Nixon resigns as U.S. president

The pressure on imperial powers to decolonize, which Woodrow Wilson first applied at the Paris Peace Conference of 1919, continued to grow as the century pressed on. In the years following World War II, the combination of internal (nationalist) and external (UN) demands for independence proved too powerful for most colonizers to resist, although the process of decolonization would be long and difficult, exacerbated by the Cold War. Former colonies provided the most fertile ground for proxy battles because their leaders were particularly susceptible to competing ideologies (after years of having their national identities defined for them) and in desperate need of money to establish their governments and build infrastructure for their nations. From 1945 to 1960, three dozen independent states were created in Asia and Africa out of former colonies, in part because the Charter of the United Nations made self-determination an international priority. By the end of the Cold War, eighty colonies had earned their freedom but not necessarily their independence. The process of decolonization in the competitive Cold War environment was fraught with violence, and it left a legacy of long-term political, economic and social devastation.

WORKING WITH THE THEMES

THE EFFECTS OF TECHNOLOGY Technological superiority is no match for old-fashioned guerilla warfare in Vietnam, the most bloody proxy battle of the Cold War.

CHANGING IDENTITIES The deep internal divisions forged by colonial policies cannot be easily overcome, even with UN support. Decolonization becomes a long and bloody process across Asia and Africa.

SHIFTING BORDERS As decolonization proceeds, new countries are pulled into the Cold War spheres of influence. Vietnam is divided in half to prevent conflict between superpowers.

GLOBALIZATION The "domino theory" leads the superpowers to directly intervene in Asia. The Non-Aligned Movement attempts to restructure the international arena during the Cold War.

The Forces behind Decolonization

The shape the Cold War took early on was as much a consequence of the post-World War II structure of the world as it was competing ideologies or the arms race. The reality was that two countries emerged from the first half of the twentieth century with relatively equally matched military strength and stable political leadership (albeit through very different methods). The world was bipolar—there were two dominant countries competing to add all the other countries of the world to their spheres of influence.

Patterns of Decolonization

After World War II, the former powerhouses of Europe—the vast British Empire and the technologically advanced Germany—and the potent Japanese Meiji regime were gone. Japan was completely reconfigured to meet U.S. strategic interests, Germany was physically divided in two with a wall down the middle of its capital city, and Great Britain and France were reliant on the United States for reconstruction, trade and military protection. Despite their desire to maintain the benefits derived from their colonies, the countries could no longer afford to administer them. There was enormous financial pressure, particularly on those countries that received U.S. aid through the Marshall Plan, to divest from the colonies and focus on rebuilding themselves. There was also enormous pressure from within the colonies as nationalist movements grew increasingly vocal and violent. The democratic values espoused in the UN Charter simply did not extend to them as colonies, and they demanded independence.

The British and French took very different approaches to the decolonization process. Whereas the fairly stable government of Great Britain preferred to negotiate reforms that gradually led toward independence (India and Ireland), the fragile French Fourth Republic, with its many ideologically driven political parties, refused to even consider losing the territory, resources and pride that its colonies provided. As a result, nationalist movements in French colonies often led to drawn-out, violent civil wars (Algeria and the Congo). And the territories where the colonial government had been defeated (either in World War II or by an internal revolution) suffered an entirely different fate at the hands of the United Nations in the Cold War world—they were divided into separate entities that better reflected the political desires of the superpowers than the nationalist realities of the territories (Korea and Vietnam).

Decolonization unfolded in the latter half of the twentieth century in many different ways but never in isolation from the nations within the region or the larger global context. The process was driven by multiple layers of influences, all interacting with one another to achieve their interests: grassroots nationalists, religious and ideological extremists, power-hungry leaders, transnational corporations, and international organizations.

The Role of the United Nations

When the United Nations was established in 1945, about one-third of the world's population lived under the direct rule of a colonial power. This ran counter to the democratic ideals espoused in the UN Charter. As Article II of the charter states: "The Organization is based on the principle of the sovereign equality of all its Members." So important was this concept of sovereign equality that Chapters XI, XII and XIII (Articles 73–91) of the charter deal specifically with the process of helping "non-self-governing territories" evolve into independent, democratic nation-states.

To assist in the process, the United Nations established an international trusteeship system, overseen by one of the main organs of the United Nations, the Trusteeship Council. For a former colony to qualify for the trusteeship system and aid from the United Nations, it had to be a territory that was never released from its League of Nations mandate, a colony of an enemy state from World War II, or a territory that was voluntarily placed in the system by its colonizer. The system sounded wonderful—the Trusteeship Council would help former colonies develop self-government based on their own cultures. But the Trusteeship Council was made up of the five permanent members of the Security Council—the United States, the USSR, China (under Chiang Kai-Shek), Great Britain and France. As a consequence, decisions were frequently made in the best interests of the superpowers and geostrategic positioning rather than the former colonies (for example, Korea).

By 1960, UN membership had doubled, and two-thirds of the new states were former colonies that struggled through the often-violent process of decolonization. In their experience, decolonization was taking too long and was not being administered in the best interests of the colonized peoples. Their presence in the United Nations shifted the power structure of the General Assembly, where a dedication to sovereign equality means each country's vote counts the same. In December 1960, the UN General Assembly passed Resolution 1514 (XV), the *Declaration on the Granting of Independence to Colonial Countries and People*, which proclaimed that all people have a right to self-determination (as opposed to it simply being a principle that ought to apply) and that colonialism should be brought to a "speedy and unconditional end." The declaration stressed that when a newly independent country was created, its structure had to be determined by the freely expressed wishes of its people. Anything else was a fundamental violation of human rights. In 1961, the General Assembly formed a special committee on decolonization with expanded membership (twenty-four), including many former colonies.

MAKE THE CONNECTION

- What effect did decolonization have on the structures and processes of the United Nations?
- What effect did decolonization have on decision making and power within the United Nations?

The Cold War Effect

While the process of decolonization was different for every colony depending on many factors—who colonized it, its natural resources, geostrategic positioning, and the degree of internal ethnic and/or religious unity—it almost never happened peacefully. In some countries, the colonizer refused to give up control, utilizing military and/or economic power to maintain supremacy. In others, the colonizer left peacefully, but there were internal disagreements about

...If Indochina falls, Thailand is put in an almost impossible position. The same is true of Malaya with its rubber and tin. The same is true of Indonesia. If this whole part of South East Asia goes under Communist domination or Communist influence, Japan, who trades and must trade with this area in order to exist must inevitably be oriented towards the Communist regime.

—Richard Nixon, December 1953

who should rule. Add to that the financial and military intervention of the world's superpowers, and the result was usually violent. A few newly independent states were able to establish stable governments and economies, but most suffered from years of civil war under a string of dictatorships, many of them financially supported by either the USSR or the United States.

The dilemma for the United States was particularly sticky because, by definition, democracy means allowing people to choose their own governments. But what if the United States freed a country from colonial status and the USSR moved in and fostered a communist revolution or direct takeover? Or worse yet, what if the people had the right to vote and they did not vote for democracy? And ideology aside, the natural resources and geostrategic position of many of the colonies were too important to risk letting them fall under enemy control. That is why they were colonized in the first place, and just because the war was now a "cold" one did not make those economic resources any less valuable to the West. Because the bipolar Cold War competition meant that a country could be *either* in the Soviet sphere of influence *or* in the American sphere of influence, losing access to a territory meant it would probably end up with the enemy, taking its resources and goods with it.

Despite the rhetoric of self-determination and democracy coming out of the United Nations, it was vital to both superpowers that they maintain economic, military and ideological control over every bit of territory they could. And an infant country struggling to establish stability was the ideal place to launch a battle by proxy.

Africa

The legacy of colonization is most markedly seen in Africa. By 1965, most of the colonizers were gone, but it would take until 1980 for all of the former colonies to pull themselves together enough to be recognized as independent states (by 1975 there were forty-five independent states, and by 1980 there were fifty-one). What happened during those years—the process of becoming independent states—as well as where they stand today is all a direct result of colonization.

As colonists, the African people were discriminated against, exploited and purposely uneducated; and the great majority of them were kept out of participating in government in any meaningful way. But when the colonizers needed help during the two world wars, they relied heavily on their colonies for troops and raw materials. After the Great War when Wilson began talking about self-determination, many colonists felt that they had earned respect and the right to sovereign equality. European resistance to granting them independence was certainly based on the economic losses they would incur in doing so, but there were also more practical problems. The goal for the colonizers was to gain tangible material and economic benefits from their colonies, not to teach the Africans how to develop stable democratic governments or coordinate economic production. Political boundaries were not drawn according to ethnicity, which made it difficult to establish cohesive nations. Just as the colonization of Africa was based on the economic interests of Europe in the late 1800s, so too was the urgency of decolonization in the 1950s and '60s.

Under pressure from the United Nations as WWII ended, Great Britain started considering how to transition its African colonies to independence. In fact, Roosevelt had included a clause in the Atlantic Charter requiring them to do so. France, Belgium and Portugal were less amenable to UN demands and engaged in violent wars to defeat nationalist revolutions in the colonies. What happened in Algeria and the Congo provide excellent examples of the struggles many African nations faced.

Algeria

The French colonization of Algeria in the 1800s was a long and messy affair, and many Europeans settled there to help defeat the indigenous Muslim Arab population. As they moved in, they dislocated the native population from the productive farmland and claimed

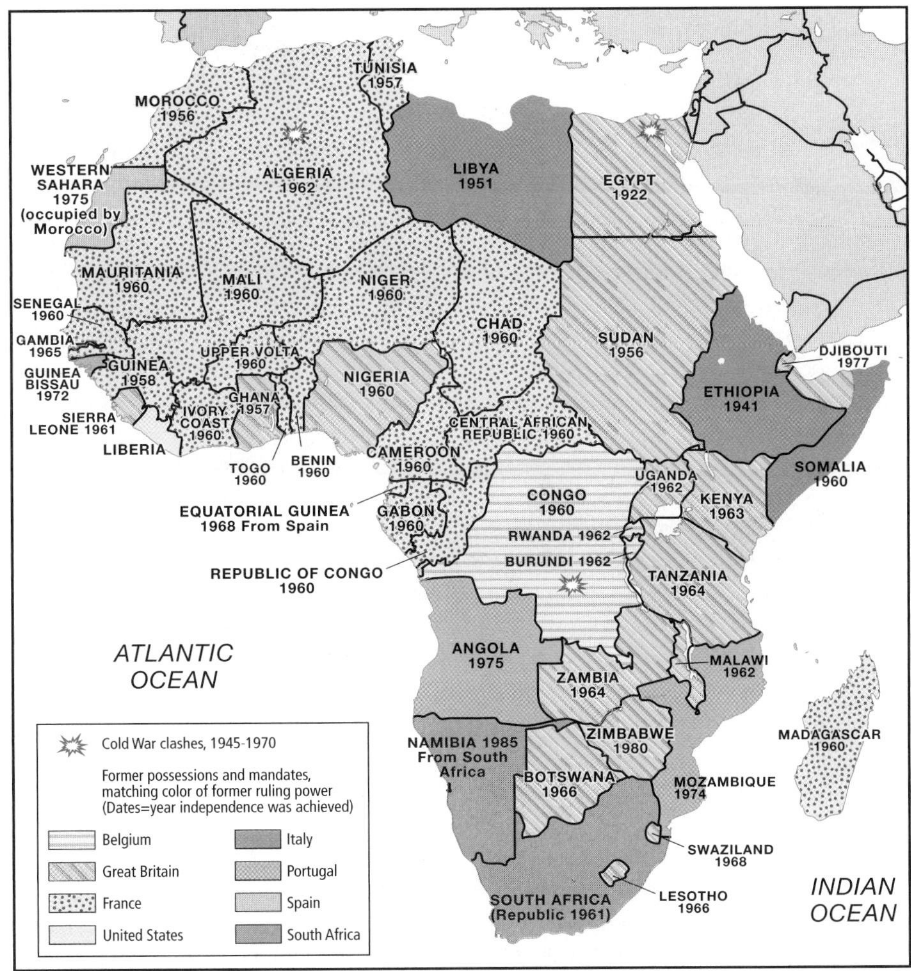

MAP 9.1 The Decolonization of Africa

Algeria as an integral part of France. The colonial government granted all people of European descent in Algeria and the native Sephardi Jews full French citizenship, but it did not extend legal or political rights to the 9 million Muslim Algerians who represented the majority of the population.

In 1954, the same year the French lost control of Vietnam, a Muslim extremist group called the *Front de Libération Nationale* (FLN) in Algeria launched its war for independence. After four years of costly and brutal guerilla warfare, the French government was in crisis and facing a credible military threat from Algeria. France was on the verge of civil war; and to prevent it, newly elected President Charles de Gaulle assured the French settlers in Algeria they would remain part of France while also promising the FLN independence. As the violence raged on, the settlers realized that de Gaulle was likely going to grant the FLN independence in order to save France from war. An extremist settler organization developed and began attacks on Paris (including at least thirty assassination attempts on de Gaulle). With the violence escalating, de Gaulle negotiated an agreement with the FLN that granted Algeria independence in July 1962. More than 1 million French Algerian settlers and Algerian Muslims serving in the French army fled to France, but an estimated 50,000 to 150,000 others were killed by the new FLN-led authoritarian government.

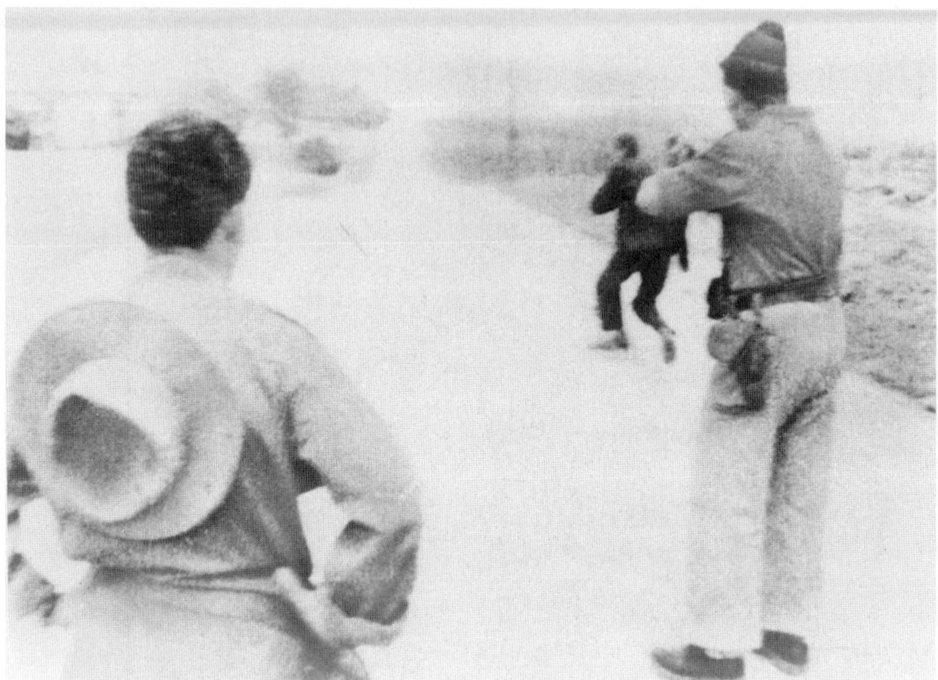

Algeria, August 1955.

Congo

King Leopold II of Belgium personally owned the Congo Free State as a corporate entity from 1878 to 1908, ruthlessly exploiting the Congolese people in order to dominate the rubber and ivory trade. He maintained control through his *Force Publique*, Belgian soldiers and mercenaries from other European countries. Whenever local chiefs tried to organize tribal resistance to Leopold's forced labor policies, the *Force Publique* responded with brutal retaliation. In the early 1900s, European and U.S. media exposed Leopold's treatment of the Congolese, and the Belgian government assumed control of the Congo in 1908. Much of the brutality ended under Belgian control, but forced labor continued as the Belgian Congo became one of the world's leading copper producers in the early twentieth century.

When Belgium was occupied by the Nazis in 1940, the Congo remained loyal to the exiled Belgian government and became the major supplier of rubber and uranium to the Allied war effort. But when World War II ended, the Belgian government reasserted its control over the Congo, and Congolese resistance movements appeared. These efforts were generally nonviolent, and the Belgian government felt no particular pressure to grant Congo independence. In 1955, government officials formulated the *Thirty Year Plan for the Political Emancipation of Belgian Africa,* estimating that it would take that long to create an educated class of Congolese who could successfully run the country. Neither the Belgian government nor the Congolese were satisfied with the plan, and a significantly more radical independence movement appeared in 1958 under the charismatic leadership of Patrice Lumumba. Although he was popular with the Congolese, the Belgian government feared it would lose substantial financial interests through "nationalization" if the leftist Lumumba took control of the Congo.

Congolese frustration reached critical mass in January 1959 with a week of heavy rioting that left several hundred people dead. The Belgian government finally understood that independence would have to be granted but still wanted a gradual and carefully planned process.

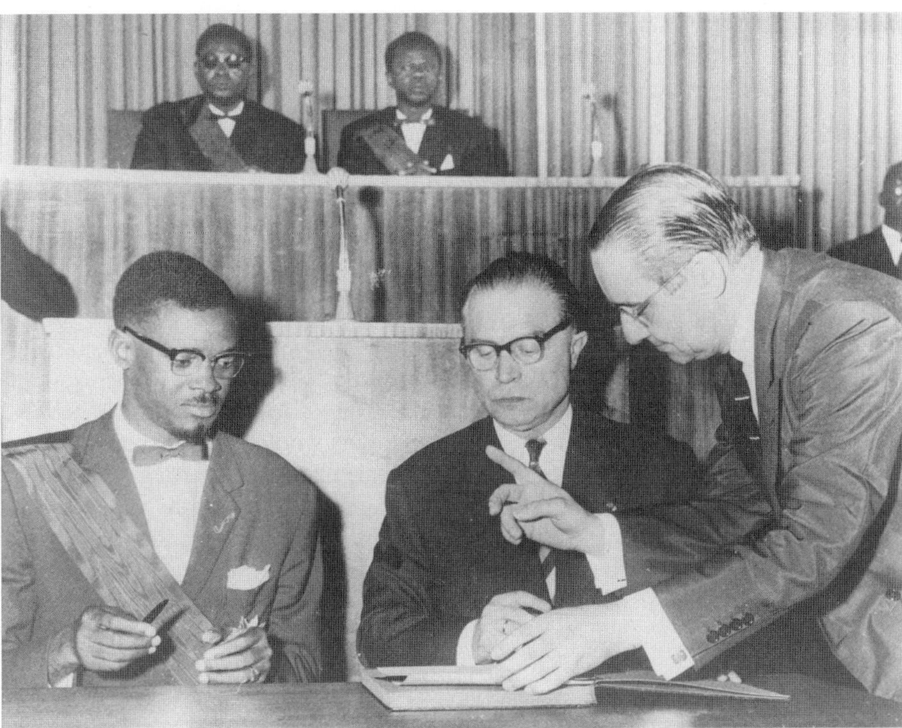

Patrice Lumumba (left) and Belgian Premier Gaston Eyskens (right) both seated at the signing of the independence pact for the Congo, July 6, 1960.

Lumumba was arrested for inciting against the colonial government, which only led to increasingly violent protests. Desperate to avoid a costly and bloody war, the Belgian government granted the Congolese full independence with a general election in May 1960. Lumumba was released from prison and became part of a fragile coalition government.

The Congo achieved independence in June 1960, and less than a week later, Europeans were targeted in violent attacks across the new country. In response, the Belgian army moved in to evacuate 80,000 Belgians still living in the Congo. Lumumba was arrested and murdered with the assistance of the Belgian government and the Central Intelligence Agency (CIA). Ongoing rebellions and separatist movements have required the presence of UN peacekeepers ever since.

So while fierce nationalist movements fueled civil wars in the colonies, defeating the colonial power generally came at a tremendous human cost. And the road between decolonization and independent nation-state was a long and difficult one.

From Independence to Statehood

At the point of decolonization, most African states were fundamentally European creations that had little to no relationship to African traditions. Their immediate problem was establishing political stability, which was particularly difficult because they had no natural tradition of democracy or any experience running a government. Before they were colonies, most functioned as tribal-held territories. One of the most important tactics colonizers used to assert their control and prevent uprisings was to exacerbate the natural tribal divisions under the policy of "**divide and rule.**" Tribal allegiance, made more intense by decades of colonial favoritism for some, was a major problem for a potential government to overcome. New governments faced incredible challenges in creating democratic institutions to reach out and overcome tribalism because their populations were largely illiterate and had no concept of representative government.

divide and rule
a political, economic and military strategy to prevent small groups from linking together to form a larger, more powerful group

There were many other divisions within national populations that created obstacles in developing new governments. In African states where individuals or European corporations owned lucrative oilfields and mines (particularly in southern Africa), those people stayed even after their governments had decolonized the territories. So there was a small minority of whites who basically controlled the economy and held onto political power, and they continued to discriminate against the majority black population through **apartheid.** Religion also created problems, with ongoing conflict between Muslims (much of northern Africa) and Orthodox Christians. Geography and climate were also major obstacles. How do you create economic self-sufficiency in the face of drought, desertification and famine? And it was incredibly difficult to establish transportation and communication lines from one end of a country to the next across the world's largest deserts (and with little money to purchase technology). Even when new governments were able to open lines of communication, schools, and a free press, which of Africa's 750 different languages should be used to reach the people?

apartheid
social and political policy of racial segregation and discrimination enforced by white minority governments in South Africa from 1948 to 1994

Watch the Video *Creating Apartheid in South Africa* on mysearchlab.com

Creating a stable, independent state under these conditions would be challenging for any government, but it was particularly difficult for former colonies that were starting with serious disadvantages. In southern African nations, apartheid maintained political, economic and social stability by extending colonial control. Many new governments in northern African nations sought regional support, getting involved in the tensions of the Middle East. Because it was the Cold War, some tried to establish socialist regimes, seeking financial assistance from the USSR.

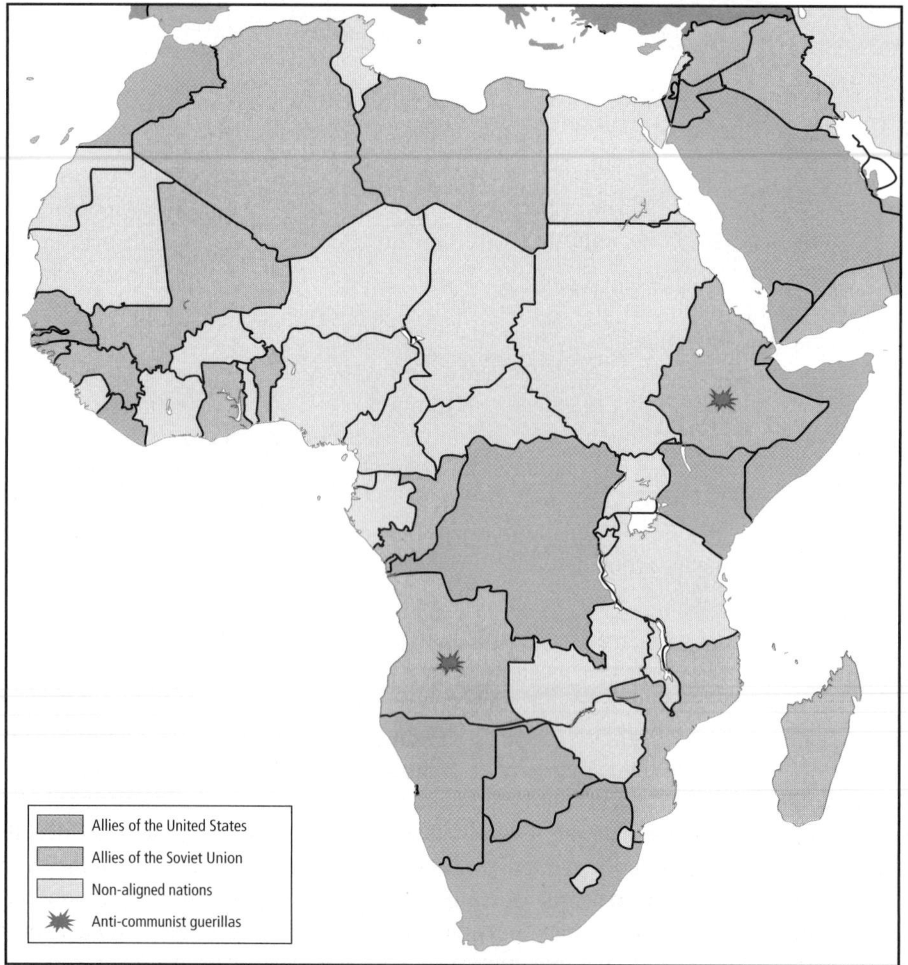

MAP 9.2 Africa during the Cold War

Others tried democracy, unifying under the only thing the people had in common—anticolonialism. Most attempts at democracy quickly turned into a "one-party state" after multiple political parties led to civil war. Only a handful of African leaders were able to establish stable governments in the early Cold War years.

No matter what the initial nationalist governments tried, they could not successfully unite the people under one government, create economic self-sufficiency, and solve the societal problems that come with rapid industrialization. Beginning in the 1960s, a wave of *coups d'état* against nationalist governments swept across Africa—in twenty-five years, more than seventy leaders were overthrown in twenty-nine different countries. Most of these coups were carried out by military leaders who saw strong control (created through fear) as the only way to unite people and create stability. The military was the only institution people respected (feared), which gave these new military dictators, who often called themselves "presidents," a whole lot of power. The result was significant political corruption, violence and outright genocide in a few cases. Civil war was the norm, and it was particularly exacerbated by the Cold War rivalry between the United States and the USSR.

Somalia versus Ethiopia

Of the many examples of how Cold War politics shaped the process of independence for African nations, the Ogaden War of 1977 and 1978 demonstrates it most clearly. Colonization, tribalism, nationalism, territorial disputes and Soviet weapons came together to ignite a war between Somalia and Ethiopia.

In the colonial era, the territory of Somalia was divided between Ethiopia, Italy, Great Britain and France. In 1948, Great Britain gave some of that territory (good grazing land) to Ethiopia, but it was not until June 1960 that Great Britain relinquished control of the colony of Somalialand. On July 1, Somalialand was reunited with the former Italian colonial holding in the south, creating the Republic of Somalia. Somalia did not, however, regain a lot of its former territory, including the pieces that went to the neighboring country of Ethiopia. Political and tribal instability in Somalia led to a military coup in 1969, which gave way to a one-party socialist regime in 1976 that was supported by the USSR.

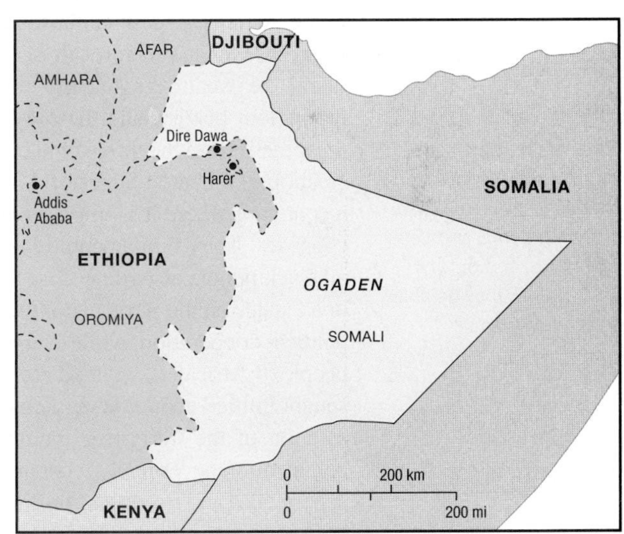

MAP 9.3 The Ogaden War

One of the oldest countries in the world, Ethiopia maintained its independence throughout most of its history, with the notable exception of Mussolini's occupation from 1936 to 1941. It was ruled (and had been since 1916) by Haile Selassie, who received millions of dollars in aid from Great Britain and the United States. But in 1974, a military Marxist coup called the Derg overthrew Emperor Selassie with the aid of the USSR. The Derg turned against the United States, closing the U.S. embassy in Ethiopia and ending the influx of U.S. financial aid, which led to economic upheaval, drought and famine. Instead, throughout 1976 and 1977, Ethiopia received increasing amounts of money and military equipment from the USSR. After a meeting between the Derg and Castro, Cuban military troops appeared in Ethiopia. To the Somali government, this could only mean one thing—Ethiopia was going to attack.

By Cold War "rules," Somalia and Ethiopia should have been allies. They were both ruled by communist regimes and sat firmly in the Soviet sphere of influence. But tribal differences and age-old territorial disputes between the Somalis and the Ethiopians overrode that communist connection, something the Soviets could never understand. The Somali government was actually angry at the USSR for helping Ethiopia and requested equal military support to wage a war against its tribal enemy and regain its rightful land.

The USSR tried to convince the Somali and Ethiopian leaders to work together to solidify Soviet control in eastern Africa but could not negotiate an agreement. Somalia decided to seek help elsewhere, but the United States would not openly support a communist country. Still, President Jimmy Carter was angry about losing Ethiopia to the Soviets and worked through his ally Saudi Arabia to provide $200 million in aid to Somalia in May 1977. Fearful of arming a communist country, Carter stopped short of providing military support.

Undeterred, the Somali government used its own military and recruited guerrilla volunteers to launch an invasion of Ethiopia on July 23, 1977. The Ethiopians were truly surprised, and the Somalis seized ten major towns in Ogaden within a few days. But the Soviet-supported Ethiopian counter-offensive in November, which included both Cuban and Russian soldiers, was powerful. By March 1978, all Somali troops were pushed back into their own country; however, the USSR forced Ethiopian troops to stop at the border rather than risk World War III.

As a proxy battle, the Ogaden War was somewhat of a draw: the USSR lost Somalia as an ally, but it gained Ethiopia. And although the United States could not openly support a communist government, Somalia did operate within its sphere of influence. This war, combined with events taking place in the Middle East, was confusing to the superpowers that saw the world in black and white. Countries could be either communist and fall within the Soviet sphere of influence or democratic and fall within the U.S. sphere of influence. Decolonization created many new countries that did not like either choice.

African Unity

Some African leaders came to believe (with good reason) that their problems establishing stable countries were a direct result of colonialism, and the Cold War conflict was only exacerbating it. To them, the wealthy countries of the East and West had used and exploited the African people throughout history, and the only way to break this cycle was to unite. Seizing on a philosophical movement from the turn of the century known as **Pan-Africanism,** the African leaders called for the creation of a United States of Africa. This would obviously be easier said than done, particularly on a continent where it is impossible to even pull together a few million people to form single, stable countries. They fundamentally disagreed on exactly who would be unified under Pan-Africanism: all black people of African descent, all people living on the African continent (including nonblacks), or all states on the African continent? Continental Pan-Africanism focused on the unity of states and political cooperation, while Diaspora Pan-Africanism demanded racial unity for black Africans and people of African descent all around the world. Others wanted unity for religious reasons, and others sought unified economic agreements. The tangible result of the Pan-Africanism movement was the creation of the thirty-two member Organization of African Unity (OAU) in May 1963, but the organization never really went anywhere in terms of creating unity. Different countries had different experiences and needs and thus pursued different paths. True African unity has been made impossible because of political instability, corrupt governments, social unrest, and abject poverty—all long-term consequences of colonialism.

Pan-Africanism
a philosophy espousing that African people share common bonds and objectives, and only by unifying will they be able to achieve them

Southeast Asia

Read the Document *American Objectives in Southeast Asia* on mysearchlab.com

The problems associated with decolonization in Southeast Asia were intricately linked to the manner in which the colonies were originally established throughout the sixteenth to early twentieth centuries. As European governments searched for trade markets in the East, the many islands and diverse inhabitants of Southeast Asia were united under the colonial empires of Portugal, Spain, Holland, France, England, Japan and the United States. The islands were continually redistributed as the imperial powers fought and defeated one another to control the lucrative natural resources and trade routes. On the eve of World War II, the dominant powers in the region were French Indochina (Vietnam, Laos and Cambodia) and Dutch-controlled Indonesia, but the United States had established a foothold in the Philippines in an attempt to limit Japan's increasingly aggressive imperialism in the Pacific. During the war, Japan seized

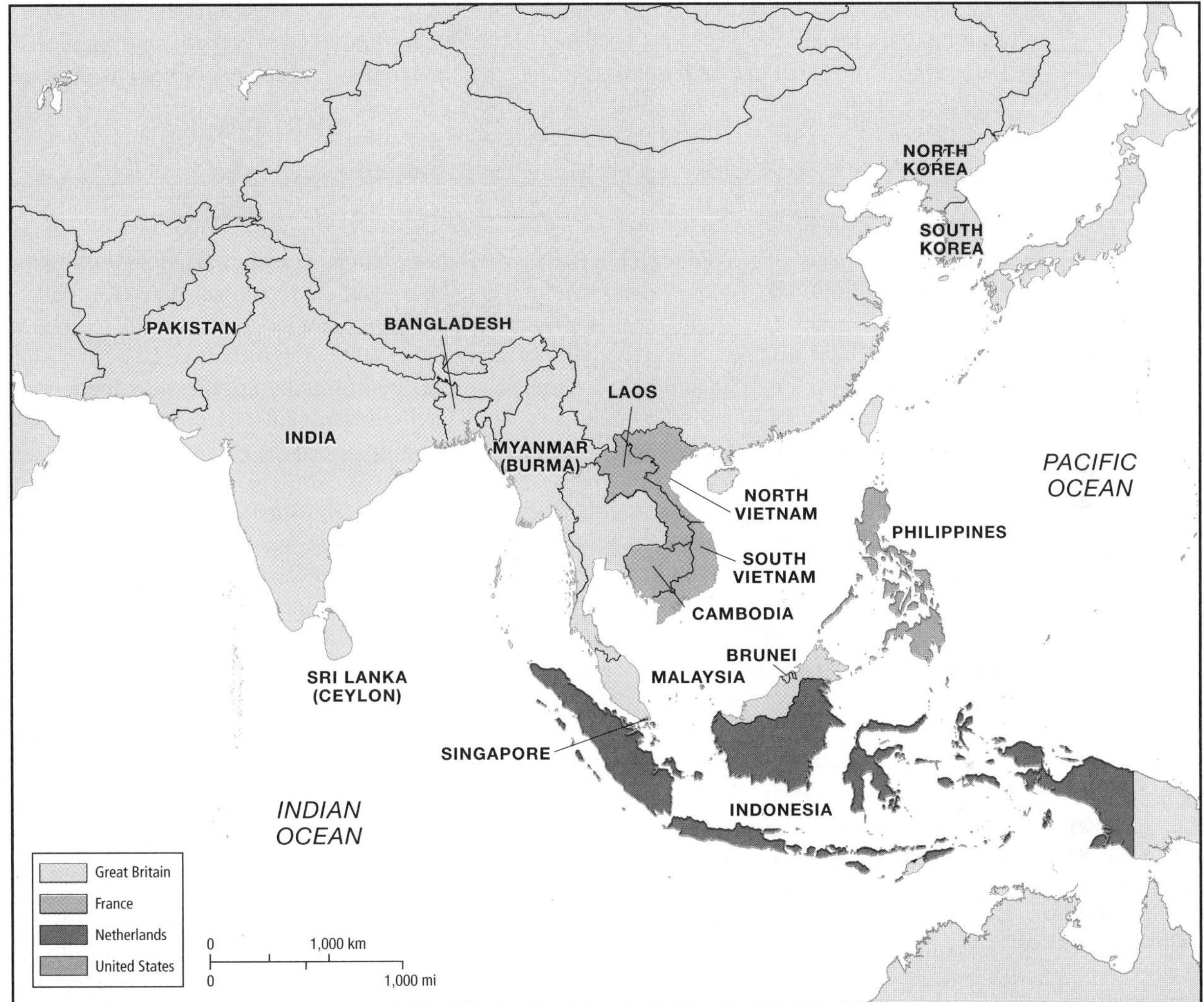

MAP 9.4 Southeast Asia

control of much of Southeast Asia and ruled by military force, sparking particularly violent resistance movements in Burma, Malaya, Indonesia and Indochina.

As a result of the many cultural impositions on the diverse indigenous people over the centuries, the decolonization process created disputes and outright wars over territorial borders, political legitimacy, resource distribution, ethnicity and religion. Unlike Africa, where there was no clear regional power to move in and fill the void left by decolonization, the USSR, Japan and China were all struggling for control in the region. Decolonization happened quickly after World War II, and these regional conflicts grew into devastating wars because of U.S., Soviet and Chinese intervention. The people of Southeast Asia were used to fighting—first against European imperialists, then against Japan—and were prepared to defend themselves against Cold War domination as well. Two case studies provide detailed insight into the high stakes of Southeast Asian decolonization in regional and global contexts.

Indonesia

Consisting of 3,600 islands spanning 3,000 miles of ocean, Indonesia is the largest country in Southeast Asia. The Dutch established control over the economy of the larger islands in the early 1600s and gradually extended their borders under authoritarian colonial rule in the 1800s. They exploited the natural resources of the islands, generating significant wealth for the Dutch economy but creating further divisions between the different ethnic and socioeconomic groups in Indonesia. In the late nineteenth century, the Dutch conquered the entire East Indies and built extensive communication and transportation systems to link their empire together in a very efficient and modern economic machine. Of course, all wealth went to the Netherlands, and the standard of living for the Indonesian people remained low.

Nationalist movements appeared in the early twentieth century, certainly as a result of economic discontent, but also largely driven by the desire to restore traditional Indonesian culture. Political movements such as the "Noble Endeavour," the "Islamic Association," the Indies Party, and a Soviet-sponsored Comintern pressured the Dutch government to allow them to participate. Because these groups all had different goals, tensions between them led to revolts that the Dutch easily quelled. But in 1926, a nationalist movement developed around the one basic thing all Indonesians believed in—the struggle for independence. Led by Sukarno, this new Indonesian Nationalist Party had a broad base of support. The Dutch arrested and exiled Sukarno, and the Indonesian Nationalist Party split apart without his leadership.

In May 1940, Holland was occupied by Nazi Germany as World War II began in Europe. Two years later, Japan invaded Indonesia and expelled the Dutch. But Japan's primary interest in the region was obtaining the resources it needed to feed its war machine, and 25 percent of its oil supply came from Indonesia. The Japanese saw themselves as liberators of the Indonesian people and promised them they would establish a nonexploitative economic and cultural arrangement. But that arrangement was established by a militaristic regime in the midst of a major war, so it was not exactly a peaceful one. The needs of the Japanese military came first, so food and necessary supplies were sent to them at the peril of the Indonesian people. Between 4 and 10 million people were sent to forced labor camps to work on defense construction projects, reinvigorating the Indonesian independence movement. As the Japanese began to lose in the Pacific war, they increasingly worked closely with the nationalist leadership of Indonesia to mobilize the people for the war effort. Sukarno viewed it as an opportunity for independence once the war was over; the Japanese government viewed it as a way to create more problems for the Allies.

In August 1945, just two days after the Japanese surrendered, Sukarno declared independence and became president of Indonesia. The Netherlands tried to reassert its colonial rule but gave up in 1949 under pressure from the United Nations. To maintain unity in the large and diverse country, Sukarno established an authoritarian government led by military rule, but he also allowed the Communist Party to exist. Frustrated by the restrictions of Cold War politics, Sukarno was a founder of the Non-Aligned Movement in 1960. A coup attempt against Sukarno in 1965 resulted in the death of 500,000 to 1 million people; and the head of the military, General Suharto, replaced Sukarno in 1968 with the support of the U.S. government. Suharto maintained a corrupt, authoritarian regime until 1998.

Vietnam

No case study exemplifies the complex intersection of decolonization and the Cold War as clearly as what happened in the former French colony of Indochina (Cambodia, Laos and Vietnam). Vietnam was a colony of France until Ho Chi Minh organized a nationalist revolution. The First Indochina War lasted for eight years, ending in summer 1954 with a crushing defeat for the French at the battle of Dien Bien Phu. Despite the United Nations' push for decolonization, the United States financially supported France during the war to help it maintain control of its colonies in Indochina. The Cold War was on, and Ho Chi Minh was receiving aid from both the USSR and the PRC. There was every reason for the United States to believe that Vietnam would become a communist country under Ho Chi Minh's leadership.

Geneva Conference 1954 meeting of the USSR, the PRC, the United States, France, Great Britain and French Indochina to deal with decolonization—the United States refused to sign the resulting agreement

Even as the Battle of Dien Bien Phu raged on, the **Geneva Conference** was convened in spring 1954 to figure out what to do with the former colonies of French Indochina. Cambodia

Sukarno in Washington, D.C., 1956.

and Laos were granted full independence and established constitutional monarchies, but there was disagreement over Vietnam. The West would agree to grant independence to a democratic regime, and the East, of course, wanted to ensure that Ho Chi Minh could establish his communist regime. The two sides were at an impasse, so, like Korea and Berlin before it, Vietnam was divided at the 17th parallel by a "provisional military demarcation line." The Vietminh retreated north of the ceasefire line, and the Vietnamese military, which had supported the French, stayed south of it. Both regrouped while awaiting the reunification of the country as the Geneva Agreements promised. Foreign militaries were ordered to leave Vietnam, and an International Control Commission consisting of India, Poland and Canada was established to make sure all parties followed the rules, but the commission had no power to take action if they did not. The Geneva Agreements made it very clear that the division of Vietnam was a temporary one designed only to prevent further military aggression while the country prepared for a democratic election (supervised by the United Nations) to be held in July 1956. When the Vietnamese people chose their government in a nationwide election, the country would be reunited.

Read the Document *"The Final Declaration on Indochina"* on mysearchlab.com

Immediately, a large-scale migration took place. Roughly 1 million civilians moved to the south, and about 52,000 went north. While the communist leadership remained in the north, many communist supporters were told to remain in the south to affect the outcome of the elections. In the meantime, the United States, the USSR and the PRC consistently violated the Geneva Agreements. In North Vietnam, the USSR and the PRC supported Ho Chi Minh's government and the North Vietnamese Regular Army (NVA). In South Vietnam, the United States stepped in to fill the political void left by the French. The CIA supported a nonviolent coup by Prime Minister Ngo Dinh Diem over Emperor Bao Dai by rigging a referendum vote in October 1955 in which Diem won 98 percent of the vote (133 percent in the city of Saigon). The United States also helped build the Army of the Republic of Vietnam (ARVN) in the south. To combat Diem's regime, communist civilians who remained in South Vietnam put together the Vietcong (VC), which was militarily supported by the NVA.

Read the Document *Ho Chi Minh on Self Determination* on mysearchlab.com

ANALYSIS

How did the wording of the Geneva Agreements affect Soviet and American actions in the late 1950s and early 1960s?

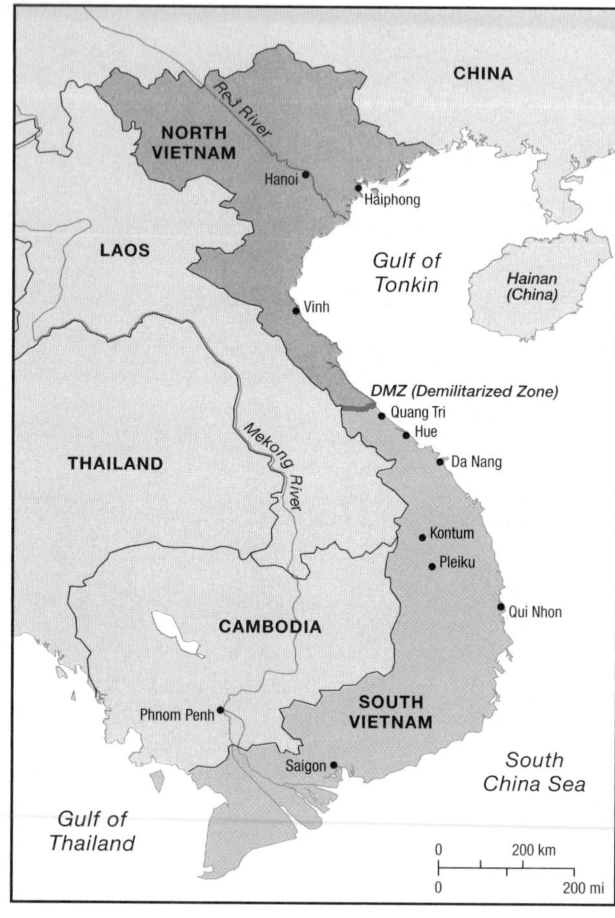

MAP 9.5 Vietnam in 1956

Despite the best efforts of the South Vietnamese government and the United States, most people in Vietnam, both north and south, loved Ho Chi Minh. He was their George Washington—he successfully led the revolutionary movement to free them from colonial oppression. To the Vietnamese, Ho Chi Minh was a nationalist looking out for the Vietnamese people, while the United States obviously was trying to recolonize them by separating them and establishing a puppet regime in South Vietnam. By the summer of 1956, it was clear that, if democratic, free elections were held, the people would vote for Ho Chi Minh, who would establish a communist regime in the reunited Vietnam.

Diem was not anxious to hold an election that would end his political career. And with the U.S. foreign policy commitment to containment and President Eisenhower's belief in the **domino theory,** there was no way the United States could allow Vietnam to reunite under a communist government. In 1956, with the full backing of the United States, Diem canceled the reunification election under the premise that the Republic of Vietnam (his government) did not sign the Geneva Agreements and was, therefore, not legally bound to uphold it. Ho Chi Minh's reaction was swift and violent—he ordered the VC to launch guerrilla attacks against the Diem regime. Several thousand communist infiltrators moved to South Vietnam to join the VC, and they created a rival political party, the National Liberation Front. Ho Chi Minh was determined to reunite Vietnam, and he ignited a civil war to accomplish it. Because it was the Cold War, that civil war was fueled by the United States, the USSR and the PRC and became the Second Indochina War.

... the military demarcation line is provisional and should not in any way be interpreted as constituting a political or territorial boundary (Article 6)

domino theory
if one country in southeast Asia became communist (Vietnam), the rest would follow (Laos, Cambodia, Thailand, Burma, Malaysia and Indonesia)

North Vietnam

Ho Chi Minh established his single-party government in the city of Hanoi. His primary concern was a nationalist one—reuniting Vietnam—but enacting communist policies was a close second. Ho Chi Minh's regime was brutal for citizens who did not hold the same values—tens of thousands of dissenters and landowners were imprisoned and executed as he strengthened his political authority and embarked on radical land reforms. Minh's many years serving the Comintern throughout Europe and Asia taught him how to balance the USSR and the PRC, so even as the relationship between the two fell apart in 1960, Minh was able to retain the financial and military support of both. His military was led by Vo Nguyen Giap, and it excelled at utilizing guerrilla tactics against the regular militaries of the French and Americans.

South Vietnam

The political situation in South Vietnam was much more complicated. The United States supported the regime of President Diem, who was really an autocratic leader rather than a democratic one, but he was an anti-communist. Where Ho Chi Minh and his supporters were focused on reuniting Vietnam, the goal for Diem and the United States was simply to prevent South Vietnam from becoming communist. U.S. President Kennedy sent 16,000 advisors (mostly diplomats, CIA and Special Forces troops) to help Diem hold on, but they faced stiff opposition. There were tens of thousands of communists in the south who carried out assassinations against

Eisenhower and Ngo Dinh Diem.

local government officials (growing from 1,200 in 1959 to 4,000 in 1961). And Diem's brutality turned many anticommunists in the south against him as well. As the political arm of the Viet Cong, the National Liberation Front was a very active anti-Diem alliance of communists, moderate political parties and religious groups.

...Finally, you have broader considerations that might follow what you would call the "falling domino" principle. You have a row of dominoes set up, you knock over the first one, and what will happen to the last one is the certainty that it will go over very quickly. So you could have a beginning of a disintegration that would have the most profound influences...

—Dwight D. Eisenhower, April 7, 1957

Like Eisenhower before him, Kennedy believed in the domino theory. He was already concerned about the spread of communism into the western hemisphere through Cuba, and he resolved to prevent it from spreading across Asia as well. The question was the best way to do it—could the United States continue to prevent democratic elections because the U.S. government would not like the outcome? Could Kennedy justify supporting a brutal dictator in Diem? And if not, would U.S. troops have to be sent to fight Ho Chi Minh? France and Great Britain, Kennedy's allies on the UN Security Council, made it clear they wanted no part of a war in Vietnam, and the USSR would most certainly veto UN action, so saving South Vietnam from communism would fall to the United States alone. In 1961, the U.S. Joint Chiefs of Staff estimated that it would take 40,000 U.S. troops to defeat both the NVA and the VC, but Kennedy resisted.

martial law
the temporary military takeover of domestic law enforcement

In August 1963, Diem declared **martial law** in South Vietnam and used troops funded by the United States to carry out violent raids against protestors. Kennedy had had enough, and he helped ARVN military officers plan a coup to overthrow Diem's government and send him into exile. On November 1, 1963, a group of Diem's top generals and bodyguards arrested Diem and his brother and then murdered them. The official cause of death for both was "accidental suicide" as they were resisting arrest, though the accompanying photographs clearly showed that their hands were tied. Kennedy was shocked, but given the level of U.S. involvement in the coup, he had no choice but to recognize the new military regime as the legitimate government of South

A document declassified in 2003 shows that torpedo fire "appear(ed) doubtful" and "freak weather effects" on radar and "over-eager" sonarmen were probably the source of the reports because there were "no visual sightings" of enemy ships. (Captain John Herrick, naval commander in the Gulf of Tonkin in August 1964)

Years after the incident, retired Admiral James Stockdale wrote: "There was absolutely no gunfire except our own, no PT boat wakes, not a candle light let alone a burning ship. None could have been there and not have been seen on such a black night...I had the best seat in the house from which to detect boats—if there were any."

In February 1968, the Senate Foreign Relations Committee held investigative hearings, charging that the Defense Department had withheld information and the Gulf of Tonkin Resolution passed because of a "credibility gap."

In 1995, Robert McNamara admitted he lied to Congress.

Vietnam. The people of Saigon initially responded with enthusiasm, but the assassination left the country with no clear leader throughout the war that followed—a series of coups put one ARVN general after another in the president's office.

The Second Indochina War

Within weeks of Diem's murder, President Kennedy was assassinated in the United States. Vice President Lyndon Johnson assumed office determined not to lose Vietnam to the communists. Johnson too feared the potentially disastrous effects of allowing communism to spread in Asia: "If we quit Vietnam, tomorrow we'll be fighting in Hawaii and next week we'll have to be fighting in San Francisco." But he also realized that sending troops to Vietnam would be unpopular with U.S. citizens. Johnson increased reconnaissance to get a better understanding of the NVA's military capabilities, and he initiated OPLAN 34-A, covert naval commando attacks on North Vietnamese targets.

On August 2, 1964, the American destroyer *USS Maddox* exchanged fire with North Vietnamese torpedo boats in the Gulf of Tonkin. The United States claimed the *Maddox* was in international waters simply to exert a U.S. presence; however, declassified documents reveal that the destroyer was there in support of covert raids on North Vietnam occurring at the time. President Johnson warned the NVA not to provoke the United States, and he sent a second destroyer, the *USS Turner Joy*, into the Gulf of Tonkin to back up the *Maddox*. On the night of August 4, both ships reported being under attack and fired back, claiming they sunk two NVA torpedo boats. President Johnson used this second attack to justify retaliatory bombings of North Vietnam, and he went to Congress requesting authority to send U.S. troops to Vietnam. On August 5, 1964, Lyndon Johnson told the U.S. Congress:

> *Our policy in southeast Asia has been consistent and unchanged since 1954: (1) America keeps her word. Here as elsewhere, we must and shall honor our commitments; (2) the issue is the future of southeast Asia as a whole. A threat to any nation in that region is a threat to all, and a threat to us; (3) our purpose is peace. We have no military, political, or territorial ambitions in the area; (4) this is not just a jungle war, but a struggle for freedom on every front of human activity...*

The Senate Foreign Relations Committee and the Armed Services Committee met in a closed session to discuss Johnson's request. There was considerable debate about whether the attacks in the Gulf of Tonkin were unprovoked, but U.S. Secretary of Defense Robert McNamara assured committee members that OPLAN 34-A was a South Vietnamese mission only. Conflicting evidence and a leak from the Pentagon led to a debate over whether the August 4 attack had even occurred. McNamara assured them that it did. Two senators expressed serious concerns about giving the U.S. president the power to effectively wage a war without Congressional oversight, as required by the U.S. Constitution. But after just two days of deliberation, the U.S. Congress overwhelmingly passed the Gulf of Tonkin Resolution—unanimously in the House and 88 to 2 in the Senate. The American people responded to Congress's support with increased confidence in President Johnson—his poll numbers rose from 42 percent to 72 percent, and he was elected president in November with 61 percent of the vote.

Read the Document *The Tonkin Gulf Resolution* on mysearchlab.com

President Johnson viewed Vietnam as a classic battle by proxy. His goal was for U.S. troops to support ARVN so that the South Vietnamese government could defend itself against communism. The situation appeared to shape up this way early on when, in February 1965, the USSR announced it would provide unconditional military support to the North Vietnamese. That month, Johnson initiated Operation Rolling Thunder, an operation that was supposed to be an eight-week bombing campaign by the U.S. air force and navy to demonstrate to Ho Chi Minh and the Soviets that the United States was supporting the south. Johnson thought that a show of the superiority of U.S. airpower would make Ho Chi Minh back off. He did not want to provoke the PRC or the USSR, so there were limits placed on the number of missions flown and the targets they could go after. But Ho Chi Minh was not deterred, and he focused his fight where he had the clear military advantage—on the ground.

Clearing the jungle in Da Nang, Vietnam, May 1970.

On March 8, 1965, the first U.S. ground troops (3,500 marines) landed in South Vietnam at Da Nang. Because of the potential for World War III, U.S. troops were to remain on South Vietnamese soil in a defensive position. Air attacks on North Vietnam escalated, with Operation Flaming Dart and Operation ArcLight added to the ongoing Operation Rolling Thunder. It quickly became obvious that ARVN needed more than just U.S. support to fight off the NVA and the VC.

American soldiers found themselves in a baffling war unlike any they had fought before. The first problem was figuring out who the enemy was. The only difference between the North and South Vietnamese people was the imaginary political line drawn by the parties at the Geneva Conference, so an NVA soldier out of uniform looked exactly like an ARVN soldier. Furthermore, U.S. troops could not assume that civilians in their own territory (South Vietnam) were friendly, because many of them were part of, or at least sympathetic to, the VC.

U.S. troops were fighting in an unfamiliar jungle against people who knew the terrain intimately because they had been fighting the Japanese (at the end of World War II) and the French there since the mid-1940s. To further complicate matters, Ho Chi Minh had built an expansive system of underground tunnels to quickly move supplies and men across Vietnam during the First Indochina War. These tunnels allowed the NVA and the VC to penetrate U.S. lines, kill American troops and then seemingly disappear. The VC was particularly difficult to fight, because the group was mostly made up of civilians who would booby trap roads and villages. These guerrilla tactics were how the NVA and the VC fought, and they were incredibly difficult for U.S. soldiers to combat.

A third and related problem for the U.S. troops and officers alike was the lack of a clear mission from their commander-in-chief. The goal of the U.S. military was not to win the war, which was completely foreign thinking for U.S. military strategists, officers and infantry. Their planning and training was geared toward offensive missions, and in South Vietnam they were sent to defend and support ARVN. But after a few crushing defeats in 1965, ARVN's morale was dropping quickly, and its desertion rate was skyrocketing (about 5,500 soldiers a month). ARVN, on its own, clearly could not defeat North Vietnam, but neither was Johnson ready to concede defeat to communism. There were 184,300 US troops in South Vietnam by the summer of 1965.

At the end of 1965, it was obvious to General William Westmoreland and President Johnson that they would have to switch strategies to be successful in Vietnam. Westmoreland believed that, with a serious commitment of troops, the NVA and the VC could be defeated by the end of 1967. As the number of U.S. troops going to Vietnam increased, the protests and questions about why the United States was involved increased as well. Journalists and photographers sent the U.S. public a

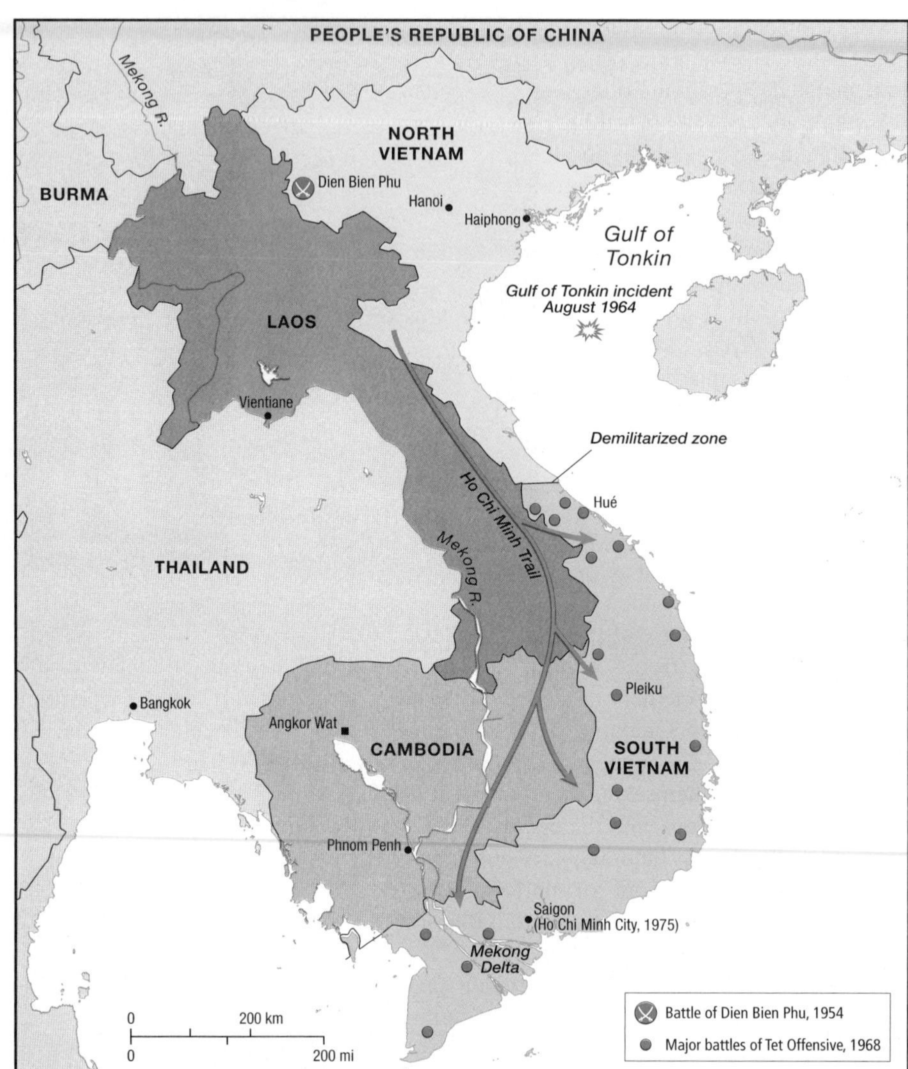

MAP 9.6 Vietnam, Laos, and Cambodia

steady stream of photographs and stories about American bombing missions, the use of napalm, and tens of thousands of villagers in South Vietnam (our supposed allies) displaced. U.S. television networks kept a running tally of the U.S. body count, and U.S. soldiers wrote home describing their frustrating experiences. These messages were inconsistent with the White House press briefings, which assured Americans that the goal was the same—to support ARVN in defending its borders—and that the U.S. and ARVN were getting closer to victory every day. With U.S. soldier and citizen morale dropping, Johnson attempted to force the North Vietnamese to the negotiating table with increased bombing campaigns targeting the Ho Chi Minh Trail, the highly effective supply line that linked North Vietnam with its armies in the South via the neutral countries of Cambodia and Laos. Ho Chi Minh refused to negotiate. By the end of 1966, there were 362,000 U.S. soldiers in Vietnam.

In January 1967, committed to taking the lead in defending South Vietnam, the United States became more aggressive about destroying the VC tunnels and hiding places. Operation Cedar Falls was a moderately successful search-and-destroy mission intended to end the constant VC raids in the capital city of Saigon. That same month, the NVA launched air attacks on U.S. bases in South Vietnam just over the border of the demilitarized zone (DMZ), drawing U.S. troops and equipment north to support them. Throughout the year, the VC stepped up its activity in the villages of South Vietnam, leading to many difficult confrontations between U.S. troops and VC but no real decisive battles in either direction.

In May 1967, amidst citizen protests and Congressional investigations about the government's conduct of the war, General Westmoreland went before a divided and angry Congress to update members on U.S. military actions in Vietnam. Some in Congress raised concerns that the shift from defensive to offensive activities would have potentially disastrous effects: "The new level of escalation marked by our bombing of the North Vietnamese airfields has brought us one step closer to World War III involving the limitless legions of [the PRC] backed by the enormous firepower of Soviet Russia" (Senator George McGovern (D), South Dakota). Westmoreland reminded them of the domino effect that a communist takeover in South Vietnam could set off, and warned: "I foresee, in the months ahead, some of the bitterest fighting of the war...It's going to be a question of putting maximum pressure on the enemy anywhere and everywhere that we can. We will have to grind him down. In effect, we are fighting a **war of attrition.**" By the end of 1967, U.S. forces in Vietnam numbered 485,000.

Watch the Video *Newsreel: Peace March, Thousands Oppose Vietnam War* on mysearchlab.com

war of attrition an attempt to reduce the effectiveness of a military force to the point of collapse by destroying its personnel and material; the war is won by the side with greater resources

1968: The Turning Point

The proxy battle in Vietnam became a quagmire for the U.S. military. The United States' original goal was to assist South Vietnam in resisting a communist invasion from the North and/or an internal coup by the VC, but as the war dragged on, the South Vietnamese government and military actually became *less* able to defend itself. President Johnson was faced with two choices: (1) abandon South Vietnam, basically ensuring that it would fall to communism along with, according to the domino theory, the rest of Southeast Asia; or (2) build up the U.S. troop presence and take the lead in defeating the NVA and the VC. By the time Johnson really committed to the second option, Ho Chi Minh was in excellent position to conquer South Vietnam because of his VC supporters operating in the south, a well-armed regular military and the frustration and dwindling morale of U.S. soldiers.

On January 31, 1968, North Vietnam struck a serious blow with the **Tet** Offensive. The NVA and VC staged a series of coordinated, surprise attacks on eighty South Vietnamese cities, including the capital city of Saigon, the provincial and district capitals, and fifty large towns. The attacks were a surprise for a few reasons: (1) a temporary cease-fire had been called to allow civilians throughout Vietnam to celebrate the Tet holiday; (2) the attacks occurred in cities, but the NVA and VC had drawn most ARVN and U.S. troops to the DMZ and out to the villages in fighting throughout 1967; and (3) the coordinated attacks involved 85,000 NVA and VC—a much stronger force than U.S. strategists thought Ho Chi Minh had.

Tet a national holiday in Vietnam celebrating the first day of the New Year

In Saigon, the NVA and VC attacked the presidential palace, the airport, the main radio station, ARVN headquarters, and even briefly seized the U.S. embassy, killing five marines in the process. ARVN and U.S. troops regrouped and retook Saigon within a week, but it took until the end of February to regain control of the other cities. The VC really dug in and held on in the former imperial capital of Vietnam, Hue. In what became known as the "Massacre at Hue," they executed thousands of civilians and a hundred thousand more lost their homes in door-to-door combat that destroyed the historic city. By pure military standards, the Tet Offensive was a victory for ARVN and the United States. The NVA and VC lost more soldiers (45,000 versus 4,000 ARVN and U.S. troops) and were unable to hold on to the territory they initially gained in the attacks. But the United States was humiliated—military strategists were obviously unprepared and had seriously underestimated Ho Chi Minh and his supporters.

Watch the Video *The Tet Offensive* on mysearchlab.com

On January 21, 1968, the NVA launched an air attack on the heavily fortified U.S. marine corps base at Khe Sanh. Khe Sanh was a vital base because its location, just a few miles from the borders of North Vietnam and Laos, provided the United States access to the Ho Chi Minh Trail. As the United States focused on defending the base, NVA and VC began infiltrating cities in South Vietnam completely unnoticed in preparation for the Tet Offensive. The assault on Khe Sanh continued throughout February and March, expanding into a full-scale ground and air siege. Keeping the base supplied to defend itself required a massive air and land operation, but the operation paid

This photograph, which shows an ARVN officer executing a VC foot soldier on the street during the Tet Offensive, outraged citizens in the West when it was published and fueled the antiwar movement. But press did not tell the story behind this scene–just before this photo was taken, the officer had discovered the beheaded body of a colleague and friend and the bodies of his wife and six children, all killed by the VC.

MAKE THE CONNECTION

- How did the media influence Western perceptions of the proxy battle in Vietnam?
- How has media coverage of war changed since Vietnam?
- Should media coverage of war be censored?

off by the end of March when the NVA began its retreat. ARVN and U.S. reinforcements arrived to relieve the beleaguered base in April, and the U.S government moved the marines to other locations, gradually reducing the number of men at Khe Sanh. In late June, the U.S. government decided that keeping the base at Khe Sanh open was too costly and ordered the base evacuated and closed. Like the Tet Offensive, the siege at Khe Sanh was a military victory for the United States (only 205 U.S. troops killed versus 15,000 NVA), but a stunning blow to U.S. troops in Vietnam and citizens at home. Why did U.S. troops lose their lives to defend a base that the U.S. government so quickly abandoned?

Another fateful event in early 1968 weakened the U.S. government's resolve to continue escalating the conflict in Vietnam. On March 16, 1968, Charlie Company, 11th Brigade, entered the village of My Lai on a search-and-destroy mission. VC had been very active against Charlie Company in the region and, in the wake of the Tet Offensive and the siege at Khe Sanh, U.S. troops were frustrated and angry. They were sure the VC was in My Lai and went into the village firing, although there was no report of enemy fire. More than three hundred unarmed civilians (men, women, children and the elderly) were killed in what became known as the "My Lai Massacre." The military investigation that followed uncovered serious problems with U.S. military leadership, discipline and morale among the troops. Lieutenant William Calley, who led his men into the village firing, was convicted of murder in March 1971.

Read the Document *Lyndon B. Johnson's Address to the Nation* on mysearchlab.com

In February 1968, just after the Tet Offensive, General Westmoreland told President Johnson that the United States could defeat the VC, but it would take several years to accomplish, require at least 200,000 more American soldiers, and probably involve U.S. invasions of neutral neighboring countries Cambodia and Laos to shut down the Ho Chi Minh Trail. Secretary of Defense Robert McNamara, one of Johnson's most trusted advisors, disagreed heartily and resigned from office. In March, his replacement, Clark Clifford, told Johnson that he did not believe the United States could win the war in Vietnam, even with more men, and convinced Johnson to provide Westmoreland with only 24,500 more troops, a fraction of what was requested. With the NVA's strength demonstrated at Khe Sanh, the VC's ability to continuously recruit and seemingly outwit U.S. strategists, and serious problems within the U.S. military, Clifford and the rest of Johnson's advisors had turned against the war and recommended Johnson seek a negotiated withdrawal. Later that month, a beleaguered President Johnson spoke to America and the world, announcing that he would unilaterally scale back the violence in Vietnam. He called on allies and enemies for support in negotiating peace. And with his approval rating at a mere 36 percent, Johnson announced that he would not run for reelection. U.S. forces in Vietnam at the end of 1968 reached 537,000, and an average of 1,200 a month were killed in action.

President Johnson, March 31, 1968.

Vietnamization

Richard Nixon was elected U.S. president in November 1968. While campaigning, he promised Americans an "honorable" end to U.S. military involvement in Vietnam. Nixon and his National Security Advisor Henry Kissinger believed that it was not possible for the United States to achieve a victory in Vietnam—the U.S. Congress and people would not allow more troops to be sent there, which is what a victory would take. But neither could Nixon withdraw all the troops, which would send a clear message to the USSR that the United States simply quit when things became difficult. Nixon's administration developed a foreign policy known as Vietnamization—focusing U.S. military efforts on preparing the South Vietnamese to gradually take over the ground war while the United States continued to provide air support and money. This would allow Nixon to gradually withdraw U.S. troops, but it would require time, money and patience.

Read the Document *Vietnamization* on mysearchlab.com

As the proxy battle within Vietnam dragged on, the Cold War changed a bit. Funding North Vietnam was a major drain on the communist economies of the USSR and the PRC. And as long as U.S. troops were on the ground in Southeast Asia, the risk for WWIII remained unacceptably high for both the East and the West. Nixon pursued a **triangular diplomacy,** using the Sino-Soviet split as leverage to improve his relationship with Mao's PRC. He hoped to encourage Mao to push North Vietnam into peace negotiations with South Vietnam, which seemed more possible because Ho Chi Minh's death in September 1969 left North Vietnam with a leadership council rather than a strong, charismatic leader.

triangular diplomacy Nixon's belief that there were two rival powers in the communist world—the USSR and the PRC—and the United States could exploit that rivalry to weaken the enemy and win the Cold War

A public opinion poll when Nixon took office revealed that most Americans supported Vietnamization policy but only if it did not take very long to achieve. Unfortunately, the methods of Vietnamization were a bit schizophrenic, leading U.S. involvement in Southeast Asia to drag on for five more years. Nixon withdrew U.S. troops from Vietnam steadily throughout 1970, but he also engaged in aggressive bombing campaigns of the neutral countries of Cambodia and Laos and lied about it to cover up U.S. involvement. In April, Nixon went on television to announce that ARVN and U.S. troops were going to invade Cambodia together to reduce the effectiveness of the Ho Chi Minh Trail. Instead, the invasion ignited a violent civil war in that country that led to the rise of a brutal communist regime called the Khmer Rouge. Still, because of Vietnamization, at the end of 1970, there were 280,000 American troops in

President Nixon on television, April 30, 1970.

FIFTEEN YEARS IN VIETNAM

- 2 million Americans served, 500,000 in actual combat
- 47,244 Americans were killed in action
- 10,446 Americans were killed in noncombat
- 153,329 Americans were seriously wounded, including 10,000 amputees
- More than 2,400 American POWs/MIAs were unaccounted for at the end of 1973
- 3 to 4 million Vietnamese were killed
- 1.5 to 2 million Laotians and Cambodians were killed

Vietnam (and another 30,000 CIA operatives), with an average of 344 U.S. servicemen killed in action each month.

In February 1971, Nixon tested the strength of his Vietnamization policy by committing only U.S. air and tactical support to an ARVN invasion of Laos. Unfortunately, ARVN proved that it could not handle the NVA on the ground. One-half of the invasion force was killed in a month, and the rest had to be airlifted from Laos by the United States at the end of March. Still, Nixon continued to withdraw U.S. troops from Vietnam—there were 157,000 troops left at the end of 1971, and the average number of men killed in action per month dropped to 123.

In February 1972, the United States reignited aggressive air attacks against North Vietnam and mined North Vietnamese harbors. On March 23, the U.S. government boycotted the Paris peace talks because Nixon did not believe that the North Vietnamese government was taking the process seriously. And that summer, the United States began bombing Hanoi again, which culminated in one of the largest bombing missions of the entire war in December 1972. But even with peace negotiations stalled, the United States withdrew 70,000 troops in early 1972, followed by another 20,000 in April and 10,000 in June. There were just 27,400 U.S. troops in Vietnam on Election Day 1972 when Nixon won reelection.

By the fall of 1972, at the urging of the PRC, the leadership of North Vietnam had generally agreed to create some sort of treaty to end the war, but they were far from hammering out the details. Furthermore, the president of South Vietnam, Nguyen Van Thieu, refused to accept any agreement that did not include a complete withdrawal of NVA troops from the south and the recognition of South Vietnam as a separate, sovereign state. Nixon was tough with Thieu: "Let me emphasize...you must decide now whether you desire to continue our alliance or whether you want me to seek a settlement with the enemy which serves U.S. interests alone." Thieu capitulated, believing that it would ensure continued U.S. support for his government. On January 27, 1973, the proxy battle in Vietnam officially ended under the following conditions: (1) a ceasefire would be in effect throughout southeast Asia; (2) the United States would withdraw its remaining troops; (3) all U.S. prisoners of war would be returned within sixty days; (4) the Thieu government would remain in power in South Vietnam; and (4) the NVA would be permitted to remain in areas of South Vietnam they had seized. Unfortunately, almost every aspect of the agreement was violated except the last one.

The final terms of the negotiated peace agreement were identical to the ones proposed by North Vietnam four years earlier at the beginning of Nixon's first term. Although the last U.S. troops were pulled out of Vietnam at the end of March, thousands of U.S. "advisors" remained in Saigon and the "secret" air war over Cambodia and Laos continued. Washing its hands of the conflict, the U.S. Congress forbade further U.S. military involvement in Southeast Asia and drastically cut funding to South Vietnam to just $700 million. From 1965 to 1975, the United States spent $111 billion on the conflict. U.S. military strategists knew that ARVN was not capable of holding off the NVA (the fifth-largest military in the world at the time thanks to Soviet funding), but they anticipated it would take about two years for North Vietnam to overrun Saigon.

In August 1974, Richard Nixon resigned as U.S. president in the face of certain impeachment for a string of illegal activities while running for reelection. When Vice President Gerald Ford took office, he became the fifth U.S. president to deal with the Vietnam conflict. That December, NVA troops attacked South Vietnam. The United States was unable to respond militarily because of the Congressional ban, despite Nixon's earlier pledge to take "severe retaliatory action" if the NVA violated the peace agreement. In January 1975, Ford stated unequivocally that the United States would not reenter the war, igniting a barrage of condemnation from President Thieu. The CIA took Thieu to Taiwan to live in exile.

With no real defense against the NVA and VC, Saigon fell in less than two months. The United States staged Operation Frequent Wind, a dramatic helicopter escape that evacuated 7,000 Americans and South Vietnamese government officials as VC and NVA looted the U.S. bases and embassy in South Vietnam. On April 30, 1975, Vietnam was reunited under the communist regime of the north. In 1976, Vietnam signed a cooperative agreement with the communist government of Laos, and it invaded Cambodia in December 1978 to overthrow the Khmer Rouge and establish a "Vietnamese-friendly" regime.

The Non-Aligned Movement

During the Cold War, the superpowers sought to divide the world into two spheres of influence, using their military and financial power to urge, force and attract countries to their particular ideological persuasion. To former empires, allying with one side afforded them a degree of ongoing power. To power-hungry leaders in smaller independent states, allying with one side gave them much-needed financial and military resources. To many former colonies, this was yet another attempt by the powerful countries of the world to exploit them, and they did not want any part of it. After a few years of discussion about the potential danger of the escalating arms race between the United States and the USSR, Indian Prime Minister Jawaharlal Nehru, President of Egypt Gamal Nasser, Prime Minister of Ghana Kwame Nkrumah, President of Indonesia Sukarno, and President of Yugoslavia Josip Tito met at the United Nations in 1960 to lay the foundation for an international organization to help countries resist being drawn into the Cold War.

They created the **Non-Aligned Movement (NAM)** in order to support "the national independence, sovereignty, territorial integrity and security of non-aligned countries." Twenty-five countries attended the first NAM conference in Yugoslavia in September 1961. By the 1964 conference in Cairo, there were forty-seven members. Given that the leaders came from different continents and different political backgrounds, the organizational structure established for NAM was nonhierarchical, and no country held veto power over any other. Initially, NAM focused on supporting newly independent countries as they were decolonized. It was a political organization that offered assistance to all in the "struggle against imperialism, colonialism, neo-colonialism, racism, and all forms of foreign aggression, occupation, domination, interference, or hegemony, as well as against great power and bloc politics." In other words, NAM opposed everything the Cold War was.

Non-Aligned Movement (NAM) a group of countries that sought independence from both the Soviet and U.S. spheres of influence during the Cold War

Conclusions

The process of decolonization was the final death toll of the imperial system that structured the world until the mid-twentieth century. And because decolonization took place in the midst of a Cold War rivalry with two superpowers vying for ideological (but really political and economic) control, the process was fraught with violence. The former colonists were nationalists—they sought independence from foreign domination—but the Cold War did not provide that opportunity any more than colonialism did.

The most violent example of how the Cold War affected decolonization was the civil war in Vietnam. The fifteen-year military conflict funded by the United States, the USSR and the PRC showed the countries of Asia, Africa and Latin America what decolonization could lead to during the competitive Cold War, and it certainly was not independence. So some political leaders in new states sought other paths, including regional unity for economic strength and military regimes for internal stability. A handful of frustrated leaders created the Non-Aligned Movement to formally protest the way the superpowers treated the other countries of the world, and its membership increased steadily throughout the Cold War.

NAM's growth indicated that many countries would not willingly participate in the bipolar power struggle. The inability of the United States to win a conventional war in Vietnam and uphold its containment policy made the fear of nuclear war greater. And the USSR's willingness to fund any government that requested help stretched its communist economy far too thin. The Cold War was changing, and the superpowers would have to change their policies to keep up.

WORKING WITH THE THEMES

THE EFFECTS OF TECHNOLOGY Why wasn't the United States able to decisively defeat North Vietnam? How did the media and expanding communications affect the decision making of the parties involved in Vietnam?

CHANGING IDENTITIES Why did the United Nations take the lead role in decolonization? What was its goal for new countries? What do you think might be the long-term effects of "divide and rule" policies? Is Pan-Africanism a reasonable goal? Why or why not? How did U.S., Soviet and Chinese intervention in Vietnam affect the images of these countries around the world? Why the difference?

SHIFTING BORDERS What do you think was the greatest challenge to creating stable states in Africa in the 1950s through the 1970s? Why did the United States, the USSR and the PRC directly intervene in new Asian states but provide only covert aid (or none at all) to new African states?

GLOBALIZATION Explain the relationship between decolonization, the Cold War, and the Non-Aligned Movement. How did NAM attempt to restructure the Cold War framework of the international arena? Do you believe the "domino theory" was credible for Asia? What might be the long-term consequences for the United States in the Cold War if it consistently bases foreign policy decisions on the "domino theory"?

Further Reading

TO FIND OUT MORE

U.S. Department of State/Office of the Historian: Foreign Relations of the United States Series. Available online at http://history.state.gov/historicaldocuments

United Nations: The United Nations and Decolonization. Available online at http://www.un.org/en/decolonization/

Ali A. Mazrui (ed.)/UNESCO: *General History of Africa, Volume VIII: Africa since 1935* (1993)

South African History Archive. Available online at http://www.saha.org.za/

Peter Leuhusen: The Vietnam War. Available online at http://www.vietnampix.com/

Vietnam War Internet Project. Available at http://www.vwip.org/

GO TO THE SOURCE

Dwight D. Eisenhower Presidential Library & Museum. Available online at http://www.eisenhower.archives.gov/research/online_documents.html

U.S. National Archives. The Pentagon Papers. Available online at http://www.archives.gov/research/pentagon-papers/

Lyndon Baines Johnson Library and Museum. Available online at http://www.lbjlib.utexas.edu/johnson/archives.hom/archives-main.shtm

Ed Blanco: Pieces: Recollections of a Rifleman. Available online at http://vietnamdiary.com/

Bernard Edelman (ed.): *Dear America: Letters Home from Vietnam* (2002)

Central Intelligence Agency: The Vietnam Collection. Available online at http://www.foia.cia.gov/nic_vietnam_collection.asp

MySearchLab Connections

Read the **Document** on **mysearchlab.com**

9.1 *American Objectives in Southeast Asia.* Under President Truman, the U.S. adopted a foreign policy doctrine called "containment," with a goal of confining communism and the Soviet Union to their existing boundaries. This doctrine led directly to the Vietnam War, in which the United States fought to prevent communist forces from attaining power in Southeast Asia.

9.2 *"The Final Declaration on Indochina."* The Geneva Conference (April 26–July 20, 1954) brought together the U.S.S.R., the U.S., France, Great Britain, and the People's Republic of China to discuss the unification of Korea and how to restore peace in Indochina, where the Vietnamese under Ho Chi Minh had just won a war of independence from France.

9.3 *Ho Chi Minh on Self Determination.* Ho Chi Minh led the Vietnamese people in their struggles against European colonialism and then American military power. Here he discusses the impact of the 1954 Geneva Conference.

9.4 Lyndon B. Johnson, *The Tonkin Gulf Resolution.* In August 1964, U.S naval vessels were confronted by North Vietnamese torpedo boats in the Gulf of Tonkin. The incident was used by President Johnson as justification for authorizing military force in Southeast Asia.

9.5 *Lyndon B. Johnson's Address to the Nation.* On March 31, 1968, President Johnson went on national television to announce new steps to limit the Vietnam War, and also, that he would not seek re-election at the end of the year.

9.6 Richard M. Nixon, *Vietnamization.* By 1969, President Nixon realized that the Vietnam War had drained American resources and prestige, and devastated morale at home. This speech outlined his plan for an honorable way out of the conflict—by reducing U.S. combat troops and strengthening the South Vietnamese armed forces so that they could be responsible for their own defense.

Watch the **Video** on **mysearchlab.com**

9.1 *Creating Apartheid in South Africa*

9.2 Newsreel: *Peace March, Thousands Oppose Vietnam War*

9.3 *The Tet Offensive*

10 The Cold War Cools: 1965–1979

CHAPTER OUTLINE

- The Brezhnev Era
- Changes in the West
- A Shift in Cold War Thinking

CHAPTER TIMELINE

1964
Khrushchev resigns; Brezhnev takes over USSR
PRC becomes a nuclear power

1965
The first U.S. ground troops arrive in Vietnam

1966
France withdraws from NATO military forces

1968
Dubcek announces Action Program in Czechoslovakia
Brezhnev announces "Doctrine of Limited Sovereignty"
Nuclear Non-Proliferation Treaty (NPT) is signed
Nixon becomes U.S. president

1969
United States and PRC open trade relations
U.S. Apollo 11 lands on the moon

1970
Allende elected in Chile

Photos from left to right: Allende supporters in Chile; The Nixons Visit the Great Wall of China; ENIAC; Sputnik 1.

1971	1972	1973	1975	1976	1979
PRC is recognized as China in the United Nations	SALT I and ABM treaties are signed Nixon visits China; Shanghai Communique is signed	Allende is overthrown; Pinochet takes over Chile Treaty officially ends the conflict in Vietnam	United States leaves Vietnam Vietnam reunited under a communist regime Helsinki Agreement goes into effect	Mao dies	USSR invades Afghanistan

By the end of the 1960s, the original "rules" of the Cold War were not really applicable anymore. The U.S. foreign policy of containment was clearly failing (in Vietnam and elsewhere), and the Soviet domestic economy was collapsing under the weight of its international obligations. The arms race had escalated out of control—five countries had nuclear weapons programs, and the superpowers had to spend an excessive amount of money to stay ahead in the race. With the successful development of its nuclear weapons program in 1964, the People's Republic of China (PRC) became a powerful world player, but it remained stubbornly resistant to falling within the Soviet sphere of influence. And as the Sino-Soviet split deepened, the United States was sinking deeper into the quagmire of Vietnam. The steep costs of the Cold War reached full impact in the 1970s in the midst of a global economic downturn, forcing the USSR, the United States and the PRC into a critical reevaluation of their goals. The results were a new method for dealing with the Cold War and some pretty dramatic changes to alliances and the arms race.

WORKING WITH THE THEMES

THE EFFECTS OF TECHNOLOGY The PRC and France start nuclear weapons programs, and the United States and USSR try to combat proliferation with the NPT and bilateral treaties. The Cold War conflict extends to the moon in the space race, and the technology revolutionizes espionage.

CHANGING IDENTITIES With internal problems in the USSR apparent, Brezhnev makes dramatic policy changes, and reformists in Czechoslovakia propose restructuring. The United States intervenes in Latin America to prevent leftist regimes from securing power.

SHIFTING BORDERS The USSR and Western Europe finally create post-World War II legal settlements along their borders.

GLOBALIZATION As détente eases the relationship between the USSR and the United States, the emerging friendship between the PRC and the United States changes the structure of the Cold War.

The Brezhnev Era

In 1964, Nikita Khrushchev was ousted from office based on his mishandling of domestic economic affairs in the USSR. He chose to resign rather than risk assassination. The coup was led by one of Khrushchev's most trusted advisors, Leonid Brezhnev, who took power in the USSR and served for eighteen years (longer than anyone except Stalin).

Domestic Concerns

Khrushchev's de-Stalinization program opened the door for reform in the USSR, but Brezhnev was the first Soviet leader to fully embrace it. The domestic economic and social problems in the USSR in the late 1960s were too big to repress. To prevent a rebellion against the government (which would demonstrate to the world that communism had "failed"), the Politburo would have to actually address the problems. The challenge was to enact enough reform to please the citizens without weakening the underlying authoritarian economic and political structure of the communist state.

The primary issue the Politburo faced was the low quality of living for the vast majority of Soviet citizens. Khrushchev's "thaw" had opened communication between East and West, and it was obvious that capitalism yielded a higher standard of living than communism did. To the Politburo, the biggest difference was the lack of consumer goods in the East, so it built economic reforms around the provision of consumer goods to the Soviet citizens. But buying consumer goods would cost money, something most Soviets did not have. The government would have to provide a cash infusion to get a consumer economy started, a particularly difficult challenge given the amount of money the USSR was spending on Cuba, Vietnam, Africa and the Middle East. And the USSR certainly could not accept financial aid from others, obviously not from the United States or its allies.

Soviet economic reform in the late 1960s and the 1970s was piecemeal and scattered. An incentive system was put in place for managers and workers so that they would receive bonus payments for producing more than expected. The idea was that they would use this "extra" money to purchase consumer goods. Travel regulations within the USSR and satellite states were eased, allowing agricultural workers from the countryside to move to cities and take factory jobs producing the consumer goods. A switch in education policy to a merit-based system created a large social class of white-collar workers who earned more money for their labor and would demand consumer goods. During the 1970s, 1 million workers were shifted into different sectors of the economy, with the goal of creating consumer demand and providing Soviet-produced consumer goods. Most of this was paid for by exploiting natural resources such as oil, minerals and gold.

In the first decade of reforms (1965 to 1975), the economy seemed to improve. The average monthly wage for workers doubled (tripled for miners and construction workers), and demand for consumer goods rose. But a fundamental problem, the centrally planned economy, prevented this economic increase from actually improving people's lives. In a capitalist economy, production is driven by what *people* demand. In the Soviet communist economy, the government determined what was produced, how much of it was available and where it was shipped. For example, even with cash in their pockets to spend, people could not buy a new house—those kinds of basic needs were doled out by the government. It was the same with food—people could afford meat and other "luxury" foods, but the government could not provide enough of

Leonid Brezhnev and Khrushchev in 1961.

Shoppers queing up to buy potatoes just delivered by truck, Uzebkistan, 1972.

the products to keep the shelves stocked. And because of the focus on industrialization over agriculture, by the mid-1970s the USSR was importing millions of tons of grain per year from the United States.

With the incentive program and the focus on consumerism, people began working longer hours to earn more money to buy more things. Family life suffered, and alcoholism became a major epidemic. But the government made production decisions based on what *the government* thought Soviet people should have and shipped goods where *the government* believed the people should have them. As a result, consumer goods and automobiles became more readily available in the cities but not in smaller towns and villages. And the Soviet-produced goods were low quality, so people turned to the ridiculously expensive black market to purchase imports from the West. Not only did the black market take money *out* of the Soviet economy, it led to a growing division between "haves" and "have-nots," which is exactly what communism is supposed to combat. Loyalty to the Communist Party earned membership in the **nomenklatura,** a very privileged social class with its own stores, resorts and even hospitals. With the extra cash in the economy, corruption and bribery became the only way to get things done. Corruption became an inherent feature of Soviet culture at all social levels and started at the top—Brezhnev owned several estates and a fleet of imported automobiles.

nomenklatura loyal Communist Party members appointed to key positions in government and industry; answered directly to the Politburo

The expansion of education beyond the privileged elite class ultimately led to a large dissident movement. University students and professionals began debating and discussing the merits of communism versus capitalism. When they began to question Brezhnev's reform policies, they were quickly driven underground by governmental regulations and harsh punishment. Many of the most vocal dissidents were Jewish, and there was a sharp increase in anti-Semitism. But unlike in Stalin's era, the United Nations was paying more attention to internal affairs in the USSR. The KGB had to be controlled, and large-scale executions were out of the question. So Brezhnev got creative with his "prisoners of conscience," as he called them. Some were kept under house arrest; others were exiled to Siberia, and the most politically dangerous were declared to be insane and held in state-run psychiatric institutions.

At the end of the Brezhnev era, the quality of life for most Soviet citizens (outside of the cities) had not dramatically improved, despite the focus on consumer goods and progress in a few

Advertisement for the Moskvitch 412, circa 1970.

industries. The reality was that Brezhnev's economic reforms were only skin deep—massive amounts of money were diverted to military spending and the huge, bloated government bureaucracy. Perhaps the most serious structural problem was that any money generated was used to create the appearance of economic health and was not reinvested in the country's infrastructure (factories, equipment, roads, transportation and communication). As the infrastructure deteriorated, so too did the quality of life. The lack of reinvestment in infrastructure prevented technological advancements in most industries (particularly transportation and communication) and set the stage for ecological disasters and social discontent related to rapidly increasing industrialization. By the end of his reign, even Brezhnev recognized that the only way to improve the quality of life in the USSR and the satellite bloc overall was to import consumer goods from the noncommunist world.

ANALYSIS

What were the short-term economic and social effects of the black market in the USSR? Can you envision what the long-term consequences might be?

Soviet Foreign Affairs

One of the largest drains on the domestic economy of the USSR during Brezhnev's era was his reform of Soviet foreign policy. He recognized the need to decrease military spending, but he could not do that unilaterally without creating the perception that the USSR was losing the Cold War. Brezhnev believed that he could only negotiate successfully with the United States from equal footing, so he devoted his resources to expanding and modernizing the Soviet military, creating a standing army much larger than the U.S. military. With American citizens growing tired of the conflict in Vietnam and increasingly unwilling to support their government's military actions, Brezhnev saw an opportunity to move ahead of the United States in the arms race.

Brezhnev extended Khrushchev's "thaw" into a permanent change in approach to the Cold War, which became known as **détente.** Brezhnev had two goals: (1) to ease tensions that were leading to ongoing and expensive military conflicts and proxy battles (as in Vietnam), and (2) to prevent what he feared was impending nuclear holocaust given how quickly the number of nuclear weapons in the world had increased in just two decades. Brezhnev worked hard to convince the United States that détente could work, promising peace even as he built up the Soviet conventional military.

détente
French word meaning relaxing or easing; in politics, détente refers to the relaxation of tension between states

Although the major participants in the Cold War are commonly depicted as just two superpowers, in reality the PRC was every bit as much of a military threat as the United States or the USSR. Because the PRC was a communist country and received aid from the USSR, the West just assumed the PRC fell under the Soviet sphere of influence. The Sino-Soviet split in the 1960s changed that perception. For détente to be truly effective in preventing war, all three military powerhouses would have to participate. And in the 1970s, all three had good reasons to pursue détente. The USSR was hoping to divert spending away from its military to save its dying economy, as well as prevent the United States and the PRC from forming an alliance against the USSR. The United States recognized that it simply could not afford (economically, politically or socially) to pursue containment through proxy battles all around the world. And the PRC felt isolated from the world (it was not a member of the United Nations) and was worried that a border dispute with the USSR might turn into a nuclear conflict.

The first action taken by the superpowers in the name of détente was achieved relatively easily. There had been discussions for years in the UN General Assembly regarding the dangers of nuclear proliferation. Most countries simply could not afford to develop nuclear weapons programs, which put them at a major disadvantage compared to those countries that could. Furthermore, at any time, countries could be destroyed by an all-out nuclear war between the superpowers that had nothing to do with them. Because it was the Cold War, these discussions went nowhere without the support of the superpowers. With détente in place, negotiations that included the United States and the USSR began in 1965, and an agreement was reached by the UN General Assembly in 1968 with the creation of the Treaty on the Non-Proliferation of

MAKE THE CONNECTION

- What is the legacy of the NPT?
- Was the NPT a useful tool during the Cold War?
- Should the NPT be maintained or abolished now that the Cold War is over?

Nuclear Weapons (NPT). As the preamble makes clear, the goal of the treaty was to stop the proliferation of nuclear weapons in order to prevent nuclear war:

> *Considering the devastation that would be visited upon all mankind by a nuclear war and the consequent need to make every effort to avert the danger of such a war and to take measures to safeguard the security of peoples...the proliferation of nuclear weapons would seriously enhance the danger of nuclear war...*

The treaty, which is still in force today, allows the five states (United States, USSR [now Russia], United Kingdom, France and China) that had nuclear weapons technology in 1968 to maintain their arsenals, but explicitly prohibits them from transferring nuclear weapons technology or usable weapons to any nonnuclear weapons state (everyone else in the world). Those five states also agree to "pursue negotiations in good faith on effective measures relating to cessation of the nuclear arms race at an early date," with the goal of complete nuclear disarmament. The nonnuclear-weapons states that signed the treaty promise never to "build, acquire, or possess nuclear weapons," but they are allowed to pursue nuclear energy as long as they allow full investigations and monitoring of their activities. That monitoring is handled worldwide by the International Atomic Energy Agency, an independent, international organization related to the United Nations, with full access to any state that has signed the NPT.

The NPT went into effect in March 1970 when both the United States and the USSR ratified the treaty (fifty-nine other countries had already signed by then), but both France and China refused to sign it until 1992, after the Cold War was over. The NPT remains the only international effort to prevent the proliferation of nuclear weapons and is reviewed and updated by member states every five years.

In keeping with the commitment to negotiate toward nuclear disarmament, U.S. President Nixon and Brezhnev agreed to engage in Strategic Arms Limitation Talks (now known as SALT I) in November 1969. Although he certainly did not admit it, Brezhnev was looking for a way to cut military spending. Nixon, who believed in Mutual Assured Destruction, was looking for a way to ease the fears of American citizens that the conflict in Vietnam would result in nuclear war between the superpowers. The talks ended in January 1972 with the first round of nuclear de-armament agreements. President Nixon traveled to Moscow in May 1972 so that he and Brezhnev could sign the agreements together. The Treaty on the Limitation of Anti-Ballistic Missile Systems (the ABM Treaty) limited the defense systems of both countries. The Interim Agreement on the Limitation of Strategic Offensive Arms froze the number of strategic ballistic missiles that both sides could have at their current (1972) levels and prohibited the construction of new intercontinental ballistic missile silos for the next five years. The SALT I agreements were a success in that they brought the nuclear capabilities of both superpowers to relative parity.

The Brezhnev Doctrine

The principle of détente did not extend to countries within the Soviet sphere of influence. Khrushchev's "thaw" had led to a resurgence of nationalism in many satellite bloc states, and Brezhnev kept Warsaw Pact troops stationed throughout to remind them who was ultimately in charge. While he allowed them to interact with the West to some extent, there were two rules that could never be broken: (1) every Warsaw Pact state must uphold that alliance above all else, and (2) only the Communist Party could hold political power. In spring 1968, Czechoslovakia was on the verge of breaking both.

By the end of 1967, there was much disagreement in the highest ranks of the Communist Party of Czechoslovakia. Communist intellectuals were disillusioned with authoritarian-style leadership that violated many of Lenin's goals. There were disagreements between nationalist groups within the party over alleged discrimination. Reformists recognized the inadequacies of the centrally planned economy and wanted to trade with the West, and intellectuals and university students demanded full democratization. Brezhnev grew concerned about the open protests against the government under Antonin Novotny and visited Prague to find out what was going on. Brezhnev warned Novotny he would have to regain control of his country, but Novotny was unable to do so.

In January 1968, reformist Alexander Dubcek became the General Secretary of the Communist Party of Czechoslovakia. He immediately began to reform the political and social atmosphere during what became known as "Prague Spring." In April, the Communist Party published an "Action Program" to "purify communism" and "build socialism in [Czechoslovakia] in a way corresponding to our conditions and traditions." Dubcek called it "socialism with a human face." His goal was essentially a nationalist version of socialism, and his ideas received widespread support from the Czech people.

EXCERPTS FROM DUBCEK'S ACTION PROGRAM

- freedom of speech, press, assembly and religious observance
- new electoral laws to provide a broader choice of candidates
- political access for non-communist parties and increased power for the government (rather than the Communist Party)
- broad economic reforms to give businesses decision-making power and allow for limited private enterprise
- trade with the West
- an independent judiciary
- independence for Slovakia

Read the Document *U.S. Reaction to Prague Spring* on mysearchlab.com

As Dubcek's popularity grew, the surrounding Warsaw Pact states became increasingly concerned that the reform movement would spread to them. They held a meeting in March, demanding that Dubcek rescind his Action Program, but Dubcek refused. The Warsaw Pact members met again in July, but this time without Czechoslovakia. They formulated a letter of demands and warned Dubcek that they would use military intervention to prevent his "counterrevolution" from spreading. Dubcek pledged support for communism but again refused to back away from reform.

Dubcek was acting on behalf of his citizens, and the governments of the Warsaw Pact nations were concerned about maintaining their own power. But Brezhnev was looking at the situation through the lens of the Cold War. If Czechoslovakia were allowed to enact a nationalist version of socialism, other satellite states could do the same (similar to the domino theory regarding communism held by the West). As far as Brezhnev was concerned, there were already too many so-called "communist" countries in the world that did not answer to him (the PRC and Yugoslavia). Not only would the spread of nationalist socialism across Eastern Europe weaken the Soviet sphere of influence, it would potentially leave the USSR militarily vulnerable to a North Atlantic Treaty Organization (NATO) attack from the West. And it could completely upset the balance of power between the United States and USSR that was so carefully maintained.

On the night of August 21, 1968, more than 200,000 Soviet and Warsaw Pact troops invaded Czechoslovakia. The invasion was a surprise to everyone, and the Czech military was basically arrested in its own barracks. Within a day, the country was completely occupied, and by the end of the week there were 650,000 Soviet and Warsaw Pact troops there. Dubcek and other Czech leaders were arrested and taken to Moscow. Although there was no organized Czech resistance to the invasion, the citizens took to the streets in protest. Violent clashes broke out, bringing death and destruction to Prague.

The UN Security Council condemned the invasion by a vote of ten to two, but the USSR vetoed the resolution, and the United States certainly could not take unilateral action in a Warsaw Pact state. In Moscow, Brezhnev "negotiated" with Dubcek and the other arrested government officials. They could return to their jobs if they accepted Brezhnev's changes to their policies. If they refused to do so, a military dictatorship led by the Warsaw Pact would be established in Czechoslovakia. Against the desire of the Czech people, their government accepted the eleven-page list of requirements and returned to Prague on August 27. Dubcek tried to continue his reform policies, but he was forced to succumb to Brezhnev's "normalization" guidelines because of the ongoing military occupation. Dubcek still enjoyed widespread public support, so Brezhnev could not risk assassinating him or removing him from office, but Brezhnev did work with other Communist Party members to isolate Dubcek politically. In April 1969, Dubcek's government was overthrown by more traditional communists; he was eventually placed under house arrest, and "socialism with a human face" came to an abrupt end.

In the middle of the crisis in Czechoslovakia (November 1968), Brezhnev gave a speech in Poland that clearly outlined his policy toward the satellite states, the "Doctrine of Limited Sovereignty." Brezhnev would use military intervention (by all Warsaw Pact forces) to intervene in any of "his" countries that did not follow Soviet rules of communism. This justified the invasion of Czechoslovakia because "...each Communist party is responsible not only to its own people, but also to all the socialist countries, to the entire Communist movement." It was a clear warning to all states within the Soviet sphere of influence (and perceived by Mao to be directed at the PRC as well) that they could not stray from Soviet principles without punishment. The West protested what they called "the Brezhnev Doctrine," but because it applied only to states within the Soviet sphere, there was little else they could do. The Warsaw Pact nations remained firmly under Brezhnev's control throughout the 1970s.

Changes in the West

As the Cold War entered its third decade, the West began to feel the economic strain of its containment policy. The attempt to build democracy in Vietnam had devolved into an ugly and expensive conflict that sapped the morale of citizens in the United States and even Europe. Droughts in the USSR, Australia, China, and Africa led to a worldwide food crisis that drove up prices and contributed to a stock market crash in the United States. When the oil-producing countries of the Middle East enforced an oil embargo against the West in 1973 in retaliation for its support of Israel in the Yom Kippur War, oil prices quadrupled in just a few months. All of these events converged to cause severe **stagflation** in the U.S. economy. People were nervous about constantly rising prices, so they tried to buy more while the price was "low." But that increased demand pushed up prices, which drove up wages, which led to unemployment. And as the U.S. government continued to fight proxy battles around the world and invest in the arms and space races, the budget deficit grew and government borrowing increased. Because of globalization, the economic downturn affected everyone who traded with the United States.

stagflation
an economic condition of both continuing inflation and stagnant business activity, together with an increasing unemployment rate

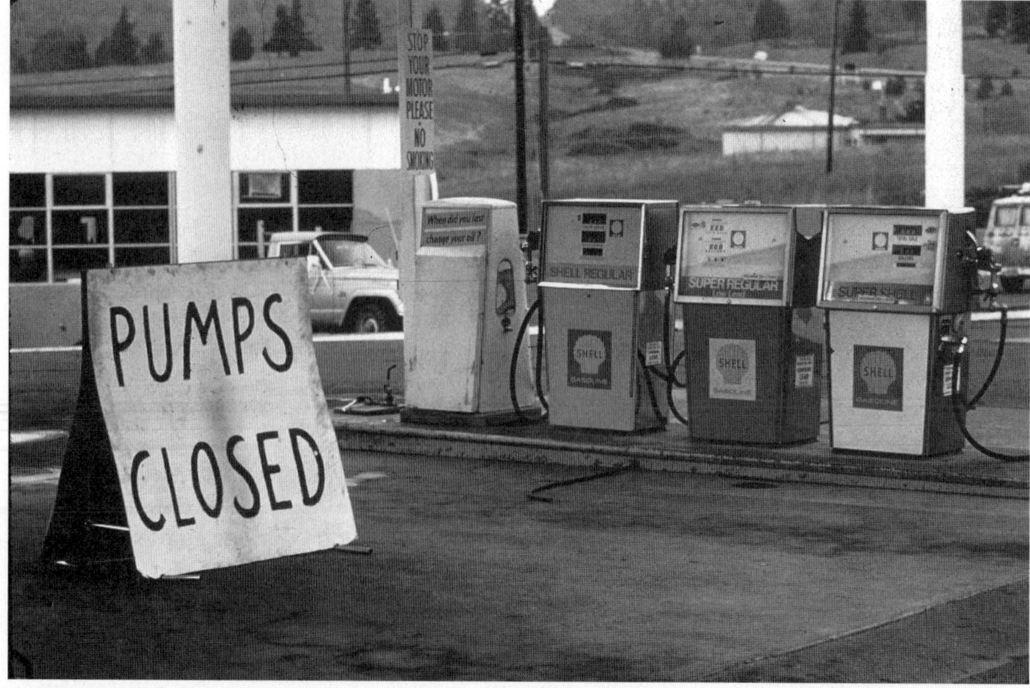

Gasoline shortage in the U.S., October 1973.

The oil embargo also demonstrated that the economies of Western industrial nations were heavily dependent on the Middle East's oil, which certainly empowered the Organization of the Petroleum Exporting Countries (OPEC), the cartel that controls the production and distribution of oil around the world. That reliance challenged the prevailing idea that global power could only be achieved through nuclear weapons and military technology.

NATO

In the early 1950s, large uranium deposits were discovered in France, enabling the government to pursue its own nuclear weapons program. France successfully tested its first nuclear weapon in 1960 and its first hydrogen bomb in 1968. Emboldened by this success, President Charles de Gaulle expressed his nation's frustration with the NATO alliance dominated by the United States and Great Britain. France, indeed all of Western Europe, was wholly reliant on the U.S. nuclear umbrella for survival, yet France's role in NATO decision making was consistently minimized. Frustrated by NATO's nuclear policy in particular, de Gaulle pulled all French military forces out of the integrated NATO military structure in 1966 and ordered non-French Allied forces and military headquarters out of the country. Although France remained a member of NATO and continued to fight the spread of communism with its own forces stationed in Germany, France's refusal to follow U.S. leadership signaled a potential rift in the U.S. sphere of influence.

U.S. Foreign Affairs

The proxy battle in Vietnam exacted an enormous political and social cost from the United States. As U.S. military involvement in Southeast Asia deepened throughout the late 1960s and early 1970s, internal support for using overt military methods to pursue the goals of containment waned. To win the Cold War, the U.S. government would most certainly have to stop the spread of communism (particularly where communism threatened the western hemisphere), but to preserve internal unity and strength the government would have to utilize different methods to do so.

By the late 1960s, the U.S. government had come to the realization that perhaps communism was not the real enemy of the United States—the USSR was. And because containing communism within the borders of the USSR had proven to be an impossible task, the way to defeat the USSR was to line up as many countries as possible on the U.S. side of the tally sheet. In that case, it would make sense to reach out to any government in the world that opposed Soviet expansion, regardless of its political ideology. This fundamental shift in Cold War thinking led to a change in methodology as well. In order to receive financial and/or military assistance from the United States, a government would simply have to demonstrate that it was anticommunist, not necessarily prodemocracy.

With Fidel Castro firmly in power in Cuba, the threat of communism spreading throughout Latin America increased dramatically. There were two reasons for this: (1) Castro and his revolutionary comrade Che Guevara were immensely popular figures among the impoverished Latin American population, and (2) the governments of many Central and South American countries were eager to rid themselves of ongoing U.S. political intervention and economic dominance, or "Yankee imperialism" as they called it. The struggle for the U.S. government was to isolate Castro as much as possible from his neighbors without violating the terms of the Cuban Missile Crisis deal in which they promised nonintervention in Cuban affairs. So the United States remained directly involved in Latin American politics throughout the Cold War, but generally in a covert way by supporting and strengthening military governments opposed to communism through financial aid and the activities of the Central Intelligence Agency (CIA).

Watch the Video Lecture *The Science of Spying, 1965* on mysearchlab.com

In an effort to spread communism and oppose U.S. **hegemony** in the western hemisphere, Castro supplied Soviet weapons to Guevara and other grassroots revolutionary movements throughout Latin America. This, of course, presented a challenge to existing governments, and as a result of pressure from the United States, the Organization of American States voted to impose economic sanctions against Cuba in 1964. As Castro was increasingly isolated from

hegemony
the domination of one state over all others within its sphere of influence

Latin America, he became even more dependent on the USSR. And although the CIA could not get to Castro, it did help Bolivian authorities execute Che Guevara in 1967.

But the larger problem the United States faced was how to prevent these revolutionary leftist movements from overthrowing existing governments and allowing Soviet influence to infiltrate Central and South America (containment). Initially, the United States responded as it always had to a communist threat, with financial support to existing governments to fight the guerilla movements and outright military action when necessary. But because overt actions might be viewed as yet another example of "Yankee imperialism" and actually encourage more of the population to rebel, the United States relied heavily on the CIA. As the United States discovered with Ngo Dinh Diem in Vietnam, it takes a strong, authoritarian regime to suppress internal grassroots revolutions. So, the United States supported and supplied autocratic and military regimes, the kind that violently suppress political and civil rights to maintain control. These regimes were certainly not democratic, but more importantly to the United States during the Cold War, they were not communist. Declassified CIA documents reveal that the U.S. government channeled supplies, money and planning assistance through the CIA to support military coups that overthrew democratically elected governments in Brazil (1964), Chile (1973), Uruguay (1973) and Argentina (1976).

MAKE THE CONNECTION

Why use the CIA to intervene in Latin American affairs instead of the U.S. military or political diplomacy?

In Chile in 1970, Salvadore Allende became the first democratically elected Marxist in Latin America, winning the election on promises of economic reform and nationalizing U.S.-owned copper mines. During the election, the CIA funded

MAP 10.1 U.S. Intervention in Latin America

Allende's political opponents, assuming that would keep Allende from office. When that did not work, the U.S. government created a two-track plan to remove Allende from power. Track one included economic, political and psychological operations designed to promote civil strife, and track two involved working with the Chilean military to stage a coup. When the military leaders were initially hesitant to do so, the U.S. government became frustrated. The CIA was ordered to do whatever was necessary to remove Allende from office and actively intervened in political, economic and military affairs in Chile. In 1973, the Chilean military and the CIA ousted Allende (who was killed in the process) and established a brutal, repressive regime under General August Pinochet.

In a few cases, where the United States feared the existing governments were not strong enough to hold on even with financial support, overt military force was used to prevent revolution. In the Dominican Republic in 1965, supporters of the militarily deposed president staged a revolution against the new military regime, igniting conflict. The U.S. marines invaded the Dominican Republic to end the revolt and occupied the country through the election of the U.S.-supported candidate in 1966.

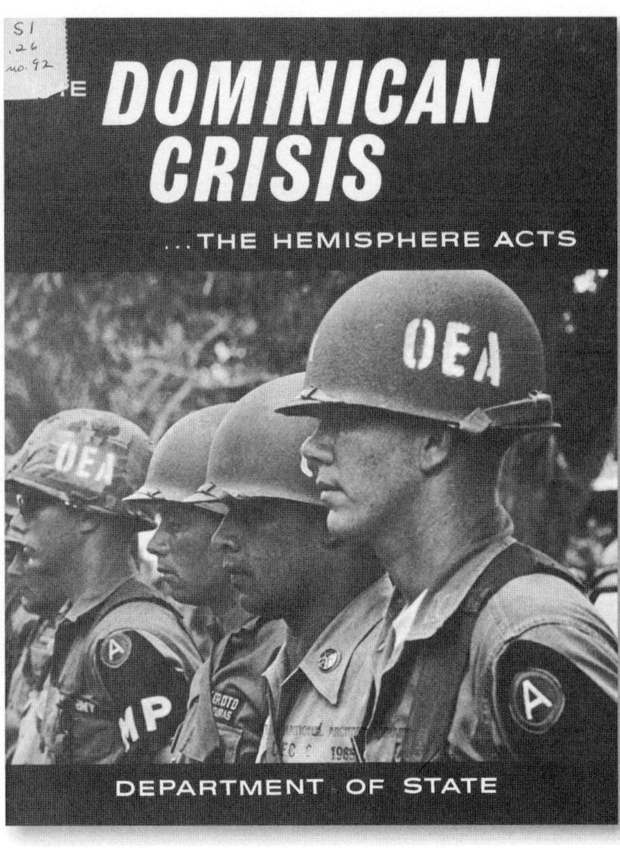

U.S. troops in the Dominican Republic, 1965–1966.

A Shift in Cold War Thinking

Three decades of combative, aggressive Cold War posturing had changed the political structure of the world. As the United States and the USSR fought to expand their spheres of influence (militarily, ideologically and financially), an increasing number of countries were drawn into the conflict against their will. Yet the Cold War resolutely marched on, seemingly destined to render economic disaster, social and political divisions, and perhaps even total nuclear annihilation for the people of the world. For a brief period, détente eased the tension, opening the door for changes in how the United States and USSR would deal with one another.

The Race to the Moon

The space race, which officially began in 1957 when the USSR launched Sputnik, grew into a heated but peaceful competition between the United States and USSR to prove scientific and military superiority. In the United States, the National Aeronautics and Space Administration whipped up public support for the race to the moon (a civilian project), which kept the government funding flowing to the secret military space programs as well. In the USSR, all space projects were top secret, and only the successful ones were announced to the people.

Throughout the 1960s, the USSR was winning the race to the moon. The Soviets brought back the first recorded images of the moon's far side in 1959 and sent the first human into space (Yuri Gagarin) in April 1961, ten months before U.S. astronaut John Glenn orbited the Earth. In 1963, Soviet Valentina Tereshkova became the first woman in space, and in March 1965 the Soviets sent the first astronaut outside of an orbiting spacecraft. But actually reaching the moon required advanced rocket technology, an area in which the United States excelled. The first two Soviet attempts to launch a rocket that would land on the moon failed (in February and July 1969). The rockets crashed just after liftoff, destroying the launch site. The U.S. mission was just three weeks behind and was much more successful—on July 20, 1969, Apollo 11 landed on the moon, where Neil Armstrong and Edwin "Buzz" Aldrin

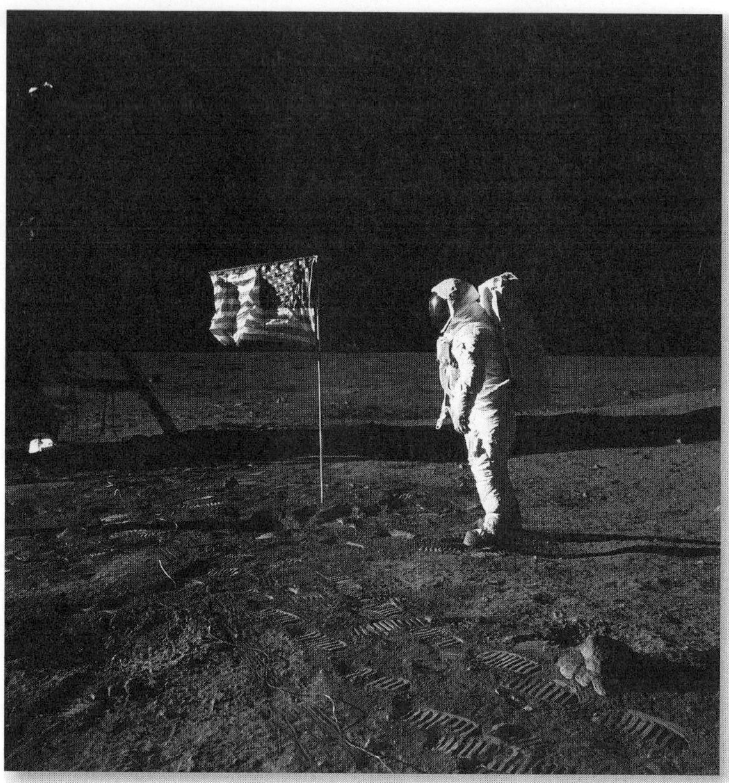

The U.S. wins the space race on July 20, 1969.

planted the U.S. flag. This much-publicized phase of the space race was over, and the United States had won.

But the Cold War continued, and the governments of both superpowers relied on the technology they had developed to pursue long-term goals such as space stations, space shuttles and the exploration of planets. Perhaps most importantly from a Cold War perspective, both countries used top-secret, space-based reconnaissance projects to photograph one another. In the West, it also fueled a communications revolution.

The Computer Revolution

With the development of satellites in 1957, the research and development behind the space race was extended to include communications technologies for espionage and data storage in the event of a nuclear war. Although governments had been utilizing computers for data analysis since World War II, the computers were cumbersome and complicated. In 1962, the U.S. government hired J. C. R. Licklider to head the new computer research program at the Defense Advanced Research Projects Agency (DARPA), the research and development branch of the U.S. Department of Defense. Licklider envisioned a "Galactic Network" in which all information could be shared around the world through computers that could "talk" to one another. By the end of 1969, the project had created the Advanced Research Projects Agency Network (ARPANET), a network comprised of four computers at different universities in the southwestern United States. ARPANET grew rapidly from there, allowing for data sharing between universities, research institutes and government agencies in the United States. In 1972, the first electronic mail was sent via ARPANET.

Because Internet technology was designed by the government for military and defense applications, it was not available commercially until 1989. By then, personal computers and desktop workstations had become available through Xerox, Apple, IBM and Commodore. In 1990, a scientist at the European Organization for Nuclear Research looking for an easier way to share information created hyperlinks. He then created webpages to store the hyperlinks, and the World Wide Web was born.

A Pacific Power Emerges

By the end of the 1960s, the Cold War had a new power player—the People's Republic of China. The PRC was powerful not only because it had developed a nuclear weapons program of its own, but because it refused to adhere to the bipolar nature of the Cold War. The PRC was certainly communist, but it would not subsume itself into the Soviet sphere of influence, which challenged the entire notion of the Cold War being a battle between communism and democracy. The PRC played a crucial strategic role in that it could tip the delicate Cold War **balance of power** by openly allying with the United States or the USSR.

balance of power
when power is divided between states to maintain equilibrium so that no state has significantly more power; the goal is to keep peace between the states

Since the Sino-Soviet split in the early 1960s, Mao had grown increasingly concerned about the negative effect that détente between the United States and the USSR would have on the PRC. By 1969, the U.S. military had troops stationed in Taiwan, as well as an ever-increasing military

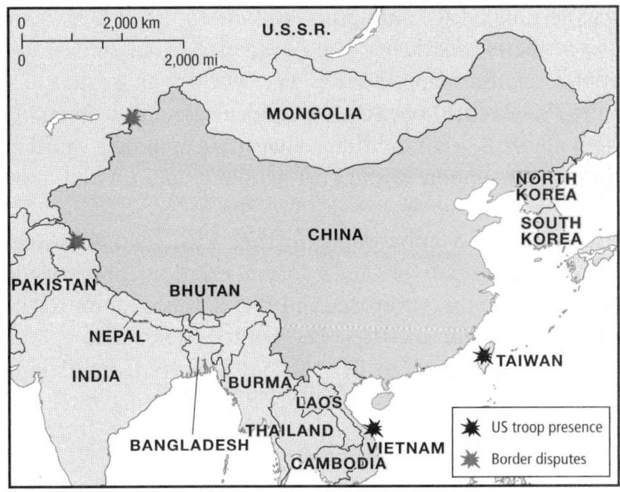

MAP 10.2 China's Border Disputes

presence in Vietnam. The military skirmishes between the USSR and the PRC that spring had resulted in a large Soviet military buildup all along the 4,500-mile border to the north, and the PRC's southwest border was still tied up in territorial disputes with India, a U.S. ally to whom the USSR had provided military assistance. From Mao's point of view, the PRC could never be a great world or even regional power with Soviet and U.S. military forces on its borders. Although the PRC had developed nuclear bomb capability, its delivery system and defense technologies lagged way behind the United States and USSR. If Mao could get one superpower to remove its military threat, the other superpower would necessarily back down as well to reduce the risk of WWIII. Furthermore, the PRC's struggling communist economy needed a financial boost, one that the Soviets were unable to provide. Perhaps the most important factor in Mao's decision making in 1969 was a matter of pride as well as power. Since its establishment, the PRC had never been recognized by the United Nations, and every attempt to change that was vetoed by the United States. Earning recognition for "his" China, and the all-important Security Council seat that would come with it, was crucial for Mao to truly take his place as a world leader. But only the United States could provide this opportunity.

Nixon and National Security Advisor Henry Kissinger had also reevaluated their understanding of the Cold War as a result of the obvious failures of the containment policy and the Sino-Soviet split. If the enemy was the USSR, as opposed to communism overall, then wouldn't it make the most strategic sense to befriend the large, military and nuclear powerhouse on its border? What was more vital to U.S. security interests—political ideology or a partner that could help contain Soviet expansion? Furthermore, the U.S. economy was reaching a standstill, competing with the growing strength of Europe and Japan for a significant share of the world trade market. Opening the PRC to trade meant adding 830 million potential consumers (almost one-quarter of the world's population) for U.S. goods. The biggest obstacle Nixon faced was how to justify changing the twenty-year policy of steadfastly supporting the nationalist regime in Taiwan and refusing to acknowledge Mao. Nixon took the first steps in 1969 by relaxing some of the trade restrictions in place against the PRC, and Mao responded positively by agreeing that the PRC could engage in informal trade discussions with the United States.

ANALYSIS

How did Mao use the bipolar tension of the Cold War to strengthen his own position?

Ping-Pong Diplomacy

The big shift came in April 1971 in the most unlikely of places—the World Table Tennis Championship in Japan. Members of the Chinese and U.S. teams became friendly, and Mao invited the U.S. team to the PRC for an exhibition event. They were the first Americans allowed in the PRC since 1949, and *Time* magazine dubbed it "ping-pong diplomacy." The U.S. team was accompanied by ten journalists (five of them American) who covered the visit, and Mao's government fully capitalized on the public relations opportunity. The world was treated to a well-choreographed perspective of the PRC's beautiful country, its rich culture and its friendly people. Chinese Premier Chou En-lai announced: "I am confident that this beginning again of our friendship will certainly meet with majority support of our two peoples," and invited more American journalists to visit the PRC.

In response, Nixon ended the twenty-year trade embargo against the PRC, and Kissinger secretly visited Beijing in July to negotiate the groundwork for a formal relationship between the PRC and the United States. Trade agreements were made, and American exports to the PRC jumped from $5 million in 1969 to $700 million in 1973. The United States also agreed to stop blocking UN attempts to transfer the recognition of the "official" China from Chiang Kai-shek's Republic of China (ROC) in Taiwan to Mao's People's Republic of China. On October 25, 1971, UN Resolution 2758 withdrew recognition of the ROC as the official government of China, declaring "that the representatives of the Government of the People's Republic of China are the only lawful representatives of China to the United Nations." Mao's PRC assumed China's coveted permanent seat on the Security Council, although the United States continued to pursue a **"two Chinas" policy** by publicly supporting both Taiwan and the PRC.

"two Chinas" policy the United States' attempt to maintain diplomatic and trade relationships with both the ROC in Taiwan and Mao's PRC

Nixon himself visited Beijing in February 1972, the first U.S. president to ever do so. The very public visit was a display of friendship and cooperation between Nixon and Mao, and it sent a clear message to Brezhnev that the Cold War had just warmed considerably in Asia. The result of the meeting was the Shanghai Communiqué, issued on February 27, 1972. In it, both the United States and China (as the PRC could now officially be called) agreed to "normalize"

President Nixon meets with China's Communist Party Leader, Mao Tse-Tung on February 29, 1972.

relations and that neither would "seek hegemony in the Asia-Pacific region." In a clear threat to the USSR, both China and the United States announced their joint opposition to "efforts by any other country or group of countries to establish such hegemony." The Shanghai Communiqué was unique in that it also contained passages in which Chinese and U.S. positions diverged sharply, particularly over ongoing U.S. military presence in Taiwan.

Read the Document *The Shanghai Communiqué* on mysearchlab.com

Mao died in 1976, and Deng Xiaoping emerged as the new leader. In 1978, China used its trade relationship with the United States to begin a gradual conversion to a market-based rather than state-directed economy. In other words, Deng started backing away from communist economics while maintaining communist politics. The transition was not smooth, and many people and some civil liberties died in the process, but the change in the economy extended China's powerful position in the military realm to the international economy as well, something the USSR was never able to achieve.

The Helsinki Agreement

The relationship between the United States and China had economic and security consequences for the USSR. Clearly, the new friendship was grounded in a common interest in limiting Soviet power. In what was obviously a veiled message to Brezhnev, Nixon told Mao: "There is no reason for us to be enemies...Neither of us seeks the territory of the other; neither of us seeks domination over the other; neither of us seeks to stretch out our hands and rule the world." Because he could not repair his relationship with Mao, Brezhnev was compelled to negotiate with the United States to keep from being marginalized.

As the US military began its withdrawal from Vietnam and Taiwan in the 1970s, the Chinese military could focus its full attention on the USSR. Brezhnev was eager to pursue the SALT I negotiations to curb the arms race, as well as secure the Soviet position on his western borders. Three decades after the end of World War II, representatives from thirty-three European countries, the United States and Canada convened the Conference on Security and Cooperation in Europe to settle the border disputes and other differences that still lingered in Europe. After two years of negotiations, they signed the **Helsinki Agreement** in August 1975, which laid out three areas (known as "baskets") of provisions.

Helsinki Agreement a declaration focused on improving the relations between communist world and the West; ratified in an attempt to reduce Cold War tensions

The first basket dealt with practical security issues such as preventing war and required the peaceful settlement of disputes for all signatories. The most important provision in the first basket was the confirmation of existing borders, meaning that the Soviet sphere of influence across Eastern Europe became official and indisputable. The second basket of provisions focused on trade agreements and cooperation in cultural, industrial and economic affairs. This led to an unofficial "economic détente" in which goods and capital investment flowed much more freely between the East and West. For example, Brezhnev signed a trade agreement that sent $700 million worth of wheat from the United States to the USSR, creating a degree of interdependency between the two rivals. The final basket of provisions guaranteed respect for human rights and political freedoms. While the USSR generally ignored the third basket altogether, the fact that the USSR signed off on the agreement would later provide a legal foundation for political dissident movements within the satellite bloc.

On the whole, the Helsinki Agreement codified the spirit of détente by solidifying the existing spheres of influence and extending the benefits of trade across the world without the risk of cultural or ideological subversion. European countries were happy that border disputes were finally settled, and both the United States and USSR gained what they needed by the economic provisions. The USSR received much-needed food, consumer goods and capital investment, and the United States opened new markets in which to sell U.S. goods.

Although the Helsinki Agreement created a measure of political and economic security across Europe, it did nothing to address nuclear proliferation and the threat of a devastating World War III. The SALT II negotiations over nuclear de-armament finally produced an accord in June 1979, but it was too late. Ongoing tension in the Middle East, which had been a threat to détente throughout the 1970s, resulted in the Soviet invasion of Afghanistan in December 1979.

In protest, the U.S. Senate refused to ratify the SALT II Treaty. Détente was over, and the Cold War was hot once again.

Conclusions

By the end of the 1960s and into the 1970s, both the United States and the USSR were feeling the financial, social and political stresses of the Cold War. To relieve that stress and address internal needs, both sides markedly shifted their foreign policies—the USSR imported money and goods from the West, and the United States embraced trade with the PRC. This period of détente was ushered in by three factors outside of Soviet or American control: (1) as decolonization progressed, new countries were created that preferred nonalignment to Cold War conflict; (2) the countries of Western Europe (particularly France) strengthened their military and economic positions and sought to cooperatively forge a "European" identity distinct from Cold War definitions; and (3) Mao's People's Republic of China became an independent and powerful state.

The result of détente was a shift away from the rigid ideological bipolar structure of the world toward a multipolar system in which decision making was based on practical security interests rather than rhetoric. The shift led to increased economic interdependence, which meant sometimes uncomfortably relying on trade agreements with "enemies" to keep economies healthy and the military machines running. For both the United States and the USSR, that meant maintaining access to affordable oil.

WORKING WITH THE THEMES

THE EFFECTS OF TECHNOLOGY How much of the "space race" do you think was political or ideological, and how much was strategic? Describe how two new members in the nuclear club (PRC and France) affected traditional Cold War alliances. What factors led to American and Soviet willingness to negotiate weapons treaties?

CHANGING IDENTITIES How do you think Soviet citizens responded to the social changes wrought by Brezhnev's reforms? What do you think was Brezhnev's biggest problem with Dubcek's Action Program—the actual policies, the public support they received, or Dubcek's independence in policy making? What did the United States fear most about the election of Salvadore Allende? Was the charge of "Yankee imperialism" justified, or was the United States simply fighting the Cold War?

SHIFTING BORDERS What were the legal foundations established by the Helsinki Agreement? Do you think Brezhnev realized the ramifications on future Soviet action but decided the agreement was more vital for the USSR?

GLOBALIZATION Did détente really *change* the nature of the Cold War, or was détente merely a sign that the Cold War structure was changing? Why did so many nations agree to sign the NPT, and what have been the long-term effects? How did economics play a role in the shifting Cold War order in the late 1970s (consider the United States, the USSR, China, and decolonization)? What do you think was the greatest threat to peace at the end of the 1970s?

Further Reading

TO FIND OUT MORE

National Aeronautics and Space Administration: 50th Anniversary of the Space Age 1957–2007. Available online at http://www.nasa.gov/externalflash/SpaceAge/

MATRIX, the Center for Humane Arts, Letters and Social Sciences Online: Seventeen Moments in Soviet History—1968, 1973, 1980. Available online at http://www.soviethistory.org/

Wilfried Loth: *Overcoming the Cold War: A History of Détente, 1950–1991* (2002)

Robert V. Daniels: *Russia's Transformation: Snapshots of a Crumbling System* (1997)

Computer History Museum. Available online at http://www.computerhistory.org/

Anne Walker: *China Calls: Paving the Way for Nixon's Historic Journey to China* (1992)

GO TO THE SOURCE

U.S. Department of State/Office of the Historian: Historical Documents. Available online at http://history.state.gov/historicaldocuments

Richard M. Nixon Library and Museum. Available online at http://www.nixonlibrary.gov/

Russian Archives Online: Available online at http://www.russianarchives.com/index.html

National Security Archive/Jaromír Navrátil (ed.): *The Prague Spring '68* (1988).

National Security Archive/Peter Kornbluh (ed.): *The Pinochet File: A Declassified Dossier on Atrocity and Accountability* (2004)

Central Intelligence Agency: Strategic Warning and the Role of Intelligence: Lessons Learned From The 1968 Soviet Invasion of Czechoslovakia. Available online at http://www.foia.cia.gov/CzechInvasion.asp

National Intelligence Council: Latin America NIEs. Available online at http://www.dni.gov/nic/NIC_foia_latin_america.html

MySearchLab Connections

Read the **Document** on **mysearchlab.com**

10.1 *U.S. Reaction to Prague Spring*. These notes, from a meeting of the U.S. National Security Council in September, 1968, describe how the NSC assessed the Soviet invasion of Czechoslovakia in August of that same year.

10.2 *The Shanghai Communiqué*. This agreement between the United States and China, signed following President Richard Nixon's historic trip to China in 1972, led to cultural and economic exchange programs between the two countries and the eventual establishment of diplomatic relations in 1979.

Watch the **Video** on **mysearchlab.com**

10.1 *The Science of Spying, 1965*

11

Conflict in the Middle East

CHAPTER OUTLINE

- Arab-Israeli Relations
- Iraq and Iran
- Soviet Invasion of Afghanistan

CHAPTER TIMELINE

1948
Israel is established; the first Arab–Israeli War begins

1952
Nasser takes over Egypt

1953
Mossadeq is overthrown and the Shah restored in Iran
United States establishes military base in Saudi Arabia

1956
Nasser nationalizes the Suez Canal

1958
Internal communist coup changes Iraqi government
UAR is created

1978
President Carter visits Iran in support of Shah
Internal communist coup takes over Afghanistan

1979
U.S. embassy in Iran seized; hostage crisis begins
Shah of Iran is overthrown
Ayatollah Khomeini takes power
Iran–Iraq War begins
USSR invades Afghanistan
Saddam Hussein takes power in Iraq

1981
Reagan takes office in United States
U.S. hostages released

Photos from left to right: Begin, Carter, and Sadat at Camp David, September 1978; Gamal Nasser; Iranian Revolution, 1979; Fatah, PLO poster.

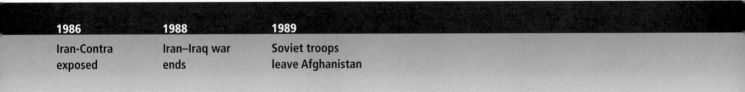

1964	1967	1970	1973	1975	1977
PLO is created	Six-Day War; Israeli settlements established UN passes Resolution 242	Nasser dies; Sadat takes power in Egypt	OPEC initiates oil embargo against the West Yom Kippur War occurs	Lebanese Civil War begins	Camp David Accords are signed

1986	1988	1989
Iran-Contra exposed	Iran–Iraq war ends	Soviet troops leave Afghanistan

As the Cold War structure was shifting with the détente of the 1960s and 1970s, events in the Middle East presented serious challenges to the existing international order and stability. There were many intersecting conflicts that had nothing to do with the fairly straightforward choice between democracy and communism that the superpowers wanted the world to make. Arab nationalism rose up against centuries of Western imperialism; Islam took on Judaism and Christianity; the age-old dispute between Shia and Sunni Muslims raged on; and ethnic and religious groups fought over territory each claimed legal and historic rights to. Caught up in the spiraling arms race of the Cold War, these regional conflicts turned violent. The superpowers tried to apply traditional proxy rules, trading money and weapons for loyalty, but neither the pan-Arabists nor the pan-Islamists cared about democracy or communism. As confused and conflicting as the situation often was, American and Soviet decision making in the region was driven by the need to maintain access to large amounts of inexpensive oil—their military and economic strength depended on it.

WORKING WITH THE THEMES

THE EFFECTS OF TECHNOLOGY Wars in the Middle East are fought with everything available: human waves, homemade bombs, imported Soviet and American heavy artillery, chemical weapons, and the threat of nuclear attacks.

CHANGING IDENTITIES The Arab-Israeli crisis ignites a massive refugee crisis. Pan-Arabists square off against pan-Islamists for regional control. Religious, ethnic, and nationalist differences lead to ongoing conflict.

SHIFTING BORDERS The creation of Israel in 1948 sets off a series of attacks and wars in the region that expands the size of the territory in dispute.

GLOBALIZATION Although the religious and ethnic differences in the Middle East do not fit into the Cold War framework, the United States and USSR actively intervene to maintain access to the oil. Jihad is declared against the West.

Arab–Israeli Relations

The relationship between Jewish communities and surrounding Arab states has been marked by violence since the early twentieth century when Jewish settlers began moving to British-controlled Palestine. Despite Israel's limited membership in the United Nations since 1949, the Arab states did not recognize Israel as a legal state; rather, they referred to it as an occupied territory. Major violent conflicts occurred between the warring factions in 1956, 1967, 1973 and 1982 and, despite several negotiated peace agreements, terrorist attacks on both sides have occurred with alarming regularity. The **refugee** crisis created by the ongoing violence and persistent foreign intervention has destabilized the entire region. When refugees move quickly and in large numbers, they often have no legal status in the country they have fled to, and the refugees are confined to camps and limited in their political, economic and social opportunities.

refugee
a person who has fled his or her country due to a legitimate fear of being persecuted for reasons of race, religion, nationality, or membership of a particular social group or political opinion

The first Arab–Israeli War in 1948 initiated a refugee crisis during which an estimated 725,000 Palestinians in the new Israeli state and almost as many Jewish people in surrounding Arab states were forced to flee their homes. Israel gained desperately needed human resources by bringing in the Jewish refugees and instituting mandatory conscription into the Israel Defense Forces (IDF) for all citizens over eighteen years of age. In the following years, the number of Palestinian refugees demanding the right to return to their homes in the "occupied" territory grew to 4 million. The Israeli government refused to allow their return because Arabs would then constitute the majority of the population and would most certainly vote the Israeli state out of existence.

As the Cold War took shape in the early 1950s, financial and military support poured into the region, adding fuel to the fire. The United States and the West allied with Israel and provided military support to Saudi Arabia, Lebanon and Jordan, and the USSR provided military aid to Egypt, Syria, Iraq and the Palestine Liberation Organization (PLO).

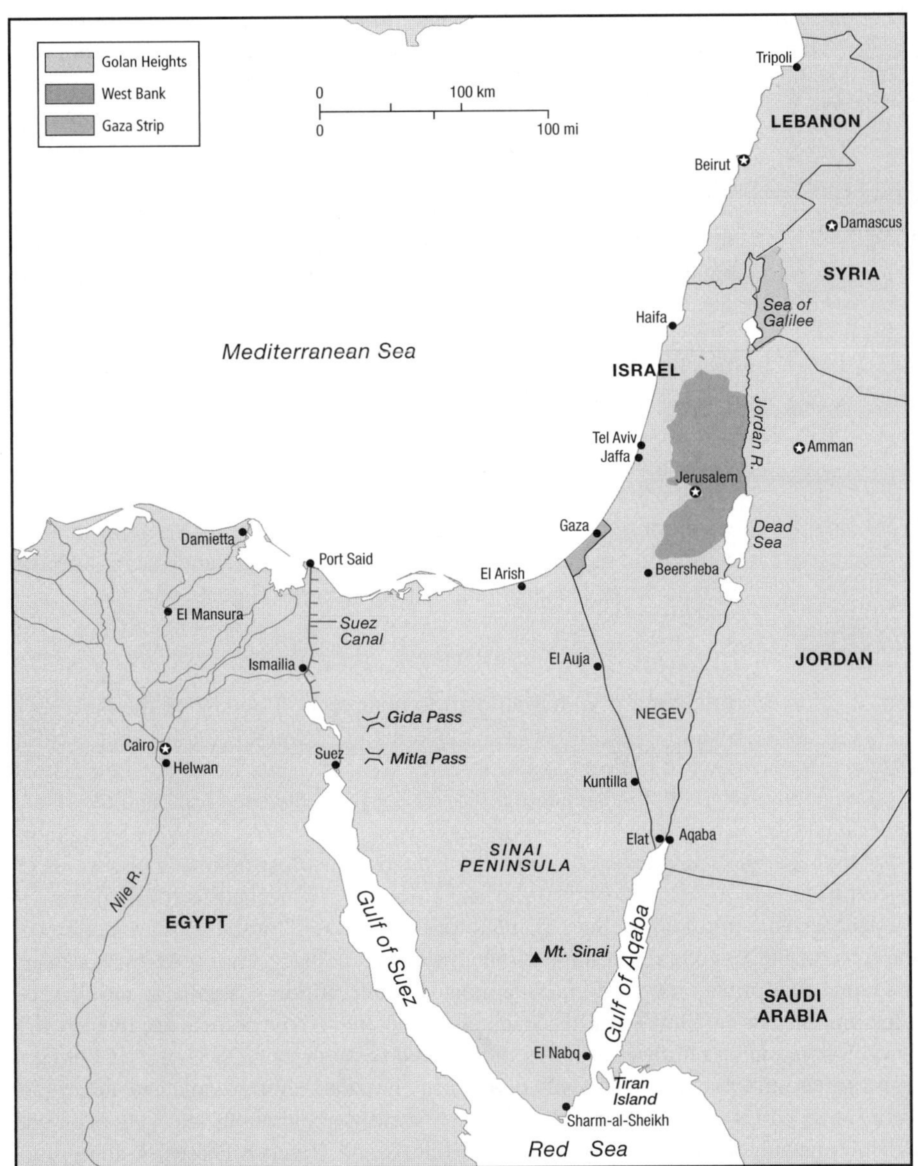

MAP 11.1 Israel and Its Neighbors, 1948

Egypt

In 1952, the King of Egypt was overthrown by an internal military coup, and the Egyptian Revolutionary Command Council took control of the government. The very popular Gamal Nasser became president of the newly created single-party state based on his Arab nationalist platform. He was adamantly anti-Western and blamed colonialism for the economic problems throughout the Middle East. He also was outraged that Israel had seized Arab land with the support of the Western world and demanded that all Arab territories be united (**pan-Arabism**), preferably under him. Nasser became the *de facto* leader of the Arab opposition to Israel, mostly because each Arab state was having its own internal economic problems exacerbated by the refugee crisis sparked by the 1948 war. Despite the many political and religious differences between the Arab states, they shared a common opposition to the continued existence of Israel.

pan-Arabism
a secular nationalist movement based on the belief that Arabs should be politically united in one Arab state

Arab Revolution poster.

In the face of this open aggression, Israel continued to build its military with support from the West, particularly France. To build his pan-Arab army, Nasser needed weapons as well. But given his vocal opposition to Israel, the United States refused to provide military support to Egypt unless U.S. troops were stationed there to supervise the situation and prevent another Arab–Israeli war. This was, after all, the Cold War, and the United States feared the spread of communism into the Middle East. If there were U.S. troops on the ground in Egypt, it would limit Soviet expansion there. But Nasser denounced the U.S. demand for a military presence in Egypt as yet another attempt at colonialism and turned to the USSR for military aid to defeat Israel.

As Soviet and American weapons poured into the region, a proxy war heated up along the Egypt–Israeli border in a region known as the Gaza Strip. Palestinian raids on Israel increased, and Israel conducted retaliatory assaults. With the situation tense, Nasser was looking for a way to demonstrate his military strength to assert himself as the leader of the entire Middle East under pan-Arabism, and he found it in the nationalization of the Suez Canal.

The Suez Crisis

Building a new Aswan dam to control the flooding of the Nile River was a crucial project for modernizing Egypt's economy, but building the dam was also a very expensive project. Nasser initially secured a loan from the United States and Britain, promising he would help alleviate the violent conflict between Israel and the Arabs. But after Nasser made the arms deal with the Soviets and went against U.S. policy by recognizing the legality of Mao's People's Republic of China, the United States lost faith that Nasser would carry out his part of the arrangement. In July 1956, the United States backed out of the loan; one week later, Nasser seized control of the Suez Canal to raise the money for the dam project by collecting all the tolls for the Egyptian government. The move was popular among Arabs, but losing control of the canal cost private investors in Britain and France millions of dollars, and they demanded retaliation. The United States, fearing Soviet involvement and the potential to ignite World War III, refused to condone a military response and worked through the UN Security Council to negotiate a repayment and use schedule with Egypt. But France secretly contacted Israel, and Israel was more than happy to participate in a military attack on Egypt. In late October 1956, France and Britain launched an air war over Egypt, while Israeli Defense Forces on the ground seized control of the Sinai region of Egypt. The United Nations, the United States and the USSR condemned the attack; invading forces were removed, and the canal was reopened under Egyptian control in April 1957.

Read the Document *Speech on the Suez Canal* on mysearchlab.com

The effect of the Suez Crisis was tremendous for Nasser's popularity among the Arab people, but government leaders in Jordan, Saudi Arabia, Iraq and Lebanon grew concerned about Nasser's expanding power over their citizens. In May 1958, Nasser ignited a civil war in Lebanon to oust its president and pave the way for pro-Nasser supporters to seize political control. U.S. and British troops participated to defend the existing governments of Jordan and Lebanon, but they could do nothing to stem the rising tide of pan-Arabism among the people.

security regime
an agreement between nations to develop principles, rules and norms to regulate state behavior, with an understanding that the peace within the community is not permanent

Both the United States and USSR watched events unfold with concern and confusion—Nasser was clearly supported by the USSR, but he was an avid anticommunist because the communist movement in the Middle East stood in the way of pan-Arabism. In 1958, to cut off a growing communist movement in Soviet-supported Syria, Nasser merged Egypt and Syria to create the United Arab Republic (UAR), and he was, of course, its president. Yet neither the

United States nor the USSR could risk alienating Nasser because of his popular appeal in the region. The growth of the UAR could solidify Nasser's control over the world's oil supply, which would negatively impact both U.S. and Soviet power. But working against Nasser could push his supporters into the enemy's sphere of influence. This made the proxy wars in the Middle East particularly confusing.

In 1958, when the pro-Western monarchs of Jordan and Iraq discussed plans to form a **security regime** to counter the power of the UAR, Nasser urged Iraqi army officers to assassinate the king and prime minister of Iraq and establish the Republic of Iraq. Though the new regime in Iraq would not join the UAR, neither would it challenge Egypt's power in the region. But Nasser continued to interfere in Iraqi politics, leading to a decade of political instability in Iraq during which leaders also received military and financial assistance from the USSR and United States to help solidify their power.

Although Saudi Arabia was a conservative Muslim monarchy (and therefore anti-Israel), it received military and economic aid from the United States to resist Nasser's pressure for political union. A U.S. military training base was established in 1953 to assist the Saudi armed forces, which were armed with U.S. aircraft, missiles, and armored vehicles. After a Saudi government-led assassination attempt on Nasser was exposed in 1958, Saudi Arabia became a leading advocate of **pan-Islamism,** opposed to Nasser's pan-Arab movement, and continued to receive U.S. support.

Within the UAR, Syria's military and political leaders began to resent their second-rate status to Egyptians. Egyptian economic policies were disastrous when applied in Syria, and communist groups, **Baathists** and surrounding Arab governments funneled money into Syria to support a growing anti-Nasser sentiment. In September 1961, the Syrian military declared its independence from the UAR and fought Egyptian forces for two days until Nasser allowed Syria to secede. Nasser admitted that he made mistakes with Syria and began enacting socialist policies in Egypt to prevent a revolution against him there.

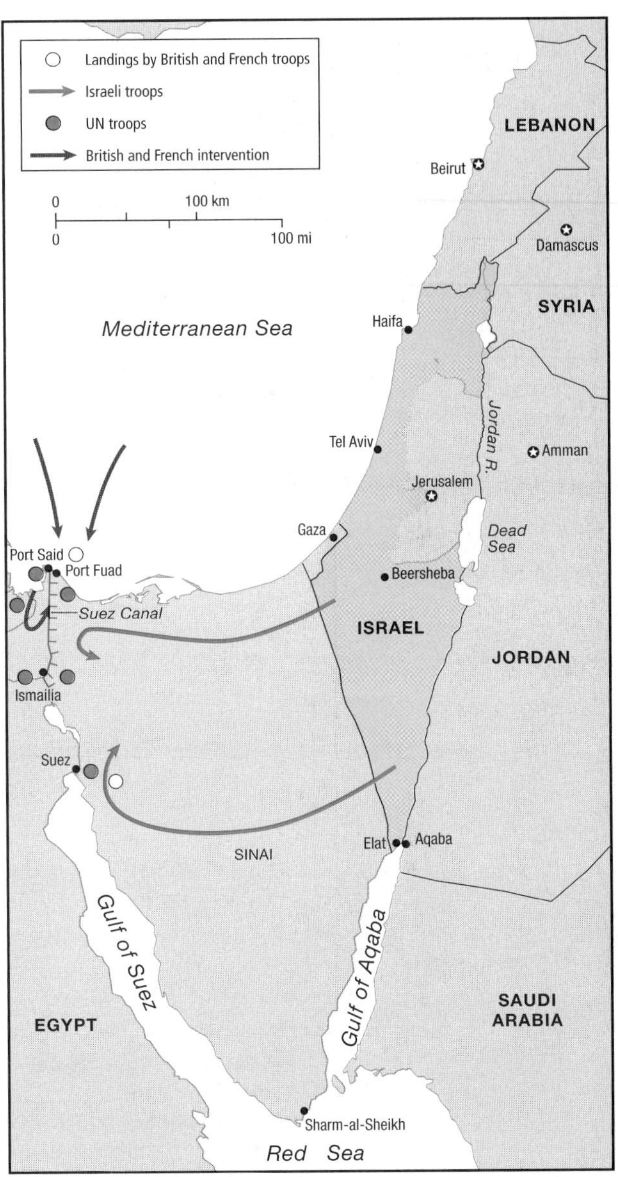

MAP 11.2 The Suez Crisis, 1956

The Palestine Liberation Organization

Palestinians supported Nasser, and he in turn helped Palestinians create several militant and political organizations to fight for the removal of the Israeli state from their territory. In 1964, Egypt worked through the Arab League to pull the various groups together as the Palestine Liberation Organization. The PLO was dominated by *al-Fatah*—a militant organization of young Palestinians who believed that guerrilla action was the only way to earn freedom from Israeli occupation. So, once again, tension heated up between Israel (supported by the United States and Britain) and Palestinians (supported by Egypt and Syria, which were supported by the USSR), resulting in terrorist attacks in spring 1967 that culminated in the Six-Day War.

The chairman of the PLO from 1969 to 2004 was Yasir Arafat, an advocate of the use of armed force to create a Palestinian state. His leadership marked a substantial shift in the goal for Palestinians, which had initially been to work with other Arab countries to remove Israel from

pan-Islamism
a political movement arguing for the unity of Muslims under one unified Islamic state, as it was during the reign of Muhammad

Baathists
a pan-Arab socialist political party founded in Syria and later spread to Iraq; Arabic for "renaissance"

the region. But Arafat wanted more, and in 1968 he led a movement to rewrite the PLO charter. After suffering a devastating loss in the Six-Day War, the PLO decided that removing Israel was not enough and demanded the creation of an independent Palestinian state. With the new charter in hand, the PLO separated itself from Egyptian and Syrian control; the PLO earned UN observer status in 1974 and Arab League membership (as a government-in-exile) in 1976.

The Six-Day War

Ongoing violence between Israel and the Arab states once again erupted in major warfare in 1967, and the Cold War climate was a huge contributing factor. When Israel completed a water project in 1964 that would greatly enhance its economy by providing much-needed irrigation for agriculture, Syria (a Baathist regime allied with the USSR) demanded that Egypt take military action against Israel to destroy the project. But Nasser resisted because his military would have to go through UN

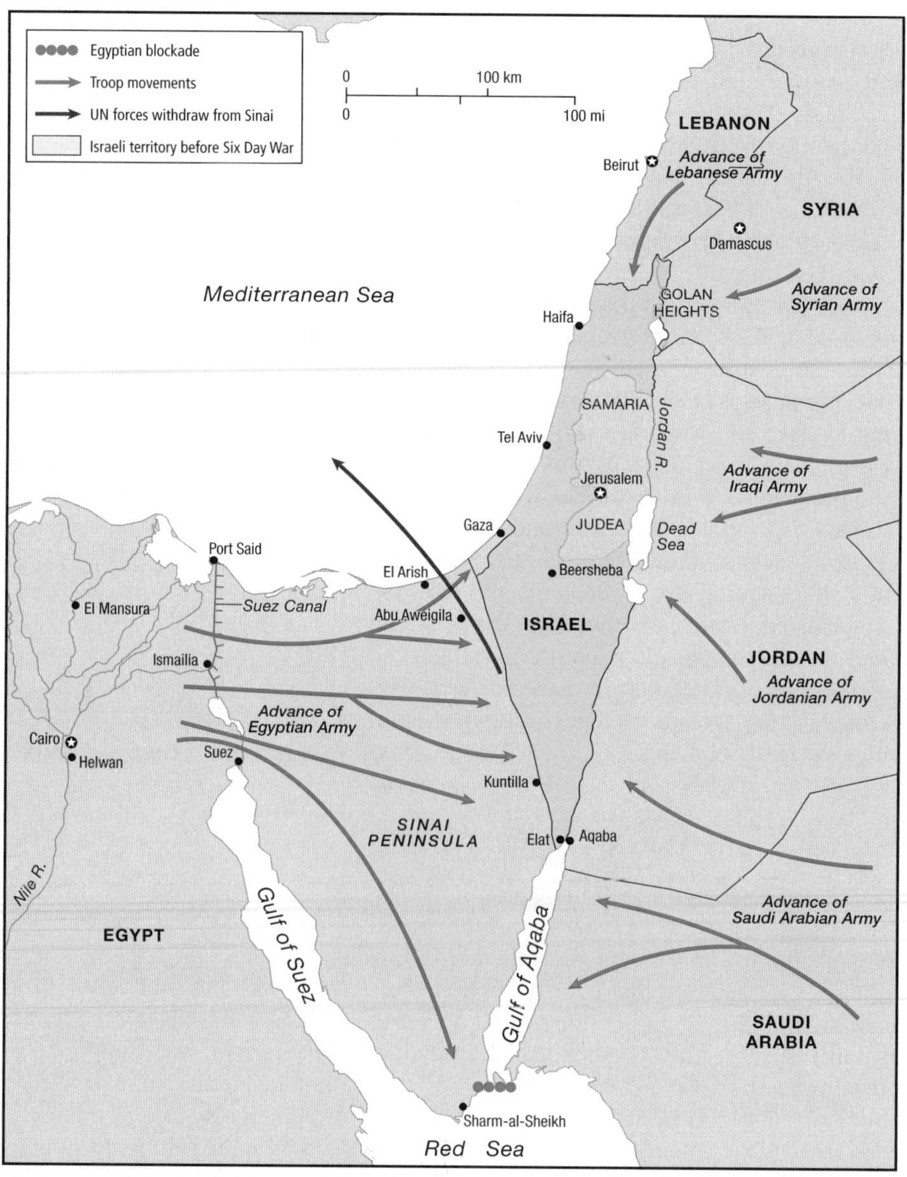

MAP 11.3 The Six-Day War

peacekeepers stationed in Sinai to get there, and he did not yet fully trust his pan-Arab "partners" to participate. To demonstrate their support, Syria and Jordan stepped up terrorist activities against Israel in 1966 as Nasser was negotiating with the United Nations for the removal of the peacekeeping force. When UN peacekeepers left Sinai in May 1967, Nasser promptly moved 80,000 troops, 550 tanks and 1,000 pieces of heavy artillery to the Egypt–Israel border. He also blockaded the Straits of Tiran, sealing off major Israeli ports from trade. As Nasser grew more aggressive, his support from the Arab states grew. Syria committed its 100,000-member army with Soviet tanks and combat planes. King Hussein of Jordan, despite his close ties to the United States and the fact that Nasser had attempted to assassinate him several times, also joined the pan-Arab military effort. Iraq sent troops to the West Bank; Syria, Lebanon and Algeria sent jet fighters (many with Pakistani pilots); and Saudi Arabia (another U.S. ally), Morocco, Tunisia, Sudan and Libya all contributed volunteer forces. The Arab oil-producing countries (Saudi Arabia, Kuwait, Bahrain, Iraq, Algeria, Qatar, and Libya) boycotted the United States, Great Britain and any other country that supported Israel in any way. Nasser threatened to close the Suez Canal; and Sudan, Algeria, Iraq, Mauritania and Yemen severed diplomatic ties with the United States.

In May 1967, Israel encompassed about 7,200 square miles, with a standing army of 75,000 troops, 1,000 tanks and 175 jet fighters, a fraction of the combined Arab forces. Israel tried to negotiate with Egypt to prevent war, but when that effort failed, Israel requested military support from its allies (France, Great Britain and the United States) and planned a **preemptive attack** on Egypt to gain an offensive position. But France's foreign policy had shifted toward reconciliation with the Arab world after granting independence to Algeria in 1962, and France refused to send any more offensive weapons to Israel. Although Great Britain was concerned about an increase in anti-West sentiment, it feared the instability that would result in the Middle East if Israel was destroyed even more and agreed to provide limited defensive weapons. The U.S. government worked furiously to find a diplomatic solution to what seemed an inevitable proxy war pitting Soviet allies against U.S. allies in a volatile region of the world. The United States, USSR and France repeatedly warned Israel not to initiate a war against Egypt and its pan-Arab army.

preemptive attack a military action designed to neutralize a potential threat or to gain a "first strike" advantage against an enemy; generally considered an offensive action under international law

As the Arabs and Israelis openly prepared for battle in May 1967, the Cold War nature of the conflict became evident. The United States had three goals: (1) to make sure that its democratic ally in the Middle East was not destroyed; (2) to maintain good relationships with its Arab trading partners to keep the oil flowing; and (3) to prevent World War III by minimizing U.S. military involvement against Soviet-supported countries. Consequently, the United States opted for diplomacy. The USSR, on the other hand, hoped to unite the Arab countries as Soviet allies, which would cut off U.S. oil supplies and expand the Soviet sphere of influence across the Middle East. To do that, the Soviets needed a war.

On May 13, the USSR told Syria and Egypt that Soviet surveillance had picked up a tremendous gathering of Israeli forces on Syria's border—Israel was clearly preparing for an offensive attack sometime that week. This was a lie that was quickly disproven by Egypt's military intelligence and the CIA, but it was enough to goad Nasser into war. Nasser's pan-Arab army surrounded Israel, increased reconnaissance missions, and blocked roads with land mines. Israel decided to go to war, even without U.S. support.

The war began on June 5, 1967, and encompassed three fronts: Egypt, Jordan and Syria. On the Egyptian front, Israel launched a well-coordinated preemptive air strike that destroyed command centers and wiped out 80 percent of Egypt's bombers and 55 percent of its fighter jets within hours. At the same time, 45,000 Israeli troops invaded Sinai and Gaza, facing 100,000 Egyptian troops with Soviet artillery. Israeli forces moved quickly, dividing the Egyptian force, and ended the war in Sinai in just four days. In a stunning defeat, Egypt lost forty times more troops than Israel, and 5,000 soldiers were captured.

Jordan concentrated the bulk of its troops in the West Bank, with four Iraqi brigades and two Egyptian battalions behind them for support. Just after the fighting began on the Egyptian front, the Jordanian army opened a second front with heavy artillery aimed at Israeli air bases and moved into southern Jerusalem unopposed. Here, the Israeli response was strategic rather than forceful—Israeli fighter jets waited until Jordanian planes were refueling and destroyed them all at once. Most of the brutal three-day ground war took place in and around the holy sites of Jerusalem and the West Bank, with Israeli forces in control by the time a UN cease-fire was declared on June 7, 1967.

Buoyed by false reports that the Israeli air force was being destroyed in Egypt, Syrian planes began bombing northern Israel in the early afternoon of June 5. That evening, the Israeli air force retaliated, knocking the Syrian air force out of the war completely. The invading Syrian ground troops were quickly defeated without air support. Israeli forces counterattacked on June 9 and 10, invading the Syrian-held territory of the Golan Heights. The Israeli government knew it would be difficult to seize control of this well-fortified area defended by natural geography (cliffs) and 75,000 Syrian troops but went forward with the attack when it realized that Egypt, Syria and Jordan were accepting UN cease-fire agreements. The Syrian military fell apart, and Israel seized the Golan Heights. The Six-Day War ended on June 10, 1967.

When the Six-Day War ended, Israel believed it had proven its strength and the Arab states would be forced to accept its existence. But the Arab nationalists and the USSR were not ready to give up yet. In early July, the USSR resupplied Egypt and Syria with heavy artillery and fighter jets. Nasser announced that he was preparing his pan-Arab army to continue the battle against Israel and its supporters who encouraged the imperialist war. Although there was no evidence that the U.S. or British militaries were involved in the war, Nasser linked them to the conflict in order to ensure ongoing Soviet support. In August, the leaders of thirteen Arab states held a summit in Khartoum, Sudan, where they pledged there would be no peace with Israel, no recognition of Israel and no negotiation with Israel.

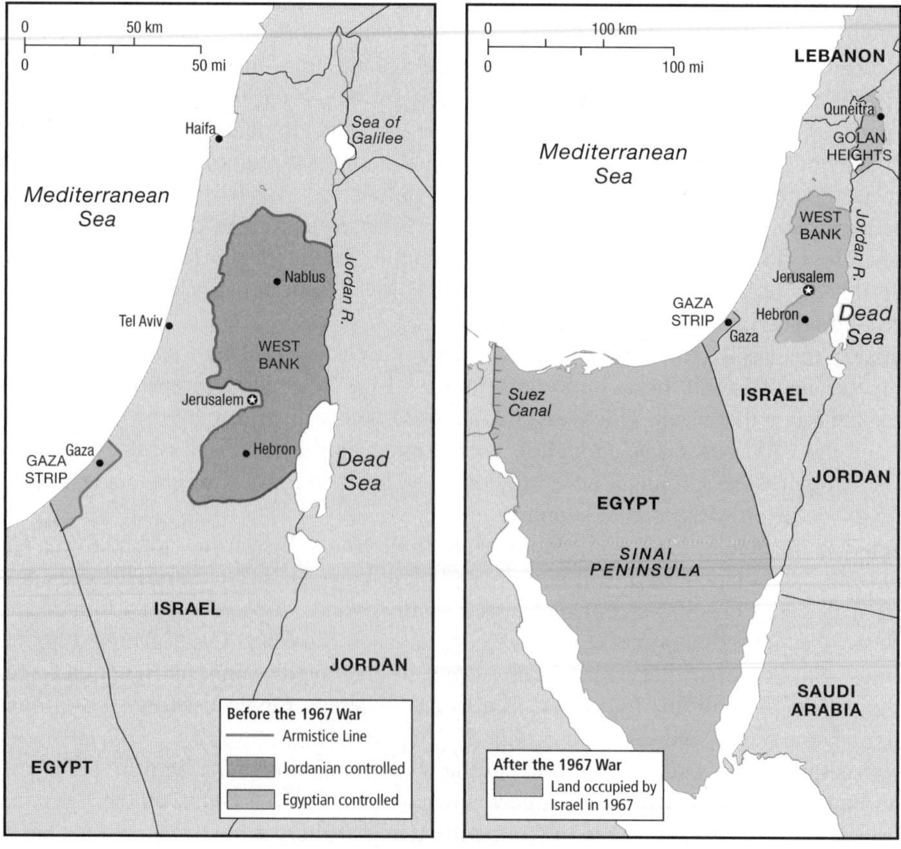

MAP 11.4 Consequences of the Six-Day War

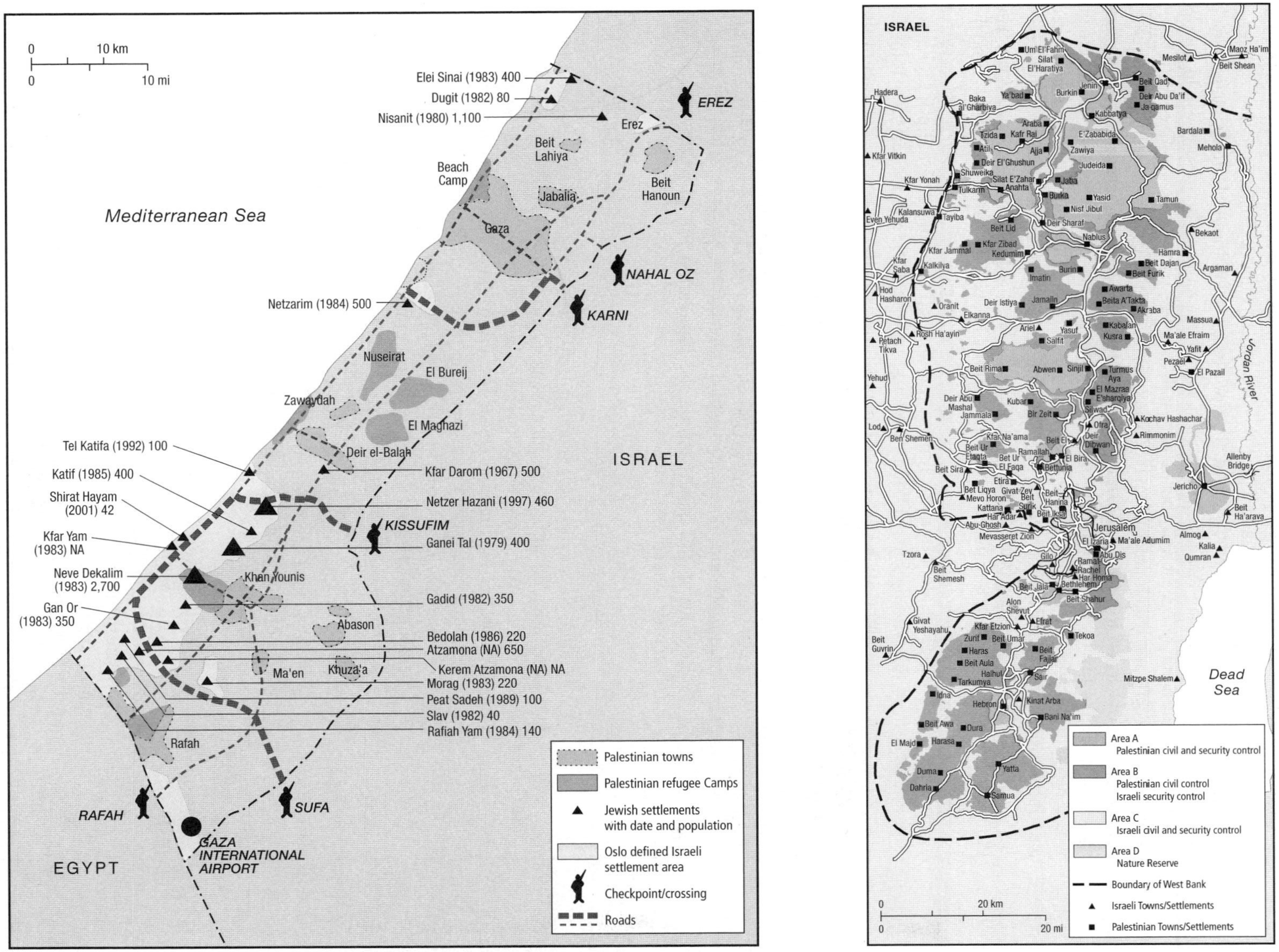

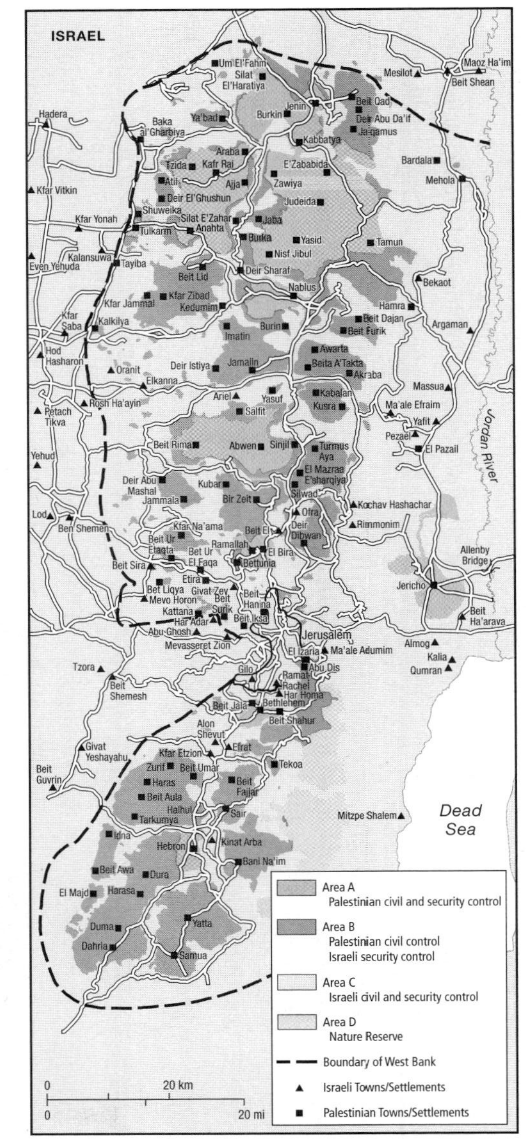

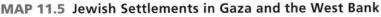

MAP 11.5 Jewish Settlements in Gaza and the West Bank

Read the Document *United Nations Security Council Resolution 242* on mysearchlab.com

The consequences of the Six-Day War were dramatic: Israel (mostly on its own) clearly defeated the much larger pan-Arab army and its Soviet weapons. Israel occupied Sinai, the Golan Heights, the West Bank, the Gaza Strip and East Jerusalem, making Israel three times larger than it was after the 1948 war. On the one hand, Israel was in a much better defensive situation with territory and a superior military; on the other hand, there were now 1 million Arabs living under Israeli government. The surrounding Arab states would not let them move in because it would further exacerbate the difficult refugee crisis, but if the Arabs stayed, particularly confined in refugee camps, it would certainly lead to internal civil conflict for Israel. The Israeli government offered to negotiate with Arab states to return some of the occupied territory (keeping Jerusalem for religious reasons and the West Bank for security reasons), but the Khartoum summit made it clear that there would be no negotiation. To help the Arabs assimilate into Israeli culture, the government created an "open bridges" program and helped "rehabilitate" them. They also established controversial Jewish **settlements** in the West Bank, Hebron, the Golan Heights, Sinai and the Gaza Strip. The PLO reacted violently, demanding that all occupied territory be returned to the Palestinians and the Jewish settlements destroyed.

settlements communities of Jewish people built in what the Arabs consider to be occupied territory

In June 1967, U.S. President Lyndon Johnson announced five fundamental principles for "durable peace" in the Middle East. Though it would involve U.S. and UN efforts, Johnson declared that "the main responsibility for the peace of the region depends upon its own peoples and its own leaders of that region. What will be truly decisive in the Middle East will be what is said and what is done by those who live in the Middle East." Given the language of the Khartoum conference, no one was terribly optimistic. On November 22, 1967, the UN Security Council passed Resolution 242 to guide the Middle East in the peace-making process. The goals and expectations of Resolution 242 have become the foundation for all Middle East peace accords since.

Youth for Settlement Strongholds poster.

Yom Kippur War

Gamal Nasser died in September 1970. His successor, Anwar el-Sadat, inherited a nation suffering from a weak economy, low national morale over the Six-Day War, and tenuous relationships with its Arab and Soviet allies. Despite the fact that the USSR had given Egypt more aid than it had given any other single country to that point in the Cold War ($4.75 million), Sadat expelled Soviet advisors in 1972 (but kept all their military equipment). With Soviet support gone, Sadat decided to pursue a better relationship with the United States, which would require him to take a much more moderate position toward Israel. He offered to sit down at the negotiating table with Israeli Prime Minister Golda Meir, but she refused any proposal that involved giving back the land Israel gained in the Six-Day War. Sadat developed an extensive economic reform program, but he did not enjoy the support of the citizens to make the program work. The only answer, then, was a military victory over Israel that would rejuvenate his people and his economy.

As Sadat began to build support for another war against Israel, he found a willing partner in Hafez al-Assad of Syria. With Soviet support, Assad had been building his military in hopes of replacing the weakening Egyptian government as the dominant power of the Arab states. In doing so, Assad had alienated President Bakr of Iraq and King Hussein of Jordan, and neither country was anxious to join another potentially doomed war against Israel. Sadat also promised to turn over the West Bank to the PLO, and Jordan and Lebanon certainly did not want to fight for that. Sadat worked hard to earn support for his war and by fall 1973 claimed to have one hundred states behind him, including Britain and France on the UN Security Council. Now all he needed was weapons. Sadat convinced the Soviets that if they did not

MAKE THE CONNECTION

There is tremendous debate over the legality of the Israeli settlements. Why? Look at Map 11.5 and read UN Resolution 242. Can you make the argument for both sides?

Three Arab heads of state: President Anwar Sadat of the UAR, Premier Lt. Col. Muammar al-Qaddafi of Libya, and President Lt. Gen. Hafez al-Assad of Syria (L-R).

provide weapons and technology for this war, he would lose political power in Egypt to a pro-American government. The Soviets did not think Sadat could win, and the Cold War had entered its period of détente. Still, the Soviets could not risk losing allies (and oil) in the Middle East, so they agreed to help.

Watch the Video Lecture *The Arab-Israeli War, 1973* on mysearchlab.com

Sadat and Assad developed Operation Badr, a plan for a surprise attack on the Jewish holy day of Yom Kippur when Israel would be most vulnerable (also during the Muslim holiday of Ramadan). In early October, the Soviet Union began sending military supplies to Egypt, Syria and Iraq. Other Arab states provided troops, weapons and/or money, including Algeria, Libya, Morocco, Saudi Arabia, Kuwait, Pakistan, Bangladesh, Sudan and Cuba. The Jewish government certainly knew that Sadat was threatening war, and King Hussein had even warned Meir on September 25 that a Syrian attack was imminent; but the Israeli government did not believe the Egyptians and Syrians would do anything the Israeli military could not handle. And Israel certainly did not want to launch a preemptive strike that would alienate the United States, its only ally. The United States told Meir to wait while Secretary of State Henry Kissinger worked through diplomatic channels.

The Yom Kippur War, which was again fairly short (three weeks), came dangerously close to open war between the two superpowers. On October 6, 1973, the Egyptian army crossed the Suez Canal and began pushing the Israelis into the Sinai while the Syrian army moved into the Golan Heights. Israel was taken by surprise in a two-front war, and both Syria and Egypt had more troops and better weapons. Egypt had reclaimed the Sinai and Syria the Golan Heights before the Israeli Defense Forces (IDF) could even mobilize. Israel was losing so badly that, on October 8, Meir authorized the use of nuclear weapons against Egyptian and Syrian targets as a last resort to prevent total defeat. The United States was unwilling to let that happen and began providing military support to Israel, totaling $800 million by the end of October. Neither the United States nor the USSR wanted this regional conflict to turn into World War III, and the UN Security Council passed Resolution 338, demanding a cease-fire go into effect on October 22, but the resolution was completely ignored by both sides. The well-armed IDF moved beyond the proposed cease-fire lines and crossed the Suez Canal, trapping the Egyptian army.

Soviet Premier Brezhnev sent U.S. President Nixon an urgent request that both superpowers should contribute troops to enforce the cease-fire resolution and threatened that the USSR

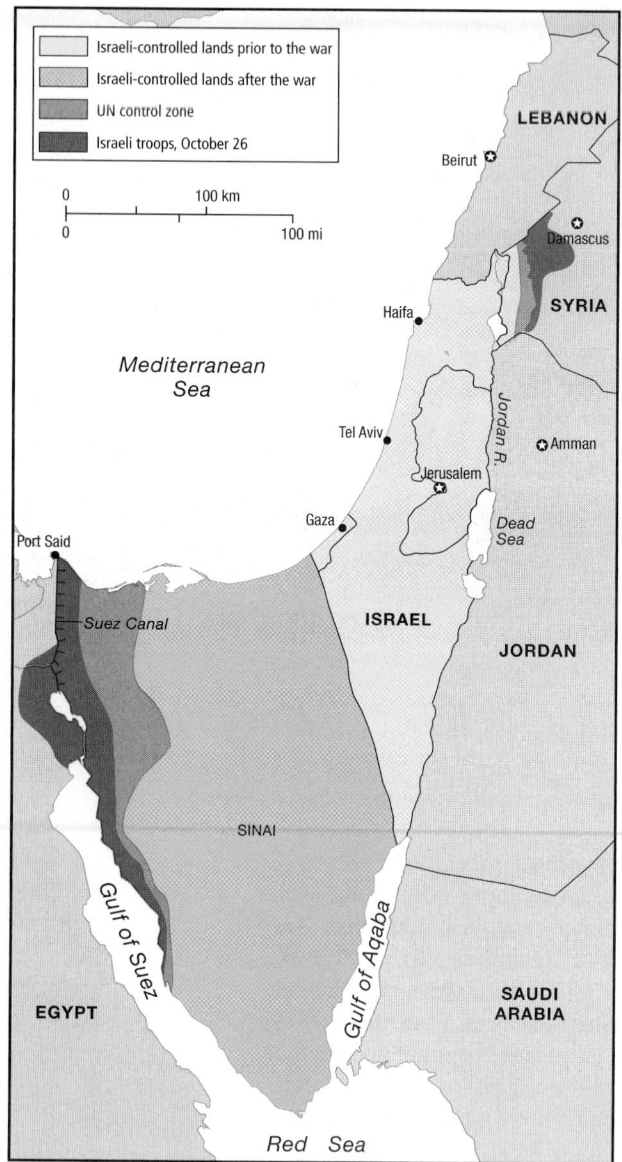

MAP 11.6 The Yom Kippur War, 1973

would act alone if the United States refused to participate. The idea of putting U.S. and Soviet soldiers on the ground in the middle of an ongoing war in the most volatile region of the world seemed ludicrous, and the United States assumed that the Soviets were simply looking for an excuse to join Egypt in destroying Israel. As the USSR moved its military into place, the United States increased its defense preparations. President Nixon warned Sadat that World War III was coming to Egyptian soil unless Sadat told the Soviets to stand down. Sadat complied; Brezhnev did not want to risk war with the United States, and the crisis was averted. On October 24, the UN Security Council reiterated its cease-fire demand, and the fighting gradually came to a close by the end of the month.

In the middle of the Yom Kippur War, the Organization of the Petroleum Exporting Countries (OPEC) imposed a complete boycott of Israel (which most of the African states later joined) as well as an embargo on shipments of crude oil to the West (targeting the United States and the Netherlands in particular). Using oil as a weapon, the Arab countries cut production, and the price of oil on the world market increased four-fold. The short-term result was the worst economic slump the industrialized countries had experienced since the 1930s; in the long term, oil-producing Arab countries grew very wealthy from the price increases and began investing in military, infrastructure and high-end consumer goods (mostly provided by the West).

With the boycott in place, Israel became dependent on the United States for military and economic assistance. As Arab countries used rising oil profits to build their militaries, Israel was forced to keep up or risk being destroyed. The U.S. government realized that if it did not help Israel, the Soviets would control the Middle East. U.S. foreign aid to Israel quadrupled, reaching over $2 billion per year, and much of that money went right back to the United States to pay for military equipment.

Although Israel was politically and economically devastated by the Yom Kippur War, its relationship with the United States had strengthened. Sadat recognized that pursuing diplomacy might be the only way to settle territorial disputes with Israel. But years of Nasser's pan-Arab rhetoric had united the people against Israel and its allies, strengthening Arab support for nongovernmental groups such as the PLO, Palestinian Islamic Jihad and Hamas, which continued their violent attacks on Israel and westerners in the Middle East.

Civil War in Lebanon

Lebanon was a nation of ethnic and religious diversity, held together relatively peacefully by a carefully crafted constitution that required the president to be Maronite Christian, the prime minister Sunni Muslim, the speaker of the parliament Shia Muslim and the deputy speaker of the parliament Greek Orthodox. But after the first Arab–Israeli War in 1948, 100,000 Palestinian refugees resettled in Lebanon, upsetting the balance and the peace. Israel would not take back the refugees; Lebanon did not want them, and a devastating fifteen-year civil war finally erupted in 1975.

The PLO capitalized on the internal weakness during the civil war and moved in, launching its attacks on Israel from Lebanon. This led to Israeli invasions of Lebanon to remove the PLO in 1978 and 1982, with U.S. troops entering the conflict in 1982 to protect Lebanon from the ongoing IDF–PLO warfare. That same year, a Shia Islamic fundamentalist organization named Hezbollah was created, supported by the governments of Iran and Syria. Calling for the destruction of Israel, the expulsion of U.S. troops and the installation of an Islamic regime in Lebanon, Hezbollah developed into a paramilitary organization. In 1982, Hezbollah began massacring Palestinians in the refugee camps, and UN troops led by the United States and France went back to Lebanon to restore order. In April 1983, sixty people were killed when the U.S. embassy in Beirut was bombed; 241 U.S. soldiers were killed by a suicide bomber at the U.S. marine headquarters the following October. U.S. troops left Lebanon in 1984, but the civil war raged on through the decade.

Remains of the bombed-out Marine barracks, Beirut, Lebanon, April 1983.

A Violent "Peace"

As the PLO gained legitimacy with the Arab people, Sadat lost it. Egypt and Syria's failure to remove Israel in the Yom Kippur War, coupled with economic and social problems in Egypt, led to rioting and the potential for civil war. Sadat had to do something and igniting another war would only exacerbate his problems. So he tried another approach—in November 1977 Sadat announced that he was willing to travel to Israel to discuss peace. Israeli Prime Minister Menachem Begin responded by extending an invitation, and the visit took place on November 19, 1977. Syrian President Assad refused to support the peace mission, and violent attacks were directed against Egyptian embassies across the Arab states. Sadat's message included the usual Arab demands for Israel to return territory from the Six-Day War and establish a homeland for Palestinians, but in a dramatic departure from anti-Israeli rhetoric, Sadat declared, "I wish to tell you today and I proclaim to the whole world: We accept to live with you in a lasting and just peace."

Israel and Egypt negotiated for almost a year before they were deadlocked. U.S. President Jimmy Carter stepped in to help, inviting Sadat and Begin to Camp David, Maryland, in September 1978. For almost two weeks, Carter mediated discussions between the two, based on UN Resolutions 242 and 338. The goal was to create "a just, comprehensive, and durable settlement of the Middle East conflict." The final agreement, known as the Camp David Accords (1979), settled the Sinai and Suez Canal disputes, created a territorial border between Egypt and Israel and, albeit less successfully, established a format for negotiations to create a Palestinian homeland in the West Bank and Gaza.

The agreement was not easy to reach, and Carter put the United States right at the center of the conflict to get it done. Once the accords were signed, both Egypt and Israel began receiving economic aid from the United States to build their military strength ($1.3 billion a year for Egypt and $3 billion a year for Israel). Although most Israelis supported the peace process, Begin received some opposition by hard-liners who did not want to voluntarily give up territory

ANALYSIS

In the context of the Cold War, why was it so important to the United States to broker a peace settlement between Israel and Egypt?

Anwar Sadat, Jimmy Carter and Menahem Begin at the Camp David Accords Signing Ceremony, September 17, 1978.

that had been earned with Israeli lives. The effect of the accords was far worse for Sadat, who was viewed as a traitor by the Arab world, including his own people. Egypt was expelled from the Arab League in 1979, and Sadat was assassinated by Muslim extremists in 1981. Rather than set a precedent for others to follow, Egypt's peace with Israel created a power vacuum in the Middle East. There was a leadership gap in the pan-Arab front, one that another Arab leader, Iraq's Saddam Hussein, was eager to fill.

Iraq and Iran

The Arab–Israeli dispute was not the only threat to peace in the Middle East. Long-simmering religious, ethnic and territorial differences were brought out by Cold War maneuvering as well.

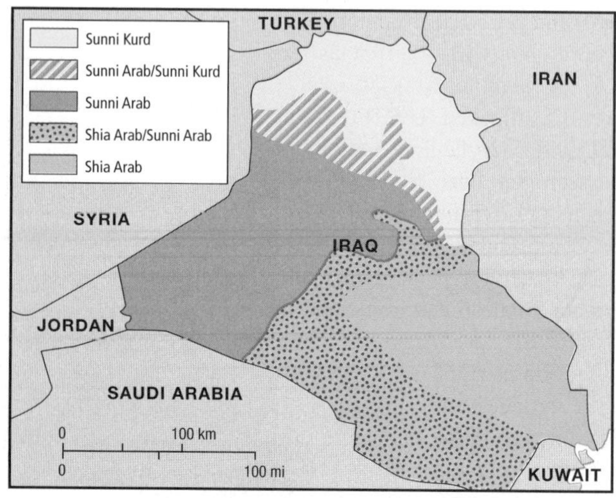

MAP 11.7 Iraq Divided

Iraq

At the urging of Nasser, General Abdul Karim Kassem seized control of the government of Iraq in 1958. It was a violent revolution in which the pro-West monarch and his supporters were executed. Kassem's communist policies changed the social structure of the country and reopened tribal, religious and ethnic conflicts, most disastrously between the Kurds and the Arabs and between the Sunni and Shia Muslims. Even with Soviet financial and military support, Kassem's government was too divided to withstand the internal pressure, and Iraq suffered from political instability throughout the 1960s as the Iraq Communist Party (supported by the USSR), the Baath Party (supported by the United States) and the Kurdish nationalists struggled for power.

In 1963, the Baathists staged a coup that removed Kassem from power, but they then immediately faced internal challenges from the Communist Party and Kurds. The new government, a one-party state ruled by the National Council of Revolutionary Command, opened negotiations with the Baathist regime in Syria to join the UAR. When an agreeable arrangement could not be made, Nasser openly challenged the legitimacy of both Baathist governments. In less than a year, the Iraqi Baathist government was overthrown and replaced with a military regime led by General Arif, a former ally of Kassem. The Kurds, supported by the pro-West government of neighboring Iran, renewed their uprisings against the Iraqi military. In 1967, Syria cut off the flow of Iraqi oil through the Syrian pipelines to Mediterranean ports over a financial dispute, causing economic collapse in Iraq. In July 1968, another CIA-sponsored Baathist coup seized control and established a government led by President Muhammad Bakr and his right-hand man, Saddam Hussein. This time, the Baath regime enacted economic development projects that made them popular with most Iraqis, and Hussein was welcomed as the president in 1979.

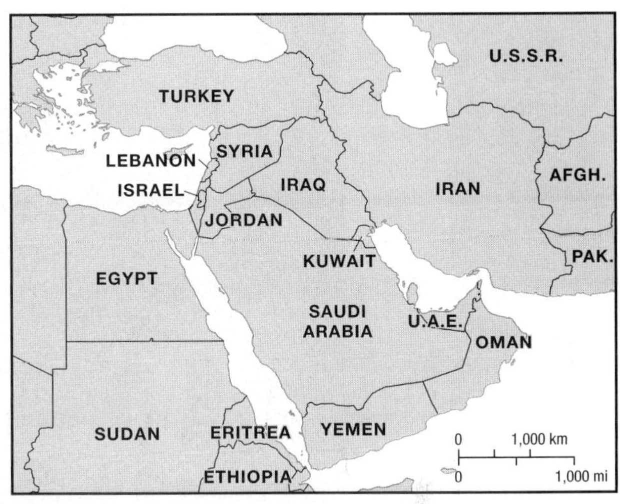

MAP 11.8 Iran and Its Neighbors

Iran

Because of Iran's location on the border of the USSR and its extensive oil fields (owned and operated by British Petroleum), it was important that the West maintain access to Iran. But a strong nationalist movement in the immediate post-World War II years led to the democratic election of Mohammad Mossadeq as Prime Minister. Mossadeq and the nationalists were determined to completely free Iran and its oil industry from British domination. In August 1953, the United States and Great Britain launched Operation Ajax, a coup that overthrew Mossadeq and gave all governmental power to the Shah (monarch) of Iran, Mohammad Reza Pahlavi. In return for U.S. and British support, the Shah openly pursued pro-Western policies (a lot of oil at a good price) and cracked down harshly on the internal nationalist opposition movement through his special national security force SAVAK.

Throughout the 1960s, the Shah became increasingly corrupt, ruling as a brutal authoritarian dictator. Despite the fact that he rejected U.S. recommendations to restore democracy in Iran, he remained an important ally during the height of the Cold War. Internally, the opposition movement against the Shah grew, spreading to Muslim religious leaders who spoke out against his Western preferences. After a particularly violent government attack against Muslim leaders in 1963, martial law was declared and the leader of the Muslim opposition movement, Ayatollah Khomeini, was exiled from Iran.

During the next fifteen years, the Shah built up his military with U.S. weapons and enacted economic reforms that led to a huge disparity of wealth between the privileged elites and the majority of the citizens living in poverty. From his exile in Turkey, Iraq and France, Khomeini launched a propaganda attack against the Shah and what he saw as pro-Western, anti-Islamic policies. What happened next is a perfect example of how events in the Middle East violated the Cold War mentality that drove U.S. foreign policy decision making.

ANALYSIS

Why did religion confuse Cold War decision makers?

What factors prevented President Carter from accurately assessing the political situation in Iran?

In January 1978, President Carter visited Iran to show his support for the Shah, publicly noting "the respect, admiration and love which your people give to you." Days after Carter left, pro-Khomeini demonstrations began across Iran, and the Shah responded with military force and martial law, killing thousands of protestors. But Khomeini's power had spread too far, infiltrating even the Shah's military, which refused to fire on Khomeini supporters. Without his military, the Shah lost control and fled Iran on January 16, 1979, taking with him two cargo planes

The Shah of Iran and his family.

Read the Document *Islam and the State in the Middle East: Ayatollah Khomeini's Vision of Islamic Government* on mysearchlab.com

Watch the Video Lecture *U.S. Hostages in Iran* on mysearchlab.com

Sunni/Shia split
a question over who would take over after Muhammad died in 632 divided the Muslim nation—Sunnis supported the election of a new leader, while Shias supported the ascension of his cousin/son-in-law; neither group recognizes the other as legitimate

jihad
Arabic word for "strive"; a religious duty to practice religion in the face of oppression and persecution

loaded with his personal wealth. On February 1, the Ayatollah Khomeini returned to cheering crowds in Iran. He hand-picked Islamic scholars to write a new constitution and created the Islamic Republic of Iran on April 1. Led by the Islamic Revolutionary Council (which was led by the Ayatollah), the new government executed almost one hundred of the Shah's military leaders and quashed Kurdish and Arab nationalist independence movements.

Because the Islamic Republic was not communist, President Carter hoped it would continue to fall under the U.S. sphere of influence. But the Ayatollah blamed the United States for the hardships suffered by the Iranian people under the Shah and rejected Carter's efforts to establish a diplomatic relationship. He demanded instead that Carter return the Shah (who was in the United States at the time for medical treatment) to Iran to stand trial for crimes against his people. When Carter refused, a group of students in Tehran stormed the U.S. embassy and seized American hostages. Although the students released the women (because Muslims do not wage war against women) and the blacks (because they were victims of U.S. oppression as well), they held fifty-two hostages who they offered to exchange for the return of the Shah and the wealth he stole from the Iranian people, an admission of guilt from the United States for its past actions, and a promise to never interfere in Iran again. In the United States, citizens were shocked to see film footage of U.S. marines and diplomats blindfolded and paraded around at gunpoint, and they demanded that the U.S. government do something. Carter cut off oil shipments from Iran and froze $8 billion in Iranian assets held in the United States, which only strengthened Iranians' support for Khomeini's case against the country he called "the Great Satan."

Meeting Khomeini's demands was clearly unacceptable, so Carter planned a rescue attempt. The top secret mission, Operation Eagle Claw, began at dawn on April 24, 1980, and fell apart almost immediately. Two of the eight helicopters were forced down because of mechanical problems due to sandstorms, and the mission was aborted. On the retreat, one of the damaged helicopters collided with a cargo plane and both burst into flames, killing eight U.S. servicemen. The survivors abandoned the scene, leaving helicopters, weapons, maps, secret documents regarding the rescue attempt and the bodies of eight dead Americans behind. Iranians rejoiced at the United States' humiliation, desecrating the bodies and parading the wreckage on international television. The hostages were finally released after 444 days of captivity, just moments after the next U.S. president, Ronald Reagan, was inaugurated into office.

Ayatollah Khomeini.

The Iran–Iraq War

The events in Iran in 1979 coincided with Saddam Hussein's rise to absolute power in Iraq, leading to a long, bloody war between two old enemies. During Ayatollah Khomeini's exile in Iraq, he reignited the ancient Islamic conflict, the **Sunni/Shia split.** Hussein was Sunni (the minority of the population in Iraq), and Khomeini pushed the Shia Muslims (the majority in Iraq) to rise up and overthrow the Baathist Party. To protect himself, Hussein expelled Khomeini from Iraq in 1977. When Khomeini established the fundamentalist Shiite Islamic Republic of Iran in 1979, Hussein feared (with good reason) that Khomeini would support the Iraqi Shia majority in a revolution against his secular Sunni government. There were ancient ethnic identities at stake as well—Iranians are Persian, Iraqis are Arab, and there is a large Kurdish population living in both countries—and all claimed rightful ownership of the land.

These reasons alone were enough to initiate conflict between the neighboring countries in 1979, but both Hussein and Khomeini knew they would need a legal reason to ensure foreign aid. The immediate issue was control of the Shatt-al-Arab, the river between Iraq and Iran that led to the Persian Gulf and was essential for trade. The two countries had engaged in border disputes over usage of the waterway for decades but came to an agreement in 1975 that established a border in the middle of the river. Iraq was bitter about the agreement and thought of it more as a temporary truce than a permanent border, but Iraq was forced to accept the agreement because Iran's military was far superior at that point.

When Hussein became President of Iraq in 1979, he was determined to become the dominant leader in the Middle East. To accomplish that, he would have to subdue the Shia majority, squash the Kurdish nationalist movement, build the economy and remove the Iranian military threat from his border. In what would turn out to be a grave miscalculation, Hussein believed that the revolution had left Iran in a significantly weakened position and he could get the Iranian Arabs to join him against the new Islamic fundamentalist regime. Hussein invaded Iran on September 22, 1980, expecting a quick victory, but the Iranian defense was much better than he had anticipated. Khomeini declared it a **jihad** that could only end when Hussein was

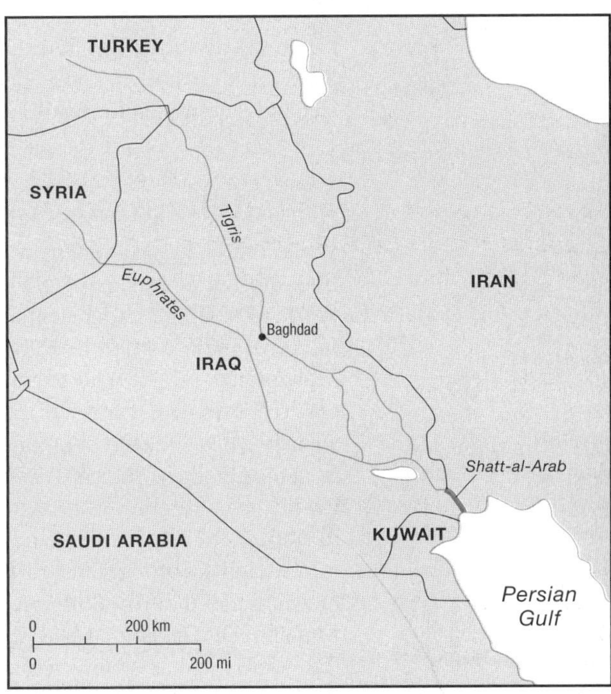

MAP 11.9 Iran, Iraq, and the Shatt Al Arab

overthrown, and the Iranians fought back with a vengeance, pushing the Iraqis out of Iran by the summer of 1982. Hussein offered to negotiate a cease-fire, but Khomeini refused to any agreement that left Hussein in power, so the war continued for another brutal six years.

Khomeini relied on volunteers—every available man and boy in Iran would be a martyr for his faith. Iran also received regional support from Syria and even covert technological aid from Israel. Hussein's military received support from the Gulf states' governments (notably Saudi Arabia and Kuwait), which feared that Khomeini would export his revolution to their people. The United States and the USSR did not want this war to spread across the Middle East and disrupt the world's oil supply and thus initially participated only to protect shipping lanes and urge acceptance for a UN cease-fire. Despite declarations of neutrality, both the United States and the USSR were supplying Iraq with money, technology, weapons and training. Hussein enjoyed this attention because it made him a world-class power player and gave him legitimacy in the Arab world. But this was the Cold War, and neither the United States nor the USSR was acting purely with Hussein's best interests at heart. With Soviet troops already in Afghanistan, the United States was wary of the expansion of the Soviet presence in the Middle East and promised to defend Iran from a Soviet invasion. So while openly providing extensive military aid to Iraq to defeat Iran, the U.S. government also began selling covert aid to Iran in exchange for the release of U.S. hostages in Lebanon in what became known as the **Iran-Contra Affair.**

Iran-Contra Affair
illegal covert plan in which money earned from the arms-for-hostages deal in Iran was funneled to contra rebels fighting against the Sandinistas in Nicaragua

Iran's primary offensive strategy was human-wave attacks, while Iraq had Soviet and French weapons, U.S. military training and chemical weapons (despite the 1925 Geneva Protocol that outlawed them). The United Nations launched an investigation after Iran charged Iraq with forty uses of the illegal weapons between 1981 and 1984. In 1986, the UN report confirmed Iraq's use of chemical warfare, despite Hussein's denials. The evidence was overwhelming, and it is estimated that Iraqi chemical warfare was responsible for more than 10,000 Iranian deaths by the time the war ended. After eight years, it was clear that neither Iraq nor Iran could decisively defeat the other, and the United Nations mediated a cease-fire in August 1988. Casualty estimates (including civilian) range from 500,000 to 1 million dead, 1 to 2 million wounded, 80,000 prisoners of war, and 2.5 million refugees, with Iran suffering disproportionately.

Although the Iran–Iraq War did not solve the religious, ethnic or even territorial disputes between the two countries, it did leave Iraq in a clear position of military dominance over the Gulf States. The Ayatollah Khomeini died in June 1989, but the Islamic Republic of Iran remained intact and determined to rebuild its military.

Soviet Invasion of Afghanistan

While the U.S. government was struggling to make sense of what was happening in Iran and Iraq, the USSR was experiencing a similar state of confusion in Afghanistan. Since the end of World War II, the leftist Afghan government had been receiving economic aid from the USSR. In April 1978, a coup in Kabul, Afghanistan, brought a Marxist regime to power under Nur Mohammad Taraki, who began reforming the predominantly Muslim country by decree. Land was redistributed, marriage traditions were overturned, and women were encouraged to stop wearing veils and start attending school. In the countryside, where local **mullahs** were respected as authority, these reforms were seen as a threat to Islam and provoked strong protests. The following year, Taraki was assassinated by his prime minister, Hafizullah Amin, and the USSR sent in advisors to help stabilize the new government.

mullah
Arabic word for "master"; a teacher or scholar of Islamic learning, or the leader of a mosque

Mujahideen
Arabic word for "strugglers"; those engaged in jihad

A civil war for control of the government began between the Soviet-supported government of Amin and the **Mujahideen,** a group of peasant protestors organized by village mullahs. The Mujahideen declared a jihad against Amin and the Russian troops in Afghanistan, who claimed they were there at Amin's request. But the more authoritarian Amin became to regain control of the country, the less the USSR supported him and the more violent the Mujahideen became. In December 1979, the Soviet military assassinated Amin and established his political rival,

Babrak Kamal, as the new Afghan leader. The Soviets immediately sent 85,000 troops to keep him in power.

Through its Cold War lens, the U.S. government saw a major threat. The Soviet military had openly invaded a country, overthrown its government and was occupying it against the will of its population. The presence of the Soviet military in Afghanistan, coupled with the overthrow of the U.S.-supported Shah in Iran and the anti-West hostility of the Ayatollah Khomeini, could allow the Soviets to seize control of the Middle East and its oil fields. The United States boycotted the 1980 summer Olympic games held in Moscow, imposed a grain embargo against the USSR and refused to ratify a pending weapons treaty with the Soviets. In his 1980 State of the Union address, President Carter announced that a new front in the Cold War had opened:

MAKE THE CONNECTION

- Why did the United States use the CIA to participate in Afghanistan?
- Why open relations with a dictator in Pakistan?
- What are the long-term consequences of these decisions?

> *Three basic developments have helped to shape our challenges: the steady growth and increased projection of Soviet military power beyond its own borders; the overwhelming dependence of the Western democracies on oil supplies from the Middle East; and the press of social and religious and economic and political change in the many nations of the developing world, exemplified by the revolution in Iran...Let our position be absolutely clear: an attempt by any outside force to gain control of the Persian Gulf region will be regarded as an assault on the vital interests of the United States of America, and such an assault will be repelled by any means necessary, including military force.*

To offset the Soviet military challenge in Afghanistan, Carter increased the defense budget, expanded U.S. air and naval bases in the region, and turned to some unlikely allies. The CIA launched its largest covert operation ever, providing weapons and training to the Mujahideen in its jihad to defeat the Soviet military. Saudi-born Osama bin Laden was recruited to transform the Mujahideen from a group of local villagers into a suitable proxy military for the United States—35,000 Muslim extremists from forty countries joined the Mujahideen in the 1980s. To hide its support, the U.S. government opened diplomatic relations with General Zia-ul-Haq, the dictator of Pakistan who hoped to install fundamentalist Islamic regimes across the Middle East. All CIA support to the jihad, including an average of 65,000 tons of weapons per year by the end of the war, was channeled through Pakistan. Financial support for the Mujahideen came largely from the heroin fields they planted on the Pakistan–Afghanistan border.

The war was ferocious and marked by war crimes on both sides. The UN Security Council condemned the invasion and tried to order Soviet forces to withdraw, but the USSR simply vetoed the resolution. By 1982, the Mujahideen controlled 75 percent of Afghanistan and the USSR was losing in every way imaginable. It had become their "Vietnam," with Soviet troops mired in an unwinnable war against citizens fighting on their own challenging terrain for control of their government, fueled by religious fervor and U.S., shoulder-launched Stinger missiles. It was not until April 1988 that the USSR agreed to a UN-mediated cease-fire, and the USSR withdrew its troops from Afghanistan in February 1989. The agreement banned further military aid to Afghanistan, but both superpowers ignored the agreement, and the supply of weapons continued as the country slipped into a civil war between rival groups of Islamic fundamentalists for control of the government.

Conclusions

Events in the Middle East confused American and Soviet decision makers who could not see beyond the "simple" dichotomy they created for the world—the struggle between democracy/capitalism and communism. But that rhetoric meant nothing in the Arab world, where the people were focused on nationalist and religious rights and were willing to die for them. The level of constant violence was extraordinary, fueled by Soviet and American weapons. The United States supported

Israel, Saudi Arabia, Jordan, Lebanon, sometimes Egypt, and sometimes Iraq; the USSR supported Egypt, Syria, Iraq, the PLO and Afghanistan. But the territorial, religious and nationalist conflicts in the Middle East intersected one another, and one day's ally could be the next day's enemy.

The bottom line for the superpowers, of course, was access to oil. They could not win the Cold War militarily or economically without it. So, despite the terrorist attacks, the hostages, the increasingly violent anti-Western sentiment, and the quagmire of war in Afghanistan, both the United States and USSR stayed active in the region. The choices they made in the Middle East during the Cold War weakened them in the short term and created issues that would continue to challenge the world in the twenty-first century.

WORKING WITH THE THEMES

THE EFFECTS OF TECHNOLOGY What were the short- and long-term effects of the use of chemical weapons in the Iran–Iraq War? How do you reconcile the prevailing Cold War arms and space races with the type of violence that is prevalent in the Middle East (terrorist attacks, suicide bombing, hostage taking)?

CHANGING IDENTITIES How did the pan-Arab movement affect national politics in the Middle East? Do you think pan-Arabism is an attainable goal? Why or why not? Why are the Israeli settlements a source of tension in the region? What are the ramifications of the refugee crisis for countries neighboring the disputed territories?

SHIFTING BORDERS Who do you think has the legal right to the disputed territory—the Israelis or the Palestinians? What about the West Bank, the Golan Heights, and the Gaza Strip? What should be done with Jerusalem? Do you think it is possible to create a cooperative regional organization like the UAR was?

GLOBALIZATION What factors led to U.S. and Soviet intervention in the conflicts of the Middle East? Did the superpowers "use" the nation-states in the region to fight the Cold War, or did the leaders in the Middle East "use" the superpowers to fight their own religious, ethnic, and territorial conflicts? The United States tried to use the same tactics in Iran that it used in Latin America but got very different results. Why?

Further Reading

TO FIND OUT MORE

ProCon.org: Israeli–Palestinian Conflict. Available online at http://israelipalestinian.procon.org/

Palestine Liberation Organization: Negotiations Affairs Department. Available online at http://www.nad-plo.org/

Israel Diplomatic Network: The Anti-Terrorist Fence. Available online at http://securityfence.mfa.gov.il/

Rashid Khalidi: *Sowing Crisis: The Cold War and American Dominance in the Middle East* (2009)

Iran Chamber Society: History of Iran, Pictures of the 1979 Revolution and the Iran–Iraq War. Available online at http://www.iranchamber.com/history/history_periods.php

GO TO THE SOURCE

Gamal A. Nasser: *Egypt's Liberation: The Philosophy of the Revolution* (1955)
Matthew Neely/Bodleian Library University of Oxford: The Suez Crisis. Available online at http://www.bodley.ox.ac.uk/dept/scwmss/projects/suez/suez.html
National Security Archive: The Saddam Hussein Sourcebook (2003). Available online at http://www.gwu.edu/~nsarchiv/special/iraq/
National Security Archive Documents/Mark J. Gasiorowski and Malcolm Byrne (eds.): Mohammad Mosaddeq and the 1953 Coup in Iran (2004). Available online at http://www.gwu.edu/~nsarchiv/NSAEBB/NSAEBB126/index.htm
National Security Archive Documents/Malcolm Byrne (ed.): 20 Years after the Hostages: Declassified Documents on Iran and the United States (1999). Available online at http://www.gwu.edu/~nsarchiv/NSAEBB/NSAEBB21/index.html Saddam Hussein: *Thus We Should Fight Persians* (1983)
Ayatollah Rouhollah Mousavi Khomeini: *Governance of the Jurist: Islamic Government* (1977)

MySearchLab Connections

Read the **Document** on **mysearchlab.com**

11.1 Gamal Abdel Nasser, *Speech on the Suez Canal.* The revolution in Egypt that overthrew King Farouk I in 1952 and brought Gamal Abdel Nasser to power in 1954 made Nasser an influential spokesman for Arab and Middle Eastern interests in a decolonizing world. One of his most important acts was nationalize the Suez Canal, a key commercial artery linking the Mediterranean with the Red Sea, from decades of British control.

11.2 *United Nations Security Council Resolution 242.* After the Six-Day War, it was apparent that the Arab-Israeli crisis had the potential to escalate into an international conflict. While all members of the UN Security Council agreed that a resolution to promote peace should be passed, there was disagreement on exactly what that resolution would require from Israel.

11.3 *Islam and the State in the Middle East: Ayatollah Khomeini's Vision of Islamic Government.* Ayatollah Ruhollah Khomeini was an activist and leader of the revolution that sought to depose the secular monarchy of the Shah of Iran. In 1979, after the Shah's downfall, he returned from exile to found the Islamic Republic of Iran.

Watch the **Video** on **mysearchlab.com**

11.1 *The Arab-Israeli War, 1973*
11.2 *U.S. Hostages in Iran*

12 The Cold War Ends

CHAPTER OUTLINE

- Reagan and Gorbachev
- The Iron Curtain Unravels
- Revolution Reaches the USSR
- The Soviet Empire Crumbles

CHAPTER TIMELINE

1981	1982	1983	1985	1986
Reagan takes office in the United States	Brezhnev dies, creating a power vacuum in the USSR	United States announces Strategic Defense Initiative (SDI)	Gorbachev takes office in the USSR; introduces *glasnost* and *perestroika* Geneva Summit	Chernobyl accident in USSR Reykjavik Summit

Photos from left to right: President Reagan giving a speech at the Berlin Wall, Brandenburg Gate, Federal Republic of Germany, June 12, 1987; Velvet Revolution in Prague, Czechoslovakia; Remains of the Chernobyl power plant, Pripyat, Ukraine; Bush, Reagan, and Gorbachev, December 1988.

1987

- INF Treaty is ratified

1988

- Bush becomes U.S. president
- New constitution in USSR separates Central Communist Party and government institutions

1989

- Soviet troops leave Afghanistan
- Solidarity is legalized in Poland–wins elections
- Hungary opens border to Austria; becomes a democratic republic
- Free elections are held in Bulgaria
- Estonia, Latvia, and Lithuania hold Baltic Way protest
- Berlin Wall falls
- Velvet Revolution in Czechoslovakia
- Romanian revolution turns violent

1990

- Gorbachev is appointed president of the USSR
- Yeltsin is elected president of Russian Federation
- Germany is reunified

1991

- Republic of Georgia secedes from USSR
- Communists stage coup against Gorbachev
- Communist Party of the USSR dissolves
- USSR ceases to exist, and the CIS is created

As the Cold War entered its fourth decade, things had changed dramatically. China's new economic policies had made it an integral part of the international economy, and Japan had quickly become the second wealthiest country in the world, dominating the electronics, consumer technology and automotive industries. The decolonization process was complete, but it had left poverty, social unrest and enormous debt in its wake across Africa, Latin America and Asia. OPEC and Islamic Fundamentalism presented serious challenges to the political and economic dominance of the West. There were seven members of the nuclear club, and the arms race between the United States and USSR raged on. In the face of this uncertainty, U.S. citizens rallied together and sought leadership that would ensure their nation would remain *the* world power, economically, politically, and militarily. But in the USSR, decades of communist economic policies and politically and socially repressive regimes had weakened internal morale and unity. It was clear that some kind of reform would be required for the empire to survive, but that worried hardcore communists. Could the USSR "win" the Cold War if it had to back away from its Soviet ideology and methodology to do so?

WORKING WITH THE THEMES

THE EFFECTS OF TECHNOLOGY The United States uses its dominant financial position to convince the USSR it has technological superiority with SDI, while the Chernobyl accident reveals Soviet incompetence.

CHANGING IDENTITIES The satellite states break out of the Soviet sphere of influence, some more violently than others. *Glasnost* and *perestroika* bring meaningful reform to political and social life in the USSR.

SHIFTING BORDERS The Berlin Wall is torn down, paving the way for the reunification of Germany. The prevailing bipolar structure of the world collapses with the dissolution of the USSR into its fifteen constituent republics.

GLOBALIZATION When the USSR ceases to exist, a regional intergovernmental organization is created to fill the power vacuum. The Cold War ends.

Reagan and Gorbachev

Decisions made by the political leaders of the United States and USSR in the 1980s would prove vital in bringing the Cold War to its conclusion. Although many internal and external factors came together to hasten the demise of the USSR, the personalities of Ronald Reagan and Mikhail Gorbachev and the relationship between these two powerful men must not be overlooked.

Ronald Reagan

Watch the Video Lecture *Reagan's Presidential Campaign* on mysearchlab.com

In the United States, no one was particularly satisfied with the way Jimmy Carter was handling events in the Middle East—the Cold War had changed, and Carter did not seem to know what to do about it. In 1980, the American people elected a new president, Ronald Reagan, who promised them "peace through strength." This entailed negotiating an end to the Cold War, which Reagan believed could only be achieved successfully from a position of overwhelming strength.

From the outset of his presidency, Reagan took a very hard line against the Soviet Union. In May 1981, he assured the graduating class of Notre Dame University that

> *...the years ahead will be great ones for our country, for the cause of freedom and the spread of civilization. The West will not contain Communism; it will transcend Communism. We will not bother to denounce it; we'll dismiss it as a sad, bizarre chapter in human history whose last pages are even now being written.*

In June 1982, Reagan addressed his closest ally, British Prime Minister Margaret Thatcher, and the British Parliament, asserting that "...the march of freedom and democracy...will leave

Marxism-Leninism on the ash heap of history as it has left other tyrannies which stifle the freedom and muzzle the self-expression of the people."

Reagan's most famous aggressive attack on the USSR came on March 8, 1983, at the National Association of Evangelicals:

> *Let us beware that while they [Soviet rulers] preach the supremacy of the state, declare its omnipotence over individual man, and predict its eventual domination over all the peoples of the earth, they are the focus of evil in the modern world....I urge you to beware the temptation ..., to ignore the facts of history and the aggressive impulses of any evil empire, to simply call the arms race a giant misunderstanding and thereby remove yourself from the struggle between right and wrong, good and evil.*

Ronald Reagan.

To back up the rhetoric, Reagan began a new phase of rearmament, increasing the U.S. defense budget by roughly 8 percent each year from 1980 (when it was $142 billion) to 1986 (when it reached $273.5 billion). He approved production of the B-1 bomber, a project President Carter had abandoned because of its cost ($200 million per aircraft), as well as the MX "Peacekeeper" missile. The size of the U.S. military grew as Reagan deployed men and missiles to Europe, Latin America and the Middle East to demonstrate exactly what he meant by American strength.

This military buildup was an integral element of what became known as the Reagan Doctrine, a very optimistic and aggressive foreign policy approach to winning the Cold War. Reagan's advisors reasoned that, because containment never really worked, the United States should focus instead on "**rollback**" to make up the lost ground both militarily and ideologically. As the USSR began to lose those "tally marks" on its "scorecard" (countries within the Soviet sphere of influence), the United States would gain a significant upper hand in negotiations. In the 1985 State of the Union address, Reagan explained his foreign policy philosophy to the nation: "We must not break faith with those who are risking their lives on every continent from Afghanistan to Nicaragua to defy Soviet-supported aggression and secure rights which have been ours from birth...Support for freedom fighters is self-defense."

rollback
helping revolutionary movements in Soviet-supported countries take over their governments; also known as "containment plus"

The Reagan Doctrine led to a marked increase in covert assistance to anticommunist groups fighting against Soviet-supported governments in Africa, Asia and Latin America. In all, nine countries that were firmly within the Soviet sphere of influence received U.S. money, weapons and/or CIA support: Afghanistan, Angola, Nicaragua, Ethiopia, Cambodia, Laos, Vietnam, Libya and Iran. The shift from containment to rollback was controversial, particularly as the shift became increasingly overt throughout the 1980s. Because this approach went directly against Soviet-supported regimes, it risked an escalation of the Cold War. The rollback approach also led to the United States supporting several very violent (but anti-Soviet) regimes, such as the Contras in Nicaragua.

Read the Document *National Security Decision Directive 32: U.S. National Security Strategy* on mysearchlab.com

"Rollback" was an essential part of Reagan's new policy toward the USSR, which was articulated in *National Security Decisions Directive-32*. The United States took an aggressive three-pronged approach to ending the Cold War that entailed: (1) cutting off Soviet access to high technology and using economic measures to keep the value of Soviet commodities low on the world market; (2) increasing U.S. military defense expenditures and troop buildup to apply pressure and strengthen the U.S. negotiating position; and (3) forcing the USSR to spend even more of its dwindling financial resources on defense to keep up in the arms race. The U.S. Department of Defense created new guidelines that called for preparations to wage a nuclear war "over a protracted period," which shifted the arms race toward defensive weapons—an entirely new technology requiring massive financial support.

Strategic Defense Initiative (SDI) proposed space-based technology to protect the United States from a nuclear attack; commonly known as "Star Wars"

In 1983, Reagan unveiled his plan for a **Strategic Defense Initiative (SDI)**, which called for a land- and space-based shield over the United States against a nuclear attack. Critics within the United States argued that SDI technology was unfeasible, and the press dubbed the program "Star Wars" after the George Lucas fictional film series. Even if the plan could work, they argued, SDI would only lead to an unreasonably expensive escalation of the Cold War. Privately, that is exactly what Reagan wanted because he believed the USSR could never sustain that kind of financial investment. The USSR would lose the arms race, and the United States would be in a powerful position to negotiate the end of the Cold War on its terms. Although many scientists argued that SDI could not be achieved, Reagan was convincing, and Congress approved billions of dollars for development.

Soviet leader Yuri Andropov responded defiantly to Reagan's "Star Wars" plan, accusing Reagan of "inventing new plans on how to unleash a nuclear war in the best way, with the hope of winning it." Andropov vehemently warned the United States against pursuing SDI:

> *[It] would open the floodgates of a runaway race of all types of strategic arms, both offensive and defensive. Such is the real significance, the seamy side, so to say, of Washington's "defensive conception."... The Soviet Union will never be caught defenseless by any threat....Engaging in this is not just irresponsible, it is insane....Washington's actions are putting the entire world in jeopardy.*

Although Andropov took a very aggressive posture against Reagan, comparing him to Hitler, his words masked true concerns over just how far the United States might go in this new phase of the Cold War. Between the Pershing II nuclear missiles deployed across Western Europe, the new missile technology in the works (the MX Peacekeeper and the Tomahawk), and the Strategic Defense Initiative, Andropov was convinced that the United States was preparing for a nuclear strike against the USSR. The USSR established a new early warning radar system, which was in direct violation of the ABM Treaty of 1972, but argued that the United States had already clearly abandoned that treaty with SDI. Convinced that the West was planning for war, Andropov ordered a worldwide alert, and the KGB monitored every aspect of life in the West. In response, the United States increased spy flights in sensitive areas along the USSR's borders. Aircraft packed with electronic surveillance gear and disguised as civilian airliners often flew close to passenger routes. The USSR was jumpy, and in September 1983 the Soviet military shot down a Korean Air Lines passenger jet when it violated Soviet airspace. NATO responded with an aggressive nuclear "training simulation" in November; arms control talks between the United States and USSR were broken off, and the world seemed to refocus on the "good guys versus bad guys" bipolar order of the Cold War.

Mikhail Gorbachev

gross national product the value of all the goods and services produced in an economy, plus the value of the goods and services imported, less the goods and services exported

By the 1980s, citizen morale in the USSR had plummeted. The Soviet invasion of Afghanistan brought an end to détente and led to terrible conditions for the ill-equipped Soviet troops fighting there in ever-increasing numbers throughout the early 1980s. The state-planned economy failed to provide basic needs, adequate income and consumer goods to the people, and the black market economy had essentially taken over for those who could afford to participate. The government expenditures on its military (up to 25 percent of the country's **gross national product**), the arms and space races, and financial aid to countries within its sphere of influence far exceeded what the Soviet economy generated. Clearly, the USSR was in decline.

A new generation of Communist Party members, many of whom entered political life during Khrushchev's de-Stalinization years, believed that political and economic reform was absolutely necessary. But the older, hardcore communists rejected what they viewed as an admission of defeat and tried to hold onto power. After Brezhnev's death in November 1982, the sixty-eight-year-old Yuri Andropov (KGB chairman) took office but was permanently hospitalized within the year and died in February 1984. Andropov was replaced by the seventy-two-year-old Konstantin Chernenko, who died just over a year later in March 1985. By then, anyone in the Communist Party eligible to become general secretary understood the necessity of reform.

Mikhail Gorbachev during his 1988 visit to New York.

When Mikhail Gorbachev took control of the USSR in March 1985, he set the country on a path of political and economic liberalization. He was guided by two key initiatives: **glasnost** and **perestroika**, both of which led to radical changes in economic and social policy. The most noticeable economic change for the people was privatization—individuals were allowed to own their own manufacturing plants, restaurants and shops, and could even engage in regulated foreign trade. Under *glasnost*, political prisoners were released, and political and social policy research centers were opened in academic institutions. Freedom of speech became legal, and restrictions on the press were lifted in an effort to publicize the reforms and build widespread support. Unfortunately for Gorbachev, the media's coverage of the reality of Soviet life—including alcoholism, pollution, government crimes and cover-ups, and the ongoing war in Afghanistan—exacerbated the existing morale problem among the citizens and had a devastating effect on their faith in the communist ideology that formed the basis of their national identity. By 1989, *glasnost* would turn against Gorbachev himself.

glasnost
Russian for "openness"; political reform that allowed for open discussion of Soviet history, politics and social issues and lifted restrictions on the press to report it

perestroika
Russian for "restructuring"; a series of slow, gradual economic reforms that attempted to save the Soviet economy, but ultimately led to its total collapse

Recognizing that economic and social freedoms must be matched by political reform, Gorbachev took on the electoral process in 1987, urging that democratic elements such as multi-candidate elections be incorporated in the USSR. At the Nineteenth Party Conference the following year, Gorbachev began the process of separating control of the Soviet government from the Communist Party of the Soviet Union. He amended the constitution to create governance positions that operated independently of the Communist Party, including a national legislative body called the Congress of People's Deputies, members of which were popularly elected by a secret ballot. Despite these progressive political reforms, Gorbachev retained his position as the General Secretary of the Communist Party of the Soviet Union, and the Communist Party held the majority of the seats in Congress.

Gorbachev's reforms within the USSR required changes in foreign policy decision making as well. In 1987, Gorbachev explained his goals to the world in *Perestroika: New Thinking for Our Country and the World*. His policies were designed to reform socialism by overturning repression and ending government corruption, while restoring personal responsibility as the hallmark of Soviet citizenship. While many of his reforms were viewed by the world as democratic in that they focused on individual rights and responsibilities, Gorbachev in no way intended that the Soviet empire would cease to be the center of political and economic life for the people. He rejected "bourgeois capitalism," arguing that communism would work well when economic policies were reformed to allow it to reach its full potential.

Read the Document *Mikhail Gorbachev on the Need for Economic Reform* on mysearchlab.com

To enact these reforms and address the many internal problems in the USSR, Gorbachev needed money. The Soviet economy operated at a tremendous deficit, so simply increasing domestic spending was not an option. He would have to cut spending in another area, and there were only two ways he could do that: (1) shift money out of the defense budget and arms race, or (2) decrease spending to support the satellite states. Either of these choices required a fundamental shift in Soviet foreign policy and put the USSR at risk to "lose" the Cold War. A move by President Reagan in March 1985 helped shape Gorbachev's path.

While in Moscow for Chernenko's funeral in spring 1985, U.S. Vice President George Bush met with Gorbachev briefly, and the two agreed that the United States and USSR would hold a summit meeting, the first in six years. Although Reagan's Secretary of Defense tried to prevent the summit meeting from happening, Reagan was committed to forging a relationship with the new Soviet leader. Gorbachev's new approach to Soviet foreign affairs focused on bringing an end to the arms race, something President Reagan was also interested in achieving, as long as the United States held the upper hand in the negotiations.

ANALYSIS

This photograph of the "fireside summit" was well publicized globally. What message are Reagan and Gorbachev sending to their own citizens? Identify the specific elements of the photo that evoke their message. Why spread it around the world?

The Summit Meetings

In November 1985, Gorbachev and Reagan met in Geneva, Switzerland. At their first face-to-face meeting, the two leaders outlined their positions in traditional Cold War adversarial terms, but they quickly realized that they actually liked one another. Reagan was optimistic about Gorbachev's *glasnost* and *perestroika* efforts and how quickly upon taking office he had begun to pursue them. Unbeknownst to his own advisors, Reagan arranged for an extended private meeting (no advisors present) with Gorbachev. What was scheduled as a fifteen-minute courtesy call became a five-hour conversation that formed the foundation for a warm, personal relationship between the two men that would evolve over the years. Gorbachev recognized that Reagan was committed to negotiating a reduction in nuclear arms,

President Reagan and General Secretary Gorbachev at the first Summit in Geneva, November 19, 1985.

against the wishes of most of his administration, and viewed Reagan as a partner in achieving that particular goal rather than an adversary.

The following January, Gorbachev proposed the complete eradication of all nuclear weapons by the year 2000. To get there, strategic arsenals would be cut in half, all intermediate-range systems in Europe would be dismantled, and both nuclear testing and space-based weapons would be banned. U.S. advisors did not trust the USSR, but Reagan trusted Gorbachev and agreed to a second summit meeting to discuss the logistics of the proposal.

Before that meeting took place, an explosion ripped apart a reactor at the Chernobyl nuclear power plant in Ukraine in April 1986, highlighting the incompetence of the Soviet system. The explosion was the result of a poorly designed reactor being operated by poorly trained personnel. An investigation revealed that the plant operators made a series of mistakes while preparing for a routine safety test, which led to a steam explosion and fires that released at least 5 percent of the radioactive reactor core into the atmosphere, downwind, and across the USSR and Europe. The Chernobyl disaster highlighted the potential dangers of unregulated nuclear energy facilities. For many in the United States, the entirely preventable disaster demonstrated that the USSR was clearly inferior in nuclear technology—here they were concerned about Soviet nuclear weapons, and the Soviets could not even keep a nuclear power plant functioning safely.

MAKE THE CONNECTION

How does the Chernobyl accident demonstrate increasing globalization by the mid-1980s?

It was in this environment that Reagan and Gorbachev met in Reykjavik, Iceland, in October 1986 for their second summit. No one expected much of substance to emerge because the United States clearly held a dominant position in the negotiations. But during the next few days, the two leaders took a series of bold and unexpected steps, each raising the ante in their mutual quest for arms reductions. They agreed on a comprehensive set of reductions of strategic arms, intermediate-range missiles and space weapons. They agreed on the complete withdrawal of intermediate-range missiles in Europe and a 50 percent reduction in ballistic missiles over a five-year period. Finally, Gorbachev stunningly suggested that the United States and USSR eliminate all their nuclear weapons within the next ten years. Reagan shocked everyone (including his own administration officials and allies in Great Britian and France) with his response—we will completely abolish all nuclear weapons around the world. Gorbachev agreed, but only if Reagan dropped SDI. The United States would not need it, he argued, if the disarmament process was underway and the two nations trusted one another. But Reagan would not budge on SDI and leave the United States at risk. Gorbachev warned Reagan that, if the United States insisted on maintaining a missile defense system, everything they had agreed to was off the table. Still, Reagan refused. The summit ended without an agreement, but the discussions certainly paved the way for future arms reductions/limits treaties.

As the leaders left Reykjavik, Reagan told the world media that Gorbachev rejected the U.S. proposals, and Gorbachev reported that Reagan's insistence on SDI "frustrated and scuttled" a historic opportunty to make the world safer for everyone. It seemed as though a crisis of trust between the two men destroyed the negotiations. Reagan's willingness to walk away from the agreement over SDI while the U.S. Congress continued to pour billions of dollars into the project signaled to Gorbachev that SDI must truly exist. The USSR could never invest the money it would take to develop the technology (if, indeed, it could be developed at all). In that moment, Gorbachev knew the USSR had lost the arms race. In December 1987, he traveled to Washington, D.C., to sign the **INF Treaty,** eradicating all existing intermediate-range missiles and banning all future production.

INF Treaty (Intermediate-Range Nuclear Forces) required the destruction of U.S. and Soviet ground-launched ballistic and cruise missiles with ranges of between 500 and 5,500 kilometers, their launchers and associated support structures and equipment within three years

The Iron Curtain Unravels

President Reagan's successor, George Bush, was elected in fall 1988 in large part because he was committed to continuing Reagan's foreign policy agenda, particularly where it concerned the USSR. Because the United States would not agree to end the arms race, Gorbachev would

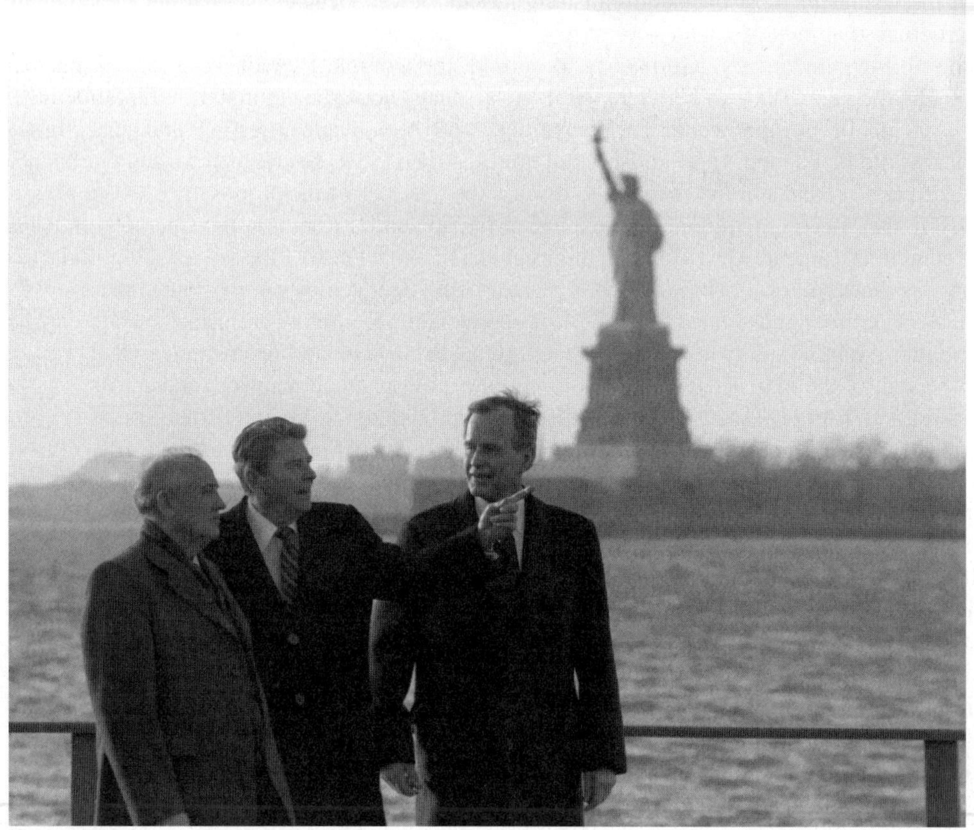

President Reagan and President-elect Bush meeting with General Secretary Gorbachev on Governor's Island, New York, December 7, 1988.

ANALYSIS

What does this staged, public relations photo tell us about the world at the end of 1988? Where is Reagan looking? Where is Bush looking? Where is Gorbachev looking?

have to find another way to cut Soviet defense spending to allow for much-needed investment in the domestic economy. To reduce military costs, Gorbachev agreed to pull the remaining Soviet troops (approximately 120,000) out of Afghanistan by early 1989 and sharply cut the number of Soviet troops committed to UN forces. The most dramatic change, however, occurred in the Soviet satellite bloc across Eastern Europe.

Nationalist movements across Eastern Europe were historically powerful and politically disruptive, as evidenced by the two world wars they helped incite in the early twentieth century. Under Soviet domination in the last half of the century, those movements were supressed, often violently. As *perestroika* and *glasnost* took root in the mid-1980s, nationalist movements began to reemerge. Combined with decades of national debt, low living standards and corruption under communist political regimes, the demand for dramatic change was swift. Gorbachev was faced with either using military force to stop the nationalist movements as his predecessors had done or using political persuasion to keep them under control. Given the financial crisis the USSR was in, Gorbachev decided to cut Soviet forces in Eastern Europe by 500,000 troops in 1988. He told the people of Eastern Europe that they had the right of self-determination but strongly encouraged them to continue to "choose" the communist party. Once they understood that the Soviets would not militarily intervene, however, the people of Eastern Europe had nothing to fear in pursuing the *perestroika* they so desperately wanted.

Watch the Video Lecture *Ronald Reagan at the Berlin Wall* on mysearchlab.com

Poland

By the mid-1970s, economic conditions in Poland had deteriorated as the foreign debt rose. The first workers' strikes began in June 1976, and the government cracked down harshly. They began again in August 1980 in direct response to a government policy of increasing prices for goods while suppressing wages. At the Lenin Shipyard in Gdansk, an electrician named Lech Walesa who had been fired in 1976 led the workers in an organized strike that demanded respect for workers' rights and the legalization of independent trade unions, among other things. The Polish government tried to contain the strike by censoring the media and cutting all phone connections between Gdansk and the rest of the country. It was not successful, and other shipyards and industrial centers around Poland joined the strike by the end of the month, effectively shutting down what was left of the Polish economy. The government was forced to negotiate with the organized strike movement, strengthening labor unions and weakening the Polish Communist Party. The Solidarity labor union, led by Lech Walesa, became the first independent labor union in a Soviet-bloc country, but it transformed itself into a social movement over the following year as it picked up 10 million members (25 percent of Poland's population), branching off into specific organizations for workers, intellectuals and students.

Tomasz Sarnecki Solidarity poster, 1989. Gary Cooper as Marshal Will Kane in the U.S. film *High Noon*. The caption reads "High Noon, June 4, 1989."

Driven by a fear of revolution and pressure from Moscow, the government was forced to suppress the growth of the Solidarity movement. Solidarity fought back with isolated strikes and the threat of a nationwide strike. In December 1981, the government declared martial law, enacted strict censorship and began arresting Solidarity supporters by the thousands. At Solidarity demonstrations against the crackdown, Polish military fired into the crowds. In October 1982, Solidarity was legally banned and its leadership arrested, but underground movements organized almost immediately, and there was intermittent violence throughout the 1980s.

Martial law was lifted in July 1983, and many Solidarity members were released from prison, but the movement remained underground until Gorbachev assumed office in the USSR in 1985. As he encouraged *glasnost* and *perestroika* policies, Solidarity began to cautiously reemerge in Polish society throughout 1986 and 1987, although its members were still harassed by the government. In 1988, a terrible economy and an increase in food prices led to organized strikes across Poland. Without Soviet military support behind it, the Polish government was forced to negotiate with Solidarity, and what began as a labor movement ten years before transitioned into a peaceful, opposition party determined to overturn communist control in Poland.

MAKE THE CONNECTION

What does this Solidarity poster tell you about the role of globalization in the unraveling of the Iron Curtain?

The February 1989 Polish Round Table Talks led to the re-legalization of Solidarity and a change in election laws that allowed the political arm of the movement to run candidates for federal office. The Communist Party would retain 65 percent of the seats of the lower house of Parliament (the Sejm), but the Solidarty Party could run candidates for the other 35 percent. An upper house, the Senate, would be created, and all 100 seats would be chosen by the voters. Both houses together would decide who would serve as president. In the elections of June 1989, the Solidarity coalition took control of the government, winning all 161 seats it was eligible for in the Sejm and 99 of 100 in the Senate. To keep both the Polish people and Moscow happy, the executive government was carefully crafted to represent both the Communist and Solidarity parties. The president was communist and, for the first time in the Soviet satellite bloc, a non-communist prime minister ran the country.

Hungary

In the late 1960s, the Hungarian government attempted economic reforms to raise the quality of life in hopes of preventing internal opposition after Imre Nagy's failed revolution of 1956. The New Economic Mechanism, as the program was called, did provide more consumer choices for the Hungarian people (albeit limited choices), but it was all based on foreign credit that the country could not pay back. The program was a disaster, and the Communist Party was steadily losing support. In 1988, a reform-minded communist prime minister took control of the government, prompting a sharp divide within the Communist Party of Hungary to surface. Despite the lack of Soviet military support, some believed Hungary should continue to rely on authoritarian communism to solve the country's economic troubles. Others invoked the spirit of Nagy, calling for reform and a closer relationship with Western Europe to solve the financial crisis.

The latter group prevailed, and on May 2, 1989, the government took down the barbed wire and electric fence along the border dividing Hungary and Austria, the East and the West. An estimated 600 people fled on the first day alone. In response to the vocal protest from Moscow and the neighboring communist regimes, the Hungarian government replied: "Not only do we need the world, but the world needs us. An era will be closed with the removal of this fence, and we hope that such systems will never be needed again."

Hungary's transition from communism to democracy was even smoother than Poland's. The government passed a "democracy package" in summer 1989 and began rewriting its constitution to allow for multiparty parliamentary elections and a direct presidential election. On October 23, 1989, the thirty-third anniversary of the 1956 Revolution, Hungary became an independent, democratic country.

At a Warsaw Pact summit meeting in July 1989, the leaders of East Germany, Romania and Czechoslovakia were alarmed by Poland's elections and the huge gap in the Iron Curtain created by Hungary. At the same time, U.S. President Bush visited Poland and Hungary, giving them moral support for democratic change but not the economic aid they hoped for. Bush was cautious, and he assured Gorbachev that the United States would not exploit Soviet problems in Eastern Europe.

1989 TIMELINE

February:
Solidarity Union legalized in Poland

May:
Border between Austria and Hungary reopened

June:
Solidarity Party claims stunning victory in Polish parliamentary elections

August:
Citizens of Estonia, Latvia and Lithuania create the Baltic Way

September:
East Germans flee to West Germany

October:
Internal coup replaces Honecker with Krenz in East Germany

Hungary becomes a democratic republic

November:
Berlin Wall falls

Bulgarian president Zhivkov resigns

Velvet Revolution begins in Czechoslovakia

December:
Romanian revolution erupts in violence; Ceausescu and wife are executed

Brandenburg Gate reopens in Berlin

Havel elected president of Czechoslovakia

East Germany

In East Germany, Erich Honecker (in power since 1971) refused to admit there was anything wrong with his system, but in reality, the country was rotting away from massive air and water pollution brought on by the economic focus on heavy industrial and chemical manufacturing. Despite a healthy trade relationship with West Germany that provided many luxury goods for Honecker and the communist elite, the economy was in complete disarray. Honecker maintained control through the *Stasi*, his security police force that ruthlessly investigated and punished dissidents and vehemently rejected any suggestions at reform. But as a Soviet satellite state, Honecker was subject to decisions made by Moscow and was displeased when Gorbachev worked out a deal with West Germany and Hungary to allow East Germans to seek citizenship in the West in exchange for economic assistance to Moscow. In the summer of 1989, tens of thousands of East Germans chose to vacation in Hungary, Czechoslovakia and Poland, eventually making their way into Austria and West Germany through the hole in the Iron Curtain. Honecker was outraged, calling the refugees "moral outcasts."

Most East Germans chose to stay and protest, hoping to create a democracy in East Germany. Weekly demonstrations soon swelled into mass protests, and Honecker ordered the police and military to open fire on the crowds. As he welcomed Gorbachev to Berlin on the eve of East Germany's fortieth anniversary in October 1989, a group of communist youth marchers

Leipzig demonstration, October 1989. The sign reads, "Gorbi, Help us!"

began to chant "Gorby, save us!" Gorbachev suggested to Honecker that the way to stop public protest was to introduce a German version of *perestroika*, but Honecker refused. Honecker's handling of a series of nonviolent protests in Leipzig led by the New Forum, a Christian protest organization, finally proved to be his downfall. On October 9, 70,000 protestors (of the city's population of 500,000) gathered; the following week the group numbered 120,000, and it doubled to 320,000 at the next protest. Honecker ordered his police and military to fire on the demonstrators, but the head of state security, Egon Krenz, ordered them to stand down to prevent a bloodbath. The demonstration was allowed to proceed peacefully, signaling to the East German people that the police were on their side and to Honecker that he was no longer in control. On October 18, 1989, members of the East German Politburo organized a coup (with Gorbachev's approval) and replaced Honecker with Krenz. Trained as a hardline communist, Krenz was desperately hoping to negotiate the wave of revolutionary activity sweeping through Eastern Europe and maintain Communist Party control. Krenz offered East Germans new freedoms, promising to lift travel restrictions to the West, but demonstrators wanted more.

Watch the Video Lecture *The Collapse of the Communist Bloc (The Berlin Wall)* on mysearchlab.com

At 7:00 on the evening of November 9, 1989, the Politburo member in charge of "Press and Information" told journalists at an international press conference that restrictions on travel to the West would be lifted. As the transcript of the interview demonstrates, he was unclear as to exactly what the changes would be and when they would go into effect but thought that it would be "immediately, without delay." As the news spread around Berlin over the next few hours, citizens from both sides of the wall rushed to see if the checkpoints were really opening. East German border guards were baffled—they had only one order, which was to stop anyone trying to escape. But the crowds were huge, and the news was reporting that things had changed, so the guards gave in and opened the barriers. West Berliners arrived from the other direction, and the citizens began to demolish the wall in front of the Brandenburg Gate.

West German Chancellor Helmut Kohl was eager to reunite his country, but only on his terms. He refused to negotiate with an unelected East German government, and the Communist Party in East Germany did not have the financial or political resources to hold onto its power. After elections in March 1989, an extension of Kohl's political party took control of the East German government, and reunification seemed imminent.

But many in the region were not ready for the sudden reemergence of a united and powerful Germany. Lech Walesa was not happy with Kohl's plan, as it potentially meant a loss of land and resources to his Polish government. Declassified documents reveal that both French President Francois Mitterand and British Prime Minister Margaret Thatcher were vehemently opposed to German reunification in private, but they could not publicly protest because they were allied with West Germany in the European Union. U.S. President Bush was cautiously optimistic about the potential to remove U.S. troops from Europe, but U.S. national security advisors feared what would happen to both Soviet and U.S. interests in the region if a reunited Germany decided to assert itself. Soviet President Gorbachev was also concerned—while he was not against unification in principle, he was worried about losing Warsaw Pact members to NATO, allowing NATO troops to move right up to the Soviet border.

In the end, a compromise was reached whereby the reunified Germany would be a NATO member, but no troops would be stationed in former East German territory. To alleviate other concerns, Kohl agreed to reduce the size of the German military overall, and signed a treaty allowing Poland to keep the land it gained in 1945. On October 3, 1990, Germany was officially reunited, and elections were held in December (easily won by Kohl's party). Though Germany was politically reunited in one year, it took the remainder of the century to truly merge its infrastructure and economies.

Bulgaria

The Communist Party leader of Bulgaria, seventy-seven-year-old Todor Zhivkov, had been in office for thirty-four years, longer than any other leader in the Soviet satellite bloc. But the revolutionary spirit spreading across Eastern Europe was too strong for even the most repressive of communist regimes. In 1986, Zhivkov attempted to ease his country's structural economic problems with a very limited "self-management" program for industrial workers, but it did not provide relief. In November 1989, the first-ever public protest in postwar Bulgaria demonstrated the public's desire for true reform, something Zhivkov refused to deliver. An internal coup at the Communist Party Central Committee led to his public "resignation," and a reformist took control of the communist nation in an attempt to prevent revolution.

With Zhivkov gone and no Soviet military for support, underground dissident groups appeared, most notably an ecological movement called *Eco-glasnost*. Ongoing protests in the capital city of Sofia led the Communist Party to step down from power and agree to hold the country's first free elections since 1931. In the June 1990 elections, the Bulgarian Socialist Party (essentially the renamed Communist Party focused on economic reform) won the majority of parliamentary seats, but the transition away from communism proved to be a long and tumultuous process for Bulgaria. As control of the government flip-flopped between socialists and anticommunists, economic policies were changed frequently, leading to massive unemployment and hyperinflation.

Read the Document *Czech Premier Ladislav Adamec Addresses the Czechoslovak Communist Party Central Committee* on mysearchlab.com

Czechoslovakia

Velvet Revolution the nonviolent coup that provided for a smooth transition in Czechoslovakia from a communist regime to a democratic republic

By the 1980s Czechoslovakia had gone from being a model of economic progress in Eastern Europe to a polluted country with outdated technology and a stagnant economy. As revolution spread through Poland and Hungary in the spring and summer of 1989, it revitalized the Charter 77 dissident movement. Charter 77, a human rights group led by playwright Vaclav Havel, had been operating underground since the Czech government went after it in 1977. Though the communist regime maintained its control of the country through the tumultuous summer of 1989, a huge student demonstration in Prague in November was met with police brutality. Under Havel's leadership, Charter 77 and other opposition groups joined together as the Civic Forum and threatened a nationwide workers' strike. The Civic Forum brought back Alexander Dubcek, leader of the 1968 Prague Spring, who once again inspired the Czech people with his slogan "Socialism with a human face." Without Soviet support, the communist party voluntarily stepped down from power in what became known as the **Velvet Revolution.** In December 1989, Havel was chosen by the Parliament (still largely communist) to serve as president, and he was popularly elected the following summer.

Romania

In Romania, the demand for change ignited violence, in part because of the violently repressive regime of Nicolae Ceausescu, who had been in power since 1965. Ceausescu was a nationalist who maintained the support of the Romanian people because he promised to keep Soviet intervention to a minimum. He was able to maintain a delicate balance during the Cold War, enough of a communist dictator to stay in the good graces of the USSR, but anti-Soviet enough to earn praise from U.S. Vice President George Bush in 1983 for being "one of Europe's good communists." He ruled over the Romanian people in a Stalinesque fashion, relying on his cult of personality to keep him in power despite their horribly low standard of living and the luxurious lifestyle he and his wife Elena openly flaunted. When occasional protests did break out, such as the workers' demonstration in Kronstadt in 1987, they were murderously shut down.

Ceausescu rejected *glasnost* and *perestroika* as the desire for reform swept across the satellite bloc in 1989, relying on his citizens' fear and his strong private security force to prevent uprisings. His grip finally fell apart in mid-December when a pastor in Timisoara was removed from his church by the government for inciting "ethnic hatred." His congregation protested and, despite the government's use of force, the demonstrations evolved into a week-long series of protests that spread across the countryside and into the capital city of Bucharest. Ceausescu relied on his security force to quell the growing revolution. Unaware that they did not have the country under control, Ceausescu gave a public address to a crowd of 110,000 people on December 21. He fully expected the usual adoration of his people, but was instead booed and insulted as the event turned into a full protest against him, broadcast across the nation on television. As the Ceausescus went into hiding, their security forces went into the streets to stop the protestors. The violence spread across Romania overnight, ultimately killing 1,100 people and wounding another 3,300.

Watch the Video Lecture *Ceausescu Clearly Loses Control of Romania* on mysearchlab.com

The Ceausescus were caught trying to flee the country on December 22. They were briefly tried (the whole thing lasted two hours) in front of an ad hoc military tribunal on December 25 and then were executed on the spot. Footage of the trial and the Ceausescus' bodies was released, but the execution itself was not filmed, leading many to question the legitimacy of the trial and sentence. After a few more days of violence, the National Salvation Front (Ceausescu's supporters) took control of the government and prevented the rise of democratic opposition parties. Of all the changes in the satellite bloc in 1989, Romania's was certainly the most violent and resulted in the least actual political and social reform.

Revolution Reaches the USSR

A single year—1989—fundamentally shifted the balance of power in the Cold War that had been carefully maintained for forty-five years. In 1990, the crisis reached the heart and soul of the Soviet sphere of influence, Moscow.

Estonia, Latvia, and Lithuania

Dissident legal scholars in the Baltic states had long argued that their incorporation into the USSR was illegal because it was forcefully imposed as a result of the "secret provisions" (which were widely published in the West by 1989) of the Nazi-Soviet Non-Aggression Pact of 1939. In November 1988, Estonia went so far as to declare itself a sovereign state. Moscow continued to deny that these provisions even existed, leading to internal conflict between Balkan nationalist groups and the local Soviet governments in Estonia, Latvia and Lithuania. On August 23, 1989, the fiftieth anniversary of the Non-Aggression Pact, more than 2 million people engaged in a peaceful demonstration called the Baltic Way, joining hands in a human chain that spanned 370 miles and linked the capital cities of all three republics. The fifteen-minute event was

The Baltic Way: On August 23, 1988, more than one million people from Estonia, Latvia, and Lithuania joined hands to create a 600 km long human chain.

organized by nationalist movements—the Popular Front of Estonia Rahvarinne, the Popular Front of Latvia and the Lithuanian Reform Movement Sajudis—that issued a joint declaration calling the Non-Aggression Pact "null and void from the moment of signing" and urging Europe to recognize that Baltic occupation was "a problem of inalienable human rights." Legally, they argued, they were independent countries living under Soviet occupation. Moscow warned Soviet citizens about the dangers of "nationalist, extremist groups" and their "anti-Soviet" agendas that would lead to "catastrophic consequences" but did not take any military action against the Baltic republics.

The Russian Federation

The dramatic political, economic and social changes that took place in the satellite bloc states in 1989 spilled over into the USSR, creating an impatient and divided Soviet citizenry. Conservatives felt that Gorbachev was moving too fast, as evidenced by the backlash against communism across Eastern Europe. As Moscow lost control of its satellite states, it seemed inevitable that it would also lose control of its republics, particularly with the widespread nationalist violence that had appeared in the Baltics, Armenia and Azerbaijan. But many other Soviet citizens began to wonder if Gorbachev's application of *perestroika* within the USSR had really gone far enough. Yes, he had made dramatic changes to the Communist Party and the institutions of Soviet government, most notably separating the two in 1988, but the USSR still functioned as a one-party state. And yes, he had begun to institute structural economic reforms by backing away from central planning, but he did not go so far as to embrace a market economy. The benefits of *perestroika* were not readily apparent to most people, and they grew impatient at the slow pace of reform.

In June 1988, a small group of radical reformists within the Communist Party of the Soviet Union began publicly demonstrating against the electoral practices dominated by the conservatives of the party. Called the Democratic Union, this group led by Boris Yeltsin hoped to transform the USSR into a multiparty democratic parliamentary system. And as the Communist Party worked to maintain control over the new legislative and executive institutions of government created in May 1989, it marginalized the radical Yeltsin and his Democratic Union, sparking outrage among the voters. The Communist Party was doing exactly what Yeltsin had accused it of doing, but now, because of *glasnost*, everyone knew about it.

In March 1990, Gorbachev was elected president of the Soviet Union by the Congress of Peoples Deputies amid charges that he used threats to ensure the two-thirds majority required for victory. He found himself in the middle of a battle between communist hardliners who wanted to resort to traditional strong-arm tactics to maintain control and radicals who wanted to give the Soviet Socialist Republics (SSRs) greater sovereignty. The task was formidable: reform the economy and government while holding the union together. And the more constitutional power he gave himself to accomplish this task, the more the citizens turned against him.

In May 1990, Boris Yeltsin was popularly elected to the newly created position of parliamentary president of the Russian Federation, making him the first democratically elected leader in Russian history. The Russian Federation was the largest of the fifteen SSRs, spanning three-fourths of the Soviet territory and containing one-half of the Soviet population, giving Yeltsin considerable national political clout. He announced that the laws of the Russian Federation would take precedence over the laws of the USSR, and he would negotiate with President Gorbachev exactly what powers (if any) the USSR would have over the Russian Federation. During the next several months, five more SSRs declared their sovereignty.

Boris Yeltsin in April 1990.

At the Twenty-Eighth Congress of the Communist Party in July, Gorbachev announced that he would allow free elections in a multiparty system, and Yeltsin agreed to cooperate with him (lending popular support) in the development of the "500 Days" plan to make the final shift to a full market economy. This angered the hardliners. But then, in the fall of 1990, Gorbachev backed away from the plan, fearing chaos, and turned to the KGB for help in maintaining control. This angered Yeltsin and even the moderates: Foreign Minister Eduard Shevardnadze resigned in December 1990 due to what he feared as the "advance of dictatorship."

In April 1991, the Georgian Republic declared its independence—the USSR was slowly dissolving. The following month, Gorbachev was able to put together a reform package that convinced leaders of nine of the fifteen republics to form a new, voluntary union. But the hardliners had had enough of *perestroika*.

MAP 12.1 The Dissolution of the USSR

The August Coup

In August 1991, Gorbachev retreated to his vacation home in the Crimea to work on the final details of the new Union Treaty. On Sunday, August 18, a delegation of Communist Party officials arrived at his home and demanded that he declare emergency rule and abandon the Union Treaty. He refused and was put under house arrest, cut off from all outside

Yeltsin speaks during the August Coup: August 19, 1991.

communication. The next morning, Monday, August 19, the people of Moscow were informed that Gorbachev was ill and that the State Committee for the State of Emergency (consisting of eight conservative communists that Gorbachev himself had appointed to power) was in control of the government. They banned all public demonstrations, disbanded the institutions of government (particularly targeting the elected republican governments), arrested political opposition leaders and sent tanks into the streets of Moscow in a show of strength.

The attempted coup was short-lived and unsuccessful, in part because its leaders were disorganized and many soldiers and civil servants refused to obey the Emergency Committee. Boris Yeltsin escaped arrest, climbed up on a tank in front of the Russian Parliament building and denounced the coup. He urged the people to defend themselves and their elected government, calling for a general labor strike and public demonstrations. On Monday night, hundreds of people joined Yeltsin in front of the Russian Parliament ready to take on the KGB and Soviet military, but there was no attack. By Tuesday night, tens of thousands of supporters had joined Yeltsin, and the first blood was spilled as three young men were killed by armored personnel carriers. After that, many of the troops turned against the coup leaders, who were either arrested or commited suicide on Wednesday, August 21. Gorbachev returned to Moscow early on August 22, ashamed and defeated, announcing, "I have come back ... to another country, and I myself am a different man now."

When the dust from the coup settled, Yeltsin was the clear victor. Even after members of Gorbachev's own government had led the failed coup attempt against him, he reaffirmed his belief in the Communist Party, which was not what people wanted to hear. He was booed in the Russian Parliament and sidelined by Yeltsin in negotiations regarding the Union Treaty. On August 24, Gorbachev resigned as General Secretary of the Communist Party and disbanded the Central Committee. Five days later, the Soviet Communist Party essentially dissolved itself as no one stepped forward to take leadership. People rejoiced, cutting up flags and tearing down statues, but no one went near Lenin's tomb at the Kremlin.

The Soviet Empire Crumbles

Even though Gorbachev was technically still the president of the USSR, most republics had declared independence and were no longer listening to him. In October 1990, Yeltsin moved ahead with a radical economic reform proposal of his own, hoping to maintain some form of economic union between the republics, preferably led by his Russian Federation. But as the republics were

MAP 12.2 The Commonwealth of Independent States

preparing to meet in December to work out the details, the people of Ukraine overwhelmingly voted for independence. In Minsk on December 8, 1991, the three Slavic states—Russia, Belarus and Ukraine—signed a pact ending the USSR and creating instead the Commonwealth of Independent States (CIS). Gorbachev was humiliated (he was not even invited to attend the meeting) and denied their right to do it, but within days the Russian Parliament ratified the Commonwealth Agreement, and eight other former republics joined the CIS.

On December 25, 1991, Gorbachev resigned his presidency and officially dissolved the Union of Soviet Socialist Republics. His speech was brief, and he did not try to hide his disappointment or concern about the security of the Russian citizens under Yeltsin's Commonwealth of Independent States. He admitted that mistakes were made during his six years in office, but he remained convinced that the "common efforts" made while he was in office would lead to a "prosperous and democratic society." Earlier in the day, President Yeltsin was respectful when he was asked to describe Gorbachev's key mistakes. "Today is a difficult day for Mikhail Gorbachev. . .Because I have a lot of respect for him personally and we are trying to be civilized people and we are trying to make it into a civilized state today, I don't want to focus on these mistakes."

Read the Document *Resolution: Soviet Unity for Leninism and Communist Ideas* on mysearchlab.com

With the USSR dissolved and Gorbachev out of power, the Soviet flag was lowered for the last time at 7:32 p.m. on December 25, 1991.

Conclusions

The Cold War conflict that dominated the world for forty-five years ended in 1991 with the dissolution of one superpower and the other claiming victory. Historians continue to debate why, exactly, the Cold War ended. Certainly, physical, economic and social conditions within the

USSR had deteriorated to the point that reform was required to prevent large-scale rebellion. Would the Soviet empire have fallen apart of its own accord if the United States had done nothing? Possibly, but the United States certainly did take actions that at least hastened its demise. Reagan's anticommunist rhetoric encouraged many Eastern Europeans to choose another path for themselves, leading to the unraveling of the Iron Curtain. As the United States poured money into its military and focused on "rollback," the resources the Soviets gained from their sphere of influence dwindled, while the costs of maintaining it rose dramatically. And while Ronald Reagan played a role in convincing the Soviets that the United States had SDI technology, Gorbachev's willingness to engage in negotiations with the United States and enact meaningful reform in the USSR, even though it meant a loss of personal power, was a marked departure from the Soviet leaders who came before him. Historically, nationalism has been a powerful force in Eastern Europe and, as we will see in the post-Cold War world, one that continues to shape the region geographically, politically and socially.

Although there is no simple answer, it certainly appeared at the end of the twentieth century that the economics of capitalism had defeated the economics of communism. In Marx's ideology, the communist revolution would be worldwide, and there would be no arms race to finance or military presence to maintain around the world. But that was not how the world functioned in the latter half of the twentieth century, and, like so many empires before it, the USSR was simply unable to bear the costs of staying on top.

WORKING WITH THE THEMES

THE EFFECTS OF TECHNOLOGY Why did the USSR believe the United States possessed SDI technology? How did the combination of SDI and the Chernobyl accident affect U.S.–Soviet arms negotiations?

CHANGING IDENTITIES How did *glasnost* and *perestroika* challenge the traditional concept of Soviet communism? Do you think Gorbachev expected the republics of the USSR to secede? Explain why the turn away from communism across Eastern Europe was so sudden. Why was it violent in some countries and peaceful in others?

SHIFTING BORDERS Why did the dissolution of the USSR create a power vacuum in central Asia? How did it change the strategic decision making of the United States and China? Why did most of the former Soviet republics agree to join the CIS?

GLOBALIZATION How much of Cold War decision making was based on ideology? On military/security concerns? On economic/trade considerations? Did the end of the USSR mean the United States was the only superpower, or did it completely restructure the international arena?

Further Reading

TO FIND OUT MORE

Jack F. Matlock Jr.: *Reagan and Gorbachev: How the Cold War Ended* (2004)

Roy Rosenzwieg Center for History and New Media: Making the History of 1989. Available online at http://chnm.gmu.edu/1989

David E. Hoffman: *The Dead Hand: The Untold Story of the Cold War Arms Race and Its Dangerous Legacy* (2009)

MATRIX, the Center for Humane Arts, Letters and Social Sciences Online: Seventeen Moments in Soviet History—1985, 1991. Available online at http://www.soviethistory.org

GO TO THE SOURCE

National Security Archive/Malcolm Byrne and Peter Kornbluh (eds.): *The Iran-Contra Scandal—The Declassified History* (1988)
National Security Archive/Tom Blanton (ed.): *White House E-Mail: The Top-Secret Computer Messages the Reagan/Bush White House Tried to Destroy* (1996)
Anatoly C. Chernyaev: *My Six Years with Gorbachev* (2000)
National Security Archive/Svetlana Savranskaya and Thomas Blanton (eds.): Reagan, Gorbachev and Bush at Governor's Island: Previously Secret Documents from Soviet and U.S. Files On the 1988 Summit in New York, 20 Years Later (2008). Available online at http://www.gwu.edu/~nsarchiv/NSAEBB/NSAEBB261/index.htm
Mikhail S. Gorbachev: *The August Coup: The Truth and the Lessons* (1991)
Boris Yeltsin: *Midnight Diaries* (2000)
The Ronald Reagan Presidential Library, the Public Papers of the President: Ronald Reagan, 1981–1989. Available online at http://www.reagan.utexas.edu/archives/speeches/publicpapers.html

MySearchLab Connections

Read the **Document** on **mysearchlab.com**

12.1 *National Security Decision Directive 32: U.S. National Security Strategy*. In 1982, President Reagan laid out his national security strategy for the Cold War, making it clear that the era of détente was over.

12.2 *Mikhail Gorbachev on the Need for Economic Reform.* Mikhail Gorbachev became the leader of the Soviet Union in 1985, and immediately launched into the reform of Soviet economic and social policy. In this document, he lays out some specific steps that the leaders of the USSR's economy must take to revitalize the socialist system and make up ground lost to the West.

12.3 *Czech Premier Ladislav Adamec Addresses the Czechoslovak Communist Party Central Committee.* As anti-communist revolutions spread across the Soviet satellite bloc in 1989, different governments chose different ways to respond. When the Czechoslovak Communist Party Central Committee gathered on November 24, 1989 to decide how to deal with the protests taking place in Wenceslas Square, Premier Ladislav Adamec made a plea for a nonviolent response.

12.4 *Resolution: Soviet Unity for Leninism and Communist Ideas*. Conservative elements in the Communist Party were particularly concerned about Gorbachev's radical policies and the devastating losses in 1989. Fearing that he would succeed in instituting capitalism in the USSR, they produced a resolution demanding that an extraordinary Party Congress be convened to remove Gorbachev from power.

Watch the **Video** on **mysearchlab.com**

12.1 *Reagan's Presidential Campaign*
12.2 *Ronald Reagan at the Berlin Wall*
12.3 *The Collapse of the Communist Bloc (The Berlin Wall)*
12.4 *Ceausescu Clearly Loses Control of Romania*

13 Restructuring Relationships

CHAPTER OUTLINE

- Restructuring Global Politics and Economics
- Restructuring the Nation-State
- Backlash

CHAPTER TIMELINE

1988
Al-Qaeda is formed in Afghanistan

1989
Students protest in Tiananmen Square
Revolutions unravel the Iron Curtain

1990
Persian Gulf War begins
Apartheid ends in South Africa

1991
USSR dissolves
United Nations takes control in Cambodia
START I agreement is signed
Civil war begins in Somalia

1992
Civil war begins in Yugoslavia

2001
China joins the WTO
9/11 World Trade Center and Pentagon attacks occur in the U.S.
United States declares "War on Terror;" invades Afghanistan

2003
Darfur genocide begins
United States invades Iraq
Yugoslavia dissolves

2004
NATO expansion adds seven members

2006
North Korea develops nuclear weapons

Photos from left to right: Rwandan refugees, 1994; Blackhawks in northern Iraq, April 1991; Yeltsin and Clinton, October 1995; Twin Towers burning on 9/11/01.

1993

Oslo Mideast Peace Accords are signed

World Trade Center is bombed

Russian constitution establishes democracy

Czechoslovakia dissolves

1994

United States and United Nations intervene in Haiti

Rwandan genocide takes place

1995

World Trade Organization is created

1997

Asian financial crisis spreads worldwide

Civil war begins in the Democratic Republic of the Congo

1998

India and Pakistan develop nuclear weapons

U.S. embassies bombed

1999

NATO expansion adds three members

United States releases Panama Canal

Because the Cold War had a tremendous impact on all parts of the world, the end of the Cold War carried major consequences as well. The most immediate result was that the United States was, by default, the "lone superpower," although political leaders around the world questioned that claim. With ongoing negotiations bringing the arms and space races to an end, perhaps a country's power in the post-Cold War world would not be measured solely by the strength of its nuclear stockpile. Countries with large traditional standing militaries (China and India) argued they had military might that was actually usable. And the wealthy (Japan and the rapidly growing European Union) argued that the forces of globalization had connected the world in ways that made military conflict undesirable for all, leaving economic strength as the true measure of global power. One thing remained clear—the sharp global division between rich and poor that was created by colonization from the seventeenth to nineteenth centuries and exacerbated by the proxy battles of the Cold War was still glaringly present. As the militarily and economically disadvantaged countries sought to improve their standing in the post-Cold War global structure, nationalism resurfaced in the ugliest of ways—civil war and genocide.

WORKING WITH THE THEMES

THE EFFECTS OF TECHNOLOGY The fear of nuclear proliferation becomes a reality; violence goes "low tech" with terrorism and genocide. The international economy recognizes intellectual property as a tradable good.

CHANGING IDENTITIES The United States is the lone superpower briefly, but China, India, and Pakistan gain power. Islamic fundamentalism is on the rise; nationalist violence sweeps across Eastern Europe and Africa, igniting refugee crises. Apartheid is abolished in South Africa.

SHIFTING BORDERS Eastern Europe is redrawn as Yugoslavia and Czechoslovakia fall apart and new countries are created.

GLOBALIZATION The WTO is created, along with several regional trade organizations. NATO expands into Eastern Europe, and the United Nations intervenes around the globe. A financial crisis in Asia spreads worldwide.

Restructuring Global Politics and Economics

The end of the bipolar structure of the Cold War in the early 1990s began a period of reassessment of how global power would be distributed in the twenty-first century. Although the United States clearly held military and economic superiority by traditional twentieth-century standards, other countries and regional organizations claimed significant power as well.

U.S. Hegemony

With the Cold War over, the American people elected a president who was focused on solving domestic economic problems. By the end of the 1980s, the United States had the largest trade deficit of any major industrialized country, which resulted in high unemployment due to the loss of manufacturing jobs and increasing social stratification. Elected in 1992, President Bill Clinton promoted aggressive pro-growth and free-trade policies during his two terms in office. During that time, the U.S. economy expanded by 50 percent in real terms, and the U.S. gross national product rose to one-quarter of the entire world economic output, although the U.S. trade deficit worsened. The unemployment rate dropped by half (to 4 percent), and 20 million jobs were created (92 percent of them in the private sector), in part because the stock market grew by more than 300 percent. The federal government paid down the public debt by $363 billion, balanced its budget, and left a $237 billion surplus. As the domestic economy strengthened, Clinton increased U.S. leadership in the international economy through the creation of the **North American Free Trade Association (NAFTA)** in 1994 and the World Trade Organization in 1995, securing $90 billion in debt relief to poor countries and stabilizing Mexican, Asian and Russian financial crises through reform of the International Monetary Fund.

NAFTA
a regional organization that removes tariff barriers between the United States, Canada and Mexico; also includes agreements on environmental and labor issues and procedures for dispute resolution between the member states

The Clintons and the Gores.

Stabilizing the international arena overall was a guiding principle of foreign policy decision making in the Clinton administration. In the 1990s, the United States perceived no major external military threat. Although communism had not been defeated (China, Vietnam, Laos, North Korea and Cuba remained communist regimes), there was certainly a strong trend toward democracy and capitalism around the world. To help push this shift along, the United States continued to engage in military and economic intervention to build democratic governments, open trade markets and promote human rights.

Clinton's foreign policy was more a worldview than a formal and coherent plan. He believed in "democratic enlargement" and "global leadership," which basically meant that the United States had a global responsibility to promote democracy and prevent human rights violations, even if fulfilling this responsibility meant intervening in sovereign nations. Critics accused the United States of being the "world's policeman," but Clinton was a strong proponent of **multilateralism** and preferred to work through international organizations rather than take unilateral action to achieve U.S. interests. Immediate foreign policy concerns for the United States in the post-Cold War world included nuclear proliferation through the black market, the interconnectedness of the international economy, and restructuring U.S. national security mechanisms to reflect the change in security concerns. These concerns led to a complex and often inconsistent approach to foreign affairs.

multilateralism multiple countries working in partnership on a particular issue

During the 1990s, 60 percent of the U.S. overseas bases built to fight the Cold War were closed down. Total military personnel were cut by 500,000, and just 18.7 percent of active-duty military personnel were stationed abroad (as opposed to 27 percent in the decade before). But U.S. military spending remained high (39 percent of the world's total) and was devoted to building technological superiority.

Despite scaling back its military presence abroad, the United States maintained hegemony (or "global leadership") through the expansion of NATO and its dominant position in the UN Security Council and international economic organizations. Although Russia, China, France and Great Britain (fellow permanent members of the UN Security Council) were acutely aware that the United States was using its military and financial power to exert its leadership, none of them was in a position to prevent it. Russia was still reeling from the dissolution of the USSR; China was working to overcome its negative image in the West to capitalize on its economic growth,

MAP 13.1 NATO Enlargement

and France and Great Britain were suffering through economic downturn and internal divisions over the expansion of the European Union.

Created in 1949 to combat Soviet expansion into Western Europe, NATO had added only a few strategically key members throughout the Cold War (Greece, Turkey, West Germany and Spain). With NATO's primary adversary gone, the organization reassessed its role in the world—should it too dissolve, or continue to expand? The reunification of Germany in 1990 spread the alliance farther east, and other former satellite bloc states were eager to make the switch to the West. Despite vocal opposition by Russia, NATO expanded to include Poland, Hungary and the Czech Republic in 1999; Bulgaria, Estonia, Latvia, Lithuania, Romania, Slovakia and Slovenia in 2004; and Albania and Croatia in 2009, with several other Eastern European states in the process of applying for membership. Because the United States dominated the military command structure of NATO, expansion of the organization extended U.S. military reach across all of Europe. In 2010, the combined military spending of all NATO

MAKE THE CONNECTION

How is the NATO expansion a continuation of the Cold War struggle for territory? Why did the expansion anger Russia?

members constituted over 70 percent of worldwide defense spending (the United States alone accounted for 43 percent).

Although Russia and NATO aim for bilateral cooperation through the Partnership for Peace established in 1994 and the NATO–Russia Council established in 2002, Russia and NATO frequently have found themselves at odds. In 1994, NATO militarily intervened against Bosnian Serb forces in the former Yugoslavia, citing regional security issues if the nationalist conflict were to spread, and in 1999 NATO military forces were actively involved in the Kosovo War. In both cases, Russia supported the Serbs. Relations between NATO and Russia were again troubled in 2008, following Russia's invasion of Georgia.

As a permanent member of the UN Security Council, the U.S. government also exerted considerable control over the council's decision making in the post-Cold War world. There were more peacekeeping operations (thirty-five) in the 1990s than any other decade due to a convergence of events: (1) domestic unrest increased when aid from the United States and USSR ended; (2) the UN Security Council was no longer handcuffed by disputes between the United States, USSR and China; and (3) Clinton insisted that intervention to promote human rights be a collaborative, international effort to avoid the legal questions surrounding the violation of sovereignty.

Read the Document The United Nations, *Universal Declaration of Human Rights, 1948* on mysearchlab.com

The largest of these operations was in Eastern Europe, where a UN Protection Force was first set up in Croatia in 1992 to "ensure the demilitarization of certain designated areas," then extended into Bosnia and Herzegovina, Macedonia, Kosovo and Georgia as civil conflict spread. These operations marked the first military effort to spread democracy into former Soviet territory, and administration and support missions remained in the region to ensure that the transition to democracy stayed on track.

One of the most challenging missions of the decade occurred in Somalia from 1992 to 1995. Operation Restore Hope was initially a U.S. military operation sanctioned by the United Nations to provide humanitarian assistance to the starving citizens of Somalia as fourteen warlords fought for control of the government. In May 1993, the United States turned the mission over to the United Nations, and a Unified Task Force of 38,000 soldiers from twenty-three countries was

U.S. Marines in Mogadishu, Somalia, January 7, 1992.

sent to monitor the tense ceasefire agreement between the warlords. The peacekeeping mission (United Nations Operation in Somalia II: UNOSOMII) was authorized to use "all necessary means" to protect the humanitarian mission, disarm rebel factions and establish a democratic government. Somalia's military government denounced UN intervention and began attacking the peacekeepers. The violence reached a peak in September 1994 when Somali rebels shot down a U.S. Black Hawk helicopter, dismembered the soldiers' bodies and paraded them through the city, igniting one of the bloodiest and most deadly urban battles since the Vietnam War. Clinton withdrew U.S. troops in spring 1994, and the entire UN mission ended in March 1995. The violence and famine in Somalia, however, raged on.

The most comprehensive UN operation occurred in Cambodia from 1991 to 1995, where the UN mission (United Nations Transitional Authority in Cambodia: UNTAC) actually took over the functions of government, organized an election, disseminated information, provided national security and assumed the responsibility of promoting human rights (rather than protecting them). Under the rule of Pol Pot, the Khmer Rouge Communist Party ruled Cambodia from 1975 to 1979, during which an estimated 2 million people died. To end the genocide, Vietnam invaded and occupied Cambodia throughout the 1980s. The Khmer Rouge reorganized as an insurgency movement, and a brutal civil war ensued. Although the UNTAC mission established a new government, it failed to effectively disarm the Khmer Rouge, and violence continued until Pol Pot's death in 1998.

Certainly the most controversial UN operation of the 1990s was the Assistance Mission for Rwanda (UNAMIR) in October 1993, which was supposed to oversee the implementation of the Arusha Peace Accord and the transition to a multiparty, democratic government. When the ceasefire failed and an all-out genocide began, the Security Council (at the request of the United States) withdrew most of the UN troops, and those remaining were barred from intervening to end the genocide. President Clinton's explanation demonstrates how U.S. interests were controlling UN decision making: "I think that is about all we can do at this time when we have troops in Korea, troops in Europe, the possibility of new commitments in Bosnia if we can achieve a peace agreement, and also when we are working very hard to try to put the UN agreement in Haiti back on track, which was broken" (June 7, 1994). Clinton did not want to commit additional U.S. troops in a violent African nation after what happened in Somalia. The UN mission returned to provide humanitarian relief in the aftermath of the genocide.

ANALYSIS

There are many legal questions about violating sovereignty in the name of protecting human rights. Can we? Should we? When? Who should do it?

Probably the most obvious example of U.S. dominance over Security Council decision making occurred in Haiti in 1995. A military coup in 1990 removed the president and violently seized control of the government, negatively impacting U.S. investments and prompting a flood of Haitian refugees into the United States. In 1994, a U.S.-led multinational force was sent to Haiti in "Operation Uphold Democracy" to, as President Clinton explained, "protect American interests and stop the brutal atrocities that threaten tens of thousands of Haitians." President Jean-Bertrand Aristide was restored to power and a UN mission (the United Nations Mission in Haiti: UNMIH) took over in March 1995, although a large contingent of U.S. troops remained and the leader of the U.S. troops in Haiti was named commanding officer of UNMIH as well.

Read the Document Deng Xiaoping, *On Introducing Capitalist Principles to China* on mysearchlab.com

The Emergence of China

Deng Xiaoping had been a loyal revolutionary during Mao's early struggle for power, but Deng's opposition to the "Cultural Revolution" in the 1960s made him an enemy of the state. After his "rehabilitation" at a manual labor camp, Deng returned to government and worked his way to the top echelons of the Chinese Politburo. As Mao's revolution came to a close with his death in 1976, Deng assumed leadership of the Chinese Communist Party, restructured the hierarchy of command, solidified the party's philosophy of **socialist modernization** and promoted vigorous economic reforms in the countryside where 80 percent of China's population lived. His

socialist modernization opening the Chinese economy to the outside world and creating special development zones, but under the control of the socialist state and legal system goal was to open China to the West to attract foreign investment and open export markets but restrict the importation of democratic political ideas. But the democratic revolutions of 1989 that dissolved the Soviet satellite bloc found a voice in communist China as well.

In May 1989, Mikhail Gorbachev and President Deng negotiated border disputes and regional territorial issues that had plagued their relationship for decades. Although they remained ideologically far apart, the renewed relationship between the two men attracted media from around the world. The crucial meeting came at the same time university students and intellectuals were demonstrating in Tiananmen Square, a memorial site and home of government offices in the center of Beijing. The protests began in April over Deng's dismissal of the secretary general of the party, but quickly took on other issues. The protestors were fighting for some version of *glasnost* in China and against the growing socioeconomic division that resulted from Deng's economic reforms. The protests took the form of public demonstrations, hunger strikes and labor strikes. Deng put off dealing with them until after the world's television cameras had left on May 18, finally declaring martial law on May 20.

The crucial thing for China is for the Communist Party to have a good Political Bureau...China will be as stable as Mount Tai. Internationally, no one will look down upon us, and more and more people will invest in China. We should seize every opportunity to develop the economy...Now the most important thing is to have a united core of leadership. If we can go on in this way for 50 or 60 years, socialist China will be invincible.

—Deng Xiaoping in a discussion with leaders of the CPC Central Committee, December 24, 1990

As the People's Liberation Army entered Beijing on June 1, 1989, residents joined the protestors by blocking off the streets leading to the square. For the next few days, hundreds of thousands of Chinese troops and an estimated 1 million protestors engaged in violent battles for control of Tiananmen Square. By the afternoon of June 4, the military had gained control. The Chinese reported that 241 people died and 7,000 were wounded (military and civilian), but estimates by NATO investigators ranged as high as 7,000 dead and tens of thousands wounded. Hundreds more were executed and imprisoned in the following weeks.

Images of the event were broadcast around the world, and the Chinese government was harshly criticized by the United Nations and Western governments. A handful of countries (notably North Korea and Cuba) openly supported the Chinese government's response, but many others took no official position. The damaging consequences for the Chinese government—the

Protestors in Tiananmen Square do battle with the Chinese military, June 3, 1989.

Most-Favored-Nation (MFN) status countries do not discriminate between their trading partners—all with MFN status receive the same treatment

suspension of foreign loans and direct investment from the World Bank and the West, the withdrawal of **Most-Favored-Nation (MFN) status** from the United States, and the arms embargo put in place by the United States and the European Union (EU)—turned out to be only temporary. The opposition movement shattered, the government continued to pursue economic reforms in industry and agriculture and quickly established its place in the post-Cold War world as an economic powerhouse.

During the 1990s, China's economy experienced one of the fastest growth rates in world history by opening itself to foreign investment and taking advantage of its plentiful, inexpensive labor force. Despite the international economic recession of the early 1990s, China's gross domestic product steadily increased by an average of 10.5 percent each year from 1988 to 1998, and its share of world exports doubled from 1990 to 2000. With a population of 1.2 billion consumers and a consistently growing share of the world trade market, it was imprudent for the West to prevent China's integration in the global economy despite ongoing charges of human rights violations. In 2001, China joined the World Trade Organization, and the Chinese economy is expected to be the world's largest by 2020.

ANALYSIS

What countries do you see as powerhouses in the twenty-first century? Why? Consider geostrategic position, military, economy, political culture, etc.

The World Trade Organization

In the uncertain international structure of the immediate post-Cold War world, countries relied on international organizations to provide stability. Both the United Nations and NATO reached around the world militarily, and regional trade blocs such as the EU and NAFTA provided opportunities for political and economic integration. The economic recession and the reverberating effects of financial meltdowns in Mexico, Russia and Asian markets of the early 1990s proved that the international economy was inextricably linked. Some countries, particularly Japan and China, and the EU engaged in **economic nationalism,** reflecting an increased focus on economic strength as a measure of power in the post-Cold War world.

economic nationalism setting economic policy in a way that prioritizes national interests above private property and profit motives; decisions are made with the goal of strengthening the nation-state foremost

The eighth round of General Agreement on Tariffs and Trade (GATT) tariff negotiations that began in 1986 (known as the Uruguay Round) was stuck in a stalemate over economic nationalism as the 1990s began. Economists grew increasingly concerned that the Cold War might morph into a trade war, similar to the tariff wars following World War I but much more global in scope. There were 123 countries involved in the Uruguay Round, many of them developing countries that were able to work as a bloc for the first time in GATT history. Negotiations stalled over trade reforms in the politically touchy areas of agriculture and textiles, which was the primary goal of the Uruguay Round. Although most countries subsidized farming in some way to maintain viable agricultural sectors, Japan and the EU had extensive tariff and nontariff protective measures that were detrimental to American agriculture. U.S. President Clinton took a very active role in the negotiations, and the United States maintained its economically powerful position after the final treaty was signed in 1994. Overall, global tariffs were cut by an average of 38 percent on industrial products, significant agricultural and textile quota were eliminated, and a new category of tradable goods, **intellectual property,** was protected under GATT regulations. But the most sweeping change to come out of the Uruguay Round was the disbanding of GATT altogether and the creation of a World Trade Organization (WTO) in 1995 in an attempt to mitigate national differences that could lead to economic warfare.

intellectual property anything created by the mind—inventions, literary and artistic works, and symbols, names, images and designs used in commerce

The WTO was created to liberalize trade by creating a forum for governments to negotiate trade agreements (which become the international trade rules) and then providing a structured mechanism by which the members can work out disputes. The stated goal of the WTO is to create an international trade system that is fair (no discrimination between trade partners or products), free, predictable, competitive and beneficial to less-developed countries so that they can benefit from participation.

Whereas GATT consisted of representatives looking out for the best interests of their own nation-states, the WTO has created a dispute mechanism system of independent judges with the power to assess penalties against any country that violates international trade laws as established by member states. A panel of three to five independent experts from different countries reviews the dispute and recommends a resolution. The panel's report is sent to the Dispute Settlement Body (the entire WTO membership), which can only reject the report by consensus. The Dispute Settlement Body monitors the implementation of the rulings and authorizes retaliation for non-compliance.

In the post-Cold War world, international institutions such as the World Bank, the International Monetary Fund (IMF), the WTO, the EU, NAFTA and a handful of other powerful regional trading blocs replaced the United States and USSR as the primary sources of financial assistance for needy countries. Because these organizations largely control international markets, most African, Asian and Latin American countries remain dependent on them and the wealthy nation-states that control them.

Restructuring the Nation-State

The dissolution of the USSR completely changed the political, economic and demographic identity of a huge chunk of the world spanning from central Europe down to Africa and over to East Asia. The experience was remarkably similar to the decolonization of Africa and Asia at the end of World War II. All aspects of political, economic and social life with the USSR and its satellite states were controlled by the central government and enforced by the military. So, much like the decolonization of Africa and Asia from the 1950s through the 1980s, the fifteen successor states of the USSR and the former satellite states had many political, economic and social obstacles to overcome to establish stable, functioning countries. And as soon as the political and military restraints were lifted, the age-old identity problem resurfaced—nationalism. Driven by the desire to participate in the global economy dominated by Western institutions, the former communist systems began the difficult transition to democracy.

Even outside the Soviet sphere of influence, the rules of the international arena had changed. The end of the Cold War meant the end of the competition for proxy states, and many countries throughout Latin America, Africa and Asia were left on their own to establish stable governance without financial and military support.

Transitions to Democracy

In the 1990s, the fifteen Soviet successor states struggled to establish political, economic and social stability. The largest of these, the Russian Federation, hoped to rebound quickly to maintain at least regional power. But in addition to the structural difficulties of switching from a centrally planned communist economy to a market-based, capitalist one, the world economy was in recession in the early 1990s. Under President Boris Yeltsin, the Russian government enacted radical economic changes that caused serious short-term economic and social problems, including inflation, corruption and a shortage of basic consumer goods. And the more the United States tried to help ease this economic transition through consultants and IMF loans, the greater the political opposition to Yeltsin's reforms grew. Yeltsin resigned in 1999, and

Vladimir Putin, second president of the Russian Federation.

sovereign democracy Russia will determine for itself what democracy means and how it is applied, and it cannot be challenged because of sovereignty

presidential power fell to former KGB officer Vladimir Putin, who referred to the Russian government as a **sovereign democracy.**

The establishment of democratic political regimes proved to be challenging, due to economic difficulties, nationalist tensions and the citizens' desire for security. Although the Russian constitution of 1993 created a democratic federal republic, Russia has continued to function in a fairly authoritarian manner. The bulk of the political power has remained in the hands of the president and, despite open elections, the winner in the presidential election has been the person endorsed by the outgoing president. The former republics closest to Russia in Eastern Europe and Central Asia retain many authoritarian elements in their governments as well, demonstrating Russia's ongoing regional influence.

MAP 13.2 Violence in the Caucasus

The other immediate problem these new countries faced was violent conflict. Territorial borders were in dispute across the former USSR, particularly where military bases, oil fields and access to deep sea ports were at stake. With the communist identity gone, nationalist secession movements appeared, particularly in the Caucasus where Christianity and Islam met. The most violent of these movements—Armenians in Azerbaijan, South Ossetia in Georgia, Romanians in Moldova and Chechnya in Russia—led to internal military conflicts. The five new countries of Central Asia—Kazakhstan, Kyrgyzstan, Tajikistan, Turkmenistan and Uzbekistan—were consumed by religious conflict as Islamic fundamentalists sought to replace Marxist regimes. The Russian military was involved in many of these conflicts, usually at the request of the government under attack by ethnic or religious factions. Despite the financial strains involved, the Russian government remained an active participant to assert its dominance in the region. And despite ongoing charges of human rights violations on the part of the Russian military, particularly in Chechnya, the United States and Russia maintained a good working relationship.

Balkan Genocide

Nationalist turmoil was a defining factor in Eastern Europe at the end of the nineteenth century and for the first half of the twentieth century. When the USSR occupied the region at the end of World War II, it militarily enforced communist regimes that squashed the nationalist movements. Communists were running the government, regardless of ethnicity. But the USSR certainly could not squash nationalist sentiment—it was simply driven underground, where it stewed and simmered for the last half of the twentieth century. As the Soviet military pulled out during 1990 and 1991 and the former satellite states earned their independence, civil wars broke out regarding who would govern, and the nationalist sentiments were cleverly manipulated by power-hungry and corrupt politicians.

The first sign of nationalist-driven conflict appeared in Yugoslavia, where differences had been mounting since Josip Broz Tito's death in 1980. Yugoslavia was formally created by the Treaty of Versailles as Austria-Hungary was carved apart, and the new state included many ethnic groups (Serbs, Albanians, Muslim Slavs, Croats, Slovenes, Slovaks, Macedonians, Hungarians and Montenegrins) who historically did not get along. As the Soviet tanks pulled away in summer 1991, the easternmost republics, Slovenia and Croatia, announced their independence from Yugoslavia. The government and military of Yugoslavia were dominated by Serbs, who represented the largest of the Yugoslav republics and the largest ethnic group (at roughly 37 percent).

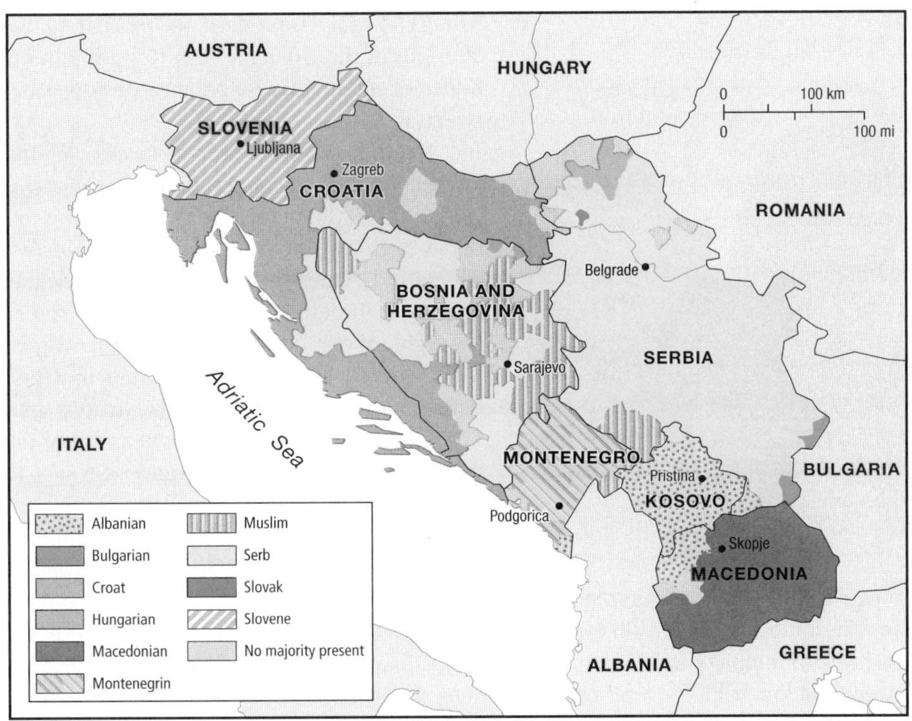

MAP 13.3 Ethnic Populations in the Balkans

When the military went into Slovenia and Croatia to prevent their secession, it was joined by the local Serb population.

In 1992, the European Community recognized Slovenia and Croatia as independent countries, and a UN peacekeeping force was sent in to uphold the cease-fire. But that recognition sparked hope in other Yugoslav ethnic groups, leading to the secession of Bosnia-Herzegovina in 1992. Because the largest ethnic group in Bosnia was Muslim (44 percent of the population), the minority Serbs (at 33 percent) feared living under a Muslim regime and declared their own independence (in the same territory). It became a civil war between the ethnic groups fighting for control of Bosnia-Herzegovina, with the Serbs unofficially supported by the government of Yugoslavia (though the Yugoslav military stayed out of the conflict). Although all ethnic groups involved certainly violated the Geneva conventions in their conduct of the war, the Serbs in particular engaged in a ruthless campaign of **ethnic cleansing.**

ethnic cleansing the attempt to create ethnically homogeneous geographic areas through the deportation or forcible displacement of persons belonging to particular ethnic groups

As Yugoslavia disintegrated, the Red Cross, the United Nations and NATO intervened in various ways but were unsuccessful in preventing the ongoing violence. Attempts to force both sides to the negotiating table failed, and peace plans developed by international organizations were rejected. NATO stepped up its military efforts in spring 1995 with U.S.-led bombing campaigns, and the Serbs responded by taking UN personnel hostage and holding them in potential bomb targets. With international organizations appearing helpless and no end in sight, Serbs in surrounding countries became violent. The government of Croatia responded with its own ethnic cleansing campaign against Croatian Serbs. In summer 1995, NATO launched a massive air strike against ethnic Serbs in Bosnia, and Serbian President Slobodan Milosevic finally agreed to peace talks. Negotiated in Dayton, Ohio, the *General Framework Agreement for Peace in Bosnia and Herzegovina* of 1995 created a separate Muslim-Croat Federation and a Bosnian Serb Republic within the country of Bosnia-Herzegovina, and it required the government to represent all three ethnic groups equally. NATO troops replaced UN peacekeepers to ensure that the agreement was upheld, and the U.S. military provided training and weapons for the

U.N. troops in Bosnia.

Muslim-Croat Federation to build it to the strength of the Bosnian Serb Republic in the hopes of maintaining a balance of power between the two groups.

But the violence was not over. Within Serbia, the autonomous region of Kosovo (90 percent Albanian) was tired of living under a Serb regime and formed the Kosovo Liberation Army to fight for independence. Milosevic ordered Serb paramilitary forces to fight them. The world again forced Milosevic to the negotiating table in 1999, but he refused to allow NATO troops into Serbia to monitor the agreement and sent the regular Yugoslav military into Kosovo to "remove" the Albanians. This round of ethnic cleansing continued for three months despite 10,000 NATO bombing missions in the region. When Milosevic finally agreed to pull his military out of Kosovo and allow NATO forces to secure its independence, 700,000 Albanian survivors and refugees violently took revenge against the Serb minority in Kosovo. In February 2002, Milosevic and more than one hundred others were put on trial for war crimes, crimes against humanity and genocide at the International War Crimes Tribunal. In 2003, Yugoslavia ceased to exist.

The only multiethnic state in the region to effectively handle the reemerging nationalist problems was Czechoslovakia. Like Yugoslavia, Czechoslovakia was a creation of the Treaty of Versailles, with multiple ethnicities within its borders. Ethnic Slovaks in the eastern part of the state wanted to secede rather than live under Vaclav Havel's Czech-dominated state. After remarkably peaceful negotiations sometimes referred to as the "velvet divorce," Havel agreed to grant their secession, and Czechoslovakia was divided into the Czech Republic and Slovakia on January 1, 1993, although Slovakia still contained a discontented Hungarian population.

What brought relative stability and peace to the region in the early twenty-first century was not the United Nations, not respect for diversity, and not peace treaties—it was the economy. After forty-five years of Soviet-style communism, the people of the former satellite bloc states were eager to join the international trade market and have access to consumer goods from around the world. But to do so successfully, they had to adopt Western political structures to support their new capitalist economies. So their governments became more transparent, cracked down on social injustice and bared their political and economic souls to the wealthy countries of the world. Most realized that, as new little countries with new little economies, they would benefit from joining the protection of a larger group such as the EU or WTO. It took a lot of work to restructure political systems to democracy, convert centrally planned production to privatization and capitalism, and replace the legacy of militarism and fear with social justice. But at the outset of the twenty-first century, most of the former satellite states had overcome these challenges and integrated into the international arena.

A Turn toward Democracy in Latin America

The end of the Cold War brought changes for the better to Latin America. The United States was less concerned about securing its authority politically over the hemisphere and focused instead on developing trade markets with its closest neighbors. Without financial and ideological support from the Soviet Union, the energy behind radical leftist movements dissipated, and bloody civil wars in Nicaragua and El Salvador came to an end. Governments did not have to rely on authoritarianism and military rule to maintain order, and there was a marked shift toward peace, democratic elections, parliamentary procedure in governance and protection of human rights.

To be sure, most Latin American governments suffered from the legacy of political corruption, unequal distribution of wealth and crushing foreign debt. But with the support of the United States and international financial institutions, the Latin American governments adopted free-market solutions to these problems. They privatized state-owned industries, reduced tariffs and, in the wake of the NAFTA agreement between Mexico, the United States and Canada, they created regional trade blocs such as Mercosur (Argentina, Brazil, Paraguay and Uruguay), the Andean Group (Bolivia, Colombia, Ecuador, Peru and Venezuela) and the Central American Common Market (Guatemala, El Salvador, Honduras and Nicaragua). In response to these efforts, the United States unilaterally reduced outstanding debts owed by Latin American countries through the Enterprise for the Americas Initiative of the 1990s.

The dissolution of the USSR had a devastating effect on Cuba's economy, which was reliant on Soviet subsidies and loans. Fidel Castro was forced to open Cuba to foreign investment to keep the economy afloat. Most of this investment came from Canada and Europe, creating a rift with the United States, which maintained its trade embargo against Cuba and its sanctions on foreign companies that did business with Cuba.

In perhaps the most symbolic move in Latin America at the end of the twentieth century, the United States returned the Panama Canal to the government of Panama on December 31, 1999, and the U.S. Southern Command (the center of U.S. military operations in the lower western hemisphere) relocated to U.S. territory (Florida).

A Power Shift in Asia

Soviet and U.S. withdrawal from parts of Asia in the late 1980s led to security concerns for many countries. Hong Kong, Singapore, South Korea and Taiwan (known as the "Asian Tigers") had made rapid economic gains through industrialization and globalization, bringing prosperity to the region. The fear that China would step in to fill the power vacuum created by the end of the Cold War led to an increase in arms shipments into the region, and the potential for conflict increased. Led by Malaysia, the Association of Southeast Asian Nations (ASEAN) created a nuclear-free, regional collective security system based on "Asian values" that embraced authoritarian government and state-controlled economic systems. But in 1997, the financial crisis that hit Thailand, South Korea, Indonesia and Malaysia (with reverberating effects throughout the international economy) left them reliant on IMF loans for survival. The **conditionality** imposed by the IMF loans restored Western-style democracy and economic control over much of the region. The devastating effects of the financial crisis led to violent conflict in Indonesia in 1999, where UN intervention was required to restore peace.

conditionality
predefined rigorous qualification criteria that must be met in order to borrow money from the IMF

The end of the Cold War caused a major political realignment in Asia. With Soviet support gone, India was forced to redefine itself. As it shifted toward free-market capitalism and joined the international economy, India developed a cooperative relationship with the United States. At the same time, U.S. ally Pakistan (also India's enemy) began supporting Islamic fundamentalist groups, causing a strain in that diplomatic relationship. With alliances broken and the concern of Soviet intervention gone, India and China resumed their ongoing border dispute and controversy over the region of Tibet. Pakistan supported a Muslim secessionist movement in India's Kashmir region, prompting renewed arguments between the bordering states that resulted in the development of nuclear weapons programs in both countries in 1998. As the twentieth century closed, India had become the world's largest democracy (by population), with nuclear weapons and the second largest standing military (behind

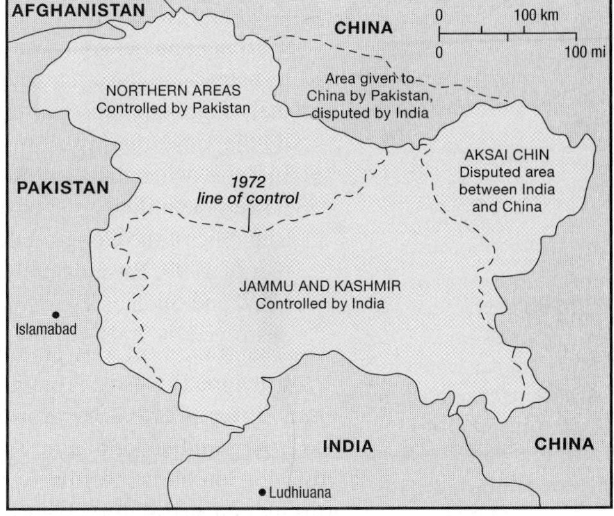

MAP 13.4 Kashmir

China). The region of Kashmir, where China, India and Pakistan come together, remains one of most volatile places in the world.

DEADLIEST CONFLICTS OF THE 1990S

1. Democratic Republic of the Congo (DRC)
2. Sudan
3. Rwanda
4. Angola
5. Somalia
6. Zaire
7. Burundi
8. Bosnia
9. Liberia
10. Algeria

Civil War and Genocide in Africa

The end of the Cold War was a mixed blessing for Africa. It was good in that foreign powers finally stopped intervening because proxy battles were over and Africa was no longer financially lucrative in modern international markets. Africa represented only 2 percent of total world trade at the end of the twentieth century. Unfortunately, that also meant that private investment and direct foreign aid passed Africa by. Most African nations were largely left on their own to figure out how to establish governments and participate in world affairs, which led to vicious cycles of civil war followed by the rise of corrupt and brutal governments to restore security. Nine of the ten deadliest conflicts of the 1990s occurred in Africa and represent approximately 90 percent of the total number of war deaths in the last decade of the twentieth century.

The underlying source of these conflicts was age-old tribal and religious differences, but the anarchy created by decolonization and the end of Soviet and American financial and military support in the post-Cold War world created the conditions for civil war.

- There were sixty-four different ethnic groups in Ethiopia when the dictator was removed in 1991, each of which wanted to secede and create its own government. When the Eritreans did, the result was civil war.
- In Somalia, the end of dictatorship in 1991 brought fourteen rival warlords and their private militias into violent conflict over control of territory and limited resources, leading to the starvation of 400,000 people.
- An ongoing civil war in Sudan between Christians in the south and the Muslim government forces of the north was exacerbated in 1989 when the National Islamic Front seized control of the government and Sudan joined the broader international terrorist movement. An estimated 2 million people died in that conflict between 1983 and 2009. A separate but related conflict broke out in the Darfur region of Sudan in 2003 between Arab livestock herders and African farmers, where an estimated 400,000 people have been killed (as of 2011) in an ethnic cleansing campaign led by Arab militias.
- A peace agreement to end the long-standing violence in Angola led to the country's first free elections in 1992. But insurgents refused to accept the outcome and engaged in guerilla warfare until 2002.
- A Hutu won the presidency of Burundi in 1993 (a traditionally Tutsi-led government), sparking another round in the Hutu–Tutsi war.
- In reaction to the attempted UN Arusha Accords, the Tutsis and Hutus in Rwanda resumed their ongoing ethnic warfare in 1994, leading to the massacre of 800,000 civilians, primarily the Tutsi minority.
- In Zaire, when dictator Mobutu Sese Seko was ousted in 1997 after thirty-two years of power, the military seized control of the government, renamed the country the Democratic Republic of the Congo (DRC) and began eradicating Rwandan Hutu refugees. In the summer of 1998, Rwanda and Uganda attacked the DRC; and Angola, Namibia, Zimbabwe, Chad and Sudan supported the DRC government. Africa's wealthiest country was all but destroyed by 2001.

child soldier
any boy or girl under 18 years of age who has been recruited or used by an armed force in any capacity, including fighters, cooks, porters, spies, or for sexual purposes

What made these conflicts particularly devastating was the recruitment of **child soldiers** and the spillover effect—the war in Sudan created border disputes with Uganda, Ethiopia and Eritrea, and it involved support from Iraq and Libya. War in the Democratic Republic of the Congo involved seven of its neighboring states, and the Hutu–Tutsi conflicts spread across four countries as refugees tried to flee. Even where civil war did not erupt, brutal authoritarianism spread violence through Cameroon, the Central African Republic, Congo, Guinea, Togo, Gambia and Niger.

There were a handful of countries on the African continent capable of instituting democratic governments in the 1990s (Zambia, Benin, Malawi, and the Ivory Coast). The only true post-Cold War success story was the Republic of South Africa, where F. W. de Klerk took office in 1989 and began systematically stripping away the apartheid system through racial reform. In 1990, de Klerk legalized the African National Congress (ANC), released its leader, Nelson Mandela, from prison (after twenty-six years) and began negotiating a power-sharing arrangement. Despite opposition from the white minority and violence between ethnic political rivals, the ANC won the parliamentary majority and Mandela became president in the first nonracial elections in April 1994. The Republic of South Africa became a multiracial, democratic country.

Child soldier in Sudan.

During the 1990s, there was an unprecedented level of international engagement in Africa in the form of UN peacekeeping missions. But the support was inconsistently applied and often limited in scope, so it was not always successful in achieving short-term peace, let alone long-term stability. The Cold War left the countries of Africa with heavy financial debt, ethnic and religious violence, and corrupt dictatorships, making it difficult to attract foreign investment. Perhaps one of the most insidious consequences of the ongoing civil violence that seeped across national borders was acquired immune deficiency syndrome (AIDS), which first appeared in the 1980s and had infected 25 million Africans two decades later. AIDS spread primarily through

Mandela and de Klerk sharing a laugh in January 1994, just weeks before the first free and democratic elections in South Africa.

soldiers who used prostitutes and drugs while engaged in regional wars, and the disease had become the leading cause of death in Africa by the early part of the twenty-first century.

Backlash

While the Cold War can perhaps be credited for preventing World War III, it also led to strong sensitivity on the part of national governments against being controlled by an outside force. After a century of colonization, international institution building and proxy wars, it became evident that there was a real resistance to being dominated by others ideologically, politically, and economically.

Nuclear Proliferation

The United States and USSR made great strides in reducing their long-range nuclear forces throughout the 1980s, which culminated in the Strategic Arms Reduction Treaty (START I) of July 1991. But when the USSR dissolved into its fifteen constituent republics just a few months later, the legality of all Soviet treaties was questioned, and the outside world could not do much more than wait to see where the nuclear weapons would resurface. Russia was recognized as the legal successor to the USSR, but the 12,000 long-range Soviet nuclear warheads were distributed between Russia, Ukraine, Belarus and Kazakhstan. Each agreed to adhere to the legal obligations of START I, but this arrangement left Russia with only two-thirds of the USSR's land-based strategic nuclear forces. After intense negotiations and promises of financial assistance, Ukraine, Belarus and Kazakhstan agreed to gradually transfer all Soviet nuclear warheads to Russia and sign the Nuclear Non-Proliferation Treaty (NPT). Further reductions in strategic arms between the United States and Russia were agreed to by presidents Bush and Yeltsin in 1993 (the SALT II), and presidents George W. Bush and Putin in 2002.

The end of the Cold War refocused attention on the importance of nonproliferation. Increased pressure was put on countries that had refused to sign the NPT, particularly those involved in regional conflicts. South Africa signed in 1991, followed by France and China in 1992. But other countries viewed the end of the Cold War as an opportunity to build their nuclear capabilities without the threat of U.S. or Soviet retaliation. India and Pakistan both refused to sign the NPT and joined the "nuclear club" in 1998. In 2003, North Korea became the first country to take its name off the NPT. North Korea developed a nuclear program and unveiled its first nuclear test in 2006.

As nuclear technology spread, there was a legitimate fear that scientists and laboratory workers would smuggle stolen supplies and sell them on the black market. By the end of the twentieth century, nuclear technology and expertise was readily available to those who could afford to buy it, and after decades of domination, many small countries were interested in joining the nuclear club. In January 2004, the head of Pakistan's nuclear weapons program, A.Q. Khan, confessed that he sold nuclear technology to Iran, Libya and North Korea throughout the 1990s, after investigators uncovered an international proliferation network based in Dubai, United Arab Emirates. The greatest fear of nuclear proliferation in the early twenty-first century, however, was that so-called **rogue states** and non–nation-states (terrorist organizations) would acquire nuclear capabilities. While it would be incredibly difficult for them to build **weapons of mass destruction (WMD)** and long-range delivery systems undetected, they could certainly use small quantities of nuclear material to create weapons that could do a lot of damage and potentially provoke a nuclear response from others.

rogue states
a Western term to describe countries that are a potential danger to world peace because they do not follow "the rules"; countries with authoritarian regimes that commit human rights violations, sponsor terrorism and/or sell weapons of mass destruction

WMD
weapons that cause extensive damage and kill large numbers of people; usually nuclear, biological or chemical weapons

Rise of Islamic Fundamentalism

For decades, the existence of the powerful Soviet military along the northern border of the Middle East kept overt U.S. military intervention in the region to a minimum. But the power vacuum created by the dissolution of the USSR, the nationalist and economic turmoil in the former Soviet states of central Asia and the frustration on the part of many Muslim extremists combined to create a volatile situation in the 1990s. Obviously, control of the lucrative oil fields and the governments whose territories the oil fields fell within was a key goal for Russia, the U.S. and Arab nationalists.

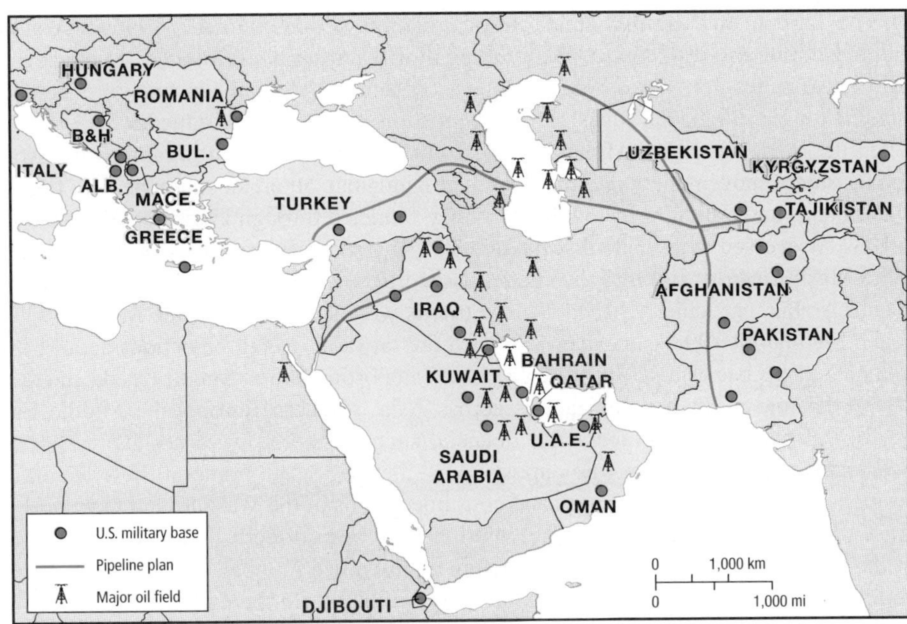

MAP 13.5 U.S. Postwar Bases in the Middle East

The United States began to build up its military presence in the Middle East in 1990 with the Gulf War. When Iraqi President Saddam Hussein invaded and annexed neighboring Kuwait in August 1990 and began committing human rights violations, Saudi Arabia requested defensive aid from its ally, the United States. Given Hussein's treatment of the Kuwaitis, disregard for laws against developing weapons of mass destruction and his efforts to control a significant portion of the world's oil supply, the United States immediately sent ground, air and sea forces under Operation Desert Shield. Russia was unable to respond militarily and did not block UN Security Council Resolution 678, allowing a U.S.-led coalition to use "any and all means available" to free Kuwait. The subsequent military action included NATO allies and powerful Arab states (Egypt, Saudi Arabia and Syria) hoping to block Iraq's military expansion. Operation Desert Storm—the devastating six-week air war and brief four-day ground offensive—freed Kuwait and established the United States' military supremacy in the region.

ANALYSIS

Why did Saudi Arabia ask for help? Why did Egypt and Syria help? Why did the United States leave bases in Saudi Arabia?

President Bush chose not to remove Saddam Hussein from power, in part because Hussein was a former U.S. ally and in part because he was a hero to many Muslims; also, Bush believed that if Hussein were overthrown, it should be by his own people and not a foreign military. The international community enacted embargos, financial penalties and mandatory weapons inspections to help spark the internal revolution against Hussein, but his military helped him maintain dictatorial powers. As a standoff over UN weapons inspections developed throughout the 1990s, U.S. military presence in the region continued to increase.

The violent backlash against U.S. intervention in the Middle East began during the Gulf War, when Hussein launched missiles against Israel in an attempt to highlight the connection between the regionally despised country and the West. In 1993, when the United States brought together Israel and the Palestine Liberation Organization to negotiate the Oslo Peace Accord, radical Islamic groups from the West Bank to Afghanistan began attracting new members who responded with violent attacks against Israelis and Americans. Organized and financed by Islamic extremist groups, the violent anti-West backlash continued into the twenty-first century.

As Soviet troops left Afghanistan in February 1989, a civil war ensued between the mujahideen and the Soviet-backed government. Without military support, the government fell in 1992, but the civil war continued among the mujahideen factions over who would take political

Al-Qaeda
Arabic word for "military bases"

control. The Taliban, an extremist Sunni political faction, seized control in 1996 and established the Islamic Emirate of Afghanistan. With the goal of fostering a worldwide Islamic revolution, the Taliban expanded its repressive religious laws across Afghanistan and into neighboring Pakistan, creating a safe haven for Islamic extremist groups such as **Al-Qaeda.**

When the Soviets invaded Afghanistan in 1979, Osama bin Laden organized the Arab mujahideen resistance movement under the Maktab al-Khidamat, an organization heavily financed by the United States and Saudi Arabia with the money funneled through Pakistan. When the Soviets left in 1989, it evolved into a jihadist movement (Al-Qaeda) against non-Islamic governments across the Muslim world. In 1996, bin Laden issued a ***fatwa,*** demanding that the U.S. military leave Saudi Arabia, particularly because those troops were stationed near the Muslim holy cities Mecca and Medina. In 1998, bin Laden extended the fatwa to overall objections against the U.S. military and citizens because of their foreign policy supporting Israel. But Al-Qaeda and the many other active Islamic militant organizations across Asia, southern Europe, the Middle East and North Africa also attracted members and financial supporters who were not expressly political. They were conservative Muslims who opposed what they saw as an immoral lifestyle confronting them as globalization spread the images and consumer goods of the West around the world.

fatwa
Islamic religious ruling, issued by a recognized religious authority in Islam

Read the Document Osama bin Laden, *World Islamic Front Statement* on mysearchlab.com

Bin Laden's words and Al-Qaeda's evolution have been directly linked to terrorist attacks against the United States and its allies. Although an unknown number of attacks have been prevented, there has been a notable upturn in terrorist activity since the end of the Cold War. Most of the attacks have been bombs (many of them suicide bombs) targeted at Jewish synagogues, U.S. consulates and hotels frequented by Americans in the Middle East, Indonesia and North Africa, which have killed and injured dozens of people. Several attacks, however, have occurred on U.S. or European soil and have targeted hundreds or thousands of civilians.

Watch the Video Lecture *President George W. Bush's Early Response to 9/11* on mysearchlab.com

In February 1993, a van exploded in the parking garage under New York's World Trade Center. In August 1998, bombs destroyed the U.S. embassies in Nairobi, Kenya, Egypt and Dar es Salaam, Tanzania. The United States responded to these attacks with cruise missiles fired by the U.S. navy against suspected Al-Qaeda training and weapons facilities in Afghanistan and Sudan. In October 2000, the *USS Cole* was bombed in port in Yemen. The escalation of violation reached a peak on September 11, 2001, when Al-Qaeda operatives hijacked four U.S. commercial airliners and coordinated attacks on both New York City and Washington, D.C. Two of the planes flew into the twin towers of the World Trade Center, causing their collapse, and a third plane flew into the Pentagon. The fourth plane, which crashed in a field in Pennsylvania, was believed to be on its way to Washington, D.C., as well.

This is not... just America's fight. And what is at stake is not just America's freedom. This is the world's fight. This is civilization's fight. This is the fight of all who believe in progress and pluralism, tolerance and freedom. We ask every nation to join us. We will ask, and we will need, the help of police forces, intelligence services, and banking systems around the world...Nations from Latin America, to Asia, to Africa, to Europe, to the Islamic world.

—George W. Bush's speech to joint session of Congress, September 20, 2001

The attack on New York in September 2001 demonstrated that the militant Islamic movement was gaining strength in terms of membership and the capability to reach around the world to do harm. The worldwide response was immediate. With the full support of the UN Security Council and NATO, U.S. President George W. Bush declared war against terrorist organizations and the governments that protect them, starting in Afghanistan:

> *...the United States of America makes the following demands on the Taliban: Deliver to United States authorities all the leaders of Al-Qaeda who hide in your land...Close immediately and permanently every terrorist training camp in Afghanistan, and hand over every terrorist, and every person in their support structure, to appropriate authorities...These demands are not open to negotiation or discussion. The Taliban must act, and act immediately. They will hand over the terrorists, or they will share in their fate.* (speech to joint session of Congress September 20, 2001)

The Taliban demanded evidence that bin Laden was behind the September 11 attacks and offered to extradite him to a neutral nation if it could be proven that he was involved. The United States rejected these offers as attempts at negotiation, and the UN Security Council issued a resolution requiring the Taliban to turn over bin Laden and close all terrorist training camps. On October 7, 2001, U.S. and British forces launched a bombing campaign targeting the Taliban and Al-Qaeda camps. The military invasion, called Operation Enduring Freedom, succeeded in removing the Taliban from power, but Osama bin Laden was not located. Although a democratic government was installed with U.S. support in January 2002, Taliban and Al-Qaeda supporters remained active in Afghanistan as an insurgency movement fighting against the government and the U.S. military that supported it.

MAKE THE CONNECTION

Why frame it as a worldwide war against freedom?

Read the Document *George W. Bush, 2001: (a) from Address to the Nation, September 11; (b) from Address to the Nation, November 8; (c) from Address to the United Nations, November 10* on mysearchlab.com

In his State of Union address in January 2002, Bush broadened the scope of his "War on Terror" to include "the terrorists and regimes who seek chemical, biological or nuclear weapons...States like these [North Korea, Iran and Iraq], and their terrorist allies, constitute an axis of evil, arming to threaten the peace of the world."

To fight this broad "War on Terror," the Bush administration adopted preemption as its foreign-policy doctrine. The premise was that, if you waited for a country or terrorist organization to attack the United States, particularly one with WMDs, it would be too late to launch a defense. Therefore, any offensive action taken against a country or group with WMDs was actually a defensive action, hence a preemptive attack rather than a preventive attack (which is illegal under international law). The first use of this preemptive strategy was against Iraq to overthrow Saddam Hussein in spring 2003.

In the first several months after the invasion and occupation of Afghanistan, the United States enjoyed the full support of the international community, its allies in the West, governments in the Middle East and Asia that were also threatened by Islamic extremist movements, and its partners on the UN Security Council. In September 2002, Bush and British Prime Minister Tony Blair presented evidence to the UN Security Council that Iraq had developed WMDs and was planning to use them against the West or allies in the Middle East (Israel). Iraq responded by presenting evidence that it had disposed of any WMDs it used to have and said it would allow UN weapons inspectors in on a limited basis. In March 2003, the United States and Britain rejected Iraq's evidence and requested authorization to use military force to disarm Iraq; but France, Russia, Germany and the Arab members of the Security Council refused. On March 19, 2003, the United States invaded Iraq with limited military support from Great Britain, Australia and Poland. Just a few weeks later, Baghdad fell, and Bush declared a victory in Operation Iraqi Freedom on May 1.

Baghdad, Iraq; April 9, 2003. U.S. Marines tie a chain around the neck of a statue of Saddam Hussein as they prepare to tear it down from its pedestal in Baghdad's Firdos Square.

During the summer of 2003, as the United States struggled to defeat the remnants of Hussein's military, capture the fallen leader and establish a provisional government in Iraq, the evidence that the United States and Britain had presented to justify the invasion was increasingly called into question. In 2005, as the U.S. occupation of Iraq continued, the CIA issued a report acknowledging that no WMDs had been found in Iraq, quickly diminishing international and domestic support for the war as well as tolerance for the U.S. policy of unilateral preemptive action in general. As time went on, many Iraqi citizens stopped supporting the U.S. occupation, despite the fact that they had been released from a brutal dictatorship. Instead, the Iraqi people and Muslims in surrounding nations viewed the U.S. occupation as an oppressive attempt to force Western values in the region.

In the eyes of Islamic extremists, the United States and its allies must be punished for their ongoing support of Israel and the military enforcement of Western democracy. In March 2004, ten bombs exploded on four trains during the morning rush hour in Madrid, Spain; and the following summer, bombs exploded on three trains and a bus in London, England. In June 2007, two car bombs in London failed to detonate, but a sport utility vehicle carrying bombs exploded the next day when it crashed into an entrance to the Glasgow Airport in Scotland. A similar car bomb failed to detonate in New York's Times Square in May 2010. All of these attacks were carried out by nongovernmental entities rather than nation-states, making retaliation incredibly difficult under existing international law. Terrorism challenges traditional Western conceptions of military conflict, demanding new approaches to war and peace in the twenty-first century.

Conclusions

In the wake of the Cold War, the international arena changed dramatically. The end of the bipolar power structure opened the door for international institutions to play a greater role in world affairs. Dominated by the wealthy Western countries, the United Nations, NATO, the EU, the IMF, the WTO and a handful of regional trade regimes integrated the activities of sovereign nation-states in unprecedented ways. But the recession of Soviet military and financial power in the 1990s also led to the violent disintegration of countries along nationalist, religious and tribal differences.

There may have been a brief period of unipolarity with the United States as the hegemonic power (certainly if you measure by twentieth-century standards), but the international arena at the beginning of the twenty-first century was once again multipolar. Europe consolidated its power through the EU, the United States maintained its military presence across the globe, and Russia regained its footing in central Asia by defining democracy "Russian style." China possessed the world's largest standing military, nuclear weapons, a permanent seat on the UN Security Council, and the world's fastest growing economy. Former underdeveloped countries such as Mexico and India began capitalizing on their human resources to become rising power players. As long as intergovernmental organizations, nongovernmental organizations, NGOs and sovereign nation-states remain the key players in the international arena, the debate about the distribution of power in the system will continue in the twenty-first century. The question is: Has humanity learned anything from the twentieth century that can help prevent violent conflict in the twenty-first century?

WORKING WITH THE THEMES

THE EFFECTS OF TECHNOLOGY What does the designation of intellectual property as a tradable good tell you about the international economy at the end of the twentieth century? Given the trend toward nuclear proliferation, do you think it is possible to prevent nuclear war?

CHANGING IDENTITIES What does the outbreak of genocide, ethnic cleansing, and terrorist bombings in the 1990s tell you about the nature of the post-Cold War world? Do you think the rise in nationalist violence and the growing number of regional and international organizations signals the end of the nation-state as the most important actor in the international arena?

SHIFTING BORDERS Why was Czechoslovakia able to handle its dissolution peacefully while Yugoslavia descended into a decade of violence? Do you think it is possible to redraw the map of Africa in a way that reduces violence and provides political, social, economic, and ethnic stability?

GLOBALIZATION Was the world at the end of the twentieth century unipolar, bipolar, or multipolar? Did the international economy take precedence over military might as a measure of power in the post-Cold War world? What does NATO expansion tell you about the goals of the West at the outset of the twenty-first century? Does the creation of the WTO and the increase in UN military activity in the 1990s signify a shift toward global governance?

Further Reading

TO FIND OUT MORE

PBS: The Impeachment Trial. Available online at http://www.pbs.org/newshour/impeachment/index.html

PBS: The Gulf War. Available online at http://www.pbs.org/wgbh/pages/frontline/gulf/

Mark Bowden: Black Hawk Down (1997). Available online at http://inquirer.philly.com/packages/somalia

PBS: Ghosts of Rwanda. Available online at http://www.pbs.org/wgbh/pages/frontline/shows/ghosts

PBS: The Gate of Heavenly Peace. Available online at http://tsquare.tv/

GO TO THE SOURCE

Roy Rosenzwieg Center for History and New Media: The September 11 Digital Archive. Available online at http://911digitalarchive.org

National Security Archive/Jeffrey Richelson (ed.): Iraq and Weapons of Mass Destruction (updated 2004). Available online at http://www.gwu.edu/~nsarchiv/NSAEBB/NSAEBB80/

The Rwanda Documents Project. Available online at http://www.rwandadocumentsproject.net/gsdl/cgi-bin/library

U.S. Department of Justice: The USA PATRIOT Act: Preserving Life and Liberty. Available online at http://www.justice.gov/archive/ll/highlights.htm

National Security Archive Documents: The Osama Bin Laden File. Available online at http://www.gwu.edu/~nsarchiv/NSAEBB/NSAEBB343/index.htm

The William J. Clinton Presidential Library. Available online at http://www.clintonlibrary.gov/digital-library.html

George W. Bush Presidential Library. Available online at http://www.georgewbushlibrary.gov/

MySearchLab Connections

Read the **Document** on **mysearchlab.com**

13.1 The United Nations, *Universal Declaration of Human Rights, 1948.* This document was one of the first acts of the newly-created United Nations. A compilation of political, social, and cultural ideals, its stated purpose was to act as a moral force that can lead the nations of the world away from oppression and toward more humane and liberal forms of society.

13.2 Deng Xiaoping, *On Introducing Capitalist Principles to China.* After the death of Mao Tse-tung in 1976, his successor, Deng Xiaoping, steered the country sharply away from the Maoist road to communism. Boldly dismantling Mao's institutions, Deng forcefully put forth his vision for China: a socialist nation that would be modern, industrial, and prosperous.

13.3 Osama bin Laden, *World Islamic Front Statement.* Before the September 11, 2001 attacks on the United States, and a series of 1998 attacks on U.S. embassies in Africa and the Near East, al Qaeda leader Osama bin Laden issued this global call to violence against Americans and their allies.

13.4 *George W. Bush, 2001: (a) from Address to the Nation, September 11; (b) from Address to the Nation, November 8; (c) from Address to the United Nations, November 10.* Following the attacks of September 11, 2001, the war against terrorism provided the U.S. with a renewed purpose and direction to its foreign affairs, as these excerpts from President Bush's speeches indicate.

Watch the **Video** on **mysearchlab.com**

13.1 *President George W. Bush's Early Response to 9/11*

14 The Legacy of the Twentieth Century

CHAPTER OUTLINE

- The Forces of Integration
- The Forces of Disintegration
- Competing Perspectives on the Twenty-First Century

The twentieth century was marked by both continuous attempts at international cooperation to prevent warfare and an escalation in the frequency of wars that fractured states and nations along religious and ethnic lines. There was an unprecedented integration of economies, cultures and political institutions in the 1900s, in large part due to advances in technology. By the end of the century, however, a strong and violent backlash to the forces of globalization had arisen. At the outset of the twenty-first century, it was not clear which force would be stronger—integration or disintegration.

Photos from left to right: EU flags; International finance; Global computer network; Jihad.

The Forces of Integration

The Evidence

Over the course of the twentieth century, the people of the world became increasingly interconnected politically, economically and culturally. This integration happened gradually and in stages, each new step built on successes and failures from previous efforts. Increasingly, nation-states chose to voluntarily align political, economic and/or social processes with others (as opposed to colonization in the sixteenth through the nineteenth centuries). Shortly after the second world war ended, philosopher Marshall McLuhan declared that the world was shrinking into a "global village," where everyone would be connected by a global communications network that functions much like a central nervous system.

In politics, the first effort at an international governmental organization was made just after World War I with the creation of the very limited League of Nations. It failed to prevent World War II, so a new and improved United Nations was formed with almost universal membership and a network of agencies to reach around the globe to promote peace and well-being. Although the United Nations to date has succeeded in preventing World War III, it has not guaranteed peace, and some argue that it should be strengthened into some version of a global government. Giving up sovereignty would have been unthinkable in the early twentieth century, but the gradual growth of the European Union (EU) provides evidence that nation-states may be willing to sacrifice a degree of sovereignty in exchange for nonviolence and economic health.

This desire for economic security has driven perhaps the most dramatic trend toward integration. The tariff wars and global economic depression of the 1920s and 1930s led to layers of multilateral trade negotiations and the creation of the World Bank, the International Monetary Fund (IMF) and the General Agreement on Tariffs and Trade. As these international governmental organizations (IGOs) ushered the world toward free trade, consumer goods moved rapidly from village to city around the world. Smaller regional trade associations appeared in almost every corner of the globe. By the end of the twentieth century, trade and finance had become globally interconnected, for good and for bad, and a World Trade Organization was created to regulate economic relationships between its members.

In military affairs, nation-states increasingly came to rely on UN peacekeeping forces and regional security regimes such as North Atlantic Treaty Organization (NATO), the Organization of African Unity and the Association of Southeast Asian Nations Regional Forum to protect and restore the peace in local conflicts. What happens within a nation-state is no longer a private affair, particularly when egregious human rights violations occur. In the latter half of the twentieth century, war crimes tribunals were held in Germany, Japan, the Balkans, and Rwanda. The success of these regional efforts led to the creation of a standing **International Criminal Court** (ICC) in 2002.

International Criminal Court an independent, permanent court that tries government and military officials accused of genocide, crimes against humanity, and war crimes

The most dramatic example of global integration has been in communications, lending credibility to McLuhan's premise of a "global village." From the first transcontinental telephone call in 1915, people across the globe began to grow closer to one another. Advancements in global communications technology progressed throughout the century, and today there is nothing that you cannot read, see, hear, play or buy on the Internet, assuming, of course, you have the political freedom and economic means to gain access to the technology. We are connected by satellite images, mobile phones, social networks, and the written word (albeit in a much more succinct format). And each time we share our experiences, ideas, values, and belief systems, we are helping others to understand the world from our perspective.

The European Union

The clearest evidence that the process of integration will continue in the twenty-first century is the expansion of the European Union. When the Iron Curtain unraveled, it opened the possibility of a unified Europe. The European Economic Community (EEC) was formed in 1967 through the merger of various economic, trade and defense treaties. The EEC was originally comprised of Belgium, Germany, France, Italy, Luxembourg and the Netherlands and doubled in size during the Cold War: Denmark, Ireland and the United Kingdom joined in 1973; Greece joined in 1981; and Spain and Portugal joined in 1986.

The 1986 Single European Act revised the existing structure and functions of the EEC institutions to allow for deeper economic integration, paving the way for the creation of a single internal market. It also expanded their powers to coordinate activities between the member states, particularly with regard to research and development, the environment and foreign policy.

The EEC created a flag and anthem, signaling a unified Europe. In early 1989, the EEC announced plans to create a European Monetary Union, with a single currency for all members.

The collapse of the USSR and the discussion surrounding the reunification of Germany had a dramatic impact on the EEC. It sparked a lot of debate about the definition of the term "European." Is it a geographic, ethnic or political identity? Should every country that wants to join the EEC be permitted to do so to encourage democracy, even if their struggling post-communist economies are a huge economic drain on the organization? A special European Council meeting in spring 1990 focused on the parameters of German reunification and established the European Bank for Reconstruction and Development to provide financial support to all Central and Eastern European countries making the transition from communism to capitalism. The EEC launched two separate conferences to investigate potential futures for Europe, one on economic and monetary union and another on political union.

Read the Document *The European Community, Treaty on European Union* on mysearchlab.com

The outcome of these two conferences was the Treaty on European Union signed in Maastricht, the Netherlands, in February 1992. The Maastricht Treaty moved European integration beyond the economic realm and toward political integration. It established a European Union built on three pillars: (1) the European Community, which replaced the EEC, expanded the power of the European Parliament and increased the number of **supranational** institutions; (2) Common Foreign and Security Policy to develop joint action in foreign policy making through the Western European Union defense alliance; and (3) Justice and Home Affairs, which provided for cooperation in law enforcement, criminal justice, asylum, immigration and judicial matters. The Maastricht Treaty included the specific rights and responsibilities of the newly conceived European citizenship (over national citizenship) and a Social Charter that addressed employment, working conditions and quality-of-life issues. It also required the coordination of member states' economic policies and the establishment of a single currency for the EU. The Maastricht Treaty required unanimous approval by its member states for ratification.

supranational having authority beyond the national borders

But not all Europeans were ready for such a dramatic change, particularly amidst the financial recession of the early 1990s. The people of Denmark rejected the Maastricht Treaty in a national referendum in June 1992, and the people of France only narrowly approved it (by 51 percent). The British Parliament was deeply divided across and within political party lines regarding the Social Charter, the single currency and, ultimately, the entire treaty itself. And in Germany, despite the support of the chancellor and parliament, the treaty faced a legal battle, with critics arguing that membership in the EU would violate Germany's constitutional requirement that "all state authority emanates from the people." The treaty was eventually ratified in 1993. Four exceptions were added that allowed Denmark to opt out of particular areas, leading to a 57 percent approval in the next referendum. In the British Parliament, the Liberal Democrats struck a deal with the Conservatives to ratify the treaty, and the constitutional court of Germany ruled that the parliament had the constitutional authority to determine EU membership.

With the ratification of the Maastricht Treaty, the fifteen member states of the newly created European Union began making progress toward their goals. The Schengen Agreement of March 1995 removed border controls between Belgium, France, Germany, Luxembourg, the Netherlands, Portugal and Spain, allowing the free movement of EU citizens. In 1997, the Treaty of Amsterdam established the European Central Bank, which assumed control over eleven of the EU members on January 1, 1999. The euro was phased in and fully replaced their currencies in 2002.

Despite the EU's success in meeting many of the goals of the Maastricht Treaty, the controversial question of EU membership remained. Austria, Finland and Sweden had joined in 1995, and accession negotiations had opened with many former Soviet satellite states and republics that were anxious to achieve the economic strength that came with EU membership. This raised concerns about the ability of the structure of the EU to handle enlargement, so the 2001 Treaty of Nice made adjustments to the core EU institutions and decision-making processes, as well as formalized the rigorous accession requirements for membership. Those adjustments opened the door for EU enlargement in 2004, as ten countries, many of them formerly communist, became member states: Cyprus, the Czech Republic, Estonia, Hungary, Latvia, Lithuania, Malta, Poland, the Slovak Republic and Slovenia.

In 2002, the Convention on the Future of Europe began preparing a draft of a Constitutional Treaty that would replace the Maastricht Treaty. The constitution extended the power of the EU institutions over national governments and merged the EEC and EU in a full political and economic union. Unification is very different than integration, however, and the proposed constitution was ratified by only eighteen members, soundly rejected by France and the Netherlands, and put on hold by the remaining members. When it became evident that it would not be ratified, the constitution was withdrawn and replaced by the Lisbon Treaty, which further amended the Maastricht, Amsterdam and Nice treaties by creating a legal framework for responding to citizens' demands. The Lisbon Treaty was ratified in 2007 and went into effect in 2009.

EU BASIC FACTS

Population: 495 million (7 percent of the world total)

Languages: 23 official

Territory: 4 million km^2

GDP: €11,785,474.9 (2009)

Motto: "United in Diversity"

Flag: twelve stars in a circle symbolize the ideals of unity, solidarity and harmony among the peoples of Europe

Trade: represents roughly 20 percent of total world trade (world's biggest exporter; world's second biggest importer)

The unification question did not stop EU progress, however. In 2007, Bulgaria and Romania joined the EU, and several other countries were in various stages of the accession process. More EU countries are adopting the euro, and the Schengen agreement has extended into Eastern Europe, promoting the movement of labor across the continent.

The EU started out in the mid-twentieth century focusing on trade issues but over the years expanded to deal with human rights, security and justice, job creation, regional development, environmental protection, and questions of identity and citizenship in Europe. It has raised living standards for Europeans, built a single, coordinated European-wide market (no tariffs or trade barriers between member countries), created a new currency, and has certainly become a power

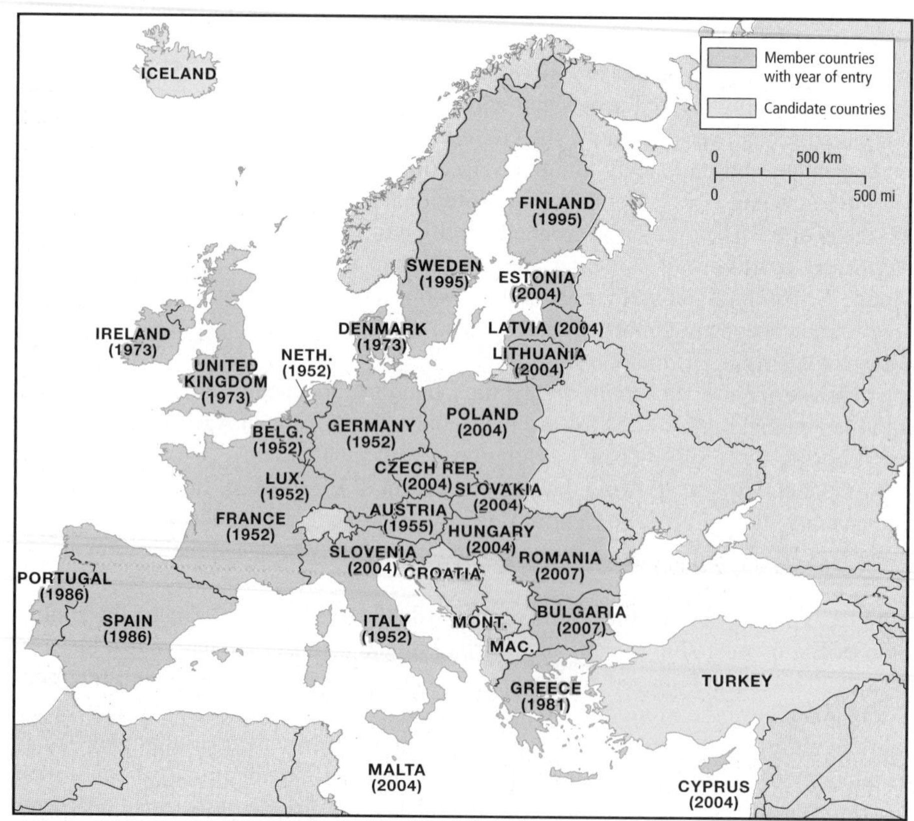

MAP 14.1 The European Union

player in world affairs because it represents so many of the world's developed, democratic countries. None of this has happened by accident; rather, it has been an often tedious and carefully worded project of compromise between diverse cultures and historically warring nations. But given the tumultuous changes European nations experienced in the twentieth century, they were anxious to redefine themselves for the twenty-first century. As the European Convention explained in its justification for a constitution:

> *In a globalised, yet also highly fragmented world, Europe must shoulder its responsibilities in the governance of globalisation, i.e. in its organisation and operation. The role it has to play is that of a power opposed to violence, terror and fanaticism, sensitive to the injustices of the world and ever ready to act. In promoting international cooperation, the European Union's aim is to change the course of world affairs in a way which is to the benefit of all. Europe seeks to set globalisation within a moral framework anchored in solidarity and sustainable development.*

By 2010, the EU was the largest economy in the world, but it took decades of ongoing negotiations to get there. To rival that growing power, the United States and its partners in the western hemisphere began drafting a plan to unite their separate regional trade agreements into a single Free Trade Area of the Americas (FTAA). The FTAA has been stalled, however, by strong protest movements throughout South America in a clear backlash against globalization. So, is the EU an anomaly, or will the forces of integration continue to work toward the "global village" in the twenty-first century?

The Forces of Disintegration

The Evidence

More humans died from violent conflict in the twentieth century than in any other century in history. In part, this is because the world population was larger, but it also most certainly was a direct effect of technology (more efficient weapons) and globalization (wars that spread across the globe). Not all of that conflict was state against state; much of it was civil war or internal violence.

Empires and colonization created artificial boundaries that did not coincide with the natural divisions between the human populations living within them. This led to two related types of warfare: the two massive global wars between imperial powers in the first half of the twentieth century and the civil wars that occurred as nationalist movements forged new nation-states out of their remains. The empires of the early twentieth century (Russia, the Ottoman Empire, the British Empire, the German Empire and the Austro-Hungarian Empire) destroyed one another in the first world war, most of them losing territory and population in the resulting Treaty of Versailles. As imperial powers gave way to democratic and authoritarian political regimes preceding and following the second world war, those ethnic and cultural differences surfaced, and nation-states were divided internally by the differences. The Balkan Wars of 1912 and 1913, Ottoman treatment of Armenians in 1915 and 1916, the Holocaust, Stalin's Great Purge, Mao's Cultural Revolution, and the Khmer Rouge in Cambodia are examples of state-sponsored violence undertaken in a misguided attempt to create unified nation-states.

Many nation-states were unable to overcome ethnic and nationalist divisions and prevent civil war. India/Pakistan violently split apart in 1947; Israel and the Palestinians have been fighting over a strip of territory since 1948; Yugoslavia ceased to exist over the course of a violent decade in the 1990s; and brutal civil wars waged across Latin America throughout the 1950s and 1960s. The decolonization process of the mid-century created instability that further divided nation-states as ethnic groups vied for control and power, particularly across Africa.

Warfare between Christians, Jews and Muslims goes back much further than the twentieth century, but an increase in Islamic fundamentalism toward the end of the twentieth century led to an increase in global terrorism. Though certainly rooted in religious values, this new brand of terrorism was part of a larger backlash against globalization. Anti-Western sentiment strengthened across many communities in the Middle East and Latin America, where trade liberalization and communications were seen as just another method of imperialism. Ecoterrorism appeared at the end of the twentieth century, arguing that capitalism, industrialization and globalization were destroying the planet. Environmental and labor-rights advocates protested against international organizations, and piracy reappeared on the high seas off the coast of Somalia.

The Polarizing Effects of Globalization

To a great extent, the Cold War hampered the ability of international organizations to maintain peace and left control of the international arena in the hands of the superpowers pursuing their own national interests. As we have seen, the end of the Cold War allowed international organizations, particularly the United Nations, to become more active in world affairs. The United Nations eagerly took on the responsibility for global security as its charter requires, providing humanitarian relief efforts in impoverished countries. But its record was mixed—success in El Salvador and Cambodia was offset by failure in Somalia and Rwanda. And where world power interests were in conflict, such as Eastern Europe and the Middle East, UN action was once again handcuffed by the veto power of the permanent members on the Security Council.

The backlash to globalization that began to appear as the Cold War wound down in the late 1980s was based on three primary arguments: (1) international organizations will take over the world and make the sovereign nation-state obsolete; (2) when we liberalize trade and ban **protectionism, transnational corporations** become wealthy and the poorest countries become poorer; and (3) the spread of Western consumer goods around the world will lead to a watering down of cultural differences. Protests against the United Nations, the World Trade Organization (WTO) and transnational corporations grew in the 1990s and early twenty-first century, picking up supporters from around the globe because of technological advancements in communications such as satellites, Internet service, digital imagery and social media.

protectionism policy of protecting domestic industries against foreign competition by means of tariffs, subsidies, import quotas, or other restrictions placed on the imports of foreign competitors

transnational corporations corporations that operate in more than one country or nation at a time; can exert significant influence over the domestic and foreign policies of the governments that host them

Critics of the United Nations argue that reform is absolutely necessary if the organization is to remain a relevant institution in the twenty-first century. It was created in the aftermath of two devastating world wars and was structured to maintain a balance of power in the latter half of the twentieth century. But the international arena has changed significantly since then, critics charge, and the United Nations must change with it. Institutional power must be restructured, financial issues must be readdressed, coordination between agencies must be improved and adherence to UN expectations must be upheld. Some critics demand the legal position of the United Nations over its member states be strengthened, while others fear it already has too much power. And because national power is at stake, there is a great deal of disagreement over how to accomplish this reform. The countries that hold power in the Security Council certainly do not want to give it up, but neither do they want to carry the financial and military responsibility of upholding the UN Charter on their own.

The sharpest criticisms of globalization are aimed at the institutions that manage international economics and trade. Critics of the WTO, primarily from the lesser-developed world and international human rights groups, argue that power politics controls the WTO far more than its guiding principles. There is too much participation from transnational corporations that have their own profit interests at heart. Because of the nondiscrimination restrictions, countries are often required to import products that they deem unsafe to people or the environment—for example, genetically engineered food, products containing lead or asbestos, and products made by environmentally unsound practices. When international trade rules undermine local laws, such as labor laws and environmental regulations, the WTO always decides in favor of upholding the trade rules (a clear violation of sovereignty). Because WTO rules protect intellectual and property rights, they often discourage innovation and increase the technological divide between the rich and poor countries of the world. The WTO argues that these criticisms stem from a fundamental misunderstanding about how it operates. A state agrees to accept these conditions when it becomes a member, and the long-term benefits of membership far outweigh the short-term costs associated with trade liberalization. Similarly, the IMF and World Bank have been criticized for imposing conditionality on countries that accept their loans, which often leads to short-term economic problems and a substantial drop in living standards for the citizens. While these institutions agree that some reform of the international financial architecture is necessary to prevent global crises, they contend that the globalization of finance works to the clear benefit of the world's smaller economies by improving the flow of capital and technology around the system. They cannot be violating sovereignty, they argue, if the country requests the financial assistance.

Supporters of globalization argue that national governments are and will always be the most important players in the international arena because an IGO is nothing more than a collection of representatives from national governments who coordinate their interests in rule making. The national government that chooses not to participate is the one that risks being hurt politically, economically and culturally. And because democracy is the underlying political principle of these institutions, free speech has ensured that they are monitored—the number of nongovernmental organizations rose from 6,000 in 1990 to 26,000 by the end of the century.

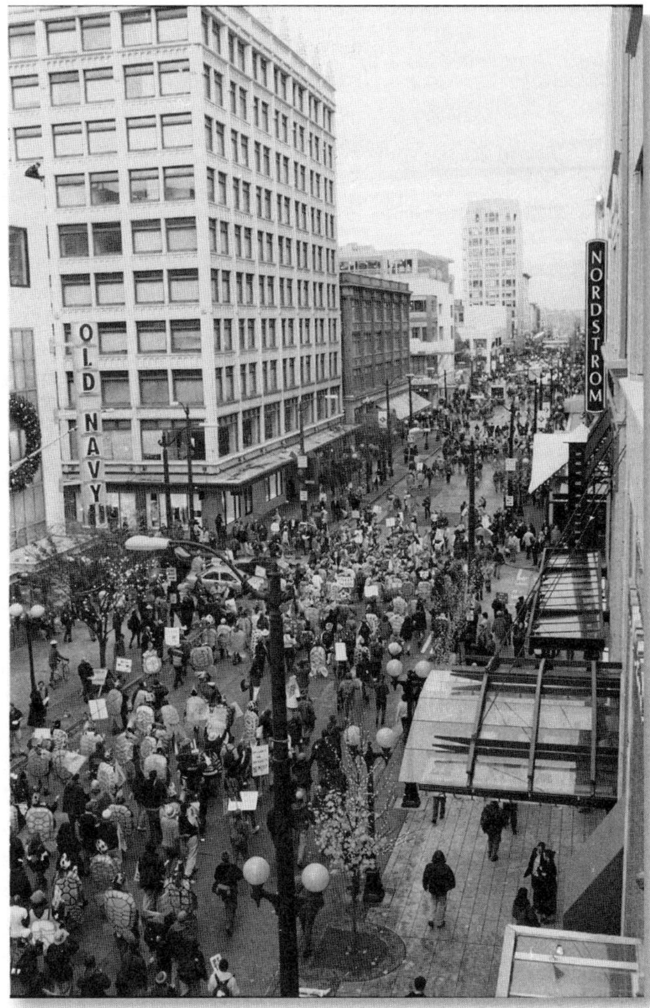

Protest march against the WTO on Pine Street, Seattle, Washington; November 29, 1999.

Competing Perspectives on the Twenty-First Century

As the twentieth century came to a close, historians, political scientists, economists, sociologists and philosophers began trying to draw connections between the diverse experiences and lessons of the twentieth century that would illuminate the path into the twenty-first century. As they sifted through the evidence of integration and disintegration to identify the overall legacy of the twentieth century, they came to different conclusions about what lay ahead for the world. What is fascinating is that they started with the same data set, but they came up with very different pictures of what the world in the twenty-first century might look like. They interpreted the events for themselves, just as you have done throughout this book, igniting debates over what might prove to be the enduring legacy of the twentieth century. The following four authors represent the prominent predictions from the Western perspective.

MAKE THE CONNECTION

What do you think is the stronger force—integration or disintegration? Why?

Francis Fukuyama: "The End of History?"

Amid the tumultuous changes of 1989, philosopher Francis Fukuyama wrote a brief essay in which he declared that that the dissolution of the USSR demonstrated the ultimate failure of communism (politically and economically). History had ended, he argued, because liberal democracy and capitalism had proven to be the superior form of governance and economics. This very controversial thesis was attacked on all sides, and Fukuyama responded in 1992 with *The End of History and the Last Man*.

Fukuyama used the phrase "the end of history" in the philosophical sense rather than as a chronological series of events, which will most certainly continue as long as humanity exists. He based his work largely on the German philosopher G. W. F. Hegel, who proposed that history is an evolutionary process of humans seeking to create the ideal sociocultural conditions that allowed them to thrive. With the triumph of liberal democratic regimes and capitalist economies at the end of the Cold War, those conditions were met; thus, the evolutionary struggle (history) has ended:

> *What we may be witnessing is not just the end of the Cold War, or the passing of a particular period of post-war history, but the end of history as such: that is, the end point of mankind's ideological evolution and the universalization of Western liberal democracy as the final form of human government.*

Fukuyama offered the events of the late nineteenth and twentieth centuries as empirical evidence—the struggle for democracy took the form of revolutions that overcame imperialism/colonialism, monarchy, fascism and finally communism. In 1900, there was not a single democratic government with universal suffrage; by the end of the twentieth century, there were roughly 120 (representing 62 percent of the world). Humans are clearly willing to fight and die for liberal democracy and, according to Fukuyama, they will continue to do so for two reasons: economics and identity.

Fukuyama warns us that we must overcome the temptation to look at the devastating events of the twentieth century and see chaos—a lack of coherence and philosophical intelligence in human beings. The one consistent trend was that violent, repressive and brutal regimes were overturned and, although stable liberal democracy often takes time to achieve, democracy "remains the only coherent political aspiration that spans different regions and cultures around the globe." As democracy has spread, so too has free market economics, leading to "unprecedented levels of material prosperity, both in industrially developed countries and in countries that had been, at the close of World War II, part of the impoverished Third World." Fukuyama argued that "modern natural science" established a "uniform horizon of economic production possibilities." In other words, technology and the free market have made it possible for all governments to meet the desires of their populations and to do so in an interconnected way, creating a "universal consumer culture."

But, as Fukuyama pointed out, man cannot be satisfied by economics alone. Unlike animals, humans need more than simply their basic survival needs met—humans are engaged in a "struggle for recognition." Self-esteem, worth and dignity, linked with anger, shame and pride, are, according to Hegel, the driving force behind humanity's historical evolution. And this is why humans universally strive for democracy—a government that provides the recognition of each citizen's dignity by granting rights and responsibilities rather than treating its citizens like subjects or slaves. Of course, it is also what drives war between nation-states (nationalism). Here again, this is where Fukuyama argues that liberal democracies excel over authoritarian regimes—liberal democracies do not engage in imperialism against one another; rather, they tend to create international organizations that extend recognition to all members. Fukuyama was careful to point out that there can certainly be conflict within liberal democracies, which often recognize people based on economic well-being and, therefore, unequally.

Criticisms of *The End of History* are based on its Western, imperialist and seemingly Christian perspective of international affairs. Muslim fundamentalists challenge Fukuyama's entire core premise that all humans share the desire for liberal democratic governance. Others agree, citing the popular power of charismatic leaders such as Hugo Chavez in Venezuela or the growing power of authoritarian capitalist regimes such as China and Russia. Libertarians believe Fukuyama has misidentified the evolution of democracy, which has actually destroyed individual rights in the name of public interest. Environmentalists argue that meeting the needs of all humans, as Fukuyama proposes, will destroy the planet and political ideology will not mean a thing. While Marxists certainly agree with the evolutionary nature of human history, they see the only viable end result as communism. And Samuel Huntington, in his 1993 *Clash of Civilizations*, famously attacked Fukuyama's claim that all people want the same form of government.

Samuel Huntington: "The Clash of Civilizations?"

In an article he wrote in 1993, political scientist Samuel Huntington envisioned a very different kind of twenty-first century world than Fukuyama's, and he expanded upon it in *The Clash of Civilizations and the Remaking of World Order* (1996). Whereas the twentieth century international arena was divided along conflicting ideological lines, Huntington argued that the twenty-first century will be divided by cultural boundaries:

> *Nation states will remain the most powerful actors in world affairs, but the principal conflicts of global politics will occur between nations and groups of different civilizations. The clash of civilizations will dominate global politics. The fault lines between civilizations will be the battle lines of the future.*

Understanding Huntington's definition of **civilization,** which focuses heavily on the concept of identity, is crucial to understanding his thesis. A civilization may involve a lot of people, or a few. It may include several distinct nation-states, or just one. Civilizations are dynamic—dividing, merging and overlapping with one another. The civilizational paradigm that Huntington created divides the world into eight major civilizations: Sinic (China and Southeast Asia), Japanese, Hindu, Islamic, Orthodox (centered in Russia), Western (Europe and North America), Latin America and Africa. These civilizations took shape over centuries of technological improvements, most notably in transportation and weapons. Western cultures excelled in this technology and expanded, dominating much of the globe with Western values and religion. A marked growth in technology and globalization in the twentieth century led to cultural interdependence and a backlash against the idea of a universal Western civilization. As Huntington tells us, "with the end of the Cold War, international politics moves out its Western phase, and its centerpiece becomes the interaction between the West and non-Western civilization and among non-Western civilizations."

civilization
according to Huntington, the highest cultural grouping of people and the broadest level of cultural identity people have; it is defined both by common objective elements (language, history, religion, customs, institutions) and by the subjective self-identification of people

Huntington argued that the West is in decline, although it is a slow process that is largely controlled by the decision makers in Western states. As the Cold War ended, political ideology became less important to people, and religion took its place. To Huntington, the resurgence of Islam "embodies the acceptance of modernity, rejection of Western culture, and the recommitment to Islam as the guide to life in the modern world." There are also examples of non-Western countries that have turned economic strength into cultural dominance (Japan, the Asian Tigers and China). They are notable because they have modernized and developed without adopting Western cultural values.

In the emerging world of ethnic conflict and civilizational clash, Western belief in the universality of Western culture suffers three problems: it is false; it is immoral; and it is dangerous... Imperialism is the necessary logical consequence of universalism.

—The Clash of Civilizations and the Remaking of World Order

The end of the Cold War created an identity crisis for countries that found themselves no longer within a sphere of influence or part of a nonalignment coalition. As the United States asserted its new multilateral approach to dominating the international arena, smaller countries began to draw together, forming regional organizations and restructuring alliances. Where these organizations have dominant cultural leaders, such as France and Germany within the EU, the civilizational connection is strong. Where there is no clear dominant cultural leader, as in the Middle East, the ability of the civilization to exert international power is hindered.

Huntington predicted that war in the twenty-first century would be among civilizations. The first, he said, would be a coalition of the Sinic and Islamic cultures to defeat the West and its cultural, religious and economic hegemony. While he believed that the conflict between the West and Islam would be fairly limited (what he called a "fault line conflict between adjacent states"), he saw the conflict between the United States and China as potentially spreading worldwide (a "global core state conflict"). The only way for the West to survive is to adapt and essentially accept its decline gracefully by acknowledging the power and influence of non-Western civilizations: "The preservation of the United States and the West requires the renewal of Western identity." And if that does not happen, Huntington says, the clash between the West and the Sinic civilizations would be "the greatest threat to world peace, and an international order."

Huntington's thesis sparked critical responses from a wide variety of disciplines. At the most basic level, many critics argue that his civilizational paradigm is too simplistic—its focus on identity overlooks political and economic causes of conflict. Others add that Huntington's conception of a "civilization" as some single, monolithic identity is completely erroneous—there are significant intracivilizational differences and conflicts that will prevent states from working together. Some critics contend that Huntington has propagated a false "us vs. them" conception of the East–West relationship that is too Western focused. They argue that, rather than construct a new perspective of the world, he is merely refitting the Cold War mentality with Islam and China as the new enemies of the United States. Critics have also called the *Clash* thesis into question based on what they see as Huntington's weak methodology and lack of scholarship with regard to Islam, China and Japan and the frequent inconsistencies in applying his own terminology. Several empirical studies indicate that Huntington has placed far too much weight on civilization and identity as causes of warfare. Finally, some critics worry that his thesis could become a "self-fulfilling prophecy" if applied to foreign-policy decision making, seeking conflict where none exists.

Benjamin Barber: *Jihad vs. McWorld*

Whereas Huntington viewed conflict as inevitable because it is rooted in identity, political theorist Benjamin Barber presented a much more peaceful vision of the twenty-first century based on the governance model of the European Union. His original essay appeared in the *Atlantic Monthly* in 1992, but his thesis found full expression in the 1996 book, *Jihad vs. McWorld: How Globalism and Tribalism Are Reshaping the World.* Focusing on political and economic questions as well as cultural ones, Barber recognized two distinct and opposite global trends that challenge democracy: jihad, which he defined as any movement attempting to preserve its own cultural values from Western imposition, and McWorld, the ever-growing, interconnected international economy.

To Barber, McWorld stems from the West (the United States primarily) creating a universal global popular culture in which everyone wears Nike shoes, drinks Coca-Cola, eats at McDonald's, watches Disney movies and listens to Lady Gaga. This is sold, particularly in underdeveloped countries, as progress and modernization because it represents an "ideology of fun." The danger, Barber said, is if the "ideology of fun" supplants political and civic ideology. When citizens become obsessed with consumption, they lose interest in public affairs, making democracy virtually impossible to practice. McWorld might bring the different cultures of the world together, but it will be under corporate leadership that has only one goal—profit.

Jihad, on the other hand, is the backlash to globalization. Barber takes it beyond its Islamic definition and applies it to any group that opposes the kind of modernization McWorld offers. It certainly includes religious extremists, but also tribalists, nationalists and separatists in all parts of the world. Jihad is willing to use violence and hamper civil liberties if it means preventing McWorld from taking over. To Barber, jihadist movements will subvert democracy, fragment the world and keep humanity in constant conflict.

In Barber's thesis, the future looks bleak for democracy, as both McWorld and jihad "make war on the sovereign nation-state and thus undermine the nation-state's democratic institutions." He fears that McWorld could ultimately win the struggle unless citizens defend the democratic nation-state. He proposes a model of global governance similar to the United States under the Articles of Confederation or the European Union under the Maastricht Treaty. The alternative to McWorld and jihad, Barber believes, is community groups of citizens working together to overcome these divergent forces and forge a global democratic civil society.

According to critics, the fundamental flaw of *Jihad vs. McWorld* is the lack of evidence to support the thesis. As one of the top American political theorists on democracy, Barber assumes that democratic government is the ultimate goal, but he never justifies why it is a preferable choice to McWorld or Jihad. Democracy is a means to an end (civil society) but certainly not the only one. Historical evidence shows that tribalism and nationalism, which are populist movements, often lead to democratic institutions. Furthermore, Barber's definition of jihad has been criticized as being prejudicial in its implication that all nationalist or separatist movements are antidemocratic;

and his characterization of McWorld devalues culture to the point of being simply an economic tool. Others find fault with Barber's assumption that human beings are so easily and mindlessly led to "dumbed-down" popular culture that consumerism becomes an overriding ideology. If that is true, they contend, the real danger to democracy is humanity itself.

Paul Kennedy: *Preparing for the Twenty-First Century*

In 1987, British historian Paul Kennedy published a sweeping history of the economic and political interrelationships in the international arena from 1500 to 1980: *The Rise and Fall of the Great Powers*. His 1993 follow-up, *Preparing for the Twenty-First Century*, built on that research to make recommendations for how societies could best prepare themselves for the future. Kennedy focused largely on the impact of technology and globalization on the natural environment, declaring that the single greatest challenge countries face is population growth. How humans deal with technology's impact on nature, Kennedy said, will dictate the shape of the world in the twenty-first century.

To establish a foundation for his prescriptions, Kennedy describes general world trends at the end of the twentieth century in what he sees as the crucial areas: population growth, shifting demographics, communications technology, agricultural technology, changes in industrial production, global warming, and the decline of nation-state with the rise of IGOs, nongovernmental organizations and transnational corporations. The most impactful one, he believes, is population growth because it depletes Earth's natural resources much faster than the planet can regenerate them. Kennedy is optimistic, however, that humans could prevent this from happening. At the dawn of the nineteenth century, Thomas Malthus predicted that the British population would outstrip its natural resources, but human activity in the form of industrialization and migration patterns intervened to "save" Great Britain. The forces of economic globalization can do the same thing in the twenty-first century, says Kennedy, but only if they are applied to all nations equitably. This is where governmental decision making comes in—in the underdeveloped world, where corrupt regimes, religious fundamentalists and transnational corporations make policies that do not spread benefits across the population, economic progress to overcome the negative effects of rampant population growth is impossible.

Kennedy then focuses on how each of these trends, if left unchecked, would impact the countries and regions of the world, specifically Japan, India, China, Russia, the European Community (as it was in 1993) and the United States. Some countries, he concludes, are in a better position to deal with the challenges of the twenty-first century than others:

> *As we move into the next century, the developed economies appear to have all the trump cards in their hands—capital, technology, control of communications, surplus foodstuffs, powerful multinational companies—and, if anything, their advantages are growing because technology is eroding the value of labor and materials, the chief assets of developing countries.*

Kennedy believes that Japan, a handful of East Asian states, and the European Community will do well in the next century, while the United States will decline because of domestic social and economic issues. All of these trends can be controlled, of course, if governments are willing to use "the power of technology" in the name of human dignity instead of profit. The countries with the greatest problems do not have the technology to overcome them, and simply applying existing technology in those places often does more harm than good. But why should wealthy countries spend their resources to create unique solutions for the underdeveloped world that cannot afford to pay? In today's globalized world, Kennedy argues, the devastating effects of resource depletion in the areas where billions of people suffer will most certainly have an impact on the rich and powerful countries as well. It will be necessary to redefine current concepts of national security if we are to have truly international security.

Criticisms of Kennedy's work focus on his application of historical events to predict what the future may look like. While his basic premise was sound—Great Powers continue to rise until they are overextended, destroying the economy and leading to an inevitable decline—critics argue that he completely misdiagnosed the United States. Kennedy treats the United States at the end of the Cold War as a traditional imperialist power that maintains and utilizes a large standing military force to expand its borders, when in fact the U.S. military in times of peace has been cut back dramatically in both size and funding. Similarly, Kennedy does not seem to understand the mercenary nature of U.S. alliances and foreign commitments. Unlike the empires of the nineteenth century, the United States would never overextend itself into decline—it would simply drop "unnecessary" relationships to protect its own interests. Others say that Kennedy focuses too much on the "big picture" in his projections for the twenty-first century and does not provide practical information for governments other than "rethink, retrain and retool." Ultimately, critics charge, Kennedy is merely a prophet of the apocalypse, predicting the end of all humanity unless governments and corporations make radical changes in their decision making.

What Do You See?

We have used the themes to trace the major events in the twentieth century with an eye on the "big picture." Hopefully, you have come to understand that history is not a series of events but rather an evolution. Peoples' ideas turn into actions and policy choices, which then shape the world we live in, affecting our ideas. History is an ongoing evolutionary process, but it is certainly not a straightforward path. History is a process driven by choices that people make about the world they live in and the world they hope to create for future generations.

Using these themes, what have you learned about the twentieth century? Certainly that the events of the century are interconnected—these themes are not discrete categories but usually intersect and interact with one another. Most of the events of the twentieth century had ramifications for multiple themes.

For example, one of most obvious developments impacting the twentieth century was technological change. Technology often seemed the impetus that pushed the world to a different level (generally in warfare). Technology created for the battlefield was turned into consumer products that sped up the processes of globalization (radios, airplanes, computers and satellite communications). Technology links us together so that we can now access news from just about every part of the world, as well as bank accounts, cultural experiences, sports and interpersonal communication. And corporations immediately put that technology to use to make money, so the exchange of information, currency, and goods happens faster than ever before, which has a dramatic effect on how business and investments take place. That, in turn, affects where things are produced and where people want to live, leading to migration. As people travel around the globe, they take their religion, music, art, literature, fashion and food preferences with them, impacting the culture of the societies they move to. This process of globalization, driven by the effects of technology, has caused a shift in borders because of migration and changing identities as different cultures come into contact with one another.

And this is where interpretation comes in. Does this process lead to a "watering down" of cultures and identities as sharing turns into adapting? Do the wealthy countries and corporations control this flow of "sharing" to their advantage? Does that lead to peace because the world is interconnected and we all prosper or die together, or does it lead to violent resistance to being dominated by others? Although the twentieth century has ended, the processes that you have been tracing through these themes certainly have not.

Conclusions

As the philosopher George Santayana famously said, "those who do not remember the past are condemned to repeat it." Have we learned from the mistakes of the twentieth century, and are we building on the progress that was made? The primary conflicts of the twentieth century were based on the need to establish superiority, whether that was nationalist superiority (Wilhelm II and Hitler), ideological/political superiority (the Cold War), religious superiority (the Arab–Israeli conflict and Islamic fundamentalism), military superiority (the arms race and nuclear proliferation) or economic superiority (colonization and trade liberalization). And if the need to establish superiority is a basic human instinct, is conflict inevitable, or is humanity capable of evolving out of it as progressive humanists suggest?

As you grapple with the events of the twentieth century and try to make sense of them, remember that you are making the choices today that will help shape the world of the twenty-first century.

Further Reading

TO FIND OUT MORE

Peter Stearns: *Globalization in World History* (2010)
Francis Fukuyama: *The End of History and the Last Man* (1992)
Francis Fukuyama: *State-Building: Governance and World Order in the 21st Century* (2004)
Samuel Huntington: *The Clash of Civilizations and the Remaking of World Order* (1996)
Samuel Huntington: *Culture Matters: How Values Shape Human Progress* (2000)
Benjamin Barber: *Jihad vs. McWorld: How Globalism and Tribalism Are Reshaping the World* (1996)
Benjamin Barber: *Fear's Empire: War, Terrorism, and Democracy in an Age of Interdependence* (2003)
Paul Kennedy: *Preparing for the Twenty-First Century* (1993)
Paul Kennedy: *From War to Peace: Altered Strategic Landscapes in the Twentieth Century* (2000)
Thomas L. Friedman: *The World Is Flat: A Brief History of the Twenty-First Century* (2005)

DIG EVEN DEEPER!

You can search for primary sources about the world in the twentieth century at the following websites:
UK National Archives: http://www.nationalarchives.gov.uk/
U.S. National Archives: http://www.archives.gov/research/
Library of Congress Country Studies: http://memory.loc.gov/frd/cs/
George Mason University, Roy Rosenzweig Center for History and New Media: http://chnm.gmu.edu/
The Legacy Project: http://www.legacy-project.org
U.S. Army Center of Military History Recommended Professional Reading List: http://www.history.army.mil/reading.html
The Cold War Museum: http://www.coldwar.org/
Woodrow Wilson International Center for Scholars, The Cold War International History Project: http://www.wilsoncenter.org/program/cold-war-international-history-project
The National Security Archive at The George Washington University: http://www.gwu.edu/~nsarchiv/NSAEBB/index.html
The University of Idaho, Repositories of Primary Sources: http://www.uiweb.uidaho.edu/special-collections/Other.Repositories.html

MySearchLab Connections

Read the **Document** on **mysearchlab.com**

14.1 *The European Community, Treaty on European Union.* In the second half of the twentieth century, Western Europe moved toward greater economic and political integration, eventually forming what became known as the European Community (EC). In late 1991, representatives from the twelve EC member states met in the city of Maastricht in the Netherlands to formulate a treaty that laid the groundwork for monetary union through a common currency (the "Euro") and established the European Union.

Index

Credits

Cover: National Archives and Records Administration (6003303); National Archives and Records Administration (542145); Library of Congress [LC-DIG-ggbain-00111]; Perspectives/Glow Images.

Chapter 1, page 2: National Archives and Records Administration (593556); **page 3:** National Archives and Records Administration (5642096/ MLR Number A1 9-E); **page 3:** Library of Congress [LC-DIG-ppmsca-25696]; **page 3:** Library of Congress [LC-USZC4-14295]; **page 7:** Library of Congress [LC-USZ62-52583]; **page 12:** Library of Congress [LC-USZ62-88790]; **page 17:** Library of Congress [LC-USZ62-94920]; **page 18:** National Archives and Records Administration (530870).

Chapter 2, page 22: Library of Congress [LC-USZ62-136100]; **page 23:** Zsolt Horvath/Shutterstock; **page 23:** National Archives and Records Administration (530713); **page 23:** Library of Congress [LC-USZ62-101877]; **page 26:** Library of Congress [LC-USZ62-55128]; **page 30:** Getty Images/Photos.com/Thinkstock; **page 36:** Library of Congress [LC-USZ62-59516]; **page 37:** Library of Congress [LC-DIG-ppmsca-13709-00160]; **page 39:** Getty Images/ Photos.com/Thinkstock; **page 41:** Library of Congress [LC-USZC4-10297]; **page 42:** National Archives and Records Administration (533726).

Chapter 3, page 46: Dorthea Lange/Library of Congress [LC-DIG-fsa-8b29516]; **page 47:** Library of Congress [LC-USZ62-106041]; **page 47:** Library of Congress [LC-DIG-ppmsca-01589]; **page 47:** Library of Congress [LC-USZC4-8341]; **page 49:** National Archives and Records Administration (530791); **page 52:** Library of Congress [LC-USZ62-10775]; **page 55:** Odin M. Eidskrem/Shutterstock; **page 56:** Library of Congress [LC-USZ62-111091]; **page 59:** Library of Congress [LC-USZ62-46692]; **page 60:** World History Archive/Alamy; **page 62:** Library of Congress [LC-USZ62-51834]; **page 63:** Library of Congress [LC-DIG-det-4a27966].

Chapter 4, page 66: National Archives and Records Administration (540153); **page 67:** Library of Congress [LC-USZ62-127379]; **page 67:** Library of Congress [POS 6 - Germany, no. 330]; **page 67:** Franklin D. Roosevelt Presidential Library; **page 69:** National Archives and Records Administration (533768); **page 70:** Library of Congress [LC-DIG-pga-01130]; **page 74:** ITAR-TASS/Sovfoto; **page 75:** Library of Congress [LC-USZ62-69527]; **page 76:** Getty Images/ Photos.com/Thinkstock; **page 78:** Library of Congress [LC-USZ62-42736]; **page 81:** National Archives and Records Administration (541929); **page 83:** Library of Congress [LC-USZ62-132747].

Chapter 5, page 88: National Archives and Records Administration (535795); **page 89:** National Archives and Records Administration (292594); **page 89:** Naval History & Heritage Command; **page 89:** Franklin D. Roosevelt Library; **page 91:** National Archives and Records Administration (559369); **page 92:** National Archives and Records Administration (540179); **page 95:** National Archives and Records Administration (541920); **page 97:** Library of Congress [LC-USZ62-75081]; **page 99:** Library of Congress [LC-USZ62-121787]; **page 101:** National Archives and Records Administration (295981); **page 105:** Naval History & Heritage Command; **page 108:** National Archives and Records Administration (531276); **page 109:** US Military Academy, Dept. of History; **page 110:** Los Alamos National Laboratory; **page 111:** Library of Congress [LC-USZ62-113253]; **page 113:** Library of Congress [LC-USZ62-94454].

Chapter 6, page 118: Library of Congress [LC-USZ62-126868]; **page 119:** National Archives and Records Administration (515906); **page 119:** Library of Congress [LC-USZ62-104106]; **page 119:** Harry S. Truman Library; **page 121:** National Archives and Records Administration (531340); **page 127:** National Archives and Records Administration (195564); **page 128:** National Archives and Records Administration (292603); **page 131:** Harry S. Truman Library; **page 133:** Library of Congress [LC-USZ62-62808]; **page 134:** Library of Congress [LC-USW33-019074-C].

Chapter 7, page 140: Library of Congress [LC-USZ62-70044]; **page 141:** National Archives and Records Administration (541966); **page 141:** National Archives and Records Administration (542104); **page 141:** Library of Congress [LC-USZ62-111093]; **page 143:** National Archives and Records Administration (520694); **page 146:** Library of Congress [LC-USZC4-3376]; **page 148:** Library of Congress [LC-USZC4-11469]; **page 151:** National Archives and Records Administration (541822).

Chapter 8, page 158: Library of Congress [LC-USZ62-129105]; **page 159:** Library of Congress [LC-USZ62-122648]; **page 159:** Library of Congress [LC-USZ62-41701]; **page 159:** Library of Congress [LC-USZ62-109608]; **page 161:** Library of Congress [LC-USZ62-120658]; **page 165:** Library of Congress [LC-DIG-ppmsca-19730]; **page 166:** Library of Congress [LC-USZ62-107627]; **page 169:** Library of Congress [LC-DIG-ds-00069]; **page 171:** Bettmann/Corbis; **page 172:** Bettmann/Corbis; **page 173:** Library of Congress [LC-USZ62-127229]; **page 174:** Cecil Stoughton, White House/John F. Kennedy Presidential Library and Museum, Boston; **page 175:** U. S. Dept. of Defense photograph in the John F. Kennedy Presidential Library and Museum, Boston; **page 177:** Everett Collection Inc/Alamy.

Chapter 9, page 180: National Archives and Records Administration (530612); **page 181:** Library of Congress [LC-USZ62-135269]; **page 181:** Library of Congress [LC-DIG-ppmsca-19765]; **page 181:** Library of Congress [yan1996002541]; **page 186:** Library of Congress [LC-USZ62-133963]; **page 187:** Library of Congress [LC-USZ62-130455]; **page 193:** Library of Congress [LC-USZ62-134160]; **page 195:** National Archives and Records Administration (542189); **page 197:** National Archives and Records Administration (532491); **page 200:** Eddie Adams/AP Photo; **page 201:** Lyndon B. Johnson Library; **page 202:** Richard Nixon Presidential Library & Museum.

Chapter 10, page 206: Library of Congress [LC-USZ62-134154]; **page 207:** NASA; **page 207:** Library of Congress [LC-U9-25538-35]; **page 207:** National Archives and Records Administration (594262); **page 209:** Library of Congress [LC-USZ62-120084]; **page 209:** Dean Conger/Historical/Corbis; **page 210:** INTERFOTO/History/Alamy; **page 214:** National Archives and Records Administration (555405); **page 217:** ALIC, National Archives and Records Administration; **page 218:** National Archives and Records Administration (593743); **page 220:** Richard Nixon Presidential Library & Museum.

Chapter 11, page 224: Jimmy Carter Library; **page 225:** Library of Congress [LC-DIG-ppmsca-19873]; **page 225:** Library of Congress [LC-USZC4-9834]; **page 225:** Library of Congress [LC-DIG-ppmsca-04919]; **page 228:** Library of Congress [LC-USZC4-3268]; **page 234:** Library of Congress [LC-USZC4-8343]; **page 235:** Bettmann/Corbis; **page 237:** Defense Imagery.mil; **page 238:** Jimmy Carter Library; **page 240:** Bettmann/Corbis; **page 241:** Hulton-Deutsch Collection/Corbis.

Chapter 12, page 246: Ronald Reagan Presidential Library; **page 247:** Hellen Sergeyeva/Shutterstock; **page 247:** CTK/Abaca/Newscom; **page 247:** Ronald Reagan Presidential Library; **page 249:** National Archives and Records Administration (558523); **page 251:** Wesley Bocxe/Photo Researchers, Inc.; **page 252:** Ronald Reagan Presidential Library; **page 254:** Ronald Reagan Presidential Library; **page 255:** mpworks/Alamy; **page 257:** picture-alliance/dpa/Newscom; **page 260:** Tiit Veermae/Alamy; **page 261:** David Fowler/Shutterstock; **page 262:** Кузьмин Валентин/ITAR-TASS/Newscom.

Chapter 13, page 266: MSGT Rose Reynolds/Defense Imagery.mil; **page 267:** PH2 Mark Kettenhofen/Defense Imagery.mil; **page 267:** Beth Dixson/Alamy; **page 267:** William J. Clinton Presidential Library; **page 269:** Library of Congress [LC-USZC4-2707]; **page 271:** PHCM Terry Mitchell/Defense Imagery.mil; **page 273:** Jacques Langevin/Sygma/Corbis; **page 275:** Vladimir Wrangel/Shutterstock; **page 278:** NATO Photos; **page 281:** Library of Congress [LC-DIG-ppbd-00348]; **page 281:** Louise Gubb/CORBIS SABA/Corbis; **page 285:** Wesley Bocxe/Photo Researchers, Inc.

Chapter 14, page 288: ojka/Shutterstock; **page 289:** Inq/Shutterstock; **page 289:** Oleg Zabielin/Shutterstock; **page 289:** Ralf Siemieniec/Shutterstock; **page 295:** Seattle Municipal Archives, ImageBank Photographs, 19991129.01.